Legal Plunder

Legal Plunder

The Predatory Dimensions
of Criminal Justice

JOSHUA PAGE AND JOE SOSS

The University of Chicago Press Chicago and London

The University of Chicago Press, Chicago 60637
The University of Chicago Press, Ltd., London
© 2025 by The University of Chicago
Published 2025
Printed in the United States of America

34 33 32 31 30 29 28 27 26 25   1 2 3 4 5

ISBN-13: 978-0-226-84115-1 (cloth)
ISBN-13: 978-0-226-84116-8 (paper)
ISBN-13: 978-0-226-84117-5 (ebook)
DOI: https://doi.org/10.7208/chicago/9780226841175.001.0001

Library of Congress Cataloging-in-Publication Data

Names: Page, Joshua, author. | Soss, Joe, 1967– author.
Title: Legal plunder : the predatory dimensions of criminal justice / Joshua
    Page and Joe Soss.
Other titles: Chicago studies in American politics.
Description: Chicago : The University of Chicago Press, 2025. |
    Series: Chicago studies in American politics | Includes bibliographical
    references and index.
Identifiers: LCCN 2024054323 | ISBN 9780226841151 (cloth) |
    ISBN 9780226841168 (paperback) | ISBN 9780226841175 (ebook)
Subjects: LCSH: Criminal justice, Administration of—Corrupt practices—
    United States. | Criminal justice, Administration of—Economic aspects—
    United States. | Law enforcement—Corrupt practices—United States. |
    Law enforcement—Economic aspects—United States. | Discrimination
    in criminal justice administration—Economic aspects—United States. |
    Discrimination in law enforcement—Economic aspects—United States.
Classification: LCC HV9950 .P34 2025 | DDC 364.973—dc23/eng/20250206
LC record available at https://lccn.loc.gov/2024054323

♾ This paper meets the requirements of ANSI/NISO Z39.48-1992
(Permanence of Paper).

CONTENTS

Introduction * *Legal Plunder*

Patrick Irving was in a bind. Imprisoned in Idaho, he desperately needed a pair of sneakers. "The plastic bag I sandwich between my two best pairs of socks . . . protects well against the rain that soaks in through [the hole in] my shoe," he wrote in *The New York Times*, "but Idaho snow is a formidable foe."[1] Irving could have bought a new pair from the commissary—a prison store that sells overpriced, low-quality goods—but that would have left him without money for other necessities like food to "stave off hunger pains," a bar of soap to wash his "parts and pieces," and "real detergent" to clean his "sweaty clothes in a toilet." Like most people in prison, Irving was broke. If he got a prison job, he would make only $0.40 an hour. The shoes cost $48.72.

Out in the community, Irving could shop around for better deals. Not so in prison. He and his peers "have only one store to choose from. It is run by a private company called the Keefe Group . . . a subsidiary of TKC, a holding company indirectly controlled by H.I.G. Capital, a private equity firm." To continue as the sole provider of goods to a captive market, Irving explains, "Keefe rewards the Idaho Department of Corrections with a revenue-sharing arrangement that guarantees a yearly minimum of $1.25 million plus 40 percent of gross beyond an annual base sales target." The company and the state agency "benefit from working closely together . . . usually at the expense of their shared clients."

For most people doing time, Irving's story is unremarkable. They know all too well that America's prisons are shot through with all kinds of revenue-generating schemes. From the get-go, most states charge people pay-to-stay fees for their own imprisonment. Ordinary activities, from sending an email to making a phone call, produce further bills. Family members and friends of the imprisoned tend to be familiar with such practices, too. Lacking funds of their own, incarcerated people usually turn to people on the outside for help. Irving, for example, depends on "two sets of recently retired parents" who "pool from their savings approximately $200 a month to help defray" the costs of living in prison. In the US today, families of incarcerated people spend approximately $2.9 billion each year on phone call and commissary costs alone.[2]

Americans who have never had such experiences, including many well-off readers of *The New York Times*, might be surprised by such facts, especially given that Irving was writing about a *public* prison. In liberal political rhetoric and popular media stories, revenue-enhancing practices are usually cast as distinctive features of private, for-profit prisons, in contrast to public facilities.[3] Some critics even claim that public prisons are too generous in providing taxpayer-funded goods and services to residents. *Free* room and board, they scoff; *free* health care and job-training programs. High-profile essays like Irving's create a breach in this conventional storyline, exposing the broad sweep of financial exploitation occurring across private and public criminal legal institutions.

Over the past two decades, tragic police killings have served as an especially powerful basis for such revelations. The most politically significant episode emerged in 2014, when Officer Darren Wilson shot and killed Michael Brown in Ferguson, Missouri. A wave of mass protests pushed the US Department of Justice to investigate the city's police practices. The agency's 2015 *Ferguson Report* was a political bombshell that generated a wave of national outrage and media coverage. For years, Ferguson police had acted, as Ta-Nehisi Coates observed in *The Atlantic*, as "agents of plunder" for a program designed to fund municipal budgets by aggressively and selectively imposing fines and fees on Black residents.[4]

Echoes of Ferguson reverberated in 2016, when Officer Jeronimo Yanez shot and killed Philando Castile during a traffic stop in Falcon Heights, Minnesota. Digging into the backstory, local reporters found that police had stopped Castile for minor driving infractions forty-nine times over the previous fourteen years, issuing eighty-two citations and leaving him with more than $7,000 in legal debt.[5] At a local rally, his mother Valerie Castile put the matter plainly: "I told my son once before he had got murdered, these people ain't even looking at you like a man, they looking at you as revenue. . . . Because every time they stop you . . . that ain't nothing but money."[6]

Similar events unfolded with regard to the pretrial process, as investigations of high-profile injustices uncovered court, jail, and bail practices that stripped resources from people accused but not convicted of crimes. In 2010, Kalief Browder, a Black teenager, was arrested for allegedly stealing a backpack. The case was flimsy, but Browder and his family could not afford the bail amount set by the court ($3,000), nor the lesser premium required by a bail bond company.[7] The state held Browder for nearly three years in the brutal jail complex on Rikers Island, where he was beaten by staff and other prisoners and spent more than 700 days in solitary confinement. Authorities eventually dropped the charges and released Browder in 2013. One year later, he told a journalist that he felt "mentally scarred." A year after that, the young man took his own life.[8]

Many journalists and activists focused on the role of financial bail in the tragic story of Kalief Browder. Shawn Carter (Jay-Z) published a *Time* magazine essay on the cruel but common dynamics at work and coproduced a documentary on the case, later writing that he had become "obsessed with the injustice of the profitable bail bond industry."[9] Along with others, Carter connected Browder's case to the death of Sandra Bland, a Black woman arrested in Texas for allegedly assaulting an officer during a traffic stop. (Notably, "the officer who arrested her was later charged with perjury regarding the arrest."[10]) Like Browder, Bland could not afford to post bail ($5,000) or pay a bond company premium, so she languished in jail. Several days after her arrest, Bland was found hanged in her cell.[11]

As Carter and others drew a direct line from Black people's deaths to the highly profitable monetary bail system, other prominent cultural and media figures staged broader interventions. John Oliver, for example, used his popular comedy news television show *Last Week Tonight* to air long-form stories on topics such as revenue-centered policing, civil asset forfeiture, monetary bail, for-profit incarceration, and contract-based prison services. Ava DuVernay's influential documentary *13th* connected extractive labor practices and financial charges in contemporary prisons to a longer history of coercive, race-targeted exploitation and the interests of powerful political and economic actors today.

Important as they are, interventions of this sort are just the most visible outcroppings of a larger and more sustained groundswell of political opposition. Across the nation, incarcerated people, artists, community activists, lawyers, journalists, scholars, advocacy groups, and others have worked relentlessly to expose and challenge the swelling tide of extractive practices in criminal legal governance. Alongside the infamous rise of mass incarceration in the US, a second change, profoundly important but less recognized, has transpired. Since the mid-1980s, government and business interests have retrofitted criminal legal institutions so that they function as generators of revenue. Today, their routine operations extract billions of dollars annually from the nation's most oppressed and exploited communities.

Legal Plunder presents a sustained analysis and critique of this development, including its origins, justifications, operations, effects, and contestations. We argue that, since the 1980s, intensive methods of financial extraction have become integral features of criminal legal governance in America and powerful forces shaping the institutions that implement them. This process has produced a distinctive new chapter in the history of what we call *criminal justice predation*. It has reconfigured the long-standing relationship between governmental operations that criminalize, police, and punish and extractive projects that use takings from subjugated groups to subsidize and enrich dominant actors and institutions.

The dramatic growth of financial predation in criminal legal governance raises a number of questions that, analytically and politically, demand attention. Why did it happen and how do the resulting operations work? How have so many powerful actors come to see such practices as desirable and legitimate? How should we understand the significance and consequences of this shift in governance? What should we make of the various forms of political opposition that have emerged, and what lessons can we draw from them to pursue justice in the years ahead? These questions guide our inquiry in the pages ahead.

Predation: A Relational Framework

Although it is common to speak of "the criminal justice system" in the singular, criminal legal governance in the US is a notoriously fragmented and decentralized affair—a patchwork of loosely connected operations, agencies, and jurisdictions.[12] Revenue-generating practices have proliferated across this landscape, but because they have emerged in piecemeal ways, there have been few signs that they fit together as parts of a larger whole. Their diversity and fragmentation have been mirrored, in important ways, by efforts to understand and challenge them.

For more than twenty years, researchers have analyzed such financial takings in detail, generally by focusing on a particular arena of action and applying an established analytic framework to the case at hand. Scholars of "monetary sanctions," for example, typically place state powers and courts at the center of inquiry, clarifying how the growing use of fees and fines fits into broader trends in punishment and systems of social control.[13] Students of prison profiteering focus, in contrast, on corporate actors and private interests, framing their analyses in terms of broader trends in business power, privatization, and public–private partnership.[14] For public finance experts, fiscal pressures and government budgets take center stage; criminal legal takings are analyzed alongside other revenue-producing policy tools and explained in terms of wider trends in public taxation and spending.[15] Without these and other productive lines of inquiry, the study presented in this book would not be possible. Indeed, our approach is directly indebted to earlier scholars, especially those who have theorized "carceral capitalism" and criminal legal means of "taxing the poor."[16]

Our goal is to complement and build on this work by developing *predation* as a more encompassing and synthetic framework for analysis. The term "predatory," as we use it, does not designate a type of actor, policy tool, or goal-oriented intention. It refers to social relations that take a particular form—and thus, can be identified by the terms on which they are organized—and to the practices that constitute and enact them. Predatory relations and practices are structured by the dominant and subordinate positions that actors occupy relative to one another and by the terms that organize and regulate their transactions. Specifically, they (1) are based on a subordinated group's subjugation and exclusion and (2) leverage the subordinated group's vulnerabilities, needs, and aspirations to pursue targeted modes of intensive exploitation or expropriation.

Relations of this type emerge through a social process that scholars such as Keeanga-Yamahtta Taylor call "predatory inclusion."[17] Most accounts of social inequalities focus on group-based exclusions and the deprivations they produce—for example, the unequal resource distributions that result when subordinated groups are denied access to advantageous jobs, schools, or neighborhoods. Working in this vein, studies of punishment and social inequality have shown how the "mark of a criminal record" can undercut access to employment, housing, and social supports.[18] Influential accounts of mass incarceration describe it as an exclusionary "warehousing" operation built to contain and manage *"a surplus population* devoid of market utility."[19]

Actions that exclude do more than just deprive, however. They position people for incorporation into predatory relations. Indeed, to the extent that subordinated groups constitute a "surplus population," they are not, in fact, devoid of market utility. People who cannot get access to decent jobs or banking services, for example, often have little choice but to accept the most exploitative and dangerous terms of work or turn to manipulative and usurious banking operations. In this regard, they share something in common with Patrick Irving, a sequestered, captive consumer forced to pay the prison commissary's inflated prices, and Sandra Bland, who from jail could only turn in desperation to the purveyors of costly bail bond services. Practices that subjugate and exclude produce the social targets and circumstances necessary for predatory inclusion to occur. From this perspective, we can see that penal operations that isolate, deprive, and control do more than just warehouse; they make incarcerated populations *productive* by ushering them into projects that generate substantial public and private revenues.

In chapter 1, we develop predation as a social scientific concept, a pivotal force in American development, and an integral facet of the capitalist social order. For now, we simply note that this conceptualization entails two key shifts in analytic and political perspective. First, the concept of predatory relations allows us to draw a wide range of criminal legal sites and practices into a common analytic frame that stems from fundamental questions of social structure and the terms of dominant–subordinate relations. Second, concepts like "predation" define general classes of social phenomena. They put what we study into dialogue with some kinds of cases rather than others. A concept like "monetary sanctions," for example, invokes theories of the penal state and invites comparisons of fine-and-fee practices to other forms of punishment. Predation points us in a different direction, calling for efforts to theorize today's extractive criminal legal practices in relation to other predatory projects, such as Native dispossession, chattel slavery, and business models that exploit people from subjugated communities through perpetual debt-and-payment traps.

Criminal Legal Governance and Predation over Time

Policing and punishment in the US today carry echoes of the predatory past. The Riker's Island jail where Kalief Browder suffered so greatly, for example, began in the nineteenth century as a collection of debtor's prisons and workhouses—institutions that served as penal threats to keep payments flowing to creditors, their architecture designed for the forced extraction of labor.[20] There is much to be learned by connecting Riker's Island's present to its past—or by tracing the lines from slavery plantations to penal workhouses, prison farming and manufacturing operations, convict leasing camps, and prison labor exploitation today. Yet there are risks as well. The idea that contemporary predatory practices are nothing more than "the same old thing again" is a distortion of reality and a misleading basis for analysis. It is also an invitation to political despair, suggesting that nothing really changes and political opposition, now as in the past, is futile. To avoid these traps, one must attend to similarities *and* differences between various modes of predation—to continuity *and* change across historical eras.

The relationship between predation and criminal legal governance in America stretches back to the colonial era. As we show in chapter 1, each has motivated, enabled, and shaped the development of the other over time. Throughout this history, their entwinement has been organized and oriented by social hierarchies of race, class, and gender. As predatory projects have made subjugated groups productive for dominant groups and institutions, they have also helped *construct* subordinated groups and intersectional inequalities.

Black enslavement and Native dispossession, for example, served as the foundational predatory projects of US history. As massive expropriations of land and labor underwrote early American political and economic development, they also constructed the material and ideological foundations of race, class, and gender hierarchies. Efforts to advance and secure the two projects fueled the early formation of state policing capacities, such as slave patrols and military police, and organized them to combat slave insurrections, flights from bondage, and Indigenous resistance to land takings. Rising capacities to police and jail, in turn, served as tools of enforcement, deployed to sustain chattel slavery and advance removal and dispossession.

In these and many other cases, criminal legal practices have provided essential supports for predatory projects operating in the broader social order. At the same time, criminal legal governance has also served as a site for predation in its own right. Penal labor during the century after the Civil War provides the paradigmatic example. Race-targeted criminalization and policing, based on "Black Codes" and other legal innovations, laid the basis for penal labor operations that served both public and private elites: the chain gang, the convict leasing system, and more. Prison manufacturing, penal farms, and forced "housekeeping" work defrayed the costs of incarceration, supported by visions of self-funding facilities that would keep government small and limit public tax burdens. Hard labor of this sort was a moral and civic imperative, authorities insisted all the while, essential for the penitence and penal rehabilitation of lawless deviants.

Socially and spatially, race-class subjugated (RCS) communities continue to define the epicenter of criminal justice predation, with other (mostly disadvantaged) communities incorporated to varying degrees.[21] As in the past, today's predatory criminal legal practices underwrite state operations and capital accumulation. They subsidize advantaged Americans and protect them from the higher tax costs that intensive policing and mass penal control would otherwise create. They perpetuate the tradition of extreme labor exploitation in carceral facilities and community supervision programs. And they continue to rely on rehabilitation, public safety, and self-funding as potent justifications.

Nevertheless, predation in the US today departs from the past in many ways. The reason, we argue, is that predatory projects always operate within and depend on the larger social structures in which they are embedded. They emerge and take shape under historically specific conditions defined by political economies, state institutions, and other key features of the social order. This observation goes some distance toward explaining why predatory criminal legal *practices* have exhibited so much historical and regional variation in the US. Political struggle, human creativity, and institutional development have, over time, transformed state laws and institutions and reorganized the workings of American capitalism. In the wake of twentieth-century social movements, class, race, and gender in the US do not operate, socially or legally, as they did in earlier eras. It is little wonder, then, that criminal justice predation in America today exhibits historically distinctive features.

Criminal Justice Predation Today

Criminal legal institutions serve many functions and goals. Their predatory practices intersect with, depend on, and, in many cases, subsidize their more commonly recognized pursuits. As these institutions divide and exclude—for example, through criminalization, imprisonment, and the policing of social and residential boundaries—they lay the groundwork for predatory inclusion. Through practices of repression, classification, and containment, they produce and position targets for resource extraction. Thus, as policing and penal operations expanded and changed after the 1960s, so too did the institutional bases of predation. Starting in the 1980s, criminal justice predation in the US began to take on a new look. Predatory practices grew in scope and scale, eventually spreading to nearly every corner of criminal legal institutions. They reached more deeply into the resources and relationships of community life. Their focus and operations were reconfigured through processes of financialization and privatization.

Historically, labor exploitation has stood at the center of criminal justice predation in America. In the late twentieth century, however, as financialization transformed political economies around the world,[22] the criminal legal field's predatory operations shifted decisively toward practices that charge prices, create debts, and pursue collections. As the form of resource extraction changed, its *reach* greatly expanded. Penal labor exploitation is limited to convicted individuals positioned at a particular site, such as a prison. The financial turn allowed extractive practices to spread across the full range of criminal legal institutions (charges could be added at nearly any point in the process) and made it possible to drain resources from legally entangled people's loved ones and communities—even in the absence of incarceration. It also expanded predation in a temporal sense: By imposing financial debts, legal authorities could lay claim to *future* resources, enhancing their ability to take what poor communities, by definition, lack.

Similarly, the wave of privatization that swept across various arenas of governance in this era transformed policing and punishment in far-reaching ways. In the criminal legal field, collaborations between public authorities and private interests have a long history. In the case of bail, for example, for-profit actors have played a prominent role since the early 1900s. Such precedents, however, pale in comparison to what emerged after the early 1980s—not only in the scope and scale of business operations but also in the kinds of authority delegated to them. Corporations emerged as major players in nearly every area of the field. At the state and federal levels, they became owners and managers of privately run prisons. In ostensibly "public" prisons, they took over as for-profit purveyors of basic goods and services. Local governments hired companies to process fine and fee payments, maintain records, operate traffic citation cameras, collect debts, monitor people on probation and parole, train police, run jail services, and more. In a short time, the field was overrun by actors who approached criminal legal governance primarily as a site of investment and profit.

In the US today, then, predatory criminal legal operations are often organized as mutually beneficial, revenue-centered, public–private partnerships and as networks of interdependent sites where authorities impose financial charges, monetize procedures, exploit captive consumers, seize assets, and collect payments. In chapters 2 and 3, we analyze the growth and operation of predatory practices since the 1980s, showing how state and market actors siphon resources from subjugated communities and convert them into revenues. Extractive procedures and practices now operate as a matter of routine. Police officers ticket drivers, bicyclists, and pedestrians and, under asset forfeiture laws, seize cash and property based on nothing more than an allegation of illicit origins. Courts impose innumerable fees and fines and funnel defendants into the bail bond industry. In jails and prisons, accused and convicted individuals are subjected to one revenue-generating practice after another. Government agencies charge fees for room and board, medical and dental care, and essential goods, such as clothing and toiletries. They generate additional revenue by selling corporations access to the human beings they control. The companies, in turn, exploit imprisoned people as a captive market for goods and services and, in return for this lucrative access, often give public agencies a slice of their profits.

Remarkably, these examples cover just a portion of the extractive practices that suffuse policing and punishment in the US today. The new operations should not be misconstrued as some kind of "unprecedented break" with the past. Nevertheless, they mark a significant new chapter in the evolving relationship between predation and criminal legal governance.

Explaining the Financial Turn

In chapters 4 and 5, we take up questions of historical change, analyzing, first, the political actions and policy developments that drove institutional conversion and, second, the frames of justification that brought key actors on board and paved the way forward. The new toolbox of revenue-centered practices emerged and spread alongside a dramatic escalation of policing and punishment in the US. This pairing in time has, for some, led to a confusion that should be put to rest at the outset. The aggressive revenue-seeking efforts that took off after the mid-1980s did not cause—and do not explain—the rise of mass incarceration and intensive policing that began in the 1970s. In fact, the inverse is closer to the actual flow of events: Growing criminal legal operations and expenditures helped fuel the adoption and spread of innovative predatory practices.

Specifically, we argue that the rise of financial predation emerged from a convergence of three developments in US politics and governance.

The first restructured public finance in ways that, starting in the 1980s, put state and local governments under severe fiscal pressures. New policies cut taxes for corporations and the rich, restricted state and local taxation, reduced federal subsidies for subnational budgets, devolved responsibilities to lower levels of government, and drove the state and local costs of policing and punishment skyward. Desperate to fill budgetary gaps and sustain their operations, state and local officials created or escalated a wide range of revenue strategies—including many, such as state lotteries, that drew funds disproportionately from poor communities. In this broader context, public officials began to reimagine their criminal legal operations as potential sources of revenue. In short order, new monetizing strategies were set in motion.

This development converged with a second: the ascendance of a racially toxic politics of law and order that demanded ever-tougher efforts to make criminals pay. At the state and local levels, the fiscal desperation of this period fueled a powerful round of austerity politics, marked by aggressive cuts to public services. In criminal legal governance, though, bipartisan tough-on-crime agendas, bolstered by powerful law enforcement and victims' rights organizations, had become a political juggernaut. Rollbacks were politically untenable yet, in the 1990s and 2000s, expenses rose ever higher. The same political pressures that blocked de-escalation, however, offered opportunities and rationales for efforts to defray costs. To get tough on crime, officials increased fines, created new violations, and embraced aggressive asset seizure tactics. To make "lawless criminals" pay for their own actions, courts and penal agencies adopted a host of new fees. Citing public safety concerns, judges began to impose larger and more frequent financial conditions of bail. As the revenue-enhancing measures accumulated, the political risks of appearing soft on crime or unsympathetic to victims deterred opposition from public officials, time and again.

The third contributing development was the global turn to public–private partnerships. As penal expenditures grew, cash-strapped public agencies needed help—and corporate leaders saw lucrative investment opportunities. Soaring incarceration rates had left state and local officials scrambling to resolve unconstitutional levels of jail and prison crowding. Entrepreneurs pitched new business models that they claimed would help public agencies solve their cost and management problems. Business interests spent millions on political action to remove barriers to entry and install for-profit operations. Governments were able to stabilize costly responsibilities through public–private contracts that, in many cases, brought them revenue through profit-sharing agreements. As corporations established themselves in the field, they showed public authorities how their penal operations could generate revenue. They also changed the field's politics. Bringing their considerable powers to bear, they worked persistently to influence elections, pressure lawmakers, and secure operations that delivered healthy returns on investment.

Changes in governance of this magnitude must somehow be justified. They have to overcome the status quo bias of institutions and transform accepted ways of doing things. They require coalitions of supporters and effective defenses against criticism. For these and other reasons, government and corporate leaders had to develop justifications for their plans and, later, for their operations. The primary audiences for such rationales were rarely the politically marginalized communities that predatory practices target. Mostly, they were designed to sway actors with greater authority and influence, such as elected officials, public managers, judges, media outlets, think tanks, and political organizations. From the 1980s to the present, such justifications have tended to fall into two broad clusters.

The first is rooted in discourses of security, criminality, and victimization. In this register, predatory practices have been framed as essential measures for securing public safety, sustaining law and order, and rehabilitating "lawless deviants." Racialized discourses that demonize and dehumanize "criminals" have cultivated social indifference to their treatment and, in many cases, support for efforts to make them pay a price. Related rationales have focused on victimization. Predatory practices, in this guise, are framed as a moral obligation to "do right by innocent victims" and, more broadly, to make sure that "taxpaying Americans who play by the rules" are not victimized yet again by "criminals," via the costly measures needed to deal with them.

The second cluster has drawn on neoliberal discourses that blur distinctions between political and economic relations, impose market-based models and standards of evaluation on governance, and treat individuals as responsible for choosing their own fates.[23] In this idiom, citizens are consumers who, in their dealings with the state, have a personal responsibility to pay for what they receive. Payments demanded from legally entangled people and their loved ones are framed as ordinary market transactions for goods and services. Public managers are charged with making prudent, entrepreneurial choices, warranted by their ability to produce savings for taxpayer-consumers and positive returns on investment.

The restructuring of public management to conform with business models and mentalities finds its complement in discourses that frame corporations as socially responsible, civic-minded partners. In this view, businesses and public agencies share an obligation to collaborate on the efficient pursuit of public goals. Presenting themselves as public-spirited partners devoted to the common good, corporate leaders have cloaked their profitable criminal legal investments in civic virtue and cost-saving governance. At the same time, neoliberal discourses have framed the targets of criminal justice predation as failed individuals who have made bad choices and engineered their own fates. Such people deserve the consequences of their personal choices. If they get into trouble with the law, it is their own fault. It is only right that they should get what is coming to them and pay the price for their mismanaged lives.

The Everyday Work of Bail Predation

In the first half of *Legal Plunder*, we apply a wide analytic lens to the relationship between criminal legal governance and predation. In chapters 6–8, we trade this breadth for the sorts of insights and observations that can only be obtained through a deeper dive into a single field of practice. Drawing on almost a year and a half of ethnographic research that one of us (Page) conducted while working as a bail bond agent, we present an extended case study of predatory bail practices, from the corporate heights of the industry to the street level of storefront operations.

The purpose of the case study is not to examine a discrete corner of the landscape in isolation from the rest. Quite the opposite. Bail practices do not operate in a world of their own; they are embedded in the larger workings of criminal legal governance. In the normal course of his job at the bail bond agency, Page interacted with judges, prosecutors, and defense attorneys; spent long hours in courts; became intimately familiar with jail procedures; and used some of the same private vendor services used by detained individuals and their loved ones. The bail industry can be thought of as a particular site within a broader web of operations that work in concert. As such, it defines a distinctive vantage point for observing, experiencing, and analyzing criminal justice predation and the actors and organizations that participate in it.[24]

In this section of the book, we return to some of the core ideas developed in earlier chapters, taking a fresh look based on a more fine-grained analysis of practices in motion. Long-term immersion in the field can reveal dynamics that are unobservable from a distance. Some kinds of insights only emerge slowly through sustained social interactions over time. Closer to the ground, for example, we can learn how race, class, and gender matter *in the doing* of predatory practice. We can extend our analysis of partnerships between governments and corporations to a different, less visible world of street-level collaborations between public and private actors.

Creating new designs for governance is one thing; carrying them out is another. Laws, policies, contracts, tools, and procedures all have to be put to use. Through an intensive analysis of commercial bail predation, we investigate how actors organize, pursue, and justify the essential work of implementation.

We begin our extended case study in chapter 6 by analyzing how industry leaders work to shape public policies and forge the conditions of street-level practice. The large insurance companies that underwrite local bail bond agencies fund and deploy professional associations to achieve desired electoral, legislative, and administrative outcomes. They build power by joining political coalitions with agendas that extend well beyond the criminal legal field. Their resulting, outsized influence allows them to defend and advance the industry, define the rules of the game that organize everyday practice, and ensure that they receive a cut from client payments to storefront businesses. Notably, this case study coincides with a wave of political campaigns demanding bail reform and pretrial justice. As a result, it allows for a close look at how corporate interests work to sustain and expand their operations in the face of opposition.

Page's ethnographic research takes center stage in chapters 7 and 8, carrying our analysis deep into the workaday world of people who make their living on commercial bail. As a participant and observer, Page was thoroughly enmeshed in the organizational cultures, routines, pressures, incentives, rules, and ethical frameworks that structure bail bond practices. He experienced managerial tactics and worker–manager relations firsthand, alongside a group of coworkers who collaborated and competed in equal measure.

Our analysis explores various forms of "regulated improvisation" at the street level, clarifying how bail agents ply their trade—and sometimes re-write the rules of the game itself. At the courthouse, the office, and other sites, agents pursue creative strategies to beat out the competition, bring in clients, and close out deals. To be effective in their jobs, they must navigate conflicts (with clients, competing agents, and public authori-ties) *and* forge collaborations based on trust and reciprocity (with actors positioned to work together for mutual gain). Extending our analysis of how social hierarchies structure predation, we show how race, class, and gender schemas frame and guide organizational and individual practices in the commercial bail sector. We also return to questions of discourse and justification, analyzing how bail agents make sense of what they do, nav-igate moments of moral uncertainty, respond to client accusations, and develop professional identities and narratives that favorably cast them, for example, as "caring service providers."

Significance and Struggle

Throughout US history, predation has operated as a productive force and a site of struggle. The predatory projects that have shaped the nation's social order and fueled its political and economic development have also underwritten fierce political conflicts, protest movements, and countless acts of individual and community resistance. Our analyses in chapters 2–8 work to clarify how dominant groups and institutions benefit from pre-dation today and how actors invested in predation win political victories. In our final two chapters, we turn to the extensive damage produced by predatory practices and to the political campaigns working to put an end to these injustices.

Chapter 9 explores the corrosive effects of predatory practices on tar-geted communities, criminal legal institutions, and democracy and citi-zenship in America. The human toll of criminal justice predation has been profound. As they strip resources and impose debt-and-payment traps, predatory practices generate hardships and crises, not only for legally en-tangled individuals but also for their families, friends, and communities. A growing body of research documents their negative effects on material well-being, physical and mental health, friendships and familial relations, and the social fabric of community life. The evidence points to a critical blind spot in many debates over poverty: In an affluent society, communi-ties suffer from poverty and hardship, in no small part, because powerful actors work creatively and continually to exploit their circumstances, take what little they have, and turn them into perpetual debtors.[25]

Predatory projects also tend to transform the institutions and organizations that enact them. Over time, revenue-generating practices have become integral to daily operations in police departments, courts, and penal facilities. Many of these institutions have become dependent on predatory revenue streams and developed organizational cultures and routines that accommodate the imperatives of revenue generation. Numerous investigations underscore the potential for self-funding arrangements to generate conflicts of interest, compromise organizational missions, foster corruption, and undermine justice and political accountability. Predatory practices are not discrete add-ons to criminal legal governance, siloed away from other operations. To the contrary, they have become so widespread and enmeshed in basic operations that an adequate understanding of contemporary criminal legal governance *requires* attending to its predatory dimensions.

The civic and political consequences of these developments have been equally momentous. To be targeted for plunder by one's government—in the name of justice, no less—is a political experience with far-reaching implications. Predatory practices teach powerful lessons about race and class, power, authority, government, law, and citizenship. They also produce what we call *indentured citizens*, governed on terms defined by a criminalized and racialized debtor's contract. Such citizens may be dogged by state surveillance and control for years—made to appear when summoned, repeatedly threatened with jail, and deprived of basic rights, freedoms, and privacies.

In chapter 10, we turn to the politics of predation and the question of what is to be done. Scholars often use a chapter of this sort to suggest reforms and reflect on their political feasibility. We do not. Predatory uses of policing and punishment are an unacceptable injustice, unnecessary for public safety or the democratic rule of law. Accordingly, they should be abolished. In principle, one could pursue this goal as part of a reformist agenda, working to isolate predatory practices and excise them from the broader workings of criminal legal institutions. The question that must be confronted, however, is whether criminal justice predation can be eliminated through reformist modifications alone. Predation has been a persistent feature of American policing and punishment from the beginning, and it is deeply woven into the operations of these institutions today. Putting an end to it will require fundamental change, on a level that is more consistent with the abolition of policing and punishment as we know them than with what most people mean when they speak of reform.[26] As abolitionist thinkers and activists have long emphasized, however, the embrace of abolitionist goals should not be confused with a principled refusal to support any reform that falls short of immediately delivering root-and-branch systems change.

To the contrary, abolitionists have called for a more discerning approach that opposes "reformist" reforms but fights for "non-reformist" reforms.[27] The orienting horizon of abolition, in this view, provides a guide for political action and for judging the desirability of reform proposals today. However much a reform might offer some people relief from immediate harms, it must also be evaluated *politically* for its potential to help or hinder the pursuit of long-term goals.[28] A desirable reform might diminish the power, functioning, and footprint of unjust systems, for example, or build solidarity by uniting affected people under shared protections that require more just and equal treatment.[29] An undesirable reform might divide affected people by bestowing special protections on subgroups viewed as more "deserving," or shore up the legitimacy of the broader regime by eliminating troubling "excesses" that have attracted condemnation and outrage.

The political logic of this approach dovetails, in many respects, with decades of empirical research on "policy feedback" in political science. Even modest reforms, these studies show, can set political dynamics in motion that lead to dramatic institutional and policy changes at later points in time.[30] Campaigns for small-scale policy changes can be used strategically to build political power, forge solidarities, and reorganize the landscape of political combat.[31] Guided by the insights of abolitionists and policy feedback scholars, we take no position on the value of incremental reform itself. The key question, as we see it, is whether a reform will protect the entire regime of criminal justice predation (e.g., by making it appear less morally troubling) or, instead, build the kinds of political conditions and capacities needed to effectively put an end to it.

We begin chapter 10 by locating struggles against predation on the broader landscape of contemporary US politics. It is not an optimistic picture. The power inequalities and institutional barriers confronted by antipredation campaigns are numerous, formidable, and deeply entrenched. The goal of our analysis, however, is not to reach this (unsurprising) conclusion; it is to specify more precisely the key political challenges that must be overcome. Guided by this analysis, we turn to the recent record of efforts to fight criminal justice predation. Against long odds, antipredation campaigns have won a surprising number of significant victories over the past two decades. Surveying these wins alongside disappointing reversals and defeats, we ask what kinds of conditions and strategies have yielded positive reforms and in what kinds of political arenas. The evidence suggests a need for humility in making across-the-board generalizations and prescriptions. Antipredation efforts have been deeply fragmented by jurisdictions, institutions, levels of government, and modes of financial extraction (e.g., prison phone calls versus court fees). Political opportunities in some cases have not existed in others; strategies that have worked here have failed there. Such patterns are far from random, however. They cluster in ways that suggest important political lessons.

We conclude by asking how our analysis might inform political strategy and action going forward. In setting directions for political struggle, there can be no substitute for listening to what people with lived experiences of predation know, understand, and prioritize. Likewise, advocates, activists, and other political practitioners possess many forms of expertise that we do not. They know far more about the landscapes they work on, the resources and opportunities available to them, and the practical challenges and trade-offs they must navigate. For these and other reasons, we do not prescribe any particular course of action. Rather, we highlight some takeaways from our analysis that we see as worthy of attention in ongoing discussions of strategy and action.

In our concluding chapter, we take up three final tasks. First, we reflect on the lessons and contributions of our study and what the concept of predation offers as a framework for critical social inquiry—and specifically, for research on criminal legal governance and social inequalities. Next, we consider how the idea of *predatory* policing and punishment might be put to practical use in organizing and advocacy campaigns, comparing its advantages and limitations to other "oppositional frames" that prevail in this political arena. Finally, we end by returning to our argument that criminal justice predation is inseparable from the broader structural inequalities and injustices that organize the social order. Emphasizing the limits of addressing predatory practices in isolation, we argue for the importance of connecting them to the freedom struggles of RCS communities, movements for systemic reparations, and campaigns for equitable systems of public finance. The fight *against* predatory criminal legal practices, we argue, should be seen as indivisible from the struggle *for* a just, caring, and democratic future.

A Note on Language

Over the past decade, a growing number of social justice organizations, activists, and scholars have stopped using the term *criminal justice system* in favor of *criminal legal system*, *criminal punishment system*, or simply *criminal system*.[32] The Vera Institute of Justice explains: "Accuracy in language matters, and these systems do not deliver justice, nor have they ever. . . . Words shape how people think, and our speech should recognize that our system of racially biased policing and draconian punishment is not just."[33]

Many academics now prefer *criminal legal* because it is a more precise term. It points to the foundations of policing and punishment in criminal law without suggesting that justice is being done (or even pursued).

In *The Courage of Compassion*, legal advocate and founder of the Bail Project Robin Steinberg offers a dissenting view. Instead of ceding the language of justice, she argues that we should lean into it and fight for what we believe it entails and requires. "I have chosen to use the term *criminal justice system*," Steinberg writes, "because the moral challenge, as I see it, is transforming what we mean and expect from justice in the first place. . . . Trading terms might evoke a sense of progress, but it does not fundamentally challenge us to think differently or work toward a new definition of justice."[34]

Throughout this book, we use the term *criminal legal* to refer to modes of governance that are based on criminalization, policing, adjudication, and punishment. We use the same language to designate criminal legal institutions, authorities, and practices. There are two exceptions to this rule, however. We use the phrases "criminal justice predation" and "the predatory dimensions of criminal justice" to remind readers that the injustices we detail are carried out in the name of justice—by institutions and actors who are charged, under their official missions, with pursuing justice. Over the chapters that follow, we hope readers will not lose sight of this unsettling juxtaposition. Predatory practices of resource stripping and revenue generation have become integral features of criminal legal governance in America. As a society, we must reckon with this fact, and with what it means for justice itself to be harnessed to an institutionalized, systematic regime of *in*justice.

1 * *Predation in Theory, History, and Practice*

Over the past four decades, resource extraction has become an integral feature of policing and punishment in America. Researchers have pursued many productive approaches to understanding the origins, operations, and effects of this development and discerning its societal and historical significance. Studies of monetary sanctions, for example, have shown how fines, fees, and related practices operate as forms of *punishment* that expand the reach of penal control and, in effect, criminalize poverty.[1] We anchor our study in a different concept: *predation*. To set the stage, we use this chapter to clarify what we mean by predation and how we understand its historical relationship to liberal political economy and criminal legal governance.

We start by defining predation and outlining its constitutive features. Next, we connect predation to the coevolving social structures of class, race, and gender, explaining how it reflects and transforms the organization of political economies over time. More concretely, we examine how predation contributed to race-making, economic development, state building, and democratic citizenship in early American history. We then explore how criminal legal institutions enabled predatory projects in earlier eras of US history and served as sites of predation in their own right. Finally, we reflect on the ways dominant-group members in earlier eras, who professed and celebrated liberal commitments, justified their predatory enterprises.

Predation: A Relational Approach

Like any analytic framework, predation serves as a standpoint for understanding and explanation. It brings some things into view more than others and establishes particular grounds for putting ideas and evidence into dialogue. As we use it, the term refers to unequal *relations* of a particular kind, the *practices* that constitute and enact them, and *projects* that operate on the basis of such relations and practices. Specifically, predatory relations and practices (1) are based on a subordinated group's subjugation and exclusion and (2) leverage the group's vulnerabilities, needs, and aspirations to pursue targeted modes of intensive exploitation and expropriation.

It is helpful to start by clarifying what our use of the term predatory does *not* entail. For one, it is not an attribution of motives. To say that relations and practices are organized in a predatory manner, we need not claim that anyone involved has "predatory" goals or intentions, as some assert.[2] Indeed, the nature of such beliefs and aims is an *empirical* question. In later chapters, we present evidence that participants understand and justify predatory practices in various ways. There is no single motive or belief that underlies predation in general and explains what it is "really about." Our account aligns instead with studies that emphasize how unjust relations and practices can be supported by diverse goals and justifications, ambivalent feelings and contradictory beliefs, states of "knowing but not knowing," and situation-specific rationales.[3]

Likewise, the concept of predation is a category of analysis, not a prediction of outcomes. One cannot determine whether certain relations operate in a predatory manner by observing whether they "pay off," as some researchers claim.[4] Such outcomes are unreliable indicators of how relations and practices are *organized*. Labor exploitation, for example, may generate handsome profits for one business yet too little for another to survive. The contrasting outcomes offer no proof that exploitative relations operated only in the first case. Like other types of relations, predatory ones can vary considerably in their results.

As a category of social relations, the term "predatory" also should not be confused with a claim about the essential nature of *things*. In the US today, for instance, fines are routinely used as tools of predation in criminal legal governance. But fines are not inherently predatory. In regulatory governance, they may be imposed on powerful elites who are engaging in industrial pollution or insider trading. Or consider the case of lending. Federal agencies in the US evaluate whether a loan is "predatory" based on traits of the loan, such as its interest rate or payment scheme.[5] In our approach, the focus shifts from the loan itself to the organization of the creditor–debtor relationship. Lending takes a predatory form when creditors exploit conditions created by a subjugated group's exclusion from services, using those conditions to impose usurious interest rates and debt-payment traps. The question of whether a lending practice is predatory, therefore, depends on how actors are positioned in social relations that operate beyond—and cannot be determined by inspecting—the loan itself.

The concept of predation, as it is used in this book, is restricted to practices that are enabled and organized by dominant–subordinate relations. Consider small-town speed traps that raise funds for local governments by ticketing out-of-town motorists. This is clearly a case of criminal legal authority being used to generate revenue. It is not a predatory practice, however, if its pursuit and targeting are not based on social structural inequalities. Or consider people who go to movie theaters and people who are incarcerated. Both groups present businesses with captive consumers who can be charged inflated prices for ordinary goods. The difference is that, unlike moviegoers, imprisoned people are positioned in this way for reasons that are inseparable from prevailing social hierarchies and societal power relations.

Finally, our concept of predation should not be confused with the concept of a "predatory state," which some scholars have used to study the emergence of early European states and contemporary polities in the global South (especially Africa).[6] In the scholarship of Douglass North and others, the *predatory state* and the *contract state* define mutually exclusive, opposing accounts of how states emerge, develop, and operate.[7] In ideal form, the liberal contract state is based on popular consent and pursues development to maximize the wealth of society. It establishes rights that are necessary to secure political freedoms and facilitate open markets, and it governs in a manner that is responsive to political competition, representation, and bargaining.

The predatory state, in contrast, is "an agent that exists to extract revenue from a group of constituents under its control in order to [enrich ruling actors and] continue its own survival."[8] Rulers work to maximize the resources they control and ward off potential rivals. As they govern, such rulers may accept compromises, work to shore up popular support, extend rights to the governed, or provide them with various forms of protection. The ultimate goals of such actions, however, are to secure rulers' power and expand their extractive operations.[9] In this guise, taxation operates as a form of extortion; security takes the form of a "protection racket."[10]

Predation, as we use the word, differs from this line of scholarship in several ways. First, it does not refer to the nature of the state as a whole, only particular relations and practices. In this regard, it operates lower to the ground of social action and suggests that diverse logics of state-led governance can coexist. Second, we do not treat predation and contract as mutually exclusive alternatives. Rather, we aim to clarify how predatory projects and liberal political economies operate in co-constitutive ways.[11] Third, our concept of predation does not assume that state "rulers" share a common set of agendas. We approach the state as an assemblage of institutional fields where actors with diverse interests engage in cooperation and conflict.[12] By analyzing predatory relations and practices, we illuminate the multifaceted nature of governance in the US, rather than reduce it to a singularly extractive enterprise.

What, then, are the key features of predatory relations, and how do they work? They begin with social processes and practices that construct *subjugated* and *excluded* social groups. Subjugated groups occupy social positions with several characteristics. First, they are distinguished as inferior and positioned on the degraded side of various social and moral boundaries. Second, their capabilities are inhibited by marginalization, oppression, and domination. Third, prevailing discourses associate them with inferior or pathological traits, values, and behaviors; stigmatize, denigrate, or dehumanize them; and portray them as threats to security, public order, or other widely held values. Fourth, such groups are disproportionately targeted for institutional and informal projects of social control, discipline, and corrective reform.

Positions of exclusion are created through processes of social closure, which involve one group depriving another of access to opportunities, resources, or statuses.[13] Such processes can operate as powerful engines of social inequality. Unequal access to education, decent housing, good jobs, and public investments can impoverish and immiserate one group as it provides wealth and superior social status to another.[14] Social closure can also reproduce social inequalities by allowing dominant-group members to hoard resources and opportunities that advantage them in competition and allocation processes going forward, sometimes for generations.[15]

Taken alone, however, such dynamics tell only part of a larger story. To see the rest, we must look to a process that scholars such as Keeanga-Yamahtta Taylor call "predatory inclusion."[16] Subjugation and exclusion create conditions that well-positioned people and organizations can exploit. People denied ordinary banking services, for example, become ripe targets for payday lenders that offer access to quick money at usurious rates. Because processes of predatory inclusion offer access to goods, services, or opportunities that have previously been denied, Louise Seamster and Raphaël Charron-Chénier explain, they are often "presented as providing marginalized individuals with opportunities for social and economic progress. In the long term, however, predatory inclusion reproduces inequality and insecurity for some while allowing already dominant social actors to derive significant profits."[17] Because processes of predatory inclusion are made possible by forms of deprivation, they sometimes allow people to satisfy significant unmet needs and wants (such as ready access to loans). Indeed, such people may, with good reason, prefer what they can get on predatory terms to having no access at all.

The history of Black urban ghettos in the US powerfully illustrates the process of predatory inclusion.[18] As Black people moved north in the Great Migration, they were blocked from entering White neighborhoods by numerous forms of social closure, including popular violence by White residents, government rules and procedures, and banking and real estate practices.[19] Though denigrated by Whites, the ghettos were, from their inception, always more than just places of exclusion. They were frequently sites of vibrant communities, and at the same time, spatial and social isolation made the ghettos *productive* for dominant groups. Deprived of other options, desperate residents filled the most exploitative jobs and bought inferior goods at inflated prices.[20] Denied prevailing mortgage rates, those who dreamed of homeownership entered exploitative bank loans, property deals, and contract-for-deed agreements.[21] Because Black residents were politically marginalized, they could be subjected to "urban renewal" projects that displaced them and their businesses to pave the way for development.[22] Today, many of these same neighborhoods are marked as primary targets for payday lenders, pawn shops, furniture rental shops, and other predatory business models.[23]

Through predatory inclusion, social groups are incorporated into intensive forms of *exploitation* and *expropriation*. The concept of exploitation has deep roots in Marxian analyses of capitalist labor relations. Forcibly separated from their common basis of survival, "free" individuals must sell their labor to those who own the means of production. Empowered in this manner, owners are able to exploit workers, paying them less than the full value of what they produce and pocketing the surplus as profits. Drawing on scholars such as Charles Tilly, we adopt a broader view: Exploitation operates when dominant actors "command resources from which they draw significantly increased returns by coordinating the efforts of outsiders whom they exclude from the full value added by that effort."[24] In this conception, the residents of urban ghettos were subjected to intensive exploitation not just as workers but also as consumers, caregivers, and more.

Expropriation refers to more direct, coercive takings, including acts of nationalization, uses of eminent domain, and colonial conquest and plunder.[25] The concept has been central to Marxian debates over primitive accumulation,[26] which guide Nancy Fraser's formulation: "Expropriation works by confiscating capacities and resources and conscripting them into capital's circuits of self-expansion." The types of "confiscated assets" that advance capital accumulation may include "labor, land, animals, tools, mineral or energy deposits—but also human beings, their sexual and reproductive capacities, their children and bodily organs."[27]

Expropriative takings come in many forms and can be productive in various ways. In some cases, such as chattel slavery, they may focus on bodily capacities and work by violently extracting productive and reproductive labor. In others, such as the uses of eminent domain in projects of "urban renewal," they forcibly seize possessions, such as community-controlled or private property.[28] Robert Nichols identifies a third variant of seizure in projects of dispossession, which *creates* property relations and ownership statuses.[29] Prior to colonization, Indigenous lands in North America did not exist, legally or socially, as owned property. "Possession does not precede dispossession" in this seizure of lands "but is its effect."[30] In other words, these lands became property only in the taking; the dispossessed were deemed "original owners" only after the fact. Closely related processes operate in debt-based predatory projects today. By imposing debts on impoverished people, governments and businesses create a form of property that they can leverage for further gain and sell to investors; they lay claim to possessions (i.e., future resources) that do not yet exist.

In sum, predatory projects can take many forms. All, however, are organized as unequal social relations in which conditions of group subjugation and exclusion enable processes of inclusion into targeted, intensive practices of exploitation or expropriation.

What, then, does a *relational* analysis of predation entail?[31] In the main, it works along two tracks, which largely define the agenda for our study. The first focuses on the "internal" relations and practices that constitute a predatory project.[32] Here, we ask: How is the project organized, what are its defining attributes, and how does it operate? How are key actors positioned in interdependent relations of cooperation and conflict? How do the various forms and sites of its operations work in complementary and contradictory ways? What logics of practice guide its enactment, and how should we understand their significance and effects?

The second track focuses on "external" relations, locating the predatory project on a broader landscape and analyzing how its operations may reflect or transform the social structures that surround it. How is a predatory project enabled, constrained, and molded by the historically specific configuration of political economy in which it emerges and operates? How are predatory practices shaped by the immediate organizational contexts—and the surrounding laws, institutions, and relations—in which they are embedded? Conversely, how might a predatory project help to reproduce and secure or transform the existing terms of a social order? In specific historical cases, how might predation play a role in reconstructing social hierarchies, shifting paths of political and economic development and generating or suppressing political struggle?

By drawing various types of extractive projects into a shared analytic frame, the concept of predation offers a way to connect seemingly disparate episodes, clarify their shared logics, and specify their similarities and differences. Their variations can be traced principally to political struggle and structural shifts in the broader social order. In the US context, liberal society and political economy have long had a co-constitutive relationship with predation. Neither can be well understood without attending to the other and to the ways they develop together over time.

Race, Gender, and Capitalism

In 1935, Ella Baker and Marvel Cooke published an article in *The Crisis* titled "The Bronx Slave Market." Reporting from the streets where Black women sold themselves as domestic day laborers, the authors explained that White women who suffered from the Great Depression also, in one sense, benefited from it. "Paradoxically, the crash of 1929 brought to the domestic labor market a new employer class. The lower-middle-class [White] housewife who, having dreamed of the luxury of a maid, found opportunity staring her in the face in the form of Negro women pressed to the wall by poverty, starvation, and discrimination."[33] The day labor jobs were rife with abuse, a fact that Baker and Cooke traced in part to "organized labor's limited concept of exploitation, which permits it to fight vigorously to secure itself against evil, yet passively or actively aids and abets the ruthless destruction of Negroes."[34] In a mere three pages, the authors paint a damning portrait of racially organized labor exploitation, its disregard by White labor leaders, and its powerful intersections with gender and care work.

Baker and Cooke's analysis exemplifies a long tradition of inquiry into the ways race, gender, and capitalism intersect and work in concert in specific times and places. In the twentieth century, this tradition advanced through pathbreaking works by scholars and activists such as W. E. B. Du Bois, Ida B. Wells, Walter Rodney, C. L. R. James, Cedric Robinson, Stuart Hall, Manning Marable, and Barbara Fields. This diverse tradition has, generally speaking, focused more consistently on race and class than gender.[35] Scholars today employ various frameworks for analysis, such as "racial capitalism" and "race and capitalism,"[36] and their engagements with gender continue to be uneven.[37] Collectively, however, this body of scholarship provides invaluable resources for understanding the social structural foundations of predation and the ways that predatory projects can transform the social orders in which they emerge.

Time and again, these studies have spotlighted what accounts of social inequality obscure when they focus narrowly on group-based exclusions:

the *incorporation* of subjugated groups into extractive relations that subsidize dominant groups and institutions. Reflecting on this history of plunder, Ta-Nehisi Coates observes: "When we think of white supremacy, we picture Colored Only signs, but we should picture pirate flags."[38] Manning Marable powerfully states the point in *How Capitalism Underdeveloped Black America*:

> Each advance in White [American] freedom was purchased by Black enslavement. . . . White state and corporate power is the product in part of Black powerlessness. . . . [Many] condemn the United States on the grounds that White society has systematically excluded Blacks as a group from the material, cultural and political gains achieved by other ethnic minorities. . . . But there is another point of view on the issue: Blacks occupy the lowest socioeconomic rung in the ladder of American upward mobility precisely because they have been "integrated" all too well into the system. . . . Capitalist development has occurred not in spite of the exclusion of Blacks, but because of the brutal exploitation of Blacks as workers and consumers.[39]

Michael Dawson and Emily Katzenstein use the term "regime of articulation" to refer to the distinctive ways that racism, patriarchy, and capitalism intersect and work together in specific times and places. Such regimes differ in many ways, but they also tend to share a more general and recurrent logic. Capitalist modes of accumulation, and efforts to justify them, have served as key sites for the production of race- and gender-based distinctions, ideologies, and practices.[40] These social hierarchies, in turn, have channeled groups and individuals into unequal positions in capitalist relations and divisions of labor.[41] Historically, the inequalities that have made capital accumulation possible—owner–worker, creditor–debtor, enslaver–enslaved, developed–underdeveloped, colonizer–dispossessed— have repeatedly been organized along racial lines.[42] Gender hierarchies have worked in concert to structure the domestic care and maintenance of exploitable labor, the types and terms of labor available to women and men, and the work of social reproduction needed to sustain capitalism.[43]

As they have dispelled the idea that capital is indifferent to social distinctions among the "interchangeable" wage laborers it exploits, scholars in this tradition have also focused attention on "hidden abodes" of expropriation and social reproduction.[44] Historically, where the necessary labors of care and social reproduction have been organized as unpaid or severely undercompensated forms of "women's work," they have served as particularly intensive sites of exploitation and violence for women marginalized by race and/or immigration status.[45] Similarly, racial markers, Dawson argues, have signposted "the division between full humans who possess the right to sell their labor and compete within markets, and those that are disposable, discriminated against, and ultimately [expropriated,] eliminated or superexploited."[46] Attention to these dynamics is essential for understanding how predatory criminal legal practices operate in the US today. As they intensively target race-class subjugated (RCS) communities for resource takings, these practices leverage the gendered organization of care to impose disproportionate financial and social burdens on women.[47]

Finally, scholarship in this tradition also frames our approach to understanding why and how predatory projects vary across times and places. This variation arises, first and foremost, because predatory projects are structured by the specific political economies in which they emerge. To make them effective, their creators must design (and often tweak) them so that they "work" on the existing legal, institutional, and social structural landscape. In this regard, Dawson and Katzenstein emphasize how racism, patriarchy, and capitalism operate as "semiautonomous" axes of structural change.[48] Major developments in one tend to reverberate through the other two. And in this manner, a "regime of articulation" that works smoothly for a period of time may eventually "develop antagonistic tendencies and conflicting demands that threaten the status quo."

Structural change, however, depends on human agency and political struggle. In *Black Marxism* and later books, Cedric Robinson directly tied what he called "racial capitalism" to the "Black radical tradition" of oppositional consciousness and action.[49] Regimes of "racial capitalism" that have functioned as oppressive social orders of accumulation have *also* operated as sites of resistance, rebellion, and efforts to imagine and build better worlds.[50] Moreover, the gendered injustices of such social orders have long been countered by the leading roles that women have played in the Black radical tradition.[51] In addition to driving changes in the structural conditions that organize predation,[52] oppositional action may also target specific predatory practices. For both reasons, predatory projects and their development cannot be well understood in isolation from the political struggles that attend them. As we will see, this insight is vital for understanding criminal justice predation in the US today.

Our discussion so far only begins to suggest the debts we owe to this tradition of scholarship, which has guided our study from its earliest stages. In the remainder of this section, we draw on this literature to more concretely develop the concept of predation through a discussion of what David Roediger calls "the intersectional convergence of slavery, settler colonialism, and women's reproductive labor" in early American history.[53]

*

From the colonial era through the Civil War, Black enslavement and Native dispossession operated in America as predatory projects on a vast scale, with Whites leveraging conquest, subjugation, and exclusionary containment to expropriate land and labor. The two projects were deeply entwined, in ways that went well beyond the practice of forcing enslaved Black workers to farm stolen Indigenous lands.[54] They also shared many features, such as long histories of resistance and struggle. Indigenous communities fought bloody battles against colonizers and resisted in ways large and small.[55] Enslaved people staged revolts, and flights from bondage known as *marronage*—undertaken not only as a path to freedom but also to pursue visions of a new kind of community—were common.[56] Indeed, as W. E. B. Du Bois demonstrated in a groundbreaking historical analysis, the end of chattel slavery depended, in no small part, on the "general strike" of enslaved people, who fled plantations to fight the Confederacy and strengthen Union forces.[57]

Nevertheless, the two projects differed in fundamental ways.[58] One focused on land and followed an eliminationist logic of removal, death, and assimilation. The other focused on labor and sought to multiply human beings in bondage as forms of wealth-generating property. Together, they help to illustrate how predatory projects in a single time and place can not only share features in common but also differ and interact. Studies of this period also provide a rich basis for showing how predatory projects operate as productive forces, capable of transforming political economies. We focus on how slavery and dispossession worked to produce racial distinctions, ideologies, and practices; fuel capitalist development; drive state building and organize the polity; and define the boundaries and meanings of democratic citizenship.

In an influential analysis, K-Sue Park calls out "the conceit that the existence of subordinated racial minorities is a phenomenon distinct from the predatory practices that plague them."[59] Slavery in North America was not initially limited to or organized by Blackness as a racial category.[60] Early interactions between European settlers and Native peoples were framed by many discourses of social contrast, but not in a manner defined as "racial."[61] As Patrick Wolfe explains, "colonizers did not set out to create a racial doctrine. They set out to create wealth."[62] In pursuit of wealth, they produced new racial boundaries, hierarchies, and ideologies.

Predatory projects in early America fueled race-making for at least three reasons: Differentiation was essential for their targeting and operation; their practices were based on social closure and acted as expressive demonstrations of unequal status and worth; and their defense depended on ideological justifications for group-based brutalities and takings.[63] Through predation, diverse peoples from Africa and North America were aggregated and delineated as racial groups. "In the sound-bite vocabulary of race," Wolfe explains, "the three points of the Atlantic triangle . . . Africa, America, and Europe became chromatized as Black, Red, and White."[64]

At all three points, predation in early America served as a crucible for the production of race- and gender-specific ideologies and stereotypes.[65] The independent, hardworking, White male citizen, taming the "wilderness" and ruling the patriarchal family, took root alongside images of White women that stressed civic virtue, moral restraint, dependence, caregiving, and domesticity.[66] Enslaved Black people were portrayed as apelike, morally and mentally inferior, devious, and less capable of feeling pain—the men framed as animalistic, aggressive, hypersexual, and dangerous; the women slotted into "controlling images" of the hypersexual Jezebel (legitimating practices of rape and forced reproduction) and the asexual mammy (happily nurturing the children of their oppressors).[67] Indigenous peoples were sometimes romanticized and fetishized as "natural" and "noble" but also portrayed as uncivilized, ungoverned, heathen, and savage in ways that justified dispossession.[68] In the settler imagination, Native women were either "Indian princesses," compliant and eager to aid White men, or overburdened, vice-prone, and sexually profligate "squaws." Native men were portrayed as barbarous, lazy, drunk, and brutal toward women.[69]

The logics of slavery and dispossession also generated distinctive laws of racial descent.[70] Under the legal doctrine of *partus sequitur ventrem*, all children of Black women were born Black and enslaved, regardless of paternity.[71] With the decline of the Atlantic slave trade, North American slavery depended ever more on the violent control of Black women's reproductive capacities.[72] Native dispossession, in contrast, advanced by making White paternity decisive. As Wolfe explains, "Indigenous people obstructed settlers' access to land, so their increase was counterproductive." Racial descent based on White paternity "straightforwardly furthered the logic of elimination. Thus, we cannot simply say that settler colonialism [and enslavement] have been targeted at particular races, since a race cannot be taken as given. It is made in the targeting."[73]

Predatory projects (and their race-making practices) were central to the construction and advancement of American capitalism in this era.

From the outset, colonial economic development was based on takings of Indigenous lands.[74] In the period between the Revolution and the Civil War, the US government acquired roughly 772 million acres through dispossession.[75] Large portions were distributed to build critical infrastructure and lay "the foundation of future American capitalism—private ownership and control of productive resources."[76] From 1787 to the Civil War, the US government transferred more than 200 million acres to White men at low or no cost.[77]

At the same time, dispossession operated as a seedbed for what Park calls "new predatory practices that shaped the market in America."[78] Analyzing the emergence of mortgage-based foreclosure, Park shows how financial innovations "racially bifurcated the colonial economy" and "advanced the development of racial ideology and the economy in tandem."[79] New lending and debt rules designed to facilitate dispossession were initially limited to Indigenous borrowers but later became common throughout colonial America.[80]

In the South, dispossession supplied the land for a plantation-based slavery economy. "Black labor," W. E. B. Du Bois wrote, "became the foundation stone not only of the Southern social structure, but of Northern manufacture and commerce, of the English factory system, of European commerce, of buying and selling on a worldwide scale."[81] Scholarship in recent decades has supported and elaborated on this assessment.[82]

Economists Thomas Piketty and Gabriel Zucman estimate that in the decades preceding the Civil War, "the market value of slaves was between one and two years of national income for the entire United States," and the total value of people in bondage (owned and traded) was greater than all the nation's factories, railroads, and canals combined.[83] Even these estimates understate the wealth produced. They do not include the riches generated by the products of slave plantations, trade in the materials they produced, slavery-dependent manufacturers and retail businesses, and slavery-based growth in the insurance, finance, and legal service sectors.

Like dispossession, slavery was a site of economic innovation. Plantation owners developed new approaches to labor surveillance, management, and accounting that spread to other sectors.[84] Eighteenth-century sugar plantations invented forms of specialization, synchronization, and regimentation that prefigured industrial factories.[85] Plantations also underwrote development in fields well beyond the pursuit of agricultural production, including medical scientific advances achieved through experiments on enslaved Black people.[86]

Dispossession and slavery were equally foundational for state building and democratic citizenship in the early republic. Enslaved workers supplied labor for government projects and generated wealth needed to expand state capacities.[87] Dispossession secured land for the development of public infrastructure at all levels of government.[88] Richard Young and Jeffrey Meiser conclude that the two predatory projects *made possible* "a prosperous, expanding, liberal-democratic Anglo-American society."[89] Precisely for this reason, dispossession and slavery played outsized roles in shaping the nation's political development.

As the framers of the US Constitution wrestled with tensions between liberal-republican political principles and their desire to protect elite wealth and power, they had little choice but to confront dispossession and slavery as existing modes of governance, central to the entire matrix of productive American inequalities. The two projects would prove critical for the framers' compromises and strategies. "The Constitution never mentions slavery . . . yet slavery is all over the document," David Waldstreicher writes, shaping its blueprint for political representation, government, and state powers.[90] Dispossession was no less important. The founders were gripped by fears that White class conflicts would generate overwhelming demands for wealth redistribution and political instability. Westward expansion and land transfers to White settlers, they came to agree, would unite the citizenry and cultivate allegiance to the state.[91]

The projects of slavery and Native dispossession also challenged the young state's limited capacities. Together, Ira Katznelson explains, they served as "pivotal driving motivations . . . shaping the small, flexible, effective American state. . . . American liberalism and illiberalism were entwined, as in a braid."[92] Pressures to secure the two projects and fears of violent reprisal stoked investments in the federal military and state and local militias, at the expense of other development agendas. In short order, these forces became "capable of achieving the greatest task of state builders: defining, expanding, and securing boundaries."[93]

The spoils of predation quickly created powerful White elites, highly invested in controlling government and its development. Southern plantation owners feared that the state's power to tax could be used to make slavery unprofitable, even to the point of abolition.[94] So, they fought relentlessly to restrict the taxes and tax-collection capacities needed to fund public investments and to block democratizing reforms that might weaken their grip on government policies. Over time, they constructed more durable political safeguards: a wealth-serving ideology that framed government taxes as existential threats to the freedoms of everyday people; constitutional limits on state taxation powers; political representation rules biased in their favor; and weak public institutions with restricted authority.[95]

Thus, as slavery and dispossession propelled state development along some paths, they hindered it along others. The same was true for the construction of democracy and citizenship in America.[96] In the colonial period, Edmund Morgan explains, the White "yeoman farmer came into his own," in a civic and political sense, only "because slavery relieved the small man of the pressures that had been reducing him to continued servitude" and land settlement allowed him to own property.[97] Through these developments, class divisions among White settlers became less stark and paramount.[98] Slavery and other forms of forced labor led many landed White elites to think that, going forward, domination of lower-class Whites might not be necessary to secure the brutal forms of labor their wealth depended on. It was only then that governing elites found common cause with their "yeoman constituency" and began to embrace the politically egalitarian ideals they championed in the War for Independence. In the pivotal state of Virginia, Morgan concludes, slavery made it possible for White elites "to nourish representative government in a plantation society," to "dare to speak a political language that magnified the rights of freemen," and to bring "Virginians into the same commonwealth political tradition with New Englanders."[99]

Before and after the founding, slavery and dispossession shaped the young nation's evolving civic ideals and laws of citizenship[100] as well as its distinctive visions of democracy, equality, freedom, consent, and sovereignty.[101] Settler colonization underwrote the development of an egalitarian "democracy of opportunity" tradition centered on honoring the productive labor of smallholder White men. Indigenous dispossession, Aziz Rana argues, "provided easy access to property, cut against oligarchic tendencies, and facilitated small-scale White producerist democracy."[102]

As Judith Shklar explains in an influential analysis, citizenship in early America developed and operated as a form of standing, not only in relation to civic peers and the state but in contrast to various inferior and excluded "others."[103] Danielle Allen goes further: In a society based on Black enslavement, Native elimination, and the patriarchal family, citizenship represented a shared standing to *participate in domination.*[104] Its meaning, per Cristina Beltrán, became inseparable from the authority to police the behaviors of subjugated groups and participate in the cruelties that such groups endure.[105]

As they underwrote citizenship, such forms of standing inhibited the expansion of democracy in America. To explain how, Joel Olson builds on Du Bois,[106] who, in *Black Reconstruction in America,* argued that white supremacy provided a "public and psychological wage"—a compensatory source of status and self-worth—to even the most impoverished and immiserated White Americans.[107] This wage, he explained, served as the basis for a cross-class White alliance that divided workers along racial lines, bonded White workers and owners, and, in various ways, impeded effective challenges to the exploitation of *all* labor.[108] A similar dynamic worked to sustain White elite dominance and impede pressures for democratization in the American polity, Olson argues. Civic standing based on superiority to racial inferiors stood in for (and dampened demands for) more empowered, participatory forms of citizenship rooted in collective self-governance.[109]

In these and other ways, slavery and dispossession operated as powerful, productive forces in early America, shaping the nation's social order and its political and economic development. The brief survey we have presented here provides a more concrete, historical basis for understanding the nature and significance of predatory projects. The object of our study, however, is not predation in general; it is the nexus of predation and criminal legal governance.

Criminal Legal Governance as a Support for Predation

Conceptually, the criminal legal domain is bounded by two contrasts: legal versus illegal and civil versus criminal. Thus, predatory criminal legal practices can be distinguished from those that are extralegal, such as the illicit methods of resource stripping that Bernadette Atuahene refers to as "stategraft."[110] They also can be contrasted with practices that operate under the auspices of civil law, such as predatory commercial lending.[111] In practice, however, predatory projects often blur and traverse such distinctions. Legal modes of predation may be sustained through illegal actions, and civil undertakings may rely on criminal legal authorities. In this section, we consider some important historical forms of predation that did not operate as criminal legal matters but were enabled, supported, and secured through criminal legal governance.

Consider again Native dispossession. Alongside military attacks and extralegal violence, land takings often advanced through strategically crafted civil laws and manipulative civil agreements such as treaties and property-sale contracts.[112] When tribes refused to leave their lands, however, brutal actions undertaken as "law enforcement" were used to force them out (or kill them) and establish social and spatial security. In such actions, "sheriffs, soldiers, and vigilante groups promoted social order through genocide and terror."[113]

As settlement progressed, policing and penal capacities grew and were put to greater use. In Texas, for instance, White colonists employed Rangers to clear out Native Americans and protect them from the threats that Indigenous people allegedly posed to their safety and property.[114] In the making of Anglo-American Los Angeles, Kelly Hernández shows, "Native American elimination" was a principal function of jails.[115] Local authorities "mostly used the county jail to cage substantive portions of the Native community, largely on public order charges. Establishing the rule of law . . . mostly meant denying Natives the 'right to *be*' in Los Angeles."[116]

A further innovation emerged in 1880, when federal officials created the US Indian Police (USIP), enlisting and authorizing Indigenous officers to police their own communities. One year later, the Annual Report of the Commissioner of Indian Affairs celebrated the USIP as a powerful new tool for projects of social control, assimilation, and elimination: "Well trained and disciplined, the police force . . . is a power entirely independent of the [Native] chiefs. It weakens, and will finally destroy, the power of tribes and bands. . . . It makes the Indian himself the representative of the power and majesty of the government of the United States."[117]

Slave patrols functioned as an early form of policing, hunting down people who ran away from their enslavers and deterring others from doing the same. To combat escapes and revolts, the patrols engaged in extensive surveillance, "assaulted rogue maroon communities, enforced the first passport system, broke up meetings of Blacks, and ransacked their homes, taking any found weapons as their own."[118] Over the long haul, Ben Brucato concludes, slavery "could not have existed or thrived without the professional and voluntary participation of all Whites in policing."[119]

As slave patrols secured human bondage, they also forged social bonds. White men of all classes, including formerly indentured servants, served together, united by the project of securing Black enslavement. The patrols supplied a firsthand, participatory experience of White identity and an affirmation of White citizenship rooted in Black subjugation. By incorporating poorer participants, the patrols also helped to make slavery and its defense into an object of personal investment for White men, even those who lacked property-ownership stakes in the institution.[120]

After the Thirteenth Amendment prohibited chattel slavery (and the Reconstruction period was put to an end), efforts to establish new forms of wealth-producing racial dominance became an overriding priority for southern White elites.[121] Criminalization proved critical in this task. Lawmakers passed "Black Codes" that severely limited formerly enslaved people's abilities to occupy public spaces and access jobs outside the most exploitative arrangements. Broad vagrancy laws criminalized Black people who did not work for White employers. Other codes made it illegal for Black people to fish, hunt, or freely graze livestock, restricting their ability to sustain themselves without working for White bosses.[122] "Apprenticeship" statutes were used to supply White families with Black child workers whose parents had died or been deemed unfit by the state.[123] The new regime of racial subjugation and exclusion facilitated the predatory *inclusion* of Black people into sharecropping and other deeply exploitative labor arrangements.[124]

Through the criminalization of Black life, many of the practices that enabled predation became technical matters of legal and penal administration.[125] Police and courts fed and served a ruthless Jim Crow regime of labor exploitation. In the state of Mississippi, police aggressively applied racially targeted laws through arrests.[126] If a detained individual could not pay the court's fine, David Oshinsky explains, "he could be hired out to any White man willing to pay it for him. Naturally, a preference would be given to the vagrant's old master, who was allowed 'to deduct and retain the amount so paid from the wages of such freedman.'"[127]

Courts played a similar role in peonage practices that forced debtors to work off what they owed to creditors. Outlawed in 1867, debt peonage continued well into the 1900s. Although a worker could not be bonded to an employer on the basis of a debt alone, White court officials held that if a worker "left service" without paying off their debt, they could be charged with fraud.[128] For the crime, debtors "could be fined, jailed, and bonded to the employer, who paid off the legal fees."[129] In Florida, courts treated any breach of the labor contract by a Black person as a crime. According to Eric Foner, transgressors were "whipped, placed in the pillory, and sold for up to one year's labor, while Whites who violated contracts faced only the threat of civil suits."[130]

In these and other ways, predation in the Jim Crow South routinely traversed the line between civil and criminal law. The same was true for the line between legal and extralegal. Predatory labor practices backed by law were routinely enforced through vigilante violence directed at Black people and their homes. Lynching was commonly seen as a noneconomic matter—a spontaneous response to egregious allegations against an individual (especially the claim that a Black man had raped a White woman). In a pathbreaking analysis, however, Ida B. Wells explained how lynching functioned as an extralegal support for a social order in which Black people served as "the wealth producers of the South—the hewers of wood and drawers of water, the servants of White men."[131] Although lynching operated outside the law, police and other government officials frequently aided White lynch mobs, participated in lynchings, or enabled them by turning a blind eye.[132] In a later work, Wells produced what Naomi Murakawa calls "a remarkably full inventory of violence" that clarified "its entangled economic, gendered, and racial dimensions," and showed how it worked through "legal and extralegal processes" to underwrite "the unearned accumulation of White economic and political power."[133]

The American South had no monopoly on racially targeted predation. In the North and Midwest after the Civil War, criminal legal practices supported predation primarily as tools of social and spatial closure and repression. During the first half of the twentieth century, millions of Black people migrated northward to escape racial terror and find steady work.[134] White business owners in the industrializing economy were eager to hire unskilled, exploitable workers and often recruited Black Southerners to make the trek.[135] Upon arrival, however, Black migrants were met by large numbers of Whites who "regarded them as inherently vile, congenitally inferior, and shorn of ethnic honor owing to the stain of slavery."[136]

Earlier, we described how the construction of Black ghettos in this period enabled various forms of predatory inclusion. Social and spatial containment, Loïc Wacquant writes, allowed well-positioned Whites to "maximize material profits extracted out of a group deemed defiled and defiling."[137] Policing and punishment were key to supporting such predatory practices and the conditions of subjugation and exclusion that made them possible.

Police were routinely deployed to contain and subdue residents of the ghetto. "Up until the 1960s," Alex Vitale writes, "this was largely accomplished through the racially discriminatory enforcement of the law and widespread use of excessive force."[138] Here, too, police supported extralegal methods of exclusion by ignoring, allowing, and sometimes contributing to violent White resistance to residential integration.[139] Of Harlem in the 1960s, James Baldwin wrote that the police "represent the force of the White world, and that world's real intentions are, simply, for that world's criminal profit and ease, to keep the Black man corralled up here, in his place. The badge, the gun in the holster, and the swinging club make vivid what will happen should rebellion become overt."[140]

The policing of "racial territory" maintained the boundaries of ghettos, marking their inhabitants as dangerous and debased and sustaining the enabling conditions of predatory inclusion.[141] In *Dark Ghetto*, Kenneth Clark analyzes the pervasive injustices that resulted: "Here is unproductive profit-making at its most virulent, using the Negro's flight from despair into the persistent dream of quick and easy money as the means to take from him what little money he has."[142] Housing offers a stark example. "Because Blacks were deprived of the mortgage bounty created by government guarantees," Mehrsa Baradaran explains, "they were ripe for exploitation by the sharks." Speculators bought cheap properties and then sold the homes to Black residents for three or four times the price. The buyers would soon learn that they had entered into a contract-for-deed agreement rather than a mortgage. And when they fell behind on payments, "they lost everything—house, down payment, and all the work they had put into the property."[143]

When Black residents rose up against the oppression and predation they endured, public officials deployed the police (and, at times, the military) to stamp out the unrest. Police and judges deemed protesters "criminals" and their actions "crimes," ignoring their political and economic grievances. Thus criminalized, disruptive challenges to predation were subdued through arrests and punishment. In the 1930s, for example, Chicago landlords who exploited the South Side ghetto saw declines in monthly payments due to the Great Depression. The "sight of landlords with law enforcement accompaniments serving eviction warrants and putting Black people out of their homes became commonplace," Simon Balto recounts.[144] In response, Black activists would wait for the authorities to leave the scene, then move the residents' possessions back into the homes. The activists described their actions as "community defense" and openly rejected "the authority of the police and sheriff's officers to actually enforce the eviction."[145] At the urging of the city's landlords, who saw the South Side as a "gold mine," the police led a violent counteroffensive that resulted in several deaths, many injuries, and a squashing of the rebellion. The mayor and police leaders blamed the violent conflict on "outside agitators."[146]

Northern and Midwestern ghettos and the labor regime of the Jim Crow South provide just two examples of how policing and punishment underwrote predation during the century after the Civil War. In the coal-rich regions of Appalachia, industrial capitalists built a brutal regime of natural resource extraction. Through violence, duplicity, and unscrupulous uses of civil law, companies separated poor rural people from their lands and established proprietary control.[147] Far more powerful than the isolated and desperate residents, they set up "company-controlled towns" and rapacious mining operations. John Gaventa uses the miner's paltry pay slip to illustrate the encompassing nature of the predatory regime, which extended well beyond the labor context. "A worker in the coal camp was reminded every two weeks [of the nexus between job and community], for from his wages were docked rent, services, goods purchased at the store, medical bills, even funeral expenses—all by the same employer. The slip symbolically fused the miner's dependence as worker, tenant, consumer, and citizen. . . . [M]isbehavior in the job could cause the loss of a home; failure to shop at the company store (where prices were often higher) could mean the loss of work; disobedience of a single rule could mean eviction from the game altogether."[148]

Mining interests went to great lengths to suppress resistance from workers and their allies, including by developing their own state-sanctioned law enforcement entities. In the late 1800s, Pennsylvania officials authorized the Coal and Iron Police, a wholly private unit, to fight union activity.[149] On behalf of employers, the private police used aggressive and, at times, brutal tactics to keep the miners in check. When hundreds of workers struck a company in Eastern Pennsylvania, they shot and killed nineteen miners and wounded many more in what became known as the Latimer Massacre of 1897.[150]

Throughout US history, government authorities and private interests (often in partnership) have used criminal laws and their enforcement to enable and secure predation. Criminal legal governance has not been limited to this auxiliary role, however. It has also served as a site of predation in its own right.

Criminal Legal Governance as a Site of Predation

Historically in the US, direct uses of criminal legal governance to pursue predatory practices have focused disproportionately on making the bodies of convicted people productive, especially through labor. Penal transportation emerged as an early example. For more than two hundred years, British authorities banished people convicted of various crimes to the American colonies. For a fee, merchants could bring the outcasts across the ocean and sell them into servitude "under private masters," generally for a term of seven years.[151] Most of the transported individuals were young men of lower class and status,[152] and they were typically sold in the colonies that were most desperate for workers.[153] Remarkably, these banished people accounted for roughly a quarter of all Brits who immigrated to the American colonies during the eighteenth century.[154]

Transportation, organized as a public–private partnership, was an innovative mode of penal governance. State authorities outsourced penal responsibilities to merchants, who profited from the sale of unfree or semi-free laborers to planters in the colonies. The planters, backed by law enforcement, profited from forced labor. Private enrichment was matched, on the other side, by benefits to government. Penal transportation allowed British officials to expand the use of criminalization and punishment for social control without needing to raise the tax-based revenues that larger penal institutions at home would have required.[155]

Transported individuals initially occupied a social position similar to indentured servants and, after completing their compulsory labor, were usually integrated into communities on similar terms.[156] In the mid-1700s, however, as rising numbers of transports arrived and "a new concern with the moral basis of citizenship" spread, their status shifted.[157] Now cast as a "form of pollution" in colonial life, they lost rights provided to "ordinary" indentured servants (including rights to vote and testify in court) and were effectively "set apart from the rest of the White population."[158]

White colonists began to associate penal workers more closely with people forced to labor through enslavement—a symbolic connection facilitated by the frequent use of both as "common field hands."[159] "By the late colonial period," Roger Ekirch observes, "thousands of convict servants . . . toiled under debased conditions not altogether different from Black slavery."[160] By the end of the colonial era, the "convict servant" designated a distinctive race-class position: below Whites in good standing, symbolically tied to the enslaved, yet still superior to Black people.

The heyday of penal labor predation in America came after the Civil War. Some of the first practices to emerge followed the logic of penal transportation, transferring control over convicted individuals to "private masters." In the South, state and local governments leased adults and children to businesses.[161] The leases were legal under the Thirteenth Amendment, which forbid slavery and involuntary servitude but sustained forced labor for people convicted of crimes. Working within the new framework, states created lease laws and procedures tailored to the needs of White elites. By the time Reconstruction ended in 1877, leasing programs had been installed in every state of the former Confederacy except Virginia.[162]

The rapid turn to leasing reflected the significant penal challenges that southern states faced after the Civil War. Northern troops had destroyed many prisons, and governments had few funds to invest in new facilities. The use of Black Codes, policing, and punishment to govern formerly enslaved people led to overcrowding in the jails and prisons that remained.[163] Leasing offered public officials a way to generate revenue, manage overcrowding, and sustain the aggressive criminal legal governance of Black people without raising taxes.[164] Ultimately, it would play a vital role in rebuilding the devastated political economy of the postwar South.

In addition to being an abusive and horribly unjust regime of punishment, the leasing system was "a system of labor recruitment, control, and exploitation particularly suited to the political economy of a postemancipation society."[165] In important respects, it dovetailed with sharecropping, tenancy, and debt peonage, all tools for turning "ex-slaves into an agricultural proletariat."[166] Christopher Muller illustrates the point by explaining how planters "gathered at courthouses and offered to pay the fines" of Black defendants so that they could force them "to work to pay off the debt. Defendants faced the impossible dilemma of choosing between the brutality of the convict lease system and the [fine-paying planters'] trap of peonage."[167]

More frequently, convict leasing supplied labor to industrial capitalists for dangerous projects such as railroad building, iron and coal mining, lumber cutting, and turpentine harvesting that were essential for rebuilding the region's economy.[168] Through such projects, the lease played a central role in the South's economic development in the decades following the Civil War.[169] At the same time, it generated millions in public revenue for state and local governments, subsidizing political development and a wide range of public projects.[170] Far from "a lag in southern modernity," Alex Lichtenstein concludes, the lease "was a central component in the region's modernization."[171]

As it remade the southern economy, leasing also produced eye-popping corporate profits. The companies worked the convicted laborers relentlessly in horrible conditions, knowing that if they got injured or died, the state would simply replace them. Importantly, the lease also weakened the position of "free" labor. Although they made up a small portion of the total corporate workforce, penal laborers "helped depress free wages [and] reduce recruitment costs, and provided a ready pool of strike breakers to confront the South's first industrial unions."[172]

Leasing mostly targeted Black men, but it ensnared Black women, too. Sarah Haley paints a vivid picture of labor camps in which women "had to cook, mend, clean, and launder and also had to hoe, plow, dig, mine, saw, pull carts, blacksmith, and grade the streets. . . . Black female labor continued to be conscripted for both production and reproduction, and their bodies were terrain for the consolidation of white supremacist ideology."[173] Convicted White women, like White men, were largely spared the lease.[174] They were not sent to the forced labor camps where Black women endured "fiendish acts of cruelty, often sexualized in nature, and [were] raped with impunity."[175]

Outside the South, penal labor predation in this era occurred mostly inside prisons. Labor was central to the modern "penitentiary ideal" of the period, which envisioned imprisonment as an enlightened penal practice.[176] Hard work, along with religious study and self-reflection, would transform wayward White men into self-disciplined, masculine citizens worthy of social and civic inclusion.[177]

Women were sometimes subjected to "reformative" programs of carceral labor as well. Michelle Jones and Lori Record describe how, starting in Kentucky in 1843, Catholic "Magdalene Laundries" emerged as "the first separate prisons for women in the United States."[178] Modeled after similar institutions in Ireland, these "religious-run, but state-sanctioned" facilities were designed to reform women whose "sexuality offended mainstream society."[179] The "fallen women" were criminalized and sentenced to the laundries, where they performed "hard labor without compensation and were subjected to cruel and sustained punishment, often for years."[180]

During the first half of the 1800s, forced labor became central to the operations of men's penal facilities throughout the US.[181] Prisons were generally subject to the principle of self-support, which prioritized keeping taxes low and government "relatively weak."[182] In pursuit of this principle, state officials entered revenue-generating contracts with private manufacturers who sought cheap, pliant labor. By the 1840s, Rebecca McLennan writes, most prisons in the US "closely resembled the great textile manufactories for which free American industry was becoming internationally known."[183] By the mid-1880s, almost 80 percent of imprisoned men provided steady labor for private interests (or a mix of private and public interests) inside prisons and in penal work camps.[184]

Like convict leasing, prison manufacturing reflected and influenced its surrounding labor conditions. Thus, as labor markets tightened during the Gilded Age, incarcerated workers became more valuable.[185] Prisons offered owners a cheap and reliable pool of workers and a way to undercut labor power at a time when unions were becoming larger and more assertive. Businesses that contracted with prisons tended to be fiercely anti-union, and they often used penal labor as a way to discipline their "free" employees.[186] In a number of Northern industries, McLennan notes, "free workers reported that, in an effort to boost production and tighten shop floor discipline, employers threatened to close up free shops and relocate to a prison unless the workers speeded up production."[187]

In the late 1800s, labor organizations fought back, targeting prison manufacturing and convict leasing operations. Their campaigns helped pass state and federal laws that imposed strict limits on private enterprises.[188] They did not, however, put an end to carceral labor predation. It was no longer legal to sell prison-made commodities on the open market, but incarcerated people could still be used as forced labor for prison construction and upkeep, as they had been since the earliest days of imprisonment in the US.[189] It also remained legal for prisons to manufacture and sell goods to other public agencies. Developed first in New York, this model quickly spread across the North, Midwest, and Far West.[190] In most of the nation, prison labor for upkeep and for production of goods sold for "state use" were considered normal operations.

Starting in the early 1900s, people incarcerated in the South were also put to work on penal farms that lowered government costs by producing food for prisons and other public facilities. Leaders such as Mississippi Governor James Vardaman championed the farms as a boon to all White taxpayers that, unlike convict leasing, would not benefit White elites at the expense of White workers.[191] In addition, Vardaman and others celebrated penal farm work as an effective way to teach young Black Southerners discipline, hard work, and deference to their racial superiors.[192] Because laws against selling prison-made commodities excluded agricultural goods, the farms allowed governments to pursue sales on the open market.[193] Thus, as they made public facilities less costly, penal farms generated extensive public revenues.[194] Parchman's farm in Mississippi, for example, quickly became a lucrative operation, generating enough money to sustain its own prison facilities and funnel resources into the state's budget.[195]

Prison farms are a useful case for illustrating how changes in the broader political economy can shift the racial targeting of penal predation. In Texas, as elsewhere in the South, penal farms were created primarily to control and exploit Black labor.[196] By the mid-1900s, they had grown into one of Texas's largest agribusiness operations, and their labor supply had largely shifted to Mexican Americans.[197] Through the Bracero Program and other developments, Mexican Americans had by this time become central to agricultural labor exploitation in the state as a whole.[198] As they were racially coded as disposable *farm* workers, they were also increasingly controlled through practices of criminalization and punishment. Soon enough, Mexican Americans made up a large portion of the labor force that toiled on prison farms without compensation.[199]

Alongside penal farms, state governments in the early 1900s adopted a practice that local governments had employed for decades: the "chain gang." In the mid-1800s, for example, White settlers in Los Angeles sentenced Native Americans (usually for low-level public order offenses) to road crews charged with public works duties, including the clearing of "horse manure, sewage, and dead animals" and the completion of "crucial road construction projects."[200] Later, Los Angeles officials would use chain gangs to control and exploit newcomers denigrated as "hobos" or "tramps," typically poor White men looking for work. In the late 1800s, stigmatizing discourses "cast White male itinerants as a new racial threat churning at the intersection of gender, labor, politics, sexuality, and kin structure within Anglo-America."[201] The chain gangs, Hernández argues, "consolidated and amplified the racialized exclusion of itinerant White men from the Aryan City of the Sun while incorporating their marginalization into the making of the modern city."[202]

As states shifted away from convict leasing, they increasingly turned to chain gangs. The transition was supported by the federal government, and it significantly changed the role that penal governance played in the southern political economy. As each state government made the shift, Lichtenstein explains, it "abandoned its role as a recruiter and seller of

forced labor . . . [for] primarily extractive industries" and began to operate as "the direct exploiter of that labor in an effort to build and maintain
transportation infrastructure."[203] Chain gangs were run by governments,
and they focused on public works, but the projects they carried out also
contributed to economic expansion and business profitability throughout
the South.

The US government adopted similar practices to advance imperial
projects abroad. When the Thirteenth Amendment was passed in 1865,
it allowed penal labor practices to continue "within the United States, *or
any place subject to their jurisdiction.*" The construction of the Panama Ca-
nal, which proved vital for the expansion of US commercial and military
might, offers a case in point. Starting in 1908, US colonial authorities
forced people convicted of crimes (mostly low-level "morality" offenses)
to carry out the backbreaking work needed to complete the project.[204] The
road crews consisted largely of migrant workers considered to be Black,
many of whom came from Barbados, Jamaica, and Martinique. Surveying
the history of such projects, Benjamin Weber concludes that the "federal
government used 'slaves of the state' to build infrastructure, establish
racial hierarchy, and consolidate power within *and beyond* US borders."[205]

Several decades later, federal authorities turned war abroad into a
basis for labor predation at home. During World War II, the US government deemed 120,000 Japanese Americans *potentially* criminal traitors,
based solely on their national ancestry, and detained them in "internment
camps." Involuntary servitude was the norm. Detainees were forced to
grow their own food, do construction work inside the camps, labor in the
fields of privately owned farms, build public infrastructure, and produce
supplies for the war effort.[206] In selecting sites for the camps, federal
officials deliberately favored locations where insufficient labor supplies
impeded agricultural production or the completion of infrastructure projects, both public and private.[207]

In this same period, state and local governments began to deploy
imprisoned workers to conserve public lands and "provide hard labor
during emergencies," such as floods, mudslides, hurricanes, tornadoes,
snowstorms, or forest fires.[208] During World War II, California created a
network of prison forestry camps that specialized in firefighting, flood
control, reforestation, and other conservatory projects. Between 1959
and 1967, roughly 18 percent of California's prison population worked
in the camps, which became common across the West but also operated in
the more urban, industrial states of the Northeast.[209] State leaders touted
the camps as demonstrations of their commitment to rehabilitative ideals.[210] Through hard outdoor work and public service, the camps would
"turn prisoners into citizen soldiers."[211]

Conditions inside prisons were so awful that performing difficult, dangerous work—at exploitative wages, in a remote camp, far from family and friends—seemed like an appealing proposition to many incarcerated people.[212] Camp labor also offered a range of valued benefits that were scarce in the prisons: the *potential* to win positive social recognition, experience a sense of civic belonging, and learn skills that might be useful after release. Seen from the grim confines on the inside, participation in the camps held great promise. The promise, however, often turned to disappointment as the harsh realities of camp life set in.[213]

Although labor has stood at the center of carceral predation for most of US history, it is not the only way that the bodies of imprisoned people have been made productive. From the 1940s the 1970s, researchers conducted thousands of experiments in US prisons, testing and developing cosmetics, drugs, and even weapons of war on their captive populations. In 1973, roughly half of all US states had one or more prisons running human experiments. Pennsylvania had nine.[214]

Here as in other cases, harsh prison conditions encouraged people to volunteer. Participation in an experiment paid more than a normal prison job.[215] For some, it was the only way to get needed medical care.[216] It offered prisoners a rare respite from the pains of prison life and, in some cases, even an opportunity to socialize with outside staff.[217] Equally important, the studies' risks were often obscured. Doctors were supposed to obtain consent, but many did not.[218] At Holmesburg Prison in Philadelphia, the men "had very little idea, if any, of what ingredient, solution, chemical, or drug they were actually testing."[219] Even so, researchers required subjects to sign release forms in order to protect themselves and their funders from legal action.[220]

The remarkably wide range of studies, Bernard Harcourt argues, played a "vital role" in the political economy of wartime America, making "unuseful bodies useful to the state" during World War II and later Vietnam.[221] At Holmesburg Prison, researchers performed "chemical-warfare tests for the army and the CIA," as well as "mind-control experiments" that aimed to turn psychoactive substances into a "truth drug" for interrogations of Soviet spies.[222] The US Atomic Energy Commission funded a prison-based study that cut and irradiated subjects' testicles in order to determine how much radiation astronauts could withstand during their missions.[223]

The researchers and their private backers profited handsomely. A "doctor with good prison contacts," Jessica Mitford notes, could "handily double or triple his regular income."[224] Some did far better. Albert Kligman became a millionaire by developing the anti-acne medicine Retin-A.[225] The studies were even more lucrative for corporations such as Dow Chemical,

Johnson & Johnson, Merck, DuPont, R. J. Reynolds, Wyeth, Upjohn, and Parke-Davis.[226] The companies bought human subjects in prisons for a small percentage of what recruitment would have otherwise cost.[227] By using prisons for dangerous phase 1 drug tests, they dramatically cut their investment costs.[228] And in many cases, prison experiments allowed for research that otherwise could not have been pursued at all, given the risks and hardships involved.[229]

Imprisoned people suffered greatly to generate such profits, enduring conditions ranging from hair loss, nail injury, and scarring to all sorts of debilitating physical and mental illnesses.[230] As they learned what had been done to them and why, many felt deceived and dehumanized.[231] Allen Hornblum reports that many of the Black men who participated in studies at Holmesburg Prison came to "regard the medical profession as torturers rather than healers" and felt that they would "never be able to trust doctors again."[232]

In the 1970s, government regulations and research protocols strictly limited human experimentation in prisons, largely in response to political mobilization.[233] Fierce campaigns for racial and economic justice had begun to focus on conditions of incarceration, and prisoners protested and rioted.[234] Bolstered by scandalous media investigations and public revelations regarding the Tuskegee syphilis study, activists and advocates turned prison research on disproportionately Black people into a target of outrage and condemnation. By the mid-1970s, there was "'overwhelming' opposition to prison medical testing," Keramet Reiter explains; government action was "the culmination of public, political, legal, and regulatory foment."[235]

In sum, throughout US history, criminal legal institutions have served as major sites of predation in their own right. From the colonial era through the 1970s, their predatory practices focused overwhelmingly on the bodies of criminally convicted people, and mostly worked to make them productive through various regimes of penal labor. The period we study in this book, from the 1980s to the present, has been marked by a dramatic shift toward practices that strip resources from legally entangled people and their communities by imposing financial charges and debts, enforcing payments, and seizing assets. Many historical precedents can be found for these practices and, as we discuss in chapters 2 and 3, some were quite important in particular times and places. Even the most substantial among them, however, pale in comparison to their contemporary counterparts. There is no equivalent in US history for the scale and intensity of financial takings today, their pervasiveness and diversity across criminal legal institutions, or their reach into the most policed and punished communities.

Conclusion

In this chapter, we have specified predation as a social science concept, an integral facet of capitalist "regimes of articulation," and a productive force in American political economy. We have explored how criminal legal governance has served as both a support for and a site of predation in US history. Throughout, we have emphasized how predatory and liberal aspects of the social order operate together, as two sides of an evolving, co-constitutive relationship.

The two have never had an entirely peaceful coexistence. Liberalism, after all, began as a modern challenge to feudal ideologies of absolutism and natural social hierarchy, championing individual rights and freedoms.[236] Asserting the equal moral worth of individuals, liberalism treats the freely entered agreement as a decisive standard of legitimacy for states and societies (via the social contract) as well as economic relations (via market exchange).[237] "The liberal individual," Charles Mills explains, "is supposed to be protected by the liberal state, and any infringement of his or her rights corrected for."[238] For these and other reasons, liberal ideals have provided important resources for challenging domination and predation throughout US history.[239] In principle and practice, this tension points to an important puzzle: How have the practitioners and beneficiaries of predatory projects reconciled them with the liberal commitments they so often celebrated in their stories of America and professed as legal, political, and economic ideals?[240]

Carole Pateman and Charles Mills suggest that an essential starting point is found in the history of liberalism itself.[241] As an "ideal theory," liberalism espouses universal principles. In practice, however, its principles have always been bounded and organized by racial and gender domination. "White men," Mills writes, "were deemed fully capable of creating the sociopolitical order, but White women and nonwhite 'savages' and 'barbarians' were not. White men were represented as morally equal to one another, but White women and nonwhites were depicted as morally unequal."[242] As it promoted individual rights, freedoms, and equalities, liberalism also served as "the exclusionary, hierarchical ideology of the racial-gendered system of modernity: racial patriarchy."[243] The social contract, in reality, took the form of a "domination contract," an agreement among White men, premised on and concerning the subjugation of "inferior" others.[244]

Specified in this way, liberalism can be seen as providing resources for challenging predation *and* for organizing and justifying it. From the outset, White colonizers tended to see conquest, subjugation, and expropriation as necessary bedrocks for liberal democracy and republican freedom—essential to their meaning and realization.[245] Predatory projects were "liberal" by virtue of what they produced and for whom: the foundations of White male citizenship and a prosperous, rights-based Anglo-American political economy. Symbolically and materially, Aziz Rana explains, White men's freedoms were understood as premised on their enabling counterparts: the servile positions of people who lived "permanently under the cloud of possible compulsion and subjection to the arbitrary will of another," including the enslaved, the dispossessed, the imprisoned, the indentured, and the dependents of the patriarchal family.[246]

Closely related discourses have justified predatory practices as necessary to defend liberal society and government. Throughout US history, White elites have promoted and exploited demonizing portrayals of menacing figures, such as the savage Indian warrior; the hypersexual, violent Black man; and the lawless, deviant criminal. They have justified predatory practices, and actions to enable and secure them, as imperative measures to eradicate existential threats or control, contain, or reform dangerous people. White fears of plantation revolts and Indigenous tribal attacks rested on something more than just the potential for losses of property and wealth: The panicked thought that a revolutionary inversion of the social order (and its predatory projects) could subject *White people* to systematic violence, enslavement, and genocide.[247]

White elites also engaged in concerted efforts to make predatory practices look like normal transactions, consistent with liberal principles. They authorized them through duly agreed upon laws and doctrines and, in many cases, dressed them up in the trappings of the freely entered contract. Indeed, legal discourses and contractual procedures run like a connective thread through the predatory histories of slavery, Jim Crow, the Black ghetto, the various incarnations of penal labor, and the consent-form ceremonies of prison experiments. They were especially prominent and important in projects of Indigenous dispossession.

From the outset, the European doctrine of "discovery" granted first-to-arrive conquerors exclusive control over Indigenous lands and their inhabitants.[248] The doctrine of terra nullius deemed Indigenous lands empty and uncultivated sites of wilderness, devoid of sovereign government. In so doing, Carole Pateman argues, terra nullius "provided an answer to one of the most fundamental questions of modernity. Why was it legitimate for Europeans to sail across oceans and 'plant' settlers in (i.e., colonize) faraway territories? . . . In the political theory and the law of nations of the seventeenth and eighteenth centuries it was argued that if land is *terra nullius* then it may rightfully be occupied."[249] Colonizers renewed and strengthened this veneer of liberal legitimacy through repeated rituals of freely entered contract. Government treaties "imposed liberal contractualism upon the tribes," Michael Rogin explains, creating "a fiction of Indian freedom to disguise the realities of coerced consent, bribery, [and] deception . . . [and allow] Indian expropriation to proceed under the color of law."[250] Later, the Dawes Severalty Act of 1887 would turn private property-sale contracts into a primary basis for deceptive and coercive land takings.[251]

Discourses that attribute inferior traits to subjugated groups have also worked to reconcile predation and liberalism. In theory and practice, proponents of liberalism have long argued that its commitments to individual autonomy and choice should be extended to people who lack certain capacities (such as young children). Historically, many of the traits attributed to subjugated groups have made it seem *unreasonable* to incorporate them into liberal rights and statuses, or to judge their management according to liberal moral and political standards. Such groups have been portrayed as lacking the capacities needed for rational action, moral self-rule, and political self-governance. The purported moral depravity of lawless "criminals," the irrationality of women, and the myriad deficiencies of uncivilized "barbarians" have made them unsuitable for social and political inclusion. Dehumanizing portrayals of racial "others" have gone even further, pushing targets of predation into a liminal status between human and nonhuman animal (or monster).[252]

As they asserted that subjugated groups lacked the capacity for liberal self-rule, discourses of group inferiority provided a powerful basis for paternalist and managerial rationales. Paternalist rhetoric cast enslaved people as childlike family members who received beneficent care and supervision for their own good, but as Walter Johnson explains, it operated more as "a pose that slaveholders put on for one another than as a praxis through which they governed their slaves."[253] Indeed, paternalist rewritings of predation have typically circulated among White elites as self-serving rationales, largely divorced from the brutality of predatory practices. In one era after another, state authorities have stressed that the forced labor imposed on imprisoned people was for their own benefit—a means of rehabilitation and uplift. In 1831, the US Supreme Court held that Native Americans existed "in a state of pupilage . . . their relation to the United States resembles that of a ward to his guardian."[254] Indigenous peoples, White elites told one another, needed to be confined to reservations and schools where they could be cared for, civilized, and assimilated.

Related rationales stressed the societal importance of enlightened resource management, often linking it to the White Christian man's duty "to bring the things of the earth to a state of usefulness."[255] "Justifications of dispossession," David Roediger explains, "connected expansion to the ability of White settlers to manage nature's gifts, including slaves."[256] White men portrayed themselves as uniquely qualified to manage the lives and labors of Black people, to make the most of Black women's reproductive capacities, and preside over land more effectively than Indigenous peoples.[257]

Finally, the coexistence of predation and liberal ideals in America has depended, in no small part, on dynamics of ignorance, indifference, and disavowal. Throughout American history, large numbers of White Americans (especially elites) have been able to go about their day-to-day lives without directly confronting or giving much thought to predation. The most jarring forms of violence, cruelty, and suffering have generally taken place in sequestered or distant sites, such as the plantation, frontier, or prison. Social and spatial isolation has made it easier for advantaged Americans to ignore, deny, or minimize predation and its harms. Most people have also received a steady diet of stories and teachings that have erased and rewritten the predatory foundations of the American social order.[258] These processes have facilitated what Mills calls "motivated ignorance"—a state of unknowing that allows dominant-group members to sustain their positive views of self and society, undisturbed by the injustices that make their life conditions possible. This type of ignorance tends be a site of deep personal and social investments. Even when confronted with powerful contrary facts, it often resists correction and "refuses to go quietly."[259]

Discourses that vilify and degrade subjugated groups have made it even easier for advantaged Americans to respond to predation with social indifference. As a general matter, the liberal social contract—based on individual responsibility for choices and their consequences—implies few obligations to come to the aid of others.[260] Against this backdrop, advantaged groups are all the more likely to look past injustice and suffering: "It is easier to be indifferent to the misery of others," Pateman explains, "if those involved are seen as having brought their distress upon themselves, or are perceived as very different, as alien, as worth less, as inferior, as barely human or as another 'race.'"[261]

Throughout American history, predatory projects have been deeply entwined with the nation's celebrated liberal ideals and institutions. The question of how the two might be reconciled has been a long-standing preoccupation for political and economic elites. Predatory practices have never been static, however; they have shifted and taken various forms over time. Political challengers have won institutional reforms and put an end to many of the practices discussed in this chapter. Well-positioned public and private actors have often adapted in response, creating new bases for predatory inclusion into extractive relations. Predation has been a perennial feature of American life, but predatory projects have come and gone. In the remainder of this book, we analyze a predatory regime that has transformed criminal legal governance over the past four decades and continues to operate throughout the nation today.

PART ONE

Operations

2 * Predatory Uses of Police and Courts

James Morrow needed dental work. His job at the Tyson chicken plant in Fayetteville, Arkansas, did not pay much, but he saved what he could. Finally, in August 2007, he had the $3,900 he needed and set off for Houston, Texas, in search of the dentist's office in a local mall. Morrow's drive took him through Tenaha, Texas, which is where he noticed the blue lights of the police car behind him. The officer said he was "driving too close to the white line," and began asking questions about his travel plans and the cash in his car. Skeptical of Morrow's story and claiming to detect an "odor of burned marijuana," the officer took Morrow to the local jail. Though the Tenaha police did not find contraband in the vehicle, they held Morrow overnight and impounded his car. No charges were brought, but police expressed suspicion that his belongings were illicit. He would not be released, they said, until he signed away the property, transferring it to the police department under the state's civil asset forfeiture law. When Morrow reluctantly agreed, the cops dropped him unceremoniously "on the side of the road with no money, no vehicle, and no phone." "Don't even bother getting a lawyer," Morrow recalled a police officer telling him. "The money always stays here."[1]

Although he may not have realized it at the time, Morrow did not just get caught up in an isolated, small-town money-making operation. Like millions of other people in the US today, he became fodder for a nationwide regime of resource extraction in which state-sanctioned authorities act as agents of legal plunder—and do so in the name of criminal justice. Over the next two chapters, we will analyze the growth, targeting, and operations of this regime.

Setting aside, for the moment, practices that work through penal custody and community supervision, we begin with the extractive operations that, in the last four decades, have taken root in policing and judicial institutions. From the biggest cities to the smallest towns, American court and police authorities strip resources from communities through predatory uses of fines and fees, asset forfeitures, and methods of private debt enforcement.

Many people from advantaged groups can relate to the idea of revenue-driven police and court practices in some way. They may have a story about getting a ticket from a small-town speed trap that seemed designed to shake down drivers from out of town. They might have heard that police give more tickets at the end of the month because they have to meet citation quotas. Or maybe they've had to appear in a criminal court at some point and walked away stunned by all the financial charges they racked up. In advantaged communities, however, people do not live their lives in a world saturated by aggressive and extractive law enforcement. Their neighborhoods are not filled with people who have been targeted by predatory practices and know firsthand the life-altering consequences of criminal legal costs and debts. Like all forms of criminal justice predation today, court- and police-centered practices target race-class subjugated (RCS) communities most intensively.[2] They incorporate other disadvantaged communities to various degrees and only occasionally ensnare the most advantaged members of society.

We begin with a discussion of how police and courts have used financial charges, debts, payments, and asset seizures in earlier eras of US history. We then analyze the practices that government authorities use today to seize cash and goods based on asset forfeiture laws. Next, we explore extractive uses of fines and fees, focusing first on police and then on courts. Finally, we show how criminal legal authorities act as backstops and enforcers for rapacious debt-and-payment operations in banking, housing, and other commercial domains.

The Past as Prologue

As explored in the previous chapter, for most of US history, penal labor and the enforcement of intensive labor exploitation stood at the center of criminal justice predation. Since the 1980s, the balance has shifted toward practices that operate through financial charges, payments, debts, collections, and asset takings. Although the changes have been historic, it is equally important to see the continuities that tie the present to the past. Penal labor predation remains common in the US today, and fines, fees, and asset seizures have a long pedigree in American criminal legal governance.

Monetary fines have served as a common penalty for crimes since the colonial era, especially for low-level offenses.[3] Methods for enforcing payments have historically included seizures of property, indentured labor, corporal punishment, and imprisonment.[4] Courts in earlier eras also paved the way for contemporary practices by using the proceeds generated by fines to cover a portion of their administrative costs.[5]

Notably, however, the most expansive and systematic use of fines as a tool of predation did not operate by turning financial payments into revenue; it worked as a supply mechanism for projects of forced labor. From the end of the Civil War through the 1940s, police and courts in southern states used Black Codes and other racially targeted laws and ordinances to shower fines on impoverished Black residents.[6] In many cases, White plantation owners stepped in to pay the fines and then, based on peonage laws, forced individuals to work for them without wages in return.[7] Incarceration for nonpayment routinely pushed people into predatory labor operations like convict leasing and chain gangs. In recent decades, governing officials have built a different kind of fine-based regime in the US—one that generates revenue more directly through financial takings and does so on a far larger scale than ever before.

Criminal legal fees have an equally long history in America. From the colonial period until the Progressive Era, public and private legal authorities were frequently paid by the case for actions such as apprehending suspects, issuing subpoenas, pursuing prosecutions, and securing convictions.[8] It was common for police and court officials to receive direct payments from individuals, and some jurisdictions even created fee schedules that listed prices for resolving types of criminal cases.[9] In the nineteenth and early twentieth centuries, justices of the peace played a central role in adjudicating low-level civil and criminal cases, and they mostly funded their pay and operations through charging fees.[10] In the main, however, individuals who accused *others* of wrongdoing and sought redress were responsible for the fees.[11] Indeed, as Michael Willrich explains, this is why the anti-corruption campaigns that bedeviled "fee-chasing" police magistrates and justices of the peace almost always charged that the officials "tipped the scales of justice in favor of their best customers: perennial litigants [especially debt collectors] and prosecutors."[12]

Although there were exceptions, it was quite rare for authorities to impose fees on accused or acquitted individuals for the costs of policing or adjudication. From the nation's founding onward, American lawmakers shielded such individuals from financial charges in the vast majority of criminal cases, rejecting practices that were routine in England and its colonies.[13] It was more common for courts to add fees to the penalties they imposed on convicted individuals. Nicholas Parillo argues that even this practice was not designed to raise revenue or intensify punishment; it served mainly as a way to protect the innocent from false accusations. With pay contingent on conviction, lawmakers reasoned, prosecutors would forgo cases that lacked strong evidence of guilt.[14] Beth Colgan contests this view, arguing that *in practice* court officials frequently pursued and valued the fees they charged to convicted individuals because of the revenues they generated.[15] While they differ on the purposes and uses of the fees, these scholars agree that criminal legal authorities rarely forced accused or acquitted individuals to pay for administrative costs, and the fees that courts sometimes added to conviction-based penalties tended to make up a small portion of the case-based payments that funded their operations as a whole.

During the Progressive Era, reformers targeted case-based payments as they fought to end corruption and make independent civil service a cornerstone of the administrative state. They created new rules and programs designed to professionalize criminal legal governance and carried out a "salary revolution" to replace fee-based funding with routinized wages.[16] Publicly financed salary systems were reinforced by rules, training programs, and ethical codes designed to end the biases and temptations of pay-for-service schemes. Fee practices persisted in some jurisdictions, but on a far smaller scale. And although progressive reformers fell well short of ending police and court corruption,[17] they established commitments to public funding and professionalization that shaped the trajectory of criminal legal governance for decades to come.[18]

Like fines and fees, asset seizure practices can also be traced back to the nation's colonial era. British customs officials during this period frequently used writs of assistance to seize "suspected contraband" and retain a substantial portion of the property they took.[19] In fact, legal scholars Eric Blumenson and Eva Nilsen argue, the "financial incentives [that the writs created for] police lawlessness and selective enforcement . . . were among the key grievances that triggered the American Revolution."[20] At the nation's founding, the Fourth and Fifth Amendments to the US Constitution established explicit protections against "unreasonable searches and seizures" and stated that no person shall be "deprived of . . . property without due process of law."

Nevertheless, federal officials quickly created new legal grounds for forfeiture practices and used them to enforce shipping restrictions related to the slavery trade, piracy and smuggling, bans on exporting particular goods, and nation-specific embargoes.[21] Throughout US history, "vice laws" have authorized targeted domestic uses of forfeiture, particularly in cases involving the illegal production and sale of alcohol.[22] In earlier eras, just as today, criminal legal authorities have also stripped people of goods that are illegal for them to possess per se (e.g., outlawed drugs) and property that they have been convicted of acquiring through theft, fraud, or some other criminal act.

In sum, asset forfeiture practices in America today have many historical precedents. But in their reach, scale, and systematic organization, these operations have no historical equivalent. In 1978, federal officials passed what is considered to be the first legislation in US history to authorize the seizure of assets deemed in some way to be the indirect "proceeds" of criminal acts, and to do so through accusations leveled at the property rather than the individual.[23] As we will see, legislative action in the 1980s dramatically expanded the scope of such takings and integrated actors at all levels of government into a common network for sharing the revenues they generated. Like fine-and-fee practices, asset seizures connect the present to the past and underscore continuities in America's long history of criminal justice predation. In all three cases, however, the 1980s and '90s marked the start of an extraordinary period of growth and transformation.

Asset Forfeiture as Legal Plunder

In October 2014, the news satire program *Last Week Tonight with John Oliver* ran a segment on asset forfeiture.[24] Mixing laugh lines with outrage and disbelief, the host explained how police officers sworn to "protect and serve" were confiscating billions of dollars' worth of people's cash, cars, homes, and other property. Remarkably, the takings were based on nothing more than an allegation that something owned by an individual had been used or obtained in a criminal manner. Lampooning the idea of a nonhuman object standing accused, Oliver ridiculed real cases with titles such as *United States v. Approximately 64,695 Pounds of Shark Fins* and aired fake footage of cops handcuffing a sofa and a lawyer interrogating a pile of cash. As Oliver made clear, though, the subject was no laughing matter. Since the 1980s, asset forfeiture has become a major tool of criminal justice predation and government revenue.

Under civil asset forfeiture, federal and state laws authorize police to confiscate property that they believe is connected to criminal activity, often without charging the owner with any crime.[25] Unlike forfeitures imposed as sentences for crimes, no conviction of the individual is needed. Accused goods are guilty until proven innocent and may be seized on the spot. The burden of proof then falls on the former owner, who can reclaim their belongings only by showing, through a costly court challenge, that their stuff has no criminal history. Many discover that the value of what has been taken from them is considerably less than what it would cost to retain a lawyer, and partly for this reason, very few asset seizures are contested.[26]

The transformation of asset forfeiture into a routine law enforcement practice began in the 1980s, when federal officials launched the "war on drugs." The call to war initially drew a tepid response from officials at lower levels of government, who worried that a greater focus on drug use and distribution would divert resources from more serious crimes, like murder and rape. Desperate to get them on board, the Reagan administration appealed to material self-interest. As part of a major new assistance program for state and local law enforcement, federal lawmakers replaced open-ended block grants with targeted funding, including sums that *had* to be used for the war on drugs.[27] They also rewarded cooperative localities with military-style weaponry and other equipment.[28] Finally, to give enforcement agencies a more direct financial stake in the drug war, federal lawmakers expanded asset seizure laws and made them more permissive.

Federal legislation passed in 1970 already authorized enforcement agencies to confiscate drugs and any property used to manufacture or transport them. The resulting revenues went directly into the US Treasury's General Fund, however, so state and local agencies did not have material incentives to pursue them.[29] Federal officials changed this calculus in the 1980s by passing laws that allowed agencies at *all* levels of government to keep substantial portions of forfeited assets.[30]

The most significant innovation was *equitable sharing*, a program that allowed state and local agencies to retain up to 80 percent of the assets they seized under federal forfeiture laws.[31] "Suddenly," Michelle Alexander explains, "police departments were capable of increasing the size of their budgets, quite substantially, simply by taking the cash, cars, and homes of people suspected of drug use or sales."[32] Equitable sharing set a spiraling dynamic in motion: Police agencies could now use seized assets to finance operational growth, which, in turn, produced greater opportunities and capacities for seizing assets.[33]

As state laws expanded on the new federal rules, drug policing operations increasingly focused on forfeiture.[34] The new incentives fueled tactical innovations like the reverse sting, in which police officers pose as drug dealers and lure people into illegal purchases.[35] Eric Blumenson and Eva Nilsen explain: "The chief attraction of the reverse sting is that it allows police to seize a buyer's cash rather than a seller's drugs (which have no [budgetary] value to the seizing agency). . . . Whether the suspects were engaged in major or trivial drug activity, and whether the strategy actually placed more drugs on the street, were of little, if any, importance. Even if a sting targeted a drug dealer, the police might defer the operation until the dealer sold some of the drugs to other buyers in order to make the seizure . . . more profitable."[36]

Eager to supplement their budgets, local leaders sometimes issued explicit directives to seize more assets. In New York City and Washington, DC, for example, officials instructed police to seize cars and cash from people who appeared to be "coming into the city to buy drugs," and specified that money was more valuable than drugs because the latter would have to be destroyed.[37] This emphasis on the *appearance* of illicit intent fueled the "profiling" of drivers, passengers, and cars for traffic stops and searches. According to Sandra Guerra Thompson, police agencies encouraged officers "to target Black and Hispanic males because of the common perception that drug dealers [likely to hold significant assets] come from those segments of the population."[38]

As police and prosecutors ramped up forfeiture practices, the revenue poured in. By 1987, the US Drug Enforcement Administration (DEA) had become a more or less self-financing operation, pulling in seizure-based funds at a rate greater than its yearly budget.[39] In total, the US Department of Justice (DOJ) seized more than $1.5 billion in assets between 1985 and 1991, a sum that rose to $2.7 billion over the next five years.[40] The new revenues helped to resolve tensions between the Reagan administration's calls to expand crime-fighting operations *and* reduce the costs of government. In 1989, Attorney General Richard Thornburgh celebrated the new funding model: "It's now possible for a drug dealer to serve time in a forfeiture-financed prison after being arrested by agents driving a forfeiture-provided automobile while working in a forfeiture-funded sting operation."[41]

With equity sharing in place, agencies at all levels of government enjoyed the spoils of plunder. From 1984 to 1994, federal agencies distributed nearly $1.4 billion in forfeiture revenue to state and local governments.[42] Local agencies topped off the transfers with revenue they produced on their own. The Los Angeles County Sheriff's Department, for example, seized around $26 million in alleged drug money in 1987 and $33 million more in 1988.[43]

After years of steady growth, forfeiture practices began to attract significant political opposition in the late 1990s, amid a spate of media stories that focused on corruption and takings from sympathetic victims.[44] The attacks of September 11, 2001 (9/11) overwhelmed these objections, however, and supplied powerful new grounds for expansion. As political leaders and media commentators stoked fears in the public, federal officials launched the war on terror and authorized enforcement agencies to seize assets from anyone who could be tied, however loosely, to domestic or international terrorism. As it shifted discourse and practice, the war on terror intersected with the war on drugs to boost forfeiture operations.[45]

As asset seizure revenues grew, they attracted for-profit firms. Businesses marketed training programs to law enforcement agencies, designed to teach officers how to be more effective and efficient in pursuing "highway interdiction" and forfeiture.[46] The industry created a new domain of public–private partnership by, in effect, promising to professionalize government seizures of community members' assets. Desert Snow, the leader in the field, reports that, in just one five-year period, its training programs helped police agencies seize more than $427 million in cash from highway stops.[47]

Its training services bringing in millions in government contracts and grants,[48] Desert Snow branched out into information systems by creating a vast, searchable database called Black Asphalt Electronic Networking & Notification System. The database allows "police nationwide to share detailed reports about American motorists—criminal and innocent alike—including their Social Security numbers, addresses and identifying tattoos, as well as hunches about which drivers to stop."[49] For law enforcement agencies, investments in Black Asphalt have yielded a healthy financial return. From 2005 to 2014, an agency's participation in Black Asphalt was associated with a 32 percent increase in asset seizures.[50]

While raking in profits and "improving" officer performance, Desert Snow also worked to build a community by turning Black Asphalt into a kind of social network. The company organizes an annual contest to see who can bring in the most forfeited assets and bestows awards on the officers who rack up the highest totals.[51] It encourages state and local agencies to post seizure data on its platform, as well as photos of police posing with assets they have taken.[52] The company's top honorific for officers, "Royal Knight," has become a status symbol in the subculture.[53] Through online socializing, collaboration, and competition, Desert Snow builds a sense of shared identity, cultivating practitioners as partners and political constituents.

Like private companies, public agencies have competed for access to the spoils of forfeiture. The dynamic is well illustrated by the case of Charles Clarke. In 2014, a DEA task force operating at Cincinnati / Northern Kentucky Airport seized $11,000 from Clarke, a twenty-four-year-old Black college student. The task force insisted that the cash came from drug trafficking, reporting that "Clarke was traveling on a recently purchased one-way ticket, he was unable to provide documentation for where the money came from, and his checked baggage had an odor of marijuana."[54] Officers found no drugs on Clarke or in his belongings, and they did not charge the young man with any crime. Clarke's cash, however, was presumed guilty and confiscated.

The two local agencies that participated in the seizure planned to split Clarke's money (minus the smaller share taken by the DEA). In short order, though, *eleven* other agencies, including the Kentucky State Police and Ohio Highway Patrol, stepped forward to claim a portion of the booty. Though they played no role in the operation, these agencies used their loose ties to the DEA task force as a pretense for demanding a cut of the proceeds. In this case as in many others, the seizure of assets marked the end of a law enforcement action and the start of a battle among revenue-seeking public agencies.[55]

Supported by government laws, symbolic ties to the wars on terror and drugs, and the material interests of public agencies and for-profit firms, forfeiture practices have grown dramatically. Between 2000 and 2019, federal and state governments seized assets worth a total of at least $68.8 billion.[56] From 2003 to 2013, the US DOJ doled out $4.7 billion to state and local agencies through the equitable sharing program, with annual payments rising from $198 million to $643 million.[57] Shockingly, and for the first time, the value of all assets seized in 2014 surpassed total losses from burglaries nationwide.[58]

The proceeds directly generated by state and local operations have been no less impressive. In 2018, for example, Florida led the country in asset seizure, bringing in $1,155,766 per 100,000 residents. That same year, Indiana was at the middle of the pack, with $91,331 per 100,000 residents.[59] From 2011 to 2013, the city of Philadelphia confiscated roughly one hundred homes, 150 vehicles, and $4 million in cash *annually*, producing about $5 million in municipal revenue per year.[60] Chicago police generated nearly $72 million in forfeiture proceeds between 2009 and 2016, retaining around $47 million for itself and splitting the remainder between the Cook County State's Attorney's Office and the Illinois State Police.[61]

Over time, the vast majority of states passed laws that incentivized law enforcement agencies to pursue forfeitures more aggressively. As of 2015, forty-three states allowed such agencies to keep, at minimum, 45 percent of seized assets, with thirty permitting such agencies to keep up to 90 percent.[62] Such policies help to explain why a 2014 investigation by *The Washington Post* found that hundreds of law enforcement agencies and task forces across the nation were relying on forfeiture proceeds to pad their budgets. Over the previous six years, 298 departments and 210 task forces had brought in amounts equivalent to 20 percent or more of their annual budgets.[63]

Seizure-based revenues are prized in particular because they take a "slushy" form, subject to little oversight.[64] Noting the lack of public accountability, a Texas state commission declared in 2008 that asset forfeiture—ostensibly a method of crime control—had "become a profit-making, personal account for some law enforcement officials."[65] A thousand miles north, the Chicago Police Department used seized assets to fund "many of the day-to-day operations of its narcotics unit and to secretly purchase controversial surveillance equipment without public scrutiny or city council oversight."[66] In 2014, the narcotics division even used forfeiture funds to purchase a money-counting machine. In Seward County, Nebraska, law enforcement used forfeiture funds to buy stun guns, bulletproof vests, a sheriff's cruiser with "paid for by drug proceeds" written on it, an $18,000 drone, and, for $15,000, two ballistic shields.[67] When a Columbia, Missouri citizens police review board asked police chief Ken Burton in 2012 to explain how his department spent the money it seized, he answered: "It's usually based on a need—well, I take that back. . . . There's some limitations on it. . . . Actually, there's not really on the forfeiture stuff. We just usually base it on something that would be nice to have that we can't get in the budget, for instance. . . . It's kind of like pennies from heaven—it gets you a toy or something that you need is the way that we typically look at it to be perfectly honest."[68]

Public officials routinely portray forfeiture as a method for capturing ill-gotten riches from the "big fish" of the criminal underworld—or to weaken the capacities of terrorists and violent drug cartels. In reality, however, it is mostly used to take small amounts of money and property from people in heavily policed neighborhoods.[69] From 2009 to 2016, for example, the median forfeiture in Illinois was just $530, with seizures occurring most frequently in Chicago neighborhoods with the largest concentrations of impoverished Black residents.[70] Studies of forfeiture practices in California, Nevada, Oklahoma, Pennsylvania, South Carolina, and Texas find similar patterns of race and class targeting.[71] In RCS communities, seizures routinely strip resources from people who have little to begin with. Faced with a costly and uncertain legal battle to regain their property, most people throw up their hands and move on.

Policing for Fines and Fees

On July 6, 2016, police officers pulled over Philando Castile in a suburb of Saint Paul, Minnesota. The cops thought the thirty-two-year-old Black man fit the profile of a person wanted for robbery. "The driver looks more like one of our suspects, just 'cause of the wide-set nose," Officer Jeronimo Yanez said before making the stop.[72] Dashboard-camera video shows Yanez walking to the driver side window and telling Castile he stopped him for a broken taillight. At Yanez's request, Castile provides proof of insurance, and then says: "Sir, I have to tell you, I do have a firearm on me." Yanez responds, "Ok, don't reach for it then. Don't pull it out." Moments later, the officer fires multiple shots into the car while shouting, "Don't pull it out. Don't move." As Yanez stops shooting and yells "shots fired" into his lapel radio, Castile's girlfriend Diamond Reynolds livestreams the incident from the passenger seat. Castile had reached for his wallet, not a gun, she explains into her camera phone.[73] Yanez would later insist he shot Castile out of fear for his life, his partner's life, and the life of Reynolds's daughter, who was in the backseat.[74] Roughly a year and a half later, a jury would acquit the officer of manslaughter.

After the fatal traffic stop, a story in the local *Star Tribune* revealed that, over the previous fourteen years, officers had stopped Castile forty-nine times, issuing eighty-two citations for minor infractions that cost more than $7,000.[75] With his license suspended for unpaid fines and fees, Castile continued driving to work, hoping to pay off his debt and get his license back. By driving without a license, however, Castile risked (and often received) more citations and legal debt.[76] It was an infuriating, expensive, and ultimately deadly cycle.

The practices that ensnared Castile plague RCS communities throughout the nation. Police routinely stop and fine people in such communities as they walk, bike, or otherwise go about their business. A 2015 investigation of Tampa, Florida, for example, found that police had written 2,504 bike tickets over the previous three years, with 80 percent issued to Black residents for violations such as riding too far from the curb, riding on the sidewalk, riding without hands on the handlebars, failing to have a bike light, or carrying a friend on the handlebars.[77] A 2017 investigation of "biking while Black" in Chicago, Illinois found that the ten community areas with the highest rates of bike ticketing did not include even one where White residents made up a majority, "despite biking's popularity in [these] areas."[78] A 2016 US DOJ investigation found that Baltimore police officers were subjecting Black residents to uniquely high rates of repetitive stops. Between 2010 and 2015, these residents made up 95 percent of the people stopped ten or more times.[79]

Because of data limitations, researchers face major obstacles when trying to conduct comprehensive national-level analyses of predatory fines and fees.[80] No national database documents how the rates, types, amounts, and collection outcomes of fine-and-fee debts vary across subnational jurisdictions.[81] Federal officials have never imposed a uniform monitoring system, and state and local agencies tend to use inconsistent recordkeeping and reporting practices. The information in available national datasets is often incomplete, poorly measured, or based on overly broad categories. Nevertheless, some scholars have used sources such as the US Census of Governments to produce a small body of studies that helps to clarify the remarkable scale and social targeting of the fine-and-fee regime that developed in the US after the 1980s.

Based on self-reported data for 2012, one study finds that 80 percent of US cities generated revenue through police-driven fines, fees, and forfeitures, with 6 percent reporting that such practices produced more than 10 percent of total revenues.[82] The 80 percent figure underscores just how pervasive these types of revenues have become. Some context is needed, however, to interpret the second figure. In the US, local governments produce only a portion of their own revenue; state and federal transfers account for a sizable share (36 percent in 2016).[83] Among "own-source" funding mechanisms, local property taxes lead the way (30 percent in 2016).[84] After accounting for these two streams, only about 34 percent is left for all other local taxes, charges for services, and so on. Viewed in this context, the evidence that 6 percent of cities in 2012 drew more than 10 percent of their *total* revenue from fines, fees, and forfeitures is stunning. This figure is almost equal to the combined percentage of local revenue produced (on average in the US in 2016) by local sales taxes (7 percent); individual income taxes (2 percent); and corporate-income, hotel, and business-license taxes (2 percent).[85]

National studies equally highlight the intense social targeting of police fine-and-fee practices. An analysis of the fifty US cities that are most reliant on this source of revenue finds that municipalities with larger Black and Latine populations rely more heavily on fines and fees for revenue. Indeed, by a large margin, these variables are the strongest predictors of local differences.[86] A separate study reinforces this finding and shows that the representation of Black residents on city councils "significantly reduces the relationship between race and fines."[87]

To understand how these fine-and-fee practices developed, it is important to begin with broader changes in US law enforcement. In the 1980s, the popularization of the "broken windows" perspective on crime and disorder combined with the intensification of punitive politics to promote more aggressive efforts to police "disorder" in "at-risk" communities. The perspective argued that minor legal infractions and evidence of disarray (e.g., the eponymous broken windows) suggest to would-be criminals that a neighborhood lacks social cohesion and constraints, and laws can be violated with impunity. In this view, minor "quality-of-life" offenses and actions that appear to flout authority must be vigorously addressed, lest they lead to far more serious forms of violence and crime. Under pressure to crack down, police departments aggressively went after people and places deemed to be "disorderly."[88]

In practice, this meant continually patrolling RCS communities, stopping and searching "suspicious" persons, and viewing nearly all residents as potential, if not likely, criminals. Some individuals, such as well-mannered elders or pastors, have been more likely to get a pass. But most residents of "the ghetto," James Foreman Jr. explains, have been "presumed guilty, or at least suspicious, and [have had to] spend an extraordinary amount of energy—through careful attention to dress, behavior, and speech—to mark [themselves] as innocent. All with no guarantee that these efforts will work."[89]

Although deeply disadvantaged neighborhoods have served as the epicenter for saturation policing, travel beyond their boundaries has rarely meant relief from the presumption of guilt. To the contrary, when police observe people who strike them as socially "out of place" in middle-class areas with larger numbers of White residents, they tend to treat them as highly suspicious. Studies of law enforcement data from cities as diverse as Minneapolis, New York City, Philadelphia, Los Angeles, Chicago, Boston, San Francisco, and New Orleans consistently find that Black and Latine individuals, especially men, are subjected to higher rates of police stops when they travel through predominantly White neighborhoods.[90]

Two kinds of stopping practices came to exemplify the approach to policing that took root in the 1980s, and both have been closely tied to racial profiling. In *pretext stops*, police pull over motorists for (often) petty traffic violations in order to look for evidence of more serious crimes.[91] In *stop-and-frisk* practices, police use claims of "reasonable suspicion" to question, and, in many cases, search people on the street, in hopes that they will find drugs, guns, or other incriminating evidence. In 2012, an astonishing report on New York City's stop-and-frisk practices revealed that "the number of stops of young Black men [in 2011] exceeded the entire city population of young Black men (168,126 as compared to 158,406)," and "90 percent of young Black and Latino men stopped were innocent."[92]

The expansion of patrolling and stopping operations significantly increased opportunities for officers to impose citation-based fines and seize assets, and both practices became more frequent and routine.[93] In police stops, the agendas of combating crime and raising revenue converged, and they continue to do so today. If a stop is initiated based on criminal suspicion but yields no incriminating evidence, it might still provide an opportunity to seize assets; barring that, the officer can often fall back on (and justify the stop by) fining the individual for a minor offense, such as jaywalking or driving with a broken muffler.

As growing law enforcement operations created funding pressures, local governments—many of which were experiencing broader fiscal crises—began to raise fine rates, create new finable offenses, and pursue more effective and efficient fining strategies.[94] Perhaps the most notorious case is the Saint Louis metropolitan area that includes Ferguson, Missouri, which became subject to investigations after the police killing of Michael Brown led to mass protests.[95] (In the city of Ferguson itself, the US DOJ found that Black residents made up 90 percent of those ticketed for public safety violations and, in 2013, payments for fines and fees accounted for one-fifth of the city's revenue base.[96]) In an analysis of the evidence and its legal implications, Henry Ordower and colleagues argue that revenue production has become so central to law enforcement in the region that fines and fees now operate as an "exercise of the taxing rather than the policing power of the municipality" and, as such, violate the state restrictions on local adjustments of taxes.[97] The use of traffic offenses to generate revenue has become so rampant, they conclude, that it is no longer clear "whether an offender is an offender at all or merely a target wearing a dollar sign."[98]

The mid-sized municipalities that surround Saint Louis are far from alone. In California, studies of Fresno, Sacramento, San Diego, Oakland, Berkeley, San Jose, and Los Angeles all find that police disproportionately target Black and Latine drivers for stop-and-search, fine-and-fee, and asset seizure practices.[99] Driving and automotive fines in California impose the heaviest burdens on low-income residents, researchers conclude.[100] And across the state, when county tax revenues drop, traffic citations tend to increase the following year.[101]

Among large cities, Chicago's predatory policing has been especially well documented. On a per capita basis, Chicago produces more revenue through fines, fees, and forfeitures than any US city except Washington, DC.[102] In 2016, auto-related practices alone generated $264 million in revenue—just over 7 percent of the city's $3.6 billion operating budget.[103] Chicago law enforcement agencies use automated cameras and police stops to issue more than three million tickets per year for violations of traffic rules, parking restrictions, vehicle compliance codes (e.g., a broken headlight), and more.[104]

When fiscal pressures have intensified, Chicago officials have sometimes responded by raising fine and fee amounts or creating new finable offenses.[105] This was the case in 2011–2012, for example, when budget shortfalls led city authorities to increase financial penalties for residents who fail to pay for a required vehicle sticker (a "wheel tax" of about $90). The $200 fine (previously $120) could now combine with other potential late fees and penalties to produce a total bill of $488.[106] City officials left the initial fee for the sticker unchanged, a subsequent report recounted, so they could reassure constituents that the new financial burdens would not fall on "soccer moms"—only "'scofflaws' who don't buy stickers or purchase them late."[107]

The burdens, in fact, have fallen most heavily on people from RCS communities, who are less able to afford the initial sticker fee and get patrolled and tagged for violations more often. Chicago police issue tickets for nonmoving automotive violations (such as vehicle sticker, parking meter, and license plate infractions) at dramatically higher rates in zip codes with lower income levels and numbers of White residents.[108] People who live in these areas also tend to have a harder time resolving the financial charges they incur through payment or dismissal. As a result, "minor" automotive citations are far more likely to push them into long-term criminal legal debts.

A substantial number of Chicago parking tickets—an estimated 13 percent of all citations between 2012 and 2018—are imposed under false premises.[109] These "tickets in error" generated over $27 million in revenue for the city during this period, plus an additional $8 million in unsettled debts that, under Illinois law, have no statute of limitations.[110] And while majority Black neighborhoods tend to be hit hardest by most automotive fines and fees, Kasey Henricks and Ruben Ortiz find that predominantly Latine neighborhoods are subjected to the highest rates of unwarranted parking tickets. "Proximity to those who lack legal residency" and "political conditions that foster threats of deportation," the authors argue, leave many residents "poorly positioned to challenge the state" and, therefore, "desirable as targets for expropriation."[111]

As policing fine-and-fee practices have expanded, for-profit firms have pitched their wares to law enforcement agencies—just as they have done with asset forfeiture. By teaming up with red-light and speed camera companies, many local governments have automated and expanded their traffic-fine operations. In its report on Ferguson, the US DOJ describes how city officials used contracts for red-light cameras to ramp up their revenue production efforts.[112] In an interview with a libertarian think tank about six months before the police killing of Michael Brown, Ferguson Mayor James Knowles boasted that the partnership was a win-win: His city did not have to purchase, install, maintain, or monitor the cameras, and its partner, American Traffic Solutions (ATS), took home a healthy cut of ticket revenues.[113] Stressing the cost-saving benefits of the camera contracts, Knowles did not mention how deeply the municipality had come to depend on ticketing revenue for its basic operations.[114] In reality, the material incentives for ATS to give out as many tickets as possible aligned well with Ferguson officials' desire to increase ticket-based revenues.

In the 1990s, ATS, Redflex, and Affiliated Computer Systems pursued aggressive lobbying and marketing campaigns to become leaders in the red-light and speed camera sector. By 2011, roughly 700 local jurisdictions in the US had traffic-surveillance contracts with for-profit companies.[115] In some cases, these contracts *penalize* cities if they approve too few tickets, adopt lenient rules for "rolling stops," or try to improve safety by extending yellow-light times.[116] To expand and defend their operations, the companies formed a lobbying group, the National Coalition for

Safer Roads, that works to defeat unfavorable local regulations, such as policies that only allow fines to be imposed for public safety reasons.[117]

In Chicago, Redflex held the contract for red-light cameras from 2003 to 2014, collecting over $400 million in fines and making more than $120 million in revenue.[118] The city ended the contract only because of a bribery scandal: Redflex had been paying a city official up to $2,000 for each camera it installed, and also rewarding him with free vacations, a condominium, and a Mercedes.[119] The exit of Redflex, however, simply opened the door for Xerox State and Local Solutions. From the start (and predictably), Xerox installed cameras disproportionately in areas where RCS communities were concentrated.[120] In 2018, Xerox inked a new five-year, $6.1 million contract with the city, not only to run traffic cameras but also to use software and data analytics to improve "the efficiency and effectiveness of the city's parking enforcement program."[121]

Like many businesses that profit from policing and punishment, traffic-camera companies operate through contracts with governments. Some entrepreneurs, however, have developed ways to profit from policing *outside* this framework. Take the mugshot industry, for example. When police make an arrest, the booking process includes a photo shoot: The suspect faces front and then turns to the side, often with a dour look befitting the occasion. Historically, mugshots were mostly for internal use, though newspapers and "true crime" magazines sometimes used them to spice up their stories.[122] This changed, however, as technological advances made it possible for local agencies to post digital booking photos and other arrest information online. (And as of 2018, only five states and the federal government treated the photos as confidential.)[123]

Tech-savvy entrepreneurs realized they could take booking photos from public databases and post them on their own websites. A new industry was born, led by companies with names like Mugshots.com and BustedMugshots.com. Citing their rights to free speech, the companies post the pictures regardless of whether an individual is charged with or convicted of any crime. The people shown in the galleries reflect the social biases of policing in America and, with good reason, many see the photos as a serious threat to their reputations and lives. Posted online, the images can easily be discovered through "people search" sites, spread through social media, and come to the attention of, say, a prospective employer, landlord, or romantic partner. Fearful that the photos could harm them (and follow them online forever), some people will pay to have them taken down.

The business model initially worked as a straightforward protection racket: The companies charged fees to remove threats that *they* created. Many people refused to pay, recognizing that a photo removed from one website could quickly appear on another. But police were producing new arrests and mugshots at a rapid pace. To make healthy profits, the owners only needed to extract payments from a tiny fraction of the people shown on their websites. Between 2014 and 2017, Mugshots.com held over thirty million records; it brought in $2.4 million in payments from only about 5,700 people.[124]

Eventually, lawmakers in some states passed restrictions on businesses that charged fees to take down the same photos that they had put up. The mugshot companies quickly adapted. Instead of charging the fee themselves, they delegated this task to third-party "unpublishing services" (also called "reputation management" agencies). The services charge fees to remove photos—or to bury them by flooding the internet with "new, positive content about the individual"—and then they give a cut of the proceeds to the owners of the mugshot sites.[125] The owner of Mugshots .com, Sahar Sarid, partnered with Thomas Keesee to start UnpublishArrest .com. Over a five-month period in 2013, Sarid and Keesee made $2 million in revenues.[126] In 2018, California Attorney General Xavier Becerra charged Sarid and Keesee with extortion. The scheme, Becerra argued, was "exploitation, plain and simple."[127]

Courts as Sites of Predation

In jurisdictions across the US today, criminal justice predation is generally organized as networks of interdependent nodes, where individuals are routinely passed from one site of extraction to another. In many respects, courts operate as centrally positioned hubs in these networks. Unlike police on patrol or penal authorities who control people under custody, courts generally do not have direct access to targets of predation. They depend on other actors, especially police, to supply them, retrieve them, and secure their compliance. Conversely, actors at other nodes depend on courts to carry out and sustain their operations. Police, for instance, depend on courts to process the citations they hand out and often require judicial threats and orders to bring in payments. Thus judges produce potential targets of predation for actors at other sites and decide how they will be distributed across sites. Their sentencing decisions deliver people to jails, prisons, and community supervision programs. As they set financial conditions of pretrial release, judges generate the "customers" that the bail bond industry requires.

In later chapters, we unravel this complex "hub" of activities. Here we analyze how courts operate as sites of predation in their own right, focusing on the proliferation of fee-based practices since the 1980s. In this period, state and local officials developed a vast array of new court fees and ratcheted up the price tags for older ones.[128] Between 2009 and 2014, as subnational governments struggled with fiscal crises unleashed by the Great Recession, officials in forty-eight of the fifty US states increased court fees, created additional fees, or both.[129] Scott Williams, a county-level manager of safety and justice operations in Minnesota, explains: "It's just an ongoing pattern where, 'Oh we have a tough budget year—we have a number of tough budget years—we have a budget hole to fill. How do we fill this? Well, we can add some [court] fees.'"[130] A 2010 Brennan Center for Justice study analyzed data from fifteen US states that, collectively, accounted for over 60 percent of all filings in state criminal courts nationwide. The authors concluded that eleven of the fifteen were "effectively turning courts . . . into general tax collectors" by using the revenues they produced to fund general budgets and public agencies unrelated to criminal law.[131]

As court fees have proliferated in recent decades, financial charges for public defense and trial costs have drawn particular scrutiny because they seem to undermine rights enshrined in the US Constitution. In *Gideon v. Wainwright* (1963), the US Supreme Court ruled that indigent defendants who face potential incarceration have a constitutional right to legal counsel. The Court stopped short, though, of requiring governments to *pay* for appointed counsel. The result was, more or less, an unfunded mandate.[132] In an effort to have "users" of court services cover some of the costs, governments across the US now charge public defense fees, essentially transforming the citizen's right to legal representation into a consumer right to purchase. The US Supreme Court ruled that this practice is legal, as the government does not deny access to public defense based on a person's ability to pay. Currently, however, forty states and Washington, DC authorize courts to bill adult indigent defendants for using a public lawyer.[133] In addition to these "recoupment" fees, many states charge up-front "application" fees.[134] Nearly all states also require representation fees in juvenile cases.[135]

The use of public defense fees varies widely, both across and within states and localities. Some courts charge a flat rate, bill defendants for "actual" costs, charge by the hour, or tie fee amounts to the nature of the alleged crime or the outcome of the trial. Recoupment fees can cost hundreds or even thousands of dollars, while application fees tend to range between $20 and $200.[136] In many places, judges can waive or reduce fees based on an individual's ability to pay. However, a nationwide study by the National Legal Aid and Defense Association "did not identify any courts using fair methods to decide what a defendant can realistically pay."[137]

Between 2014 and 2024, courts charged $150 million in lawyer fees.[138] As with other types of court debt, governments collect a small portion of the amount produced through public defense fees. The money they do bring in, however, can prove crucial for funding legal services. Mary Fox, Missouri's state public defense director, told *The Nation*: "I'm not thrilled that someone who is indigent has to pay for the right to counsel because that is not consistent with *Gideon*. But on the other hand, trying to balance our budget, we use those monies that come in exclusively for training our staff and other necessary expenses that allow us to provide representation." Mary Pollard, the executive director of North Carolina's Office of Indigent Defense Services, said similarly, "We would be strapped without it. . . . We're spending everything we take in."[139]

Fees for public defense also serve a rationing function. Across the country, defendants are required to agree to a version of the following statement when applying for public counsel: "*I understand that I may be required to repay the state for all or part of my attorney fees and costs.*"[140] Faced with unknown and potentially large expenses (in addition to other criminal legal charges), people with limited resources likely feel immense pressure to forgo representation.[141] The temptation to waive legal representation is even more intense when court officials insist that defendants pay fees up front. Although it is unconstitutional to condition public defense on payment, it sometimes happens. For example, before California outlawed charging for public counsel in 2020, the American Civil Liberties Union (ACLU) of Southern California found that indigent defendants across the state were routinely told that they *had* to pay a $50 application fee in order to receive legal representation. A public defender in Los Angeles demurred: "I am essentially required to say: 'Hi, if you pay $50, I can work with you.'"[142] When people could not pay up, they had to take a plea or represent themselves—thereby easing (however slightly) public defense caseloads and costs.

Financial charges for trial costs have similarly worked to commodify and weaken an established right of citizenship (in this case, protections afforded by the Sixth Amendment to the US Constitution). As John King explains, charges for trials vary extensively across jurisdictions:

> Several states explicitly add a fee for the election of a jury trial. Delaware, for example, imposes an additional $78 per charge if the defendant elects a jury trial instead of a bench trial. Colorado, Illinois, Mississippi, Missouri, Montana, Nevada, Ohio, Oklahoma, Texas, Virginia, West Virginia, and Wisconsin all provide expressly for an additional charge to be assessed against a defendant who elects a jury and is convicted. Other states have general statutes authorizing assessment of the costs and fees of the prosecution against a defendant, which could be read to include a larger fee if the defendant was tried by a jury.[143]

In Washington state, defendants have a choice. They can pay $125 to be tried in front of a six-person jury or twice as much for a twelve-person jury.[144]

The vast majority of criminal cases in the US today do not go to trial. Prosecutors and defendants enter plea deals that establish a judgment of guilt without the costs (in time, labor, and resources) that a trial would require. Little is known about whether a desire to avoid the steep financial costs of going to trial might, in some cases, make defendants more willing to accept plea deals. In some jurisdictions, though, even pleading out costs money. In Pennsylvania, for example, courts are authorized to impose "plea fees" on defendants, and some counties charge nearly $200.[145] Defendants can avoid the fee by refusing to admit guilt, but if they do so and then are found guilty at trial, the court adds a further charge to its standard trial fees.[146]

In some jurisdictions, criminal cases that produce convictions provide courts with an additional opportunity to generate fee-based revenue. As of 2016, courts in sixteen states charged individuals an application fee to expunge a conviction from their public record, with prices topping out at $550 in Louisiana.[147] An amicus brief filed in *Timbs v. Indiana* (2019) notes that Tennessee "established a $450 [fee for] criminal record expungement [in 2012] for the principal purpose of raising revenue for the state general fund."[148]

In addition to all these fees, which are based on the individual's case, courts also impose surcharges (or "assessments")—essentially, fees used for the express purpose of generating revenue, typically in cases of conviction.[149] In California, the first surcharges were created in the 1960s, as small levies added to traffic citations to help fund driver education programs and other driver-related services.[150] In the early 2000s, however, public agencies and program directors across the state began to push for their own surcharges. Legislators obliged, and the fees stacked up. The cost of running a stop sign in California illustrates the effects. The base fine for the infraction averages around $35 across the state, but the ticket comes with a litany of assessments that help to fund various state and local agencies, many of which have no relationship to processing the violation itself. After all the add-ons, the fine is not $35; it is $238.[151] Similar charges increase a DUI infraction in California from a base fine of $390 to a total cost of $2,024.[152]

Assessment practices of this sort are now standard in courts across the US, and they subsidize a wide range of government agencies and services.[153] Michigan, for example, generates roughly $418 million from surcharges per year, a third of all funding for the state's trial courts.[154] In Arizona, courts require convicted individuals to pay a surcharge equivalent to 83 percent of the total amount of fines and fees they have incurred. Half of the resulting revenue goes to criminal legal agencies, and the remainder to help fund elections administration, state medical services, and other government functions.[155] Local departments of education in North Carolina draw substantial funding from surcharges levied on people who are found guilty of operating "improper equipment" (e.g., a car with a broken speedometer or taillight).[156] Georgia, Missouri, and California use assessments to raise money for their "brain and spinal injury funds," among a host of other things.[157]

Unlike case-based fees and surcharges, court *fines* are explicit punishments—monetary sanctions justified on penological grounds. As noted in chapter 1, there is nothing inherently predatory about imposing a fine. In some contexts, in fact, progressive reformers have advocated for them as "an enlightened alternative to incarceration or other harsh penalties."[158] In the US today, however, court fines are typically imposed *on top of* such punishments, not as substitutes for them.[159] Fines are used most often in low-level (e.g., "quality-of-life") cases that disproportionately involve people from RCS communities.[160] And like fees and surcharges, they generate substantial revenues for state and local governments. For this reason, as well as the pressures of punitive politics, officials have strong incentives to push fine amounts ever higher.[161]

Since the 1980s, court fines have followed roughly the same trajectory as court fees, police fines, and asset forfeiture practices. In 1991, roughly 11 percent of adults held in state and federal prisons had received fines as part of their sentences; by 2014, this figure had more than tripled to 34 percent.[162] For three reasons, though, data for adult prisoners capture only a small portion of the overall growth. First, courts routinely impose fines when sentencing people to probation and other forms of community supervision.[163] Second, fines are the predominant form of sanction imposed for low-level offenses, which rarely result in imprisonment. And in recent decades, fines for misdemeanors have risen dramatically.[164] Third, fine rates have risen in juvenile cases, where courts impose them not only for criminal violations but also for status offenses. Rhode Island, for instance, fines juveniles for "habitually spending time in poolrooms, bars, and houses of ill-repute." Some states also fine parents for their children's actions. In seven states, parents can be fined for their child's "absenteeism" at school, and in six, they can be fined if their kid writes graffiti.[165]

Funds produced by court fines are used to finance a wide range of government agencies and programs.[166] In Tennessee, the same law that designates "mandatory minimum" fines for drug offenses ($250 to $5,000) also states that 50 percent of the money collected must be paid to "the general fund of the governing body of the law enforcement agency responsible for the investigation and arrest which resulted in the drug conviction."[167] In New Orleans, fine proceeds became so central to the funding of public defense that when Hurricane Katrina sharply curtailed them, city officials reduced the staff of attorneys from thirty-five to ten.[168] In North Carolina, fines became such an important source of school funding that, in 2015, dozens of county governments joined a lawsuit arguing that the use of such funds to "pay for housing inmates . . . wrongfully siphoned off fines for traffic violations that should have been earmarked for public schools."[169]

Because the vast majority of people who pass through criminal courts are poor, few are able to pay the full costs of the fines, fees, and surcharges imposed on them. In all too many cases, extractive court practices push people into long-term debt-and-payment cycles in which new financial charges get piled on top of what they already owe. In nine of the fifteen states studied by the Brennan Center, courts set this process in motion by charging fees *just to set up* payment plans for people who cannot pay their full bill at once. Thirteen charged interest or late fees to people who fell behind on payments, regardless of whether they had the necessary resources or had other financial obligations, such as child support.[170] If payments came too slowly and courts initiated collections efforts, nine of the fifteen states allowed local governments to bill individuals for this cost as well.[171]

Debts can rise even faster when courts partner with for-profit collections companies. In addition to the court's bill for collections, many states allow the companies to add their own fees, often based on the *total amount* owed by the individual. State laws allow the companies to charge fees equal to as much as 30 percent of the full debt in Illinois, 40 percent in Florida, and 50 percent in Washington.[172] In these and other ways, governments and their business partners can greatly increase the debts that predatory court practices create. Alexes Harris recounts how "Kathie," a low-income mother of three in Washington state, saw her initial $11,000 in court obligations spiral into a $20,000 debt due to interest on the amount owed, court charges for collections costs, and private collections fees.[173]

Through aggressive practices such as wage garnishment, private collectors and public courts work collaboratively to squeeze resources from legal debtors. Unable to resolve all the legal debts they owe, many people become stuck in a coercive routine of financial extraction and criminal legal surveillance and control. Later in the book, we return to these dynamics in order to analyze their consequences for legally entangled debtors, their loved ones, and their communities.

Backstops and Enforcers for Consumer Exploitation

In chapter 1, we described how criminal legal institutions have served throughout US history as sites of predation and as *supports* for predatory projects in the broader society. In America today, such projects frequently operate through creditor–debtor relations and use what Devin Fergus calls methods of "financial fracking" to extract resources from marginalized communities.[174] Since the 1980s, experiences with demanding debt burdens and debt collectors have become increasingly common for all but the most elite Americans. And the most exploitative and extractive practices have disproportionately targeted RCS communities.

In 2017, consumer debts in the US totaled more than $13 *trillion*.[175] A number of developments help to explain this astronomical figure. As the richest Americans acquired ever-greater shares of wealth and income after the 1970s, it became harder for most other people to cover living expenses. Wages for middle- and lower-income Americans stagnated; work became more precarious; policy changes weakened social protections; and governments and employers shifted a growing number of risks and responsibilities onto families and individuals.[176] As deregulation freed corporations to shift their investments from production (and jobs) to financial markets, it also paved the way for businesses to develop new tools of financial exploitation.[177] Growing numbers of Americans took on sizable debts for things like medical bills, student loans, and the use of credit cards to help make ends meet.[178]

As these developments unfolded, people in RCS communities were positioned as especially ripe targets for "predatory inclusion" into the most rapacious business schemes and debt traps. People in these communities had long been deprived of access to credit by banks and other businesses, and their own resources were often insufficient to meet their needs and goals.[179] They tended to have a much harder time getting approved for the kinds of credit that growing numbers of Americans were using to manage household costs, buy houses and cars, and start or invest in businesses.[180] People in RCS communities frequently had low credit scores that could be used to justify usurious terms of credit, and few were well versed in the arcane terms of contract that unscrupulous lenders often use to lure people into exploitative debt agreements.

As deregulation unleashed a wave of profitable and risky innovations in finance, RCS communities were inundated with credit card offers that held out a lifeline in the short term but generated debts that rose steadily through the compounding effects of elevated interest rates, fees, and penalties.[181] Credit needed to buy homes and cars became more available, but frequently in the form of subprime loans that led to ruinous debts and property forfeitures.[182] The same communities that were subjected to a growing number of criminal legal financial charges, debts, and collections in this period were simultaneously saturated with predatory payday lending, pawn shop loan, and check cashing operations.[183]

The debt burdens that became widespread in this era took a far more intense form in the most marginalized communities. As of 2021, median debt-to-asset ratios were estimated to be 50 percent higher for families with Black and Latine heads than for families with White, non-Latine heads.[184] The *kinds* of debts people acquired also tended to differ. People in RCS communities continued to be deprived of access to what Louise Seamster calls "good debts" that can be used to make profitable investments in homes or businesses, accumulate wealth, smooth spending during tough times, raise one's quality of life, and move into a more advantageous position going forward.[185] Far more frequently, they have been saddled with "bad debts" that drain their limited resources, cut into their future paychecks, and leave them worse off down the road.[186] Because their incomes tend to be more limited and less predictable, people from RCS communities are also far more likely to fall behind on payments—and into the clutches of debt collectors.

Valued at over $20 billion in 2022, the US collections industry encompasses collections agencies, law firms that specialize in legal enforcement, and a thriving market of investors who package, buy, and sell debts.[187] In 2017, wealth fund managers invested roughly $107 billion in private debt markets, working through 346 different investment vehicles to pursue $456 billion worth of opportunities worldwide.[188] In the US, a field of more than 6,000 collection agencies is dominated by a handful of large private and stock exchange–listed companies.[189] It is a notoriously aggressive industry, with agencies continually developing new ways to locate debtors, increase fees and penalties, and extract payments. To maximize profits, many are willing to risk being fined for violations of consumer protections, such as those established by the Fair Debt Collection Practices Act (FDCPA) and Fair Credit Reporting Act (FCRA). The cost of a fine is, in many cases, negligible compared to the additional profits that companies can generate through illegal pressure tactics, false filings, fraud, and misrepresentation.[190]

The consumer debts pursued by the industry are civil matters, not criminal. In fact, criminal prosecution and punishment for such debts is prohibited by federal and state laws and the Fourteenth Amendment to the US Constitution. The FDCPA forbids debt collectors from even *threatening* to pursue criminal arrest, prosecution, or punishment. Yet, despite these and other formal protections, criminal legal institutions in the US have become key players in the enforcement of consumer debts.

When people fall behind on payments, debt collectors can turn up the heat by filing a case in civil court. Use of this tactic rose sharply starting in the 1990s, driven by developments inside the industry. As debt-trading markets grew, investors pressured collections agencies to become more efficient. In response, the businesses turned to law firms that specialize in securing payments.[191] In New Jersey, the number of court judgments on debt cases rose from 500 in 1996 to 140,000 in 2008.[192] Debt buyers accounted for 48 percent of all judgments in New Jersey's lower-level civil courts in 2011, and for more than one million judgments between 2001 and 2011.[193] And New Jersey is not alone. In a 2018 report, the ACLU described the breakneck pace of debt adjudication in civil courts across the country:

> Millions of collection lawsuits are filed each year in state and local courts that have effectively become collectors' courts. The majority of cases on many state court dockets are debt collection suits, and in many state courts, debt purchasers file more suits than any other type of plaintiff. Debt collection lawyers can file hundreds of suits a day . . . [with] the overwhelming majority of [debtors] not represented by an attorney. . . . Many courts churn through collection lawsuits with astonishing speed and little scrutiny. Over 95 percent of debt collection suits end in favor of the collector, usually because alleged debtors do not mount a defense.[194]

Predictably, the people subjected to these proceedings come disproportionately from RCS communities, and their cases can easily carry them into criminal legal arenas.[195] Civil court judges can bolster collection efforts in a variety of direct ways, such as ordering the garnishment of wages or bank accounts or subjecting personal property to lien or seizure. Once a civil case has been brought, however, the criminalization of unpaid debt is an ever-present possibility. The most common pathway operates through a "failure to appear" for court proceedings. Forty-four states explicitly authorize judges, magistrates, and justices of the peace to issue arrest warrants for debtors who "fail to appear," despite the fact that defendants do not need to be in attendance for these officials to enter judgments. Legally, failure to appear qualifies as "contempt of court," a criminal offense subject to arrest based on a "body attachment" order or "capias warrant," but judges have substantial discretion in such cases.[196]

It might sound easy to avoid arrest and possible incarceration: just show up for court. But civil courts process collections cases at a blistering pace, and many debtors do not receive advance notice of the proceedings. That risk is greatly enhanced by the fact that collections agents often file multiple suits in separate venues and at different times.[197] In cases where notice *is* received, debtors may still be unable to attend due to work or childcare obligations, disability, lack of transportation, or illness.[198] And even if the court delivers a judgment, the risks may not end there. Creditors can ask the court to impose post-judgment proceedings, wherein defendants undergo "judgment debtor examinations" regarding their wages and assets. Failure to appear for these proceedings, too, can result in an arrest warrant and, potentially, jail time.[199]

A second pathway to criminalization operates through civil court judgments that impose payment plans, which sometimes mirror the schedule demanded by the creditor.[200] In these cases, judges convert private payment plans into public judicial orders. From that point forward, failure to pay on time becomes a contempt of court violation, subject to a criminal arrest warrant and punishment. The only way a debtor can remedy this type of "offense" is by satisfying the creditor.

Since the 1990s, the use of debt-based arrest warrants has become so common that instructional materials on debt collection law now advise lawyers that "body attachments are usually rather effective, as most debtors do not like to be imprisoned and suddenly find funds for bonds."[201] A 2018 study of 1,000 court cases in twenty-six states found arrest warrants issued for consumer debts ranging from medical bills, student loans, and rent payments to payday loans, gym fees, daycare center fees, ambulance services, and online classes from for-profit colleges.[202]

The arrest warrants set criminal legal processes in motion in multiple ways. When police pull over a car, stop a pedestrian, or enter a home, a quick check of a database can inform them of the outstanding debt-based warrant, which they can then leverage to extract information or take individuals into custody.[203] Debt-based warrants are also sometimes used to authorize police sweeps of public housing or homeless shelters. The details of the resulting arrests make for a harrowing read. In a report on the criminalization of consumer debt, the ACLU recounts numerous cases, such as this one from September 2015: "Gordon Wheeler was arrested by seven or eight US marshals at his Texas home for failure to appear at the US District Court for the Southern District of Texas. Wheeler was unable to show up in court because he had just had open-heart surgery. . . . The original $2,500 federal student loan he obtained to pay for trucking school in 1983 had mushroomed into $12,000 with interest and fees. Wheeler is retired and subsists on social security and disability, and says he cannot pay it, noting, 'You can't squeeze blood out of a turnip.'"[204]

When debtors are sent to jail, judges sometimes set bond at the exact amount owed to the collection agency. This practice ensures that release cannot be obtained for an amount less than payment of the debt and, in some cases, the bond payments are given directly to the creditor.[205]

In practice, critics argue, such actions violate the legal ban on incarcerating debtors. "If, in effect, people are being incarcerated until they pay bail, and bail is being used to pay their debts," legal scholar Alan White explains, "then they're being incarcerated to pay their debts." The "contempt" justification is simply a pretext, former Illinois Attorney General Lisa Madigan argues: It "gives the lawyers the ability to say [debtors] aren't being thrown in debtors' prison, they're being thrown into prison for contempt of court. To me, that's disingenuous."[206]

Arrest and jail tactics provide a powerful basis for threats designed to motivate payments.[207] In fact, threats of this sort have played a prominent role in supporting a third pathway to criminalization: In payday lending and some other cases, failure to pay can be framed as a "bounced check" crime. In cases of this sort, prosecutors and debt collectors have increasingly operated as "business partners." Overwhelmed by the number of debt cases brought to criminal courts, some district attorneys have simply handed over enforcement to collection firms, signing contracts that authorize them to threaten criminal legal action for nonpayment. "Some collectors with these contracts," the ACLU reports, "send letters on the district attorney's letterhead to threaten people with criminal prosecution, jail, and fines—even when the prosecutor hasn't reviewed the case to see if a criminal violation occurred."[208]

Beyond the collections industry, many other private interests mobilize criminal legal authorities as enforcers when payment-related problems arise. This is particularly true in the arena of residential housing. Lucrative, high-interest subprime mortgage agreements—and the foreclosures they frequently produce—tend to be heavily concentrated by race and class, with older women in RCS communities serving as especially frequent targets.[209] Similarly, landlord profits from rental properties tend to be substantially higher in neighborhoods that have larger numbers of low-income and racially marginalized residents.[210] Evictions, which allow owners to pursue more profitable arrangements and also send a payment-motivating message to nearby residents, are routine in such neighborhoods, and police and courts often play a critical role.[211] Between 2007 and 2016, a landmark national study finds, "Black Americans made up only 18.6 percent of all renters yet accounted for 51.1 percent of those threatened with eviction and 43.4 percent of those who were evicted."[212]

The criminalization of payments owed for housing can occur in various ways. Only one state in the US, Arkansas, treats the failure to pay rent as a criminal act per se.[213] Once authorities deliver notice of a violation, Arkansas residents who are behind on their rent have just ten days to pay in full or risk up to ninety days in jail. Remarkably, prosecution is based solely on the landlord's claims. Arkansas law does not require investigation into how much rent is actually owed and provides no mechanism for the tenant to dispute the asserted amount.[214]

In all other states, nonpayment of rent is a civil matter, but landlords often turn to criminal legal authorities for enforcement. In 2018, the practice drew national attention when journalists revealed that Sean Hannity (Fox News) and Jared Kushner (President Trump's son-in-law) held ownership in companies that routinely filed civil claims to extract money from low-income tenants.[215] Property managers repeatedly sought court-ordered evictions for late payments, often in cases where tenants were only a few days behind or had failed to pay because of medical emergencies or disputes over mold removal. Discussing one of the companies, Susan Reif of the Eviction Prevention Project explained that by "serially filing against the same tenants, they are using the courts as collection agencies [and] trying to increase their profit margin by demanding fees under the threat of being evicted."[216] If tenants do not pay up and a court orders eviction, law enforcement officers are hailed to the scene, where they present renters with an immediate threat of criminal arrest.

The case of Juanita Fitzgerald illustrates this process, while also highlighting the notorious practices of for-profit nursing homes and assisted living facilities that extract profits from poor residents and, in some cases, deliver them to private equity firms.[217] A longtime resident of the Franklin House in Eustis, Florida, Fitzgerald struggled to make payments and eventually fell behind. In 2017, just before her ninety-fourth birthday, Franklin House took action to evict Fitzgerald. When police officers arrived, Fitzgerald refused to cooperate: "Bodycam footage from the arrest showed her screaming and sliding to the ground in an apparent attempt to avoid being taken away. A police report obtained by the *Miami Herald* noted that Fitzgerald had told officers, 'Unless you carry me out of here, I'm not going anywhere. . . .' The police report stated that Fitzgerald was transported to jail without handcuffs because of her age. However, she can be seen wearing handcuffs and ankle restraints at the jail in an on-camera interview with WCMH-TV. Her wrists and forearms appear deeply bruised."[218]

Government agencies also look to courts and police to compel payments and secure revenue. Child support enforcement offers a stark example, underscoring how forced "repayments" to the state drain resources from subjugated communities. Child support enforcement is mandatory for children who enter many poverty-focused programs, such as Temporary Assistance for Needy Families (TANF), foster care, and Medicaid. Under federal law, families that apply for TANF benefits, for instance, must cooperate with paternity establishment and child support enforcement efforts *and* must transfer their rights to the payments to the state. Officially, government agencies collect child support on behalf of TANF-receiving families (typically mothers and children). In practice, the majority of collected funds get split between state and federal government.[219]

People who owe child support debts to welfare-involved families (disproportionately men from RCS communities) confront significant risks of criminal legal action. Nonpayment can lead to incarceration, directly through criminal prosecution or indirectly through contempt proceedings in civil courts. Under federal law, nonpayment can be prosecuted as a criminal misdemeanor subject to fines and up to six months in prison; child support debts over $10,000 or overdue for longer than two years can result in felony charges punishable by up to two years in prison.[220] In larger US cities, roughly 15 percent of Black fathers are, at some point, incarcerated for a failure to pay child support.[221] Political debates over child support frequently focus on images of "deadbeat dads" who fail to make payments despite being able to do so;[222] in reality, criminal punishments are far more likely to be imposed on men from RCS communities who lack the ability to pay than on noncustodial parents who have substantial resources but withhold payments.[223]

Indeed, the interplay of child support debt and incarceration runs deeper than just enforcement. Roughly 25 percent of the people held in state and federal prisons have open child support cases, and at least fifteen states treat incarceration as a form of "voluntary unemployment" that merits no adjustment in child support payment schedules.[224] In all other states, imprisoned people must discover for themselves that they can petition for a revised plan and then successfully navigate the process. As a result, large numbers of people accrue child support debts during their prison stays, and, upon release, must immediately make payments on the arrears (plus any interest).[225]

In many cases, these payments do not go to the children but rather to government institutions, which claim them as "repayment" for expenditures on public assistance programs. If the released individual does not keep up with the court-imposed schedule for paying off their accumulated and ongoing child support obligations, they can be charged with a willful failure to pay and become subject to punishments up to and including re-imprisonment.[226] In effect, courts use the threat of incarceration to force noncustodial parents to pay for *public* benefits. In this regard, they bear a striking resemblance to the Tenaha police officers who used threats of jail to pressure James Morrow into handing over his belongings.

Conclusion

Do the kinds of police and court practices analyzed in this chapter actually pay off for the actors who pursue them? Many activists and advocates claim that they do, and, in this chapter and the remainder of the book, we argue that they are right. However, scholars who study monetary sanctions and the legal financial obligations (LFOs) they generate have sometimes drawn conclusions that seem to contradict this contention. Some have even argued that the practices they study cannot be conceptualized as "predatory" because they generate so little revenue.[227]

Skepticism about revenue production is generally based on a sound observation: Legally entangled people tend to be quite poor, and collecting money from them can be costly and difficult. In a groundbreaking study of five Washington counties, for example, Alexes Harris finds that government authorities recovered only a small portion of total outstanding debts and the sum of money they collected was no greater than what it cost them to secure the payments.[228] Total collections from LFOs added up to less than the public costs of processing and convicting defendants, monitoring their payment status, and penalizing them for nonpayment.[229] On this basis, Harris concludes: "The system of monetary sanctions serves little economic purpose."[230]

How can this view be reconciled with our own? Because monetary sanctions scholarship is framed by the concept of *punishment*, it has focused on a set of practices that is narrower than what we define as criminal justice predation. The fines, fees, and restitution orders that stand at the center of this research program define a distinctive standpoint for evaluating the payoffs of predation. First, relative to most predatory criminal legal operations, these practices tie revenue production to some of the greatest challenges of debt collection. Second, the focus on court-imposed sanctions places the lucrative operations of for-profit firms, as well as the extractive practices of police agencies, custodial facilities, and community supervision programs, outside the scope of analysis. Third, as it analyzes court practices *inside* the criminal legal field, this line of research sets aside the various ways that actors *outside* of the field use law enforcement, courts, and penal facilities to extract payments and generate revenues.

The practices left out are far more likely to involve direct and immediate resource takings. For example, asset seizures carried out by law enforcement do not require debt collection efforts, and they generate substantial revenues for institutions at every level of US government. Police take cash and goods on the spot, and it is rare for targeted individuals to pursue challenges in court. Police citations (made more cost-efficient by technologies such as red-light cameras) and related practices such as car impoundment reliably generate significant municipal revenues.[231] In chapter 3, we analyze numerous carceral practices that operate through on-the-spot payments, mandatory deductions from prison wages, or deposits into individuals' bank accounts. Private interests generate vast profits from criminal legal governance, as participating partners, investors, and beneficiaries of criminal legal debt enforcement. In fact, when scholars who study monetary sanctions turn to these corporate operations, they tend to reach conclusions similar to our own. In an article on "privatization within [the] public system of justice," for instance, Harris and coauthors conclude that "private corporations are running many key justice system programs and generating large profits from captive populations."[232]

Even in the case of fines and fees, however, available evidence is hard to square with the idea that predatory financial practices "serve little economic purpose." In this chapter, we have described a wide range of cases in which fine and fee revenues subsidize public agencies, as well as episodes in which threats to these funding streams provoked alarmed opposition. In an amicus brief filed in *Timbs v. Indiana*, a group of leading scholars concludes: "Today, the system of targeting the poor with fines and then imposing 'poverty penalties' generates huge sums for states and localities, as do forfeitures."[233] In 2019, *Governing* conducted "the largest national analysis to date of fine revenues," and its findings were unambiguous: "In hundreds of jurisdictions throughout the country, fines are used to fund a significant portion of the budget. They account for more than 10 percent of general fund revenues in nearly 600 US jurisdictions. In at least 284 of those governments, it's more than 20 percent. Some other governments allocate the revenues outside the general fund. When fine and forfeiture revenues in all funds are considered, more than 720 localities reported annual revenues exceeding $100 for every adult resident."[234]

Monetary sanctions scholars make a vital point when they stress how difficult it can be to collect on LFOs—or better said, how hard it is for deeply impoverished people to pay off these debts. It is equally important, though, to recognize how dogged and creative government agencies have been in pursuing such debts. Many courts that have trouble collecting on LFOs hire businesses that specialize in wringing payments from debtors. In some localities, courts have responded by designing installment-based payment plans, aggressively garnishing wages and tax returns, or even shutting off people's home utilities to make them pay up.[235] Threats and practices of incarceration play an important role as well.[236] In some jurisdictions that limit collections based on ability to pay, policymakers have authorized public agencies to keep tabs on debtors going forward and activate collections if and when their financial situations improve.

For reasons that have as much to do with political action as social analysis, it is essential to appreciate the remarkable scale of public and private revenues generated by predatory criminal legal practices in the US each year. A wide range of corporations and government agencies have developed a significant material stake in predatory revenues, and, in chapter 10, we explain how this reliance poses significant challenges for political struggles to end criminal justice predation. In this regard, the Brennan Center for Justice observes: "With local governments and law enforcement agencies increasingly dependent on revenue extracted via the criminal legal system, any cost-benefit analysis they perform will likely favor more, not less, enforcement. So what is to be done to rebalance the scales of justice?"[237]

As we will see, advocates, activists, and their allies are developing creative strategies for overcoming resistance from invested defenders of the status quo. While arguments about the "fiscal irrationality" of certain predatory practices may win over some policymakers and government officials, they tend to hold little sway with politicians and public administrators who believe (often with good reason) that without tax increases and other changes in public finance, predatory revenues provide a lifeline. So, for researchers who hope to understand and explain the growth and staying power of criminal justice predation, as well as the forms of struggle needed to reform or end it, it is imperative to identify how—and for whom—extractive practices "pay off."

3 * Predatory Uses of Custody and Supervision

On June 8, 2023, Judge Thomas Whitney sentenced Esmeralda Ahumada to serve twelve to twenty-two years in an Idaho prison. Several months earlier, Ahumada, a thirty-five-year-old woman, pled guilty to second degree murder for killing her eighty-one-year-old grandfather.[1] During sentencing, the judge and prosecutor acknowledged the tragic nature of the case. Like many women sent to prison, Ahumada had suffered years of sexual abuse and mental health struggles.[2] She told police that she shot her grandfather in the chest to stop him from sexually abusing her.[3] Judge Whitney praised Ahumada for taking personal responsibility "from start to finish."[4] Still, in addition to sending her to prison, he made her pay a $1,000 fine, surcharges, and a fee for using the services of a public defender.[5]

Ahumada's story recalls several points from our analysis in chapter 2. The court operated simultaneously as a site of adjudication and financial extraction. Ahumada's personal ordeals reflected her subordinate position in the nation's matrix of social structural inequalities. And in sentencing Ahumada to prison, the court performed its role as a "network hub" that produces and distributes subjects for other sites of criminal legal governance and predation.

In this chapter, we extend our analysis of predation from police and courts to incarceration, community supervision, and related programs (such as diversion and reentry). In these arenas, public agencies use financial extraction and penal labor to keep costs down, supplement budgets, manage legally entangled people, and subsidize a wide range of government operations. They do not, however, act alone. More often than not, custodial and supervisory modes of predation in the US are organized as public–private partnerships that operate for mutual benefit.

Race and class targeting are fundamental to the forms of predation analyzed in this chapter, baked in from the get-go by the social concentration of jail, prison, and community supervision populations in America.[6] Indeed, today as in the past, predatory practices that operate through penal custody and supervision disproportionately target race-class subjugated (RCS) communities.[7] The form and focus of these practices, however, have shifted over time. For most of US history, penal forms of predation overwhelmingly focused on labor extraction (see chapter 1). Since the 1970s, coercive and exploitative labor practices have declined in US prisons, and since the 1980s, financial modes of predation have soared.

Between 1974 and 2004, the average number of hours worked by an imprisoned individual in a week dropped by more than 50 percent.[8] "The market for the products of prison labor," Adam Reich explains, "has declined dramatically, and incarcerated people, on average, are working less [today] than ever before, yet inequality in the distribution of work and [its] rewards has sharpened over time."[9] On an average day, roughly one-third of people held in state prisons do not work at all; of those who do, 20 percent work ten or fewer hours per week.[10] Moreover, incarcerated people in the US have become far less likely to supply labor for private companies. In fact, the vast majority of people who work in prisons, jails, and detention centers perform "housework" for the custodial facility itself (e.g., laundry or food service). Wendy Sawyer and Peter Wagner are succinct: The idea that US prisons today are "'factories behind fences' that exist to provide companies with a huge slave labor force" is a myth.[11]

As we show in this chapter, substantial amounts of labor exploitation continue to take place under the auspices of penal custody and supervision. Private companies still profit from penal labor in various ways, particularly through community supervision and related programs. The scale of these practices, however, bears little resemblance to the labor-supply operations that made penal institutions major engines of economic development and capital accumulation in some earlier eras of US history. Conversely, as mass incarceration advanced after the 1970s, penal governance became a growing site of public revenue production, corporate investment, and private profit. Extractive practices based on financial charges, debts, and payments became pervasive, routine features of carceral and supervisory operations.

We begin our analysis with penal labor exploitation, first in prisons and then in the context of community supervision programs. We then turn to the various ways government agencies produce revenue through direct financial charges and takings and via commissions paid by corporate partners. Next, we explore how public and private actors work to maximize revenues flowing from "voluntary" purchases made by imprisoned people and their loved ones. We analyze how corporations profit from incarceration by tapping into public funding streams. And finally, we examine how charge-and-payment practices operate in community supervision programs.

Public Uses of Prison Labor

Throughout the US today, incarcerated people are subjected to intensive labor exploitation, often under threat of losing vital privileges and suffering other penalties.[12] Because they labor under the auspices of criminal punishment, incarcerated workers are not "employees." Consequently, Erin Hatton explains, they are largely stripped of the "rights and protections that define free-world labor: [There is] no minimum wage, no overtime, no unemployment, no workers' compensation, no social security, no occupational health and security protections, and no right to form unions and collectively bargain."[13] For extraordinarily low pay (and in some states, no pay at all), incarcerated workers generate substantial benefits for governments and, in a much smaller number of cases, for private businesses as well.

On any given day, roughly two-thirds of the people held in state and federal prisons have job assignments.[14] The large majority of these workers perform various kinds of "prison housework" that enable and subsidize the daily operations of carceral facilities.[15] They "cook and serve food in prison mess halls; they clean prison dorms, bathrooms, schoolhouses, hospitals, and recreation yards; they fix prisons' electrical and plumbing systems; they paint prison walls and wash prison windows."[16] Typically, these are monotonous, remedial, "dead-end" assignments of the lowest status[17] and they pay horribly—on average in 2004, just $5.88 *per week*.[18] Currently, in Alabama, Arkansas, Florida, Georgia, Mississippi, South Carolina, and Texas, the workers who do these jobs get paid nothing at all. Notably, the percentage of incarcerated workers assigned to these facility-sustaining "housework" jobs *grew* by 18 percent from 1974 to 2004.[19]

In many states, agricultural forms of penal labor also help to underwrite prison operations. Nationally, only about 2 percent of imprisoned people do this kind of work, but the percentage is much higher in some states (e.g., 17 percent in Arkansas).[20] Imprisoned workers grow crops and raise animals that allow state departments of corrections (DOCs) to feed the people they incarcerate at a fraction of the cost that market suppliers would charge. From 2014 to 2018, for example, the Texas DOC saved $160.3 million "by producing food and fiber items instead of purchasing those products externally."[21] Some DOCs also generate revenue through sales to other public agencies and private businesses. The federal law that prohibits selling prison-made goods on the open market exempts agriculture,[22] and this carve-out has helped to make penal labor an important link in the nation's food supply chain. An Associated Press investigation of prison-farmed goods and livestock identified almost $200 million in sales between 2018 and 2023.[23] The buyers included major retailers such as Walmart, Target, Costco, Aldi, and Whole Foods as well as the makers of food and beverage brands such as Ball Park hot dogs, Gold Medal flour, Coca-Cola, and Riceland rice.

The old American tradition of forcing incarcerated people to toil on penal farms continues in places like Louisiana's Angola prison, where every incarcerated resident (74 percent of whom are Black) is initially assigned to work in the fields. Angola is one of a handful of contemporary penal farms whose operations can be traced back directly to chattel slavery, with some located on the same lands as pre–Civil War plantations.[24] Some southern states force imprisoned people, disproportionately Black men, to work the farms without pay.[25]

Practitioners and professionals in the field value prison work for multiple reasons. It helps authorities manage prison populations by keeping residents busy and integrating them into supervised work routines. Many also see it as an effective way to reform individuals convicted of crimes.[26] Although this idea has a long history in the US, Reich argues that its focus has shifted since the 1970s. In earlier eras, penal labor was generally touted as a tool of personal transformation—a way to foster better habits, self-control, and respect for authority. Today, "reform" focuses more on the cultivation of *market* mentalities and forms of discipline. Toward these ends, prison administrators emphasize "the importance of making the job market inside the prison as similar to the one outside as possible, so that incarcerated people can learn to respond to market incentives—and can behave as disciplined market subjects inside."[27]

Prison labor also offers administrators a way to avoid the higher costs of paying market wages to workers from surrounding communities. A report by the American Civil Liberties Union (ACLU) and the Global Human Rights Clinic at the University of Chicago Law School (GHRC) concludes that penal labor exploitation "saves state governments billions of dollars a year in prison upkeep. One conservative 2004 estimate placed the nationwide value of these cost-saving services at about $9 billion."[28] To put this figure in perspective, consider that from 2002 to 2010, *total* state corrections expenditures in the US were roughly $48–$53 billion per year.[29] Penal labor subsidizes prison operations, helping to shield taxpayers from the full costs of mass incarceration.

In 2017, a Louisiana county sheriff underscored this reality as he spoke out against a law that threatened to reduce the number of people under state custody who were held in local jails. Unlike pretrial defendants, these convicted individuals could be legally forced to work. The sheriff publicly complained that the new law would take away "some good ones that we use every day to wash cars, to change the oil in our cars, to cook in the kitchen, to do all that where we save money."[30] Similarly, a Florida public official told a local newspaper: "There's no way we [could] take care of our facilities, our roads, our ditches, if we didn't have inmate labor."[31]

As this list suggests, penal labor subsidizes a wide array of government functions and projects beyond the operations of carceral facilities.[32] Imprisoned people in the US today clean courthouses, construct government buildings, remove deer carcasses from roadways, tend graveyards, repair public water tanks, answer phone calls for departments of motor vehicles, make hand sanitizer (a critical service during the COVID-19 pandemic), and clear homeless encampments. Pay for these work assignments varies considerably. In some states, Hatton finds, "prisoners on work crews earn the same as they would in prison maintenance jobs (including nothing in no-wage states); in other states, depending on the job, they may earn closer to correctional industry wages," as discussed below.[33]

Some incarcerated people travel to "work camps," living and laboring away from prisons for extended periods of time. In California, roughly 4,000 convicted individuals do time at state-run prison fire camps, working alongside other firefighters.[34] For this dangerous work, they earn "good time" credits that reduce their sentences, $2 per day, and an additional $1 per hour when actively fighting fires.[35] The wage is a tiny fraction of the $27.77 per hour paid to other wildland firefighters, but given the penurious wages usually paid for penal labor, the California DOC can rightly describe it as "lavish pay by prison standards."[36]

When a court ruling threatened to shrink the program in 2014, the state attorney general's office warned that doing so "would severely impact fire camp participation, a dangerous outcome while California is in the middle of a difficult fire season and severe drought." Other firefighters could be hired at regular wages, but the state of California saves about $100 million each year by using prison labor.[37] Speaking of these firefighters in 2017, Governor Jerry Brown framed penal labor as a state resource that needed to be systematically managed: "It's very important when we can quantify that manpower, utilize it."[38] In 2018, during peak fire season, the California DOC adopted a more civic-minded frame, proudly announcing that fifty-eight *juveniles* were among the 2,000 incarcerated firefighters who served "a vital role, clearing thick brush down to bare soil to stop the fire's spread."[39]

The "state use" system of penal labor that began in the early 1900s (see chapter 1) is still operational. In 2004, just under 5 percent of incarcerated workers were assigned to "correctional industries," down from 13 percent in 1974.[40] Paid an average of $27.39 per week (450 percent more than "prison housework" pay), industry workers produce a wide range of goods and perform services that DOCs sell to other public agencies.[41] In 2021, state use programs produced goods and services worth a little over $2 billion.[42] The system operates as a command economy: "Many states require all state agencies, political units, and public institutions to purchase manufactured goods, including furniture, cleaning supplies, and uniforms, from their state correctional industries."[43] Under the same model, federal agencies must buy goods from UNICOR, the federal prison system's correctional industries program.

The programs occasionally generate substantial revenues. In 2020, DOC sales of goods and services brought in over $33 million in Illinois and more than $191 million in California, while UNICOR generated $404 million in proceeds at the federal level.[44] As a general matter, though, correctional industry programs are not big moneymakers. In fact, as Christian Parenti observed in 1999, "most prison industries end up *costing* the government money, or at best break even."[45] The vast majority of state use programs today are able to self-fund operations.[46] However, some still operate in the red, at least periodically.[47] The federal UNICOR program, for example, was not profitable for eight years in a row, 2009–2016.[48]

Private businesses directly employ only a small percentage of incarcerated people, generally through two kinds of arrangements. In work-release programs, people held in prisons and jails leave to work for a business or nonprofit during the day and then return at night. Public agencies, which pay very little overhead for these programs, generate revenue by garnishing substantial portions of work-release employees' "free-world wages."[49] An Associated Press investigation found that Alabama officials brought in more than $30 million over a five-year period by taking 40 percent of work-release participants' earnings. In Louisiana, sheriffs, who receive "about $10 to $20 a day for each state prisoner they house in local jails to help ease overcrowding . . . can deduct more than half of the wages earned by those contracted out to companies—a huge revenue stream for small counties."[50]

The second arrangement operates inside custodial facilities. From the 1930s through the 1970s, federal law prohibited the sale of prison-made goods on the open market. In 1979, however, federal lawmakers created the Prison Industry Enhancement Certification Program (PIECP), which allows businesses to set up shop inside prisons (in order to directly oversee production) or delegate managerial duties to prison staff, who supervise incarcerated workers as they fill company orders. Today, prison laborers do everything from computer coding, data entry, and telemarketing to metal fabrication and product construction, packaging, and assembly. These are the highest status prison jobs; they pay the most and "typically include job training in marketable skills."[51]

PIECP programs in the US today are very small, however, not only in comparison to the prison industries of earlier eras but also relative to the other penal labor practices discussed in this section. As of September 2021, they employed only 4,860 individuals nationwide.[52] By law, prisons and their business partners must pay the "prevailing wage" for a category of work, consult local unions, and show they will not displace nonincarcerated workers—all of which suggests that the terms of PIECP employment should align with local labor markets. In reality, workers in the program tend to receive little for their labors. Private employers, Hatton explains, "often pay only the minimum wage, not the prevailing wage, and legal loopholes [sometimes] allow them to pay even less."[53] In addition, the law allows prison officials to deduct up to *80 percent* of PIECP workers' wages for various purposes. From 1979 to 2018, penal authorities garnished $272 million "to cover costs of incarceration."[54]

Labor Predation and Community Supervision

Beyond the confines of jails and prisons, community supervision programs compel individuals to work for free or very low wages under *threat of incarceration*. The precise number of people subjected to such practices is unknown. But even if that number included only a fraction of the roughly 3.7 million Americans on probation and parole (in 2021), it would run to the hundreds of thousands,[55] and that's before factoring in the many people forced to work under community service sentences and court-mandated treatment programs.

"Work requirements are ubiquitous conditions of parole, probation, and supervised release," Noah Zatz explains. "This means that, in principle, parolees [and probationers] can be incarcerated for failing to find a job, for quitting or refusing a job, or for working at a job that fails to maximize earnings."[56] This is no idle threat. Zatz and colleagues report that on any given day in the US, about 9,000 people—disproportionally Black and Latine—are incarcerated for violating work requirements under community supervision.[57] Compared to prison labor exploitation, which primarily subsidizes government operations, supervision programs play a far greater role in supplying highly exploitable workers to private employers. Indeed, to avoid getting locked up, people in these programs are often forced to accept the worst kinds of private-sector jobs and working conditions.

Formerly incarcerated people confront significant barriers in their efforts to secure decent employment.[58] Nevertheless, most parole programs pressure them to secure a wage-earning job as quickly as possible.[59] The result, Gretchen Purser argues, is that people are routinely "channeled toward, and relegated to, the bottom segment of the labor market."[60] Through ethnographic research, Purser shows how parole programs funnel participants into day labor jobs marked by "deplorable pay and exploitative working conditions."[61] Day labor agencies, she explains, "offer parolees an opportunity to acquire the documentation of gainful employment that is stipulated as a condition of parole and that thereby functions as a form of extra-economic coercion in the workplace. This is something to which employers, dispatchers, and laborers readily attest. One dispatcher matter-of-factly stated that one of the reasons workers come to his agency is 'because their parole officer sent them and they work here because of that. Many POs,' he continued, 'communicate directly with me.'"[62] In these arrangements, Purser finds that employers exercise extensive control over workers, acting as de facto parole agents, who can set parole-violation processes in motion with a phone call.

In a separate ethnographic study, Susila Gurusami explores Black women's experiences with parole and probation supervision in Los Angeles.[63] Across the two contexts, she finds a shared emphasis on requiring and monitoring work. Job-seeking and employment serves as a major focus of interactions with parole and probation officers. Backed by the threat of (re)incarceration, the officers pressed the women in Gurusami's study to find formal, documentable jobs, put in longer work hours, and forgo investments in long-term goals in favor of immediate work.

While parole and probation push people into highly exploitative jobs, community service programs generate free (or very cheap) labor for governments and nonprofit organizations. Among penal professionals, community service is often viewed as a favorable alternative to incarceration or probation for people convicted of low-level crimes. However, a national study finds that community service is frequently mandated as a *supplement* to probation and that "manual labor is by far the most common type of service work."[64] To participate, individuals must sign "volunteer" contracts in which they agree to waive the safeguards of minimum wage and labor protection laws. In some jurisdictions, they are also required to pay signup and maintenance/monitoring fees.[65]

In some cases, court officials force people who are unable to pay off their legal financial obligations to "volunteer" for service (e.g., as an alternative to jail). Zatz and colleagues report that in "Los Angeles alone, 50,000–100,000 people each year must perform unpaid, court-ordered community service, often to work off criminal justice debt. State and municipal governments and nonprofits get a stream of free labor from individuals who may have to work for hundreds of hours."[66]

Local, state, and federal governments all promote the societal and fiscal benefits of forcing juveniles and adults to do community service work.

On its website, the Missouri DOC announces that "probation and parole staff oversee the completion of more than 385,000 community service hours annually, which translates into nearly $3 million in free labor and services."[67] A key "benefit" of the program, a federal agency's website explains, is that it "gives the community free labor and provides services that otherwise might not be available due to lack of funding."[68]

Sometimes, labor is also required as a condition of pretrial diversion programs that allow accused individuals to avoid prosecution (and potentially probation or incarceration). In an investigative series published by *Reveal*, Amy Harris and Shoshana Walter show how judges in Oklahoma, Arkansas, Texas, Missouri, and North Carolina use drug diversion programs to channel thousands of people into exploitative labor projects. In Oklahoma, courts send about 280 men to Christian Alcoholics & Addicts in Recovery (CAAIR) each year. Under CAAIR's supervision, the men are required to work without pay for chicken processing companies, participate in Bible study, and attend Alcoholics and Narcotics Anonymous meetings.[69]

Men who complete the CAAIR program are eligible for a $1,000 stipend, but a 2014 report finds that only one in four makes it to the end. The rest either quit or get expelled for infractions such as relapsing or not being dutiful enough in their work. Brad McGahey is one who didn't make it. McGahey was sent to CAAIR (instead of prison) after stealing a horse trailer and violating the terms of his probation. Although McGahey did not have a substance abuse problem, the judge argued that the program would teach him a better "work ethic" and help him stay out of prison in the future. During a shift at the poultry processing center, McGahey's hand got stuck in a conveyor belt, leading to a "severe crush injury." Doctors told him not to work while his hand healed, but CAAIR supervisors held the line: "You can either work or you can go to prison." McGahey responded, "I'll take prison over this place. . . . Anywhere is better than here."[70]

Indeed, by refusing to work, McGahey violated his diversion agreement and soon found himself in prison. He was now free of CAAIR and the chicken processing racket, but in reality, he had only entered a different chamber of the predatory criminal legal labyrinth.

Incarceration, Financial Extraction, and Public Revenue

In our analysis of courts and law enforcement agencies in chapter 2, we charted the dramatic rise of predatory financial practices that began in the 1980s and '90s. Developments in the carceral sector followed a similar path. From the 1980s onward, public officials searched relentlessly for ways to generate revenue from penal institutions and the people they held captive.

Government efforts to make mass incarceration fiscally productive have taken many forms. Local politicians, especially in struggling rural areas, have often competed to bring jails and prisons to their towns, in hopes that they might offer residents jobs, jumpstart economic development, and increase tax revenues.[71] In the penal "bed market," local jail administrators essentially rent out their unused spaces, charging a price to "take in people from overcrowded state prisons . . . jails in neighboring counties" or federal detention centers.[72] These contracts can sometimes be lucrative, and some counties now depend on bed rentals to finance their jails.[73] Since the 1980s, however, the most pervasive and consequential efforts to generate public revenue from mass incarceration have focused on reconfiguring operations inside jails and prisons.

Across the US, people in custody are treated as consumers of public services and forced to pay a wide array of "pay-to-stay" fees for their own incarceration, such as booking fees, per diem "rent," and bills for necessities such as medical and dental care, food, clothing, and toiletries. Although a handful of jurisdictions charged for a small number of services in earlier decades, pay-to-stay fees were quite rare until the 1980s.[74] In the years that followed, one state after another adopted new rules that forced imprisoned people to "pay for their crimes" in financial ways that went beyond their formal sentencing.[75] As the size and costs of penal populations grew, mandatory charges for "custodial services" promised to generate sorely needed revenue. Today, all fifty states contain some jurisdictions that levy jail or prison pay-to-stay fees, and forty-three authorize prisons to charge them on a statewide basis.[76]

Pay-to-stay fees routinely saddle incarcerated people with debts, which then need to be collected. To do so, many state DOCs deduct payments from prison labor wages and from funds that family members and friends deposit into imprisoned individuals' accounts. Government agencies in some states have used lawsuits to collect on such debts, targeting resources that incarcerated people have received through inheritance, trust funds, legal settlements, or even intellectual property such as artwork or a book.[77] In 2018, for instance, Curtis Dawkins received a $150,000 advance for his acclaimed short story collection, *The Graybar Hotel*. When he tried to put the money in an education fund for his children, the state of Michigan sued to seize 90 percent of it as payment for his imprisonment.[78]

Often, the collections efforts continue after individuals are released from prison. This is especially the case in juvenile systems, where parents can be billed for years after the end of a child's incarceration.[79] But as of 2015, at least eight states held formerly incarcerated adults legally liable for financial obligations incurred in prison, with many partnering with debt collectors to bring in payments.[80] In Florida and Wisconsin, liability for the debts continues even after death, so that government agencies can demand payments from the individual's estate.[81]

Because there are no systematic reporting requirements for pay-to-stay fees and collections, there are no national estimates of how much revenue they generate. Given how poor incarcerated people and their kin tend to be and how little prison jobs pay, it seems likely that the national total is very modest (especially in comparison to budgetary needs). In some instances, though, charges imposed for room and board, health care, food, clothing, and other basic needs can generate meaningful sums.[82] In 2013, a single local jail in Macomb County, Michigan collected $1.5 million in room and board.[83] The state of Michigan brought in $3.7 million in 2017,[84] and from 2001 to 2005, Connecticut generated $5 million in revenue through pay-to-stay fees.[85]

For businesses that claim they can increase collections, the difficulty of extracting payments from people who own and earn so little presents an opportunity. In Ohio, Intellitech Corporation created specialized software for pursuing pay-to-stay fees. The company keeps 70 percent of the money it collects (after delivering 30 percent to the county), so it has strong incentives to be aggressive. As a result, the ACLU of Ohio explains, "many of the counties [with] the highest pay-to-stay fees . . . utilize Intellitech to administer their collections policy."[86] The company's president, John Jacobs, refers to Intellitech as the "Walmart" of the pay-to-stay world and insists that it is "a win for the taxpayers and a win for the sheriff."[87]

In addition to pay-to-stay fees, which *impose* financial charges on individuals, some penal agencies also generate revenue by selling "pay-for-upgrade" packages that allow people with sufficient means to improve the terms of their custody. In California, people held in some local jails can pay about $75–$127 per night to do their time in a more comfortable facility. The upgrade in Seal Beach, for example, offers TVs, computers, and newer beds.[88] Because payments must be made up front, programs of this sort require no collection efforts. In local lockups, they work to deepen the already-severe social inequalities that suffuse public custody in America. They allow people with greater resources to buy their way out of the most unhealthy, chaotic, and potentially dangerous conditions, which other jailed individuals are forced to endure.

The lion's share of public revenue generated by jails and prisons does not come from fees directly charged to incarcerated people, however. It comes from selling businesses access to the human "assets" that penal agencies control—captive markets held in carceral facilities, where "consumers" can be charged inflated prices for low-quality goods and services. Consider the case of carceral banking, a service that has become increasingly essential as public officials have attached fees and prices to more and more aspects of custodial life. Very few people in jails and prisons can pay for their day-to-day expenses on their own. Most depend on people from the outside community to send them money.

Until the early 2000s, friends and family members made deposits in prison accounts either in person or by mailing in paper money orders.[89] In 2002, entrepreneur Ryan Shapiro proposed an electronic banking system that would allow people to put money in such accounts via computers (and eventually smartphones).[90] To entice cash-strapped jail and prison administrators and establish his operations, Shapiro offered a deal that was hard to refuse. His company, JPay Corp., would cover all transition costs and then pay government partners up to 10 percent of its fee-based revenues.[91]

As the carceral banking sector grew and competing companies emerged, government agencies were positioned to choose the most advantageous deals. In evaluating bids for contracts, they have frequently prioritized the size of commissions. The Florida DOC, for example, explicitly states that "The department will make an award, by region, to the responsive, responsible bidder submitting the highest percentage commission."[92] For carceral banking companies to be seen as viable bidders, then, a healthy commission offer is often essential. The sizable cuts given to governments, however, are generally well worth it to the company. Once the contract is inked, the business enjoys a monopoly. Community members cannot shop around for the best deal; they must deposit money through the facility's chosen vendor.

The arrangement has paid off handsomely for JPay. In 2013, JPay processed roughly seven million transactions, yielding total revenue of more than $50 million.[93] By 2014, the company had "grown to provide money transfers to more than 1.7 million offenders in thirty-two states, or nearly 70 percent of the inmates in US prisons."[94] In 2014, JPay reportedly took in $53 million in deposit fees.[95] The big numbers reflect JPay's dominant market position, which it owes, at least in part, to the generous commissions it pays: As of 2014, government agencies received $0.50–$2.50 from JPay for each and every money transfer.[96]

Commission payments align the financial interests of public and private partners, giving governments a material incentive to allow companies like JPay to charge exorbitant rates. And because public officials have largely declined to regulate carceral banking, price-setting is subject to few external constraints. Providers can charge friends and family members as much as the "market" will bear—sometimes upward of 45 percent of each deposit.[97] JPay's rates vary across jurisdictions and depend on the amount and mode of transfer (e.g., computer versus phone). In Minnesota, for example, JPay charges $3.95 for a $0.01–$20 deposit, $6.95 for $20.01–$100, $8.95 for $100.01–$200, and $10.95 for $200.01–$300 (plus $1 for phone deposits).[98] Because the fees make up a higher percentage of smaller transfers—almost 50 percent of a $10 deposit by phone—they hit the poorest users the hardest.

The companies are quick to point out that people do not *have* to use their banking services; they can still send money orders through the mail. In practice, though, friends and family have strong incentives to use the fee-based electronic system. To mail a deposit, individuals must fill out a form and send it with the money order, instructing JPay to put the money into a specified account. This hard-copy process can take days, weeks, or even months.[99] To push friends and family toward the more costly electronic option, JPay highlights the delay right on the deposit form: "Did you know? Money orders can take days to mail and process? There's a Better Way. Send money without a money order—and get the funds there faster!"[100]

Carceral banking is usually thought of as a form of *private* profiteering. In reality, it is a predatory public–private partnership. Governments make money, in effect, by selling companies monopoly rights to access captive markets; commissions function as the price of sale for opportunities to exploit the human beings that governments hold in custody. Desperate to supplement their budgets, many public agencies collaborate with their corporate partners to sustain inflated prices and push depositors toward choices that maximize revenue. In fact, in addition to commissions from the company, many penal agencies claim a further cut of deposits as payment for the pay-to-stay fees they impose—and do so *before* the intended recipient can access the funds.

With slight modifications, this model—the contractual exchange of monopoly access for commissions—generates public revenue across a wide range of carceral functions and operations. Consider commissaries, where imprisoned people spend a sizable portion of the funds deposited in their bank accounts (after public and private partners claim their shares). Commissaries are often run by a for-profit company such as Keefe Group, Oasis, Trinity, or Aramark. To become the sole provider inside a carceral facility, the firms pay commissions to governments that can exceed 45 percent of revenue.[101] Once established, they are able to sell products to incarcerated people at inflated prices.[102] A 2018 study of Illinois, Washington, and Massachusetts found that individuals spent an average of $947 per year for commissary goods (primarily food and hygiene supplies).[103] Nationwide, commissary sales in prisons and jails total roughly

$1.6 billion per year, generating significant profits for industry leaders and steady revenues for governments.[104]

People held in jails and prisons—who commonly struggle with isolation, boredom, stress, and social deprivation—also must pay fees to maintain relationships with people on the outside. Until the 1990s, phone call rates inside and outside carceral facilities were roughly similar.[105] Over the ensuing decades, corporations and governments restructured phone services to advance their shared revenue interests. Today, jail and prison phone calls are often very expensive, sometimes costing upward of $17 for fifteen minutes.[106]

For telecom companies, large commission payments have not only secured government cooperation; they have also provided a justification for exorbitant prices. Citing the large commissions public agencies take (typically 20–63 percent), companies such as Securus and Global Tel-Link (GTL) insist that they have no choice but to charge high per-minute rates and add-on fees.[107] In 2013 alone, telecom companies delivered $460 million to their public partners.[108] Between 2004 and 2014, a single leading company, Securus, paid over $1.3 billion in commissions to governments.[109] The companies are not suffering, though. After the payouts, they collectively take in about $1.6 billion per year.[110] They are so lucrative that powerful private equity firms have singled them out for acquisition in recent years. In 2011, American Securities purchased GTL for $1 billion, and six years later, Platinum Equity bought Securus for $1.5 billion, taking control of JPay as well (which Securus had acquired in 2015).[111]

Under the Obama administration, the Federal Communications Commission (FCC) moved to regulate prison and jail phone services, setting caps on prices and, thus, limiting revenues for corporations and state and local governments. Industry leaders turned to the courts, filing legal challenges to block implementation. In 2017, under the leadership of a new chair appointed by President Donald Trump, the FCC chose not to defend the phone rate caps in court, bringing the brief stint of regulation to an end. (Tellingly, it was *after* the FCC made this decision that Platinum Equity moved forward with its plan to acquire Securus.[112])

As they put an end to the FCC's rate caps, the leading telecoms also branched out in new directions. Many prisons now provide dedicated kiosks where individuals can exchange electronic messages with friends and family for a fee.[113] This low-quality imitation of email typically costs around $0.50 per message, with additional charges for attachments. Messages are limited in length, ranging from 1,500 to 6,000 characters, and are closely monitored by authorities. In 2014, the kiosks generated $8.5 million for JPay, roughly 12 percent of its total revenue.[114] In this case as well, governments take a cut of the action. For instance, Washington's prison system receives commissions set at 5 percent of JPay's e-message earnings.[115]

Investments in video visitation have produced a particularly robust area of growth. Bolstered by arguments that the old practice of free, in-person visitation posed a security risk, public and private actors established a more profitable digital format for meeting social needs. In 2015, the Prison Policy Initiative reported that over 500 penal institutions in forty-three states and Washington DC tested out video visitation.[116] The price for such visits varies but in some places costs $1 a minute, plus additional fees.[117] For penal administrators, video visitation offers a way to generate revenue from commissions and an opportunity to reduce or reassign in-person visitation staff.[118]

Generating "Voluntary" Purchases

Some forms of carceral predation, such as pay-to-stay fees, work by imposing financial charges. Others require imprisoned people or their friends and family to make a "voluntary" choice. For JPay to turn a profit and pay its commissions, for example, substantial numbers of people must decide to deposit funds in carceral bank accounts. In this section, we explore two ways that public and private partners work to maximize such purchases: channeling and nudging.

Channeling works by positioning actors, structuring options, and shaping circumstances so that imprisoned people and their loved ones become more likely to make revenue-generating choices. In some cases, successful channeling requires little more than the establishment of a monopoly provider. Where basic needs such as toilet paper or tampons are involved, for example, the elimination of alternative providers is generally sufficient. As of 2022, jails and prisons in thirty-eight states had no legal obligation to provide menstrual products to incarcerated women.[119] In these states, payments to a facility's sole, for-profit vendor may be the only way for a woman under custody to obtain basic, routinely needed healthcare products.

A company that operates as a sole vendor may not hold a true monopoly, however, if a publicly run prison already supplies similar goods or services free of charge. In such cases, for-profit providers have a clear financial stake in making sure that publicly provided alternatives are more limited, inferior in quality, or harder to access. Public agencies' incentives are often aligned: Restricted prison offerings of sub-standard goods can help keep budgetary costs down, and elevated sales by a corporate partner can boost commission payments.

Prison commissaries provide a good example of this dynamic. Throughout the US, the small amounts, low quality, and severely limited variety of prison-provided food and toiletries motivate incarcerated people to spend money at commissaries. April Grayson, a woman imprisoned in California, explains: "The bar of soap dissolves after one shower. . . . And the deodorant burns your underarms. . . . Everyone who is locked up is hungry. . . . They don't provide enough food."[120] To stave off hunger, Grayson used the scant earnings from her prison job to buy ramen noodles. The ramen packets are available only for purchase, and as Michael Gibson-Light explains, they are so valued behind bars that they now serve as "the de facto form of informal money" that people trade for other goods, such as clothes, coffee, or tobacco.[121] In a study of formerly incarcerated people in New York, Tommaso Bardelli and colleagues report that "most people agreed that one needed to spend at least $50 on food every other week to supplement paltry meals served by the prison mess hall and avoid feeling constantly hungry."[122]

A similar dynamic underwrites profits in the large and growing market for prison e-tablets. Tablets are increasingly available for purchase in US jails and prisons, though some companies play the long game by giving them to imprisoned people for free.[123] In both cases, the provider's main goal is to secure a basis for ongoing tablet-based purchases. For a price, incarcerated people can use the tablets to "email" with people on the outside and access music, books, movies, podcasts, or videogames. The sales generate corporate profits and commissions for governments.

To channel people toward tablet purchases, some state facilities have confiscated radios and MP3 players, forcing a shift from free entertainment devices to those that charge a fee.[124] Similarly, some administrators have pushed people to pay for ebooks on their tablets by restricting free prison library services or banning the receipt of books through the mail.[125] Custodial facilities have used the same tactic to promote the use of "debit release cards." When people leave prison or jail, they often have funds left in their carceral bank accounts (from working, family deposits, or government-provided "gate money"). Before the early 2000s, facilities transferred these funds by check or cash.[126] Seeing an opportunity, for-profit firms advocated for a transition to "release cards," preloaded with individuals' funds. Many jails and prisons made the switch and ended the use of checks and cash, effectively channeling released individuals into an arrangement where fees may be charged for balance inquiries, withdrawals, transfers to separate accounts, or even inactivity.[127] The for-profit release-card system has now become widespread across the US.[128]

States and counties have used similar channeling methods to facilitate transitions to fee-based video visitation, compelling usage by restricting in-person visits. A 2015 study found that 74 percent of jails that adopted video visitation did away with face-to-face visits entirely.[129] In the early years of the transition, Securus contractually *required* some jails to end in-person visits once video visitation was installed.[130] Although contracts no longer require jails to shut down in-person visitation, authorities have strong incentives to do so. In some counties, jails receive a portion of video visitation revenues (rather than or in addition to fixed commissions). In St. Clair County, Michigan, for example, Securus gives the jail 50 percent of the money it makes from video calls.[131] A complaint filed in a class action lawsuit against St. Clair and Securus details: "The county's proceeds from phone and video calls have grown to occupy a significantly larger portion of the jail budget. From 2015 to 2017, during the three years immediately preceding the elimination of jail visitation, jail call revenue averaged a 4 percent share of the jail's revenue. From 2017 to 2022, the most recent five years for which data is available, that share more than tripled to 14 percent of jail revenues. In 2021, revenue from family jail calls was over 18 percent of all jail revenues."[132] Given the financial motivations for channeling people into using video calls, it is perhaps unsurprising that all sixteen jails in Michigan jurisdictions no longer allow in-person visitation.[133]

While channeling works by structuring people's circumstances and options, nudging involves efforts to tempt, guilt, incentivize, or otherwise motivate people to make purchases. When users in prisons or jails turn on a tablet, for example, they are presented with images and messages designed to entice them into buying a popular band's new hit single, renting a must-see movie, or sending an electronic message to a loved one. Companies offer must-act-now "deals" to bring a sense of urgency to purchasing. Advertising tactics of this sort are not so different from what many people experience in the broader society. But given the monotonous, grim conditions of life inside prisons and jails, even small nudges can lead users to hand over what little they have for a bit of entertainment or a chance to communicate with loved ones.[134]

Friends and family members of incarcerated people are especially likely to be targeted for nudging tactics. Located outside the custodial facility, they are less affected by channeling practices and more likely to have the means to pay for goods and fee-based services. For example, once a community member uses a phone or computer to deposit money into a prison bank account, they are likely to receive a stream of emails encouraging them to do so again *and* to check out other goods and services offered by the firm. JPay sends follow-up emails that urge customers to try out the company's "VideoGram" service, which they can use to send thirty-second cell phone videos to an imprisoned loved one for a fee. JPay even offers special deals on the first message to entice people into sampling the service, and, ideally, becoming a repeat customer.

Nudges often take the form of emotional appeals designed to tug on people's heartstrings and leverage ethics of care. An email from JPay, for instance, urges recipients to "discover the emotional impact of sharing a thirty-second video clip—try JPay's VideoGram service today! [. . .] VideoGrams give your loved ones a glimpse into your life and forge a connection of caring."[135] In their messaging strategies, companies often frame themselves as caring partners trying to help families maintain their loving bonds. The tactic is common around holidays, which tend to be particularly hard times for many incarcerated people and their loved ones. In December 2017, JPay wrote to its community customers: "We know it's important for you to support your loved ones with emails and other communications . . . especially during the holidays! So to celebrate the holiday season, we are offering 10 percent off of your [email] stamp purchases starting today."[136]

The "care package" industry nicely illustrates how channeling and nudging can work in concert. Since the 1990s, many state DOCs have partnered with firms that charge fees to deliver care packages to incarcerated people. Orders are placed online, and the packages may include items such as food, beverages, toiletries, electronics, and clothing.[137] To channel demand, the companies have often worked with prison officials to eliminate community members' alternatives, such as personally mailing or hand-delivering a box of goods to a prison. Where such options remain, people who send their own packages often must navigate "byzantine gifting rules."[138] Because any misstep can lead staff to toss a package in the trash, friends and family members typically order from the companies and pay marked-up prices for a limited array of preapproved items.[139]

Channeling sets the stage for nudging, mostly through industry websites designed to pull people into more frequent and costly purchases.[140] The central motif of recruitment is telegraphed by company names such as iCare, MyCarePack, Golden State Care Pack, and Care-a-Cell. Buying a package is a form of loving care work, the companies suggest, a material demonstration of affection, especially meaningful to the recipient. The websites are filled with affirming images and messages that associate purchases with positive emotions. The unstated but ever-present prod to action, however, is guilt. The websites, in effect, financialize what it means to care and turn pricey package orders into an imperative for doing right by loved ones. In this framing, those who do not pay for a delivery, however unaffordable it might be, fail their loved one in a desperate time of need.

Images of dignified, happy families of color abound on the websites, suggesting that for-profit care packages strengthen family bonds and are the kind of thing that a "decent" family does.[141] Pictures of smiling, package-purchasing women evoke gendered beliefs about caring roles and responsibilities and the moral expectation that a *good* woman makes sure her husband or son does not go without.[142] Customer testimonials stress how personally meaningful it is to fulfill this role. "This program is so wonderful," Janice testifies on Care-a-Cell's site; "it allows me to send messages of encouragement and a little something to let my son know that I am thinking of him."[143] For a mother who is struggling to make ends meet and worried that she cannot afford the company's prices, the not-so-subtle message is that a son who does *not* receive a care package might believe that no one is "thinking of him" and feel forgotten and alone.

Private Profits from Public Funds

Companies like Securus, GTL, and JPay make money by extracting resources from incarcerated people and the communities they come from. They depend on government contracts to set up their operations, but little of their revenue comes from government payments. Many companies in the carceral arena, however, profit directly from public expenditures. Architectural firms design prisons, for example, and the leader in the field, DLR Group, has raked in more than $3.5 billion in government payments for its work.[144] Big banks underwrite the bonds needed to fund many prison construction projects, and they make hefty profits as governments pay off those bonds.[145] The contractors that build custodial facilities make out well, too. From 2007 to 2012, Turner Construction brought in an average of $278 million per year through prison and jail projects.[146]

Once they are up and running, the vast majority of US prisons, including those that are publicly managed, use for-profit vendors to provide a host of goods and services. As of 2015, Corizon Health was bringing in roughly $1.5 billion annually from healthcare provision contracts in a mix of public and private penal facilities.[147] Food service companies such as Aramark and Trinity have prison-based contracts that "run into the hundreds of millions of dollars."[148] Bob Barker Industries produces a wide array of goods for prison staff and imprisoned people, generating millions in profits from government payments as well as sales to people behind bars.[149]

The "prisoner transport" industry nicely illustrates how businesses have turned basic penal operations into publicly funded profit streams. In the US today, a large number of federal, state, and local agencies pay businesses to move people (often hundreds of miles) from one custodial site to another, with typical prices running about $0.75–$1.50 per person per mile.[150] To maximize profits, the firms pack their vans full and make as few stops as possible, "relentlessly shaving time and costs on the road."[151] As one former executive stated: "You route the prisoner like a package, but miss a single deadline, and you lose money."[152] Operating with little regulatory oversight, the transport industry is rife with abuse (and lawsuits).[153] Still, the sector remains highly profitable, especially for TransCor America, a subsidiary of CoreCivic, which brought in total revenues of about $8 million in 2014–2015.[154]

The most thoroughgoing case of privatization in the carceral field has also been the most publicly debated: prisons run entirely for profit. As mass incarceration strained state capacities in the 1980s, a growing number of corporations positioned themselves as civic-minded partners, eager to help relieve government burdens. Public officials turned to outsourcing as a way to resolve capacity crises, stabilize expenditures, and shed costly responsibilities (see chapter 4).

From the mid-1980s to the late 1990s, prison companies struck major deals with state governments and a handful of federal agencies. Contracts to house state prison populations fueled most of the industry's early growth, with Corrections Corporation of America (CCA) leading the pack. Three years after its founding, CCA became a publicly traded company, initially valued for investors at $18 million. From 1991 to 1997, the firm's total revenues grew from $50 million to $462 million, as the number of beds it controlled rose to over half of the private prison market.[155] Following CCA's lead, Wackenhut Corrections Corporation (WCC) went public in 1994 with an initial valuation of nearly $20 million.[156] By 1997, the private prison industry included roughly a dozen companies that collectively brought in more than $1 billion in revenue by incarcerating roughly 85,000 people in 120 private prisons and jails (75 percent of which were managed by CCA and WCC).[157] Just ten years earlier, only about 3,000 people had been housed in such facilities.[158]

The boom was *almost* followed by a bust. In the late 1990s, the industry faced a crisis so significant that CCA teetered on the brink of bankruptcy. Throughout the decade, companies had built facilities "on spec" (without a contract in hand), in hopes that governments would fill them. Amid significant budget shortfalls, however, some state officials began to express skepticism about the idea that private prison contracts were saving governments money.[159] Under pressure from a broad coalition of advocacy organizations, religious groups, and activists, some also began to question the legitimacy of imprisoning people for profit. At the same time, a series of escapes and violent episodes in for-profit facilities undercut industry claims about the high quality of business management.[160] As a result, public officials in many states became more reluctant to enter new agreements and fill the "spec prisons."[161] Investors stepped away in significant numbers: Shares of CCA stock lost 93 percent of their value between 1998 and 2000, and WCC stocks fell by more than two-thirds.[162]

The leading firms searched for ways to adapt, and immigrant detention offered a way out. Federal lawmakers had begun to pass tough new laws that criminalized immigration and ramped up detention and deportation operations—a trend that would intensify sharply after September 11, 2001. Struggling to house the growing number of noncitizen detainees, federal agencies turned to private firms.[163] Just as their fortunes were fading, CCA and WCC secured huge new contracts.[164]

In the years since, the US government has held steady in its aggressive approach to immigrant detention, and carceral companies have profited handsomely. Between 2008 and 2016, contracts with Immigration and Customs Enforcement (ICE) generated revenues of about $700 million for CCA and $1.18 billion for GEO Group (WCC became GEO Group in 2004).[165] Under the Trump and Biden administrations, federal authorities have housed about 80 percent of immigrant detainees in for-profit lock-ups. In 2022, contracts with ICE generated more than $555 million for CoreCivic (CCA became CoreCivic in 2016) and over $1 billion for GEO Group.[166]

As they moved into new arenas, prison companies also took steps to ensure and boost their profits. Learning from the industry's earlier crisis, they prioritized "guaranteed minimum" contract provisions offering protection against risks such as scandals, political attacks, and sharp turns in governance. Such provisions require governments to pay for a set percentage of prison beds (typically 80–100 percent), regardless of whether they are filled.[167] To raise returns on investment, the big firms also cherry-picked the most profitable carceral "holdings." At the individual level, the firms worked to minimize the number of high-need, high-cost occupants held in their facilities.[168] They focus today on operating minimum- and medium-security lockups, Marie Gottschalk explains, "leaving the comparatively more expensive maximum-security inmates on the government's tab."[169]

Cashing In on Community Supervision

Earlier, we described how community supervision programs operate as sites of labor predation. Financial extraction is pervasive in this arena, too. Like prison pay-to-stay fees, charges imposed for the "use" of parole and probation services have become common. Thirty-seven states authorize parole supervision fees, with all but twelve adopting the enabling laws after 1990,[170] while forty-seven states authorize probation fees, with charges in most ranging from $10 to more than $200 per month.[171] In some states, probation agencies also charge an up-front fee for enrollment, intake, or processing that can add anywhere from $25 to $600 to an individual's bill.[172] Beyond these charges, many people placed on probation and parole are ordered to participate in and pay for more case-specific programs and services.[173]

Together, the payments can add up to substantial amounts of public revenue. In North Carolina, probation and parole fees generated over $14 million in 2014.[174] As of 2016, Massachusetts was bringing in roughly $20 million a year in probation fees based on charges to people who resided mostly in the state's poorest areas.[175] In Texas, Alexes Harris and colleagues find, "supervisory and program participation fees [account for] 33 percent of local probation office budgets statewide [and in some places up] to 60 percent of local office operating costs."[176]

Similar extractive practices have taken root in pretrial diversion programs intended to help people charged with low-level crimes avoid convictions.[177] Court officials have wide discretion over when to offer diversion, and depending on the case, *The New York Times* reports, prosecutors are "willing to adjust their diversion policies for the right price."[178] In such transactions, relief from prosecution becomes a consumer good, available only to those who can afford hundreds of dollars in fees. In some places, people have to pay up to $250 (nonrefundable) *just to find out if they are eligible* for diversion.[179] Diverted individuals typically declare their guilt and agree to accept formal conviction if they fail to complete the program. To stay in the program, they must adhere to conditions such as class attendance, community service, counseling, and drug testing—with a fee usually charged for each.[180] Officials emphasize that the fees make the programs possible but, in practice, some jurisdictions use diversion revenues as general-purpose "piggy banks."[181]

Court-ordered diversion programs are often run by for-profit providers, based on contracts that require commission payments to governments. In many jurisdictions, when a prosecutors' office sends people to a diversion company, it receives a cut of the payments made by each individual.[182] In 2012, Corrective Solutions, a leader in the field, brought in $8.8 million in revenue through admission fees plus a host of itemized charges for things like "class rescheduling, payment plans, late payments, underpayments and even overpayments."[183]

In some cases, companies have cashed in on diversion in ways that bypass governments entirely. In 2010, two Harvard business graduates founded Corrective Education Company (CEC), a diversion enterprise that focused solely on shoplifting and worked through direct partnerships with retailers.[184] To build a clientele, CEC offered retailers free technology (e.g., proprietary software to track offenders) and a cut of revenue (about $40 per enrollee).[185] The business model was simple. When on-site staff accused individuals of shoplifting, they presented them with a choice: pay for CEC diversion or face arrest and prosecution. Leaving little to chance, CEC supplied retailers with scripts and instructional videos, emphasizing that on-site staff should stress the dire consequences of arrest and conviction. To avoid this fate, the accused would need to sign CEC's "restorative justice agreement" and complete six-to-eight hours of "rehabilitative" therapy.[186]

The new business model quickly attracted major retailers, such as Abercrombie & Fitch, Bloomingdale's, Burlington Coat Factory, DSW, and Walmart.[187] From 2011 to 2015, roughly 90 percent of the 20,000 people asked to choose between arrest and CEC opted for the latter.[188] Enrollees had to pay $400–$500 for the program, and although the company had promised to provide need-based "scholarships," less than 2 percent actually received them.[189] CEC became an attractive venture capital investment and, in 2017, generated $7.6 million in revenue. That same year, however, a superior court judge ruled that CEC was engaging in a form of extortion and forbid the company from operating in California.[190] Indiana's attorney general lodged similar charges.[191] As negative publicity mounted, Walmart and other companies cut ties with CEC, significantly cutting into its profits.[192] Not long after, CEC ended its diversion operations.

For-profit probation companies, which derive their revenues entirely from individuals' fine and fee payments, have also become commonplace.[193] At least ten states (including more than 1,000 court systems) now assign people who owe *misdemeanor* fine debts to private probation services.[194] The companies collect fine payments for the courts and make money for themselves by charging fees that, in some cases, can more than double an individual's total bill.[195] In Georgia (a leader in private probation, where about thirty companies collect over $100 million in payments per year), people are frequently put on private probation simply for traffic violations, which are treated as criminal offenses in the state.[196]

Probation companies tend to be very aggressive in pursuing debt collections, with many using tactics similar to those described in chapter 2, such as threats of incarceration and letters bearing the seal of the local district attorney's office.[197] Consider the case of Harriet Cleveland. In 2008, Cleveland received traffic tickets for driving without a license or insurance in Montgomery, Alabama. The mother of three earned $7.25 an hour as a custodian. Because she lacked the money to pay her fines, the judge ordered two years of probation overseen by the for-profit firm Judicial Correction Services (JCS). Cleveland was initially relieved to stay out of jail, even at a cost of $200 per month ($40 of which went to JCS). But relief turned to desperation when she lost her job and could no longer make payments.[198]

Seeing that Cleveland was broke, JCS agents began calling her daughter, her estranged mother, and her daughter's paternal grandmother, saying that if payments were not made, Cleveland would go to jail. When these tactics fell short, JCS reported that Cleveland was "willfully" declining to pay her debts, and the court sentenced her to thirty-one days in jail.[199] Human Rights Watch reports that probation firms like JCS routinely "approach jailed probationers' families and negotiate with them for payment."[200] An agent from one of the firms outlines: "Once [the families] know you are serious, they come up with some money. That's how you have to be. They have to see that this person is not getting out unless they pay something. I'm just looking for some good faith money, really. I got one guy I let out of jail today and I got three or four more sitting there right now. . . . It's hard. You get cussed at, you get called every name in the book, you get people crying."[201]

Over the past two decades, community reentry services have served as a growing site of for-profit operations, even in states that have rejected private prisons.[202] Since 2010, GEO Group and CoreCivic have invested heavily, buying up smaller companies and cornering the market for state and federal reentry service contracts. Today, they are the controlling interests behind a large complex of residential "halfway houses" and nonresidential "day reporting" facilities that manage reentry services. In 2017, GEO Group acquired a major competitor in the halfway house industry for $360 million.[203] To keep pace, CoreCivic invested over $270 million in reentry acquisitions.[204] The two firms' rising investments in reentry are part of a broader strategy to diversify operations and change their image from prison profiteers to public-spirited partners—"good citizens" helping governments and communities to reintegrate the hundreds of thousands of people who leave prisons and jails each year.

Conclusion

It was the beginning of the end for private prisons, or so it seemed. In August 2016, the inspector general for the US Department of Justice (DOJ) issued a damning report on conditions at for-profit facilities under federal contracts.[205] One week later, the DOJ announced it would phase out contracts with prison companies. Deputy Attorney General Sally Yates explained: "Private prisons served an important role during a difficult period, but time has shown that they compare poorly to our own bureau facilities. They simply do not provide the same level of correctional services, programs, and resources; they do not save substantially on costs; and . . . they do not maintain the same level of safety and security."[206] Adopting a state-versus-market frame, Yates contrasted the troubling for-profit operations with superior conditions at government-run lockups: "These steps would be neither possible nor desirable without the bureau's superb and consistent work at our own facilities." Reformers celebrated. An anti-privatization organization, In the Public Interest, cheered: "This is *huge* news . . . a major setback for the private prison industry, which pulls in hundreds of millions of taxpayer dollars in profits each year."[207] US Senator Bernie Sanders agreed: "It is an international embarrassment that we put more people behind bars than any other country on earth. Due in large part to private prisons, incarceration has been a source of major profits to private corporations."[208]

More cautious observers noted the phaseout's limitations. The new rule would affect just thirteen private facilities, less than 12 percent of the total population incarcerated by the federal Bureau of Prisons, and only about 1 percent of the US prison population as a whole.[209] It would not reduce the number of people incarcerated; it would not apply to people held in privately run state prisons (a much larger group); and it left out federal agencies, such as ICE and the US Marshals Service, that make far greater use of private prison facilities.[210] For-profit incarceration would remain prevalent in the US, and so would contract provisions guaranteeing minimum payments to private prison operators, regardless of how many of their beds are filled.

Important as they were, these critiques left the DOJ's tidy opposition of state and market actors—and public and private motivations—largely unchallenged. In the DOJ's telling, the problem is corporate involvement, and the solution is a restoration of government control. The analysis presented in this chapter is deeply at odds with this narrative. Custodial and supervisory forms of predation in the US today are most commonly organized as public–private partnerships. They braid together what the DOJ's narrative treats as separate and opposite. *Publicly* run prisons are sites of extensive and highly profitable *private*-sector activity. They are designed at the outset by architecture firms, built by private contractors, and financed with bonds underwritten and purchased by large commercial banks. They hire corporations to run basic operations in areas such as health care and food service. They invite for-profit vendors into their facilities and allow them to exploit captive markets of imprisoned people who can be charged exorbitant prices for phone calls, video visitation, care packages, financial services, and commissary goods.

Beyond the large-scale integration of private firms into publicly run facilities, however, the DOJ's framing of government control as the solution fails in the context of penal predation in a more fundamental way. Throughout the US, governments are primary actors in custodial and supervisory predation—full participants in all its various forms and, in many cases, the creators of its extractive operations, just as they are in police- and court-based forms of predation (see chapter 2). Public agencies at all levels exploit penal labor and extract financial resources from convicted individuals and their loved ones. They relentlessly impose financial charges on custodial and supervisory populations and aggressively pursue collections. They sell corporations monopoly access to the human "assets" they control, offering the opportunity to exploit imprisoned people in exchange for commissions that generate sizable public revenues.

Legal scholar Hadar Aviram has argued that contemporary US prisons challenge "the distinction between the public and private sector . . . [and the assumption] that private actors are motivated by different incentives than public ones."[211] Publicly and privately run prisons, Aviram concludes, operate according to a shared market logic that conceives of prisons as firms, people under custody as consumers, and administrators as businesspersons.[212] Indeed, as we have shown, state and market managers alike work to make the populations they control *productive*, leveraging them to lower costs; maximize returns on investment; and achieve their revenue goals.

The thorough *marketization* of America's public institutions of criminal legal governance is, in many ways, historically distinctive. Public administrators in earlier eras cut costs and generated revenue from penal populations and operations in various ways, primarily by enforcing carceral labor and supplying it to business partners. Since the 1980s, however, government officials have greatly expanded their entrepreneurial pursuits by implementing a wide array of new predatory practices based on financial charges, debts, and payments. These practices, rather than labor exploitation, now generate the lion's share of financial rewards, for public and private actors alike. In the two chapters that follow, we present an explanation for the dramatic rise of financial predation in criminal legal governance. We begin by analyzing how broad changes in political economy combined with specific political and policy developments to drive institutional conversion. We then turn to political discourse and the framing strategies that public and private actors used to establish, legitimize, and defend their criminal legal projects of financial plunder.

PART TWO

Development

4 * Reconstructing Criminal Justice Predation

America's criminal legal institutions have been entwined with race, gender, and capitalism from their inception. Their predatory operations, however, have grown and taken new forms since the 1980s. Older modes of penal labor predation continue, but they have been surpassed in scale and consequence by practices that charge prices, impose debts, collect payments, and strip communities of assets. To understand how and why these changes occurred, it is insufficient to view criminal legal institutions in isolation, through the lens of crime and punishment. In important ways, these practices progressed as elements of a broader reworking of the social order in the late twentieth century. This is a tale of dramatic, historically specific institutional change.

In this chapter and the next, we build on a long tradition of efforts to understand how changes in penal practices relate to historical shifts in the organization of capitalism and social inequalities.[1] Today's extractive practices are diverse and, in some respects, so are their origins. The entrepreneurs who created carceral banking, for example, had no hand in the proliferation of court fees. The US Congress was central to the rise of asset forfeiture but had little to do with the growth of for-profit probation programs. Even so, such changes are best understood as connected developments that emerged together in time and moved in shared directions.

We proceed at two levels. First, we connect changes in criminal justice predation to broader shifts in political economy that swept across governing institutions after the 1960s. Next, we move closer to the ground to specify the actors, institutions, and policy developments that worked more directly to drive changes in criminal legal governance. Here, we focus on a powerful conjunction of three factors: intense fiscal strains created by anti-tax politics and policy devolution to lower levels of government; the rise of an intensely punitive and racialized tough-on-crime politics; and the large-scale entry of private businesses that saw profitable opportunities in the field.

The changes we explain in this chapter cannot be traced to a single, coordinated political campaign. They emerged in piecemeal ways, as variously situated actors managed and took advantage of shifting conditions. Institutions, organized interests, and unequal power relations play important roles in this story, as do "policy feedback effects" that transformed political landscapes and made some paths of action easier to follow than others.[2]

The Neoliberal Turn

Like many concepts used for social analysis and critique, *neoliberalism* has been defined in various ways for particular intellectual and political purposes.[3] We use the term "neoliberal" broadly to refer to actions and processes that (1) extend market logics, rationalities, and standards of evaluation to new spheres of social and political life and (2) shift or blur the boundary between state and market, drawing their institutions and actors onto common ground and restructuring their relationships in ways that are more favorable to capital accumulation. In key respects, neoliberalism can be seen as elevating principles of economic liberalism (e.g., market competition, consumer choice) over principles of political liberalism (e.g., equality of standing, participation in the collective exercise of authority) and reorganizing political relations on economic terms (e.g., treating citizens as paying consumers and their politically established rights as commodities).

Our analysis focuses on four historical developments that have reshaped liberal political economies since the 1970s. The shift toward criminal legal practices that focus on charges, debts, assets, and payments closely tracked the more general *financialization* of political economies. In turning public costs into personal responsibilities and public functions into sites of corporate investment, criminal legal governance moved in lockstep with global projects of *privatization*. New criminal legal practices that positioned citizens as consumers and government actors as entrepreneurs reflected a broader *marketization* of the state. And the growing reliance on criminal legal institutions to carry out public revenue functions progressed as part of a more general process of *securitization*.

FINANCIALIZATION

Over the past half century, "financializing" processes have transformed political economies around the world. In the resulting social order, scholars such as Nancy Fraser argue, financial charges, debts, and payments become more central to projects of capital accumulation and "global financial institutions pressure states to collude with investors in extracting value from defenseless populations." Such practices have played an increasingly prominent role in how "peasants are dispossessed and rural land grabs are accorded a veneer of legality in the capitalist periphery." Inside wealthier nations, too, financialized capitalism has been marked by a proliferation of rapacious, racially targeted practices that operate through exploitative charges and terms of debt.[4]

From this perspective, new directions in criminal justice predation since the 1980s—including the methods adopted and their timing and targeting—can be seen as instances of a more general development. In the 1980s, corporate investments in the US started to shift decisively from labor and production to financial markets, responding to the more audacious and lucrative investment vehicles allowed by financial deregulation.[5] In this same period, America increasingly became what some call a "debtfare state," in which most people carry burdensome, long-term debts, and the creation and enforcement of such debts generate vast private wealth.[6] From the start of this era, the most intensive methods of financial exploitation disproportionately targeted race-class subjugated (RCS) communities.[7] Consequently, the same communities that began to endure widespread criminal legal financial takings and debts were *simultaneously* inundated with payday lenders and other establishments that operated on financially predatory business models.[8]

In this same period, public and private actors also developed new ways to use government welfare programs as a basis for siphoning financial resources from impoverished Americans.[9] New rules turned public aid recipients into debtors by requiring them to "repay" the state for social expenditures. State officials began to routinely divert federal dollars for programs such as Medicaid and Temporary Assistance for Needy Families—officially designated for people below the poverty line—into general funds and use them for unrelated purposes. Eldercare became an expansive site of financial extraction for both public and private providers. Foster care agencies filled budget holes by seizing assets left to children by deceased relatives, including veteran's benefits, survivor benefits, and even burial plots—all in the name of repaying the state. Child support enforcement, mandatory in many poverty programs, seized resources from parents (mostly poor fathers), too.

New financial-takings practices inside and outside the criminal legal arena not only rose side by side; they became integrated. Over the past forty years, businesses that profit from consumer debt-and-payment traps have come to rely ever more on criminal courts and threats of jail to enforce collections (see chapter 2). Private equity firms have turned companies that exploit captive markets of imprisoned people into lucrative investment vehicles (see chapter 3). Predatory bail practices that connect courts, jails, and bond agencies now generate sizable financial returns for big insurance companies (see chapter 6). And corporate prison operators, such as CoreCivic and GEO Group, are publicly traded companies that generate substantial wealth for shareholders (see chapter 3). In these and many other ways, criminal legal governance in the US operates today as an integral component of financialized (and racially organized) capitalism.

PRIVATIZATION AND MARKETIZATION

Starting in the 1980s, privatization and marketization advanced in tandem. Growing numbers of businesses established themselves as partners in criminal legal governance, turning many of its operations into profitable enterprises. Embracing business models and entrepreneurial mentalities, government managers marketized their operations, working to turn the people and practices they controlled into revenue generators. Public and private partners came to treat both accused and convicted individuals as consumers, obligated to pay for "services used."

Here again, the timing and direction of change in criminal legal governance closely tracked broader developments. Since the 1980s, privatizing "reforms" have swept the globe, transferring public assets, functions, responsibilities, and authorities into business hands and establishing public–private partnerships.[10] Through outsourcing initiatives, governments have given corporations authority over critical functions such as fighting wars, administering welfare, maintaining infrastructure, providing utilities, and managing public lands.[11] Through sales to for-profit bidders, governments have stripped public assets, such as transportation and energy systems, and commodified access to essential collective goods, such as water.[12]

In the US, privatization transformed government operations into a productive basis for capital accumulation. In the criminal legal field, corporations became owners and managers of carceral institutions as well as vendors of goods and services in nominally public lockups. Municipalities and counties hired companies to operate citation-generating speeding cameras, process fine and fee payments, collect debts, monitor probationers and parolees, train police in asset seizure, run jail services, and more. As they did so, however, these same governments were *also* hiring for-profit firms to handle waste management, road construction, personnel records, retirement benefits, fishing licenses, and a host of other functions.

As privatization brought business *interests* into governance, marketization established business *models* as frameworks for organizing and evaluating public institutions.[13] In the 1990s, this development advanced rapidly under the banner of "reinventing government."[14] Public officials embraced pay-for-performance and other elements of the New Public Management that made governments run more like businesses, focused on efficiency and bottom-line results.[15] Cost-benefit analysis and return on investment became more central to the selection and evaluation of public policies. Rather than shrinking the state, as small-government rhetoric promised, institutional and policy changes turned state capacities more aggressively toward market-creating and market-supporting purposes, such as ensuring supplies of low-cost labor, bailing out corporations, and opening new sites of investment.[16]

More and more, visions of "good governance" called on resource-deprived public managers to think like entrepreneurs, look for ways to monetize their operations, and leverage the "assets" they held. Criminal legal officials were no exception in this regard. Routine police patrols could focus more intensely on seizing assets through forfeiture and handing out revenue-generating citations. Courts could charge fees to cover costs for all manner of judicial and administrative operations. Departments of corrections (DOCs) could charge pay-to-stay fees and bring in commissions by selling companies access to their captive consumers.

As elected officials cut taxes and turned away from equitable, civic visions of public finance, government agencies increasingly addressed citizens as paying consumers and funded operations through "user fees." Government allocations for public universities dwindled, and individual tuition costs ballooned. Funding for parks declined, forcing visitors to pay entry fees for a day out in nature. Against this backdrop, the widespread adoption of user charges in the criminal legal field hardly raised an eyebrow. Early in this period, in fact, a 1988 report on probation supervision by the Massachusetts Legislative Research Bureau stressed the connection: "As user fees proliferate and a pay-your-own-way philosophy of government holds sway, the question begins to change from whether to charge [supervision fees], to how much."[17]

SECURITIZATION

Fourth and finally, as investments in military, policing, and penal institutions grew dramatically during this era, practices of surveillance and punishment spread into new arenas of public life, and military and policing operations intensified and became more deeply entwined. Scholars use the term "securitization" to describe and connect these developments.

The core promise of modern government—to protect people's well-being in exchange for their funding and support—can take various forms.[18] In the last decades of the twentieth century, the basis of this promise shifted away from an active welfare state (protecting against life's risks and hardships) toward an aggressive security state (protecting against various threats, internal and external, through police and military powers). Ascendant ideologies cast government assistance as illegitimate and identified law enforcement and social control as the state's primary constitutional obligations.[19] These developments, Jackie Wang argues, constituted a significant shift "in how racialized populations in the United States would be managed."[20]

Securitization intersected with predation in at least two important ways. First, it escalated and integrated projects at home and abroad that used force to manage groups marked as threatening racial others. The line between foreign and domestic security blurred as military interventions became long-term policing operations with their own infamous prisons, such as Abu Ghraib and Guantanamo Bay, and as police departments across the US made increasing use of military hardware, tactics, and veterans.[21] Domestic policing strategies were taken abroad as models for US military operations, refined and intensified, and then returned to American cities in more martial forms.[22] The racialized "folk wisdom" of domestic law enforcement leaders in the late twentieth century was captured by Los Angeles Police Chief Daryl Gates when he observed that "the streets of America's cities had become a foreign territory."[23]

As David Harvey shows, military forces were also increasingly used in this period to facilitate processes of "accumulation by dispossession." More and more, their capacities to threaten, coerce, and secure served as tools for accessing and controlling resources (like oil) and carrying out the work of global debt enforcement.[24] At the same time, a growing number of US military operations were turned into profitable sites of corporate investment and contracting.[25] As security operations inside and outside the nation's borders grew and converged, both became more entwined with private profiteering, resource extraction, debt enforcement, and expropriation.

Second, as securitization advanced inside the US, it wove policing and penal practices into other state functions. On one side, it spread criminal logics of rule violation, policing, and punishment to new arenas, intensifying surveillance and discipline in sites such as schools, workplaces, and welfare programs.[26] On the other, it drew criminal legal institutions into the management of a wider array of public functions and problems. Police were increasingly expected to act as social workers on the street, serving as points of contact for assorted public health and social welfare interventions.[27] As public housing assistance dried up, jails and prisons became sites of residence for growing numbers of destitute people.[28] And as public investments in psychiatric hospitals and community-based treatment centers dwindled, they became the nation's largest public mental health facilities.[29] "Though intended for punishment," Bruce Western concludes, carceral facilities "had become the backstop for the American welfare state," stepping in "where the welfare state [had] failed."[30]

It was in the midst of this broader process that criminal legal institutions came to play a more central role in public revenue functions. Extractive penal practices increasingly operated as what Mary Katzenstein and Maureen Waller call "a new form of taxation," shifting the "costs of essential government services . . . to the poor."[31] Indeed, legal scholars have argued that some local practices have become so focused on revenue production that they "effectively [turn] courts, clerks, and probation officers into general tax collectors"[32] and, therefore, should be treated as an "exercise of the taxing rather than the policing power of the municipality."[33] In other words, the migration of revenue functions into the criminal legal field did not occur in isolation; it tracked broader developments during a period of far-reaching securitization.

In sum, the transformation of criminal justice predation that began in the 1980s cannot be well explained as an isolated, field-specific development. Its timing, targeting, and directions were all closely aligned with broader processes of financialization, privatization, marketization, and securitization. Predatory innovations in policing and punishment ran with, rather than against, the grain of sweeping changes that operated throughout the political economy.

Explaining Institutional Change

The connections we have drawn so far provide vital context for understanding the shifts in criminal justice predation that began in the 1980s. But they do not constitute a satisfactory explanation in their own right. To complete the work, we need to combine them with a more focused analysis of how specific actors, institutions, and policies combined to drive change.

The task would be easier if the relevant developments all stemmed from a single piece of legislation, or if actors spread across disparate arenas followed a shared, coherent plan. But that did not happen. Instead, the contemporary regime took shape through the accumulation and interaction of many developments, as various public- and private-sector actors responded to changes in their circumstances. These conditions, in turn, were largely produced through political mobilization, contests to control the use of state power, and downstream "feedback effects" generated by policies and governing strategies adopted at earlier times.[34] Against the backdrop of a racialized political economy, our explanation focuses on a conjunction of political and policy developments in public finance, policing and punishment, and privatization.

PUBLIC FINANCE

Primary responsibilities for criminal legal governance in the US fall mostly to state and local governments. Starting in the 1980s, successful campaigns to restructure public finance pushed these governments into fiscal crises that fueled desperate efforts to develop new revenue-generating practices. Our story begins at the federal level.

In 1971, as US corporations confronted tougher regulations at home and stronger competition abroad, Lewis Powell—a former president of the American Bar Association (ABA) who would later become a US Supreme Court justice—wrote a sharply worded memo to business leaders, arguing that the "American economic system is under broad attack." "There should not be the slightest hesitation to press vigorously in all political arenas for support of the enterprise system," he insisted, "nor should there be reluctance to penalize politically those who oppose it."[35] Powell's memo expressed and galvanized a growing sentiment among business elites, helping to spur a fierce political offensive. From 1974 to 1978, corporate political action committees (PACs) rose in number from 89 to 784, with another 500 emerging to represent trade associations and business interests.[36] The groups mobilized around a broad political agenda that included deregulation, rollbacks of workplace and environmental protections, and efforts to weaken labor unions. They invested heavily in campaigns to rewrite tax policies and restructure public finance.[37]

Organized business interests forged a powerful political coalition with racial and religious conservatives, and following the election of President Ronald Reagan in 1980, set to work in earnest.[38] In Washington, the pressure groups and their elected allies pursued three interrelated pathways of fiscal retrenchment: cutting federal taxes on corporations and the affluent, reducing federal spending obligations through a process of policy devolution to state and local governments, and paring back federal financial supports for subnational governments.

Working along the first path, the Reagan administration drew on bipartisan support in the US Congress to pass huge tax cuts in 1981 and again in 1986, slashing top rates for corporations and the wealthy.[39] In short order, federal revenues fell, deficits rose, and the burdens of taxation became far less progressive. These developments became durable features of federal policy over the next several decades, producing a massive redistribution of wealth to the richest Americans.[40] And as rising deficits became a source of bipartisan alarm, business and government leaders called for sharp reductions in federal expenditures and responsibilities for social welfare programs.[41]

Racial politics played an important role in these developments. In the wake of civil rights victories in the 1960s, conflicts over race and taxation converged to define a major axis of party competition.[42] Racist discourses that demonized "welfare queens" and other "freeloaders" cultivated anger in White constituencies at "what was perceived as a coercive redistributive tax state that pandered to minority interests."[43] Race also structured the distributions of benefits and burdens: Tax cuts at the top overwhelmingly enriched White Americans; the funding shortfalls they created for social investments and protections disproportionately harmed RCS communities.[44]

Federal deficits helped to spur action along the second path: policy devolution. Bolstered by fierce attacks on "big government in Washington" and celebratory images of subnational governments as "laboratories of democracy," deficit hawks argued for shifting numerous federal policy responsibilities down to states and localities. Again, racial politics played a key role. "States' rights" arguments have been used to support racial domination in the US since the era of slavery and, in the decades that preceded the 1980s, they served as a rallying cry for opponents of the civil rights movement and its legal and policy victories.[45] As a candidate and as president, Reagan proudly endorsed the doctrine.[46] At the start of his 1980 campaign, Reagan gave a speech in Neshoba County, Mississippi, infamous as the site at which, in 1964, three civil rights workers (attempting to register Black voters) were murdered "in the name of states' rights."[47] Speaking to a crowd that included members of the Ku Klux Klan—a group that soon endorsed him—Reagan pledged to "restore to states and local governments the power that properly belongs to them."[48]

During the 1980s and '90s, federal-to-state devolution advanced through a mix of explicit policy changes, unfunded mandates, and federal inaction.[49] States, in turn, passed many of their new responsibilities down to local governments through "second-order devolution."[50] City and county officials now had to shoulder a mounting number of fiscal responsibilities and burdens.[51]

As their obligations multiplied, state and local governments were rocked by developments along the third pathway of fiscal retrenchment: sharp reductions in federal transfers and new restrictions on how they could use federal dollars. Between 1980 and 2002, the proportion of municipal and county revenues supplied by the federal government declined by 54 percent.[52] The federal dollars that continued to flow were increasingly designated as individual rather than institutional supports.[53] As a result, federal transfers to fund state and local *government operations* fell by a remarkable *77 percent* between 1980 and 2004.[54]

Rising obligations and falling transfers combined to usher in a new era of "fend-for-yourself federalism."[55] More and more, state and local governments were left to their own devices as they suffered chronic fiscal shortfalls. An obvious solution for these governments would have been to raise more revenue through taxes. So, why didn't they?

The answer, in a nutshell, is that there were powerful obstacles blocking their way. Starting in the late 1970s, conservative activists had stoked racial resentments toward "government handouts" to mobilize White support for radical anti-tax measures.[56] In 1978, California voters passed Proposition 13, which imposed sharp limits on local property taxes. Soon, nearly every state restricted local tax-raising abilities, with many imposing similar limits at the state level.[57] Between 1978 and 1980, forty-three states adopted some kind of property tax limitation or relief and ten indexed income taxes to inflation.[58] States and localities throughout the US also imposed tax and expenditure limitations to tightly constrain public officials' abilities to raise tax rates, assessments of taxable property values, overall tax levies, general revenue amounts, and levels of public expenditure.[59] The Great Recession that began in 2007 brought the revenue woes of states and localities into sharp relief—and made them substantially worse.[60] But long before this time, the fiscal crisis of subnational governments had become less an event than a chronic structural condition.

The result was a sharp turn toward austerity politics, with efforts to shed burdens imposing the greatest harms on the most oppressed and marginalized communities. Austerity, Jamie Peck explains, "is something that Washington does to the states, the states do to cities, and cities do to low-income neighborhoods." It is "the means by which the costs of macroeconomic mismanagement, financial speculation, and corporate profiteering are shifted onto the dispossessed, the disenfranchised, and the disempowered."[61] Public officials moved to reduce public expenditures by chopping investments in welfare, education, and housing and working to drive down public-sector labor costs.[62] At the same time, they embarked on a relentless search for ways to raise revenue, adopting a new stance that David Harvey calls fiscal "entrepreneurialism."[63]

Many cities turned to private financial institutions to pay for operations, making themselves dependent on bond markets in ways that frequently exacerbated racial inequalities and constrained self-governance.[64] They created new fees for public goods and services, requiring residents to pay for access to licenses, permits, administrative actions, and public facilities. City leaders, pressed to act as "fiscal entrepreneurs," competed to attract private investments and secure access to various resources. They developed a host of new strategies for enticing businesses and wealthy residents to move to town, such as tax abatements and tax increment financing (TIF) bonds, cultural investments designed to appeal to upper-class tastes, and development projects that offered businesses hard-to-pass-up opportunities and infrastructures tailored to their needs.[65]

Fiscal entrepreneurialism also produced new efforts to draw public revenue from poor and working-class people. A growing roster of "sin taxes," for example, boosted revenues from alcohol, tobacco, gambling, and foods and beverages deemed unhealthy.[66] State lotteries were also created at a breakneck pace in the 1980s and '90s. The lotteries, which disproportionately attract players disadvantaged by race and/or class,[67] generated $31.2 billion in revenues for state and local governments in 2021.[68] As these examples suggest, the adoption of new tools for generating revenue from lower-income communities was not restricted to criminal legal institutions. For several reasons, though, such institutions presented public officials with especially salient and attractive sites for innovation, where revenue production could be pursued with great intensity.

To begin with, state and local officials have direct control over these institutions. So, the political actors who faced the worst fiscal pressures were also well positioned to change criminal legal practices (and in most cases, without seeking legislative permission or alerting the public). Moreover, revenues generated through policing and punishment would be relatively impervious to economic downturns, promising some stability under conditions that typically diminish other public revenue streams.[69]

Criminal legal institutions also loomed large as targets for revenue-generating innovations because they were generating some of the most extreme budgetary challenges. We analyze this dynamic in greater detail in the next section. For now, we simply note that throughout the 1980s and '90s, state and local leaders of criminal legal agencies struggled to manage skyrocketing operational costs and, in some cases, even lost previous sources of funding. Many began to look for ways they might use their own routines and procedures to fill the budgetary gaps. In a case study of Iowa and Nevada, Karin Martin finds that less than one year after federal officials stopped using Law Enforcement Assistance Administration grants to distribute funds to state agencies (in 1982), both states imposed their first surcharges on convicted individuals to help fund operations.[70]

At the local level, the costliest expansions of policing and punishment often occurred in the same communities that suffered the worst fiscal crises. This colocation has been central to the social and spatial patterning of predatory criminal legal practices in recent decades. Studies show, for example, that communities with larger Black populations tend to spend more on policing activities; confront tougher budgetary challenges; use fines, fees, and forfeitures more intensively; and create rules that allow local agencies to retain higher percentages of sanction-generated funds.[71] These are disproportionately the places where racially biased public policies and business practices have deprived public institutions of adequate funding and investment.[72]

The most intense combinations of this sort tend to occur in communities of people who are subjugated by *both* race and class. But they can also be found in lower-income, predominantly White communities and in middle-class communities where residents are mostly people of color. Josh Pacewicz and John Robinson underscore and develop this point in an important analysis of "pocketbook policing" and municipal "opportunity structures" in the Chicago suburbs.[73] In 2016, they report, "eleven Chicago suburbs collected more in fines and forfeits per capita than Ferguson [Missouri]. These suburbs generally collect revenue via a repertoire of plainly entrepreneurial strategies . . . [including] aggressive impounding of vehicles, DUI checkpoints, and use of red-light cameras in conjunction with altered timing of stoplights."[74]

Against this backdrop, Pacewicz and Robinson focus on what they call the "puzzle" of high pocketbook-policing rates in predominantly Black middle-class suburbs. Based on administrative data and interviews with municipal officials, the authors conclude that public managers in predominantly White and Black suburbs largely held the same views about which kinds of revenue sources are more versus less desirable. Because of racial discrimination and segregation, however, their *opportunities to act* on these preferences differed considerably. Predominantly Black suburbs were far less successful at attracting large businesses, and therefore "enjoyed little access to sales and other point of sales taxes." As they struggled to stave off or manage deep service cuts and make use of their limited revenue choices, administrators in Black suburbs embraced pocketbook policing. Although they saw "fines and forfeitures as 'bad revenues,'" they felt they had little choice and began to pressure law enforcement to use these tools more aggressively.[75]

The social and spatial unevenness of pocketbook policing, Pacewicz and Robinson argue, "reflects how racism is baked into the fiscal mechanics of local government."[76] Indeed, as we have seen, race and racism played important roles in the national restructuring of public finance that began in the 1980s. Across the country, state and local officials turned to criminal justice predation, in part, to cope with crises that policymakers created through fiscal retrenchment.

Developments in public finance provide an important first step toward explaining why the focus of criminal justice predation shifted so significantly starting the 1980s. The state and local officials who controlled most of the nation's criminal legal operations needed *financial* infusions in this period. Although penal labor exploitation continued to be useful for some purposes, it did little to address authorities' dire revenue problems.

POLICING AND PUNISHMENT

In response to chronic fiscal shortfalls, state and local officials routinely imposed cost-saving cutbacks. Criminal legal operations and expenditures, however, continued to rise throughout the 1990s and 2000s. To understand this distinctive trajectory, and its role in promoting extractive practices, one must turn to the politics of crime and punishment. In so doing, our goal is *not* to explain the dramatic growth of policing and punishment in the US after the 1960s. It is to clarify how the arms race of "tough-on-crime" politics and the rise of punitive modes of governance intersected with the restructuring of public finance to fuel the construction of a new predatory regime.

Criminal legal governance expanded so rapidly after the early 1970s that the US soon locked up more people per capita than any other country on earth. From 1975 to 2005, the number of state and federal prisoners rose from roughly 240,000 (111 per 100,000 residents) to over 1.5 million (491 per 100,000 residents).[77] Jail populations nearly doubled between 1985 and 1995, and then rose by half again over the next decade.[78] The combined probation and parole population increased by 239 percent between 1980 and 2016.[79] Criminal court dockets swelled, especially in larger urban areas. In New York City, the epicenter of zero-tolerance policing, the number of misdemeanor cases handled by courts increased by nearly 400 percent from 1980 to 2010.[80] Today, state courts in the US process roughly thirteen million misdemeanor cases each year.[81]

Together, these developments produced staggering increases in operational costs. National public spending on corrections, policing, and judicial expenses rose from $65 billion in 1985 to $112 billion in 1995,[82] then to an eye-popping $265 billion in 2012.[83] Most of the costs fell to states and localities. Thus, while federal spending on incarceration rose from less than $1 billion in 1980 to almost $7 billion 2013,[84] state spending was already close to $7 billion in 1985 and rose to $51.4 billion in 2010.[85] Local jail expenditures grew from $5.7 billion in 1983 to $22.2 billion in 2007.[86] The story was similar for police and court operations. Together, cities, towns, and counties pay for about 75 percent of the total public costs of policing, which more than doubled between 1982 ($44.6 billion) and 2002 ($100.6 billion).[87] Over this same period, court costs, about half of which are funded at the local level, increased from $18 billion to $51 billion.[88]

Nearly everywhere in the field, operational growth outpaced available funding. State and local investments in incarceration rose sharply but could not keep pace with the growing costs of building and operating facilities.[89] Public allocations for courts were nowhere near sufficient to fund the processing of so many new cases. In a series of reports, the ABA sounded the alarm and documented how, due to funding gaps, courts had been forced to furlough personnel, delay filling judicial vacancies, freeze salaries, accept long-term layoffs, and limit hours and days of operation.[90] State and local officials were caught in a bind, on a scale that far exceeded their fiscal challenges in other areas. Something had to be done, but what?

The most obvious response would have been to pare back operations, incorporating policing, adjudication, and punishment into the prevailing "austerity" strategy. There were some efforts to do so. Courts, in effect, rationed indigent defense by increasing public defenders' caseloads. Jails and prisons reduced spending on goods and services such as health care, rehabilitation programs, and recreation and entertainment (all of which made the conditions of confinement even harsher). Some states tried to stem the costly tide by adjusting policies for the revocation of parole and probation and creating specialized courts (e.g., drug courts). But initiatives of this sort came nowhere close to solving the problem. As Marie Gottschalk points out, the "only way to make major reductions in corrections budgets is to close penal facilities and reduce correctional staff."[91] The same is true for courts and policing, where major cost savings all but require large reductions in operational (and especially personnel) expenditures.[92]

Several formidable barriers stood in the way of such steps. The first was party competition over law-and-order issues. Michael Campbell and Heather Schoenfeld use the apt phrase "captured crime politics" to describe the partisan one-upmanship that occurred in most states and localities during the 1980s and '90s.[93] Republicans made race-coded law-and-order agendas a centerpiece of their electoral brand. To fend off Republican claims that they were "soft on crime," Democrats backed funding increases for police and prisons, supported "legislation that targeted a wider net of criminals (including juveniles), ensured imprisonment for even minor crimes, and established new mandatory minimum sentences."[94] By the 1990s, few politicians in either party were willing to take positions that an electoral opponent could plausibly label as anti-victim, soft on crime, or unsupportive of law enforcement.

A second, related constraint came from powerful organized interests pushing for heavier investments in policing and punishment. As policy feedback studies emphasize, policies sometimes produce groups of beneficiaries that mobilize to defend and expand them.[95] In the 1990s and early 2000s, this process played out across the employment sectors of the criminal legal field. As the ranks of police and prison officers grew, unions representing them gained members and resources. The increasingly robust unions joined forces with prosecutors' associations and victims' rights groups.[96] By the 1990s, loose coalitions of such interest groups had become a serious political force advocating for tougher penalties and expansions of policing and penal operations.[97]

The third constraint arose from the nation's notoriously fragmented political institutions. There was no central mechanism for *coordinating* cutbacks in criminal legal operations. As John Pfaff explains, the "criminal justice system" in the US is actually "a mismatch of independent, often competitive bureaucracies, all attentive to different constituencies and facing different political and economic incentives."[98] Even when their operations are functionally interdependent, such agencies (and their budgets) tend not to be centrally managed. As a result, it is generally easier to pass costs on to someone else than to reduce operations and expenditures as a whole—and actors in one arena rarely have reason to fret over the costs they create for others.[99]

The pattern is well illustrated by a dynamic that Franklin Zimring and Gordon Hawkins call the "correctional free lunch," where county officials make decisions that fill state prisons and leave the resulting bills to others.[100] State administrators are generally powerless to control prison entry rates, and local prosecutors and judges have few incentives to consider state-level expenditures. As punitive pressures mounted in the 1990s and 2000s, the latter aggressively pursued and imposed felony convictions, overstuffing state prisons even as crime and arrest rates declined.[101] "With shrinking local resources, few alternative programs, overcrowded local jails, and overburdened probation departments," Mona Lynch explains, shifting responsibilities to the state level made "financial sense for the county as well."[102] Responding to similar tough-on-crime pressures, state legislators compounded the problem by creating longer "mandatory minimum" sentences and more restrictive conditions for prison release. Federal judges, in turn, limited state-level administrators' efforts to spend less per capita on the people they imprisoned: Goods, services, and living conditions can only deteriorate so far before they violate the constitutional prohibition of cruel and unusual punishment.[103]

In these ways and many others, the *institutional structure* of criminal legal governance blocked the path toward serious cutbacks in operations and costs. The pursuit of new revenue streams offered an alternative path, and here public authorities had several things going for them.

First, the most heavily policed and punished communities were deeply marginalized in power relations and political processes, and legally entangled individuals were widely stigmatized and demonized in the broader society. For both reasons, criminal legal agencies had access to large numbers of people who were politically vulnerable to resource extraction.

Second, criminal legal actors had powers to *compel* resource transfers few actors possessed elsewhere in the administrative state. Financial charges could be forcibly imposed on accused individuals, with payment schedules tied to the threat of incarceration. Police could do the same by issuing citations and using forfeiture laws to seize people's money, cars, homes, and other goods. Prisons and jails could levy "pay-to-stay" fees and take payments directly from, among other things, deposits in incarcerated people's spending accounts. Caught in desperate circumstances, people accused or convicted of crimes had little choice but to "voluntarily" pay the prices authorities set for public defense, jail and prison canteen products, and the like.

Third, many criminal legal institutions directly controlled human beings as "holdings" that could be turned into revenue-generating assets. Courts, for instance, could hand people on probation over to for-profit supervision companies for a fee. Jails, prisons, and immigrant detention centers held substantial populations in custody. For a price, public managers could grant companies access to them as captive consumers or, in some cases, workers.

Fourth, in many cases, heads of policing and penal agencies had the authority and tools needed to *independently* pursue predatory revenue strategies, without any additional legislative or budgetary approval (see chapters 2 and 3). In an era of austerity politics, independence of this sort was highly prized. Public managers were well versed in the risks of funding models that depended on contested political decisions, shifts in government control, the vicissitudes of economic cycles, and hard-to-predict swings in public opinion.[104] Criminal legal authorities were unusually well positioned to buffer against such risks by retooling operations they already controlled.

In a 2010 *Police Chief* magazine article titled "Generating New Revenue Streams," Paul LaCommare expressed the entrepreneurial spirit that became common among criminal legal managers. In the mid-1980s, his police department in West Covina, California embraced the "concept of developing a police revenue service."[105] After years of funding volatility, LaCommare wrote, West Covina now "focused on revenue-generating programs that offer side benefits to the department."[106] For police leaders across the country, he argued, it was imperative to "broaden the traditional definition of police responsibilities and include a proactive approach to developing new revenue streams in the current economy. Those agencies that are willing to envision the future and then plan and act to provide future financial resources will be in the best position to provide public safety."[107]

Finally, by the 1990s, the criminal legal field had developed substantial new institutional *capacities* for pursuing financial extraction. As Theda Skocpol has long argued, administrative capacities and policy innovations tend to have a reciprocal relationship.[108] Available capacities for implementation can limit or channel policy choices and, in turn, can be built up or undermined through the pursuit of new governing initiatives. This perspective points to an underappreciated observation regarding the massive growth of US policing and penal operations after the 1960s: It built substantial new capacities for revenue-generating practices based on financial extraction.

The smaller criminal legal operations of earlier eras were generally sufficient to serve as sites of supports for labor predation. They could easily supply fifteen workers for a chain gang, fifty for a prison industry contract, or 150 for a convict leasing agreement with a company pursuing a local project. Equally important, many of the predatory labor models they enabled and supported—such as slavery, debt peonage, and sharecropping—operated in the community, under "private masters," and thus were compatible with smaller, less costly criminal legal institutions (see chapter 1).

To generate revenue streams large enough to matter to public managers and business entrepreneurs, however, financial extraction must occur on a fairly high scale. In poor communities, labor pools are often sizable; financial resources are generally sparse and thinly spread. A great many small takings are needed to generate meaningful revenues for a firm or government. From this perspective, even the local-finance crises of the 1970s happened a bit too early for direct financial extraction to work effectively at scale. The explosive growth of policing and punishment was, at that time, just getting underway. By the 1990s and 2000s, however, the implementation capacities were in place. Sprawling institutions of mass penal control made it possible to integrate criminal legal operations into a process of financialization that was, in these decades, remaking the US political economy as a whole. Financial charges could now be imposed on vast numbers of people, at one point of contact after another, as they were stopped, arrested, accused, or convicted. Community members could be saddled with debt, and the coercive powers of the penal state could be marshaled for collections.

PRIVATIZATION

The wave of privatizing projects that swept the globe in the 1980s and '90s created favorable conditions for the entry of for-profit firms into criminal legal governance in the US. But it did not necessitate their entry or make their integration inevitable. These were hard-won achievements that required significant political work. Corporations fought aggressively to gain access and establish lucrative public–private partnerships. Their successes changed not only the structure and practice of criminal legal governance in America, but also its politics. They help to explain not only why policing and punishment now operate as significant sites of private investment and accumulation in the US but also why so many *public* agencies in the field adopted revenue-centered mentalities and practices after the mid-1980s.

In chapters 2 and 3, we showed that for-profit businesses established themselves as governing partners in nearly every corner of the field. The breadth of this development makes it far too unwieldy to analyze here in its entirety. To make the task manageable and allow for necessary detail, we present a more focused analysis of the corporate role in imprisonment.

Public–private partnerships have existed in some form since the earliest days of penal governance in America (see chapter 1). Nevertheless, the contemporary era stands out for its more thorough integration of for-profit firms into core operations, the transfer of more fundamental forms of governing authority into private hands, and the greater scale of financial investment and profiteering.

Corporate entry did not just coincide with the two developments discussed so far. In important respects, it was enabled by them. As carceral expenditures rose, profit-seeking corporations began to look for ways to tap into them. And as operational costs outpaced funding, DOCs desperately needed to find solutions. The ranks of incarcerated Americans swelled so rapidly that, by the 1980s, many jails and prisons were filled beyond capacity. When legal advocates successfully challenged the inhumane conditions, court orders to relieve the overcrowding accelerated the need for more facilities and threatened to push costs beyond the already unmanageable status quo.[109] For reasons explained earlier, significant funding increases and operational cutbacks were both highly unlikely. Public managers were eager for outside help (to put it mildly), and business interests jumped at the opportunity.

Companies like Corrections Corporation of America (CCA) and Wackenhut—backed by Wall Street brokerage houses such as Merrill Lynch, E. F. Hutton, Prudential-Bache, and Shearson Lehman Brothers—offered to build new facilities using private funds that required no legislative or public approval. Starting in 1985, a growing number of state agency heads decided that the deal was too good to pass up. Carceral firms built new prisons based on "lease back" agreements with governments, and often did so *without* prior agreements ("on spec"), based on the expectation that criminal convictions would continue to rise, and more prison cells would be needed.[110] For public managers, outsourcing promised to relieve capacity strains, satisfy court orders, and potentially stabilize or lower expenditures. Privately owned and operated prisons spread across the nation.

Early successes that focused on prison construction and management sent a clear market signal with broad implications: Public agencies were overwhelmed, and creative entrepreneurs could make money by devising solutions for their problems. In short order, criminal legal authorities of all sorts received a dizzying array of offers. By entering public–private partnerships, government agencies could shift costs and responsibilities to companies for things such as court diversion, probation supervision, police administration, and ticket writing (in the case of red-light cameras). In nominally "public" prisons, for-profit firms took over food and healthcare provision, telecom services, and much, much more. Playing the long game, many companies offered to upgrade and run operations at no immediate cost to the state, so long as they received contracts on favorable terms. And, as we described in chapter 3, some promised to generate new revenues to public agencies as well.

JPay cornered the carceral banking market by offering not only to convert states' paper-based banking systems to new digital formats for free but also to pay public agencies significant commissions going forward. Other companies offered similar deals. In 1995, MCI installed phones and phone service throughout California's prisons free of charge and agreed to pay the DOC 32 percent of revenues from calls.[111] By 1999, the department was bringing in $16 million annually from its phone contracts.[112] Telecom companies would later use the same strategy with e-tablets, supplying them to imprisoned people for free and then charging fees for their usage and sharing profits with governments through commissions.

To make such profitable operations possible, corporations spent millions on political action, worked closely with privatization advocates in government, and formed coalitions with business pressure groups and conservative think tanks. As Loïc Wacquant explains, carceral companies advanced their interests "within the framework of a campaign for all-around privatization launched by the Reagan administration and encouraged conjointly by neoconservative think tanks and big Wall Street brokerage houses." In 1988, the Heritage Foundation "presented private imprisonment as a 'new economic and technological frontier' and predicted—the better to produce—the imminent engagement of the country's largest firms."[113]

To land their first contracts, prison companies targeted conservative states, such as Tennessee and Texas. They spent heavily on campaign contributions and recruited well-connected lobbyists from the public sector. As Lauren-Brooke Eisen documents, the firms brought on "consultants (usually former corrections directors) who could gauge state leadership and correctional trends," alerting them "if an impending criminal justice reform might cut the demand for prison beds or facilitate inmates' early release."[114]

Between 1987 and 1997, prison companies won legislation in twenty-six states to explicitly authorize their contracts and protect them from legal challenges.[115] Specific legislation of this sort helped to secure operations, but it was not always necessary for gaining access. Eight states and the federal government simply expanded their interpretations of existing partnership statutes. With no statutory bans to constrain them, other states moved forward without any such legislation. Thus, at the state level, carceral companies largely focused their political efforts on swaying government decisions about which public functions to privatize, which firms to select for contracts, and what terms to set for corporate performance and profit. Over time, such efforts turned public–private partnerships into a lucrative (and "normal") feature of state-level penal governance.

At the local level, the companies pursued similar goals by working to sway elections for sheriffs, judges, and district attorneys. In these smaller political arenas, corporate resources and pressure tactics can rarely be matched by community members or civic groups. In many cases, their main political opponents are their market competitors, who already hold or hope to win desired contracts. From 2012 to 2014 in California, for instance, the telecom company Securus used three $10,000 donations to establish itself as one of the Sacramento County Sheriff's largest political contributors. At the time, Sacramento County partnered with ICSolutions for telecom services, and the existing contract period was about to run out.[116]

Since the 1990s, political contributions have also served a key tool for corporate efforts to sustain or enhance the profitability of carceral contracts. A Prison Policy Initiative report recounts, for example, how Global Tel-Link used "$85,000 in campaign contributions to two Orange County, California county supervisors [to flip them] from being opponents of [the company's exorbitant] phone rates into supporters." In exchange for the supervisors' commitments to the rates, the company agreed to pay $4 million per year into an "Orange County slush fund [that the county misleadingly] called the 'Inmate Welfare Fund.'"[117]

Political influence at the federal level has required heavier investments. Between 1989 and 2015, the two largest for-profit prison companies (GEO Group and CCA) funneled more than $10 million to candidates for federal offices and spent nearly $25 million on federal lobbying efforts.[118] In the 1980s and '90s, the companies' political efforts focused mostly on privatizing federal prison operations. Later, they used their political influence to secure a dominant role for for-profit firms in the detainment of non-US citizens. After the attacks of September 11, 2001, federal officials' responses signaled that there would be growing opportunities to profit from immigrant and refugee detention. The big prison firms quickly ramped up political contributions to key lawmakers as well as efforts to build trust and influence with relevant federal agencies. Between 2000 and 2004, CCA's spending on federal lobbying efforts rose from $410,000 to $3 million.[119]

To increase their political influence, carceral companies supplemented their direct actions with coalition work. Many became active members of the American Legislative Exchange Council (ALEC), supporting conservative agendas beyond their immediate interests in order to bring additional allies and resources to bear in their own political campaigns.[120] Through participation in ALEC, Eisen argues, "the industry has grown more profitable." The group's criminal justice task force, cochaired by a CCA official, "drafted model state laws [to promote] a more draconian stance on sentencing and [strengthen] the private prison industry. This opened the door to the industry and played an important role in ensuring a long-term need for their facilities."[121]

From the outset, carceral companies strengthened their political hand by recruiting former elected officials and high-level public managers to work for them or serve on their boards.[122] This revolving door advanced penal privatization in a number of ways. Most directly, it provided the industry with well-connected, knowledgeable agents positioned to identify opportunities, secure access, and bargain effectively. It also sent a powerful message to elected officials and senior administrators that, if they treated the industry well, they too might secure lucrative private-sector positions down the road. By bringing respected former leaders of public corrections onto their boards and into their managerial teams, prison companies also enhanced their legitimacy as public-spirited partners.

Indeed, this dynamic played a critical role in helping the industry transition from its early position on the political Right to a more secure position in the bipartisan middle. CCA, for example, recruited onto its board of directors Thurgood Marshall Jr., the son of Supreme Court Justice Thurgood Marshall and former cabinet secretary to President Bill Clinton.[123] Dr. Reginald Wilkinson, former director of corrections in Ohio, known as a champion of rehabilitation, joined the board of the prison operator Management and Training Corporation (MTC). When asked about the move, he explained: "State directors of corrections struggle with the same issues the private industry faces. . . . I'm the same person I was in government. We need to get past people's ideologies."[124] In some cases, recruitment into the industry has reached into the highest levels of government. Upon retiring from the White House, for instance, John F. Kelly, former Marine Corps general and chief of staff for President Donald Trump, joined the board of Caliburn International, a for-profit operator of detention centers for immigrants, including unaccompanied and separated minors.[125]

Through contractual partnerships and shared personnel, the integration of government and business entities grew deeper over time. As it turned punishment and incarceration into powerful engines of private capital accumulation, this integration also promoted shifts toward revenue-centered logics and practices in public penal agencies. A substantial body of scholarship has explored the many ways that *learning processes* can contribute to changes in policy and governance. Elected officials and civil servants puzzle over problems, learn from their governing experiences, and develop new understandings through interactions with actors in their networks.[126] Through such interactions, Peter Hall concludes, actors positioned outside government can influence the "interpretative frameworks" that prevail among actors inside government and, in stronger cases, may even produce a "paradigm shift" in how public authorities make sense of their work and define appropriate and desirable courses of action.[127]

Over time, revolving doors and penal partnerships served as a powerful basis for change in the "interpretative frameworks" that guided the work of public agencies. Some managers who took positions in the private sector later returned to government. During their stints in the for-profit arena, they were steeped in organizational cultures that normalized the pursuit of revenue and encouraged them to see carceral populations and operations as assets and opportunities. More generally, experiences with cross-sector collaborations exposed public administrators to a world of entrepreneurial ideas and projects that suggested possibilities for public-sector analogs.

From the 1980s onward, for-profit firms showed that it was possible to generate substantial revenues from penal populations and operations. They also showed, in various and specific ways, *how* new revenue streams could be created by, for example, exploiting jail and prison populations as captive markets, charging them prices, tapping into resources held by their friends and family, using debts to lay claim to future income, and aggressively pursuing payments.

Privatization also drew public managers into contract negotiations, where they learned to be shrewd bargainers, fighting over terms and maximizing commissions received in exchange for access to their "assets." In some cases, they became so adept that companies began to complain that *they* were being exploited. In 2019, Securus Technology sued its longtime partner, the Florida Department of Corrections, in federal court, claiming the Florida DOC forced the company to pay for "a panoply of goods and services that had nothing to do with inmate telephone services . . . such as inmate tracking technology, security upgrades and iPhones for its staff . . . because it wasn't getting [the funding] it needed from the state legislature."[128] In its coverage, *The Florida Times-Union* noted the irony that "Securus, which is known for charging steep fees of its own, accused the department of [obtaining its wish list] 'on the backs of some of Florida's most vulnerable citizens: the state's inmates and their families.'"[129]

In sum, the restructuring of public finance and the rapid expansion of punishment helped pave the way for corporations to flood the criminal legal field. To maximize profits, these businesses aggressively pursued opportunities for financial gain and projects that focused far less often on labor exploitation than on financial investments and returns, prices and payments, and various methods of monetary extraction. The confluence of policy developments that brought corporations into the field also transformed power relations in the politics of punishment itself. As for-profit firms poured resources into building political influence, they shifted the balance of policy networks and political contests. They forged new alliances, reshaped legal and institutional frameworks, and helped shift public agencies toward revenue-centered, financially extractive business models.

Conclusion

Why did the trajectory of criminal justice predation shift so dramatically in the US starting in the 1980s? Our answer to this question reflects a broader perspective developed throughout the book: Criminal legal governance operates and evolves as an integral part of the broader political economy. Its institutions, practices, and uses reflect *and* produce developments in the surrounding social order. In this chapter, we employed this perspective as an approach to explaining historical change, working across two levels of analysis.

At the level of social structure, we clarified how shifts in criminal justice predation over the past four decades advanced as part of a broader transformation of political economies—running with the grain of historical change rather than against it. In a global era of financialization, privatization, marketization, and securitization, the path that criminal legal institutions followed shared a great deal in common with developments in other arenas of governance. Closer to the ground, we showed how the adoption of new predatory practices emerged from a confluence of political and policy developments in three areas: the reorganization of public finance and the production of fiscal crises; the highly racialized intensification of punitive politics and governance; and corporations' successful efforts to become major players in the criminal legal field.

In many ways, our analysis complements previous efforts to understand why mass penal control advanced together with the neoliberal restructuring of political economies after the 1960s. However, in focusing on the predatory dimensions of policing and punishment (rather than the expansion of penal control itself), our analysis suggests some different perspectives on how the two fit together. Indeed, in the US context at least, it suggests grounds for reconsidering some prominent accounts of the "neoliberal penal state."

Loïc Wacquant's influential analysis distills a number of the key issues.[130] For Wacquant, "punitive containment as government technique" emerged as a response to some of the defining conditions of neoliberal rule—most notably, capital's declining needs for low-skilled labor, the erosion of the welfare state, and the unsettling of ethnoracial hierarchies.[131] Together, these developments generated powerful new social insecurities, centered on groups at the bottom of the social order. "The enlargement and exaltation of the police, the courts, and the penitentiary" allowed elites to manage the new insecurities and "shore up the deficit of [state] legitimacy" produced by neoliberal uses of government (such as rolling back social and regulatory protections and more actively serving capital interests).[132] Thus, from the 1970s to the present, Wacquant argues, the primary function of criminal legal governance has been to contain and control "the dispossessed and dishonored populations [that represent] the living and threatening incarnation of the generalized social insecurity."[133] Prisons have operated as "warehousing" facilities that serve three main purposes: the "negative economic function of [storing] a surplus population devoid of market utility,"[134] the "social and moral excommunication [of] a polluting group,"[135] and the maintenance of "ethnoracial division and domination."[136]

Material and symbolic exclusions stand at the center of this account. The neoliberal penal state operates as a segregating technology of control, securing the social order against threats that come from the "other" side of economic, racial, and moral boundaries. This logic applies even to the practices we conceptualize as "predatory." Wacquant explains that measures that make "the inmate or his kin pay . . . are pursued less for their financial fallout, which is negligible compared to the pharaonic expenditures demanded by [penal governance], than for the message they send to prisoners and their families [and] the rest of the population. . . . What matters . . . is [visibly expressing] the fact that prisoners are 'paying their debt' to society and [accentuating] the symbolic boundary that demarcates and isolates them from the citizenry."[137] Jan Rehmann elaborates a more orthodox Marxian variant of this view, writing that "most of the prisoners [in the US today] are not overexploited but rather warehoused. . . . What is primarily at stake is not direct economic exploitation but rather . . . controlling the devastating social consequences of [neoliberal] capitalism."[138]

Undoubtedly, contemporary policing and imprisonment *do* function as tools of exclusion, containment, and control. But that is not all they do. Since the 1980s—relatively early in the rise of the neoliberal penal state—governing authorities have routinely designed and deployed policing and penal practices as tools for making the allegedly superfluous, unuseful populations they target *productive*. As they exclude and quarantine, criminal legal institutions also exploit and extract. Or put more precisely, the practices that governing authorities use to exclude, deprive, and control *have enabled and facilitated* the incorporation of legally entangled people into extractive relations. This is the process of "predatory inclusion" that we discussed in chapter 1, and it is a core feature of criminal legal governance in America today. Analyses that connect processes of exclusion to predatory inclusion allow for a fuller, more accurate understanding of how the neoliberal penal state actually works.

Second, we agree that criminal legal governance since the 1970s has played an important role in managing various social insecurities generated by neoliberal restructuring. But this story of complementarity—with one controlling what the other produces—captures only a part of the relationship. From the 1980s onward, criminal legal governance has been a site of neoliberal reorganization in its own right. Its internal developments have closely tracked broader processes of financialization, privatization, marketization, and the securitization of surrounding governmental functions. Actors throughout the field have embraced more entrepreneurial approaches to management, searching for ways to exploit their "assets," reconfigure procedures to generate revenues, and forge financially productive partnerships with for-profit firms.

Third, like Wacquant and others, we emphasize the importance of connecting changes in criminal legal governance to broader shifts in social structure. When taken too far, however, structural analyses can lead scholars into functionalist explanations based on what disembodied social forces (allegedly) necessitate.[139] Such analyses tend to skirt what we have emphasized: that political economies operate as fields of human possibility, creativity, and struggle. An explanation based solely on structural change and functional necessity would have erased the *contingencies* involved in public managers' adaptive searches for solutions to fiscal crises, JPay's innovative appeals to state agencies' needs, the strategic choices that drove partisan electoral strategies, CCA's creative investments in reshaping the politics of criminal legal governance, and more. Emphasizing the open-ended nature of political conflict and adaptation, we have worked to incorporate prevailing trajectories of structural change into what William Sewell calls a more "eventful" approach to historical explanation.[140]

If the neoliberal penal state (including its predatory dimensions) functions to "meet the needs of the class system and the class society in general"[141] (or any other social structural necessities), it does so because of contingent choices and outcomes of political struggle. How and why those choices and outcomes emerged—as opposed to others—are questions of great analytic and political importance. We hope to have demonstrated in this chapter the value of pursuing explanation in a way that attends to the effects of broad structural forces but also analyzes how contingent events (driven by people working to navigate specific social constraints and political circumstances) produce significant shifts in institutions and governing practices.

Finally, scholars who ignore what we call predatory practices have omitted a crucial explanatory factor from their accounts of how and why the neoliberal penal state developed in America as it did. As we have emphasized, the aggressive revenue-seeking efforts that took off after the mid-1980s did not cause—and do not explain—the rise of mass incarceration and intensive policing that began in the 1970s. Nevertheless, over the past four decades, revenue-generating pressures and priorities have shaped countless governmental decisions about how to organize and implement policing, adjudication, and punishment. Indeed, as we argue throughout this book, the official "core" operations of criminal legal governance in the US today are inseparable from, and cannot be well understood apart from, its predatory dimensions.

5 * *Justifying Criminal Justice Predation*

Global Tel-Link (GTL) has created a miracle machine, or so their promotional materials for the Inspire tablet would have you believe. The Inspire streamlines bureaucracy, for instance, "allowing staff more time to focus on what's important—security and control." By "offering new insight into inmate activity," it brings surveillance into the twenty-first century. Through its video visitation and e-commerce capacities, the Inspire limits "the opportunity to distribute contraband and improves facility security by reducing the need for inmate movement," thereby lowering staffing costs for cash-strapped prison managers. And by focusing prisoners on "small, safe areas of choice and responsibility," the Inspire "promotes positive behavior, has a calming effect on inmate social dynamics, and reduces overall risk for staff." The evidence, GTL insists, speaks for itself: "Facilities that have deployed tablets have noted decreases in inmate-on-inmate violence, inmate-on-staff assaults, and behavior code violations."[1]

According to GTL, the Inspire works wonders for imprisoned individuals too, easing the pains of confinement and preparing them for life on the outside. Its video and email interfaces offer "productive and innovative ways for inmates to stay connected with friends and family;" its "educational videos, exercises, courses, and more help inmates transition into the next phase of their lives, secure employment, and break the cycle of reincarceration."[2] By offering access to the latest music, movies, and books, the tablet's e-marketplace allows individuals to escape the boredom and stress of life behind bars. Jailhouse lawyers can even use the tablet's "electronic law library" to research cases without leaving their cells. Truly, when it comes to this knock-off iPad, everybody wins. Or so it seems.

It's tempting to dismiss sales pitches like GTL's as empty words of little consequence, especially when trying to explain something as monumental as the growth and transformation of criminal justice predation over the past four decades. In the previous chapter, we explained these developments as products of social structural change, the restructuring of public finance, the rising pressures of law-and-order politics, and mass corporate entry into criminal legal governance. Compared to such potent forces, what difference does it make what companies like GTL have said about their products? More generally, why should we care about the ways corporate and governmental actors have portrayed themselves and their predatory criminal legal practices?

As should be clear by now, today's predatory regime did not emerge all at once. It was built over time, through the accumulation and interaction of many legal and institutional changes, all of which, in one way or another, had to be *justified*. To make its profitable prison business possible, for example, GTL had to convince government officials that it would be a trustworthy partner and give them good reasons to contract for its e-tablet services. And what about the people who work at companies like GTL? To motivate and sustain operations, corporate leaders generally need to provide their personnel with some kind of morally acceptable account of what they do for a living—ideally, one that affirms the value of their work and imbues it with a sense of purpose. Indeed, the need for such stories is no less pressing in government agencies and the lives of public administrators.

In this chapter, we analyze some of the key rationales used by governmental and corporate actors to justify criminal justice predation since the 1980s. Our agenda is intentionally one-sided: It focuses only on the *enabling* frames that have helped to establish, expand, and secure predatory practices. We reserve our discussion of *oppositional* frames for the final two chapters of this book, where we incorporate them into a broader analysis of political resistance and struggle.

The rationales we analyze here have been deployed to enlist the support, or undercut the opposition, of various actors and audiences. Outside these contexts, they have typically targeted decision-making authorities or actors who are well positioned to influence them—especially elected officials, agency heads, judges, journalists, and leaders of powerful organizations. In contrast, they have rarely been designed or deployed to secure buy-in from the communities that make up the primary targets of criminal justice predation. Now as in the past, legal plunder is largely imposed on subjugated communities through authority and force, without much effort to persuade them of its virtues. When community opposition does escalate to the point of posing a threat, the priority for defenders is usually to convince institutional authorities to stay the course.

Invested participants tend to directly appeal to mass publics on a more episodic basis, mainly when highly visible developments threaten to destabilize the status quo. Such appeals may be deemed necessary to manage the fallout from a damning investigative report, major protest, policy defeat, or judicial ruling. In these sorts of cases, messaging strategies are usually designed to pacify rather than mobilize mass publics. The goal is to dissipate the troublesome spike in public attention and, along with it, any possibility that elected officials will start to see their support as a political liability. In chapter 10, we discuss a notable exception: To undermine an unwanted reform, defenders of predation sometimes stir up fears that change will endanger the public, hoping that anxious and outraged community members will pressure their elected officials to stand firm. Important as they are, however, such episodes tend to be brief departures. Predatory criminal legal practices rarely draw much attention from the public at large—a situation that suits practitioners and beneficiaries just fine.

Since the 1980s, corporate and governmental actors have used an adaptable but fairly stable set of rationales to legitimize criminal justice predation. The most prominent can be grouped into two general categories. *Neoliberal, market-centered discourses* portray corporations as public-spirited civic actors and necessary partners in efforts to achieve the common good. They frame the state as a place of business, the citizen as a consumer, and predation as an ordinary market transaction. And by treating personal responsibility and self-management as fundamental civic obligations, they cast the targets of predation as failed deviants who rightly pay a price for the choices that they have freely made. *Security-centered discourses* frame predatory practices as essential tools for protecting public safety and maintaining law and order. They criminalize and vilify targets of predation, and they portray criminal legal takings as a way to "do right by" victims, families, and communities harmed by crime.

Public-Spirited Partnerships

Business and political elites have routinely used discourses of public-spirited partnership to justify the participation of for-profit firms in criminal legal governance. Such enabling frames have smoothed the political path for for-profit diversion and probation programs, outsourcing contracts for fine-generating traffic cameras, commercial bail bond operations, and a great deal more. Here, though, we home in on the epicenter of public–private partnerships in criminal legal governance: incarceration and penal management. By analyzing this single sector, rather than skimming a wider range of operations, we are better able to detail how various aspects of partnership discourses have worked in concert, the course of their deployment over time, and the kinds of political work they have accomplished.

Early justifications for corporate entry into the carceral arena drew heavily on the neoliberal discourses that animated wider challenges to the activist state in the 1980s and '90s. Calls to transfer public functions to private actors were, in some cases, openly hostile to government itself. On the Right, many political voices attacked government in sweeping terms, as inherently inept and inefficient. Grover Norquist, founder of the powerful group Americans for Tax Reform, famously declared his desire to "reduce [government] to the size where I can drag it into the bathroom and drown it in the bathtub."[3] Calls to privatize penal governance in the US sometimes echoed this rhetoric, framing for-profit firms as an antidote to woeful government incompetence. In an essay published in 1985, for example, Joseph Fenton (then CEO of his own security company, later the president of Criminal Justice Solutions, LLC) claimed that the government's "record of apparent failure" at rehabilitation made business an attractive alternative. Because the private sector "has a vested interest in the success of its program," he wrote, they "can reestablish the intended purpose of corrections."[4]

Arguments that condemned government and framed corporations as a superior *alternative* were soon surpassed, however, by discourses of public-spirited *partnership*, designed for bipartisan appeal. In this formulation, government was not the problem per se; the problem was the idea that government could effectively "go it alone" without the help of the private sector. "We know big government does not have all the answers," President Bill Clinton declared in his 1996 State of the Union address; "the era of big government is over."[5] Clinton and other neoliberal reformers conjured a more hopeful and less conflictual vision of the future, in which public, private, and nonprofit leaders would join forces to solve big problems; governments and corporations would cease to work at cross-purposes; and efforts to serve the public interest would harness the strengths of organizations from every sector of society.

Celebratory visions of cooperative partnership were bolstered by the related discourse of "corporate social responsibility" (CSR) that— especially after 1989, when President George H. W. Bush called for "a thousand points of light" in service to the nation—swept across economic, political, and academic institutions.[6] At the center of CSR was "the notion that companies should accompany the pursuit of profit with good citizenship within a wider society."[7] Corporations created CSR offices, and universities added CSR courses to the curriculum.[8] Business communications blurred the distinction between for-profit and nonprofit actors, encouraging governments to see them as trustworthy partners with civic (rather than profit-minded) motives.

The new discourses of responsibility and partnership ascended as business interests waged a fierce offensive against the "countervailing powers" of the activist state.[9] As governments became more favorable to capital and rolled back regulations and protections, CSR discourses offered reassurances that corporations took their civic obligations seriously and would effectively monitor themselves.[10] Visions of partnerships devoted to the common good put a public-spirited gloss on successful efforts to turn government operations into lucrative sites of investment.

Inside the carceral sector, justifications for corporate entry tailored these general themes to fit the growing crisis of penal management. By the mid-1980s, aggressive policing and punishment had overwhelmed the nation's carceral capacities, and rates of criminal conviction showed no sign of slowing. Overcrowded prisons became targets of litigation, and courts placed numerous states and counties under orders to improve conditions of confinement.[11] Lacking additional facilities and unable to raise tax-based funding to build new ones, governments were in a bind.

Seeing a golden opportunity, construction, finance, and prison management companies presented themselves as civic allies with the capacity to help. They advertised their abilities to "solve . . . overcrowding quickly and economically" and deliver prison construction funding "without voter referendum."[12] Preparing to go public on the stock exchange in 1986, Corrections Corporation of America (CCA) emphasized its readiness to help out "federal, state and local agencies . . . in their efforts to comply with federal and state court orders on a cost-efficient basis."[13] In a 1987 advertisement in *American Jails* magazine, McCarthy Building Companies offered a more finance-centered version of the prevailing message: "Handcuffed by jail-building delays? . . . We'll finance it, guarantee the cost, build it, and lease it to you. . . . This is the turnkey, bond-issue-free solution that more and more communities are using to replace overcrowded, old, and outdated justice facilities . . . we can provide you with the facility you need today without the delays and surprises you typically encounter with the traditional building process."[14]

As the companies pitched solutions to immediate needs, they and their allies in government drew on a ready stock of economic ideas to argue that public–private partnerships would be a boon to penal governance in general.[15] Market competition for government contracts, they promised, would lower costs, increase efficiency, and free up funds for other public purposes. The quality of operations would improve as private competition pushed public agencies to perform better. Relentlessly focused on bottom-line results and efficiency-enhancing innovations, businesses would also be nimbler than governments. Unconstrained by public-sector employee unions, entrenched bureaucracies, or institutional procurement processes, carceral companies could more easily restructure staffing and wages and invest capital where it was most needed.[16]

In this manner, discourses of public-spirited partnership drew strength from culturally resonant claims about the benefits of free-market competition. Along with prison construction and management, such arguments helped pave the way for a wide range of for-profit penal operations and services, such as health care, food, commissary, banking, and telecommunications. Penal rehabilitation programs illustrate the pattern. Amid the tough-on-crime politics of the 1980s and '90s, policymakers soured on the postwar "rehabilitative ideal"[17] and reduced funding for traditional correctional programs (most notably, education).[18] Still, many academics and criminal legal practitioners remained committed to the correctional enterprise. To retool and implement rehabilitation in such a tough political environment, influential leaders came to view public–private partnerships as essential. For instance, Francis Cullen, former president of both the American Society of Criminology and the Academy of Criminal Justice Sciences, published an article in 1986 promoting the "privatization of correctional treatment." Through partnering with public-spirited businesses, Cullen argued, the government could "enhance the political viability of correctional treatment." He encouraged fellow "progressives" to "capitalize on the current privatization trend and to explore ways in which this movement can be used to help humanize prison environments."[19]

Government officials continued to design and fund programs for subgroups they viewed as deserving, such as juveniles and people convicted of low-level crimes. And over time, as mass incarceration gave rise to growing problems of community reentry, political pressures pushed them to fund new post-release programs.[20] Most of the programs adopted a neoliberal approach to reforming the individual rather than investing in the kinds of opportunities and supports that people released from prison need.[21] Even so, they required capacities that few public agencies had. Business interests saw a lucrative opportunity to tap into public expenditures *and* to increase their profits by charging "user fees" in post-release halfway houses, day reporting facilities, and rehabilitation centers. Companies, armed with the rhetoric of business acumen and public allyship, professed their commitments to the civic projects of reducing recidivism and turning "criminals" into productive members of society.

Damon Hininger, the CEO of CCA reassured officials in 2014: "We are determined to prove that we can play a leadership role in reducing recidivism and that we have every incentive to do so. The interests of government, taxpayers, shareholders, and communities are all aligned."[22] As Hininger's statement suggests, discourses of public-spirited partnership remain vulnerable to criticisms that emphasize profit-maximizing motives and the substantial wealth generated for corporations and shareholders. To neutralize this vulnerability, carceral companies have typically leaned into narratives of interest alignment and altruistic care. Government contracts base payments on performance, they claim, so their profits depend above all on meeting *policy goals*. This alleged alignment of material incentives and public purposes means that, ultimately, *we are all in this together*.

In reality, few carceral contracts make business profits conditional on the achievement of specific policy goals. In many cases, such as contracts for telecom, commissary, and food services, government agencies simply charge companies a price for monopoly access to a reliably profitable captive market. Contracts to run for-profit prisons sometimes even include "guaranteed minimum" provisions that ensure payments for a set percentage of beds (typically 80–100 percent) regardless of whether the beds are filled. And despite what business leaders may claim, the interests of shareholders and taxpayers are rarely aligned in contract negotiations that decide how the spoils of predation will be split between public agencies and private firms.[23]

Carceral companies have also fended off charges of profit-driven self-interest by doubling down on claims of caring and dutiful service. Telecom companies, for example, emphasize their commitments to keeping families together and helping imprisoned people stay connected to the outside world. Challenged to justify their profits, their executives insist the commissions they generate for governments help to fund health care, entertainment, and other forms of "inmate welfare." In the salutary view of Rick Smith, CEO of Securus Technologies, these and other uses of commissions demonstrate that his company performs "a noble service for society."[24]

Corporate providers of other carceral services offer similar rationales. JPay's founder and CEO, Ryan Shapiro, told *Time* magazine in 2014: "We go out of our way to make sure that [families who use JPay] feel comfortable—that, you know, you're spending money with a company that cares about you."[25] Leading firms like JPay stress that, while they naturally charge a price for services, they are more than *just* businesses. They are caring organizations that make it possible for community members to convey their loyalty and love to a parent, child, sibling, cousin, or friend who is trapped in a lonely and difficult world behind bars. "We're not trying to make an extra dollar everywhere we can," JPay's Shapiro claimed in *Time*.[26]

In this framing, private interests naturally align with public goals. Businesses are caring, public-spirited actors devoted to the common good. G4S, the largest private security firm in the world and a major corporate

partner of police and prison agencies in the US, offers a useful example. David Taylor-Smith, a top official at the company, complains: "The
thought that everyone in the private sector is primarily motivated by
profit and that is why they come to work is just simply not accurate . . .
we employ 675,000 people and they are primarily motivated by pretty
much the same as would motivate someone in the public sector."[27] G4S
routinely extols the virtues of CSR, touting it as a central pillar of its
organizational culture and identity: "We understand the importance of
working in a way that is sustainable, ethical, and that generates social
value for communities. This is why we have embedded social responsibility into our business strategy and approach."[28]

Normal Market Transactions

As shown in earlier chapters, the state enables and directly participates
in criminal justice predation. Governments produce targets for extractive
projects by criminalizing behaviors, people, and social spaces, and they
authorize predatory practices as matters of law enforcement. State actors
use their coercive powers to seize assets, impose financial obligations, and
demand payments under threat of punishment. Through public–private
contracts, they enable their corporate partners to profit as well. Government officials organize predatory relations through policy designs and
legal-institutional procedures. By channeling the people they control toward points of extraction and structuring their circumstances and options,
they push and entice individuals into making revenue-generating choices.

All of these actions fade from view, however, when criminal legal takings get framed as "normal" free-market exchanges. In chapter 1, we
discussed the importance of liberal-contractual discourses and rituals for
efforts to legitimize predatory projects in earlier eras of American history.
Updated and adapted in various ways, these discourses play an equally
significant role in criminal justice predation today. Indeed, as neoliberal
discourses and reforms blurred the distinction between states and markets
in the late twentieth century, the reimagining of corporations as public-
spirited civic partners advanced alongside a marketizing reconceptualiza-
tion of the state.

Starting in the 1980s, a wave of reforms applied "business models"
to governments in the US, imposing expectations of market efficiency,
return on investment, and entrepreneurial management.[29] As progressive
modes of tax-based funding declined, Americans increasingly had to pay
"user fees" to access public facilities, goods, and services. More and more,
government agencies referred to and treated the people they served as
"customers."[30] Against this backdrop, the idea that accused and convicted

people *should* be billed for criminal legal "services" resonated with a growing body of social experience and common sense. The extension of market models to the state paved the way for discourses that normalized predatory criminal legal practices—both corporate and governmental—as ordinary market transactions.

Rationales of this type are particularly striking in the context of government-mandated financial charges, such as court fees, carceral "pay-to-stay" fees, and community supervision fees. Government actors set the amounts of these fees and impose them in the absence of any decision to purchase. The state arrests individuals and then orders them to appear in court, serve time in jails and prisons, and complete terms on community supervision. Throughout, it requires legally entangled people to pay criminal legal fees and uses its penal powers to enforce debt collections. There is no competition for "buyers" nor any calibration of "prices" to supply and demand. Nevertheless, government officials routinely use sales-transaction frames as justifications.[31]

Consider a Washington state lawmaker interviewed by Alexes Harris. To help Harris see court and supervision fees as normal and natural, the official compared them to price tags at a department store: "If you go to Nordstrom's to buy a dress, I assume you're going to pay for it. It's not like I get it free just because I feel like it. So, there are costs that [the defendants have] incurred through choices of their own. So, [the fee is] not punishment so much, it's just, that's the cost of the decisions they've made."[32] In this framing, criminal legal fees are not about retribution, moral penance, or the production of revenues. They are simply the cost that consumers must pay for using government services.

This storyline implies that the customer's financial obligation is a product of their own free choice. But what choice? The court appearance is required by the state, and the arrest that led to it was not optional. The prison pay-to-stay fee is imposed on a person whose stay under custody is physically enforced. No, the choice in question lies farther back in the causal chain, in the individual's decision to break the law. In a discussion of community supervision fees, a probation officer put it this way:

> You don't get anything for free. . . . This was a choice you made. You know, you chose to do the crime, you chose to take probation, of course you're going to. . . . I mean you can't go to the doctor's office and get an office visit without having any money, so you're not going to be in a courtroom where you're . . . where you've got a judge, DA, probation department— everybody in there—without having a fee assessed to it. There are consequences to every action, that's where the bond comes into play. You have an attorney that represents you, that's where the court-appointed attorney

fee comes [in]. We spend our time with you working with you to help you get [in] compliance with the [judge's order]. So, you know, your probation fees—I think it's all very just—I think it's fair.[33]

In presenting financial charges as the market price for bad decisions, state authorities do more than apply a generic model of consumer exchange; they adopt a defining trope of predatory business models in the broader economy. To justify exploitative home and auto loans, for instance, lenders point to borrowers' low credit scores (and other risk indicators) and explain that, under the circumstances, the market dictates higher fees and interest rates and stricter terms of payment.[34] If borrowers had wanted loans on better terms, lenders point out, they should have made better choices in the past. Transferred to the criminal legal context, this framing becomes: To avoid steep fees, people should not have committed crimes or even put themselves in a position to face accusation. Bad decisions carry financial consequences. That is just how the market works. And increasingly since the 1980s, it is how criminal legal institutions operate.

As one would expect, for-profit actors also frame predatory criminal legal practices as normal market-exchanges. Consider again the prison telecom companies that make their profits by exploiting conditions of penal control and isolation. The companies sign contracts with governments, but their services are not paid for with public funds. In most places, incarcerated people and their loved ones cover the costs. They cannot shop around for better deals because telecoms have no competitors in jails and prisons. Their only choice is to pay the monopoly provider or forgo communication.

Yet, as they have weathered decades of accusations of price gouging in carceral institutions,[35] companies such as Aventiv (formerly Securus) have routinely responded that they are no different from any business operating in the free market. Aventiv's primary goal, its CEO explains, is "developing innovative technology products and services that will better serve customers and consumers."[36] Aventiv's profits are thus the fruits of superior performance amid stiff market competition.

Because telecom companies have no competitors inside prisons, their legitimizing appeals to market *competition* depend on shifting attention from the incarcerated consumers of their services to the government partners who share their profits. To secure a government contract, the companies emphasize, they have to win a "competitive bidding process" by offering better products on superior terms than their competitors offer to government.[37] When called upon to justify the high rates, fees, and penalties they charge, they explain that "current market dynamics and costs" leave them no choice.[38] To criticize their profits as ill-gotten gains, they imply, is to condemn free-market competition—and by extension, a system of economic freedoms widely valorized as central to "the American way of life."

Justifications of this sort draw their power from an ideological model of markets as free and fair sites of competition that, by definition, produce legitimate outcomes. Even if this portrait of markets was not misleading in general (and it is), it would be tough to reconcile it with the realities of the prison telecom industry, which is largely controlled by three corporations. "The dominant firms," Stephen Raher explains, "attempt to paint a picture of competition by referencing other, smaller, competitors." However, "the presence of a 'competitive fringe' does not overcome the anticompetitive effects of market concentration." Because the start-up costs are so high, aspiring "competitors face prohibitive barriers to entering the market."[39]

In addition to high barriers to entry, contracts with public agencies usually insulate prison telecom companies from competition for extensive periods. Once GTL or Aventiv inks a deal with a government agency, it typically operates competition-free for several years (and may also receive noncompetitive contract extensions). When a new round of bidding begins, the company is likely to enjoy significant advantages based on its existing position, greater access to operational information, and established relationships with government personnel. If public managers receive a better offer from a rival company, they still have to weigh the potential benefits of changing providers against the costs of transition, including potential disruptions of service. In practice, penal agencies have few options for alternative providers. They also have strong incentives to prioritize the size of their own commissions, which can lead them to prefer bidders that plan to charge incarcerated people and their kin *higher* prices.

Given the absence of provider competition inside jails and prisons, telecom companies typically do not frame their sales as normal market transactions, in which customers shop around for the best deals. Instead, they emphasize individuals' decisions to use their services (rather than forgo communication). GTL, for example, explains that the fees it piles on top of basic rates are "optional payment and billing methods exercised solely at the direction and convenience of the consumer or end user."[40]

By focusing narrowly on customers' *potential* for choice, this framing deflects attention from the *conditions* of choice that structure and motivate purchases. In this framing, the company's monopoly disappears from view, and so do the desperate circumstances of isolation and boredom that make e-tablet purchases and communications with loved ones on the outside feel like a necessity to people locked up in jails and prisons. The frame erases, too, how government and corporate actors structure the options available to imprisoned people. As discussed in chapter 3, they frequently restrict free alternatives in order to channel the people they control into fee-based services—and where free or nearly free options are available, they work to ensure that the expensive alternatives are far superior. Businesses can also be relentless in "nudging" imprisoned people and their loved ones; they tempt, guilt, and incentivize people on both sides of the walls into making revenue-generating choices.

Yet despite all of this, carceral businesses insist that the people they extract payments from are no different from consumers in the rest of society. Asked to justify the high prices GTL charged for e-tablet services, a company executive deflected: "The inmates [were] not forced to use [the e-tablets]; they chose to use them."[41]

Failed Deviants in Need of Reform

Neoliberal discourses underwrite a third set of enabling frames by depicting targets of criminal justice predation as deviants who violate societal norms and values. The symbolic figure that anchors this type of rationale is not the ordinary market consumer, nor is it the "criminal lawbreaker" per se. It is the failed and irresponsible market actor who lacks prudence as a consumer and diligence as a worker. Dividing society into "makers and takers," this discourse defines *deviant persons* by applying the market-based expectations of neoliberal citizenship.[42]

As new modes of predation spread across criminal legal institutions in the 1980s and '90s, a "personal responsibility crusade" swept American society.[43] In the name of promoting prudent and disciplined personal choices, this moralistic movement undermined collective protections against social risks. Each individual, this view holds, is "charged with managing themselves as a potential source of risk."[44] Self-sufficient citizens who play by the rules should not have to pay the costs of cleaning up after other people's mismanaged lives.[45] "Care and discipline of the self is portrayed as necessary for the good of the social body," Julie Guthman explains, and anything less is considered an unjust "cost to the taxpayers . . . the nation and state."[46] People who violate this moral and civic standard deserve to pay a price.

Discourses of personal responsibility have drawn a strict symbolic line between the nation's good, self-regulating citizens and various demonized figures constructed at the intersections of race, class, and gender stereotypes: "street thugs," "welfare queens," "illegal immigrants," "deadbeat dads," and other "parasites" who take what they have not earned and

thereby violate the social compact.⁴⁷ "Underclass" narratives have played
a particularly important role in defining the neoliberal citizen's symbolic
opposite. Since the 1980s, Loïc Wacquant argues, these discourses have
fixated on "the assumed 'pathologies' of ghetto residents, namely . . . behaviors that so-called middle-class society considers abnormal, offensive
or unduly costly, from violent crime, school 'dropouts,' teenage pregnancy
and labor market 'shiftlessness,' to the proliferation of 'female-headed
households,' drug consumption and trading, and 'welfare dependency.'"⁴⁸

When challengers attack predatory criminal legal practices, they often
tell stories about powerful perpetrators of injustice and sympathetic victims. In response, defenders regularly draw on neoliberal discourses to
recast the so-called victims as irresponsible deviants who expect others to
pay for their bad choices. They seem especially apt to do so when justifying practices that generate debt and punish people for nonpayment. Consider, for example, the testimony of a county collections and compliance
supervisor during a debate over jailing debtors in Texas: "I can tell you
as a collector for the last ten years that I have seen multiple defendants
that say they cannot afford to make payments but [I] literally have gone
to lunch and seen them getting a full set of nails ($45) at the local nail
salon; or they have been incarcerated for public intoxication over and
over, so they have money for their beer but not money to pay their fines
and fees? I just think that we are taking way too much into consideration
for these defendants."⁴⁹ In the same debate, a chief court clerk similarly
framed defendants as people with pathologically misplaced priorities and
mismanaged lives who *willfully* refuse to pay their debts: "When these defendants make the choice to break the law they know they do not have the
means to pay the court cost and fine. Although they do have the means
to pay for alcohol, cell phones, cigarettes, nails and other wanted—*not
needed*—items. . . . Remember [the] day in Ferguson when the Payless
shoe store got looted? Well guess what: [not] a single pair of work boots
were taken. Go figure!"⁵⁰

To bolster the story of intentional nonpayment, public officials have
often repeated the empirically dubious claim that judges generally waive
fines and fees for indigent people (see chapter 2). As it dispatches the
most morally troubling cases, this rhetorical maneuver also implies that
everyone in question could pay their bills if they chose to do so. By "refusing" to pay—in effect, demanding a free ride—such people flout their
financial obligations and disrespect legal authorities. It is justified, therefore, to charge such "deadbeats" interest on criminal legal debts or even
lock them up, as an official insisted during a debate in the Illinois Senate:
"Now, if you're just going [to] thumb your nose at a court ruling, and not
pay the fine, then by golly, it only stands to reason, fine, we'll charge you

with a little interest. And if that doesn't work, I'll join with the majority leader next session and if [the debtors] continue to thumb their nose at the court and show total disregard for what they have been convicted of, and refuse to pay their fine then fine, let's just lock 'em up."[51] This narrative, Brittany Friedman and Mary Pattillo explain, presents audiences with "an autonomous individual who is in full control of their circumstances . . . and acts with clear purpose."[52] Debtors, in this view, are unprincipled rational actors. They have (or could get) enough money to pay what they owe, but they choose instead to spend it on frivolous personal pleasures—effectively "thumbing their nose" at the state as well as society's most basic expectations of economic responsibility.

Legitimizing rationales that frame targets of predation as irresponsible, free-riding economic deviants may be especially common when debts and payments are at issue, but they are not limited to this context. On a larger scale, they facilitate social indifference toward criminal justice predation as a whole.[53] A striking example can be found in the US Department of Justice's (DOJ's) influential report on predatory policing and court practices in Ferguson, Missouri. The investigators pointedly observe: "City officials have frequently asserted that the harsh and disparate results of Ferguson's law enforcement system do not indicate problems with police or court practices, but instead reflect a pervasive lack of 'personal responsibility' among 'certain segments' of the community. . . . [This] personal-responsibility refrain is telling: It reflects many of the same racial stereotypes found in the emails between police and court supervisors."[54] The overwhelmingly poor and Black neighborhoods targeted by Ferguson police were, in the eyes of local authorities, filled with people who refused to work and exercise self-discipline—the kinds of takers who had long received more than their fair share from government handouts and preferential treatment. In being forced to pay up at the courthouse, they not only got what was coming to them, they were forced to repay the system for what they had received but not deserved.

Neoliberal stories of deviant people with disorderly, mismanaged lives have also supported justifications that frame predatory practices as reformative. Like many of the arguments used to promote welfare reform in the 1990s, these rationales weave together neoliberal conceptions of the mismanaged life and paternalist agendas that call for using state powers to teach "the dysfunctional poor" restraint, probity, and diligence.[55] In this framing, practices that impose and enforce debts are lauded as teaching tools: Legal financial obligations (LFOs), authorities assert, provide *opportunities* for debtors to learn how to manage themselves more effectively. A Washington state lawmaker emphasized to Alexes Harris, for example, how "reachable" debt-payment goals cultivate a disciplined striking toward worthy ends: "We don't see legal financial obligations as a punishment at all. We do see it as a potential motivation to work their way out of bad decisions. So that's the reason we looked at trying to make [the debt amounts] reachable. So that people could crawl their way out of it."[56]

Efforts to frame predatory practices as reformative efforts are especially common in the case of penal labor. The work requirements imposed in carceral facilities, community service, and reentry programs are similarly portrayed as tutelary efforts to promote strong work ethics, personal responsibility, and self-discipline. One of the largest actors in the field is UNICOR, a government-owned company that, in 2007, employed 19,720 federal prisoners at wages ranging from $0.23 to $1.15 an hour.[57] In UNICOR's public reports and statements, this meager pay is downplayed through a steady emphasis on the goal of creating productive, self-sufficient worker–citizens.[58] Incarcerated workers, the company argues, receive something far more valuable than money: an opportunity to better themselves. As Dennis Dunsmoor, the director of UNICOR's Colorado program, says: "These guys are going to get back out on the street. A lot of these guys have never worked a job, never clocked in, never worked eight hours, and just that skill alone is very valuable, so we teach them that kind of work ethic."[59]

Or consider a 2016 report on the Center for Employment Opportunities (CEO), written by the Manpower Demonstration Research Project (MDRC).[60] CEO is a multicity reentry business that provides people released from prison with temporary low-wage, unskilled work and a one-week course on "job readiness and life-skills." The MDRC report sets aside questions of worker compensation from the outset, focusing instead on CEO's potential rehabilitative benefits. Likening the program to "cognitive behavioral therapy," the authors echo company rhetoric in touting post-release labor as a way to "change individuals' behavior" by modifying "core 'criminogenic needs,'" such as "impulsivity, lack of self-control, antisocial thoughts, and antisocial peers." By "reporting for work each day, cooperating with colleagues, and following supervisors' directions," participants are said to cultivate the "habits and competencies that make for a good employee."

Protecting Public Safety

In studies of monetary sanctions, scholars have emphasized how a racialized "culture of punishment" in the US has fueled and justified the growth of fines, fees, and other criminal legal takings.[61] In the remainder of this chapter, we build on their work by analyzing three groups of security rationales that focus on the state's obligation to defend the nation and protect its citizens.

The first set frames predatory practices as necessary to secure public safety and social order. Since the 1980s, the state's obligations in this regard have served as a powerful and adaptable rationale for expanding the reach and intensity of criminal justice predation. In the name of getting tough on crime, government officials created new violations, added fines, and raised fine levels. In the name of making criminals pay, they piled on fees at every stage of the legal process, from pretrial through parole. In the name of precaution for the community, they applied financial conditions of bail more often and in larger amounts. In the name of the war on drugs and, later, the war on terror, they strengthened and deployed asset forfeiture laws to seize cash and goods. Throughout, state officials and their business partners have presented predatory takings as measures designed to preserve public safety and social order. To allow for a deeper and more detailed analysis, we focus again on a single operational trajectory: the dramatic growth of seizures based on asset forfeiture.

In chapter 2, we described how police use asset forfeiture laws to seize cash and property from people who are rarely charged with a crime, let alone convicted. Since the 1980s, public officials have promoted and defended this practice as an essential weapon in the nation's "wars" against crime, drugs, and terror. Asset seizure, they argue, is an efficient and effective way to strip criminals of ill-gotten gains and, often, use the resources to strengthen law enforcement. In 1990, US Attorney General Dick Thornburgh celebrated this dual function: "The Department of Justice has been and will continue to aim at drug dealers where it hurts them most—in their pocketbooks. It is poetic justice when money seized from drug dealers is . . . used to wipe out the stain of drug trafficking. Our new message to drug profiteers is, 'You make it, we'll take it.'"[62]

Through a series of laws passed in the mid-1980s, federal officials expanded and promoted asset seizure as a way to get "tough on crime." In *United States v. Property Known as 6109 Grubb Road* (1989), Judge Morton I. Greenberg stressed how the politics of "law and order" and the war on drugs shaped asset forfeiture's new meaning and purpose: "In legislation ranging from the Controlled Substances Penalties Amendments Act of 1984 to the Narcotics Penalties and Enforcement Act of 1986 to the Anti-Drug Abuse Act of 1988, Congress has sent out a clear message that narcotics offenses are to be dealt with harshly. *Congress's provision for civil forfeiture of real property in the Comprehensive Crime Control Act of 1984 is a critical part of its legislative drive to wipe out drug trafficking.*"[63] In the years that followed Greenberg's dissent, actors at all levels of government shared in the bounty of forfeiture revenue through the equitable sharing program (see chapter 2). When critics challenged the practice, its defenders rolled out security justifications time and again.

The war on drugs offered an especially potent vehicle for weaving threats at home and abroad into a single legitimizing rationale for seizures. Through the lens of the global drug trade, internal and external dangers appeared inseparable. On one side, the story went, weak border defenses failed to protect the nation against foreign drug cartels and traffickers. On the other, "soft-on-crime" policies failed to defend communities against domestic drug gangs and street dealers. Stefan D. Cassella, the US DOJ's assistant chief of asset forfeiture and money laundering (who would later become CEO of the company Asset Forfeiture Law, LLC), illustrated this rationale in a *Federalist Society* article published in 1997. Forfeiture, he insisted, is used to "take the instrumentalities of crime out of circulation." Blending global and domestic threats, he continued: "If drug dealers are using a 'crack house' to sell drugs to children as they pass by on the way to school . . . we can shut it down. If a boat or truck is being used to smuggle illegal aliens across the border, we can forfeit the vessel or vehicle to prevent its use time and again for the same purpose. The same is true for an airplane used to fly cocaine from Peru into Southern California, or a printing press used to mint phony $100 bills." In these and other ways, asset seizure "provides both a deterrent against crime and a measure of punishment for the criminal. Many criminals fear the loss of their vacation homes, fancy cars, businesses, and bloated bank accounts far more than the prospect of a jail sentence."[64]

Casella's focus on "vacation homes, fancy cars . . . and bloated bank accounts" is deeply misleading. Over the past four decades, most asset forfeitures have involved small-scale takings from poor and working-class people (see chapter 2). Security rationales obscured this reality, and from the start, they enjoyed bipartisan support. This framing made it possible and politically useful for Republicans to incorporate the expansion of asset forfeiture into their broader pro-military, border-security, and law-and-order agendas. It also made the promotion of forfeiture inviting for Democrats eager to reposition their party on issues of race, poverty, welfare, and crime.

By the 1980s and '90s, Democratic Party leaders were desperately looking for ways to neutralize Republican accusations that they were soft on crime.[65] To shore up the support of disaffected White voters, many saw it as politically necessary to pursue and publicly champion law-and-order policies. In 1989, when President George H. W. Bush delivered a speech calling for "more prisons, more jails, more courts, [and] more prosecutors," then–US Senator Joe Biden (D-DE) used a televised response to tell the public: "The president's plan does not include enough police officers to catch the violent thugs, enough prosecutors to convict them, enough judges to sentence them, or enough prison cells to put them away for a long time."[66] In 1994, Biden would tout the Violent Crime Control and Law Enforcement Act, championed by President Bill Clinton, as clear evidence that so-called liberal Democrats now stood for law and order: "Let me define the liberal wing of the Democratic Party. The liberal wing of the Democratic Party is now for sixty new death penalties. That is what is in this bill. The liberal wing of the Democratic Party has seventy enhanced penalties. . . . The liberal wing of the Democratic Party is for 100,000 cops. The liberal wing of the Democratic Party is for 125,000 new state prison cells."[67]

In the 1980s, the rarely used practice of asset forfeiture presented centrist Democrats such as Biden and Clinton with an opportunity to present themselves as breaking new ground in the pursuit of law and order. Biden contributed so much to this effort that some critics today consider him "the architect of the government's asset forfeiture program."[68] Working closely with former Dixiecrat Senator Strom Thurmond (R-SC) and the Reagan administration, Biden coauthored the Comprehensive Forfeiture Act of 1983 and the Comprehensive Crime Control Act of 1984. Together, these laws abolished seizure exemptions for multiple categories of property, allowed substitute property to be seized if assets deemed illicit could not be located, lowered the burden of proof needed to seize property (suspicion would now suffice), and created the equitable sharing program to distribute forfeiture revenues across all levels of government.

Echoing narratives advanced by the political Right, Biden crowed in a 1991 Senate speech, "We changed the law so that if you are arrested, and you are a drug dealer, under our forfeiture statutes, the government can take everything you own. Everything from your car to your house, your bank account, not merely what they confiscate in terms of the dollars from the transaction you just got caught engaging in."[69] By pushing to expand forfeiture and publicly claiming credit, Biden and other centrist Democrats sent a message to voters that they could be just as tough as Republicans. In the process, they legitimized asset forfeiture as something it demonstrably was not: an essential tool for securing the safety of the American public.

The Vilification of Targets

Security discourses have also enabled and secured predatory criminal legal practices by vilifying what some scholars refer to as their "target population"—criminalized people and communities.[70] Reflecting on the politics of punishment in the 1980s and '90s, David Garland writes:

"The recurrent image of the offender ceased to be that of the needy delinquent or the feckless misfit and became much more threatening—a matter of career criminals, crackheads, thugs, and predators—and at the same time much more racialized."[71] In key ways, this shift in discourse marked a resurgence of old storylines. In the early twentieth century, Khalil Gibran Muhammad shows, scientific racism and the nascent field of criminology were deeply entwined. Together, they "scientifically" established a discourse of Black criminality replete with profiles of inherently and, in some cases, monstrously threatening racial-criminal others.[72]

In the last decades of the twentieth century, a series of popular and academic publications resuscitated this "scientific" discourse. In *Crime and Human Nature*, James Q. Wilson and Richard Herrnstein claimed to find new evidence of a racial-biological basis for criminality.[73] In books with inflammatory titles, like *Body Count: Moral Poverty . . . and How to Win America's War Against Crime and Drugs*, academics and social critics spun tales of juvenile delinquents destined to become brutal, habitual criminals.[74] Influential experts such as John DiIulio conjured images of an impending wave of hyperviolent "superpredators . . . born of abject moral poverty [in] fatherless, Godless, and jobless settings."[75] Mass media portrayed hardened criminal youth as "amoral, radically impulsive, and brutally cold-blooded preadults who murder, assault, rape, burglarize, deal deadly drugs, engage in gang warfare, and generally wreak communal havoc."[76]

Such talk played a critical role in justifying some of the period's most draconian changes in penal governance, such as lifetime sex offender registries, life sentences without the possibility of parole for juveniles, "habitual offender laws" (e.g., Three Strikes and You're Out), and long-term solitary confinement in ultra-austere "security housing units."[77] It's worked in a similar manner to facilitate the growth of predatory criminal legal practices.

Security-based rationales turn depictions of an irredeemable, racial-criminal underclass into a singular basis for imagining the people targeted by predation. Reports that police, courts, and penal facilities are forcing *these* sorts of people to pay financial charges are unlikely to provoke much outrage. When questioned about asset seizures in 2015, US Senator Jeff Sessions (R-AL) dismissively responded that most of the people affected by it had "done nothing in their lives but sell dope."[78] That same year, the DOJ's *Ferguson Report* revealed more shocking examples of how municipal authorities viewed the groups they subjected to predation: "We discovered emails circulated by police supervisors and court staff that stereotype racial minorities as criminals, including one email that joked about an abortion by an African American woman being a means of crime control."[79]

In the late 1990s, an assortment of social justice and libertarian groups challenged asset forfeiture practices and, bolstered by sympathetic media stories about people wrongly stripped of their belongings, began to gain momentum.[80] By calling attention to how asset seizure had harmed "ordinary Americans," activists and journalists destabilized the established image of its targets (villainous criminals) and purposes (protecting the public from local crime). The attacks of September 11, 2001, provided authorities an opportunity to change the game by focusing attention on a different threat: foreign "terrorists."

As political leaders called for a global war on terror, they presented asset forfeiture as essential for securing the homeland and taking the fight to America's enemies. In late 2001, US officials moved to freeze assets and block financial transactions for actors allegedly connected to terrorist activities.[81] The war on terror, they argued, had to be "fought in the halls of our financial institutions" and "won by the destruction of checkbooks rather than on a battlefield."[82] By shifting the focus to foreign villains, public officials sidestepped charges that innocent US citizens were being victimized and reasserted the narrative that asset seizure was critical for public safety.

Practitioners of predation and their supporters also exploited the political demonization of immigrants as a way to extend target-group rationales. Nativist and racist portrayals of immigrants as threatening and contaminating invaders have a long history in the US.[83] Scholars argue, however, that the 1980 Mariel Boatlift of Cuban and Haitian refugees marked the onset of a historically distinctive turn toward the *criminalization* of immigration.[84] In rhetoric and practice, public authorities increasingly treated immigrants as presumptive threats to public safety and unauthorized border crossings as felonious behaviors warranting incarceration (although the latter constituted only a misdemeanor under the Immigration and Nationality Act of 1965).[85]

Rising political discourses suggested that such immigrants were doubly criminal: first, for "breaking and entering" (as unwanted invaders of the homeland), and second, for "stealing" from American taxpayers who fund government services and institutions. Immigrant women were portrayed as illegally crossing the border in order to have "anchor babies" and take undeserved government handouts.[86] Such narratives have played a key role in justifying sweeping border-enforcement projects that capture and warehouse immigrants in detention facilities, large percentages of which have been set up as for-profit operations (see chapter 3).

Under the Trump administration, efforts to demonize and detain immigrants grew more intense. Ignoring contrary social scientific evidence,[87] Trump repeatedly described immigrants as violent criminals who threaten public safety.[88] His characterization of Mexican immigrants as rapists and drug dealers signaled a resurgence of white nationalist discourse, in which hordes of dangerous immigrants threaten "real Americans." In 2019, a Texas sheriff echoed Trump in a speech at the White House, asserting that immigrants are "drunks [who] will run over your children" if released from custody at the border.[89]

Who should pay to hold off the "foreign invasion" became a central question. Trump's repeated insistence that Mexico should pay for a "big, beautiful wall" along the southern border struck all but his loyal followers as extraordinary and absurd.[90] In its core logic, though, his demand was not exceptional. It fit comfortably into a major rationale for criminal justice predation writ large: At the border, as in the courtroom or prison, *they*—those threatening others who willfully do wrong, not law-abiding American taxpayers—should be made to pay the bill. The dangers *they* pose to the public, after all, are the reason why the bill exists at all.

Indeed, while Trump did not complete a border-spanning physical wall, his administration *did* impose financial charges on migrants. By aggressively denying entry requests and pursuing deportations, enforcement agencies forced large numbers of would-be migrants to navigate appellate procedures, for which the administration began to charge fees.[91] Few migrants could afford the process needed to stay in the country. Others paid the fee and, in so doing, helped to fund the very dragnet that had ensnared them. In the summer of 2020, the Trump administration expanded these methods a by instituting a $50 fee to apply for asylum.[92] Through these financial charges and other administrative burdens, Rachel Morris concludes, Trump effectively "got his wall after all."[93]

Doing Right by Victims

Along a third dimension, security discourses have supported predatory criminal legal practices by framing them as ways to protect, honor, and serve victims. Some victim-compensation arguments take a literal form, promoting financial takings as a way to directly remunerate crime victims and their families. The only LFO that provides such compensation, however, is restitution—a "monetary sentence assessed to compensate victims for lost wages, hospital bills, or loss of property."[94] Although some convicted individuals accrue substantial restitution debts, the amount of money victims and families receive is generally quite small.[95]

Nevertheless, restitution has played an outsized role in efforts to legitimize criminal justice predation. Alexes Harris reports in her study of monetary sanctions in Washington state that "every court official I interviewed highlighted the importance of restitution to victims in the imposition and enforcement of LFOs [in general]."⁹⁶ Symbolically, restitution operates as a synecdoche—a part that stands in for the whole as if it were a faithful representation. Proponents return to it time and again as a way to justify a wide range of extractive practices, the vast majority of which do not assist victims or their families in any direct way.

In 1992, for example, the state of New York passed legislation making a wide range of court fees and surcharges mandatory. Judges could not waive financial charges, legislators held, due to "the important criminal justice and victim services" they funded.⁹⁷ In reality, the mandate provided very little funding for victims' programs. In 2018, Jeff Sessions, by then the US attorney general, made a similarly unfounded rhetorical move in defending asset forfeiture: "The women and men of the DOJ's Money Laundering and Asset Recovery Section play a central role in finding and restoring forfeited funds to crime victims."⁹⁸

Notably, the 1980s and '90s saw the emergence of a powerful wave of victims' rights advocacy in the US. The new groups often told a story of double victimization: Law-abiding citizens were victimized first by the perpetrators of crimes and then by a callous legal system that treated them little better than "criminals." Advocates demanded stronger efforts not only to fight crime but also to respond to victims' needs. Elected officials soon began to invoke crime victims to justify all sorts of new punitive measures *and* institutional changes. Lawmakers created new federal and state agencies focused on victim compensation and services. They passed laws such as the Victims of Crime Act (1984) and the Crime Victims' Rights Act (2004), designed to provide victims with fair treatment, dignity, and privacy.

The push for victims' rights called not only for more to be done *for* victims but also for more to be done *to* people convicted of crimes. David Garland explained in 2001: "The need to reduce the present or future suffering of victims functions today as an all-purpose justification for measures of penal repression, and the political imperative for being responsive to victims' feelings now serves to reinforce the retributive sentiments that increasingly inform punitive legislation."⁹⁹ In the 1990s, politicians routinely presented themselves as honoring crime victims by passing tough-on-crime laws in their names. Sometimes they did so literally—as in the case of "Megan's Law," which created a public "sex offender" registry.¹⁰⁰

Advocates and politicians together framed penal policy in a way that pitted victims against "offenders."¹⁰¹ In this zero-sum setup, anything that allegedly helped "criminals" (e.g., financing higher education in prisons) was deemed harmful and offensive to victims, while efforts to crack down on the accused and convicted were framed as self-evidently beneficial to victims.[102] Though such measures provided little to no material benefits to crime victims, aggressive fines, fees, and forfeitures were portrayed as a way to "do right" by them.

Victim-based frames have traveled widely, sometimes to cases, such as unauthorized immigration, that involve no personal experience of victimization at all. Starting in the late twentieth century, Jonathan Simon argues, crime victims in the US came to serve as stand-ins for all rightful, law-abiding citizens.[103] In this storyline, "criminals" victimize upstanding citizens once by wreaking havoc on their communities and then again by, in effect, *making* the state take larger shares of their hard-earned money to fund expansive (and expensive) policing, prison, and court operations. Dutiful taxpayers are thus secondary victims, who must be safeguarded by practices that impose financial charges on accused and convicted people.

At times since the 1980s, public officials have suggested that the nation's criminal legal institutions can and should be "self-financing," echoing similar discourses from earlier eras of US history (see chapter 1). In 1989, Attorney General Richard Thornburgh championed asset forfeiture in precisely these terms, describing how a "a drug dealer [could] serve time in a forfeiture-financed prison after being arrested by agents driving a forfeiture-provided automobile while working in a forfeiture-funded sting operation."[104]

Similarly, in a 2004 *New York Times* article, a sheriff from Macomb County, Michigan celebrated the fact that pay-to-stay jail fees allowed the local department to "bring in a substantial amount of money"—nearly $1.5 million collected from about 22,000 individuals in the preceding year.[105] "The public loves them," he told the *Times*. "What we say is, 'Why should we as taxpayers have to pay the whole cost of incarcerating these people who break the law?'" The sheriff's phrasing is noteworthy given the significance of jails in the pretrial process. In 2023, roughly 83 percent of people held in local jails had *not* been convicted of a crime.[106] The leaders of the West Tennessee Violent Crime and Drug Task Force (largely underwritten by asset seizure revenues) invoke the same trope when they proudly proclaim: "We exist because we are funded by the *criminals*, not the *taxpayers*."[107] Reflecting on jail-based fees in a 2019 interview, a local Alabama official mused about the cushy "benefits of being an inmate," including how "you don't have to work to pay for anything." As he put it, "Every time a person goes to jail, the average taxpaying citizen is being penalized. We have to fund that jail. . . . The average citizen is out there working to fund that." "You've got to have" pay-to-stay fees, he concluded, "inmates need to pay something."[108]

As they legitimize predation, arguments of this sort can also pay political dividends for elected offices and public managers. In a 1988 report (early in the period of transition), the Massachusetts Legislative Research Bureau emphasized how probation supervision fees "pay costs that would otherwise fall upon the taxpayer." For precisely this reason, the bureau went on to explain, they had proven immensely helpful "in garnering public and legislative support" for probation agencies in a number of other states.[109]

In sum, security-centered discourses have smoothed the path for predatory criminal legal practices in three interrelated ways since the late 1980s. They have portrayed such practices as essential tools for protecting public safety and order. They have vilified the targets of predation as a collection of enemies, at home and abroad, who threaten the American people and necessitate a forceful response. And they have valorized predatory practices as efforts to honor and support crime victims, prevent their double victimization, and (by funding criminal legal institutions) protect law-abiding American citizens from being victimized as taxpayers. Weaving these strands together, governing authorities portray legal plunder as a win-win proposition—a meeting of virtue and necessity. They provide a way to get tough on criminals, pursue public safety, honor and serve victims, and meet the pressing fiscal needs of criminal legal institutions, all in one fell swoop.

Conclusion

In *Every Twelve Seconds*, an ethnographic study of a slaughterhouse, Timothy Pachirat analyzes how the concealment of distasteful and troubling realities helps to sustain a "civilized" society's positive self-regard, as well as its social inequalities and injustices.[110] Slaughterhouses are physically remote. Few people who rely on them for food and goods think much about their practices or observe them in person. The actors "who profit directly . . . actively seek to safeguard the distance and concealment that keep the work of industrialized killing hidden from larger society."[111] In this regard, Pachirat argues, the slaughterhouse shares much in common with the prison, the psychiatric ward, and the nursing home. The same can be said for the predatory practices that have spread throughout America's criminal legal institutions.

People in heavily policed and punished communities experience such practices firsthand. Stories of criminal legal debts and payments, and the hardships and bitter injustices they entail, circulate as common knowledge in the most heavily policed and punished communities.[112] For most Americans, however, criminal justice predation has been more like the violence of the slaughterhouse: sequestered elsewhere and easy to ignore. Since the 1980s, predatory criminal legal practices have spread and operated, in the main, as what Mary Katzenstein and Maureen Waller call a *hidden* system of taxation.[113] This has been the case not only for the public but also for the vast majority of elected officials, whose attention is typically focused elsewhere and who, by virtue of their privileged status, rarely have personal roots in targeted communities or social ties to affected people.[114]

Inattention and active concealment are vital starting points for understanding the recent political history of criminal justice predation in America. The actors who built the contemporary regime did so mostly behind the scenes, through processes that scholars refer to as "subterranean" or "quiet" politics.[115] Their efforts to develop and sustain these operations have been well served by the disengagement of others, and they have generally worked to keep their dealings out of the spotlight. The rationales analyzed in this chapter were put to extensive use in the 1980s and '90s, as revenue-seeking actors worked to bring institutional decisions-makers on board and set up their operations. Once established, these rationales circulated mostly among practitioners and their elite supporters, as taken-for-granted worldviews. Concerted messaging campaigns were pursued on a more targeted and episodic basis, mainly to expand operations or neutralize threats.

The punitive politics that fueled mass incarceration in these decades frequently worked by whipping up demands for aggressive policing and punishment. The discourses that underwrote predatory practices typically did their work at a lower temperature. They normalized and reassured. They framed carceral profiteers as trustworthy, public-spirited partners who provided reasonable solutions; coercive resource-stripping practices as ordinary market transactions; and ruinous takings and debts as just deserts for people who led deviant, irresponsible lives. Predatory criminal legal practices were presented as beneficial for reforming lawbreakers, protecting public safety, and helping crime victims and their families. Vilifying portrayals of "criminals" encouraged social indifference toward legal plunder and its devastating consequences.

Over the past two chapters, we have explained why the trajectory of criminal justice predation in America shifted so dramatically after the early 1980s and how the political work of institutional change was accomplished. Throughout, we have focused on the creation and justification of new laws, partnerships, procedures, and tools that can be used to extract resources. To generate revenues, however, such capacities must be put to use. Designs for governance, predatory or otherwise, have to be *implemented*. In the three chapters that follow, we analyze how predatory practices get structured, enacted, and legitimized at the street level through a case study of the commercial bail industry.

PART THREE

Making Bail

6 * The Predatory Dimensions of Pretrial Release

The Luxor Hotel in Las Vegas is teeming with bail agents. They have traveled from far and wide for the 2016 winter gathering of the Professional Bail Agents of the United States (PBUS), the "national voice of the bail agent." Protecting for-profit bail is the meeting's unofficial theme, and the vibe in the lobby is tense and energized. Agents gather here and there, nervously discussing lawsuits and legislative efforts that threaten their livelihood. There's lots of chatter about legislation in New Jersey that will make defendants less reliant on commercial bail and push some bond companies out of business. With PBUS's presidential election just a couple days away, Beth Chapman (of TV's *Dog the Bounty Hunter* fame) is running a slick campaign. Her slogan, "Secure Our Future," is a none-too-subtle nod to the industry's rising sense of threat. Her glossy campaign brochure touts her willingness to sacrifice for the cause, noting that she and her husband recently suspended their TV series, *Dog and Beth: On the Hunt*, so that she can "spend time fighting against legal challenges and policy changes that are adversarial to the bail industry." In a few days, Chapman will emerge victorious and set forth as PBUS's wartime president.

At a well-attended, two-hour session, "Lessons Beyond New Jersey: Understanding the Arguments and Solutions of the New Generation of Bail Reform and Pretrial Release," panelists address the threats to their business head on. The moderator, Nick Wachinski, CEO of Lexington Insurance, says it's time for a new approach. Campaign contributions and arguments for the superiority of money bail are, he says, "not working—anywhere." The time has come for "solutions-based thinking." The commercial bail industry must be positioned not as a business alternative to a public system, but as government's public-spirited partner offering taxpayers a cost-effective way to ease jail overcrowding and protect public safety.

The president of Crime Victims United of California (CVUC), former prosecutor Nina Salarno, takes the microphone. Having enhanced the legitimacy and power of California prison officers in the 1990s and

2000s (by wrapping their union's political efforts in sympathetic images of victims), CVUC is an attractive partner for the oft-maligned bail industry[1]—an industry, Salarno stresses, that needs a public relations makeover. Prosecutors and police typically "associate you with defendants," she notes, insisting that the industry must respond "No, [bail agents] actually protect the victims, because they ensure that the system moves, the person gets to court, I can prosecute my case, we're done." Efforts to reframe the industry as a boon to public safety and an ally in fighting crime are already paying dividends, she says: "We're actually starting to get law enforcement involved." In fact, David Clark Jr., the "African American sheriff [of Milwaukee County] that speaks on Fox News," is "willing to come in and help, because he understands the importance of bail. And he's a very powerful national person; he will bring in law enforcement."

Salarno encourages the audience to get behind victim-friendly legislation in their states. This strategy will open doors at the legislature for efforts to protect commercial bail, and "it's really good PR." Cheering the rhetorical turn to public safety and victims' rights, Lexington CEO Wachinski interjects: "It has nothing to do with bail, and it has nothing to do with that P word: profit." By partnering with victims' groups and embracing victims' rights, the industry can shift attention away from financial practices that are increasingly seen as predatory. It can show that bail companies help victims, governments, taxpayers, and even defendants who, without them, would linger in jail and suffer personal and legal hardships. The agenda seems to strike a chord with the audience, with many nodding their approval. During Q&A, a man in the audience affirms: "That is probably one of the best things I've heard. . . . I really appreciate what you've just said."

Who will pay the lobbyists and lawyers and make the campaign contributions? Who will supply the political capacity and coordination needed to successfully rebrand and defend the industry? Such questions never arise at the PBUS panel session, because the answers are well understood: The companies that make big profits from insuring bail bonds will provide the financial muscle and political connections. While Beth Chapman and local mom-and-pop storefronts may be the public face of commercial bail, Wachinski's Lexington Insurance and its peers are the industry's largest and most powerful beneficiaries.

The conference at the Luxor was just one stop along the way in an ethnographic study of the bail industry that one of us, Joshua Page, conducted in 2015–2016. For roughly a year and a half, Page worked as a bail bond agent at "A-Team Bail Bonds" in "Rocksville," participating and observing as a frontline employee.[2] (See appendix A for a discussion of methodology and ethics.) Based on this research, chapters 6–8 present a case study of commercial bail. In earlier chapters, we explored the broad landscape of criminal justice predation, clarifying how contemporary practices work, what they have in common, and why many emerged at the same time. Our study of the bail industry allows for a more fine-grained, empirically grounded analysis of predatory practices in motion. Connecting the high-finance world of corporate insurance to the low-finance world of bail and jail, we show how pretrial processes extract resources from subjugated communities and turn them into public and private revenues.

"Bail" simply refers to a process of pretrial release on conditions set by the court. In the US, the decision to set *monetary* conditions is largely a matter of judicial discretion, but it is extremely common.[3] Since most defendants cannot afford the full payment, they often turn to a bail bond company to gain pretrial freedom. The business charges a nonrefundable premium, typically 10 percent of the bail, to post a bond (i.e., a promissory note). To secure the bond, "cosigners" usually agree to assume responsibility for ensuring that the defendant makes it to court. If the accused fails to appear, the court, in theory, moves to collect the full amount of the bail from the company. In response, the company works to return the defendant to custody, sometimes using "bounty hunters." Failing that, it tries to recoup the full amount of the bail from the bond's cosigners.

In this manner, the bail bond industry extracts billions of dollars from impoverished communities each year, often in cases that do not result in any finding of guilt.[4] From a cross-national perspective, this is a highly distinctive arrangement: The US and the Philippines are the only two countries in the world that permit a for-profit bail bond industry. And from a historical perspective, commercial bail can be seen as a forerunner of many of the for-profit appendages to criminal legal governance that operate in the US today. Since the early 1900s, it has been a powerful example of how business interests can profit from turning citizens' rights into exploitative consumer exchanges. Indeed, many of the predatory practices that have emerged in this arena since the 1980s can be seen as elaborations on a model pioneered by commercial bail: the use of financial charges, payments, and collections to generate private profits from those subject to criminal legal governance.

For this reason and others, a close study of the bail industry sheds substantial light on criminal justice predation as a whole. Throughout the next three chapters, we will return to themes developed in earlier chapters, putting them into dialogue with on-the-ground insights that can only be obtained through long-term immersion in the field of practice. Although the bail industry can be seen as emblematic, it is not a "representative case" of criminal justice predation that allows for empiri-cal generalizations to the whole. Rather, it is a particular site, positioned within a larger web of intertwined operations—a distinctive vantage point for analyzing predatory practices in multiple arenas of criminal le-gal governance.[5] As a bail bond agent, Page (like other bail agents) spent long hours in courtrooms, navigated jail operations, used jail services, and developed relationships with defense attorneys, prosecutors, and other legal professionals. As a participant, Page *had to* become intimately famil-iar with such actors, institutions, and processes. Indeed, beyond our case study of bail, insights from Page's research inform and guide many of the analyses presented in this book.

In chapters 7 and 8, we explore the work of implementation, analyzing how predatory business models in the bail bond sector get put into prac-tice. Ultimately, the industry could not succeed without effective street-level actors. If bail bond agents did not pound the pavement, work the phones, build trusting relationships, and close deals, profits would not flow to bail companies and their insurers. Such practices emerge through a complex interplay of structure and agency. They are bounded by laws and norms, subject to codes of competition, and organized by a host of rules and routines. In chapter 7, we consider how bail agents develop effective strategies for landing clients on this terrain and make sense of their work in ways that feel personally and socially valuable. In chapter 8, we analyze some of the major ways that race, class, and gender structure perceptions, choices, actions, and justifications in the daily work of bail predation.

We begin in this chapter with the powerful actors who structure, operate, and defend the bail bond industry. Commercial bail in the US is organized as a public–private partnership—an interdependent, mu-tually enabling division of labor. In popular and scholarly discourses, bail is often portrayed as a "privatized" domain, in which public func-tions have been handed off to the commercial sector. In reality, it is a field of ongoing, dynamic collaborations between state and market actors who jointly turn jail and bail into wellsprings of public and private revenue.

Building a Field of Extraction

Commercial bail has existed in the US for more than a century, but its political origins are largely forgotten. Like many institutions, it enjoys something of a taken-for-granted status. Bail bonds are "naturally" sold by businesses, in this view, and purchased by customers in order to get out of jail. Certainly, bail *is* among the most commercialized legal functions in the US today. As we will explain, however, it is far from a "free market" operation.

The roots of the American bail system stretch back to the colonial era, when Pennsylvania officials established a right to bail in all but capital cases. After 1776, most states adopted constitutional language based on the Pennsylvania model.[6] The "right to bail" was not an absolute right to release.[7] Rather, defendants were entitled to release *if* they could produce acceptable sureties—i.e., reputable people who promised to pay the court a specified amount of money if the accused did not return to court. At the time, courts did not require defendants or their sureties to deposit money as a condition of bail.[8] Originally, the US Constitution did not include a right to bail. In 1789, however, federal officials created a statutory right to bail in noncapital cases. Then, in 1791, they enacted the Eighth Amendment, providing citizens with constitutional rights against "excessive bail," "cruel and unusual punishment," and "excessive fines."[9]

The use of monetary bail (often called "cash bail") conditions, paid through up-front deposits or commercial bonds, first emerged in the 1800s. Scholars speculate that this practice was adopted to reduce unnecessary pretrial detention, especially on the frontier and in urban areas, where defendants might lack "reputable people" to serve as sureties.[10] In response, judges increasingly placed "secured money conditions on defendants hoping they could 'self-pay.'" As early as 1898, entrepreneurs began to set up commercial sureties—businesses that allowed accused individuals to leave jail for a fee set well below the full bail amount. Commercialization took off so quickly that in *Leary v. United States* (1912), the US Supreme Court observed that "the distinction between bail and suretyship is pretty nearly forgotten. The interest to produce the [defendant] in court is . . . wholly pecuniary."[11] The court ruled in *Leary* that private companies could create legally enforceable contracts with bond-seeking guarantors.[12] In essence, it used state powers to enable and certify the creation of a new market: the bail industry.

From then to the present era, state powers have operated as the engines that produce consumer demand for the bail bond market. As judges hear individual cases, they decide who should be eligible for release and on what conditions. They can set nonmonetary conditions, for example, or release individuals on their own recognizance, based on a stated commitment to show up for court. In some states, they also have the option to require an "unsecured" bond that imposes no financial cost unless the accused fails to appear in court. Judges only produce potential customers for local bail businesses when they choose to set "secured" monetary conditions.

For this reason, bail industry profits always depend on the forces that influence judicial discretion. In recent decades, such forces have been a boon to business. In large US counties from 1990 to 2009, the percent of felony defendants given monetary bail conditions rose from 53 to 72.[13] Average (mean) bail amounts rose by 46 percent, driven mostly by growth in the "upper tail of defendants [who soon faced] bail payments in the hundreds of thousands of dollars."[14] As median bail amounts also increased, the proportion of defendants that depended on commercial bail more than doubled.[15]

There is little evidence that trends in felony offenses drove this surge.[16] It is far more likely that judges changed their behaviors as a risk-averse response to shifting political conditions—specifically, to the rising tide of tough-on-crime pressures and concerted efforts to vilify court officials as liberals who coddled criminals and cared little about victims (see chapter 5). Like sentencing decisions, choices regarding release conditions increasingly came with political risks, especially for elected judges. By imposing hefty bail amounts and restrictive conditions (such as monitoring and drug testing), judges could insulate themselves from damaging "soft-on-crime" accusations.[17]

Policy changes mattered as well. Historically, bail's official purpose in the US was "to enable persons accused of crime to remain at liberty while preparing for trial. . . . [T]he only lawful reason for requiring defendants to post bail [was] to [ensure] their presence for required court appearance."[18] Some judges had also considered defendants' alleged dangerousness when setting bail, but only on an informal basis. In 1984, however, federal legislation made protecting public safety an official purpose of federal bail and authorized judges to detain defendants they considered dangerous.[19] Then, in 1987, the US Supreme Court ruled that pretrial detention *without* bail was constitutional, deeming it a form of regulation, not punishment. Soon, states began to align their laws with federal policy, "allowing more arrestees to be detained because of potential dangerousness."[20]

The new laws were not mandates, of course, but the zone of discretion they created—to use dangerousness to deny bail or make its conditions harder to meet—further exposed judges to the racially charged pressures of law-and-order politics. Judges became more vulnerable to groups that might scour the public record for evidence of their commitments. These groups included victims' rights organizations, bail industry associations, prosecutors, and police unions. In the ensuing decades, concerns about "dangerousness" became even more central to bail decision-making, justifying and fueling the growth of tough monetary conditions for pretrial release.[21]

From Desperation to Dollars

Public laws make the bail industry possible, and judicial decisions supply potential buyers. Monetary conditions of bail, however, do not force defendants to go to bail bond companies. In principle, accused individuals can skip the expense by waiting for trial in custody. In practice, though, pressures to turn to a bail bond agency tend to be intense.

Local jails are notoriously terrible places, even worse than prisons. They are frequently dangerous, dirty, chaotic, and mind-numbingly boring.[22] Many defendants are desperate for relief from these conditions. Equally important, they are eager to get out so they can work on their cases or, at a minimum, keep their lives from falling apart. Accused individuals who remain in jail tend to get convicted at higher rates, receive longer prison sentences, and fare worse in plea-bargaining processes than similarly situated defendants who are released pretrial.[23] By staying in jail, they also raise the odds that a stigmatizing criminal accusation will become visible in the community. Stuck in lockup, parents cannot fulfill their obligations to children and partners. Absences from work or school can quickly accumulate, with dire consequences. Legal scholar Bill Quigley explains: "Once a person has spent more than twelve hours in jail, even if they are later determined to be innocent, they start losing ground. [In the worst cases, people] lose their job, after losing their job they lose their apartment, with no job and no apartment they lose custody or visiting rights to their kids."[24]

Thus, the basic recipe for creating commercial bail customers consists of pretrial detention, the imposition of monetary bail conditions, and pressures that make defendants desperate to leave jail. Two more ingredients are crucial as well: severely limited personal resources and bail amounts beyond what defendants and their loved ones can pay. The Eighth Amendment forbids excessive bail but, in practice, courts rarely limit bail amounts based on defendants' ability to pay.[25] The high bail amounts they set, especially in gross misdemeanor and felony cases, are usually well beyond defendants' financial reach. Research suggests that roughly 80 percent of accused individuals are poor enough to qualify for public defender services.[26] Lacking personal resources, they routinely turn to family and friends. The problem, studies repeatedly show, is that people who live in poverty tend to have family and friends who are also poor.[27] Even when loved ones are willing to pitch in, few defendants are able to raise anything close to their full bail amount on short notice.[28] Into this impasse step bail agents, eager to offer a way out.

Commercial bail, then, is a market in the sense that businesses compete and consumers make purchases. Its operations, however, bear little resemblance to an arena of voluntary exchange in which actors freely enter mutually beneficial agreements. The bail industry works more like a mining operation, created, organized, and supplied by government and carried out on a financial landscape that holds only the thinnest of resource deposits.

The big moneymakers in this operation are not storefront businesses; they are large insurance corporations. The reasons, once again, can be traced to government. By law, some states require bail companies to carry insurance, and almost all states forbid them from taking on bond obligations beyond what they can cover with assets on hand. Without insurance, most storefront businesses could only write bonds for small amounts. Outside the wealthiest companies in the field, the vast majority have to underwrite their bonds by partnering with an insurance corporation, usually selected from a field of about thirty major players.[29]

In exchange for their backing, the insurers take a cut of every bail premium.[30] In the US today, insurers underwrite about $14 billion in bonds each year, generating estimated annual revenue between $1.4 and $2.4 billion.[31] In this manner, a sizable portion of the resources taken through bail predation migrate up and out, eventually finding their way to the rarefied world of high finance. A 2017 report explains: "Bail insurance is increasingly part of larger, often global companies, and it is a small part of their businesses. Traded in London, Tokyo, and Toronto, or registered in tax havens like the Cayman Islands and Bermuda, these corporations and executives operate far from the influence of the people and communities over whom they hold power."[32]

Commercial bail has grown larger and become more integrated into global finance in recent decades, but its status as a reliable and lucrative site of investment is nothing new. In 1975, Forrest Dill observed that "the sale of bail bonds is . . . an immensely profitable, low-risk arena of enterprise within the insurance industry."[33] The risks are no greater for the insurance firms that underwrite bonds today. The reason is simple. In the minority of cases where a defendant skips court and triggers the forfeiture of a bond, corporate underwriters are rarely forced to absorb the costs. In auto and property cases, insurance companies typically have to pay out 40 to 60 percent of their revenue in losses each year. In the bail industry, sureties pay out *less than 1 percent* in bond losses.[34] Courts rarely demand payment on a forfeited bond and, when they do, the local bail company (not the corporate insurer) typically covers the cost.[35] Local businesses carry the financial risks and serve as the visible face of the industry. The sureties and their investors reap a steady flow of profits outside public view.

Pretrial Predation as a Partnership

Pretrial governance in the US is organized as a public–private partnership where state and market actors jointly carry out judicial functions, govern subjugated groups, and extract community resources. The arrangement pays handsome dividends for public institutions. From the outset, commercial bail allows governments to shed costs and responsibilities by placing released defendants under the supervision of bail companies. Today, non-convicted defendants make up roughly two-thirds of the nation's total jail population.[36] In the absence of bail agencies, this group would be far larger, and jails would be much more expensive. As they reduce jail expenditures, bail agencies also shoulder some of the costs of ensuring that defendants show up for court.[37] When defendants flee, bond companies often work with bounty hunters to bring them back at no additional public cost. (Law enforcement also picks up many defendants who miss court—either by executing failure to appear warrants or through unrelated encounters, such as traffic stops.)

Cost savings, however, are only the beginning. Government agencies are collaborators in bail predation, controlling the field of play and actively claiming their share of the spoils. To gain entry at all, bail companies and agents typically have to pay licensing fees to state and local governments. Many counties also charge "filing fees," which they add to the defendant's bail amount.[38] If a defendant posts cash bail without a bond company, the court may secure this fee by taking payment out of the bail amount itself, subtracting it (and other fees) from the money it later returns to the defendant. Bail companies typically pay different fees when they post bonds. In Alabama, for example, agents pay a fee for each bond, plus an additional fee if the defendant has multiple bails. In 2012, Alabama lawmakers raised the per-bond fee from $20 to $35. According to the sponsor of the bill (which also increased other court fees), the state had no choice: "If it doesn't pass, [the court system is] going to have an immediate layoff of 500 more [people]." He continued, "It's a user fee. Those that use the court pay for it. We didn't have to pass it on to the general public."[39] Bail companies typically add the costs of these administrative fees to their clients' premiums, acting as de facto bill collectors for the government.

One might think that bail forfeitures provide a substantial source of government revenue. The risk of forfeiting funds to the state is, after all, the linchpin of commercial bail, recognized by all actors involved. If the accused fails to appear for court and a judge forfeits the bond, the bond company is legally responsible for paying the full bail amount to the court. Because they shoulder this risk, the theory goes, companies will exercise greater care in evaluating potential customers, assessing the odds that defendants will show up for court and monitoring clients throughout the pretrial process in order to protect their investments.

As noted earlier, insurance corporations rarely incur losses when defendants fail to appear in court. Local bail agencies are typically on the hook. Even so, consistent research findings suggest that courts rarely force bail agencies to pay the full amounts of forfeited bonds—a remarkable fact given how aggressively they pursue revenue in general.[40] Their willingness to leave money on the table, in this case but not others, can be traced to the interdependent relationship that binds courts to bail companies. When defendants fail to appear for court, this relationship often shifts toward conflict. Bail companies employ attorneys to fight forfeiture rulings through repeated appeals, making collection a costly endeavor.[41]

Cooperation is as important as conflict for forfeiture outcomes. In their daily work, court officials work collaboratively with bail companies and, in many ways, depend on their contributions. In their classic studies of pretrial governance, Forrest Dill and Malcolm Feeley each emphasize the many ways bail bond agents help legal professionals meet their obligations and objectives.[42] Above all, bail businesses allow judges to set monetary bail amounts beyond what defendants can pay on their own while also limiting overcrowding.[43] In the current era, jails routinely operate at or above capacity, and judges face intense political pressures to impose high bail amounts. Partnerships with bail companies make both challenges more manageable. In this respect and others, judges have good reasons to listen when bail companies claim that repeated forfeiture payments will put them out of business or force them to limit their operations to a small number of defendants who pose little or no flight risk.

Instead of full payment, courts may opt to take a much smaller cut by levying "delinquency fines" against bond companies. In Rocksville, the site of Page's study, the delinquency penalty is usually 10 percent or less of a forfeited bail. A-Team does not contest such charges and, while courts receive a small fraction of what they are owed, they do so at little cost to their budgets or their relationships with bail agencies. A-Team comes out unscathed as well: It simply adds the amount of the fine to the client's tab. (Similarly, when A-Team contests a forfeiture ruling, it bills clients to compensate its in-house lawyer for time spent drafting and filing motions.) In the end, the costs of back-end fines, like front-end filing fees, are only nominally incurred by bail companies. Passed along to defendants and cosigners, they ultimately transfer resources from low-income communities to government budgets.

When courts allow individuals to leave jail on bond, they also frequently charge fees for services that they mandate as nonmonetary conditions of release, such as drug and alcohol testing and electronic surveillance. In recent decades, counties have increasingly relied on for-profit providers for such services. The costs are charged to defendants, sometimes with an additional increment that goes to the court. A 2016 report explains: "In all states except Hawaii and the District of Columbia, defendants are charged a fee for electronic monitoring. Defendants may also be charged a monthly fee for pretrial services supervision, drug or alcohol testing, or participation in counseling or anger management classes. In some cases, a defendant who is ordered released with conditions like electronic monitoring may be forced to wait in jail until he can pay a fee to set up the GPS monitoring, or may be sent back to jail if he cannot continue paying fees."[44]

Condition-of-release fees can be quite costly, especially for the race-class subjugated (RCS) communities most heavily affected by policing practices. In Rocksville, for example, Page worked with courts that mandated daily alcohol monitoring (usually for charges of driving while intoxicated). Defendants had to pay for one of three monitoring devices, on a scale that offered greater convenience for a higher price. For $220 per month, defendants got a breathalyzer, which they had to blow into three times per day and regularly bring to court so staff could download the data. For $250 per month, they got an ankle unit that continually tested for alcohol transmitted through the skin. This eliminated the hassle and risk of needing to "blow" three times per day, but it still required trips to court for data downloads. For $280 per month, defendants could get a continuously monitoring ankle unit that also transmitted data remotely, making repeated trips to court unnecessary. No matter which type of monitoring they "chose," defendants who failed to make payments for their required monitoring devices were subject to incarceration until the conclusion of their case. A 2020 report by the American Bar Association (ABA) identifies a variety of similar practices across the country and notes that mandatory drug tests "are rarely free" for defendants, "regardless of who runs the pretrial services program."[45]

In the pretrial process, contracts with corporations also generate public revenues in ways that mirror prison-based predation (see chapter 3). Like convicted prison populations, accused individuals held in jails can be exploited as captive markets, and access to them can be sold to private bidders by local officials burdened by the high costs of their jails.[46] Some arrangements of this sort are not directly related to bail; others are related in nonobvious ways.

Consider contracts with telecom companies. In jails, as in prisons, such contracts generate big corporate profits and sizable commissions for governments. People held in jail routinely pay for phone calls to stay connected to people on the outside and arrange for visitation. They pay for tablets for entertainment, education, job searches, and interpersonal communications. For accused individuals, paying inflated prices for these services is often a necessary step in the process of obtaining commercial bail services. To secure the premiums and cosigners they need to be released on bail, most defendants have to repeatedly reach out to friends and family.

A striking example of how local governments use contracts to capitalize on commercial bail involves paid agreements to allow advertising inside jails and police departments. The California-based firm Jail Advertising Network (JAN) bills itself as providing "fair, affordable, and equal opportunity advertising to qualified bail bond agencies and criminal defense attorneys in the form of signboards that can be installed in local and county jails."[47] By contracting with JAN, local governments can turn the bare walls of their jails and police departments into valuable ad space for bail companies competing for customers in an overcrowded industry. For JAN and its government partners, the walls of incarceration are literally financially productive.

JAN charges bail companies between $500 and $2,150 for six months of advertising in a single lockup.[48] For the same service, it charges private attorneys between $500 and $1,850.[49] Local governments claim 70–80 percent of the profits, with JAN retaining a much smaller portion.[50] Summarizing the benefits of a partnership with JAN, Lieutenant Greg Clifton of the Stanislaus County Sheriff's Department explained: "This service is free to us and provides a great revenue stream for our department. Plus, I no longer have to argue with bail agencies over posting their own bail bond boards or advertisements at our jails."[51] JAN, of course, presents itself as a public-spirited partner, eager to help local governments: "Since our inception [in 1999], we have seen downturns in the economy lead to more severe financial issues for jails than ever before. Jails are being asked to do so much more with so much less. Our purpose is to provide jail administrators with a solution to help meet their ever-increasing financial needs and overcome shortfalls from lack of government funding or changes in legislation that limit means of revenue."[52]

In sum, the pretrial process in the US is organized as a dense, interconnected network of public–private partnerships, large and small, diverse in their terms, and spread across a host of sites. Bail predation does not take place on the "business" side of a boundary between state and market; it operates in ways that complicate and renegotiate the boundary itself.

Profitability and Political Action

The profits generated by commercial bail depend on government laws and policies that establish the ground rules for pretrial release. For corporate bail interests, the clarity of this fact provides powerful incentives to build political capacities, recruit allies, monitor government agendas, and take political action. In this section and the next, we return to some of the political themes pursued in chapters 4 and 5, based on a more focused analysis of how the bail lobby has worked to expand, secure, and reconfigure extractive pretrial practices.

In chapter 4, we explained how rapid growth in policing, incarceration, and related expenditures drew large numbers of corporations to the field, which transformed the politics of criminal legal governance in ways that accelerated the growth of financial predation. Over time, as public and private actors invested in and became dependent on predatory revenues, they developed material stakes in defending and enlarging such operations. Similar dynamics have been central to the politics of bail predation since the 1980s, and especially the hardball tactics adopted by insurance companies and their well-heeled lobbying groups.

In recent decades, commercial bail interests have spent millions on political action, working aggressively and creatively to expand existing operations and establish new frontiers.[53] At the center of these efforts stands "the bail lobby," a loose assembly of groups that work across local, state, and federal arenas to influence policy decisions and rewrite the rules of the game.

The composition of the lobby reflects the hierarchical structure of the field. Down at the front lines of the field, the high levels of risk and competition that drive aggressive bail practices (see chapter 7) work to impede solidarity and coordination. Some states and counties have politically active bail agency associations, but their resources and influence tend to be limited. On the few occasions when Rocksville businesses tried to work together on political action, Page observed, the efforts usually fell victim to the distrust and antagonism that years of competition had produced.[54] At the top of the field, in contrast, insurance companies came together in the early 1990s and established themselves as a powerful and durable political force.

The American Bail Coalition (ABC), the most prominent advocacy organization in the bail lobby, was founded in 1992 by a group of insurance company executives. The origin story merits retelling. A 2010 ABC newsletter recounts that the executives came together because of concerns about the development of alternatives to commercial bail, especially "government pretrial services," a model they described as spreading like an "incurable AIDS-like virus." Anxious to protect their profit streams, they organized to discredit the alternative of "tax-dollar supported institutions" as a leftist invention of "the so-called bail reform movement of the sixties, conceived during the *haut baroque* period of the criminal as victim of society."[55]

Backed by the insurers' deep resources, ABC invests in a wide range of political strategies. It supplies county officials with information and arguments they can use to tout the benefits of commercial bail and cast doubt on alternatives; it lobbies local, state, and federal politicians; and it funds and fields campaigns to pass (or defeat) laws for the benefit of the industry. ABC's political influence has been greatly enhanced by its participation in the American Legislative Exchange Council (ALEC), a conservative, federally organized advocacy network.

By building networks of interest groups, corporate leaders, and politicians, developing strategies to exploit American federalism, and writing and disseminating model legislation, ALEC has become a powerhouse in US politics.[56] As we discussed in chapter 4, it has an impressive record of political victories in the promotion and defense of criminal justice predation. For good reasons, ABC's advocates believed that their goals "meshed neatly with those of ALEC."[57] Expanding commercial bail fit within ALEC's broader policy agenda, and several of ABC's leaders gained positions on ALEC committees.[58] In 2010, ABC celebrated the fruits of this political collaboration: "During its two-decade involvement with ALEC, ABC has written twelve model bills fortifying the commercial bail industry. In addition to the model bills, ALEC has issued ABC-sponsored state factors, legislative briefs, and studies related to the bail issue."[59]

When the bail lobby goes on the offensive, its goal is often to weaken or remove regulations that constrain predatory bail practices or, in a small number of jurisdictions, forbid commercial bail altogether.[60] In Oregon and Wisconsin, two states that have banned commercial bail, the lobby has waged campaigns to bring it back. As Shane Bauer explained in 2014: "[Dennis] Bartlett [former executive director of ABC] and the lobbyists he hired were recently active in Oregon, a state that banned bail bondsmen in 1978. They came close to relegalizing them last year after, an ABC executive told me, the association spent $250,000 to promote the idea. That same year, ABC succeeded in slipping a provision into a Wisconsin budget bill that would have brought back bondsmen and bounty hunters, now banned in the state [Wisconsin outlawed commercial bail in 1979]. (Under pressure from Wisconsin judges, prosecutors, and sheriffs, Governor Scott Walker issued a last-minute line-item veto.)"[61]

To promote profitability, the lobby also works to minimize financial risks and losses. Even in the case of bond forfeitures, where bail companies are rarely forced to pay the full amounts of their obligations, the lobby pushes to write formal limits into law. Working with ALEC to distribute model legislation, the lobby has sought to make forfeiture rules more permissive.[62] A working group in Santa Clara, California, which included law enforcement officials and reform advocates, described how such policy victories made it harder for courts to collect forfeitures: "California's forfeiture statute contains language promoted by the pro–bail bonds industry group [ALEC] that requires the court to follow strict notification rules and deadlines in order to collect a forfeited bail from a bail bond agent. The procedures required to collect on a forfeiture are so burdensome and costly that they are often not pursued."[63]

Political action can also be used to support corporate innovation and efforts to establish new footholds for profitable operations. For example, teaming up with ALEC once again, industry leaders mounted a campaign to convince policymakers to create a new system of "post-conviction bonds." Extending the conventional pretrial model, where bail bond companies take responsibility for ensuring that defendants show up in court, post-conviction bonds shift responsibility for monitoring convicted people under community supervision from the state to the private sector.[64] The fee-for-service model transfers costs from taxpayers to convicted individuals and generates profits for the industry. "As with pretrial bail," Shadd Maruna and colleagues explain, "the individual pays a percentage of [the post-conviction bail] amount as a nonrefundable charge in order to be released to the responsibility of a commercial bail agency. Persons in the participant's release environment, such as parents or guardians, voluntarily sign 'agreements of indemnity,' whereby they, along with the individual, would have a monetary incentive as indemnitors to the surety."[65] Lawmakers have authorized versions of this model in Mississippi, South Dakota, and Michigan.[66]

Defending Bail Predation

Commercial bail has no shortage of opponents. It is frequently targeted by activists, journalists, justice organizations, and others who deem it unjust and demand change. In this environment, the industry must invest in political capacities to survive. As challenges emerge, the bail lobby mobilizes time and again to defeat policy reforms and undercut pretrial alternatives that might weaken or eliminate the bail market.

The industry's decades-long campaign against pretrial service (PTS) agencies offers a particularly helpful case for illuminating the range of tactics involved. PTS agencies conduct risk assessments to inform judges' bail decisions, supervise released defendants (on conditions such as electronic monitoring, timely check-ins, or pursuing drug or alcohol treatment), and report back to the court on defendant compliance. According to the ABA, there are an estimated 300 to 400 PTS programs in the US, with the vast majority operating alongside commercial bail in cases where multiple conditions have been imposed.[67] Bail reform advocates have often touted arrangements based on the PTS model as potential substitutes for the monetary bail system. The bail lobby, as one might expect, views the model as a dire threat.

To fight it, the industry has poured resources into conventional interest group strategies, such as making campaign contributions to elected allies and lobbying officials to undermine or eliminate PTS agencies.[68] The lobby also works to shape various audiences' perceptions of the PTS model. For example, it places ads in local newspapers, claiming that PTS agencies enable dangerous criminals,[69] and it sends anti-PTS informational materials to policymakers, local organizations (e.g., chambers of commerce), and law enforcement officials.[70] The bail lobby's demonstrated willingness to pour money into small local elections, in amounts that usually dwarf what rival candidates can raise, lends an air of warning to such informational letters. Elected officials—including judges, district attorneys, and sheriffs—would not have to be especially savvy to see the politics risks of failing to heed the message.

The lobby also works to impose burdensome rules on PTS agencies to hobble their operations. In 2008, for example, ALEC developed the "Citizens' Right to Know: Pretrial Release Act" (CRTK). In the name of public accountability and transparency, the model legislation requires PTS agencies to gather wide-ranging data and produce onerous reports.[71] When Florida adopted a version of CRTK, it required PTS agencies to complete *weekly* reports with detailed information about every defendant they processed. It is unlikely that the heavy reporting obligations served any public purpose other than burying PTS workers in unproductive tasks. According to the National Association of Pretrial Services Association, Florida's PTS agencies "were already tracking their results before the law passed, and because of Florida sunshine laws, the data have long been available to the public. At the time of the bill's passing, not a single request for the information had been made."[72]

CRTK laws can weaken PTS agencies in several ways. First, as the Florida case illustrates, they create burdens that detract from core responsibilities, like tracking defendants. Second, by raising administrative costs, they make agencies look less efficient and, thus, bolster the bail lobby's claim that the PTS model wastes taxpayer money. Third, they produce detailed information that critics can use to discredit PTS agencies—while bail companies, as private entities, do not have to report their processes or outcomes. The resulting asymmetry gives the bail industry a major advantage in high-stakes political comparisons between the two. Fourth, ALEC's model CRTK legislation stipulates that PTS agencies that do not comply with stringent reporting requirements may lose 25 percent of their funding. When US Representative Ted Poe (R-TX) introduced a CRTK-style bill at the federal level in 2017, PBUS, the insurance-driven "national voice of the bail agent," openly acknowledged that the main goal of targeting PTS agencies in this manner was to "stop the 'bail reform' movement in its tracks."[73]

For the political defenders of commercial bail, the fight against PTS is just one battle among many. As serious legal and legislative challenges have targeted the bail industry in recent years (see chapter 10), corporate bail interests' political investments have been both deep and wide. A 2017 *New York Times* story recounts how Lexington National Insurance Corporation, a Maryland-based bail underwriter, responded to reforms in its home state by paying for top-shelf lawyers with elite credentials, political connections, and a wealth of high-stakes experience.[74] "Lawyers for the industry have also submitted amicus briefs in recent months in cases in Atlanta, Houston, New Orleans, and San Francisco," the *Times* noted, "trying to stop civil rights groups from suing in the federal courts to overhaul bail in those cities." In addition, the lobby filed its own lawsuits in New Jersey and New Mexico to roll back reform in those states.[75]

Alongside its legal battles, the industry has invested heavily in campaign contributions and direct lobbying, hoping to shore up political support and defeat pretrial reforms.[76] In 2021, insurers "spent $17 million to defeat proposals to weaken or abolish the for-profit bail industry. . . . The spending has jumped more than tenfold since 2010 as insurers have led the industry's lobbying efforts, targeting laws in more than a dozen states."[77] These maneuvers have fended off or rolled back major reform campaigns in states such as California, Connecticut, Maryland, and New Mexico.[78] Even with these successes, industry leaders continue to sound the alarm that a "perfect storm" now threatens to wash away the industry.[79]

In the past, such portrayals may have seemed hyperbolic. Today, however, the industry's crisis is real. With a growing cadre of influential groups lined up against it, the bail lobby has become increasingly isolated.[80] In a growing number of jurisdictions, government officials and community leaders have begun to openly question the legitimacy of for-profit bail *in principle* as well as practice. It has become reasonable to wonder how—if at all—the industry can continue to fend off would-be reformers, despite the political advantages that stem from its vast material resources and long-term integration into the criminal legal field.

These, of course, are the same questions that echoed through the halls of the Luxor Hotel when Page attended the winter meeting of PBUS in 2016. As noted earlier, the answers tended to focus on rebranding the industry through a "public image makeover" and trying to build new political partnerships. Indeed, industry leaders have become particularly keen to recruit allies that they hope will provide moral cover. Alongside prominent crime victim advocates, industry strategists have cultivated relationships with individuals who claim to speak on behalf of low-income communities of color. A good example is Reverend Jesse Lee Peterson, a self-described Black conservative who publicly argues that bail reform measures "threaten the already frayed fabric of our inner cities."[81] As to the rebranding, the industry is now trying to appear less as a free-market alternative to government management, and more as a solutions-oriented partner in public administration. Promoting this narrative, Lexington's Wachinski writes:

> Without question, the populations in both state prisons and county jails across the United States have seen a boom in growth. With the creation of new technologies, have come the creation of new classes of crimes and criminals. The simplest solution to this problem is to create a professional, transparent, and responsible bond between private industry, the bail industry, and the public sector that will resolve this crowding issue and minimize the number of days that a defendant stays in jail after arrest while awaiting trial. In addition to resolving the pretrial detention and pretrial release problem, the public–private partnership option offers a bail-type alternative for the release of convicted defendants or diversionary track defendants who enter into a treatment-based program through the courts.[82]

In this framing, bail companies are socially responsible, committed partners in good governance, interested above all in promoting justice and public safety. To demonstrate these commitments and show that they stand with the communities that supply their customers, industry representatives have endorsed policy changes with little direct connection to bail (and thus, with no implications for their profits). The ABC, for instance, has "called on state policymakers to pursue fair-chance or ban-the-box policies to ensure that citizens with a criminal record have every fair chance to attain a job and stable employment."[83] As Wachinski explained at the 2016 PBUS meeting, efforts to paint the industry as an eager participant in solving social problems might help to shift public debates away from the dreaded "P word" (i.e., profit).

The rebranding has had a public safety component as well, but one that has required only modest changes to long-standing narratives. In practice, the bail lobby has simply foregrounded partnership and common-good themes while carrying on its long tradition of stoking fears of crime and prejudices against criminally accused people. The wave of reforms designed to scale back commercial bail, the lobby argues, will inevitably increase the victimization of law-abiding citizens. Because this claim is not supported by empirical research,[84] the industry has been especially eager to publicize isolated cases in which defendants released on nonmonetary bail commit a new crime.[85] A press release opposing bail reform in California states, for example: "Bail Reform in NJ is getting negative results. Christian Rodgers was shot and killed by Jules Black who was released with no bail or recourse early into bail reform being active. Other cases of shootings, carjackings and theft have also been reported about recently released suspects under bail reform."[86]

As it stirs the public's fears of violent crime, the industry warns lawmakers against challenging its interests. In some cases, this strategy works in concert with efforts to recruit allies who have greater moral standing and can supply a more sympathetic public face. At the Luxor in 2016, Nina Salarno touted the benefits of partnering with crime victims' rights organizations like her own: With for-profit bail identified as a "victims' issue," policymakers would have to think twice before supporting bail reform. "Nobody wants blood on their hands, nobody wants to be the cause of another victim. Nobody wants that responsibility," she said. The message was clear: Politicians who refuse to be good partners of the bail industry (by opposing reform) should expect to be publicly excoriated by victims' rights groups. They will pay a political price for their alleged betrayal of victims.

Conclusion

The storm of opposition facing the bail industry has grown more intense as critics have increasingly focused attention on what we term *predation* in the pretrial process. In the field of bail, arguments against two-tiered justice, wealth-based detention, and profit-making are nothing new. Recently, however, a growing number of advocates have emphasized how bail bond companies and their insurers profit from the harms inflicted on defendants, families, and communities—and how the industry deepens social inequalities and racial wealth gaps. *Color of Change*, a national civil rights organization, states that activists "across the country are organizing to fight against bail bond profiteers that are preying on low-income Black people who are disproportionately impacted by every aspect of the criminal justice system. The bail industry is making billions from our nation's slave-like bail practice that is forcing people to buy their freedom.

And as the industry gets wealthier, it is financially crippling the Black families they exploit."[87] The Bail Project, a national bail fund and advocacy organization, similarly asserts that "the $2 billion bail industry, with its well-documented predatory and exploitative practices, extracts money from precisely those communities that have the fewest resources."[88]

Extractive bail practices operate as part of the broader web of pretrial predation (see chapters 2 and 3). In contemporary struggles for bail reform and pretrial justice, tactical questions about whether and how to connect the two loom large. One strategy isolates and seeks to eliminate the for-profit bail bond industry. States such as Illinois, Kentucky, Oregon, and Wisconsin have taken this path, prohibiting commercial bail within their borders. Bans and strong policy constraints that target for-profit bail in this manner undoubtedly make a difference for many defendants—as well as for people who earn their living in bail businesses *and* those who, behind the scenes, generate great wealth from their work. For communities ensnared in the system, however, reforms that target businesses and aim to de-privatize the field may yield less relief than some imagine.

In this and earlier chapters, we have repeatedly seen how public and private actors adapt and innovate when confronted with new obstacles to predation—and how constraints on some actors can pave the way for others to step in. The repeated pattern should worry reformers whose agendas focus solely or primarily on imposing tight regulations on bail businesses. The industry has often proved resilient, finding creative ways to sustain or reconfigure their practices and playing the political long game to weaken or remove barriers down the line.

Reform agendas that aim to abolish commercial bail offer greater protection against such possibilities. They also carry the political advantage of targeting the for-profit interests that have evoked the greatest public condemnation and outrage in conflicts over bail provision. Such agendas, however, come with their own risks. If only some jurisdictions pass bans (and others do not), the new laws will do little to reduce the national political power of the commercial bail lobby, which can be counted on to wage persistent, well-funded campaigns to reinstate its operations (as it has in Oregon and Wisconsin).[89] Beyond this likelihood, agendas that seek only to banish business operations also take a dubious gamble: They wager, at least implicitly, that public provision will be more just. As we have shown, government agencies and officials are *already* active participants in bail predation. They are full partners in commercial bail, collaborating with businesses to extract resources, and they establish their own processes for wringing money from defendants.

For criminally accused people and their communities, then, such reforms may simply favor one partner over the other, shifting the who and how of financial takings without offering relief from predation itself. By making governments responsible for managing released defendants, such reforms would produce substantial new costs for public institutions. The costs, in turn, would create pressures to generate revenue. With commercial bail swept aside, local officials could impose hefty monetary bail conditions of their own, accompanied by sizable fees. In fact, suggestive examples of this scenario already exist. Prior to 2023, when Illinois eliminated monetary bail, counties across the state collected 10 percent of each bail deposited with the court, justifying the "service fee" in ways that echoed traditional bail company arguments.[90] In 2016 alone, Illinois courts took in $15.1 million in bail filing fees.[91]

A more ambitious challenge to pretrial predation can be found in reform agendas that aim to end monetary bail.[92] Such reforms would abolish the financial conditions of release that make the for-profit bond industry possible. At the same time, they would forbid the imposition of publicly managed cash bail conditions and, in so doing, deprive courts of a key mechanism for imposing "premium-like" fees. These would all be significant accomplishments.

The catch is that, unlike bail businesses, courts do not need monetary conditions to extract revenue from pretrial release. Nonmonetary conditions provide a wide array of opportunities to charge defendants fees. Many courts already make defendants pay for electronic monitoring, drug and alcohol testing, and other pretrial release requirements. With the end of money bail, the government agencies that take over the management of released individuals could easily create and impose new ongoing fees for the "service" of supervision itself. In fact, a report from Harvard University's Criminal Justice Policy Program warns that "moving away from a money bail system that penalizes the poor is a good thing, but policymakers and reformers should be wary of a new hazard that may emerge: 'offender-funded' supervision."[93]

Priorities for bail reform take a different shape if we begin with the fundamental injustice of criminal justice predation and locate pretrial release within this broader ecosystem. From this perspective, extractive cross-sector collaborations can be recognized as the norm; the bail industry can be seen as a collection of business interests that has many counterparts, spread across and entwined with most of the nation's criminal legal institutions. Across all these arenas, bail included, a one-sided focus on the professed evils of handing state functions off to the market is unlikely to chart an effective path toward justice. Even if one's concerns are limited to pretrial predation, an elevated focus on privatization may actually have counterproductive effects through a process the political scientist E. E. Schattschneider called "the substitution of conflicts": Efforts to connect *all* predatory pretrial practices and focus political organizing and messaging on their abolition can be crowded out by battle lines and alliances drawn to target particular actors (who can be replaced) or particular tools of extraction (which have substitutes).[94]

As we detail in chapter 10, advocates are winning important reforms related to bail and pretrial processes. The fact that many of these reforms are incremental, targeted, and vulnerable to subversion is not surprising given the power of the public and private actors invested in the status quo. In our view, the goal should be to understand and selectively pursue reform efforts in ways that help move us toward the political horizon of justice. The critical question to ask about any reform that targets bail-based or bail-adjacent resource extraction is then: Will it advance and strengthen or divert and dissipate the struggle to *abolish* bail predation, the broader workings of pretrial predation, and ultimately criminal justice predation as a whole?

Some organizations are already asking versions of this question and suggesting ways forward. In a document titled "After Cash Bail: A Framework for Reimagining Pretrial Justice," the Bail Project grounds its strategic work in the principle that "no accused person should be charged fees or assessed costs for any release conditions or pretrial detention imposed by a court, as this would again replicate the economic inequity of cash bail."[95] The end goal, then, is not simply to end monetary bail, but to stop governments and businesses from using the pretrial system to extract resources from legally entangled persons, their families, and their communities.

7 ∗ Regulated Improvisation at the Front Lines

Predatory designs are never self-enacting. Legal and institutional arrangements, business models, policies, and procedures all must be put into practice. Actors at many levels contribute to this work, but none are more essential than the people who fill street-level jobs. In the criminal legal context, effective resource extraction depends, in the first instance, on the activities of frontline workers. No matter how successful corporate and government leaders are in setting up the game, the game itself must be played. The daily work of extraction must be carried out by police officers, prison administrators, judges, court clerks, probation and parole officers, collections agents, and others who interact directly with targets of criminal legal governance. Such individuals have to turn rules and tools into action, making choices and working out strategies as they go.[1] Thus, to understand predation in the commercial bail industry, we must investigate not only its construction and defense but also the day-to-day labor that constitutes its ground game.

Bail work can be seen as a form of what Pierre Bourdieu called "regulated improvisation."[2] Like a jazz musician riffing in and around a chord progression, bail agents work creatively on a structured field of play. The field is organized by criminal legal institutions and processes; industry-specific laws, rules, contracts, and norms; and network ties that connect offices and actors in the pretrial process. For bail agents, the prevailing terms of the game make some actions sensible and others unattractive, unacceptable, or even unthinkable. That translation of structures into practices, however, is far from automatic. Bail agents work creatively with the resources they have, sometimes in ways that remake the rules of the game. They devise strategies for beating out the competition, bringing in clients, and closing deals. They cultivate personal networks of collaborators. Individually and collectively, they develop beliefs and stories about what they do—frames that enable and guide their daily practices and help to justify what they do as ethical, reasonable, and even noble work.

For those who hope to learn about the everyday realities and "regulated improvisations" of a work environment, there are few substitutes for methods that insert the researcher directly into the world of practice. Ongoing immersion in the field offers unparalleled opportunities for encountering the unexpected and questioning—based on a steady flow of direct observations and experiences—one's understanding about how and why the game works as it does. In chapters 7 and 8, we explore predatory bail practices from an insider's perspective, drawing heavily on Page's ethnographic research as a bail agent at A-Team. Instead of observing the business as an occasional visitor or using interviews to ask staff what they thought and did, Page experienced the daily routines and challenges of the bondsperson firsthand. His field notes reflect the standpoint of a participant and practitioner—a teammate to his coworkers and a bail agent like any other as far as clients were concerned (for further discussion, see the methodological appendix).

On the job, Page learned that the bail hustle operates on two levels. The short game consists of immediate efforts to find, recruit, manage, and secure paying clients. The long game involves cultivating the social infrastructure that bail agents need to be consistently successful: *networks of relationships* with actors in the field that can be leveraged to get referrals, obtain desired actions at the courthouse, and provide valued services to potential clients. To be effective, bail agents have to balance the two, sometimes making hard choices between immediate sales and the need to build or preserve relationships that they depend on in their work.

We begin by analyzing how bail agents' conditions of employment and experiences of market competition structure their field of action. Next, we consider the short game, exploring the techniques and strategies that agents use to recruit clients and close deals with cosigners. We then turn to the long game, analyzing how agents construct and sustain the networks they need to reliably contribute to the business's bottom line. Fierce competition in the field, we show, operates through a moral economy of reciprocity, loyalty, and trust. We conclude with an analysis of how, from the agent's perspective, for-profit bail operates as a service industry, providing valuable guidance, assistance, and caring support to accused individuals and their loved ones.

Organizing the Ground Game

At the front lines of the bail industry, resource extraction is organized as a fierce competition. In the hierarchical relationships that underwrite bonds (see chapter 6), revenues reliably flow up to the insurance companies; risks run down to the storefronts, where they push workers and managers to scramble at every turn. As they navigate these narrower profit margins and higher risks, bail companies strain to beat out their competitors and continually search for ways to increase revenue. Positioned at the lowest level of all, bond agents operate under intense pressures.

Bail agents are typically employed as independent contractors. Paid on commission rather than salary, they receive a cut of each premium, which is generally set at 10 percent of the bond. (At A-Team, agents receive 25 percent of the premium, so for a $5,000 bond with a $500 premium, they get $125.) To make enough money to live on, most agents have to prioritize volume, working relentlessly to recruit clients, get signatures, and secure payments. Some bond companies create additional pressures by setting up gamelike competitions among their agents. At A-Team, for example, the owners held in-house sales contests and posted rankings based on the dollar amounts of the bail contracts that agents wrote each month. Exhortation also plays an important role. At monthly meetings, A-Team managers pressed agents to adopt aggressive sales strategies and stay focused on the financial bottom line. Page's field notes from one such meeting illustrate the dynamic:

> We're discussing defendant and cosigner paperwork. . . . An agent asks the bosses about the amount of detail we should get into when going through contracts [with clients]. The boss says, "Not like an attorney. We're trying to close a deal." Another boss adds that we "don't want to scare them off." We agree that we want defendants and cosigners to understand their responsibilities . . . [and] that they're on the hook. But we don't want to get into the nitty-gritty details in the contracts, such as the permission it gives the company to get all sorts of personal records.

Managerial practices of this sort amplify pressures that flow, first and foremost, from the structure of the street-level market. New agents quickly discover that the field is jammed with competitors; if they hope to keep up, they will need to be aggressive at every step.[3] If they hope to earn a living, they must continually fight to beat out other agents vying for the same clients.

In the contest for profitable cases, not all clients are created equal. Bail companies generally try to avoid posting smaller bonds ($1,000 or less) because owners perceive them as offering lower payouts at higher risks.[4] At A-Team, managers and agents tended to think that defendants with low monetary bail had too little "skin in the game" and, thus, would be more likely to skip out. Such individuals, they assumed, had little to lose if they failed to appear in court. Because this view is common, bail businesses tend to underserve people who are too poor to pay even a small bail amount but, no less than other defendants, are desperate to avoid waiting for trial behind bars. Some, like A-Team, occasionally take on such cases because "small bonds can turn into big bonds" down the road. But in general, managers press agents to avoid the "small stuff" and, in this manner, make the competition for high-dollar bonds all the more intense.

The pool of desirable cases tightens further as agents evaluate potential clients' abilities to pay. Bail companies typically offer payment plans to make bond premiums more affordable. Managers strongly prefer full up-front payments, though, worrying that long-term arrangements can make profits less certain and debt collection efforts more likely. Page's supervisors generally discouraged payment plans. Accepting half now and half later, they told Page, would be acceptable only if the bail amount was large ($5,000 or more) and the payment period was short. In such cases, A-Team took aggressive steps to secure the full premium within thirty to sixty days. To minimize the risk of nonpayment, agents were told to press for authorization to make direct withdrawals from clients' bank accounts. "*Think loan shark*," one manager instructed, as he told Page to resist any request to stretch a payment plan beyond two months. At monthly meetings, managers sent a clear message: Expressions of sympathy are useful for recruiting clients, but customers take advantage of agents who are *too* sympathetic, and compassion cannot be allowed to put revenue at risk.

The primary target of recruitment is generally not the accused individual. Typically, it is a family member, romantic partner, or close friend who, if all goes well, can be convinced to cosign for the bond and take responsibility for paying the premium. ("It's like cosigning for a loan," agents explain.) The poverty conditions that leave so many accused individuals unable to make bail without a bond company also tend to make bond premiums unaffordable for defendants who cannot find a willing and qualified cosigner. At minimum, A-Team requires cosigners to be at least twenty-one years old and have a "decent-paying" full-time job. People who can meet the criteria tend to be scarce in defendants' social networks, and those who do may be reluctant to take on the significant risks and responsibilities of cosigning.

Indeed, for most people who sit down across the desk from a bail agent, the cosigning decision carries great stakes and significance. The people who sign on the dotted line are typically poor or near poor, and they are disproportionately women of color (see chapter 8). By signing, they agree to be held legally and financially liable if the defendant fails to appear in court. The potential losses can be devastating for a person who is just scraping by, and for loved ones who depend on them. Partly for this reason, cosigning decisions can raise difficult social and moral questions. What does one person owe to another, and why? How fully have favors been repaid in the past? Which betrayals can be forgiven? How much, ultimately, is too much to ask?

Cosigning can create new dynamics of debt, guilt, or resentment in a valued relationship, or reestablish ties to a defendant that were severed long ago. Hesitation is especially likely when former romantic partners worry that they will become re-entangled with a defendant's life in unwanted ways. A significant number of accused individuals (overwhelmingly men) ask their past partners (typically women) to serve as cosigners.[5] Many women who are reluctant at first ultimately agree, often out of a concern for children they have with the accused (see chapter 8). In other cases, a person who is qualified to cosign will decline, and the accused individual, like defendants who cannot muster any suitable candidate for this role, will remain locked up. Through this process, the pool of viable and desirable targets that agents compete over shrinks even further.

Competition in the bond sector is not limited to the initial contest over who will land the big premiums, however. It extends all the way to the final steps of getting cash in hand. In the struggle to secure payments, bond businesses do not only compete with one another. Businesses like A-Team have to vie with a variety of other actors seeking to cash in their own claims on the meager resources held by defendants and their loved ones. Attorneys and court officials may demand payments for services and fees. Defendants or cosigners may carry debts incurred through earlier criminal cases or owe payments to child support agencies.[6] They may be under intense pressures to pay off private lenders, businesses, or collections agencies. Bail companies work to make sure they will not be last in line, left empty-handed when the money runs out. Collections specialists, who take aggressive action to secure delinquent payments (through legal proceedings if necessary), are highly valued in the industry. In some cases, they have firsthand knowledge of the competition, based on careers that have spanned the public and private sectors. During Page's fieldwork, A-Team strengthened its collections capacities by hiring a former county clerk who had honed his skills recouping delinquent fee payments for the Rocksville government.

The Gentle Side of Cutthroat Competition

Relentless competition pressures bail agents into adopting aggressive strategies, and it often provides a rationale for unethical or even illegal practices. To make a profit for the company and a living for themselves, agents have to *hustle*. People in the field have little respect for agents who sit at the office and wait for clients to walk in or call, a practice they dismissively term "counter service." *Real* agents "live bail," perpetually making phone calls, building relationships, and marketing their services out in the field.

Traditional ground zero for the bail hustle is the courthouse.[7] In Rocksville, agents can usually be found plying their trade at first appearance court, where people are charged with gross misdemeanors and felony crimes.[8] Here, the competition among agents may be aggressive but, ideally, solicitation is not. Conventional wisdom in the field holds that the overeager salesperson is unlikely to land a deal. Skilled agents studiously avoid any appearance of having interests of their own, applying pressure, or swooping in to take advantage. Their presentation of self tends to be low-key, strategically tailored to convey that they are available allies of defendants and, importantly, that they "know the ropes." They are experts who can help a worried newcomer make sense of and navigate the process. Amid the swirl of confusing procedures and legalistic jargon, they offer themselves as well-versed interpreters and sympathetic guides.

Agents develop their own personal style for "pulling bonds out of court." They adopt and cultivate particular techniques for warding off competitors and shepherding clients out the door, over to the agency, and into contracts. In general, though, the process unfolds something like this: The agent sits or stands in the courtroom, perhaps looking over the court roster (which lists defendants' names, charges, and bail amounts) or carrying out some other business. Making sure to be visible, the agent aims to come across as an integral part of the scene, with a purpose in the courtroom that is unrelated to any specific defendant. Ideally, a family member or friend of a defendant will assume that the agent works for the court and see them as someone who might be able to answer a question, such as when the session will begin or how long it will last. In this preferred scenario, the potential client will initiate contact, allowing the agent to take on a helpful, responsive role. If no one steps forward in this manner, the bondsperson will survey the room, sidle up to someone, and look for an opening to ask what brings the chosen person to court that day.

As the conversation progresses, the agent will mention their job and their substantial experience in an offhand way, then offer to answer any questions the person might have during the proceedings. The focus on information is intentional. People who go to court to support a defendant rarely know much about the process and rarely have a private attorney to consult. Even people who have been to court many times can find its procedures and legalisms befuddling. They almost always have questions about the particular case, typically related to charges, bail amounts, or the reputation of a particular judge, prosecutor, or public defender. The agent tries to fill in the gaps in a reassuring manner, turning confusion and anxiety into opportunity. In the effort to reel in clients, the calm conveyance of trustworthy information is the lure. Typically, right after the judge sets bail, the agent will explain what has happened and, if the case seems worth pursuing, will assure the individual that, yes, they *can* get the defendant out of jail. When all goes well, the agent quickly escorts the potential client out of court, continuing to gently close the deal while shielding them from competitors who hope to make their own pitches.

A smooth process of this sort is an agent's best-case scenario. Solicitation at court is a competitive process, however. On a number of occasions, Page observed shouting matches between bail agents, particularly when one felt that another had violated an unspoken rule of the game, such as not forcefully pursuing a potential client who is already "with" a competitor. At such moments, the veneer of helpful, disinterested civility falls away, and the ferocity of street-level competition erupts into the open. In one instance, a competing agent chased Page and a client out of court. Claiming that she had spoken to the client the night before, the agent angrily accused Page of stealing her business. In other cases, frustrated agents shoved business cards into the hands of potential clients as Page talked with them, writing a discounted price on the card to undercut Page's offer. (Agents sometimes offered to charge less than 10 percent of a bond in order to "steal" a potential client.) Even without such fireworks, the intensity of agent competition sometimes shone through the overlay of gentle solicitation tactics. A lightly edited entry from Page's field notes illustrates:

The morning before an afternoon court session, I called Gina, the sister of a defendant, to ask if she could meet me at the A-Team office so we could walk to court together. A-Team had bailed out the defendant on an earlier case, and I hoped that entering court with Gina would keep potential competitors at bay. If she parked in the lot near A-Team, I offered, I could give her a validation card to save her the fee. She agreed to the arrangement.

When Gina and I walked into the courtroom, she pointed out the defendant's girlfriend, Ashley, seated next to a competing bail agent named Erik. Gina did not like Ashley and was irritated to see her there. When we sat down, I indicated Erik and said, "He's going to try and get the bond." She replied, "Don't worry, I'm rolling with you guys." After the judge set the defendant's bail at $35,000, Gina and I stepped out into the lobby, followed soon after by Erik escorting Ashley. At this point, Gina and I stood about forty feet away from Erik and Ashley in a lobby that was empty aside from the four of us. As we looked at each other, the scene reminded me of a duel: a bond duel.

Because Erik was one of my main competitors, I told Gina right then that she and the defendant could take a couple months to pay the 10 percent premium. To make our deal more attractive, I said they could just put half down and then do half in payments. At this point, Ashley began to walk toward Gina and me, and Gina stepped up to talk with her. Ashley told Gina that Erik had offered a cut-rate bond: a 5 percent premium (instead of 10) with no payments. I quickly called my manager and received permission to match Erik's offer. Gina would need to pay $1,750 up front but would not have to make payments afterward. Thinking that was doable, Gina told Ashley that she was going with A-Team. And because Ashley did not have money to put toward the bail, Erik was essentially cut out of the deal.

Gina and I then walked back to the A-Team office. I poured Gina a cup of coffee as she made calls to get the money together. After striking out with several friends and family members, Gina said she would need a few days to come up with the money. She would also need a cosigner, I reminded her. I checked in with Gina several times over the following week but eventually realized the bond was not going to happen. Although I had won the duel with Erik, I did not win the bail.

In the field note, one can see several common elements of competitive bail predation. The agents target two impoverished Black women who have no choice but to work with a bond company if they want to get the defendant out of jail. Page and Erik work to outflank each other, win the trust and loyalty of one of the women, and tap into whatever resources she might be able to access. As the agent's "duel" becomes more evident, it exacerbates tensions between the defendant's allies, Gina and Ashley. The two women become surrogates for the agents in a conflict that is ultimately about who will get to take *their* money. Yet, given the slim resources available to Gina and Ashley, there was a good chance that neither agent would profit. When hard-won "victories" turn to ash in this manner, as they often do, agents can feel pressed to put in longer hours and squeeze potential clients harder for business.

Such dynamics are far from unique to Rocksville. In Connecticut, for example, a 2003 legislative report concluded: "Bondsmen aggressively solicit clients at police stations and in the courts. The solicitation has led to confrontations and altercations . . . between bondsmen. It also has confused clients and disrupted court proceedings."[9] Similarly, a California news story reports: "It's not unusual for bail companies to subtly skirt the law and troll for customers near the courthouse, where inmates' families and jail visitors constantly stream by."[10] Some A-Team agents rarely attended court, and a couple avoided it altogether, because the aggressive and sometimes openly antagonistic interactions made them too uncomfortable. Erik, Page's opposite in the "duel," felt so burned out by the cutthroat courthouse market that he left the bail business a short time later.

Courthouses do not have to operate as such aggressive sites of predatory competition, even in the context of a commercial bail industry. It all depends on how governments approach policy questions of regulation and enforcement. Some counties closely monitor courtroom solicitation to restrain predatory bail practices and prevent them from disturbing judicial proceedings. Toward the end of Page's fieldwork, in fact, Rocksville authorities began to enforce state rules against courtroom solicitation, with regulators even attending court in street clothes to monitor agents. Bail agents quickly adopted a less aggressive posture at the courthouse, limiting themselves to the "gentler" methods described earlier and developing recruitment strategies that worked outside the court context entirely. The rapid shift illustrates, once again, one of our key themes in chapter 6: Terms of competition in "private" bail markets—from the size of potential client pools to the rules and sites of the game itself—are set by government policies and practices.

In Rocksville, the most prominent alternative to the courthouse is what agents call "prospecting," a euphemism for telemarketing. Over the past few decades, new technologies have made it possible to post criminal legal data online, and political pressures have pushed public agencies to do so. Data transparency advocates have used Freedom of Information Act requests (and related tools) to force administrative units to publish information online, including individual-level crime records.[11] Victims' advocates and tough-on-crime political leaders have similarly used pressure tactics and policy changes to expand public access. Such efforts have been facilitated by a broader "culture of control" that suggests criminal threats are ever-present and exhorts communities, families, and individuals to protect themselves.[12] The assumption behind online data publication efforts is that community members need information about people who have been arrested, charged, or convicted of crimes in order to avoid victimization. (Sex offender registries provide the most notorious example of this logic.[13]) Such demands have unintentionally paved the way for new predatory tactics in the bail industry.

Prospecting works like this: When an individual is arrested, the county publishes their name, birth date, and reason for arrest online. When a defendant is charged and initial bail is set, many (though not all) counties put this information on their website as well. Bail agents monitor the electronic jail roster, searching for potential clients. When they find good leads, they enter the defendant's name and birth date into a proprietary software program that retrieves contact information for the defendant and their family members. (Bail companies pay a small fee to the for-profit provider of this software for each search.) Agents then cold-call defendant's family members and say something like this: "My name is

—— from A-Team Bail Bonds. I'm calling about ——. They are in jail here in Rocksville, and we'd love to help them get out." In prospecting, as in the courtroom, the agent pursues bail solicitation through expressions of sympathy, efforts to provide information, and signals that they are willing and able to help.

Throughout the prospecting process, bail companies try to make things as easy as possible for customers. If clients have access to the internet, they can fill out paperwork online. If they use a debit or credit card, they can pay over the phone. If they want to wait until after the first appearance hearing to decide about bail, the agent will be happy to meet them at court, or at the bail office if they prefer. Importantly, the relative ease of this transaction is not limited to the client. For bail agents, prospecting offers a low-investment alternative to courtroom solicitation. With a phone, computer, and internet connection, they can ply their trade from almost anywhere. They can also avoid the stressful machinations of the courthouse and any monitoring and enforcement efforts that public agencies might pursue there. Given its convenience and profit-making potential, some agents choose to focus most of their efforts on prospecting. It's the same hustle with a lot less hassle. Like public and private actors who pursue predatory revenues at higher institutional levels, bail agents adapt and innovate in response to changing structural conditions. In the process, they change the sites and terms of the bail game itself.

The Collaborative Side of Cutthroat Competition

It would not be hard to tell a story about street-level bail bond work that conforms to classic economic models of individualistic competition: *Lone bail agents in an unforgiving marketplace work relentlessly to drum up customers in a contest of each against all.* This sort of portrait, however, would mislead in significant ways. The bail hustle unfolds in a social world where interpersonal relationships and shared expectations matter a great deal. In this sense, it is more consistent with a sociological tradition of scholarship that emphasizes the "social embeddedness" of market transactions and economic life.[14] As Mark Granovetter observed decades ago, "there is evidence all around us of the extent to which business relations are mixed up with social ones."[15] At the front lines of the industry, the ability to turn criminal accusations into profits depends, in many ways, on social ties. Local bail actors work continually to build relationships of trust and reciprocity that can be used to bring in clients and facilitate resource extraction.

As Page learned on the job, success in the bail market depends on cooperation as much as competition. It is shortsighted to simply put your head down and plug away, fighting to land one bail after another and cajoling individuals to sign contracts. Successful agents invest significant time and effort in the long game, cultivating social relationships and providing help to other actors in the field. Even the most skillful bail agent would find it hard to make a living by going it alone. To be consistently effective, they have to build a "social infrastructure" capable of generating referrals and favors on a regular basis over time.[16]

Hanging around at the courthouse, for example, serves more than one purpose. As they scan the scene for potential clients, bail agents also work to cultivate good relationships with clerks, bailiffs, police officers, lawyers, and judges. They do what they can to become a recognized and positively regarded member of the workplace community. As Malcolm Feeley observed in a classic ethnographic study of courts in 1979: "Bondsmen find it advantageous to remain on the good side of the police who can direct business their way, and to ingratiate themselves with judges and prosecutors who can pass cases, grant continuances, stay bond forfeitures, and facilitate reductions through compromises."[17] Success at the street level often depends on favors from people who work at the court, up to and including judges' decisions to release bail companies from their financial obligations when defendants do not show up (see chapter 6).

More powerful court officials can offer distinctive kinds of help, but people with no formal authority may prove just as useful. A classic example is the "jail runner"—a person locked up and subjected to the state's judicial and penal powers who can solicit new clients for the agent. A major 2014 report on commercial bail in New Jersey details the practice:

> [B]ail agencies have come to rely heavily on accused criminals in the form of county jail inmates to drum up business and gain customers. . . . Indeed, the commission found that in New Jersey it is quite common— and has been for years in some instances—for bail bond agents to recruit prisoners as freelance subcontractors acting at their behest and to offer cash and other incentives to those who steer new clients to them. These arrangements, sometimes initiated via flyers mailed directly to inmates, are maintained through the jail telephone system with agents openly striking deals with those who agree to serve as "runners" behind bars. This occurs even though it is a regulatory violation for non-licensed individuals to solicit bail and despite the fact that both parties to such conversations are on notice that their phone traffic may be monitored and recorded by jail authorities.[18]

In Rocksville and nearby counties, agents usually recruit jail runners by offering nonmonetary forms of compensation—for example, by proposing to pass messages back and forth between the person in jail and their friends or family members. Like many bail agencies, A-Team has contracts with telecom companies that allow jailed individuals to call them for free. To avoid the exploitative costs of phone calls from jail, defendants routinely dial up bail offices in hopes that staff will help them communicate with their relations. Bail agents suggest that referrals to potential clients at the jail would be a suitable way to compensate them for this unrequired assistance. If defendants fail to come through with solid leads, they generally lose this line to the outside world.

The jail runner is just one of many actors positioned to strike up mutually beneficial partnerships with bail agents. Criminal defense lawyers are among the most important. Like bail agents, these attorneys make a living based on the needs, fears, and vulnerabilities that arise from criminal charges and jailing practices. The interplay of the two fields illustrates how cooperation and competition can work as complements, not just opposites. In the scramble to extract resources from the criminal accused, competition *within* each field drives cooperation *between* fields.

Similar to bail agents, private defense attorneys pursue clients in a competitive market, where they must vie for business from a resource-poor population. The two also resemble each other in a second way: They are positioned as repeat players in an iterative game, with incentives to take the long view when it comes to economic gain. By investing in mutually beneficial partnerships, each can get a leg up on the competition in their own sector.

Referrals stand at the center of this relationship. Bail agents send potential clients to attorneys, who then (ideally) return the favor. To cultivate a steady flow of new clients in Rocksville, Page and his coworkers needed to build relationships that made attorneys happy to send business their way. In so doing, they pursued a form of cooperation that, due to its utility for both parties, has a long history.[19]

Cooperation in this case takes the form of what Marcel Mauss called a "gift economy."[20] The giving of the referral obligates the recipient to return the favor at a later point in time. As Mauss explains, each gift shows that the giver is generous and, therefore, deserving of reciprocity. Acceptance of the gift conveys respect for the giver as well as a willingness to take on an obligation in return. In this manner, gift giving operates simultaneously as a moral and a competitive-strategic form of action. By giving more referrals to a particular lawyer than their competitors do, bail agents can establish themselves as especially worthy of reciprocity and (if all goes according to plan) ensure that they will be first in line when the lawyer has referrals to give in the future.

Thus, gift giving between lawyers and bail agents works through a kind of moral code—what we can call a "moral economy of predation." Lawyers and bail agents enter an unwritten compact that resides, so to speak, "above the heads" of the people they mine for revenue. Clients are not parties to the compact; they are the objects of its agreements and the "gifts" that its creators give and receive. In this sense, the gift economy constructed by lawyers and bail agents operates as what Carole Pateman and Charles Mills call a "domination contract" (see chapter 1): It is an agreement among actors in superior positions that is premised on—and serves as a basis for—the mutually beneficial exploitation of people in subordinate positions.[21]

At the same time, the gift economy is an arena of competition in its own right. In Rocksville, agents from rival shops (or even the same company) compete to establish referral-based relationships with specific attorneys—and then work to fend off anyone who tries to cut in. In the eyes of agents, a successful referral to a lawyer is almost as good as landing a quality bail, because they expect it to pay off down the road. When talking with potential clients, agents always look for opportunities to make a referral. Framing their offer as an act of service ("If you'd like, we can provide a free attorney referral."), they work to steer clients away from court-provided public defenders and toward fee-based private counsel. A-Team's agents routinely touted the benefits of the latter, claiming that while some public defenders are good at their jobs, they are too overwhelmed with cases to provide effective counsel in the manner a private attorney would.

Consistent with Mauss's analysis, bail agents feel pressure to make sure that the gifts and referrals they send to attorneys are "high quality." Private attorneys from established, well-known firms can be especially demanding. On a Friday afternoon at A-Team, Page answered a phone call from a partner at one of Rocksville's leading criminal defense firms who asked to speak to a manager. None was available, so Page asked if he could take a message. The attorney forcefully reminded Page that his firm recently sent A-Team a $30,000 bail. A-Team needed to reciprocate, he insisted, and he would not accept "junk"—he wanted "blue bloods." Only defendants who could afford his firm's high prices would suffice. Page informed the staff and, later that afternoon, agents received an email from management requesting that they channel suitable customers to the firm.

As this episode suggests, bond company owners and managers tend to be as eager as agents to nurture relationships with attorneys. Many companies highlight lawyer referrals as a valuable "service" on their website and pursue long-term relationships with specific firms. Gift economies, as Mauss noted, depend on social solidarities that go beyond reciprocal self-interest and have to be shored up from time to time. A-Team threw expensive parties to strengthen its ties to lawyers and law firms. A rival company had a full-time employee paid to entertain lawyers in various ways. Likewise, law firms invited bail company owners to their holiday parties and lawyers came bearing small gifts for the bail agents (like donuts or bagels) when they dropped by the shop.

Through these and other tactics, bondspersons and attorneys work to build a shared, durable compact in which each side feels they *already* owe a debt to the other. The force of this compact becomes clear when one party feels that the other has failed to uphold its side of the bargain. The frustrated law partner who called A-Team to demand more "blue blood" referrals offers a case in point. On numerous occasions, Page observed agents cursing the names of attorneys who, in their eyes, had failed to honor their debts by sending over high-quality customers.

Gift-giving relationships with lawyers can be time- and labor-intensive and are sometimes frustrating. Over the long haul, though, they support and stabilize bail agents' efforts to make a living. Sometimes they even allow agents to earn what they need without hustling quite so hard for business at the courthouse and over the phone. Compared to other options, such as using jail runners, relationships with lawyers also carry lower risks of getting in trouble with state regulators.

Some states, such as California and Texas, ban bail agents from referring clients to attorneys, but these rules are hard to enforce (unless, say, an agent's referral is captured by a phone call recorded at the jail).[22] The difficulty of observing rule-breaking makes it similarly difficult to enforce laws that ban attorneys from making referrals exclusively to one bail company. In Rocksville, attorneys and bail agents rarely try to hide their relationships. They openly attend each other's parties, arrive at court together, and drop by each other's offices. At most bail agencies and law firms, the gift economy is largely taken for granted as a necessary response to the realities of intense business competition.

Relationships between lawyers and bail agents exhibit many features of predatory criminal legal partnerships observed in earlier chapters. By forging a gift economy, law firms and bail agencies create more favorable landscapes for resource extraction in their respective fields. Each, in effect, piggybacks on the other, turning the foothold established by one profit-generating operation into an opportunity for another. All too often, the referrals function as just one step in a longer cascade of expensive entanglements that passes defendants and their families from police to courts to jails to bail agencies and lawyer's offices, all before any trial even begins. As it flows onward, the predatory cascade also grows outward, pulling into its grasp an ever-widening swath of family and community members tied to the accused individual.

In fact, law firms are far from the only private interests that work to establish partnerships with bail agencies and get in on the profitable pretrial action. Businesses of many kinds peddle fee-for-use or contract-based goods and services that they claim will allow bond companies to make more money. Owners, managers, and agents usually warm to the idea if they think the product will give them a leg up on the competition and boost their bottom line.

Some companies sell telemarketing programs designed to make bail-prospecting practices more efficient. Others specialize in tracking "no show" fugitives. In Rocksville, there is a business that charges fees to bail companies and law firms in exchange for getting them listed in a catalog that authorities give to defendants in jail. Various tech companies also compete to sell or rent electronic devices that bail agencies can use to monitor defendants out on bond. A-Team contracts with one that specializes in supplying the "House Arrest Bit" (HABIT). Defendants wear it on their wrist like a Fitbit, and bail agents use the company-provided app to keep tabs on them around the clock. When A-Team forces clients to wear the HABIT, it also makes them pay for the full cost of the service, over $100 per month.

At the front lines of the bail industry, as in so many other arenas we analyze, partnerships emerge when the parties see potential benefits from collaboration. Frequently, such business relationships intensify resource extraction from subjugated communities. Bail companies are generally on the lookout for ways to make their operations more efficient and effective at generating revenue. In some instances, their owners and managers may also come to perceive an acute need or problem—or a game-changing development on the horizon—that, as they see it, calls for immediate investments in an outside solution. Entrepreneurs with knowledge of the bail industry work continually to devise tailored solutions, pursuing strategies similar to the for-profit prison firms that, in the 1980s, inundated state and local governments with offers to help resolve the penal overcrowding crisis (see chapters 4 and 5). One after another, the entrepreneurs try to persuade bond company owners that what they have to offer is essential for surviving and profiting in such a cutthroat business environment.

Service and Street-Level Justification

People who work at bail businesses are well aware that their job is to extract resources from vulnerable people caught up in desperate circumstances. They know that they use aggressive tactics and that the contracts clients sign could, in some cases, prove ruinous for them. They recognize that some of their practices—such as cold-calling potential customers, hounding defendants' family and friends in court, and striking quid pro quo deals with private attorneys—are unscrupulous (and in some cases, illegal). This recognition is made manifest in the metaphors that agents and supervisors use to describe their work and in the "jokes" they make to one another. It is expressed in the common slang of the trade, as when Craig, a more seasoned agent training Page into the job, commented that "there wasn't much meat" at the courthouse that day and then, remembering Page was a novice, clarified his meaning: "families with money." It was on stark display when the A-Team manager told agents to "think loan shark" when setting up payment plans. Hanging out in the court lobby one day, Page said to a veteran agent that the work sometimes "makes me feel like a vulture, a used car salesman." Laughing, the experienced bondsman replied, "Yeah, it *is* like that. We're like ambulance chasers. We're bond chasers. You should call your book that: *Bond Chasers: Josh Chasing Bonds in Rocksville.*"

Despite all of this, bail agents and managers rarely see their work as morally wrong or worthy of condemnation. The apparent contradiction returns us to questions of ideology and justification that occupied our attention in earlier chapters. In this instance, however, we have an empirical advantage that we lacked in other contexts: Field notes from a sustained period of ethnographic research that allowed Page to participate, day in and day out, in the organizational culture of A-Team and in relationships with practitioners beyond it. As a working agent at A-Team, Page was able to *be there* for ordinary conversations and spontaneous conflicts, for coworkers' casual expressions of pride and doubt, and for occasions when A-Team employees were challenged to explain their actions or statements.

In chapter 6, we analyzed some of the key messaging strategies that leaders of the bail lobby use to defend and justify the industry in political conflicts. Bond companies, they argue, are invaluable partners of government, easing public fiscal burdens and promoting public safety. However effective such frames may be for swaying policymakers, they do not resonate or circulate much at the front lines of bail predation. Over the course of his research, Page rarely heard echoes of these justifications. Instead, for bail agents in Rocksville, the enabling frames that mattered most were based on narratives of *service*—stories about the assistance, counseling, and care they provided to clients.

The central aim of the bail business is to make money. The tactics agents use to land bonds often entail manipulation and aggressive efforts to pressure desperate people into putting themselves at risk. But as we have explained, bail predation also has a gentler side, perhaps most visible in the offers of reassurance, help, and guidance that bail agents use to win the trust of potential clients. Bond work is multifaceted.

Its various aspects can be used to tell very different tales. Frames that focus on care and service imbue the bail agent's work with a higher purpose: helping confused and vulnerable people who have gotten caught up in "the system." In a published reflection on his time as a Virginia bail agent, Dan Barto captures the common refrain: "I can say that in the several years I've been writing bonds, most bonding agents, myself included, derive satisfaction in helping people get through this legal process. We provide a service to people. While there may be some bondsmen who care only about the money, there are many who take pride in performing this service well."[23] Similar to Barto, one of Page's coworkers at A-Team liked to describe himself as "part drug and alcohol counselor, priest, and cop."

Early in his fieldwork, Page asked some of his coworkers how they got into the trade. A senior agent, Jamie, recounted that she joined A-Team to help with the "business side" of the operation, but eventually began writing bonds. One of her first cases opened her eyes to something she had not anticipated. She met the mother of a defendant in the parking lot of a jail located on the outskirts of Rocksville. The woman's son had been arrested for driving while under the influence. As Jamie led her through the paperwork for cosigning, the woman explained through tears that her son was in a terrible state, having recently watched his father fall from a cliff to his death. She feared that her son was spiraling out of control and did not know what to do. A mother herself, Jamie did what she could to comfort the distraught client. Grateful, the woman gave Jamie a big hug. The experience was a turning point for Jamie, who recalled thinking: "Oh, I can see how this would have real meaning, the job." Bond work, she began to see, was a *helping* profession.

Like all stories about the self, the bail agent's tale of care and service is selective and partial.[24] It pushes the more troubling parts of the job into the shadows, focusing attention on activities that make bond work seem socially valuable and morally sound. Some might dismiss this sort of account as nothing more than a bad-faith rationalization. Surely, the terrible realities of bail predation must be obvious to someone who routinely engages in the sorts of practices described in this chapter. In fact, as we have already noted, most bail practitioners *do* recognize, at least at some level, that there is a dark side to the business. That the two understandings can coexist in a single person, however, should not be surprising. Research on political psychology has frequently emphasized how people maintain contradictory beliefs, compartmentalize them, and make use of them at different times.[25] Scholars of political ideology have stressed how social injustices can be sustained by people "knowing but not knowing" the morally troubling conditions they benefit from—and how participants can "know" abundant contrary facts "yet nevertheless" carry on performing roles and embracing justifications *as if* they did not.[26]

As a participant, Page learned firsthand how narratives of caring service can be warranted by bail agents' firsthand experiences. He also developed a perspective on why so many bail agents selectively emphasized certain experiences as they tried to make sense of their jobs and interpret them so that they fit the caring-service narrative. From the start, new bail agents' perceptions of events are shaped by their socialization into the field. When they arrive for their first day on the job, they enter a field in which care-and-service narratives are already firmly established. As they learn the ropes and become invested in their work, they are taught to see service provision as a professional ethic and imperative. As the new employee's coworkers talk about hand-holding and counseling, they frame the meaning of the job itself. Primed to interpret their own experiences through this lens, newcomers see daily evidence that supports and reinforces it. Contrary events get dismissed as exceptions to the rule, downplayed as secondary to the heart of the work, or massaged into narratives more consistent with the frame. Bail agents know that their offers of assistance are a means to an end—landing clients, getting paid, and making money for the company. But they *also* know that, day in and day out, they work hard to help and support desperate clients who have nowhere else to turn, and that such efforts make them feel good.

As a legitimating device, service imagery works along three pathways. First, by focusing attention on care and assistance, it allows agents to sidestep their active role in exploiting vulnerable people. Self-reflection centers on the help and support they provide along the way; the ultimate stripping of resources fades from view. Second, service imagery functions as a basis for "moral licensing," a process in which good deeds are treated as expressions of an individual's true nature and, equally important, as actions that earn them moral leeway in other regards.[27] In this way, care-and-service work makes it possible for bail agents to see the troubling aspects of their work as "balanced" by the good they do and secondary to who they really are. Third, the heavy emphasis on what bail agents do for clients helps to legitimize bail predation as a "normal" business transaction in which payments are freely exchanged for services. Cosigners, in this framing, are not desperate people forced to hand over what little they have in order to free a loved one from custody. They are (or should be) the grateful recipients of a host of valuable services beyond the bond itself, including expert guidance through the pretrial process and significant amounts of counseling and care. Like any business, the bail company simply requires its customers to pay for services rendered.

The prominence of care and service, in practice and as a legitimizing narrative, originates in a pretrial system that reliably generates unmet needs for defendants and their relations. The court's imposition of financial bail creates a need for bond services. Holding the keys to the jail (because most defendants cannot afford bail on their own), agents are positioned as essential providers of a desperately desired form of aid. The friends and family members of defendants, in most cases, know little about the bewildering pretrial process and rarely can afford a private attorney to shepherd them through. Court personnel, including public defenders, generally lack the capacity needed to offer individualized information, advice, or support. So, defendants' families and friends tend to be left adrift, grasping for clues in an effort to figure things out for themselves. Bondspersons hoping to secure clients are eager to fill the vacuum by serving as unofficial legal guides who provide advice and personal support to the accused's kith and kin.

Early in his fieldwork, Page attended court with Sean, a relatively seasoned, decidedly avuncular agent. As usual, they arrived at court a half-hour before the session and began to approach people who were there to support defendants. They warmly asked if these people needed help, for instance, with locating the correct courtroom. Sean struck up a conversation with a tense, worried looking family and, after a few minutes, escorted them into the courtroom. Page sat directly behind them, taking notes, which he summarized later at the office:

> Today, Sean advised a family at court to provide records to the public defender showing that the defendant was mentally ill. The defendant is accused of assault. The lawyer then used that information in the bail hearing, and the judge gave the defendant (a young Black man) a conditional release without monetary bail; the main condition was to get a psychological screening. Sean sat with the family and explained the proceedings, and when the defendant received a conditional release, he acted like that was great news (even though he would not make any money from the case). I heard him say to the mom, "God bless you." The mom then realized that she had not gotten the mental health paperwork back from the public defender. During a pause in the court session, Sean instructed her to go up and ask for it. She was clearly grateful for his advice. Sean was a little bummed he didn't get the bond, but he was confident that the family would call on him in the future if they needed help getting somebody out of jail.

Like most agents, Sean worked strategically to meet a potential client's needs and felt good about the gratitude he received. As in most cases, the defendant's family knew little about the formal and informal rules of the court and found "court speak" befuddling: What's the difference between "conditional" and "unconditional" bail? Does an "in custody mental health evaluation" mean that the defendant can or cannot bail out today? Will the accused have to stay in jail until after the probation violation hearing? Agents like Sean try to demystify the court process and, equally important, offer reassurance: "Don't worry, we'll get him out so he can fight this case." Some agents carry tissues to offer to defendants' distraught relations, and most are careful not to leave an impression of moral judgment. Knowing that defendants' family members and friends often feel that court and jail personnel blow them off or treat them like they are guilty by association, bail agents try to come across as well-informed, compassionate, and nonjudgmental helpers.

The self-presentation is designed to reel in the client or, if things do not work out, leave a good impression (in case the individual or someone they know needs a bond in the future). The various acts of help, however, also create a material record of good deeds and an evidentiary basis for the agent's positive self-regard. *I helped. I listened. I offered comfort to someone in distress. I made sure they didn't feel judged. I explained what was happening and gave them good advice about how to take care of the situation.*

After defendants get bailed out, agents have additional opportunities to reinforce this narrative. Upon release, defendants typically came to the A-Team office straight from jail. As a result, they often interacted with bail agents before seeing (or perhaps even speaking with) loved ones. Although happy to be out of jail, they were often despondent and depleted. In this emotionally fraught situation, A-Team's agents were positioned to provide reassurance, support, and advice directly to the accused individual. Agents with good social skills could emerge as something like a trusted ally—and feel pride in being one of the very few "friendly faces" in the legal system, as one of Page's bosses liked to refer to agents.

As cases advanced in the pretrial process, A-Team's agents and office staff often kept defendants informed about court dates and locations, contacted court staff on defendants' behalf (especially if they missed court or were at risk of doing so), and sometimes even drove defendants to their court dates. By helping clients show up for court, the agents helped protect A-Team's investments. But the agents also knew that defendants could make their situations dramatically worse by missing a court date. They did not have to squint very hard to see their efforts as a form of care that had the accused's best interests at heart.

At the street level of the industry, service-centered discourses do not always work through narratives of help and care. At times, favored images of benevolence can be hard to sustain. Some clients refuse to act like grateful recipients of care and may even openly charge agents with exploiting their terrible predicaments. When potential clients get turned away as high risk and/or low reward, they are sometimes forceful in declaring their feelings of betrayal. Some bitterly complain that earlier kindnesses were just deceptive ploys and argue that agents are discriminating against them in ways that prove they only care about getting paid. And of course, there are cases in which agents are so brazen in their efforts to maximize profits that it becomes virtually impossible for them to interpret their own actions as benevolent forms of service.

In such circumstances, bail agents tend to fall back on an emotionally cooler free-market frame that invokes the societal legitimacy of freely entered market agreements and the normalcy of expecting payment for service. Defendants, Page's coworkers insisted, are not forced to work with A-Team or any other bond company. They *voluntarily choose* to purchase the company's services. In turn, A-Team, acting as any business would, offers its services to some (but not all) customers on terms of its own choosing.

When pressed to justify their actions in individual cases, Page's coworkers would often appeal to the literal signing of contracts. One day, an older defendant came to A-Team's office to ask why the company continued to ask him and his cosigner for payments. Having paid half of the premium, the man thought he no longer owed A-Team money. A manager explained that his brother (the cosigner) had signed a form guaranteeing payment of the other half. The man insisted that the agent had not explained the payment plan to him or his brother. The agent duped them, he said, and he was now "broke," with no way to pay off the debt. The manager pulled out the paperwork to show that the brother had, in fact, voluntarily signed the contract, even if he did not understand the agreement at the time. So, the defendant's claim that the company was "scamming" him was baseless, as far as A-Team was concerned. As a practical matter, the voluntary signing of the contract gave the man no option for recourse. As a legitimating frame, the decision to freely enter into the contract negated any claim that A-Team committed an injustice by exploiting the man's desperation and lack of knowledge.

In this regard, the defendant's predicament resembled many homebuyers who lost their life savings during the subprime mortgage crisis: With little understanding of the threats they posed, homebuyers knowingly signed mortgage contracts with ballooning loan rates. As the contracts eventually drowned them in debts, homebuyers were simply (and forcefully) reminded that they had voluntarily agreed to a contract.[28] As discussed in chapter 1, dominant groups have used contracts to pursue and legitimize predatory projects in similar ways for centuries, including the dispossession of Native Americans, extreme exploitation of Black sharecroppers, and "recruitment" of participants in prison-based medical experiments.

At A-Team, however, appeals to literal contracts were often unnecessary. Even the toughest tactics used to strip resources from poor and vulnerable cosigners were sometimes made acceptable through a simple reminder: *Hey, we're a business, not a charity.* Defendants made choices that landed them in jail, A-Team's staff offered their services, and the customers were now free to choose their next move. They could check prices at other companies or forgo bail altogether. A-Team went out and competed for customers and, like all businesses, it tried to get the best terms it could when bargaining over contracts. In the rough and tumble world of business, Page's coworkers largely agreed, there was nothing untoward about any of this.

Conclusion

When he started his job at A-Team, it took Page some time to learn the ropes. As one week turned to the next, though, his work shifts became more routine. He settled into the rhythms of the field and became a reliable performer of an established role. Inside A-Team and out in Rocksville, Page's work was structured by norms and expectations, policies and procedures, and the unforgiving logic of a competitive market. Just like his coworkers (and agents throughout the industry), he adapted to the organized routines that shape commercial bail at the street level.

To say this, however, is not to reduce bail agents to dutiful creatures of the structures they inhabit. Scholars have shown how routines that make particular modes of social action predictable and persistent *also* operate as sites of creative performance and generators of change.[29] Bond companies and their agents have to adapt general procedures to fit specific cases. Competitive pressures push them to innovate. Shifting constraints and opportunities encourage them to modify established routines. As they do so, they sometimes restructure the field of play itself.

Consider, for example, the partnerships that bail company owners and agents forge with criminal defense attorneys and firms. Structural conditions provide an important starting point for understanding these relationships. They are motivated by intense market pressures and constrained by surrounding laws and institutions. Even so, the defining features of these dense networks are not necessitated by structural forces, nor are they dictated by government authorities, corporate sureties, or national leaders of the bail industry. They are the creative inventions of street-level actors, who sustain and adjust them to meet their needs and goals. By constructing a gift economy grounded in moral codes of reciprocity and loyalty, bail agents transform an individualistic competition of each against all into a field that runs on social ties and solidarities, where collaborators succeed by sharing favors and referrals. They reconfigure local routines and, in important ways, rewrite the terms of bail predation from the bottom up.

The cat-and-mouse games that workers and state regulators play can also spur innovation, as illustrated by the shifting routines of bail solicitation in Rocksville. Early on in his fieldwork, Page learned that soliciting business at court is legally shady but "everyone does it." Only a rogue agent, however, would show up at the home of a defendant's family without permission from the defendant. State regulations prohibit this practice, and Page quickly learned that people in the bond business considered it "out of bounds." Thus, industry norms in Rocksville drew a sharp line between courtroom solicitation (shady but normal and expected) and showing up unannounced to pitch bonds to a family at home (inappropriate and unacceptable).

As noted above, about six months into Page's research, state regulators started their crackdown on courtroom solicitation in Rocksville. They attended court to catch agents in the act and began to issue more fines for violations. In response, some agents started to rely more heavily on "prospecting," making cold calls to defendants' family members and, in effect, arriving unexpectedly to sell them on bonds. Their actions led other bail agents, who had previously resisted prospecting, to feel that they had to adapt. Cold-calling spread. It became an accepted, then an *expected* focus of bail competition in Rocksville. Regulators reacted, in turn, by sending letters to bail companies, reminding them that prospecting violated state policy and would result in sanctions. To stay one step ahead, prospecting agents developed new ways to avoid detection. Some, Page learned, even began to use fake names when leaving phone messages for potential clients.

Examples such as these return us to a key theme from earlier chapters: Predatory relations and practices are dynamic sites of adaptation and change. Public authorities and private firms innovate to produce new opportunities, expand their operations, and defend their revenues. When reforms close off one mode of extraction, they quickly devise way to sidestep the impediment. When significant threats arise, they roll out new political strategies and pivot to different justifications. As we showed in chapter 6, the bail industry is no exception. Industry leaders continually adapt to changing conditions, retooling their business models and political tactics to sustain and enlarge their profits. In some cases, they restructure the bail field from above by imposing new rules on bail companies and agents.

Powerful actors at the top of the industry, however, are not the only producers of profitability and change. Down at the street level, bail companies do the necessary and challenging work of turning business designs into effective practices. Industry profits depend on what bail agents do at their jobs each day—and thus, also depend on the stories of service that allow agents to see their jobs as morally acceptable and right. At the front lines, owners and agents experience intense pressures and, sometimes, rapid changes in circumstances. They rarely have the luxury of resting easy in comfortable old routines. More often, they are on the lookout for new ways to gain a competitive edge and, on occasion, they must scramble to adapt to unexpected developments. In ways that encompass both continuity and change, profits at the top of the bail industry depend on the creativity and diligence of people who work at the bottom.

8 * The Intersectional Logic of Bail Predation

In *Seeing like a State*, James Scott explains that "officials of the modern state are, of necessity, at least one step—and often several steps—removed from the society they are charged with governing."[1] As a result, their powers depend on their ability to make communities and environments *legible* from a distance—to see and make sense of them in ways that enable effective intervention. Legibility, Scott explains, depends on the construction and use of rational schemas that allow outsiders to comprehend and act upon the social and physical world. Bail companies are not states, of course, but they and their employees confront a similar challenge: how to "see" clients' lives and relationships in ways that facilitate revenue-extracting interventions.

Among the bail agent's core skills, few are more important than the ability to use limited information to size up potential clients and get a fix on their circumstances quickly. Indeed, as Page learned during his first weeks in the field, the process of becoming a bail agent is inseparable from *learning to see* people's lives in discerning ways. In commercial bail, distinctions based on race, class, and gender play an especially central role in such efforts to see and make sense.

In chapter 7, we analyzed the front lines of the bail industry as a site of "regulated improvisation." Bond agents experience the powerful pressures and constraints of a field structured by criminal legal institutions and industry rules and norms. But agents develop creative strategies for navigating and even reorganizing this social terrain. In this chapter, we complete our case study of for-profit bail by analyzing how race, class, and gender organize and orient bond work at the street level. Distinctions among "social kinds" frame agents' perceptions and guide their practices in ways that reflect power relations in the broader society.[2] Here as elsewhere, however, bail agents do not simply enact culturally or institutionally determined scripts. As social and mental structures, race, class, and gender do not dictate specific courses of action. Rather, they give the bail game a particular shape, operating as interpretive schemas deployed and adapted in everyday practice.

At A-Team Bail Bonds, race, class, and gender are taken-for-granted ways to make sense of events and distinguish various sorts of clients and cases. Their heuristic prominence is, in no small part, a reflection of real social and material conditions. In a society of stark class inequalities, bail work is firmly anchored in poor and working-class communities. Throughout the US, race greatly affects who lives where and with what resources, who gets charged with crimes and how court and jail authorities treat them, and who needs bail bond services and how much they can pay for them. Gender is equally salient in a field where men swell the ranks of the accused and women routinely shoulder the financial burdens of pretrial release. For bail workers *not* to see race, class, and gender, they would have to ignore highly visible and consequential features of the pretrial landscape.

Bail bond practitioners, however, do far more than recognize and adjust to such realities. They see them through the lens of social stereotypes and experience them in ways that conform to social prejudices. Beliefs about group differences frame the ways agents make sense of events and interpret social cues. They provide rubrics for judging moral worth, estimating case-specific risks, offering bonds on "appropriate" terms, and justifying daily practices.

We begin by exploring how race and class intersect and operate in the organizational culture of A-Team. Next, we analyze how bail bond managers and agents use race and class distinctions as rubrics of evaluation and guides for decision-making. We then analyze how gender intersects with race and class to orient commercial bail practices, showing how bail predation is structured by the "gendered organization of care" in American society.[3] Finally, we return to questions of ideology, detailing how beliefs and prejudices related to race, class, and gender help to justify street-level bail predation.

Race and Class in Organizational Culture

For-profit bail companies are free to pick their own clients, but they do not do so under conditions of their own choosing. The consumer markets they compete in are largely constructed by others. Patterns of crime, policing, and prosecution in the US produce pools of accused individuals that skew strongly toward poor men of color.[4] Pretrial jail populations also disproportionately consist of poor and racially marginalized men.[5] Judicial bail-setting practices exacerbate these biases. In cases where defendants are identified as Black or Hispanic or as men, judges are significantly more likely to set financial bail conditions (a prerequisite for using a bond to secure release) and to impose higher financial bail amounts.[6]

Local variations notwithstanding, markets for bail bond services in the US are highly concentrated: Policing and judicial practices practically dictate that bail industry revenues are drawn disproportionately from the limited resources held by race-class subjugated (RCS) communities.[7] This fact is a vital starting point for understanding many aspects of bail predation, but it tells us little about how race and class operate inside the bond industry itself. Page's ethnographic research offers a particularly strong basis for analyzing race and class as elements of bond company culture and as frames of interpretation, decision-making, and action.

When he started his research, Page thought his coworkers would tread lightly around race, treating it as a sensitive subject, at least in open conversation. He was wrong. Racial talk was an overt and routine feature of his workplace. Bail agents and bosses at A-Team were mostly middle-class White suburbanites (though a few were middle-class people of color). Some avoided making derogatory racial remarks and, on occasion, racist comments would elicit nervous laughter or a joking reproach. But Page rarely saw anyone outright object to such comments or engage in a pointed conflict over racism.

At the office and in the field, A-Team personnel commented on "what race" clients were and what that meant, helped each other suss out the race of defendants and cosigners, and sometimes talked about more general issues of race, crime, and punishment. In such contexts, though, they rarely treated race as a dimension separate from class. Race, for Page's coworkers, generally implied class in a double sense: People from racially marginalized groups were presumed to be poor in the sense of lacking assets and income. And even among the most materially impoverished clients, they were presumed to be less "classy" in their behaviors, cultural values and dispositions, and commitments to honoring obligations.

In casual conversation, agents and managers sometimes explicitly trafficked in racial stereotypes regarding intelligence, physical features, laziness, violence, trustworthiness, sexual behavior, and personal irresponsibility. Page's field notes recount informal discussions with coworkers like this one with Nancy, a middle-aged White woman who identified as a liberal: "I got a call from a woman to check on the amount owed on a payment plan. I asked Nancy to look up the amount, and she told me that the debt had been paid off. 'Wow, that's really responsible,' I said. I was surprised that they paid it off so quickly and double-checked that they didn't owe more. Nancy replied, 'Yeah, the Mexicans hold to their commitments . . . more than the Blacks.'"

Group-based beliefs of this sort did not define hard, inescapable categories of client treatment or perceived deservingness. Agents would sometimes adjust their views based on experiences with specific clients (a process we explore later in this chapter). As a point of departure, though, Page's coworkers tended to assume the worst about poor clients of color, particularly Black men. When taking notes during court hearings, for example, a senior coworker used "GB" (shorthand for "gangbanger") to indicate young, Black, male defendants accused of "street" crimes. The veteran agent advised her novice colleague Page to do the same because, in her experience, GBs were irresponsible, high-risk clients. Such individuals were presumed to be guilty of poor personal character *and treated accordingly* until something, in the agent's estimation, proved them innocent.

Most agents, including some coworkers of color, held views about group culture that echoed "underclass narratives."[8] "The ghetto" was rife with social pathologies, they believed, and the reasons why had a lot more to do with dysfunctional norms and values than oppression or discrimination. Both self-described liberals and conservatives on the staff generally agreed that "the culture" of lower-class Black communities generated destructive, self-defeating behaviors. A White woman at A-Team routinely explained how the "baby daddy" problem in such communities could be traced to a culture of welfare dependency.

Bail agents frequently commented on the injustices of the legal system and criticized the failures of police and courts. As they counseled and accompanied clients, they saw that many people were getting raw deals from these institutions. Nevertheless, on questions of race, culture, and social order, A-Team personnel often identified with police officers and court officials as people who occupied positions similar to their own: They too were constantly forced to deal with the chaotic, mismanaged lives of a disorderly "underclass." A conversation between Page and a senior agent at A-Team, for example, took place as protesters filled the streets in response to the police killing of Michael Brown in Ferguson, Missouri. Why, the owner wondered aloud, do Black people "always have to riot?" The agent identified with Darren Wilson, the officer who shot Brown, and expressed sympathy for his plight. He was certain that Brown had been high on drugs and, in essence, responsible for his own death. Contemplating his own question about why Black people "always have to riot," the agent wondered aloud whether it had to do with their "heritage" or "ethnicity."

The views Page encountered at A-Team are largely consistent with research on racial attitudes in the American public, especially given the staff's demographic profile.[9] But agents' beliefs and prejudices are more than just reflections of the broader society. They are also constructed through and sustained by bond workers' immediate field of labor. On the job, agents work with defendants who are stigmatized as deviants by criminal charges, encountering them at what are often disastrous low points in their lives. These workers form impressions of accused individuals and their kin just as their lives have been thrown into disarray. And for reasons we have explained, the people agents encounter in these degrading and tumultuous situations are disproportionately from RCS communities. In many cases, bail agents have few or no meaningful relationships with lower-income people of color in their own neighborhoods or social lives. Experiences on the job become their primary source of personal "evidence" for thinking about what people from poor, racially marginalized communities are like.

One night at the A-Team office, talk turned to a bus driver from a local African-immigrant community who allegedly solicited sex from a pregnant teenage girl. One of Page's coworkers commented to another: "You can't do this job and see the same cultures do the same things over and over and not come to the conclusion that some groups have major problems." People like to say that everyone is the same, she continued, but in this job "you see that some groups just do worse things." Most people from the bus driver's community could not be trusted, the agents agreed, and they always seemed to be mixed up in illegal things. Like these two coworkers, many A-Team agents expressed and defended their racial beliefs as nothing more than empirical descriptions—summaries of firsthand experiences that provided a reliable basis for "knowing" a group. The lessons that agents draw from their day-to-day experiences, however, depend on how they interpret them.

During his time in the field, Page never saw a bail agent describe an experience with a White client as evidence of "the true nature" of Whites in general. In fact, White clients' circumstances were often seen as a product of some unfortunate turn of events or fall from grace. One day, for instance, Page watched as a coworker used details from the court docket (which did not specify race) to guess that a defendant must be White and, based only on this assumption, make up a story about her. Noting that her current address was at a local shelter, the agent surmised that she had moved from a more rural area, gotten into drugs, and ended up living on the streets. The presumption that White defendants were "normal and unremarkable people" who had fallen on hard times or gotten caught up in bad situations was common at A-Team, especially when defendants had drug issues. Similarly, agents were more likely to see White defendants as accidental or spontaneous lawbreakers—people who had messed up in the moment, but were not, in any essential sense, *real* criminals.

White clients were the exception in this regard. Experiences with individuals from other racial/ethnic groups were far more likely to be viewed through a cultural-pathology lens and treated as telling evidence of the group's true nature. Black people, in particular, were seen as following an expected and even natural path into criminality. Bail agents defended comments to this effect as simply stating the truth of what they regularly saw, *political correctness be damned*. For the most part, it did not occur to Page's coworkers that they might be selectively remembering and interpreting events in ways that affirmed their prior beliefs. As race-class stereotypes framed how agents perceived, explained, and drew lessons from their work experiences, they reliably produced "firsthand evidence" of various groups' failures in comparison to White normalcy.

Race, Class, and Risk

Established as "obvious" in A-Team's organizational culture, shared assumptions about social groups provide a kind of social compass for agents, orienting practices in the field and guiding decisions about how specific cases should be handled. Racialized assumptions about class and class-inflected conceptions of race function as rubrics for sizing up a client's character and ability to pay. They suggest from the get-go whether a person is likely to be trustworthy, responsible, able to pay, and, in other ways, a good or bad risk. White clients are typically seen as better bets for bail contracts in all these regards.

A conversation Page had with a senior agent, Mark, is a good example. It was Monday morning, and Page asked whether Mark had checked the jail roster for DUI cases. For two reasons, bail agents in Rocksville tend to prioritize felony DUIs: They believe that middle-class Whites are as likely as anyone to get arrested for this offense (raising the odds of finding such clients), and they know that people charged with DUI violations typically receive relatively large monetary bails. Mark commented that Monday morning is not a good time to look for DUI cases because Black people go drinking downtown on Sunday nights. "So, they don't have money?" Page asked. "Even if they do, do you even want to write [the bond]?" Mark continued, "There's a difference between these [people] and, say, Josh Page." Lower-class Black people were just different from middle-class White people, in Mark's view, less reliable in dealing with the courts and honoring their obligations to A-Team.

The extent to which bail agents depend on race and class categories can be seen in how they respond when the relevant social cues are ambiguous or absent. Page repeatedly saw how coworkers read texts and contexts for bits of information that might be assembled to render a race-class verdict. In chapter 7, we described how, shortly after his arrival at A-Team, Page shadowed a more seasoned agent, Craig. On a slow day at the courthouse, Craig observed that "there wasn't much meat" and then, remembering that Page was a rookie, clarified, "families with money." Afterward,

Craig suggested he and Page head over to a government building where charging documents are kept. There, Craig showed Page how to scan the documents for promising cases, focusing on information like names, addresses, and case descriptions that might suggest bail amounts and the odds that potential clients would be able to cover A-Team's premium. As he read, Craig commented to Page that, with so little information, you have to use "stereotypes" to size up the cases. Flipping through the pages, he took note: "White," he said, even though there was no indication of race on the page. When Page asked how he knew, he said the name just "sounds White."

In addition to names, residential segregation allows agents to use geographic locations as indicators of race and class. Seasoned agents develop mental maps of the county (and in some cases, the state) and use street addresses to surmise people's race and class. While perusing the county jail roster one day, Page pointed out a defendant with a decent-sized monetary bail and suggested to his coworker Sean that perhaps they should pursue the case. After a quick glance at the address, Sean stated the name of a neighborhood that agents often described as "the ghetto." Sean needed no further information. He suggested that he and Page move on and try to find a more promising case, ideally, with an address in a "good" part of town.

If agents know an address but cannot place it, they often enter it into a navigation app or website, such as Google Maps. By locating addresses on a map of the city or county, such technologies allow agents to locate potential clients on a social matrix of race and class. Their "street view" functions can be used to ferret out additional clues. Finding a well-kept single-family home at the address, for example, an agent might think it more likely that the individual is part of a "decent" family with access to resources. Or they might come to a different conclusion and decide to move on.

As some of the preceding examples from Page's field notes suggest, agents seek out race and class cues, in part, because they expect to have more problems when they take on what they perceive as "ghetto" clients. The primary reason why they do so, however, is that they see race and class as reliable bases for evaluating *risk*. As many criminal legal agencies adopted formal risk assessment tools as guides for decision-making in recent decades, bail bond companies did not. Bail agents and their bosses mainly rely on "gut" judgments to size up potential clients. As they estimate the likelihood that defendants will show up for court and cosigners will pay their bills, many openly rely on stereotypical beliefs regarding race, class, geographic locales, and criminalized social types (e.g., "sex offenders" or "meth heads"). Most of Page's coworkers saw such categories as practical, reliable bases for pursuing legitimate, job-relevant risk assessments.

An episode from Page's fieldwork illustrates the centrality of race in this regard. The case involved a middle-aged truck driver, Ryan, who got arrested and charged with assault while driving through Rocksville. Page arranged bail with the defendant's wife, who lived a few states over. The wife agreed to pay the $1,000 premium and cosign the bond. Because Ryan lived out of state—a status that agents tend to associate with a higher flight risk—Page had Ryan's parents cosign the bond as well. Excited about lining everything up, Page asked one of his superiors, Chet, for permission to post the bond. Chet told him to get a mortgage for collateral, just to be safe.

A demand for collateral, especially a mortgage, would require a new round of negotiations and could ruin the deal. Page huffed out of frustration and asked if a mortgage was really necessary for a $10,000 bail. Chet asked, "Is he Black?" Page responded by describing Ryan as "a burly White dude." After thinking it over, Chet allowed Page to post the bond without collateral. Chet's appraisal of Ryan clearly changed when he learned the defendant's race. Had Ryan been Black, and had his family lacked a mortgage (or refused to risk losing their home), he likely would have remained in jail while his family tried to secure his release with another company.

As this example suggests, racial profiling in the bail industry can have serious consequences. It raises the odds that people from RCS communities will be denied bond services or offered such services only on terms that are harder to afford or put them at greater financial risk—any of which could leave them unable to secure pretrial release. Here, it is important to recall that however exploitative a bond contract may be, it is far worse for a defendant to be deprived of bail and forced to remain in jail (see chapter 6). A judge's decision to order monetary bail becomes moot if bond companies elect to take a pass or will post a bond only on terms that defendants and their loved ones cannot afford. Even in cases where clients are able to sign bond contracts and obtain pretrial release, being perceived as "high risk" can result in serious negative consequences. The risks, costs, and hardships of bail predation all grow more intense when clients are forced to put up greater collateral and accept other undesirable terms of contract in order to secure a bond.

It is also crucial to remember that, despite these race and class preferences for client recruitment, RCS communities remain the central targets of bail predation. Bond companies could not survive and profit without them. The potential client pools that police and courts generate from more advantaged communities are simply too small. As they work to land bonds, agents use race and class cues to be more selective. They try to avoid cases they see as more likely to produce hassles and headaches and, especially, customers they perceive as presenting greater risks. In the contract process, they use such cues as guides for when to apply stricter scrutiny and offer to post bonds on tougher terms. In cases where potential clients are profiled as higher risks, agents are more likely to require multiple cosigners (seeking to obligate "decent," responsible people with higher-quality jobs), impose more stringent payment plans, or require more substantial collateral (typically a house or car title). In some cases, the more demanding conditions put bail out of reach. In many others, the price of the defendant's exit from jail is an agreement that carries potentially ruinous risks and costs—but is deemed worthwhile by the defendant and their loved ones, given the risks and costs of remaining behind bars.

The Gender Basis of Bail Predation

While men of color are disproportionately arrested, convicted, and incarcerated in the US, the financial burdens generated by criminal legal practices tend to fall heaviest on women of color (see chapter 9). In commercial bail, cosigning procedures serve as the main mechanism for turning women into targets of predation. Because so few defendants have enough resources to secure bail contracts on their own, most function as a starting point (or "lure") for efforts to land qualified cosigners. Women, and especially mothers, sit at the top of the pecking order in this process because they are seen as most likely to have the requisite means and motives—the financial wherewithal needed to pay for a premium and the feeling that they have a personal *duty to care* in relation to the jailed individual's predicament. In this way, gendered beliefs and understandings intersect with race and class schemas to guide predatory bail practices at the street level.

The bail agent's search for a cosigner begins with the question: Who will feel obliged to take care of this person? Whether the individual will be able to pay premium costs can, at first, be treated as a secondary matter. (People who are desperate to free a loved one, Page learned early on, can be surprisingly resourceful in their efforts to raise funds.) No, the first and most critical task is to find someone who feels a personal duty to take on the costs and risks that come with cosigning. In this regard, the bail bond industry's ability to generate revenue from pretrial custody depends significantly on agents' efforts to leverage *ethics of care.*

To understand why and how women get selectively targeted and pulled into cosigning roles, one must begin with what Evelyn Nakano Glenn calls the *social organization of care*: the "systematic ways in which care for those who need it is allocated and how the responsibility for caring labor is assigned."[10] Women ultimately bear the heaviest financial burdens of bail predation in the US because bond agents work on a social terrain where gender structures caring relations.

Dispositions to care for others—whether they involve feeding and cleaning at home, providing emotional support, or bailing someone out of jail—are cultivated through practices of social training that have deep political, economic, and legal roots.[11] Historically, marriage and family laws in the US have constructed care as a private duty of wives and mothers, and family socialization processes have generally assigned caring roles and expectations to girls and women.[12] Gender ideologies have further framed the unwaged forms of care work performed in family and community settings as women's natural vocations and as personal acts of devotion that promise intrinsic, feminine rewards.[13] Occupational exclusions and cultural and institutional biases have channeled women into low-wage or no-wage care work, with poor women of color and immigrants generally being forced to work the most demanding, lowest paid jobs.[14]

The rise of socially and spatially concentrated policing and punishment that began in the 1970s has generated new human needs on a vast scale, especially in RCS communities. Such needs take multiple forms (physical, financial, emotional, spiritual, and social), all of which raise hard questions about caring responsibilities. Who should be expected to travel to visit a loved one in prison or deposit funds into the commissary account that an incarcerated person depends on to meet vital daily needs? Why should one person rather than another (or *any* person other than the legally entangled individual) take on the significant costs and risks of getting involved with the bail industry, the prison system, or the courts? As people, including bail agents, reckon with such questions, they tend to be informed by the more general ways they have experienced and come to understand the social organization of caring roles and responsibilities.

In conversations with Rocksville bail agents, Page sometimes commented on the fact that most cosigners seemed to be women.[15] Without exception, agents agreed on this point, but few found it interesting. The prevalence of women struck these workers as unremarkable because it fit into their own assumptions about who would (and should) step up to take care of defendants. The gendered lenses they saw through made it seem natural to look to women first, and to some women more than others. One A-Team boss instructed agents to immediately ask defendants: "What's mom's name and number?" Mothers, nearly everyone assumed, would care enough to bail out their children and make sure they showed up for court. Grandmothers and long-term romantic partners were viewed as second best—solid options, but not quite as reliable. Short-term "girlfriends" tended to be seen as a riskier bet. In such cases, supervisors told agents to find out what they could about the length and stability of the relationship, so as to gauge the potential cosigner's commitment to the defendant before moving forward. Men occupy a lower spot in the pecking order. They cosign for bonds often enough that bail agents are not surprised by their involvement. But A-Team's owners and employees rarely mentioned men when discussing primary options for turning a defendant's case into a bond premium.

The gendered care frames used when targeting and evaluating potential cosigners find their counterpart in bond workers' conceptions of the cosigning role itself. Agents commonly refer to cosigners as "babysitters" for defendants—and see and treat them as such. The metaphor evokes a role that is traditionally filled by teenage girls and women and carries strong expectations of caregiving, monitoring, and safeguarding.[16] Like a parent's agreement with a babysitter, the bail contract turns cosigners into accountable agents of the bond company, responsible for keeping their wards in line and safely returning them at the end of a specified period of time.

Such frames play an equally important role in the meanings that accused individuals and their significant others attach to cosigning. Typically, it is viewed not only as an instrumental way to obtain pretrial release but also as an expressive act that conveys something meaningful about loyalties and commitments. As cosigners arrange premiums, take on contractual obligations, and make themselves responsible for the defendant in various ways, they often see themselves as *taking care of* the defendant. Here, it is important to remember that pretrial release matters for defendants in ways that go far beyond freedom from jail (under terms of continued surveillance and obligation). Cosigning tends to be perceived as an act of care that makes it possible for the accused individual to take care of themselves and others. Locked up, they cannot earn money, attend school, or take care of people who depend on them. They are rarely able to meet their own needs or fulfill their obligations to children, employers, family members, or friends. Getting out on bond does not guarantee that defendants can satisfy such needs and responsibilities. It does, however, give them a fighting chance to do so.

For many potential cosigners, however, such hopeful visions are accompanied by more worrisome thoughts and feelings. They feel conflicted about helping the accused and emotional about the whole process. Decisions about whether to cosign raise hard questions about what one person owes another, who has done favors for whom in the past, which betrayals can be forgiven, and how much is too much to ask. Many people become anxious when asked to cosign for a bond, for reasons that go beyond the financial costs and risks. This is especially likely when former romantic partners worry that they will become re-entangled with a defendant in unwanted ways.

When bail agents sense ambivalence and hesitation, they usually double up on the "gentle" tactics of care and counseling explored in chapter 7. Seeking to close the deal, they express sympathy for the cosigner's plight and an appreciation for their sacrifice. They listen attentively to clients' worries, help them through conflicts of the heart, provide emotional support, and offer reassurances to allay their anxieties. They stress that they are looking out for the cosigner and find ways to indicate that, in their own way, they care about the defendant too.

On the day that Page first encountered Angie in the courtroom, for example, he learned that her husband Johnny was accused of statutory rape—specifically, of having sex with a fifteen-year-old friend of their daughter on the couple's wedding anniversary. Angie cried off and on and told Page she felt exhausted. She lived about eighty miles away and had been staying nearby with Johnny's mom so she could follow the case in person and try to help Johnny make bail. Page expressed sympathy and did his best to explain how the confusing legal proceedings would work. Later, outside the courthouse, when Angie lamented, "I don't even know what questions to ask," Page reassured her that she could call him any time. He would be there for her. In this case and many others, the most strategic approach to recruiting the client presented itself, simultaneously, as the most humane and sympathetic response to someone in Angie's position.

When they met next, Angie said she had visited Johnny the night before, and he told her he was having a breakdown and felt suicidal. After noting that Johnny said he felt better after she met with him, Angie stressed to Page that she did not show up at court because of her *own* feelings for Johnny. She was there "for the kids" that she and Johnny co-parented. In Page's experience, it was common for cosigners to feel that they needed to offer "good reasons" for taking care of a person accused of a crime. This dynamic was especially common in cases such as Angie's, where defendants were charged with highly stigmatized crimes, and in cases where the cosigner was the alleged victim (or victim's relative).

In moments of this sort, caring responsibilities tend to become favored elements of what C. Wright Mills called *the vocabulary of motives*—the range of situationally acceptable bases for accounting for one's conduct.[17] Bailing out the defendant "for the kids" retains the focus on caregiving (as a frame for the situation) but shifts its referent to people seen as more deserving than the defendant. Angie wanted Page to know that her actions were taken *as a mother*; they were not about caring for the man who had betrayed her so terribly. She needed to take care of Johnny so he could help take care of their kids. However, with her children eighty miles away, Angie was, at that moment, struggling to meet her kids' needs partly *because* she was tending to Johnny's situation. Crying at Page's desk, she described what amounted to a catch-22 of caring obligations.

Although Johnny had harmed her and stood accused of statutory rape, Angie still felt duty-bound to visit him, put money on his books, and bail him out. In such cases, Page's supervisors expected him to offer support and try to forge a bond with the women, so they would feel an obligation to him rather than the competition. When Johnny's mother and Angie cosigned, they lost $700 on the spot (the first installment of a payment plan) and placed themselves in A-Team's service. In addition to their remaining payments, they were now financially responsible to the company if Johnny missed court or accrued additional costs (e.g., if the agency needed to employ a bounty hunter). Made responsible for "babysitting" Johnny, the women became the watched and watchful agents of A-Team, surveilled from a distance as they tended to the company's investment.

When friends or family members prove less willing than Angie to cosign for a bond, agents often try to motivate them through more intensive appeals to ethics of care. By focusing attention on horrible, dangerous, and unhealthy jail conditions, for example, they ramp up the potential cosigner's fears for the defendant and feelings of guilt. Sheila, one of Page's coworkers, would warn mothers that their daughters were locked up with "prostitutes, murderers, and thieves." Another, Sean, routinely used variations on the line, "Listen, there's no jail worse than Rocksville County in the state. And I've been to all of them." That was a lie. He had not been to all (or even most) of the jails in the state. In fact, he had never been inside Rocksville's lock up. But the point was not to be truthful; it was to use fear and guilt to pressure a potential cosigner into taking care of the accused.

Some defendants pursue a similar strategy, hoping to pressure a reluctant cosigner into bailing them out. Defendants routinely call bail companies from jail to ask whether agents can contact potential cosigners. When they do, some suggest or state that the agent should stress the risks and hardships of remaining in jail, such as losing a job, getting victimized by guards or fellow prisoners, not receiving medications, or not being able to work on their case. They encourage agents to paint a picture of desperation and despair and convey that their safety and hopes depend on the person who has received the call. The following summary of a field note excerpt illustrates:

Page got to the office a little before 9 a.m. and received a call from the local jail. The young woman, Veronica, was charged with drug possession and her bail was $5,000. She wanted to bail out and go to detox. Her voice shook and her breath was ragged. At her request, Page called her mother, who was divorced from her father. When the mother didn't pick up, Page left a message. Veronica called back around 11:15 a.m. Sounding slightly hopeful, she asked if Page had reached her mother. When he said he hadn't, she exhaled deeply and went silent. "Who else might be able to help?" Page asked. She gave him her dad's number, but her tone clearly suggested that he was unlikely to bail her out. Then she had an idea: Page should tell her dad that she needed to go to detox because she was pregnant. Confused and concerned, Page responded, "He doesn't know?" He didn't, she replied. "Do you really want me to be the one to tell him?" She said she had just found out and feared that her withdrawals would kill the baby. Page agreed to call her dad but didn't commit to unveiling the news about the man's future grandchild. A powerful combination of caffeine and anxiety sent Page's heart racing. Before dialing, he took several deep breaths and got a glass of water. When Page reached the father, the man seemed to have expected the call and stated matter-of-factly, "I'm not bailing her out." He'd done so several times in the past and his daughter had gone right back to using. Page didn't tell him about the pregnancy; in fact, he didn't push at all. He simply thanked the man for his time.

The experience of this case led Page to reflect on his own assumptions about gender and care, as a participant in the field. He realized the extent to which *he* assumed women would be more open to bailing out defendants. He expected men to be more reluctant and, when they were, he was less likely to push in the manner he did with women. Pressing the men just struck him as unlikely to produce results. This was especially true if men acted aloof and disinterested or, like the father in the example above, stated plainly that they would not offer help. Page was rarely surprised when men (including fathers) felt they were not obliged to cosign a bond agreement. Indeed, in cases where men took up the burdens of cosigning, they were far more likely than women to act as if they had done something extraordinary. Such cases resonated in a telling way with bail agents' descriptions of cosigners as "babysitters." Like fathers who get special recognition for "babysitting" their own children (in contrast to mothers, who are seen as merely parenting), men were far more likely than women to see the act of cosigning as bestowing a special gift that exceeded their obligations to the defendant.

The significance of gender roles and ideals can also be seen in the rare cases where a defendant did not want someone to feel that they had to bail them out and, for this reason, chose not to call A-Team from jail. While prospecting for clients one day, Page reached a woman whose son, Paul, a Black man in his mid-thirties, was accused of drunk driving and had a bail set around $10,000. The mother, who worked full-time as a nurse's aide, agreed to cosign and pay the premium (half up front, half later). About an hour later, Paul came in to fill out his paperwork. Page cheerfully greeted him at the door and offered bottled water and coffee. But unlike most recently released defendants, Paul did not seem relieved. In fact, he appeared dejected.

Reading through the bond contract, Paul sighed, "My mom came down, didn't she?" Surprised by his unexpected release, Paul wondered aloud who in his "circle" had told his mother about his situation. Knowing that she would try to help him if she found out he was in jail, he had tried to keep her in the dark. He was hoping the state would drop the charges but, if it did not, he was sure he could handle the jail stay: He could do time, as he put it, "standing on his head." The last thing he wanted was for his mother to have to fork over hundreds of dollars just because of his "bullshit case." When Paul found out his mom had paid hundreds of dollars *and still owed* hundreds more, his frustration turned to sadness. Since the deal was done, he figured, all he could do now was try to pay her back and "say thank you."

Though exceptional (defendants generally do not get upset when people bail them out), Paul's case is instructive. Paul *knew* his mom would feel obliged to take care of him by posting bail, even if it placed her (and perhaps others she took care of) at risk. He responded by withholding information and trying to bear the burdens of his situation alone, out of a feeling that he needed to protect his mother. Both the expectation and the response suggest Paul's understanding of how gendered caring relations structured the situation. Paul's actions and statements can also be read as an assertion of independent, adult masculinity: *I am a man, capable of taking care of myself without calling my mother to the scene. I'm willing to endure hardships to protect her.*

In these and other ways, bail bond work is structured by and operates through the gendered organization of care. Despite the far-from-ordinary circumstances involved, caring roles and responsibilities operated in this corner of the criminal legal field in a gendered manner that nearly everyone involved—from bail company personnel to cosigners and defendants—took for granted. Without careful attention to such dynamics and how they intersect with race and class, one cannot understand how resource extraction gets accomplished at the front lines of the bail bond industry or how and why its burdens get distributed as they do.

Underclass Narratives and Street-Level Justifications

Predatory bail practices are enabled and justified in many ways. In public relations and political campaigns, industry leaders and advocates present bond companies as public-spirited partners, easing government burdens and promoting the collective good. At the street level, bail agents are far more likely to frame bail bond work as a helping profession of care and service or, in circumstances that require a fallback position, as a business just like any other. Our focus on race, class, and gender in this chapter points to an equally important set of justifications that focuses on the targets of bail predation and draws heavily on cultural constructions of "the underclass." In Rocksville, shared beliefs and narratives about the "kinds of people" who made up the clientele framed judgments about client deservingness and the morality of commercial bail practices.

Earlier in this chapter, we analyzed how underclass narratives frame bail agents' perceptions of risk and guide their selections among potential clients. The same narratives underwrite rationales for bail predation, particularly as they relate to violence, crime, dishonesty, and irresponsibility. Target-group justifications of this type operate at the collective level, through constructions of the clientele, and at the individual case level, as they attach to particular clients.[18] In both contexts, pathologizing images of "the underclass" supply bail bond workers with a repertoire of rationales that can be adapted to specific situations on the fly.

Attributions of social deviance and disorder help to justify predatory bail practices, first and foremost, by minimizing the moral significance of any client suffering they may produce. One way they do so is through the idea that people should get what they deserve, based on the choices they have made and the actions they have taken. If bail bond clients are harmed in some way, this framing suggests, it is certainly not a case of bad things happening to good people. No one should feel sorry for people who have broken laws, scoffed at work, and left others to suffer the consequences of their actions—people who refuse to get their act together and repeatedly make choices that are harmful to themselves and others. When bail bond workers deploy this frame, they do not downplay the severity or experience of client hardships; they turn them into just deserts. In a fair system, they tell themselves and others, people should get what they deserve, for good or for ill.

Stereotypes of a disorderly underclass also make the harms of bail predation less morally troubling by normalizing client suffering. The principle here is that people's experiences of life events depend on what they are used to and have come to expect. Agents tend to assume that clients' lives are dramatically different from their own. Disruptive crises, material hardships, and severely strained family relationships are, agents believe, routine in their clients' lives. In "those neighborhoods," people are used to such things as utility shutoffs and threats of eviction; they have dealt with them before and can manage them now. Thus, when agents become aware that a bond contract has had disastrous consequences for a client, they tend to see the situation differently than if it had happened to them or those in their social circles. Such problems, as they see it, are par for the course in "the ghetto." The source of turmoil today is the bail bond contract, but it was something else yesterday and will be something different tomorrow. In this manner, underclass narratives provide bail agents with a ready-at-hand basis for social indifference toward the harms they produce.[19]

A second logic of justification does not minimize the significance of harms; it attributes responsibility for them. Again, bail agents typically see clients' predicaments as products of their own free choices and, for this reason, as signs of their character. Bail bonds are expensive, agents agree, but clients have no one but themselves to blame for the costs: *They made their bed, and now they have to lie in it.* "Those kinds of people," agents tend to believe, are always getting into trouble and blaming others for the fallout. This framing is especially important when agents know that they have pressed to take every dollar they can from a client or when a client makes it clear how deeply they will suffer. In such cases, attributions of moral responsibility allow agents to acknowledge harms done and then sidestep blame.

The moral responsibility frame is, in turn, often used to shore up the defense of bail predation as a normal market transaction that we discussed in chapter 7. A-Team workers routinely emphasized that, however bad the contracts might be, bail companies do not force defendants to use their services; clients, as consumers, choose to do so. Page would occasionally question this free-market defense by noting that clients do not have much of a choice if the only alternative is to suffer the harsh consequences of staying in jail. In response, coworkers would usually shift to the moral responsibility frame by saying something like: "Then don't go to jail." In this way, each frame offered a fallback position for the other. In one, the consumer has freely chosen to enter a market contract and, therefore, is to blame for their predicament. In the other, the lawbreaker has freely chosen to violate the social contract and consequently bears responsibility for the fallout. When Page would comment that defendants are "alleged" lawbreakers, his coworkers would remark that the people in question were still guilty of making morally questionable choices that, the agents assumed, led to their arrests—such as hanging out with the wrong people, going to the wrong places, and so forth.

The final way that bail agents draw on underclass narratives to shield themselves from moral blame takes the form of what philosopher Miranda Fricker calls *testimonial injustice*: the kind of injustice that occurs "when prejudice causes a hearer to give a deflated level of credibility to a speaker's word."[20] At the bail bond agency, it typically involves discrediting clients' stories and complaints as untrustworthy attempts at manipulation. People from "the ghetto," in this view, are always trying to game the system. They have had lots of practice lying to get what they want and will not hesitate to try to put one over on the bail agent. In this frame, being tough is really about not being a dupe, and clients' claims of hardship should always be taken with a grain of salt.

A more detailed look at a case from Page's fieldwork helps to illustrate this frame and how it works in concert with the others we have described. Toward the end of an afternoon shift, a senior worker, Chet, asked Page to take over the case of a defendant named Rob, who was charged with domestic assault and assigned a bail of $40,000. Chet said the bail premium ($4,000, with $1,500 paid up front) was coming together smoothly and Page just needed to tie up loose ends. Rob had $1,000 in his bank account, his girlfriend would kick in the other $500, and family members in a nearby state had agreed to cosign the bond. Page could post the bond once he secured the $1,500 and a cosigner, and Rob would pay the rest ($2,500) in installments.

Happy to land a relatively large bond, Page got to work on the phone. Quickly, though, he found his case unraveling. Contrary to Chet's assurances, the cosigners were not lined up. Rob's aunt was willing to help but did not have a job; his grandmother agreed to cosign but did not have email or a fax for the paperwork; and his father was in the same position as the grandmother. Eventually, Page arranged for the family members to use the fax services of a check cashing business but, when the documents arrived at A-Team, they were incomplete.

Exasperated, Page silently cursed Chet for "giving" him the case and sought advice from a manager, Jamie. When Page said the family had no access to email, Jamie (who knew from Chet that the family was poor and Black) responded sarcastically, "Of *course* they don't." Chet had given a misleading description of the family's situation, but Jamie placed blame squarely on the family members. Her frustration with the family was wide-ranging. How could they not have a computer or email—or jobs? Why couldn't they complete the simple forms? How would A-Team collect from these out-of-state residents living off Social Security checks if Rob went on the run? The whole situation, Jamie suggested, made the family seem unreliable. She insisted that Page find a more dependable cosigner, one who lived in state and had a decent job. When this effort failed, Jamie and Mark, a senior agent, told Page to go ahead and charge Rob's bank card $1,000. That way, at least, they could confirm that Rob had the money in his account before continuing to pursue a solid cosigner.

As Page drove home from the office, a coworker asked him to take a call from Rob, who was clearly confused and upset. He had put up the $1,000 and his family had faxed in the cosign forms. So why was he still in jail? Page explained that he still needed to collect the remaining $500 and find a cosigner who lived in state and had a job. Rob was dismayed. Chet, he said, had told him that $1,000 up front plus later payments would get the job done. He'd said nothing about an in-state requirement. Chet had manipulated him, he said, and Rob now felt betrayed by the sympathetic way Chet had listened to his "life story" and acted like a "stand-up dude." At this point, Page felt confused too and asked Rob to call back in twenty minutes. Unable to reach Chet, he called Jamie, who would not budge on the terms: $1,500 and an employed in-state cosigner. *Rob* was lying, not Chet, she said. "They always say 'Chet told me such and such.' Who are you going to believe? Chet or some dude in jail?"

When Rob called back, he was angry and incredulous. Why in the world did A-Team run his card? How long would it take to refund the money? Why did Chet jerk him around? He was panicked that he would lose his job while sitting in jail. None of his "people" had any money; he was the "breadwinner." Page did not know what to say, especially since he was beginning to suspect that Chet *had* misled Rob. He assured Rob that he would keep working the bail, and, if things did not work out, he would refund the $1,000 so Rob could go to a different company.

When they hung up, Chet called. Rob needed to "relax," and Page needed to "stay firm," he said. He then revealed his "play." He *had* told Rob that $1,000 would be enough, while angling all along to get another $500 from Rob's people and then another $2,500 in eventual payments. Chet seemed peeved that Page had mentioned the extra $500 to Rob, saying that Page should have told him they were just waiting on a co-signer (while continuing, behind the scenes, to press people for the extra $500). Approaching the situation as a teachable moment, Chet instructed Page not to let "street dudes push you around." They need to know that "manifest destiny is in our hands," he said, and if Rob continued to press, Page should just "tell him to get lost and refund his money." A half-hour or so later, Jamie called to let Page know that Rob had called the office to complain and, after talking with him for a while, she had transferred the call to Chet, who took care of the situation himself. Chet told the young man to "fuck off," Jamie said without further detail. Later, when Page asked Chet what had happened, he replied, "I just had to show him who ran the show, and it isn't him."

Over the course of this episode, A-Team personnel drew on negative constructions of the company's "underclass" clientele to interpret Rob and his family's actions and deploy a variety of protective rationales. The prejudicial discrediting of testimony emerged as soon as the client began to say that he had been wronged. When Rob complained about Chet's deception, Jamie dismissed his story as untrustworthy, pointedly clarifying (through a rhetorical question) that Chet's version of events was obviously more credible than "some dude in jail." When Rob got angry and demanded redress, Chet only saw confirmation that A-Team was dealing with a "thug" who needed to be put in his place. Otherwise, the defendant would continue his manipulative and bullying ways. Chet suggested that, like a lot of A-Team's poor Black clients, Rob thought he could cry foul and game the system. Page should not let clients get away with it, Chet believed, and without any apparent sense of the historical weight of his words, he urged Page to make it clear to such clients that "manifest destiny is in our hands"—to leave no doubt about whose story will be believed, who holds the power to control whose fate, and who, as a suspect subordinate, should gratefully accept what they were given.

The defenses and rationales explored in this section are widely deployed at A-Team. Because they are all built on group constructions of "the underclass," however, their application across individual cases is decidedly uneven. Bail agents sometimes temper or set aside their presumptions about the clientele by applying to individuals what Elijah Anderson calls a distinction between "decent" and "street."[21] Based on speech, dress, and other markers, agents come to see some clients from RCS communities as "decent" folks who embrace "middle-class values," moral propriety, and the active pursuit of a better future. Such people are seen as more deserving of sympathy, and perhaps even a helpful break in the terms of their bond contract. When clients present themselves as upstanding cosigners or desperate and grateful defendants, agents sometimes become more willing to believe their stories and less prone to see suffering and hardship as their just deserts.

For bail bond clients, however, the achievement of "decent" status is always precarious. A single act that strikes the agent as irresponsible, manipulative, or suspect—anything that reads as "underclass" or breaches the unspoken expectation of grateful compliance—is likely to be treated as evidence that the person is really just another client from the "street" way of life after all. Underclass narratives set default assumptions that can be reinstated at any time. One coworker at A-Team (Mark, a White man from the suburbs) described himself to Page as a reasonable "pessimist" about Black defendants—someone who "thinks the worst and waits to see what happens." This stance was a point of pride for Mark. He was not "naive," he said, because he "grew up playing ball" with Black people. Working bail, he told Page, had cemented the distrust he developed back then. When poor Black defendants or cosigners showed defiance or broke script in some way, they immediately confirmed his assumptions and returned Mark to his default.

As this example suggests, the decent/street boundary can operate as a site of high-stakes symbolic interaction. Some clients adopt strategic presentations of self, designed to fit the mold of a "decent" community member. Through clothing choices, mentions of civic work, or expressions of devout faith, they try to distinguish themselves from the "street" clientele. Convinced that most clients are manipulative, agents sometimes ignore early favorable cues (based on a gut feeling) and, as the process unfolds, watch for signs that the person is putting on an act. Clients may respond, in turn, by trying to shore up their "decent" status, perhaps by joining in the denigration of "street thugs" or expressing dismay at behaviors in their community.

Gender matters for these social-classification dynamics as well. Initially, agents tend to lump cosigners (mostly women) and defendants (mostly men) together, on terms defined by their assumptions about the bail industry's "underclass" clientele. Usually, this lumping will persist for the duration of the case, serving as an anchor for the rationales and legitimizing frames discussed in this section. Defendants, who typically have limited interactions with bail agents, rarely have much of an opportunity to show that they are something other than a stereotypical "street dude." Cosigners have more chances to make a good impression, and they make up a large majority of clients that bail agents come to see as morally respectable and deserving of sympathy. In such cases, the agent's initial lumping is replaced by a splitting: the cosigner is recast as the defendant's more "decent" opposite.

Splitting complicates the use of underclass-centered protective rationales, especially when agents can see that their work has created financial and emotional distress for women they view as upstanding and good. To resolve the tension, agents sometimes turn to gendered narratives of victimization. As we discussed in chapter 1, stories that provide ideological cover for predatory practices by charging subjugated groups with uniquely objectionable forms of gender-based oppression and exploitation have a long history in America. A-Team personnel continued this tradition when they blamed the harms of bail predation on an "underclass culture" in which "street" men routinely exploit and mistreat more "decent" women—living off their incomes, mistreating and manipulating them, and taking advantage of their love.

If the distraught cosigner is, in fact, being victimized, who is the victimizer? To bail agents, the answer is clear: they did not put her in this situation, the defendant did. If the money paid to the bail bond company causes her to suffer, blame surely lies with the defendant—who, agents often assume, has probably been taking advantage of this woman for many years. Bail agents, in this rendering, are powerless to change the costs and burdens of bail. The true measure of their actions and their character can be seen in the practical assistance and emotional support they provide. Far from exploiting the cosigner's situation, they see themselves as allies of the victimized cosigner.

Conclusion

Language, Ludwig Wittgenstein famously argued, tends to be misunderstood if it is observed only as an abstract set of symbols and structures. "The speaking of language is a part of an activity, or of a form of life," he explained; in the language games we play, "the use of the word in practice is its meaning."[22] Confusions, he suggested, mostly "arise when language is like an engine idling, not when it is doing work."[23] Much the same can be said of criminal justice predation. To understand it well, one must observe its machineries in motion and analyze how its designs get put into practice. In the first half of *Legal Plunder*, we analyzed the broad landscape of criminal justice predation in the US today, explaining its growth and transformation and showing how its various operations strip resources from communities and turn them into corporate and governmental revenues. Over the past three chapters, we have pursued the challenge of analyzing predatory relations and practices "in gear" (to use Wittgenstein's metaphor) through a case study of commercial bail.[24] Starting at the top, with the powerful actors who construct and defend the industry, we moved down to the field's lowest arenas, where it is possible to experience and observe the frontline work of resource extraction *in the doing*.

In this chapter, we have drawn on Page's ethnographic research to analyze the roles that race, class, and gender play in the cultures and practices of storefront bail operations. Up to now, most studies of bail have focused on courts and judicial decision-making and analyzed race, class, and gender through a group-disparity lens. Such studies have demonstrated significant ethnic and racial disparities in the rates at which judges grant release and require financial conditions.[25] Far less attention has been given to the commercial side of bail. Few studies have analyzed how race, class, and gender help to organize and legitimize industry practices—or how they figure into frontline workers' understandings, choices, and actions. The analysis in this chapter addresses these matters directly and clarifies how and why they matter so greatly for bail predation today.

At A-Team and companies like it, predation gets performed *through the active use* of social structural inequalities. The intersecting axes of race, class, and gender frame bail workers' perceptions, interpretations, decisions, and justifications. Bail agents put them to use as rubrics of evaluation and rely on them to develop baseline assumptions about their clientele. In the competitive world of commercial bail, race, class, and gender operate—socially, spatially, symbolically, and materially—as defining features of the field of play.

PART FOUR

Significance and Struggle

9 * What Do Predatory Criminal Legal Practices Do?

In February 2002, California State Senator Richard Polanco (D-Los Angeles) convened a public hearing at the Trinity Baptist Church in South Los Angeles.[1] Polanco chaired the state legislature's Joint Committee on Prison Construction and Operations, and the hearing focused on an issue that had him inflamed: the state's prison phone policy. At the time, California only allowed people in prisons to make expensive collect calls to the world outside. WorldCom and Verizon, the contracted providers, charged a $3.50 connection fee for each call, plus $0.15 to $0.89 per minute (based on destination).[2] The charges were a boon to the companies *and* the state. Public officials required the firms to hand over about 40 percent of all phone call revenue. In an interview with the *Los Angeles Times*, Polanco decried the policy: "This is profiteering on the backs of the innocent. It is just wrong to have a state policy that gouges the families of inmates."[3]

The hearing offered community members an opportunity to speak out about the hardships they endured because of the phone policy. That morning, the *Los Angeles Times* reported that "African American churches from throughout Southern California are busing in members—as many as 1,000 are expected—to protest the policy. Other groups that work on behalf of prisoners also are sending emissaries."[4] Indeed, at the hearing, people described being forced to choose between accepting expensive collect calls from their incarcerated loved ones and paying rent and other bills.[5] Vicki Ricotta Nicholson testified that she paid over $400 a month to talk with her husband. "These calls are necessary," she explained, because of her husband's "serious medical condition" and his needs for "constant legal consultation." To pay for the calls, Nicholson had to find a second job.[6]

Phone bills, it became clear, were straining relationships. Tamika Casey recounted how she had to limit her uncle to one call per month. It was painful to ration his calls, especially since he could no longer call his children's home directly. "Their phone has been disconnected," she said, "because of the costs of making these collect phone calls." But there was nothing unusual about this situation, Ms. Casey stressed to the legislators. "This has put a great hardship on our families. And it's tearing families apart. This is happening to the families that can least afford to have these types of tragedies happen in their families."[7]

By 2002, the direct beneficiaries of such hardships—the telecom companies and the government—had a well-established partnership. For roughly a decade, private firms had paid for the state's prison phone system and its administrative costs (in exchange for being able to charge steep prices for phone calls) and they had given the government millions of dollars per year in commissions. In 2001, the telecoms had taken in $85 million, $35 million of which went to the state.[8] In just five years (1996–2001), government revenue from the contracts had *doubled*.

At the Trinity hearings, Paul Jennings gave expert testimony that the spike in revenue was no accident: "Contracts that have been issued [to prison telecoms] in recent years have focused on the company that will pay the highest commission. . . . The best provider would mean who's going to pay the most money."[9] The state now expected (and budgeted for) commission-based revenue, pumping it directly into the general fund, where it became available for non-prison expenditures. Faced with a $20–25 billion budget deficit, the state desperately needed money for its operations.[10] A representative from the department of finance confirmed at the hearings that "budget cuts to other areas" would be required if the state lost revenue from prison phone calls.[11] It was "impossible," Senator Debra Bowen (D-Los Angeles) explained, to reduce costs and hardships so long as the telecoms insisted on big profits and the state continued to require large commissions.[12]

For people living in the most policed and punished communities in the US today, stories like the ones told at the Trinity hearings are all too familiar. They may often go unheard, but collectively they testify to the far-reaching effects of criminal justice predation. The revenue-generating practices that have proliferated since the 1980s have transformed criminal legal institutions. At the same time, they have served as powerful forces of marginalization, disruption, and immiseration in race-class subjugated (RCS) communities.[13]

In earlier chapters, we showed that predatory criminal legal practices generate very substantial private and public revenues. The resources they siphon from communities underwrite corporate profits, CEO salaries, shareholder dividends, and lucrative returns for private equity firms, Wall Street banks, and their financial investors. They fund middle-class jobs in the public and private sectors. They ease the tax burdens of advantaged

Americans by subsidizing the costs of governance. In these and other ways, criminal justice predation shapes life conditions for large numbers of privileged Americans who are scarcely aware of its existence.

In this chapter, we shift our focus from the benefits that predatory practices generate for dominant groups and institutions to the corrosive effects they have on targeted communities and criminal legal governance. First, we examine how predatory projects transform the institutions and organizations that carry them out. Our analysis shows how the daily work of extraction reconfigures organizational cultures and routines, undermines the "justice" missions of criminal legal agencies, enables corruption, and erodes political accountability. Next, we turn to the effects on communities, exploring the socioeconomic deprivations, hardships, and crises that communities experience as a result of criminal justice predation. Finally, we consider the civic consequences of legal plunder for RCS communities, focusing on how extractive practices shape what Evelyn Nakano Glenn calls "substantive citizenship."[14]

Institutional Dependence and Organizational Missions

The social psychologist Gordon Allport once observed that "as a man does something, he becomes something."[15] The same may be said of organizations. "In ways both large and small," Donald Moynihan and Joe Soss write, "bureaucracies may slowly mold their culture, routines, and authority relations around the exigencies of a particular policy."[16] Predation is not an official policy, but it has become a major function of criminal legal institutions. As a result, public agencies now raise questions once reserved for private firms in the field: To what extent do revenue pressures and agendas compromise official missions to seek justice and ensure public safety? How does the dogged pursuit of revenue affect the ordinary workings of policing and punishment?

Relevant studies and experts in the field have been remarkably consistent in their appraisals. "The pursuit of revenue," Karin Martin and colleagues assert in a review of monetary sanctions research, "makes debt collectors out of law enforcement officers."[17] A 2012 report by the Conference of State Court Administrators states that revenue pursuits have "recast the role of the court as a collection agency for executive branch purposes."[18] In a study of misdemeanor punishment, Alexandra Natapoff argues that "bureaucratic self-preservation and profit" have become so central to petty-offense operations that "the revenue objective calls into question the true purpose of the criminal misdemeanor apparatus."[19] Based on a fifteen-state study of legal financial obligations (LFOs), The Brennan Center for Justice concludes: "An overreliance on criminal justice debt coupled with aggressive collection practices . . . undermines the traditional functions of the courts and criminal justice agencies enlisted to collect debt."[20]

As police, courts, and penal agencies have pursued predatory revenues, many have become dependent on them. As early as 1998, roughly 40 percent of the officials who led local police departments and sheriffs' offices agreed or strongly agreed that their agencies had become "dependent on the revenue generated from civil asset forfeiture."[21] To make the costs of public projects politically viable, many government agencies (inside and beyond the penal field) exploit the cheap labor of people controlled by carceral facilities and community supervision programs.[22] A 2019 study found that in more than 720 localities in the US, criminal legal fine and forfeiture revenues alone contributed general funds in excess of $100 for every adult resident.[23]

The state of Michigan offers a well-documented example. In 2019, the state's Trial Court Funding Commission (TCFC) reported that fees accounted for roughly one-third of all court funding ($418 million per year in assessments alone) and delivered $30 million in funding to non-court agencies in the state.[24] The state legislature had created the TCFC in 2017, two years after the Michigan Supreme Court ruled that the state's courts lacked the independent legal authority to impose fees to pay for their operating expenses.[25] The ruling set off a panic, and state lawmakers rushed to pass legislation that allowed courts to continue levying such charges until October 2020 and gave the commission time to formulate alternative plans for financing the many agencies that relied on fee revenue.[26]

The state's dependence on legal fee revenue put Michigan judges under enormous pressure to keep it coming.[27] District Judge Thomas P. Boyd recalled how a county administrator pointedly reminded him in 2005 that the "district court is the cash cow of local government."[28] When Judge Boyd failed to bring in as much money as his colleagues, county officials demanded that he explain his negligence. Two years later, Boyd recounted, "the chair of the county commission's finance committee told me that the county would like about $300,000 revenue in excess of expenditures from the court."[29] Similarly, Judge Sheila R. Johnson testified that city officials "inquired about why our revenue had decreased and what we were going to do about it," making it clear that "the court should be a self-supporting money maker for the funding unit and that we must be responsible for funding ourselves and doing whatever is necessary to increase revenue."[30]

Such pressures have become commonplace in criminal legal governance. In a study of Texas probation programs, for example, Ebony Ruhland and colleagues describe how self-funding expectations drive personnel to maximize fee collection. One manager told the researchers: "I will tell you it's something that's pushed very hard. . . . I mean it's how our department is funded. And we depend on collection of fees. So, monthly . . . our officers are under a lot of pressure to do whatever we can to collect fees. Period. End of story."[31] Probation agents, the authors show, clearly understand that their jobs depend on wringing payments from the people under their supervision.[32]

Recognition of this sort can have significant consequences for organizational culture, service motivation, and staff morale in criminal legal agencies. As we showed in earlier chapters, predatory self-funding practices have many champions at the front lines of policing and punishment. Some agencies and task forces openly celebrate the fact that their operations are paid for, to a significant degree, by "criminals" rather than taxpayers. But many people who work in the field feel more conflicted about pressures to raise funds and express doubts about whether revenue-generating agendas are appropriate for agencies that ostensibly aim to pursue justice.

For these personnel, daily work often requires a resigned acceptance of troubling practices that are needed to sustain operations. A probation officer in the Texas study, for example, described financial charges and collections as a "necessary evil"—an unsettling but inescapable fact of life for an under-resourced agency.[33] Similarly, municipal officials who view police-generated funds as "bad revenues" (that they would prefer to avoid if they had other options) nevertheless pressure police agencies to increase funding streams through fines, asset seizures, and other tactics.[34]

In some cases, criminal legal officials openly condemn the extractive practices that have become integral to their jobs. Professional training and socialization encourage many people who work in criminal legal agencies to see themselves as public servants, impartial upholders of the law, and protectors of their communities. These occupational identities and values can clash with practices that forcibly strip resources from legally entangled people in ways that lead some officials to speak out. Judges, who take solemn oaths of office and have extensive legal training and professional prestige, have been particularly vocal critics.

In Michigan, for instance, judges explicitly protested to the TCFC that self-funding practices undermined the official mission of criminal courts by creating inherent conflicts of interest, threatening the legitimacy of legal proceedings, and distorting justice.[35] The Michigan District Court Judges Association argued that the "constant pressure to balance the court's budgets could have a subconscious impact on even the most righteous judge." The "possible temptation" to fill funding gaps by ramping up convictions, the association warned, threatened to undermine constitutional guarantees of due process.[36]

The association's public statement powerfully testified to the dangers of revenue-centered adjudication—and to the forces that push judges into a resigned acceptance of predation. Put simply, they need the money.

Since the 1980s, judges' organizations and the American Bar Association (ABA) have repeatedly raised alarms about how funding shortages and massive caseloads overwhelm courts and undermine justice. Because self-funding offers some relief, judges confront a devil's choice.[37] They can participate in the injustices that arise from a resource-poor, understaffed court or the injustices that stem from using courts to produce revenue.[38] The first option carries professional risks as well, such as developing a reputation for backlogged dockets, trial delays, and administrative errors; provoking complaints from public managers who depend on court-based revenues; and even getting voted out of office. Against this backdrop, it is not surprising that so many judges participate in the self-funding project.

Concerns that revenue seeking can compromise justice and violate constitutional safeguards are well founded. Some kinds of extractive practices directly undermine *access to justice* for people who lack sufficient resources to pay.[39] For example, the hefty fees that states charge for expungement deprive many people of the ability to clear their name and participate in the community free of the stigma and obstacles that burden people with a criminal record.[40] Similarly, court fees charged for public defender services or going to trial can deter people from exercising their constitutional rights.

In other instances, predatory practices generate tiers of *unequal treatment* under the law. For instance, incarcerated people who cannot pay for phone calls, basic supplies, reading materials, and other fee-based goods do their time under markedly harsher conditions. In some locales, people with the means to do so can buy less burdensome conditions of confinement.[41] Defendants who cannot afford commercial bail services lose their liberty and suffer the negative consequences of pretrial detention. And, as we will discuss later in the chapter, nonpayment of LFO debt can result in probation violations, extended periods of community supervision, and even incarceration.

As the US Department of Justice (DOJ) stressed in a 2023 letter sent to jurisdictions across the country, extractive fine-and-fee practices can threaten and, in some cases, breach constitutional protections.[42] When governments "incarcerate individuals solely because of their inability to pay a fine or fee," the DOJ reminded legal officials, they violate the "due process and equal protection principles of the Fourteenth Amendment."[43] Self-funding court practices can also lead to unconstitutional conflicts of interest.[44] In a 2019 ruling, the US Court of Appeals for the Fifth Circuit considered a case in which local Louisiana courts raised funds from pre-trial bond processes. When defendants used a bail company, courts received a percentage of the payment: the higher the bail, the more money for the courts. Because the funds paid for essential judicial costs (e.g., staff salaries), the court ruled that judges were playing a "dual role" as "the source of essential court funds and an appropriator of them." The "direct, personal, and substantial interest" in outcomes, the court held, "would make the average judge vulnerable" to revenue-enhancing biases in a way that pushed "beyond what due process allows."[45]

The infamous case of Ferguson, Missouri, provides a particularly stark example of how predatory agendas and practices can reconfigure police and court operations and subvert legal protections. The DOJ's 2015 report concludes: "Ferguson's law enforcement practices are shaped by the city's focus on revenue rather than by public safety needs. This emphasis on revenue has compromised the institutional character of Ferguson's police department, contributing to a pattern of unconstitutional policing, and has also shaped its municipal court, leading to procedures that raise due process concerns and inflict unnecessary harm on members of the Ferguson community."[46] Here again, though, Ferguson stands apart more for its notoriety than for its injustices. In Wisconsin, for instance, court data reveal that changes in fee-based funding formulas for district attorneys' offices incentivized prosecutors to significantly increase revenue-enhancing felony charges.[47] Similar developments have played out in New York state, where local governments shifted operations in order to claim larger shares of fine-based revenues. A 2006 analysis revealed that 33 percent of lower courts in New York converted moving violations, which generate revenue for the state, to lesser parking violations that funded localities in roughly one-third of cases. A separate study showed that, in 2009, plea deals were used to turn half of all state speeding charges into local fines that generated $23 million for municipalities.[48]

Criminal legal institutions that prioritize revenue generation also tend to downgrade efforts to protect communities from violence and other forms of harm. Surveying national evidence, Beth Colgan argues that "the revenue-generating capacity of fines, fees, and forfeitures risks perverting governmental incentives. [B]y promoting policing and adjudication methods that are most likely to increase revenue, governmental actors may fail to consider, or even implement policies that directly conflict with, public safety needs."[49] In earlier chapters, we presented numerous examples of this dynamic. The growing emphasis on asset forfeitures in the 1980s and '90s, for example, spurred the development of police tactics such as the reverse sting that target drug buyers (who are easy to apprehend and carry cash that can be directly converted into revenue) rather than distributors (who are more likely to be involved in violence but also to possess drugs that have to be destroyed). The more time police spend on revenue-related practices, such as doling out fines and executing warrants for nonpayment, the less time they have to spend on efforts to curb violence and build the community relationships so critical for preventing and solving crimes.[50] And when probation officers "spend much of their time reminding their clients to pay unaffordable fees and fines, they have less time to work with people to help them break the cycle of repeated contact with the criminal justice system."[51]

Predation also jeopardizes public safety by promoting conditions that can make police violence more likely.[52] In a 2023 study, Brenden Beck finds that municipalities "that collect 1 percent more in fines and fees than the typical municipality experienced 4 percent more police killings."[53] Devon Carbado suggests how this dynamic might work in a broader discussion of police violence against Black people: By incentivizing stops, "predatory policing" increases "the frequency with which African Americans have contact with the police." The "possibility for violence exists not only at the moment the officer initially issues the citation," he explains, but also later, when officers stop "individuals on the assumption that they may have an outstanding warrant for [an unpaid] citation that would justify an arrest."[54] Beck's findings and Carbado's interpretation dovetail with our broader argument: As criminal legal agencies pursue predatory practices, they shift priorities and adapt operations in ways that undermine justice, public safety, and equality before the law.

Corruption and Political Accountability

The routine implementation of predatory practices also creates hospitable environments for various sorts of corruption, including personal enrichment, corporate rule-breaking, and the illegal state takings that Bernadette Atuahene and Timothy Hodge refer to as "stategraft."[55] Here again, an organizational perspective is essential for understanding the connection. As organizational cultures and routines adapt to support day-to-day practices of predation, they cultivate the perception that targeted groups' resources are available and suitable for the taking and normalize the use of authority, coercion, and manipulation to strip people of what they have (or can obtain under duress). As public and private organizations aggressively exploit legally entangled people, they can leave their personnel less certain about ethical constraints and blur the line between legal and illegal takings. The risks are especially high when frontline actors have broad discretion, are subject to limited oversight, and experience intense pressures to bring in revenue.

Enmeshed in the organizational pursuit of predatory takings, personnel can come to see extralegal methods for stripping resources as nothing more than ramping up or tweaking standard practices. Unauthorized uses of detainment provide a common example. Bail bond agents and bounty hunters sometimes seize (in essence, kidnap) defendants for failing to pay their bills—an illegal but self-enriching extension of their authority to apprehend defendants who fail to appear for court.[56] Some bail companies also charge illegal fees and then, without any legal authority to do so, threaten to return defendants to jail if they fail to pay.[57] Similarly, as we discussed in chapter 2, law enforcement officers sometimes abuse their legal powers of detention as a way to "break" individuals who resist forfeiting their assets.

Extortionary threats are effective, in part, because targeted people are often uncertain of their rights to resist. Private probation companies in Alabama, Georgia, and Mississippi, for example, threatened to throw clients in jail for nonpayment of fees, despite lacking the legal authority to do so. The clients scrambled to pull together the money because they assumed that the companies could legally make good on their threats.[58] The same tactic worked to compel payments in a separate case where Georgia probation agents charged illegal fees for electronic monitoring and drug and alcohol tests.[59]

Predation creates opportunities for public authorities to engage in practices of self-dealing as well. For corporations that depend on public–private partnerships, the use of money and other resources to *legally* curry favor with public officials can come to seem normal and routine—nothing more than the ordinary "cost of doing business," of gaining an edge on the competition and securing profits. Campaign contributions, pricey social events, and lobbying investments are standard fare. Offers of bribes, kickbacks, personal vacations, and other forms of self-enrichment can develop as their illegal counterparts.

Local scandals have revealed cases in which public officials have been paid off by private companies seeking to win or renegotiate contracts to run prisons, probation programs, and red-light camera services.[60] In a widely reported incident, a pair of Pennsylvania judges accepted millions of dollars in bribes and other illegal payments to increase the sentences of juvenile defendants and send them to specific for-profit detention centers.[61] Behind the scenes, bail agents, bounty hunters, private probation agents, and debt collectors sometimes pay government employees under the table for information or access that gives them an advantage over competitors.[62]

Within law enforcement agencies, asset seizures and other predatory practices have generated large pools of discretionary funds that can be used in self-dealing ways. In Tennessee, a homeland security agency illegally spent over $110,000 in federal forfeiture funds on catering and banquet tickets.[63] The US Marshals Service created an "Asset Forfeiture Academy" in an exclusive Houston high-rise but rarely used it for "academic" purposes at all. In Ohio, a prosecutor's office spent nearly $30,000 in forfeiture funds on office furniture and briefcases for attorneys. And in Philadelphia, police used asset seizure as a "clandestine revenue source" to fund $2.2 million in salary increases and pay for expenses such as a raccoon-removal service.

Organizational self-dealing can, in turn, encourage individual practices of self-enrichment. The spoils of predation supply ample opportunities for individuals to pad their pockets. And research suggests that when workers see their organizations engage in corrupt or unethical practices, they often feel less compunction about doing so themselves.[64] Police officers involved in asset seizures sometimes take a bit for themselves, reporting and delivering only a portion to their departments.[65] In some cases, they go further, using the legal practice of asset seizure as cover for what amounts to robbery. In St. Paul, Minnesota, officers on the Metro Gang Strike Force seized cash and goods from individuals (mostly people of color) who could not be linked to gang activity in any way.[66] In addition to keeping televisions, computers, jewelry, and other valuables for themselves, officers sold some of the goods they stole to colleagues and family members.[67]

The full scale of predation-related corruption is unknown, partly because illicit activity often goes unreported. Government oversight tends to be weak and irregular; targeted individuals tend to have limited power to expose the wrongdoing and may reasonably believe that filing a complaint will be risky or futile.[68] As a result, exposure usually depends on extraordinary efforts by journalists, litigators, whistleblowers, or watchdog groups.

When exposure does occur, accountability is often elusive. Corporations use legal maneuvers to avoid major penalties or settle lawsuits without admitting wrongdoing, and government officials use legal loopholes to deny responsibility and dodge punishment.[69] Judges and prosecutors have immunity from civil prosecution for corrupt actions taken in their official capacities.[70] Police can invoke "qualified immunity" in many cases, a doctrine that shields government employees from civil lawsuits unless they violate "clearly established statutory or constitutional rights."[71] For instance, officers in Fresno, California successfully used the doctrine to avoid personal liability after pilfering more than $225,000 seized in a police raid.[72]

Criminal justice predation, in both its authorized and corrupt forms, tends to be insulated from legal and political accountability. In some respects, this is nothing new. Historically, RCS communities have been policed and punished in America with authoritarian impunity.[73] The lack of effective mechanisms for community control is a perennial theme in criminal legal politics, starkly illustrated by decades of demands for civilian oversight, community policing, and, more recently, calls to defund the police.[74] Since the 1980s, predatory criminal legal practices have weakened political accountability further still.

Contemporary modes of criminal justice predation rely heavily on public–private partnerships—a mode of governance well known for making democratic accountability more difficult.[75] The cross-sector structure of predation, writ large, makes it hard to answer even basic questions about criminal legal debt. The ABA observes in a 2020 report: "Right now, courts across the country cannot determine or report the full costs paid by an individual as a result of a criminal charge because private companies impose and collect so many of the fees/costs without any court involvement."[76] Unlike public agencies, private companies are not bound by open records laws or obliged to answer requests under the Freedom of Information Act. Exercising their legal rights, they guard information that could be used to hold them accountable.

Take bail companies, for example. Because they are private entities, they can withhold information about which people they choose to serve (versus turn away) and how they set prices and conditions for different clients. Community groups and government regulators are generally limited to personal complaints when they seek evidence of discrimination and mistreatment. There are no public records to document bail agents' relationships with defense attorneys and other legal professionals or the ways bail companies monitor clients and pile on fees for various "services." In fact, Page pursued the ethnographic research analyzed in chapters 6–8 partly because public information about the bail bond industry is so scarce. In the field, he quickly learned that government regulators and court actors—judges, defense attorneys, prosecutors, and clerks—knew surprisingly little about bail company operations.

Or consider the secretive mugshot industry discussed in chapter 2. When people discover that their arrest photos have been posted online, they rarely know whom to contact to get their picture taken down or how to navigate the expensive removal process. Many do not realize that, even if they pay for removal, their pictures will likely pop up on another site, forcing them to go through the costly process again. Due to weak oversight and regulation, targeted people generally cannot turn to government for information, much less for assistance removing their mugshots from the internet or holding the mugshot companies accountable.[77]

Privately held information is especially troubling in the context of carceral facilities, where imprisoned people are subject to near-total control behind closed doors. Because private prison companies serve public functions and receive public funding, critics have long argued that they should be subject to the same open records laws as public agencies. Since 2005, members of the US Congress have repeatedly introduced the Private Prison Information Act to impose such a requirement.[78] But prison companies have blocked the bill every time, arguing that information about their contracts and operations is available from their government partners (e.g., state departments of corrections). Corporate filings with such agencies, however, rarely include the types of information needed to hold them accountable, such as incident reports and grievance logs.[79]

Private firms are vigilant, too, in denying researchers and members of the press access to their penal facilities—arguably even more so than government penal agencies, which also tend to carefully restrict entry to carceral facilities.[80] Journalist Shane Bauer went undercover as a prison officer at a Corrections Corporation of America facility because, he concluded, it was the only way to develop a trustworthy, directly observed account of how for-profit lockups operate.[81] Because companies guard information so closely, communities, advocates, and public officials typically have to speculate about how profit incentives shape daily life inside the facilities. As Lauren-Brooke Eisen notes, "We know next to nothing about the product other than how Wall Street values these companies." Should an incident threaten the company's reputation and bottom line, a private prison has "every incentive to cover it up."[82]

Equally important, there are few avenues for holding criminal legal businesses accountable. Unlike government agencies, bail companies, prison firms, and other for-profit entities are not required to hold public hearings about their budgets, expenditures, or policies and practices. And unlike state officials, leaders of these firms are not subject to elections or legislative confirmation hearings (as is generally the case with prison wardens, directors of corrections, and other high-level public administrators).[83] Corporate CEOs and other business leaders typically answer only to shareholders and investors or, in the case of bail agency owners, insurance companies.

Contemporary modes of criminal justice predation further threaten accountability by creating opportunities for illegitimate or illegal forms of self-financing. Asset forfeiture practices have drawn harsh criticism in this regard because they supply so many police departments with substantial, largely unregulated pools of resources. As described earlier, there are numerous examples of police departments using seized money in ways that have no connection to public safety. In other cases, such funds have been used to strategically evade political control and accountability. An investigative report in 2016, for example, revealed that the Chicago Police Department used forfeiture-generated funds to "secretly purchase controversial surveillance equipment without public scrutiny or city council oversight."[84] Eric Blumenson and Eva Nilsen argue that law enforcement self-financing through forfeiture "raises serious accountability concerns, and threatens to establish a sector of permanent, independent, and self-aggrandizing police forces." As such, it is not a "legitimate organ in a democracy."[85]

Radley Balko sounds similar alarms about prosecutor-led diversion programs. In an article in *The Washington Post*, Balko tells the story of John DeRosier, district attorney of Calcasieu Parish, Louisiana. DeRosier allowed people in pretrial diversion and misdemeanor probation programs to *buy their way out of* community service by giving him gift cards and money orders. He used these "discretionary" proceeds to support law enforcement organizations and other politically aligned groups; to convey his affection for friends, campaign supporters, and friendly journalists; and, allegedly, to reward members of his staff. All these actions violated a Louisiana rule stating that DAs can only charge fees for the costs of diversion programs. Balko explains, however, that DeRosier and other prosecutors pay the rule little mind because there is almost no chance of accountability. Clarifying the broader context, he summarizes: "Because diversion programs tend to be run entirely by DA's offices with no oversight from the courts or outside agencies, there have been myriad problems with accounting, transparency, and allegations of grift."[86]

Similar problems of accountability arise throughout the criminal legal field as authorities use predatory practices to build up their own pots of resources outside of the budget process. Some courts put fee proceeds into judicial funds, subject to little oversight, while jails and prisons often deposit the commission payments generated by phone calls, commissary purchases, and the like into vaguely defined and largely unmonitored "inmate welfare funds." When journalists at *The Sacramento Bee* were able to uncover how the inmate welfare fund was being used by the Sacramento Sheriff's Office, they found that the money had been spent on employee vacations, equipment, salaries, and other expenses that had little or no connection to the well-being of imprisoned people.[87] Mary Katzenstein and colleagues show that lawmakers in multiple states have altered statutes to give jail administrators wide discretion over inmate welfare funds. For example, California loosened its law so that jail officials must use the funds "primarily" rather than "solely" for inmate welfare. Through the strategic deployment of "verbal modifiers," Katzenstein and colleagues show, lawmakers and administrators engage in a process of "concealment," hiding or obscuring information in ways that severely limit public accountability.[88]

Across the landscape of US criminal legal institutions today, predatory practices generate autonomous resource pools with weak ties to public processes of budget allocation, fiscal oversight, and democratic accountability. Crucially, decisions about how to use such resources are made with virtually no accountability to the communities that are the primary sources of the funds and are disproportionately subjected to the practices they pay for.

Social and Economic Consequences for Communities

The consequences of criminal justice predation for RCS communities are profound. To understand their socioeconomic dimensions, one must begin with the fact that predatory practices never generate effects in isolation. Their consequences depend on the surrounding circumstances of people's lives. Fees that would be an annoyance for one person, for example, can be life-altering for another. Predatory takings that some families or communities can weather without disruption will, for others, set in motion cascades of hardships and crises.

The RCS communities that serve as the epicenter of criminal justice predation in the US are generally sites of concentrated social and economic disadvantage where, all too often, the margin between making ends meet and watching one's life unravel is razor thin. People in these communities disproportionately suffer the effects of racism, poverty, precarity, food insecurity, environmental toxins, health problems, and other debilitating conditions—as well as the effects of evictions, experiences of violence, losses of loved ones to incarceration, and other destabilizing events. Incomes tend to be low and assets nearly nonexistent.[89] The terms of available work are often defined by low compensation, no job security, limited hours, and unpredictable schedules.

The roots of these community conditions can be traced, to a significant degree, to practices of subjugation, exclusion, and predation in earlier eras, including a steady stream of discriminatory and exploitative business practices and government policies pursued throughout the twentieth century.[90] The predatory business models that saturate RCS communities today play a key role too, in ways that often work through consumer debt and sometimes rely on criminal legal authorities as enforcers (see chapter 2). People with low incomes frequently have too little cash on hand to cover their basic needs and bills or invest in their future. To fill the gaps, they often engage the services of exploitative payday lenders, take out usurious pawn shop loans, make needed purchases through high-interest payment plans, sign risky subprime mortgage agreements, and turn to other businesses that offer fast cash or goods on unfavorable terms. In the process, they can become ensnared in long-term debt-and-payment traps that leave them worse off still.[91]

Like predatory business models, extractive criminal legal practices systematically drain resources from RCS communities, intensifying social and economic disadvantage. A study in Maryland, for instance, reports that bail bond companies "extract tens of millions of dollars from Maryland's poorest zip codes, contributing to the perpetuation of poverty."[92] A 2017 study of New Orleans similarly finds that "the burden of paying bail, fines, and fees is borne primarily by Black residents, most of whom are struggling economically."[93] An analysis of LFOs in Minnesota concludes that they "exacerbate existing poverty and spatial isolation in rural areas, compounding and further entrenching historical, systemic disadvantages that Native communities already face."[94] And an innovative longitudinal analysis in Washington state argues that the "LFO burden (re)produces poverty over time," contributing to "racial differences in the accrual of household wealth and community resources."[95]

Criminal legal takings can have devastating consequences for individuals and families in RCS communities, whose circumstances already tend to be precarious. Even relatively small asset seizures and LFO obligations can strip people of funds that they desperately need to buy medicine, pay bills, make rent, or secure childcare.[96] In a study of traffic fines and personal finances in Florida, Steven Mello finds that people who receive a $175 citation "accrue unpaid bills and delinquencies on their credit reports while also reducing consumption, suggesting an inability to cover the unexpected expense." Low-income drivers, Mello explains, experience "financial distress observationally similar to a $950 income loss following a $175 ticket."[97]

Many people with LFOs are also weighed down by other types of debts (e.g., from medical bills, credit cards, or student loans).[98] As they experience a widening gap between their nominal incomes and the funds that they have available to live on, such people are also forced to decide which debts to pay down first. The pressures to pay LFOs ahead of other expenses can be enormous. Bankruptcy rules prohibit individuals from discharging most types of criminal legal debt.[99] And when people fall behind on payments for LFOs, they often rack up additional charges (e.g., late fees and collection fees) that push them into a "never-ending debt loop."[100] When people do not pay down their LFOs, criminal legal agencies and their private partners often take actions that "damage credit scores and directly compromise access to credit" and pursue "civil judgments that result in liens, wage garnishment, and tax rebate interception"[101] Recall, too, that many jurisdictions treat LFO payments as a condition of parole or probation. Authorities can revoke supervision status for nonpayment, which, in turn, can lead to a loss of eligibility for benefits such as food stamps, social security, and housing assistance.[102] In La Grange, Georgia, the local government has taken to shutting off water service to the homes of "delinquent" legal debtors in an effort to squeeze payments.[103] Authorities in San Francisco have towed and impounded cars that belonged to people with unpaid LFOs (even in cases where the owner was living in the car) and have imposed additional fees for the length of time the car remained impounded.[104]

As we discuss later in the chapter, many jurisdictions have also embraced the infamous tradition of "debtors' prisons," banned by federal law in 1833 and ruled unconstitutional in 1983.[105] Using procedural workarounds and contempt of court charges, judges threaten to jail people who fail to pay their LFOs—and often follow through. In an extreme case of coercion, an Alabama judge in 2015 told hundreds of debtors that they could make payments in blood, money, or jail time: If they could not afford to pay their LFOs, they could donate to a blood drive outside the court and exchange their receipt for a $100 credit on their debt. For those unwilling to give blood and unable to pay cash, the judge grimly asserted: "The sheriff has enough handcuffs."[106]

Fearing reprisals, many people are forced to confront agonizing choices about which of their debts, bills, and other financial obligations to pay down first. In a study of monetary sanctions and LFOs in Texas and New York, one participant described a common predicament:

> It has been very stressful and it's been a burden. Because then you have to choose between getting something maybe I really need for my kids and paying this and taking care of it to try to get it cleared and off my back. So it's been really hard. Especially when I wasn't working and didn't have resources at the time. . . . I was just trying to maintain and that's why I kind of put it off for a while 'cause I was just really struggling. So from that particular fine, other fines came. Then it just multiplied and multiplied and multiplied.[107]

When individuals feel that they have to prioritize LFOs over other debts and expenses, the consequences can be severe.[108] In a statewide survey conducted by Alabama Appleseed Center for Law and Justice in 2018, about 83 percent of people with LFOs reported giving up "necessities like rent, food, medical bills, car payments, and child support in order to pay their court debt."[109] In a study of probation in Texas, one interviewee explained: "I do without sometimes. I pick and choose what I eat. When I've worked in fast food, I'll take home what we didn't use. Get on the ramen noodle diet. Get a box of twelve for $2. . . . Don't buy shoes. Don't buy extra clothes. I need two hearing aids. I've been taking the money I have saved up for hearing aids to pay for this [probation]."[110]

To make LFO payments, legal debtors turn over tax refunds, recycle goods, and sell their plasma.[111] All too often, they take out high-interest, short-term loans. In the Alabama study mentioned above, 44 percent of respondents reported using payday loans to cover LFOs—a finding that is unsurprising given that a majority of families with LFOs lack access to full banking services.[112] Jailed defendants and their families also rely on these costly loans to cover bail bond premiums, sometimes at the encouragement of bail companies.[113] In this manner, people struggling to pay off LFOs take on additional bad debt, strengthening a cycle of payments to various creditors that reinforces poverty and generates repeated hardships.[114]

The family members and friends of legally entangled individuals bear a large portion of the costs and suffer various "symbiotic harms" generated by LFOs and other criminal legal costs.[115] To cover LFO costs, some family members drain retirement savings and skip utility, rent, and mortgage payments.[116] In a study of bail, one former defendant recalled that his mother, who put up money for the bond premium, "didn't pay her light bill a couple times. She didn't pay her rent a couple times."[117] In another study, a formerly incarcerated person recounted: "Everything that was put into bailing me out was everything my mother had in savings, and she borrowed some money from my grandparents. She was back to working paycheck to paycheck. Eventually, about a year and a half after being locked up, my mother had to give up the house she loved and move back to an apartment."[118]

In chapter 8, we explained how gendered caring roles and expectations guide bail agents' efforts to secure cosigners for bonds. As a result, women from RCS communities wind up responsible for the lion's share of bail-related costs and burdens. Similar gender dynamics play out across the nation's criminal legal institutions.[119] Older women, especially mothers, are disproportionately called on to care for the children of imprisoned adults, send packages to incarcerated loved ones, pay for phone calls, fund visits to prisons, house and feed formerly incarcerated relatives, cover the costs of bail premiums and court fees, and more. The Ella Baker Center for Human Rights finds that women make up 83 percent of family members who pay fines and fees stemming from convictions.[120] In its 2018 report, Alabama Appleseed concludes: "While other Alabamians are saving for retirement, paying off mortgages, and helping their children with payments for higher education and other expenses, African American women with no criminal histories are paying other people's court debt."[121]

Although older women bear the heaviest burdens, family members of all sorts can wind up on the hook.[122] Indeed, this can happen in some cases *without* the family member's consent. In Florida and Wisconsin, legal responsibilities for some LFOs are automatically transferred to family members in the event of the debtor's death.[123] In some states, laws allow government agencies to take LFO payments from a debtor's family members without their authorization. In a 2011 study, Katherine Beckett and Alexes Harris report that county clerks in Washington state were authorized to garnish "up to 25 percent of the earnings of the debtor *or his/ her spouse* and . . . seize jointly held bank assets, home equity, and tax refunds."[124]

In juvenile cases, parents are generally held responsible for LFOs.[125] The financial drain can produce significant hardships, including "spillover effects on the juveniles' siblings. Forced to pay off one child's court fines, families may not have enough money for their other children's school clothes or tuition."[126] In adult criminal cases as well, children are likely to suffer consequences when outlays for things like LFO payments, bail premiums, and prison expenses strip resources from custodial parents and guardians or limit noncustodial parents' ability to pay child support.[127]

All too often, resource takings and the hardships they create strain the bonds that hold families and friendships together.[128] Tensions can arise when legal expenses leave partners and parents unable to meet their other obligations (such as paying rent, bills, or child support).[129] The same is true when people sacrifice scarce resources to pay for debts that are not of their own making. In chapter 8, we described such dynamics in the context of Page's ethnographic research as a bail bond agent. At A-Team, some family members and friends embraced the role of provider and caregiver for the defendant, viewing it as an expression of their loyalty, affection, and generosity or, in some cases, as a way to strengthen or renew a relationship. Others resented the financial losses, risks, and responsibilities involved, including having to take care of adult children, spouses, and exes. This was especially the case when they felt forced back into a relationship or role they no longer wanted.

Such negative frustrations may be immediate, or they may emerge over time. Helping loved ones with legal expenses is a form of gift giving and, as in many contexts, there is often an expectation that the recipient will eventually reciprocate.[130] Some people simply want their money back. Others, Page found, expect the recipient to change their behavior in some way: to get help with chemical dependency, depression, or anger, get a job (or a better job), pay child support, help with childcare, or, in some other way, *honor* the giver's financial and social sacrifice. If reciprocation does not come, dashed expectations can lead the giver to experience disappointment or anger.[131] The recipient of the gift may also feel ashamed or upset at themselves for failing to follow through, even if they believe that circumstances made it impossible to do so. Negative emotions on both sides can lead people to doubt, avoid, or even abandon important relationships. In *Doing Time on the Outside*, Donald Braman describes a similar dynamic in the context of incarceration: "Most inmates do not earn much money and are unable to reciprocate the material sacrifices their partners must make. Girlfriends and wives often send money and care packages, accept expensive phone calls, spend money traveling to visit inmates, and support their children. For poor women, the marginal costs are quite high because they have less disposable income and time; as a result, incarceration has an especially corrosive effect on the relationships that poor women enter into."[132] In these ways, predation can fray social ties that are vital for survival in poor communities, weakening structures of mutual aid and making future assistance less available.[133]

The hardships created by criminal justice predation are not just material and social; they are also psychological and physical.[134] For legal debtors, perpetually looming threats of life disruption and state violence can be stressful and terrifying. A respondent in one study described legal debt as "overwhelming" and said, "I go to therapy because you are always scared they will be knocking at your door. I have started using [drugs] because of the anxiety."[135] Legal debtors move through their lives with the weight of the state pressing down on them, fearing that the authorities might burst through the door. This feeling of being haunted by state power is likely to be especially fraught for Black Americans, who have endured racist and authoritarian state violence for centuries and seen time and again how quickly ordinary interactions with the police can turn deadly.[136]

The fears and anxieties that surround legal debts can contribute to health problems, too.[137] In a national study of young adults, Elizabeth Sweet and colleagues report that "high financial debt relative to available assets is associated with higher perceived stress and depression, worse self-reported general health, and higher diastolic blood pressure."[138] There is little reason to think that debts to the state are an exception to this general pattern. In fact, a 2012 study of reentry experiences in Missouri concludes that legal debts directly contribute to physical and mental health problems.[139] In a multi-state study, interviewees told Harris and colleagues that struggles to pay off LFOs had negatively affected their health.[140] Some respondents said that debt-related stress and negative self-appraisals reinforced chemical dependency.[141]

Health effects of these sorts can undermine employment, community involvement, and schooling and add to the social and economic barriers associated with having a criminal record.[142] But obstacles can arise from LFOs in more direct ways as well. In some states, people who fail to pay their legal debts are banned from obtaining occupational licenses needed for certain jobs, such as commercial driving and funeral services.[143] When courts and companies (e.g., private probation firms) report legal debtors to credit agencies and garnish their wages, they mark people in ways that can make employers less willing to hire them and landlords less willing to rent to them.[144]

When a person falls behind on LFO payments, courts in many states often revoke or suspend their driver's license.[145] The frequency of such suspensions is astonishing: In 2020, roughly eleven million people in the US lacked a valid driver's license because they owed money to courts. Between 2006 and 2015, California alone suspended the licenses of more than four million residents (17 percent of the state population) for this reason.[146] In 2015, one of every six drivers in Virginia had a suspended license due to unpaid court debts.[147] Between 2016 and 2018, New York issued nearly 1.7 million driver's license suspensions related to nonpayment of traffic tickets.[148] Government actions of this sort are concentrated among the poor and, as state-level studies of California, Florida, and New York show, among Black Americans.[149] In some states, debtors also have to pay a "reinstatement fee" (typically $100 or more) to get their licenses back.[150]

The case of Ashley Sprague, a young woman from Lebanon, Tennessee, illustrates the cascading effects of a driver's license revocation.[151] In 2015, Sprague received $477 in tickets for speeding and not having proof of insurance. When she could not keep up with payments, the court suspended her license. After receiving additional citations for driving with a suspended license, Sprague's bill climbed to $946. She then learned that she would have to pay an additional $388 to have her license reinstated. At the time, Sprague earned only $2.13 plus tips as a server at Waffle House. Unable to drive or get rides to work, Sprague could not pay her legal debts and lost her job. Without steady income, she had to send her kids to live temporarily with relatives.[152]

Disruptions of employment and earnings also result from administrative hassles. In a study of LFOs in Washington and Illinois, Michelle Cadigan and Gabriela Kirk show that debtors must routinely update the court in person about their financial situation, a process that can take hours and lead to lost earnings.[153] Some interviewees "noted that their employers were suspicious as to why they had to continue taking time off to attend court, leading to a strained relationship with employers who might have already accommodated a stigmatizing criminal record."[154] Few legal debtors have a choice, however. If they fail to appear for a hearing, the court can issue a bench warrant, potentially leading to additional fees and even jail time.

Through these and other dynamics, criminal justice predation functions as a de facto mechanism of labor discipline.[155] Legal debtors are often under intense pressure to take the worst positions in the gig economy or work off the books in informal jobs that are dangerous and extremely exploitative. In some cases, the pressure is explicit, as when court officials direct debtors to pursue *any* available money-making opportunity. Harris found that in Washington state, "court officials encouraged debtors to seek illegal 'under the table' day labor, ask family or friends for loans, or even beg for money by the side of the road in order to service their LFOs."[156] Court officials need not be so direct, however. People with LFOs understand that if they do not pay their debts, they risk further court appearances, fines and fees, arrest, and incarceration.

There is growing concern that such pressures may reinforce cycles of crime and punishment that tend to have corrosive effects on communities. Although limited, some research argues that people may engage in criminal behavior to get out from under legal debt.[157] One study finds that LFO burdens increase the risk of recidivism among juveniles, especially Black youth.[158] Legal debts can also undermine the kinds of life conditions that support crime desistance and successful community reentry: stable housing, supportive relationships, mental and physical well-being, and decent-paying, steady work.[159] Through these effects, predation can accelerate the cycling of people back into the criminal legal system, where they become subject to further resource takings at the hands of police, courts, carceral institutions, supervision agencies, and profit-seeking corporations.

Civic and Political Consequences for Communities

As predation generates cascading social and economic effects, it also restructures citizenship. By citizenship, we refer to both the equalities and inequalities that define people's positions in the social order—their civic standing in relation to the state and other members of the polity.[160] The formal status of citizenship defines a key component, of course. But some people who have such status may live as "second-class citizens," while select others who lack it may enjoy greater degrees of power, recognition, and standing to be heard in government and beyond. In brief, civic standing depends not only on legal status but also how people are positioned in less codified structures of social, economic, and political relations.

The prevailing terms of the civic order in a society evolve over time, Evelyn Nakano Glenn writes, in response to political movements, legal change, and "everyday practices and struggles."[161] They are reconfigured on an ongoing basis "through face-to-face interactions and through place-specific practices that occur within larger structural contexts."[162] As in the past, predatory projects today help to construct people's experiences of civic standing.[163] In this section, we focus on how predation contributes to legal and political estrangement and various forms of marginalization. In chapter 10, we analyze how the injustices of extractive criminal legal practices give rise to resistance, community mobilization, and political struggle.

Consider first the depredations of resource stripping and social disruption discussed in the preceding section. In one of the twentieth century's most influential accounts of citizenship, T. H. Marshall argued that poverty and social degradation set groups apart as civic inferiors and undercut people's abilities to exercise their civil and political rights.[164] Indeed, decades of empirical studies have documented how resource deficits and related forms of social isolation and strain can weaken civic engagement and political participation.[165] Poverty can also push people into means-tested public assistance programs that treat them as failed citizens, subject them to directive and supervisory forms of governance, and sometimes further depress civic and political engagement.[166]

The individual-level dynamics are often compounded by neighborhood-level effects, particularly when economic disadvantage is concentrated by racial segregation.[167] Traci Burch shows that community-level resource deprivations produced by penal governance—e.g., through the costs of supporting incarcerated loved ones and negative effects on employment and public benefit eligibility—tend to deepen political marginalization.[168] Like other forces that intensify community hardships and disruptions, predation can also weaken the forms of collective efficacy that support collective civic and political projects at the neighborhood level.[169]

Predatory criminal legal practices also produce what policy feedback scholars call "interpretive" (or "political learning") effects.[170] For people in RCS communities, police and other criminal legal officials often serve as the most visible and proximate face of government.[171] Encounters with these authorities are highly salient experiences of the state that can play an outsized role in defining, subjectively and objectively, the lived realities of a citizen's rights, protections, obligations, claims to recognition, and standing to speak. Personal entanglements with criminal justice predation can convey powerful lessons about what government is and does, how the rule of law works, and where one stands in the social and political order.

To be subjected to plunder by one's government—in the name of law and justice, no less—is to experience firsthand what Bennett Capers calls "the state assigning worth."[172] Community members' perceptions that they are being singled out because of who they are and where they live make such experiences a powerful basis for what Benjamin Justice and Tracey Meares describe as "race- and class-based lessons on who is a citizen deserving of fairness and justice" and who is not.[173] Criminal justice predation makes clear that, even in the US today, the ability to be legally secure in one's property remains a function of race and class position. In this sense, it helps to construct the symbolic and material significance of race and class themselves.[174]

Thus, as predatory practices have become more integral to criminal legal governance in the US, they have come to play a more prominent role in shaping how people in RCS communities experience and perceive law, legal institutions, and state authority.[175] In an innovative study, Vesla Weaver, Tracey Meares, and Gwen Prowse arranged unguided, cross-city conversations between people from intensely policed communities. Individuals communicated via "portals"—shipping containers converted into "immersive audiovisual environments that allow distant people to talk as if in the same room."[176] Many participants spoke about encounters with predatory policing and the lessons they drew about race, class, and citizenship. One explained, for example: "[Police] look at us as nothin' but paychecks. That's all we is to them. Nothin' but paychecks. They like eat you. . . . 'Oh yeah. We got them. Then we gonna get paid as soon as we take 'em in.' They don't care about us."[177] Another elaborated: "You Black man and you young, they don't care about you . . . ya dig? They want to keep you behind the walls so they can get paid. See they get paid from you good money, man, you know good money."

In a study of misdemeanor courts in Texas, Ilya Slavinski reports corroborating evidence. One respondent told him: "It's just money coming in from every mother fucking way. Yeah, you've got people lining up at six o'clock, seven o'clock in the morning, ready to go pay their fucking ticket. . . . It's just a big ass business for people who. . . . Whoever has their hands tied into this, whatever you want to call it, they're the ones gaining from it. They're the ones getting all the money, they're the ones benefiting. Screwing the citizens over type shit."[178] Findings from these and other studies suggest that predation contributes to what Monica Bell terms "legal estrangement." Intensively targeted groups come to "see themselves as essentially stateless—unprotected by the law and its enforcers . . . marginal to the project of making American society . . . [and] subject only to the brute force" of government authorities.[179]

By turning the public spaces of heavily policed neighborhoods into "takings zones," predatory practices also erode people's basic freedoms of movement and civic interaction.[180] In such neighborhoods, costly citations—and perilous interactions with the cops who issue them—have become a pervasive risk attached to ordinary activities such as walking, biking, and driving (see chapter 2).[181] Debt-based driver's license suspensions further undermine residents' abilities to drive to work or pick up a child at school without risk of further costly criminal penalties.[182] Five years after the DOJ published its damning report on the Ferguson Police Department, *The New York Times* reported that Black Ferguson residents continued to carefully regulate their behavior in response to the risks of predatory policing: "They avoid main roads. They maintain good posture. Sometimes they choose not to drive at all."[183]

Extractive practices inside prisons degrade lived experiences of citizenship in ways that are more severe. In a comparative study of coercive employment, Erin Hatton analyzes dynamics of power and civic standing in carceral labor programs.[184] In capitalist economies, all workers experience some form of *economic coercion*. Because they cannot get by without money, people are compelled to seek, accept, and remain in undesirable jobs. Incarcerated people experience similar pressures: Given the cost of necessities, imprisoned people often have little choice but to work for shockingly exploitative wages (see chapter 3).

In carceral facilities, however, labor extraction is based more directly on *status coercion*—the threat of being stripped of one's position as "a prisoner in good standing."[185] This status, Hatton explains, is the basis of "all the rights and entitlements that become privileges behind bars, like being able to buy food from the commissary, or being able to go to the recreation area and exercise and socialize with friends, or being able to have visits from your family or use the phone to call your spouse and your children." If incarcerated workers refuse to perform a task, like "having to clean up feces with nothing more than a tissue," prison officers can strip them of "good standing," deprive them of "privileges," and even send them to solitary confinement.[186]

In interviews, people who have worked in carceral institutions detail the cruelties of authoritarian overseers and the emotional toll of being treated as second-class citizens. One of Hatton's interviewees explained why he referred to being treated "like a slave" in this context: "It's the human decency they don't really have. No human respect for you. They figure, if you got the state greens on, then you are below them. You are a peasant. They are upper class; you are lower class. You're poverty. You are nothing. They talk to you in any kind of way. Sometimes, they put hands on you, they put feet on you."[187]

Within and beyond carceral facilities, criminal justice predation also constructs civic inequalities through the production of debt. As a general matter, debtors occupy inferior positions in unequal power relations that may subject them to a variety of coercive actions, reformative programs, and punishments.[188] At various levels of scale—from indebted nations forced to adopt austerity measures down to municipal governments, organizations, and individuals—debtor status can enable and justify social control and resource extraction.[189] For these and other reasons, Michael Feola observes, debt "is not simply an economic standing, but a mode of governance."[190]

Debts imposed by criminal legal institutions establish particularly severe forms of debt-based governance, characterized by intensive state surveillance, managerial supervision, and, in many cases, incarceration. The state-citizen relationships defined by LFOs are distinctly criminalized and racialized. They are imposed and managed as a matter of law enforcement, and their meaning is colored by the punitive trope of "owing a debt to society." LFOs are debts to the state and its designated partners, explicitly defined by government authorities as "criminal" matters. Moreover, because criminality is such a race-coded concept in US culture *and* because criminal legal debts are imposed in such racially concentrated ways—LFOs underwrite a deeply *racialized* as well as criminalized form of debt-based governance.

For these and other reasons, people with LFOs occupy a distinctive position vis-à-vis the state that we conceptualize as *indentured citizenship*: a form of civic and political standing that is modified by the terms of a criminalized and racialized debtor's contract. Indentured citizens occupy an inferior status—marked by distinctive obligations and curtailments of freedom and privacy—that sets them apart from the others in the polity. The terms of their citizenship are refracted through the lens of debt in ways that reconstruct the moral and the material dimensions of civic standing. Legal debt itself becomes the marker of a degraded status, rooted in violation of the social contract and therefore punishable in its own right.

The terms of indentured citizenship today differ considerably from systems of indentured servitude in early eras of American history. Criminal legal debtors do not need a "master's consent" to marry or travel; they are not subjected as a class to a fixed term of "bound labor;" and they retain formal rights far beyond what existed in the early American context.[191] In key respects, however, legal debtors today are "semi-citizens," subject to distinctive obligations, curtailments of rights, and modes of power that flow (directly and indirectly) from their debts to the state.[192] Indeed, their debts are often *sold* as a form of property in transactions that grant new owners—banks or private debt collectors, for example—control over their lives, rooted in rights to extract ongoing payments.

In the US today, people are often subject to criminal legal surveillance and social control for years after they have completed terms of imprisonment, probation, or parole, solely because of LFOs imposed through predatory practices. Many people are swept into this net of criminal legal management based on nothing more than a parking ticket, the inability to pay a legal fee, or a consumer debt that a business has chosen to pursue in court (see chapter 2). As Alexes Harris explains, LFOs routinely "relegate impoverished debtors to a lifetime of punishment . . . [and operate as] a method of social control that symbolically, physically, and perpetually punishes the poor."[193] Such debtors, Harris argues, become "perpetual subjects of the criminal justice system who at any time can be called to answer for their nonpayment and may even be reincarcerated."[194]

Put simply, for indentured citizens, liberty is always tenuous.[195] In many states, LFO payments define a condition of community supervision, which can be revoked in favor of imprisonment if individuals fall behind. In some states, legal debtors can be incarcerated simply because a court deems their nonpayment to be "willful." Authorities in some jurisdictions can arrest people for failing to pay an LFO or appear at a debt hearing, jailing them until the court determines their ability to pay. In a small number of states, people who are unable to pay their LFOs can choose to spend time in jail to lower the amount owed. In Mississippi, authorities have forced debtors to live in state-run centers and work hard, dangerous jobs for corporate employers until they complete their payments (this takes about four months, on average, but can last for up to five years).[196]

Private collections agencies also serve as important agents of social control in these relationships, either because they are hired to secure payments for public agencies or because they purchase LFOs from such agencies and work to maximize their return on investment. In chapter 2, we explained that many jurisdictions delegate authority to such businesses, enabling them to add their own charges (and steep interest rates) to people's LFOs. For legal purposes, these private charges become part of the LFO itself, extending the terms of social control in a manner similar to the charges that governments tack on. In these cases, compounding interest, mounting fees, and financial penalties often combine to turn indentured citizens into long-term subjects of for-profit businesses, backed by the authority of the state.

The restrictions and degradations of civic standing that LFOs set in motion begin in criminal legal institutions and then spread outward. In criminal courts, Harris explains, "debtors are unable to receive certificates of discharge . . . to have their records sealed, to receive pardons, or to request deferred prosecution."[197] In many cases, people with LFOs "cannot regain certain rights lost upon conviction, such as the right to vote, carry a weapon, serve on juries, or run for elected office, until their account is paid in full."[198] Across the nation, governments deny legal debtors social welfare protections, occupational licenses, and other services.[199] On the basis of unpaid LFOs, individuals can be excluded from need-based income and food assistance programs, including Supplemental Security Income for the elderly and disabled.[200] And, as we noted earlier, when failures to keep up with LFO payments damage credit scores, they can significantly limit people's access to employment, rental housing, auto and home loans, and all but the most predatory financial service operations.[201] Such barriers tend to be especially damaging when LFOs are imposed at a young age and create discrediting markers that follow individuals for years (if not lifetimes).[202]

Among the many ways that LFOs degrade civic standing, voting restrictions are distinctive in their political significance. The vast majority of US states permit some form of "wealth-based penal disenfranchisement" that disproportionately leaves people from RCS communities unable to exercise their right to vote.[203] Some states impose an outright ban, turning requirements to pay off LFOs into a kind of poll tax.[204] In a notorious case, when Florida voters passed a ballot measure in 2018 to restore voting rights for people with felony records, Republican lawmakers responded by making restoration conditional on the full payment of LFOs.[205] The legislative change barred about 8,000 people from voting. Moreover, because government agencies do not have to notify people of their ineligibility, many people with criminal records do not know their voting status. Rather than risk illegally casting a ballot and facing felony charges, many potential voters in Florida appear to have opted out of the electoral process.[206] Arizona also bars people with felony convictions from voting until they pay off their legal debts.[207] And in a telling expression of civic hierarchy, the state funds elections for eligible voters with revenues generated by the very same fees that produce LFOs.[208]

LFOs also facilitate race- and class-targeted voter suppression in less direct ways. People who lose their driver's license as a result of unpaid LFOs may have trouble getting to a polling place, especially in rural areas that lack public transportation. In jurisdictions that require photo IDs for voting, the loss of a driver's license can create a substantial barrier to electoral participation.[209] And in states that only bar people with felony records from voting if they reside in prison, LFO-based revocations of parole and probation function, in effect, as tools of disenfranchisement.

In Alabama, unpaid LFOs can be deemed a violation of the Definition of Moral Turpitude Act, which bans otherwise-eligible people from voting because the state has determined that they have an immoral character.[210] In 2018, Alabama authorities barred Alfonzo Tucker Jr. from voting because he owed the state $4 in legal debt.[211]

The right to vote, Judith Shklar argues, has been a key marker of full citizenship throughout US history, signposting superiority to groups excluded on the basis of race, class, and gender.[212] Today, LFO-based exclusions diminish the political influence of RCS communities *and* convey a powerful message about civic standing. Karin Martin and Anne Struhldreher write: "Withholding voting rights because of debt tells those with a criminal history: *You don't get a say.* It means that, after having otherwise paid their debt to society, individuals with previous convictions are cut off from civic engagement. And when regaining this right is tied to paying—in full—the frequently onerous debt that accompanies a conviction, voting restrictions hit low-income communities and communities of color hardest."[213]

In sum, as predatory criminal legal practices subsidize groups and institutions at the top of the social order, they construct inferior forms of civic standing, deepening political marginalization and subjecting community members to intense regimes of surveillance and social control. Since the 1980s, the spread of new revenue-centered modes of criminal justice predation has played an important role in reconfiguring the interplay of race, criminalization, and citizenship that has long been central to US history. Predatory takings and legal debts criminalize people and places in highly targeted ways; they strip communities of resources that support political engagement; and they teach powerful lessons about government, law, and social hierarchy. Through these and other processes, criminal justice predation operates as an active force in the ordering of civic and political relations.

Conclusion

Back in South Los Angeles, at Trinity Baptist Church in 2002, State Senator Richard Polanco (D-Dist. 22) described the struggle for phone justice as "a long journey."[214] Imprisoned people and their families, advocates, religious organizations, and a handful of legislators had been pushing for change for quite some time. Just two years earlier, they had successfully pressured the legislature to pass a bill that would require the state to offer contracts to prison telecom companies based on the lowest phone rate offered. The bill likely would have reduced prison phone rates, corporate profits, and state revenue. Although it would not have eliminated commissions to government, Governor Gray Davis (D-CA) cited this concern when he vetoed the bill. The state of California, he said, simply could not afford a "$30 million loss in revenue."[215]

Questioned about the veto by the *Los Angeles Times*, Davis spokesperson Byron Tucker defended the commissions as "revenue that California is receiving rightfully for the services being provided."[216] Tucker did not specify who received the services in question. He likely meant imprisoned people and their families, who paid dearly to stay connected, but just as easily could have referred to telecom firms, which depended on the state for monopoly access to captive markets. Either way, Tucker affirmed, the state had a right to get paid.

Undeterred by Davis's veto, communities kept organizing for phone justice. "After years of pressure," the *Los Angeles Times* reported on the morning of the hearing at Trinity Baptist Church, "California officials this month signed contracts that will cut phone rates by 25 percent for most inmate calls—and also trim the annual commission the government pulls in" [to $26 million].[217] These changes did not go far enough for community leaders such as Reverend Richard Byrd, who demanded a phone rate reduction of at least 50 percent and a new policy to "redirect all of the [state's] profits, above the actual costs of monitoring the calls, into community-based reentry management programs for ex-offenders and their families."[218]

The hearings at Trinity Baptist Church were organized to push state legislators to change policy, but they also served a more expressive purpose: They gave church leaders, family members, and formerly imprisoned people an opportunity to make their frustration and suffering *public*. They wanted people in power—elected officials, telecom executives, agency heads, and journalists—to confront and acknowledge the hardships they endured as a result of phone policies that prioritized revenue over justice. As Reverend Jalani Kafela explained, the people in attendance came to "bring some sense of what our pain is really about at a local level."[219]

As shown throughout this chapter, the pains of criminal justice predation are all too familiar to people in RCS communities. As they drain resources out of poor neighborhoods, extractive practices strain the social bonds that hold families, friendships, and communities together. Their targets are trapped in poverty, burdened with "bad debt," hounded by collections agencies, threatened by state authorities, and subjected to years of surveillance and social control. Their life prospects are limited by damaged credit scores, exclusions from public programs, and pressures from judges, probation officers, and other state actors to accept any job that will allow them to keep up with payments. Fearing that missed payments will result in additional fees, fines, or even incarceration, they use the limited money they have for necessities like food, rent, utilities, and health care to keep the public and private holders of their criminal legal debts at bay.

The resulting strains are felt across myriad arenas of personal experience, from bouts of emotional and physical pain to public rituals of economic and civic degradation. Some of the most powerful forms of shame and pain, speakers at the Trinity hearings emphasized, take root in people's most valued and immediate social relationships. Predatory criminal legal practices turn legally entangled people into the reason for a friend or family member's misfortune. LFOs leave individuals less able to fulfill existing social obligations and, at the same time, create new social debts and expectations that can seed resentments and erode support networks.

Community members at the Trinity hearings were equally eager to convey their outrage at what they perceived as a lack of political representation and accountability. Their grievances focused particularly on Representative Roderick Wright (D-Dist. 35), chair of the state Assembly's Utility and Commerce Committee, who had refused to hold a committee hearing on phone justice and then declined to attend the Trinity event in South Los Angeles. "It is a sad day for us," Reverend Byrd testified, "when a public servant from one of the poorest communities in California, one that's suffering the most from this problem, is unwilling to find relief for his own constituents."[220] Reverend Kafela insisted that Wright's "failure to call the public hearing is reprehensible and must be held up as an example of a legislator that is out of touch with the needs of his constituents. And we hope that everyone will let him know that."[221]

The frustrations expressed by Kafela and others focused on an individual representative. As we have shown, however, predatory practices have deepened the political marginalization of RCS communities and diminished the political accountability of criminal legal institutions on a national scale since the 1980s. Revenue-centered projects have reshaped organizational cultures and routines in ways that subvert publicly stated agency missions and compromise public safety. They have subjected people in RCS communities to a steady stream of experiences that lead them to believe that state authorities see them as marks for plunder rather than citizens entitled to equal representation and protection.

To convey this feeling, many of the community members who spoke at Trinity Baptist Church protested that they were being treated as "criminals." Speaker after speaker included in their prepared remarks some version of this statement by Reverend Byrd: "It is my hope that you will remember that the families of offenders have not committed crimes. The only crime is being a family member of someone who is incarcerated."[222] At one level, the refrain expressed an objection to processes of criminalization that are unjustly applied to RCS communities as a whole: Inflated phone charges are unjust, in this rendering, because they punish people who have committed no crime *as if* they were criminals.

At another level, the refrain asserted something more general about the relationship between predation and citizenship. Community members and religious leaders wanted their representatives to know how it felt to be treated—by one's own government and under cover of law and justice—as a target of plunder. Refusing to silently accept this role, they demanded recognition as citizens of equal worth, with equal rights to be heard, represented, and protected from rapacious financial takings.

Criminal legal predation operates, in many ways, to reinforce the civic and political marginalization of RCS communities. The hearings at Trinity Baptist Church serve as a reminder, however, that perceptions of injustice can also generate powerful demands for change.[223] The year of the hearings, 2002, also underscores that community members and organizations have been mobilizing to fight criminal justice predation for decades. Indeed, they and their allies have won many significant victories. Just a couple years after the Trinity hearing, the state of California changed its phone policy so that, instead of being limited to collect calls, imprisoned people could make slightly less expensive prepaid phone calls. In time, the struggle for phone justice in California would produce much more substantial wins.

In 2007, Governor Arnold Schwarzenegger (R-CA) signed legislation to phase out the commissions that telecom companies paid to the state.[224] Since 2011, California's state government has not received a cut of corporate revenues from prison phone calls. (The telecoms still pay commissions to local governments. As of 2023, Los Angeles County was bringing in roughly $30 million a year.[225]) State officials went even further in March 2021, locking in a six-year contract with Global Tel-Link (GTL) that eliminated the $3 fee to establish a GTL account and significantly reduced prices for phone calls. As a result, the California Department of Corrections and Rehabilitation said, "a normal fifteen-minute telephone call anywhere in the US [would] cost just 37.5 cents" and imprisoned individuals would receive one free fifteen-minute call every two weeks.[226] The state predicted that the new contract would save imprisoned people and their loved ones roughly $17 million a year. Karen McDaniel, executive director of the reform group Place4Grace, celebrated the victory: "It wasn't long ago when the cost of phone calls was just prohibitive. . . . Literally, we as families had to choose between 'are we going to have phone calls, or are we going to have milk?'"[227]

After the state and GTL inked the contract, Kathleen Allison, secretary of the Department of Corrections and Rehabilitation, predictably gave credit to government leaders and affirmed her agency's public service values. Secretary Allison did not mention the community groups that had waged long, arduous campaigns for phone justice, nor did she try to explain why their demands had been ignored and sidelined for so long. Like many leaders in the criminal legal field, Allison presented a vision of reform scrubbed clean of opposition groups and their struggles to force change upon reluctant governing authorities. Notably, the fierce, sustained efforts of California activists and advocates would eventually lead the state legislature to make prison phone calls free in 2022.[228] It is to these groups and the political campaigns they wage across the nation that we now turn.

10 * Political Struggle and the Fight to End Predation

In May 2017, the state of California charged Kenneth Humphrey, a sixty-three-year-old Black man, with burglary, robbery, elder abuse, and theft for stealing $5 and a bottle of cologne from a neighbor.[1] At the arraignment, the public defender asked the judge to release Humphrey without financial bail, noting his age and poverty, community ties, and willingness to seek treatment for chemical dependency. Humphrey had a record, the defense acknowledged, but he had not been charged with a crime in twenty-five years. In the past, he had always shown up for court. A restraining order, his attorney argued, would suffice to protect the alleged victim. The prosecutor, citing Humphrey's record, the current charges, and a pretrial assessment, argued that Humphrey posed a danger to the public and, therefore, should have to post a hefty bail.[2] The judge agreed and set bail at $600,000 (later reduced to $350,000). Unable to pay the price or secure the services of a bail bond company, Humphrey was stuck in jail.[3]

Jeff Adachi, the elected public defender of San Francisco, saw the case as an injustice—and an opportunity to challenge the state's pretrial system, in which judges routinely set high monetary bail conditions and bond companies and other entities extracted revenues from defendants and their families. Adachi's office partnered with Civil Rights Corps, a legal outfit that contests predatory criminal legal practices nationwide. Together, they filed a habeas petition with the state court of appeals, arguing that the judge failed to consider Humphrey's ability to pay before setting a bail amount beyond his means. The judge, they said, had effectively ordered pretrial detention, and he had done so without considering whether noncustodial release conditions were adequate to protect public safety and ensure an appearance at court, as the law required. These actions, the team argued, violated Humphrey's constitutional right to equal protection and due process.

In January 2018, the court of appeals sided with Humphrey, who, by then, had been detained for six months. The court ordered a "new bail hearing at which the court inquires into and determines [Humphrey's] ability to pay, considers nonmonetary alternatives to money bail, and, if it determines [the] petitioner is unable to afford the amount of bail the court finds necessary, follows the procedures and makes the findings necessary for a valid order of detention."[4] Shortly thereafter, San Francisco District Attorney George Gascón asked the state supreme court to review the case and explicitly state that judges still held the authority to remand defendants in the interest of public safety.[5] Three years later, the California Supreme Court ruled for Humphrey, effectively affirming a right to affordable bail in California—something the US Supreme Court has never done. The decision also confirmed, as Gascón had hoped, that judges *could* detain defendants if they determined that no other options would sufficiently protect public safety or ensure appearance at court.[6]

After four years of struggle, the victors celebrated. "This landmark ruling is one of the most important decisions in recent history in terms of racial justice and #MassIncarceration," Civil Rights Corps tweeted.[7] But some advocates underscored the tough fight still to come. After all, the *Humphrey* ruling was a process reform. It only set procedures for judges to follow. It did not define "ability to pay" or establish criteria for deciding which defendants could afford bail. It also did little to curb existing practices of pretrial surveillance and social control. Under *Humphrey*, judges could still order pretrial detention or highly restrictive release conditions, such as electronic monitoring. Moreover, they retained the ability to order monetary bail and, depending on how they defined "affordable," push defendants into the waiting arms of bail bond companies.

To win broader change, Civil Rights Corps and other groups established the Care First Coalition. Rooted in abolitionist principles, the coalition advocates for a state law to ban cash bail, limit pretrial detention, curb restrictive release conditions, and end court-based financial takings. These groups understand that their work will be contested at every step by powerful opponents such as Crime Victims United of California, law enforcement organizations, and the bail bond lobby. For instance, in 2018, these opponents were so successful at pressuring lawmakers to water down a statewide bail reform bill that even liberal groups like the American Civil Liberties Union (ACLU) ended up opposing the measure. And though the bill passed into law, it was scrapped before it could be implemented, killed off by a ballot initiative pushed by the bail bond lobby in 2020.[8]

The uneven story of pretrial reform in California raises dispiriting questions. Why has it been so hard to win victories that curb or end predatory criminal legal practices? Why have so many policy wins produced far less positive change than they initially seemed to promise? Yet the same story can be read as a *challenge* to political cynicism and despair. It shows that efforts to fight predatory criminal legal practices can succeed in nontrivial ways. *Humphrey*, for instance, stands as just one among many victories won by antipredation campaigns across the country in recent years.[9] These successes raise important questions, too: What kinds of smaller wins are needed to move toward the ultimate goal of ending criminal justice predation? What kinds of political conditions and strategies make sizable victories more likely? And how can advocates respond to the significant obstacles they confront?

In this chapter, we start with the barriers to change, before digging into the remarkable growth of organized antipredation groups and efforts in the past two decades. Undaunted by disappointments, these groups have won important victories; we take stock of both, analyzing the lessons learned from the activists' efforts and considering how they might inform political action going forward.

Barriers to Change

To understand the politics of criminal justice predation today, we must begin with the people who endure its greatest injustices. Predation, as we've shown throughout this book, targets marginalized populations, finding its epicenter in race-class subjugated (RCS) communities and radiating outward to other (mostly disadvantaged) groups.[10] In various ways, all such communities stand at the intersection of two richly documented sources of distortion for democratic ideals in America: race and class.

RCS communities are deeply disadvantaged in electoral-representative politics. A thick web of institutional barriers curtails their ability to exercise voting rights.[11] They hold few of the resources—wealth, political connections, or institutional positions of authority—needed to succeed in political arenas, leaving them underrepresented and outgunned in the battles waged by organized interest groups,[12] and they are often sidelined in strategic efforts to build coalitions and recruit people into action.[13] Electoral and policy contests rarely focus on the issues that matter most to RCS communities (such matters are, in effect, organized out of the prevailing terms of conflict).[14] And, of course, RCS communities' civic and political marginalization is deepened by the pernicious effects of criminal justice predation.

Research testifies to the far-reaching consequences of these disadvantages. Empirical studies find that policymaking is so attuned to upper-class influence that the preferences of people in the lower third of the income distribution register little to no effect.[15] The US has fallen into an "inequality trap," in which stark disparities of wealth and political power reinforce each other in a feedback loop.[16] Racial biases are equally severe. White Americans remain greatly overrepresented in elected offices and wield outsized influence over electoral and policy outcomes.[17] Black Americans, among all racial/ethnic groups, fare worst of all in the political arena: They "lose more on policy; they lose more consistently across policy areas; and they lose more consistently over time."[18]

For RCS communities, conventional modes of political participation have rarely been sufficient to win relief from social injustices and practices of authoritarian rule.[19] On matters of policing and punishment, political obstacles have been especially formidable. Communities associated with crime and disorder are widely pathologized in US politics—portrayed as unworthy of social empathy and deserving of whatever harsh treatment they receive. As discussed in chapter 5, long-standing sociopolitical discourses have woven Blackness and criminality together, making each central to the other's meaning. And when RCS communities decry policing and penal practices, elected officials often engage in a kind of "selective hearing," calibrated to support their own political agendas. As Elizabeth Hinton, Julilly Kohler-Hausmann, and Vesla Weaver observe, "when Blacks ask for *better* policing, legislators tend to hear *more* instead."[20]

The prevailing structure of two-party competition presents additional obstacles. Although bipartisan support for mass policing and punishment has a long history,[21] crime and punishment remain powerful tools of partisan combat. For Republicans, debates over efforts to limit predation are opportunities to sow division in the opposing party's coalition and frame "liberal agendas" as a threat to public safety. Democrats trying to weather such attacks have strong incentives to water down reforms, and some take hardline positions, hoping to preempt or refute charges that they are soft on crime. Such strategies have been inviting, in part, because RCS communities have been positioned as "captured minorities" in the Democratic coalition: Party leaders and officeholders have usually seen them as reliable supporters (unlikely to cast their ballots for Republicans) and worried that visible efforts to relieve their hardships might alienate the White supporters they depend on for votes and campaign contributions.[22]

In the fight against criminal justice predation, these obstacles have been compounded by two kinds of policy feedback effects.[23] First, the growth of financial extraction has combined with the growth of criminal legal operations to multiply and strengthen actors with material stakes in predatory revenues. Threats to these revenues tend to mobilize coalitions of law enforcement unions, professional associations, and agency leaders as well as actors elsewhere in government who have come to depend on predatory takings to supplement their budgets. The corporate partners of public criminal legal agencies now fight to defend and expand their operations. For example, the profits flowing to telecom companies (see chapter 3) and to bail bond insurance companies (see chapter 6) fund highly organized political lobbies with the deep pockets and political clout.

Actor-centered effects have been reinforced by institutional forms of policy feedback. Extractive practices have become deeply entrenched in the criminal legal field, justified by organizational cultures and normalized as just "how things work." Predatory revenue has allowed operations to grow beyond what could be afforded by tax-based funding alone. Thus, many of the institutional actors best positioned to influence change have strong incentives to protect the status quo. In the absence of substantial increases in other sources of public funding, agency leaders are likely to view restrictions on predatory practices as costly and disruptive.

Similarly, heavy reliance on for-profit partners has allowed criminal legal operations to grow far beyond what could be sustained via public administrative capacities alone. The federal government, for example, now holds so many noncitizens in private detention centers that a dissolution of these partnerships would require a radical change in immigration policy or a massive investment of public funds in government-run facilities.[24] Federal officials cannot significantly reduce the flow of profits to CoreCivic and GEO Group, the industry leaders in private detention, without incurring massive costs or abandoning their current approach to immigration.[25] In this area and many others, government dependence on for-profit capacities now poses a significant barrier to rolling back revenue-enhancing modes of criminal legal governance.

Partly for these reasons, even modest reform proposals tend to draw fierce resistance. Moreover, the powerful actors who fight to sustain predatory operations enjoy significant institutional advantages. In cross-national perspective, the US political system is particularly geared toward preserving the status quo.[26] The system's structural features—often celebrated as institutional "checks and balances"—create an extraordinary number of veto points where a single win by a well-positioned opposing group can scuttle a proposal with broad support.[27] In the US Congress, for example, a string of committee and subcommittee victories is usually needed before a floor vote; passage requires a majority in both chambers; and filibuster rules often make a supermajority (sixty of one hundred votes) necessary for a victory in the Senate. For these and other reasons, political scientists often describe Congress as "the graveyard of reform."[28] If a proposal survives these obstacles, the president must agree to its passage and, even then, it may still be overturned by a court or undermined by implementing agencies. At all levels of government, antipredation

campaigns compete on a "terrifically difficult" field where "once a program is implemented and takes root, it is almost as difficult to repeal."[29]

Federalism exacerbates these disadvantages. Because criminal legal
governance is largely a state and local affair in the US, the political struggles that surround it take place on a highly fragmented field of jurisdictions and institutional venues. Across these arenas, big corporate actors
(like CoreCivic) and national pressure groups (like the American Bail Coalition) are repeat players. In addition to resource advantages, they typically enter state and local conflicts with experienced personnel, materials,
strategies, and arguments honed through earlier battles. In subnational
arenas, organizations representing police, prosecutors, and other criminal
legal authorities also tend to be veterans of the game who have cultivated
allies, learned how to exploit technical procedures, and demonstrated
their ability to reward or punish officeholders. State and local challengers
rarely possess such political advantages.[30]

Because RCS communities are often spatially segregated and socially
isolated, they also tend to be systematically disadvantaged in efforts to
win support from mass publics. Few people outside RCS communities are
aware of the predatory injustices they endure, and stigmatizing narratives
of "underclass pathology" provide a powerful basis for social indifference.
Awash in racialized discourses about violent crime, many Americans are
primed to take the bait when defenders of the status quo work to gin up
fear-based resistance to reforms.[31] After decades of neoliberal rule, many
are also prone to accept claims that criminal legal financial charges are
normal consumer transactions, similar to what they experience in their
daily lives (recall chapter 5).

If and when reform campaigns gain traction, defenders of predation
often enjoy structural advantages in broadcasting their messages through
media outlets due to the institutional positions they hold (e.g., police
chiefs and heads of departments of corrections). Public and private actors
invested in predation roll out the full range of legitimizing rationales
analyzed in chapter 5. Frequently, they turn to two forms of what Albert
O. Hirschman calls the rhetoric of reaction: the perversity thesis and the
jeopardy thesis.[32] The first argues that a proposal meant to improve a
situation will, perversely, make it worse. For example, when Virginia
lawmakers considered a proposal to improve prison health care by eliminating a $5 copay (which deterred medical visits), opponents argued the
plan would "lead inmates to abuse the program just to get out of their
cells" and, thus, overwhelm and imperil the healthcare services upon
which such individuals depend.[33]

The jeopardy thesis asserts that, beyond its intended goals, a proposed
action will threaten some other highly valued state of affairs. In just this

way, defenders of monetary bail argue that even if bail reforms help defendants, they will endanger public safety by releasing "dangerous criminals."[34] When proposals target predatory practices, defenders frequently argue that the changes will force the government to levy unacceptable taxes on people "who play by the rules." For instance, when a group of New York Democrats tried to raise the minimum wage for imprisoned workers to $3 an hour, Republican State Senator Daphne Johnson predicted dire effects: "[With this] higher minimum wage for incarcerated criminals . . . the senate Democratic majority are driving New York even deeper into the fiscal ditch. Worse still, senate Democrats expect law-abiding, hardworking taxpayers to foot the bill."[35]

All of these factors help to explain why campaigns against predation are so hard to win—and why their victories are so impressive. Some also help to explain why many celebrated policy victories have proved to be ephemeral or far less consequential than expected.

After reforms are passed, opponents often fight to unravel them. Bail reform in New York offers a case in point. When advocates secured a state law that abolished monetary bail for most misdemeanors and nonviolent felonies in 2019, the bail industry lobby, law enforcement groups, opposing lawmakers, and media outlets mobilized public outrage by framing the reform and its supporters as serious threats to public safety.[36] Under political pressure, prominent Democratic proponents of the reform, such as Governor Andrew Cuomo and New York City Mayor Bill de Blasio, pivoted to calling for a rollback of key provisions.[37] State lawmakers quickly passed ancillary legislation.[38] Thus, only a few months after it took effect—and despite ample evidence that nonmonetary conditions of release do *not* put public safety at risk[39]—the statewide reform was substantially undercut.

The New York case illustrates one way that policy victories can come undone: backlash and reversal. Bureaucratic resistance or subversion is another. That is, once reforms are enacted, opponents inside or outside government may try to undercut their implementation. For instance, they sometimes work to pressure or weaken the implementing agency.[40] Administrative and judicial actors may also have their own reasons to pursue what Daniel Carpenter calls "institutional strangulation," especially when they perceive change as threats to their operational resources, reputations, "turf," or professional autonomy.[41] In many instances, discretion in individual cases can also be used to deny individuals legally guaranteed protections and benefits.[42]

In Atlanta, for example, Mayor Keisha Lance Bottoms passed an ordinance to shift courts toward the use of (nonfinancial) signature bonds and set new ability-to-pay rules when it came to monetary bail conditions.

A subsequent study of 700 court hearings revealed that judges failed to follow the new rules about 40 percent of the time.[43] A retrospective assessment concluded: "Politicians' promises and legislative victories grab headlines and buoy our spirits. But the hardest work comes after."[44]

The struggle to implement the Humphrey ruling discussed at the beginning of this chapter offers another good example. A report released in October 2022 found that the ruling had not led to reductions in pretrial detention or made bail more affordable for defendants in California.[45] Rachel Wallace, a coauthor of the report, explained: "All of the records and data we received point to the alarming conclusion that many judges are not following the mandates of the Humphrey decision."[46] Judges continued to set unaffordable bail and "often ignore[d] the requirement that they consider less restrictive alternatives to detention."[47] There is little evidence that judges were under political pressure to subvert the intent of Humphrey. More likely, they simply resisted changes to established court routines, norms, and assumptions (e.g., the idea that defendants need financial "skin in the game" to show up for court and that, absent strict control, they will harm themselves or others while on pretrial release).[48]

Policy victories can also be undermined by administrative burdens— onerous procedures that make it hard for legally entangled individuals to receive what has been promised by law.[49] For example, many jurisdictions have passed ability-to-pay reforms that create graduated monetary sanctions (imposed on a sliding scale) or shield people from driver's license suspensions, revocations of probation or parole, or expensive bail conditions.[50] In some cases, however, individuals can only obtain relief if they are able to bear substantial administrative burdens. Theresa Zhen writes that "The intrusiveness of the [financial] determinations" can be uncomfortable and hard to endure and "the documentation requirements create enormous burdens for low-income individuals," who must assemble proof of their economic circumstances.[51]

Intergovernmental challenges can also undercut reforms. When California lawmakers banned for-profit detention facilities throughout the state, the Trump administration sued, arguing that the state's ban discriminated against the federal government and obstructed its ability to carry out vital operations.[52] And when district court judges in North Carolina made a pact to waive certain court-based fines and fees, state lawmakers sought to undercut the agreement. They directed the Administrative Office of the Courts to monitor and report local judges' waiver rates and required the judges to provide a fifteen-day notice to all agencies at risk of losing revenue—from jails and county offices to school systems—*before* issuing a financial waiver to a defendant.[53]

Local officials sometimes challenge state-level reforms as well. For example, when the New Mexico legislature effectively banned civil asset forfeiture in 2015, the city of Albuquerque "argued the state law didn't apply to its own city codes and continued to seize cars."[54] When the predatory regime in Ferguson, Missouri became a subject of widespread protest and condemnation, the state legislature capped the percentage of total revenue that local governments could generate from tickets and fines and the state supreme court made it illegal to pursue debt collections by jailing people for nonpayment. Forced to end their jail-based collection efforts, local officials adapted by hiring aggressive private collection agencies.[55] Several municipalities even sued to overturn the state's cap on fine and citation revenue.[56]

Private companies respond to reforms with similar tactics of adaptation, evasion, and confrontation. "When reforms threaten . . . revenue streams," Alex Kornya and colleagues note, "predatory industry actors will not simply disappear—they will devote their resources first to resisting the policy changes, and then (where that fails) adapt their business models to extract wealth within the new system."[57] For example, when reforms have cut into the profits generated by state and federal prisons, private prison companies have successfully pursued new sites of investment, such as immigrant detention and prisoner reentry (see chapter 3).

For all these reasons, battles against criminal justice predation are always uphill. And yet, organized opposition is making strides, continually and creatively working to effect—as well as to protect and to institutionalize—change at all levels of criminal legal governance.

Mobilization Against Predation

Across the nation, people and communities subjected to criminal justice predation are fighting back. This observation may seem to contradict our argument in chapter 9 that predation operates as a powerful force of civic and political marginalization. The dynamics are not mutually exclusive, however. Oppressive and exploitative regimes often give rise to complex political responses. The same practices that subjugate and marginalize can also spur collective resistance.

Responses to oppression and hardship depend, first and foremost, on how people interpret their experiences.[58] This insight stands at the center of scholarship on "collective action frames." Reviewing this literature, William Gamson stresses that *injustice* frames are particularly critical to political mobilization.[59] "Different emotions can be stimulated by perceived inequities," he explains, but "injustice focuses the righteous anger that puts fire in the belly and iron in the soul."[60] Perceptions of injustice do not always lead to action. But when they connect personal travails to collective inequities and identify "motivated human actors that carry some of the weight bringing about harm and suffering" (putting "heat into the cognition"[61]), they can provide a powerful basis for resistance.[62]

Building on these insights, scholars such as Hannah Walker have developed a complementary counterpoint to research demonstrating how criminal legal encounters contribute to political marginalization.[63] As we discussed in chapter 9, such encounters can convey powerful lessons that cultivate legal estrangement and political withdrawal. Like all social experiences, though, such encounters are open to interpretation. "To be politicized by interactions with the [criminal legal] system," Walker explains, "one must believe not only that what happened . . . was unfair . . . but also that [the] unfair experiences were a result of systematic targeting on the basis of race, place, or class."[64] The seedbed of political mobilization in the criminal legal context, Walker concludes, is a sense of systemic, collective injustice.

From this perspective, our analysis of predation suggests several spurs to community mobilization. Because predation is socially and spatially concentrated, people in RCS communities repeatedly see evidence that *their neighborhoods* and *people like them* are singled out for coercive takings. All the worse, these takings are justified in the name of public safety and law. If a community member has not directly experienced predation, someone close to them likely has. The pervasiveness of such experiences in RCS communities seeds perceptions that the system selectively targets people because of who they are and where they live.

Equally important, the people who endure predatory takings have not, in many cases, been charged with or convicted of any crime. No charge is needed when police use forfeiture laws to seize money and goods. Defendants and their loved ones can pay hundreds or thousands of dollars in bail costs in cases that do not lead to convictions. Friends and family members, accused of no violation, are forced to pawn their belongings, take out payday loans, and spend what little they have to pay mounting criminal legal bills. It is little wonder, then, that some come to see their plight as part of a profound collective injustice.

The "heat" in such cognitions arises too from the ways that predatory practices threaten the material and social foundations of community life. In an ethnographic study of popular resistance in Bolivia and Mexico, Erica Simmons explains that ordinary people are especially likely to rise up in opposition when governments and corporations threaten "subsistence goods . . . that [they] see as essential material resources, symbols of cultural tradition, and anchors for highly valued social practices." When people believe powerful actors have "put relationships with [such] goods at risk," Simmons concludes, "material and symbolic worlds are both at stake; citizens take to the streets to defend not only their pocketbooks but also their perceptions of community."[65]

Simmons's analysis encourages attention to how predation operates as a socially *meaningful* act of governance. Practices that strip people of resources needed for material survival also tear at the social fabric of community life. When police routinely impose tickets on drivers, bicyclists, and pedestrians, they imperil shared public space, turning ordinary movements through the neighborhood into perilous ventures. Financial takings undercut people's abilities to meet social obligations to children, elders, romantic partners, and peers. Driver's license suspensions—and jail stays for people who cannot afford to pay for bail or debts—have a similar effect, as they jeopardize jobs and incomes. In these and many other ways, predation threatens the resources, social practices, and norms of reciprocity so foundational to communities.

Local organizations and organizers are key in fostering shared feelings of systemic injustice and turning them into collective action.[66] In her study of criminal legal contact and political action, Walker stresses the mediating role played by community-based organizations (CBOs). Churches, nonprofits, local advocacy groups, service providers, and other CBOs "help individuals overcome efficacy and resource barriers to participation."[67] They provide "a natural point of contact for those who are already mobilized and are looking for a way to participate."[68] And they create opportunities for interactions that encourage other community members to see their personal travails and crises through "a larger frame of injustice."[69]

CBOs are not the only organizations that have strengthened opposition to criminal justice predation in recent years, however. Across the country, organizations with justice-centered missions have been recruited into the fight by community activists or, for other reasons, have come to see predation as fitting within their missions. Against a backdrop of mass protest, the US Department of Justice's (DOJ's) 2015 *Ferguson Report* (and the media attention and public outrage it helped to generate) proved critical for many such organizations.

For decades, advocacy groups have worked to reform unjust sentencing laws, police practices, probation and parole conditions, and prison operations. As activists, researchers, and journalists drew attention to predatory practices in this domain, many justice-centered organizations developed new initiatives that focused on fines and fees, cash bail, and asset forfeiture. Such groups span the political spectrum, from liberal stalwarts like the Vera Institute of Justice and the ACLU to libertarian-conservative outfits like the Cato Institute and the Justice Policy Institute. In many cases, such organizations supply resources, promotional capacities, and forms of legal and technical expertise that CBOs and activists need to covert "heat" into effective political action.

More radical groups devoted to prison and police abolition have made similar moves. Since its founding in the 1990s, for example, Critical Resistance has fought to dismantle the "prison industrial complex" based on guiding principles that center racial and economic injustices. For years, it focused on blocking carceral expansion and shrinking existing operations. More recently, it has launched new efforts to fight predatory practices, such as cash bail and court fines and fees.[70] "Bail reform," Critical Resistance argues, "must be used as yet another way to expose the white supremacist foundations of policing and work to abolish policing and the use of fines and fees that force people into jail in the first place."[71]

As protest movements joined the fight against predation, they connected it to broader networks of activists and organizations. Some advocates came from the Occupy movement against economic inequality, corporate greed, and money-driven politics. In 2015, four years after police forcibly ended the occupation of Zuccotti Park (the heart of the movement), Michael Levitin insisted that Occupy Wall Street had not faded away; it had "splintered and regrown into a variety of focused causes."[72] Scholars refer to this process as "spillover," the tendency for movements to transition into new issue areas and organizational forms after they have peaked.[73] In the case of Occupy, spillover gave rise to the Debt Collective, a "union for debtors" that "fights *against* predatory financial contracts and *for* the universal provision of public goods . . . so that people don't have to go into debt to access them."[74] The group came to see criminal justice predation as integral to its mission and began to provide aid to legal debtors, help cosigners of bail contracts challenge unlawful debts, and work with coalitions to end criminal legal fees.[75]

Movements that center racial justice have also supplied essential activist networks and organizational support. From early on, the Movement for Black Lives (M4BL) approached police and vigilante killings of Black people through an intersectional lens and treated them as an anchor for broad agendas of societal transformation.[76] When the M4BL and allied groups issued a policy platform in 2016, they demanded "an end to money bail, mandatory fines, fees, court surcharges and 'defendant funded' court proceedings" and "an immediate end to the privatization of police, prisons, jails, probation, parole, food, phone and all other criminal justice related services."[77]

Racial justice advocacy organizations—including older operations like the NAACP and Southern Poverty Law Center and newer ones like Color of Change—also incorporated predation into their agendas. Color of Change was founded in 2005, a response to the racial injustices surrounding Hurricane Katrina. Initially, the group's efforts to hold governments and corporations accountable for the harms they caused in RCS communities included little predation-related work. Today, however, its platform includes "ending money bail [and] profit incentives fueling mass incarceration," "decriminalizing poverty," and stopping "prison labor exploitation."[78]

Rising opposition to criminal justice predation in the twenty-first century has emerged through a confluence of developments. As predatory practices generated compounding harms in RCS communities, they supplied a powerful basis for shared perceptions of systemic, group-based injustice. Community organizing and activism, policy advocacy, and the *Ferguson Report* all helped to raise media coverage and public attention. Social movement networks, justice-oriented organizations, and progressive political leaders took note, and a growing number began to integrate criminal justice predation into their struggles for social justice.

Victories and Disappointments

Antipredation campaigns take many forms, and they are spread across a fragmented field of conflict. It can be hard to "see" the full scope of opposition, and so, analytically and politically, it helps to step back from particular contests and take stock of the whole. In this section, we explore what Charles Tilly calls the prevailing "repertoire of contention"—the range of actions that, in a time and place, activists and advocates experience as imaginable, practical, and efficacious.[79] Our goal is to understand how challengers have made headway and why specific tactics have gained more traction in some areas than others.

Bail reform efforts have been widespread in recent years, and litigation has become a prime means of contention.[80] The *Humphrey* case is just one of many examples. In 2016, Civil Rights Corps partnered with state-level organizations to file a lawsuit against Harris County, Texas, alleging that its bail procedures produced "automatic wealth-based detention."[81] Harris County judges set misdemeanor bail amounts based on a fixed schedule that ignored ability to pay, leading to extensive pretrial detention.[82] A federal court ruled in 2017 that the "policy and practice" violated the equal protection and due process clauses of the US Constitution.[83] Two years later, the county accepted a consent decree that rescinded the fixed schedule, set new procedural safeguards, and mandated nonmonetary release for most misdemeanors.[84] As a result, the percentage of misdemeanor cases in which financial bail was set fell from 92 percent in 2015 to 14 percent in 2020.[85]

In 2019, legal advocates in San Francisco used an innovative "crimsumerism" strategy to sue Bad Boy Bail Bonds (BBBB), arguing that the business's debt-payment plans qualified as "consumer credit arrangements" and were, thus, subject to consumer protection laws. BBBB had violated cosigners' rights, they claimed, by failing to provide written notification that its plans defined contractual obligations and liabilities. The court agreed and barred BBBB from collecting existing bail debts estimated at roughly $38 million.[86] This local win effectively expanded the repertoire of contention, establishing a new basis for challenging other bail practices that run afoul of California's consumer protection laws, such as threatening cosigners with arrest and aggressively harassing debtors. This new "crimsumerism" strategy holds promise for challenges to commercial bail in other states and may offer a way to contest a broader range of criminal legal business practices. The National Consumer Law Center has since published a how-to manual to help advocates apply "consumer laws to commercial bail, prison retail, and private debt collection."[87]

The prominence of litigation in the bail arena partly reflects the difficulty of winning legislative contests, wherein opponents often have powerful allies and can use an abundance of veto points to block criminal legal reforms.[88] Such obstacles are not insurmountable, however. In recent years, reformers have scored legislative victories in a handful of states.[89] In Illinois, advocates won a blanket prohibition of monetary bail conditions. In some other states, advocates secured bans on cash bail for people charged with minor offenses (Colorado) or specific sets of misdemeanors and "nonviolent" felonies (the scaled-back outcome in New York). In New Jersey, a 2017 law mandated release on recognizance for defendants deemed "low risk" and limited financial conditions to "extreme" cases. Two years after it took effect, judges set financial bail conditions in only forty-three cases *statewide*.[90] With so few potential clients, the state's bail bond industry is crumbling.[91]

Although they are modest in number, such legislative wins underscore the important role that elections can play in setting the stage for policy change—a dynamic that has been equally important for bureaucratic and judicial advances. In recent years, elected prosecutors in cities such as Los Angeles and Philadelphia have taken significant steps to curb cash bail practices. In San Francisco, Chesa Boudin (a former public defender who at one point represented Kenneth Humphrey) ran for district attorney as an outspoken reformer; after winning, he used his position to establish a policy forbidding "prosecutors from requesting money bail under any circumstances."[92] (Notably, Boudin was later recalled from office through a campaign that blamed his reforms for crime.) In the Harris County case discussed earlier, county officials agreed to sign the bail settlement only after a slate of reformist candidates, *all* Black women, swept the judicial elections.[93]

Outcomes over the past two decades also highlight the vital roles played by community-based activists and organizations in bail reform. Protests, often tied to broader calls for justice, have helped to push the issue onto government agendas and raise political pressures for action.[94] Organizers have mobilized community members to vote for reformers and to monitor and hold court officials accountable.[95] Local groups have also intervened directly in the financial machinery of bail predation. Community bail funds, which have existed for over a century but have grown dramatically in recent years, raise money to release defendants (typically with modest bonds) from jail. The Bail Project, a national fund, reports that from 2017 through June 2021, it "posted over $46 million in bail for nearly 18,000 people."[96] The Minnesota Freedom Fund, which received a huge influx of donations after the police killing of George Floyd, now pays for the release of defendants with sizable bails.[97] By paying for bail directly, such organizations offer relief to legally entangled people and potentially deprive bail companies of clients and profits.

Challenges to *civil asset forfeiture* (CAF) have worked a bit differently. In this area, liberal and left opponents, who tend to see CAF as an oppressive tool of social control and exploitation, have often been joined by libertarian-conservative groups, who tend to view CAF as a big-government assault on property rights and individual liberty. The resulting opportunities for bipartisan advocacy have made legislative strategies more promising for CAF than for bail.[98] Between 2014 and the end of 2021, thirty-six states and the District of Columbia reformed their forfeiture laws.[99] In 2017 alone, over one hundred CAF-related bills were introduced in legislatures across all fifty states.[100]

The enacted reforms have varied greatly in scope and ambition.[101] Four states abolished CAF, while a larger group made them conditional, in some or all cases, on prosecutors securing a conviction. Over a dozen states passed laws to make it easier to challenge seizures in court, shifting the burden of proof to governments so that individuals do not have to prove the "innocence" of their assets to get them back.

In some states, legislators took an incentive-based approach, limiting law enforcement agencies' abilities to directly benefit from the assets they seize. Seven states and Washington, DC now limit the use of all such funds to non–law enforcement purposes. Other states have set percentages that can be delivered to local law enforcement,[102] hoping that limits on self-funding through CAF will shift police agencies' focus from revenue seeking to public safety goals. The strategy carries risks, however. By spreading the proceeds, it expands the number of government entities with a stake in forfeiture-based revenue. Effectively, more actors acquire new material reasons to defend CAF—or even to pressure law enforcement agencies to seize more goods (see chapter 9).

The most common legislative actions have imposed softer, process-centered reforms designed to promote transparency. Twenty-six states and Washington, DC now require public agencies to keep and report records regarding forfeitures. When Alabama made the change in 2019, Jennifer McDonald of the Institute for Justice noted that reporting mandates might facilitate bigger victories down the road: "By itself, improved transparency cannot fix the fundamental problems with civil forfeiture— namely, the property rights abuses it permits and the temptation it creates to police for profit. [Still, it is] a welcome first step for keeping both the public and legislators well-informed."[103] Reporting requirements, in this view, can provide advocates with helpful ammunition for legislative campaigns, lawsuits, and mobilization efforts in the future.

Despite their many differences, CAF and bail reform campaigns have been equally dependent on electoral politics. Under the Obama administration in 2015, for example, US Attorney General Eric Holder forbid federal agencies from "adopting" and distributing the assets that state and local law enforcement agencies seized under federal law—a practice that had ballooned under the equitable sharing program.[104] After President Trump won office in 2016, however, Attorney General Jeff Sessions reversed the rule, explicitly to "increase forfeitures."[105]

In Philadelphia, where voters elected former defense attorney Larry Krasner as district attorney in 2017, electoral, legal, and bureaucratic tactics converged with community action to create a powerful force for change. Litigation set the stage when the Institute for Justice filed a class action suit to challenge Philadelphia's forfeiture practices in 2014.[106] Grassroots organizations pushed CAF onto the public agenda, partnered with the Krasner campaign, and worked hard to bring voters to the polls. Decarcerate PA, a coalition of reform organizations, threw its support behind Krasner and pushed him to oppose CAF.[107] Krasner embraced the issue on the campaign trail and, after taking office, pushed for a settlement of the class action suit, which included major reforms and $3 million in restitution payments.[108] He also made good on his promise to reduce the use of CAF and direct a portion of proceeds to nonprofit organizations. Philadelphia's CAF program was not abolished, but it became smaller and less rapacious.[109]

Of the tactics used to challenge CAF, litigation has produced the most discussed victory to date: the 2019 US Supreme Court decision in *Timbs v. Indiana*. Tyson Timbs was arrested for selling small amounts of heroin to an undercover agent. The court sentenced him to one year of home detention and five years of probation, and it charged him $1,203 in fees. The police, acting under Indiana's CAF law, seized a Land Rover that Timbs had purchased for $42,000, using funds he received from his father's life insurance policy. Timbs sued the state, claiming the seizure violated the excessive fines clause of the US Constitution. The Indiana Supreme Court ruled against him, holding that the clause pertained only to federal government, not to states. In 2019, however, the US Supreme Court overruled, affirming that states must adhere to the excessive fines clause and that its protections cover civil forfeitures as well as criminal fines.

The effects of the ruling have been subject to debate. Some argue that it will produce little change because the Court did not declare forfeitures "excessive" or even provide lower courts with guidance for making such determinations.[110] Others are more optimistic.[111] Lisa Foster, codirector of the Fines and Fees Justice Center, argues that the ruling gave advocates "a new tool [they can] use to end . . . the imposition of fees and excessive fines and forfeitures. . . . They can go to state and local governments and talk about the Supreme Court opinion and if necessary [use it to sue them for imposing] excessive fines, fees, and forfeitures."[112] Emma Andersson, senior staff attorney at the ACLU, sees the decision as "an invitation [for advocates] to litigate these claims more often and push courts to make the excessive fines clause a more robust protection."[113] Veterans of the struggle over predation, Foster and Andersson emphasize the potential for creative litigators to turn precedents like *Timbs* into bigger wins down the road.

Like CAF, predatory *fine-and-fee* practices have sometimes drawn opposition from coalitions that bridge political divides—especially in the case of sanctions imposed for unpaid legal financial obligations (LFOs). Free to Drive, a coalition of "over one hundred ideologically diverse organizations," leads a national campaign to end state practices that suspend or revoke the driver's licenses of legal debtors. Since 2017, it has helped push twenty-four states and Washington, DC to pass laws to "curb debt-based driving suspensions."[114] Some members of Free to Drive have also joined the fight against LFO-based incarceration. Here, as in the case of bail, legal advocates have often built litigation around the idea of "ability to pay." The charges of willful disobedience that courts use to justify debt-based incarceration presume that debtors have enough money to pay what they owe; they just choose not to (see chapter 9). Litigators have argued that judges routinely fail to check whether this is true and, in so doing, violate people's constitutional rights.

In 2015, ArchCity Defenders, an advocacy organization based in St. Louis, Missouri, joined forces with Civil Rights Corps and the St. Louis

University School of Law Legal Clinic to file class action lawsuits against the cities of Jennings and Ferguson, Missouri. In both cities, they argued, officials illegally locked up individuals for nonpayment of LFOs without considering their ability to pay or the possibility of imposing alternative (i.e., non-imprisonment) sanctions.[115] Alec Karakatsanis of Civil Rights Corps describes the depth of injustices challenged by the lawsuits: "When I went to Ferguson, Missouri, in 2014 in the wake of the murder of Michael Brown, my clients in Ferguson told me about how they were sleeping on top of each other on the floor in jail cells covered in feces and mold with no access to natural light or fresh air because they could not pay old tickets to the city."[116] In 2016, officials in Jennings settled their case, agreeing to pay out $4.7 million, cancel unpaid debts and related warrants, and adopt reforms such as ability-to-pay hearings.[117] The city of Ferguson fought the lawsuit until 2024, when it finally agreed to a $4.5 million settlement.[118] Advocates have won similar victories in several other jurisdictions, including the state of Idaho; Maplewood, Missouri; Montgomery, Alabama; and New Orleans, Louisiana.[119]

Compared to debt-based sanctions, the fine-and-fee practices that produce LFOs have proven more resistant to reform. Legislative wins have been, for the most part, limited to juvenile cases. The movement began in California and initially focused on very progressive counties. In 2012, a group of University of California, Berkeley law professors and students began studying juvenile LFOs in Alameda County (home to Berkeley and Oakland) after hearing stories about families receiving huge bills for court fees.[120] In 2016, the group published a report that documented the widespread, racially disparate use of fees and their negative effects on low-income families. Based on the findings, the group called for an immediate fee moratorium.[121] Shortly thereafter, the Alameda County Board of Supervisors voted to eliminate fees imposed in juvenile cases for using public defenders, probation supervision, electronic monitoring, and drug testing.[122]

The local victory helped to kickstart a statewide fight.[123] Debt Free Justice, a coalition of legal advocates and "movement building organizations led by impacted people," spearheaded the effort. Once again, legal advocates paved the way for political action by publishing a damning report on the use of juvenile fees across California.[124] In 2017, the coalition won state legislation that prohibited counties from charging or collecting administrative fees in future juvenile cases. To cement the victory, advocacy organizations sent an "implementation packet" to county boards and relevant agencies, spelling out their new legal obligations, and then worked to verify whether counties had ended fee assessments.[125] In 2020, California lawmakers made the provisions of the 2017 legislation retroactive, eliminating all outstanding juvenile fee debts (roughly $350 million).[126]

Over time, the struggle against juvenile fines and fees has become a national and, to some extent, bipartisan campaign. In 2023, for example, the conservative American Legislative Exchange Council adopted model legislation that would eliminate juvenile LFOs.[127] As of 2024, twenty-three states had passed laws that significantly reduced or eliminated fees and fines for juveniles, and twenty additional states had active reform campaigns. The policy changes relieved juveniles and their families of an estimated $28 million in costs.[128]

Efforts to produce similar results for adults have gained less traction and achieved far less policy change. Nevertheless, there have been some notable victories. In Missouri, state lawmakers—acting under intense political pressure five months after publication of the *Ferguson Report*—capped the percentage of total revenue that municipalities could draw from traffic fines. Municipal court revenues based on traffic tickets declined by almost 40 percent in Missouri over the next three years.[129] Lawmakers in Ramsey County, Minnesota (home to Saint Paul) ended fees for probation supervision, electronic monitoring, and some medical co-pays charged to people in jail.[130] And in 2023, New Jersey's governor used a budget procedure to end state-imposed public defender fees and allocated over $4 million to cover the state's estimated losses in fee-based revenue.[131]

As with juvenile LFOs, California has taken the boldest steps toward reducing fees for adults, and here again, advocates began their campaign in an especially progressive local venue. In 2018, San Francisco's board of supervisors voted to make theirs the first county in the nation "to eliminate all locally controlled fees assessed from people exiting jail or the criminal legal system."[132] County residents would no longer have to pay for their own incarceration, probation, assessments, or electronic monitoring. The board's pathbreaking action resulted, in part, from steady, effective efforts to secure support from the county's district attorney, public defender, sheriff, and chief of adult probation.[133] After Alameda and Los Angeles counties followed suit less than two years later, advocates took their fight to the state legislature. The efforts led to a series of new laws that, together, "permanently repealed forty local administrative [criminal legal] fees, backfilled $65 million in lost local revenues with a state appropriation, and discharged an estimated $16 billion in fee debt."[134] To advance on these successes, advocates have built a national network of organizations called End Justice Fees to connect and facilitate political campaigns across the country.[135]

To strengthen their hands in the state and local venues where policies regarding fees, fines, and LFOs are controlled, advocates have also worked to draw federal authorities into the fight. In response, the US DOJ issued a "Dear Colleague" letter in 2023 regarding "the importance of conducting a meaningful ability-to-pay assessment before imposing adverse consequences for failure to pay, considering alternatives to fines and fees, guarding against excessive penalties and ensuring due process protections, including the assistance of counsel when appropriate."[136]

The detailed statement of federal expectations and legal interpretations strengthened an earlier letter issued by the Obama administration in 2016 and revoked by the Trump administration in 2017. Although it changed no policies on its own, the revived letter sent a powerful political signal. Lisa Foster of the Fines and Fees Justice Center argues that the federal intervention "helps litigators sue jurisdictions engaged in unconstitutional and illegal conduct, . . . gives advocates and policymakers a strong argument when they pursue legislative action, . . . [and] gives judges and courts a road map for reform."[137] As a high-profile statement by the Biden administration, the letter also provides elected state and local Democrats with some political cover and encouragement (from the top of the party) to take on fine-and-fee reform.

Like fine-and-fee campaigns, challenges to extractive carceral practices have made headway by focusing first on progressive local venues. For example, in 2020, advocates moved the San Francisco Board of Supervisors to unanimously pass the "People Over Profits" ordinance, making the county "the first in the country to permanently stop generating revenue from incarcerated people and their families through phone calls, commissary markups, or other services."[138] Notably, the board framed its measure in expansive terms, targeting *revenue generation* pursued at the cost of incarcerated people and their families. This holistic approach diverged from the national norm of narrowly targeted reforms focused on isolated practices (e.g., phone call charges) and actors (e.g., corporations), while leaving the broader whole undisturbed.

Credit for the framing largely belongs to an effective outsider-insider collaboration. It was initially promoted by the San Francisco Jail Justice Coalition, a mix of advocacy groups that includes several with presently or formerly incarcerated leaders (e.g., All of Us or None of Us, Berkeley Underground Scholars, and Young Women's Freedom Center).[139] The Coalition worked closely with the Financial Justice Project (FJP), a unique governmental entity housed in San Francisco's Office of the Treasurer and Tax Collector. The FJP's mission is "to assess and reform how fees and fines impact our city's low-income residents and communities of color."[140] In addition to investigating and reporting predatory practices, the FJP works with community organizations to provide a bridge between the grassroots and the halls of government. Beyond its work on the "People

Over Profits" ordinance, the FJP is an active member of coalitions such as Debt Free Justice California and the Free to Drive campaign.

At the state level, campaigns against *carceral predation* have won important victories for "phone justice." Coalitions such as #ConnectFamiliesNow and Campaign for Prison Phone Justice have secured laws that make prison calls free in California, Colorado, Connecticut, and Minnesota. Advocates also scored a big win in 2023, when Massachusetts used the budget process to make calls free in prisons *and* jails.[141] Responding to political pressure, a handful of other states have reduced or eliminated the commissions that telecoms pay governments.[142] By targeting commissions, advocates weaken public agencies' incentives to support exorbitant phone rates and undercut telecom claims that their high rates are necessary to cover payments to governments. States that took this step, the American Bar Association reports, "saw immediate and drastic price decreases with no impacts on service availability."[143]

State and local victories against carceral telecom companies have gone beyond the pursuit of phone justice. In 2021, for example, advocates won legislation in Connecticut that bans the use of any communication services "to supplant in-person contact visits" with incarcerated people.[144] The provision blocks restrictions on in-person visits, which increase reliance on fee-based video visitation and email services. Perhaps the biggest win to date occurred in 2023, when San Francisco launched the nation's first public program to provide all jailed individuals with free e-tablets *and* tablet-based services—including "access to e-books, audiobooks, movies, and music provided through a first-of-its-kind collaboration with the San Francisco Public Library."[145]

At the national level, advocates moved the Federal Communications Commission (FCC) in 2021 to lower rate caps for interstate prison and jail phone calls by as much as 44 percent. As Worth Rises noted at the time, the new policy provided meaningful but quite limited relief: It applied only "to interstate calls and only to prisons and jail populations with over 1,000 people, leaving out millions."[146] Advocates valued it mostly as an incremental step toward bigger changes, and their persistence paid off. In January 2023, President Biden signed the "Martha Wright-Reed Just and Reasonable Communications Act," clarifying that the FCC had the authority to cap rates for all prison and jail phone *and* video calls and instructing the FCC to set "just and reasonable rates."[147]

Advocates fought to include video calls in the law because they saw how telecom companies had adapted to earlier reforms that threatened profits. "The companies rapidly pivoted to this [video] technology," the Prison Policy Initiative (PPI) explained, "when the FCC began to restrict what could be charged for phone calls. As a result, video calling rates are much higher than phone rates today."[148] Here, as in the "Dear Colleague" letter on fines and fees, advocates worked strategically to bring a federal agency's powers to bear on state and local practices. Indeed, their efforts substantially *expanded* the FCC's authority to regulate communications in state and local carceral facilities and limit telecom-based resource extraction.[149]

In some cases, efforts to curb carceral predation have targeted corporate operations directly, without seeking policy change through government. Nonprofits such as Flikshop and Ameelio, for example, operate as direct service providers, subsidized by donors. Flikshop offers an alternative to predatory telecom services by allowing community members to send free or low-cost postcards to imprisoned people.[150] Through donor support, Flikshop has been able to offer its service free of charge to thousands of people.[151] Ameelio offers governments a nonexploitative alternative to telecom companies like Securus and Global Tel-Link (GTL). Backed by large donations, the nonprofit has secured agreements with carceral facilities in four states to provide imprisoned people and their loved ones with free video-conferencing and other communications.[152]

Divestment campaigns take a more contentious approach to expanding the scope of conflict and working outside government policymaking processes. Across the US, they have been waged by college students, labor unions, racial justice organizations, immigrant rights groups, criminal legal reform coalitions, and abolitionists. Through "naming and shaming" tactics, activists in this vein work to stigmatize prison profiteers and pressure partners and investors into withholding or withdrawing support. These sorts of efforts have pushed a variety of banks, corporations, hedge funds, mutual funds, and city governments into severing ties with for-profit prison companies.[153]

Divestment campaigns have also targeted private firms that invest in carceral profiteering. For instance, Worth Rises, a "nonprofit advocacy organization dedicated to dismantling the prison industry,"[154] has waged a pitched battle against Platinum Equity, which bought telecom giant Securus for $1.6 billion in 2017. After closed-door appeals for divestment failed, Worth Rises publicly went on the offensive. First, it mobilized public pressure to successfully stop the Pennsylvania State Employees Retirement System from investing $150 million in Platinum Equity.[155] Then, it targeted Tom Gores, Platinum Equity's chair and CEO and owner of the Detroit Pistons.

With the NBA printing "Black Lives Matter" and other social justice messages on basketball courts and jerseys around the country, Worth Rises took out a full-page ad in *The New York Times* that pointedly asked NBA leaders and team owners: "If Black Lives Matter, what are you doing about Detroit Pistons owner Tom Gores?" The group also worked with artists and activists to force Gores to resign from the Board of Trustees for the Los Angeles County Museum of Art. The campaign attracted the attention of comedian Samantha Bee, who ridiculed Gores and Platinum Equity on her show, *Full Frontal*: "It sounds like the shell company of a bad guy in a Marvel movie."[156] The naming and shaming efforts have publicized the injustices of carceral predation; stigmatized Securus, Platinum Equity, and Tom Gores; and put a range of relevant market actors on notice that profitable investments in incarceration can prove costly in other ways.

Compared to campaigns against financial predation, efforts to challenge *penal labor exploitation* have been less successful. But there have been some wins. For example, legal advocates sued GEO Group for illegally exploiting people held in immigrant detention centers. GEO Group paid the detainees $1 a day, regardless of their hours or the work they did. The payments, GEO claimed, were a stipend for "voluntary work," not a wage. But in 2021, a federal court in the state of Washington rejected this claim, ruling that GEO was violating the state's minimum wage law. The decision obligated the company to pay roughly 10,000 detainees a total of $17.3 million and, going forward, to pay detained workers in the state at least $13.69 an hour.[157] The victory was important not only because of what it meant for detainees and for GEO Group, but also because it shined a spotlight on the injustices that suffuse carceral labor predation in general.

Achieving similar legal victories for people sentenced to jails, prisons, and community supervision programs has been extremely difficult. In these penal settings, labor predation is secured against legal challenge by constitutional, statutory, and administrative provisions. Partly for this reason, activists have turned to disruptive protests designed to raise public awareness and pressure policymakers. Since 2015, activists inside and outside carceral facilities have co-organized prison strikes in numerous states.[158] Cultural interventions have stirred public outrage as well—most notably in the case of Ava DuVernay's celebrated documentary, *13th*. Yet, there have been few changes to law and practice.

Perhaps the most ambitious effort is a growing movement to abolish the exemption of penal labor practices from the Thirteenth Amendment's prohibitions on slavery and involuntary servitude. The Abolish Slavery National Network, a coalition of at least sixty organizations, is at the forefront of this struggle.[159] The group calls for a constitutional Abolition Amendment to "end the exception," a step that would require approval by the US Congress and three-fourths of the states. The odds are long, but activists have moved several state governments to take related actions. Between 2018 and 2024, seven states abolished their penal exceptions to state constitutional provisions that forbid slavery and involuntary servitude, and there are active campaigns in numerous other states to do the same.[160] On their own, these measures do not require governments to increase pay or improve working conditions for incarcerated workers.[161] Their value is largely symbolic: They express commitments, at least in principle, to ending coercive and intensive forms of labor exploitation in carceral institutions. Advocates hope that such state-level actions will create momentum for "ending the exception" nationwide.

The Political Road Ahead

So far, we have analyzed three key aspects of the fight against predation: barriers to success, processes of mobilization, and patterns of tactics and outcomes. Here, we ask how this analytic work might be useful for thinking about political strategy and action going forward. On these matters, as we explain below, there can be no substitute for listening to what people with lived experiences of predation know, understand, and prioritize.

Advocates, activists, and other political practitioners also possess many forms of expertise that we do not. They know far more about the landscapes they work on, the resources and opportunities available to them, and the practical challenges and trade-offs they must navigate. For these and related reasons, we do not prescribe any particular course of action. Rather, we clarify some takeaways from our analysis that strike us as worthy of attention in ongoing discussions of political strategy and action.

One such takeaway is that the results produced by specific tactics and institutional pathways have varied greatly across political contexts. "What works" has depended on the predatory practice at issue, the level of government, jurisdiction-specific laws and political conditions, partisan and ideological factors, and more. Instead of a one-size-fits-all solution, our analysis suggests opportunities to strategically match tactic-and-venue choices to political circumstances. State legislative campaigns, for example, have been most effective when challengers have been ideologically diverse and coalitions have been able to credibly persuade and pressure officials across party lines (e.g., in the fight against asset seizure). Litigation strategies that have worked in some areas (e.g., bail reform) have proven untenable in cases where legal authorization is more entrenched and formidable (e.g., penal labor exploitation). As seen in California, advocates have sometimes used early wins in very progressive counties to build momentum for statewide campaigns. The political conditions that supported this strategy may have analogs in other "blue" states, but they are unlikely to be found in "deep red" states.

Another notable observation is that substantial victories have often emerged through a confluence of political efforts and advances, such as successful litigation, grassroots political pressure, victorious election campaigns, and strategic uses of bureaucratic powers. This pattern suggests the potential value of bringing together advocates with different specialties to develop overarching strategies and coordinate efforts for constructing the building blocks needed to achieve more ambitious goals.[162]

The fact that big wins so often arise through the interaction of diverse campaigns and tactics also has implications for long-standing debates between reformers and radicals that tend to pit contentious "outsider" actions (that challenge governing institutions) against conventional "insider" tactics (that work through them). In some cases, these conflicts reflect significant differences in political principles, strategies, and goals—as, for example, when abolitionists oppose "reformist reforms" that they believe will dissipate or divide political opposition and ultimately shore up an unjust regime.[163] These issues are rightly seen as matters of serious political disagreement and debate. Nevertheless, radical activists, including abolitionists, support a wide range of "non-reformist" reforms aimed at reducing the footprint and functioning of the regime and serve as effective steppingstones toward systems change. In such cases, the empirical record suggests that outsider-activist and insider-reformer tactics can combine in powerful ways. Indeed, as we discussed in the preceding section, electoral victories have sometimes proved critical for policy wins prioritized by social justice activists, and community activists have sometimes played a key role in producing the election outcomes that paved the way.

On a larger scale, disruptive and contentious mass actions have played a crucial role in producing antipredation reforms in recent years.[164] The wave of street protests that followed the police killing of Michael Brown, for example, moved the US DOJ to publish its damning investigation of predatory police and court operations in Ferguson, Missouri. The protests and the report, together, pushed predatory criminal legal practices onto government agendas, pressured public officials to act, and drew larger, established justice organizations into the fight. It was hardly coincidental, however, that the US DOJ's response occurred during the Obama administration, as justice protests began to sow divisions in the Democratic Party's center-to-left coalition. Recall as well how the US DOJ's "Dear Colleague" letter on fines and fine-and-fee practices was first issued under the Obama administration, rescinded under the Trump administration, and then forcefully restated under the Biden administration.

The importance of community activism and protest leads to a more fundamental point. For reasons that flow from democratic moral and political commitments, we believe that campaigns against predation must be rooted in and shaped by the most heavily policed and punished communities. But this view is also supported by our assessment of the political record, which suggests that these communities' efforts have been (and will be) indispensable for effective campaigns to end predation. RCS communities emerged early on as sites of extensive political mobilization and organization, at a time when few people beyond their bounds were aware of the scope and depth of predatory injustices. Most of the larger advocacy organizations that have won significant reforms were drawn into the fight through a process that began with the political voices and actions of people from such communities. (Again, it was mass protests instigated by RCS communities that eventually pushed the US DOJ to produce a bombshell investigative report that focused media attention, provoked national condemnation, and moved policymakers to action).

Time and again, organizers and activists from neighborhoods where personal experiences of predation run deep have been vital participants in efforts to sway public officials, elect allies to office, name and shame corporate profiteers, and formulate political and policy strategies. In a study of "ground-level discourse" in RCS communities, Mihir Chaudhary, Gwen Prowse, and Vesla Weaver reinforce this point as it relates to political campaign principles and what Robin D. G. Kelley calls "freedom dreams."[165] Connecting their findings to "a central tenet of abolitionist discourse," the authors conclude that "to center the most impacted communities in the process of creating change promises the most capacious rendering of freedom."[166]

For these and other reasons discussed in our section on political mobilization, community organizing has played a vital role in antipredation campaigns. Organizers and CBOs have developed many effective models for bringing affected people together and targeting predation as a systemic, actionable, and collective injustice. We are particularly struck by the effectiveness of tactics that work not just through efforts to explain and convince, but by providing personal support and material assistance in conjunction with educational and organizing efforts. Some bail funds, for example, go beyond paying for pretrial release and providing relief from related debts, adopting an approach that Hahrie Han calls "transformational organizing" to simultaneously reduce harm, build power, and strengthen the fight for system change.[167]

These organizations, Jocelyn Simonson explains, work to forge connections between the people they serve and "local social movements aimed at changing criminal justice practices."[168] In many places, the funds "cultivate organizers and leaders among the people they bail out."[169] Emancipate NC, based in Durham, North Carolina, integrates its bail relief work into community organizing efforts that aim to end prevailing bail practices and "dismantle structural racism and mass incarceration."[170] Its Freedom Fighter Bond Fund connects the two levels of action by bailing out activists arrested for protest and civil disobedience.[171] As a movement-oriented bail fund, Emancipate NC is not unique. "In city after city, county after county," Simonson notes, "community bail funds and bailouts build out their presence as part of vibrant networks of groups, often led by directly impacted and incarcerated or formerly incarcerated people, to build power and push for change."[172]

By providing immediate help and support in ways that connect people to systems-level injustices and struggles, models of this sort offer a powerful way for antipredation campaigns to mobilize and incorporate people from heavily targeted communities. The organized collectives they produce can strengthen a wide range of tactics that target courts, legislatures, public agencies, election campaigns, and corporations, in part by grounding those efforts in people's experience-based knowledge.

In our analysis of barriers, we noted cases in which reforms designed to limit predation were undermined at the implementation stage. This pattern suggests the importance of developing concrete strategies for what Peter Edelman calls "persistence, despite victory."[173] Here again, organizations in the field have already developed effective models that can be elaborated and pursued more widely. Groups such as Debt Free Justice work to secure faithful implementation by educating public officials and businesses about what reforms require them to do and tracking their compliance. Other organizations use court- or jail-watching practices to monitor implementation and let authorities know that community-based *groups* are keeping tabs on how they use their discretion.[174]

Mitali Nagrecha and colleagues note that steps should be taken to prepare the ground for implementation *before* reforms get passed. Advocates can work to secure "buy-in" from key administrative and judicial actors and develop plans to pressure, monitor, and expose post-reform practices. Focusing on judicial discretion, the authors outline an agenda for shifting the cultural and material conditions of courts in ways that facilitate the faithful enactment of future reforms.[175] Advocates can also work to set favorable terms of implementation at the policy design stage, fighting to include strong monitoring and reporting provisions and funding for oversight. In a study of prisons, Ann Chih Lin has also shown how the fates of new programs can depend on how they fit into (or alter) the preexisting cultures, routines, and needs of implementing organizations.[176] Lin's analysis suggests the value of tailoring policy designs to what advocates know (or can learn) about the specific organizations charged with turning policies into practice.

Certainly, our analysis also highlights how the fragmentation of anti-predation campaigns across jurisdictions, institutional venues, and practices (e.g., phone justice, bail reform) comes at the political advantage of well-resourced defenders of the status quo. Over the past two decades, however, network-building efforts have demonstrated effective ways to span these divides. By connecting diverse activist, advocacy, and research organizations, networks facilitate the diffusion of ideas, strategies, and materials across political arenas and campaigns. They provide infrastructure for transfers of political resources, experienced personnel, and lessons from previous battles.[177]

Antipredation networks—such as Free to Drive, Debt Free Justice, Care First Coalition, End Justice Fees, #ConnectFamiliesNow, and the Abolish Slavery National Network—have been on the rise in recent years, often driven by bottom-up, community-based efforts. In addition to strengthening ties among themselves, local groups have enlisted large, established advocacy groups (e.g., the ACLU, NAACP, and Vera Institute of Justice), foundations (e.g., MacArthur, Open Society, and Arnold Ventures), and research entities (e.g., the Justice Collaboratory at Yale and the Brennan Center for Justice at New York University). In some cases, these groups have organized events and funded initiatives that bring together activists, advocates, researchers, and policymakers. Such efforts can help to build flexible infrastructures that connect, inform, and assist disparate issue- and jurisdiction-specific campaigns.

Some organizations make network development a key priority. For instance, as the Fines and Fees Justice Center archives and disseminates research and other materials to support antipredation campaigns across the country, it also works to create and strengthen ties between scholars, political powerbrokers, legal practitioners, and community organizers.[178] The PPI, a research and advocacy outfit, has excelled at efforts to inform and connect disparate state and local struggles.[179] And Worth Rises has a remarkable record of bringing together groups with diverse political, legal, and economic capacities—including many led by current or formerly imprisoned people and their families—to fight a wide range of private and public actors "who have a financial interest in maintaining our carceral state and our crisis of mass incarceration and mass surveillance."[180]

The development of networks that allow organizations to draw strength from one another across arenas illustrates a more general dynamic observed in our analysis: the potential to change the political game by *expanding the scope of conflict*.[181] A striking example can be seen in the fight against predatory telecom practices. In the midst of their uphill battles in state and local arenas—where officials directly control operations and, in many cases, are materially invested in predatory revenues—advocates expanded the scope of conflict by drawing federal authorities into the fight. At the federal level, they operated on a more favorable terrain, made headway with the FCC and Biden administration, and mobilized the powers of the US government to impose new constraints on public and private actors at the state and local levels.

The most fundamental way that antipredation campaigns have expanded the scope of conflict—and can continue to do so—is by recruiting growing numbers of justice-oriented advocacy and movement organizations. This allows campaigns to increase their capacities for political communication and mobilization, acquire more substantial and varied political resources, and become capable of pursuing influence through a wider range of political networks.[182] It also helps to *redefine* issues and goals in politically advantageous ways. When organizations such as the NAACP incorporate criminal justice predation into their agendas, they usually do so by identifying it, internally *and publicly*, as an instance of broader social injustices. As they promote these broader frames, they shift the terms of conflict away from the toxic politics of crime and punishment. The dynamic operates as a discursive form of political incorporation, integrating vilified "criminals" into larger groups of oppressed people who demand freedom, justice, and full standing as equal citizens.

Among the examples discussed earlier, the Movement for Black Lives (M4BL) has been especially significant. As Deva Woodly explains, M4BL is far more than "a reaction against police brutality"; it is a movement with a distinct political philosophy (what Woodly calls "radical feminist Black pragmatism") that aims to reconceive and transform "all of the forces that inhibit Black people's ability to live and thrive."[183] The events in Ferguson, Missouri that triggered the transition from #BlackLivesMatter to a full-fledged uprising represented a "confluence of injustice," stitching together the devaluation and destruction of Black lives, state and corporate practices of race-targeted financial predation, and "the horrors of . . . racial capitalism."[184] In the years since, M4BL has elevated a political agenda for achieving racial justice, healing, and care.[185] In the process, it has helped to push criminal justice predation onto other organizations' agendas and tie its meaning directly to societal regimes of domination, devaluation, extraction, and oppression.

The Debt Collective, which organizes debtors to fight rapacious credit practices and debt-based injustices, offers another good example. This group works to build solidarity across different groups of debtors, emphasizing the shared logic and consequences of various debt-generating practices and institutions. The collective insists that criminal legal debts are not distinctive matters of crime and punishment, but further instances of the widespread imposition of life-altering debt burdens.[186] Americans, the group argues, now live in a "debtfare state" that turns "what should be publicly financed goods" into "individual debt obligations" that are ruthlessly exploited by creditors.[187] The Debt Collective's agenda points to the political value of deepening the connections between antipredation campaigns and struggles over public finance—a subject we return to in our concluding chapter.

Conclusion

A handful of corporations are especially well known among people who study and struggle against criminal justice predation. Companies like CoreCivic, GEO Group, JPay, Global Tel-Link, Securus, Keefe Supply Company, and Aramark generate huge profits—and in many cases, hefty public revenues for their government partners. Their political power and prowess can make them seem like unconquerable Goliaths. So, it is big news when financial and political troubles close in and the ground beneath them begins to shake.

This was the case in April 2024, when news broke that the carceral telecom giant Securus was on the verge of bankruptcy. Even with annual revenues of $700 million, the company held over $1 billion of debt, and potential investors were keeping their distance. "Securus has been in the red for the last few years," Dana Floberg and Morgan Duckett wrote in *The Appeal*, "due in part to huge interest payments on debt taken out by Platinum Equity when it acquired the corporation, as well as management fees it must pay to the firm." Platinum had eight months to come up with the necessary financing or sell off Securus.[188] Once a prized acquisition for the private equity firm, Securus had become a millstone.

The telecom's dire situation surely came as a shock to many, but not to the advocates who had, for years, fought against carceral profiteering in general and Securus in particular. The forces that pushed Securus to the brink of demise coalesced through an accumulation of smaller victories achieved through diverse tactics and institutional pathways. As described earlier, Worth Rises and other groups used naming and shaming campaigns to stigmatize Securus, Platinum Equity, and Platinum's founding CEO Tom Gores; this served as a potent warning to potential investors, reinforced through direct communications to key business leaders that purchasing or investing in Securus would carry significant reputational risks. Advocates also lobbied the Federal Trade Commission to block Securus's efforts to shore up its financial position by acquiring other telecoms.[189] The advocacy groups' three-pronged approach of public protests, behind-the-scenes negotiations with business insiders, and political lobbying cut off Securus's access to financial lifelines.

Such company-specific actions were all the more effective because they converged with a steady drip of wins that threatened to limit profitability in the carceral telecom sector as a whole. In addition to expanding the FCC's regulatory authority, advocates have won an assortment of victories in state and local jurisdictions that make prison and jail calls free, cap prices for phone and video calls, outlaw commissions to governments, and ban replacing in-person visitation with fee-based video alternatives. For potential investors, the market signal has been crystal clear: Campaigns across the country are on the march, and they have the potential to significantly erode the profits that Securus and other telecom companies generate from mass incarceration.

Concerns about the financial and reputational risks of investing in the industry have deepened as influential artists have heaped scorn on Securus and its peers. DuVernay's 2016 documentary, *13th*, described Securus as a nefarious big-time player in the "prison industrial complex." In a 2019 episode of *Last Week Tonight*, John Oliver took on JPay and Securus, detailing how the businesses exploited imprisoned people and their families—and calling Securus's efforts to increase profits by limiting in-person visitation "evil." In 2020, rap artist Drakeo the Ruler released an album, *Thank You for Using GTL*, recorded over the phone while confined in jail. The album, National Public Radio reported, "dragged GTL into an artistic endeavor, and in so doing required every outlet that engages with it to delve into the business practices of [an] industry being challenged on multiple fronts."[190] As they worked to raise public awareness and challenge social indifference, these cultural interventions reinforced the idea that it was publicly perilous to invest in carceral telecom investments.

The Securus episode is not only an example of the ways campaigns against powerful, entrenched interests can succeed by using diverse, interlocking tactics, but a reinforcement of a second general point about struggles for justice: Significant victories are often won through cumulative processes that unfold over years or even decades.[191] Developments that may appear as sudden, shocking ruptures are frequently the results of long-term, persistent political action. In *Breaking the Pendulum*, Philip Goodman, Joshua Page, and Michelle Phelps argue: "Struggles over punishment are long and laborious, and challengers often feel like they are pushing Sisyphus's boulder up the hill. Nevertheless, tireless contestation often pays off over the long haul. It creates fissures in the penal landscape that help generate larger shifts under the right conditions."[192] It took advocates at least six years to imperil Securus and just as long to eliminate cash bail and transform the pretrial process in Illinois.[193] The battle to make California's prison phone calls free took more than *a quarter century*.

The slow road to meaningful change can easily lead to a politics of despair—a collective sense that injustice is perennial, change never comes, and political struggle is a fool's errand.[194] To keep this despair at bay, abolitionist scholars stress the importance of seeing and celebrating the "small wins." As Keeanga-Yamahtta Taylor argues, "small victories can empower one to fight larger battles."[195] They can inspire collective joy, which advocates and scholars argue is critical for solidarity building and movement success.[196] Small changes that seem minor in the moment can also alter the political landscape in ways that allow for radical change down the road.[197]

It was in this spirit that many advocates celebrated Securus' troubles as a "monumental win."[198] They knew all too well that the powerful telecom might yet find a lifeline, and even if it went under, another corporate profiteer might take its place. But the campaign against Securus *succeeded* in ways that few would have thought possible less than a decade earlier, and it may well have taken a consequential step toward ending carceral telecom predation. It also offered a path forward. Worth Rises and its allies argue that "the same tactics that brought Securus down—narrative change, policy campaigns, regulatory efforts, and investor activism—offer a roadmap for tackling exploitative prison profiteers across the prison industry." For Bianca Tyler, Worth Rises' executive director, the winning campaign was a "warning to all those with no scruples about how they make their money: hands off our communities."

Conclusion * *Predation, Inquiry, and Politics*

In August 2014, people filled the streets of Ferguson, Missouri to protest the police killing of Michael Brown. Some broke into stores and took merchandise. As often happens at such moments, politicians and pundits rushed to decry the "looting," with many fixating on it as the key issue at hand and wielding it to justify repressive state action. The "looters in Ferguson," Beckett Adams wrote in the *Washington Examiner*, are "shameless criminal opportunists . . . holding that community back."[1] Because of their "ugly behavior . . . a police presence is now required." The irony of such public condemnations was soon laid bare by the US Department of Justice's report on police and court practices in the city of Ferguson. For years, Black city residents, many of whom were among the protesters, had been subjected to a predatory regime that used fines and fees to, in a word, *loot* their communities and fill municipal coffers.

In this book, we have presented a critical analysis of criminal justice predation, focusing on the origins, operations, and consequences of its contemporary forms and the political struggles that surround it. As we close, we want to step back and reflect on the concept that anchors our study, predation, and elaborate on some of its analytical and political implications. First, we look beyond our analysis of legal plunder to consider what a *predatory perspective* contributes to the broader study of criminal legal governance. Next, we turn to the potential uses of predation as a way to frame campaigns against extractive criminal legal practices, exploring the relative strengths and limitations of this approach. Finally, we ask what a predatory perspective suggests for political efforts to put an end to legal plunder and repair its harms.

Predation and Criminal Legal Governance

In chapter 1, we drew on a long history of critical thought to develop predation as a general analytic concept. The question that drove this work, however, was much more specific: How should we think about the various practices that criminal legal authorities use to strip resources from communities in the US today, locate them in historical perspective, and subject them to analysis? For years, monetary sanctions scholarship has defined the prevailing approach to this question and demonstrated its value. Its frame of inquiry was developed by extending concepts and theories from the study of punishment and society. The rising use of court fines and fees, for example, has been explained, like mass incarceration, as one of the excesses produced by punitive politics. In this view, such practices function as monetary forms of punishment that extend the reach of criminal legal surveillance and social control. The targeting, scale, and consequences of financial charges and debts are studied as inequitable *by-products* of a punitive regime centered on low-income communities of color.

The concept of predation offers an alternative, complementary approach. Instead of extending established ways of thinking about policing and punishment, it brings a different kind of framework to bear—one that begins outside the realm of criminal legal governance—in efforts to understand how structural inequalities relate to projects of exploitation and dispossession. Our earlier chapters present the results of this approach to studying *extractive* criminal legal practices. Rather than summarize them here, we take up a different question: What might the study of criminal justice predation contribute to—and what are the implications of our study for—broader efforts to understand criminal legal governance in the US?

A starting point can be found in our use of the phrase "predatory dimensions" in the subtitle of this book. Predation is an aspect of something larger and more complex. It does not define the essential nature or overriding purpose of policing and punishment. Its dimensions are entwined with many others. Its neglect has had important implications for the study of criminal legal governance, in part, because it has impeded inquiry into how predation intersects with and matters for *other* operations, functions, and uses of policing and punishment—including those that anchor research agendas in the field. Consider, for example, the various penological and disciplinary functions of criminal legal governance;[2] its uses for broader modes of governance that operate through surveillance, containment, and social control;[3] its role in labor market regulation;[4] and its significance for functions typically associated with the welfare state.[5] A predatory perspective on criminal legal governance invites new questions about how the operations of legal plunder intersect with each and how their interplay is configured.

Indeed, while the central goal of this book is to illuminate how police, court, and penal operations have served as sites of and supports for predatory projects, our analysis also underscores the significance of predation for criminal legal governance itself. In the early American republic, slavery and Native dispossession played defining roles in the organization and development of policing and penal operations. In the Jim Crow South, few if any aspects of policing were left untouched by the projects of enforcing labor extraction in the community (e.g., sharecropping) and, together with courts, forcing Black workers into various forms of penal labor exploitation (e.g., convict leasing). In this period, labor predation was not only a core function of penal administration in the South; it was central to the management and operation of Northern and Midwestern prisons.

A substantially different configuration accompanied the intensive exploitation of Black residents in urban ghettos during the mid-twentieth century, and yet another has prevailed over the past four decades. Across these eras, the predatory dimensions of criminal legal governance shifted in form and purpose many times. Their centrality (relative to other dimensions) rose and fell, and so did the extent of their reach into other aspects of operations. Such changes in configuration—and the reasons why they have occurred—merit far more scholarly attention than they have received.

Indeed, efforts to compare criminal legal formations across eras and locales and explain why they change might both be enhanced by paying closer attention to their predatory dimensions. Pressures to secure slavery and dispossession fueled and shaped the early development of policing and penal capacities in the US, and after slavery was abolished, the project of creating a new regime of race-based labor predation in the South drove dramatic shifts and expansions once again. Developments after the 1960s followed a different storyline. As we have stressed, the pursuit of predatory revenues did not produce the massive expansion of policing and punishment that took off in the 1970s. At the same time, our analysis suggests that it is hard to understand many aspects of criminal legal governance in the US today—including how they came to work as they do—if one ignores its predatory dimensions.

By pushing the frame of inquiry beyond punitive politics and toward structural shifts in political economy and their implications for projects of exploitation and dispossession, a predatory perspective allows for a fuller explanation of how and why new modes of resource extraction proliferated in the criminal legal arena starting in the 1980s (see chapter 4). The prioritization and pursuit of these new practices (amid growing dependence on predatory revenues), in turn, transformed police, court, and penal operations in far-reaching ways (see chapters 2, 3, and 9). As they responded to new needs and expectations, criminal legal agencies reconfigured their operations. Revenue pressures reoriented police patrols, changing priorities, practices, and routines in ways that compromised public safety missions. Courts spent more and more time on processing and collecting fines and fees. Pressed to raise their own funds, they retooled their procedures as well as their terms for pretrial release and penalties for conviction. The management and operation of penal facilities and programs changed in similar ways, as organizational routines and cultures evolved in new directions throughout the field. The normalization of criminal legal takings helped to facilitate corruption. The spoils of self-funding practices and the growing participation of businesses in predatory partnerships further eroded public transparency and democratic accountability to communities.

A predatory perspective also shifts our understandings of policing and punishment in the US by changing how we understand the *boundaries* of the criminal legal field and the ways they change over time.[6] On one side, it suggests a different vision of who participates in, shapes, and has stakes in criminal legal governance. On the other, it offers an alternative view of who is "legally entangled" and directly targeted by public and private governing authorities.

The importance of corporate partners in criminal legal governance today is well recognized. Even so, a predatory perspective yields some distinctive insights into the sources, scope, and significance of this expansion of the field. Our account of why public officials opened up penal governance to corporations in the 1980s includes a number of well-known factors, such as rising promarket ideologies, political pressures, capacity shortfalls, and public funding constraints. At the same time, our analytic approach highlights a widely neglected factor that played a key role in paving the way for for-profit actors.

The remarkable scale of corporate entry was facilitated, in no small part, by the growth of revenue-generating agendas and predatory financial charge-and-payment schemes *inside* government agencies. Fee-based operations, in particular, were ready-made for outsourcing to companies, and they provided entrepreneurs an established model for developing lucrative new business operations (e.g., fee-based private probation). Financial charges imposed on accused and convicted people for "using" public courts and community supervision programs and "staying" in public carceral facilities helped to legitimize private operations that did the same. Growing reliance on predatory revenues sometimes motivated officials to seek out business partners, such as private debt collectors, and to outsource the provision of goods and services in ways that would bring in contract-based commissions.

By enlisting and enabling predatory business operations, government officials have substantially bolstered state capacities for criminal legal governance. Commission payments have helped state departments of corrections sustain and expand operations. New prison and detention facilities have been funded by private financiers and run entirely for profit. Electronic monitoring and drug testing companies that charge fees directly to accused and convicted people have expanded government surveillance capacities. Based on the same model, halfway houses, reentry facilities, and for-profit probation companies have expanded state capacities for supervising formerly incarcerated people. And the list goes on.

Such partnerships account for only some of the ways that predation has redefined the boundaries of the field and the scope of its influential participants over the past four decades. The full breadth includes not only direct participants but also the diverse beneficiaries of predatory revenues. The consequences for criminal legal governance flow not only from direct involvement but also from how the field's expansion has reshaped its politics. In earlier chapters, we emphasized how predatory partnerships brought powerful corporations into the field that invested heavily in political action and exerted outsized influence in electoral contests and conflicts over policy and law. Some are more visible than others, however.

Few people think of insurance companies as important players in criminal legal governance. But it is hard to grasp how pretrial processes operate in most states today without attending to the corporate sureties that profit from underwriting bail bonds, fund the powerful "bail lobby," and write and rewrite policies that structure the bail game and greatly affect pretrial governance in many other ways. Similarly, private equity firms likely do not come to mind when people think about how criminal legal governance works in the US. But Securus and JPay are widely recognized as powerful players in carceral administration and penal politics, and they are owned by Platinum Equity, whose managers and investors have no small say in how they go about their business.

Predation has also expanded the field to include a wider array of consequential government actors. Commission-based contracts with carceral telecom companies turned the Federal Communications Commission (FCC) into an important site of conflict over penal operations and revenues. In 2021, this expansion of the political terrain allowed advocates to harness the FCC's regulatory powers for change. At the same time, the distribution of predatory revenues to public agencies has dramatically expanded the number and variety of government actors that have a direct material stake in the ways criminal legal governance operates. In many cases, these actors have been eager to weigh in on policy matters to protect their share.

Likewise, a predatory perspective encourages a broader view of who is "legally entangled," in the sense of being a direct subject of institutional actors in the field (beyond just interacting with, say, police in their community). In official statistics, common perceptions, and most scholarship, this category is limited to people who are arrested, accused of crimes, or convicted. The people who immediately surround them, such as family members, friends, and neighbors, are generally seen as experiencing *collateral consequences*—subsequent effects on people who are not the direct targets of criminal legal action. In contrast, when a predatory framework is adopted, community members and their capacities and resources are defined, from the outset, as direct targets of important dimensions of criminal legal governance.

At the level of practice, we have analyzed many cases in which the friends and family members of accused and convicted people are directly targeted for criminal justice predation. Because imprisoned people rarely have significant resources of their own, for example, carceral telecom, banking, and care package companies target their loved ones in the community. They work to exploit emotional bonds and feelings of obligation in order to push them into making purchases and depositing funds—and of course, into generating private profits and public revenues. For similar reasons, industry profits in the bail sector depend on convincing the loved ones of an accused individual to pay premiums and sign onerous contracts. The detained individual is, in many respects, the enabling condition for predatory practices that primarily target their associates. Through the cosigning process, such individuals (primarily low-income women of color) become directly entangled in the pretrial process and *personally* responsible for meeting the expectations of courts and bail companies.

Finally, a predatory perspective expands how we think about criminal legal governance as a source of social inequality in the US today. There is a diverse body of scholarship on this topic, but most leading works focus primarily on processes of *exclusion*. People who are marked with a criminal record, for example, experience formidable barriers to accessing employment, decent wages, secure housing, and public assistance.[7] Negative experiences with policing and punishment lead many people to hide from and avoid contacting institutions that make important decisions about their lives and, in some cases, could provide them with protections, material supports, opportunities, or services.[8]

Without an analysis of these and other exclusionary dynamics, it is impossible to understand how criminal legal governance contributes to societal inequality. Indeed, we have suggested in previous chapters many ways that legal plunder generates exclusions and deprivations. To cite a straightforward example, payments of criminal legal fines, fees, and debts leave many people unable to acquire desperately needed goods and services, or even to maintain stable access to food and housing. In our analysis, however, exclusion tells only one half of a larger story.

The other half explains how criminal legal governance operates as a site of and support for *predatory inclusion* (see chapter 1). By putting the two sides together, it becomes possible to see how researchers may underestimate the full effects on social inequality produced even by the forms of exclusion they analyze. When the mark of a felony record blocks people's access to what they need, it often facilitates their inclusion into intensely exploitative arrangements. They cannot get a regular loan, so they have to turn to a predatory pawnshop or payday lending operation that charges exorbitant fees and usurious interest rates. They cannot get a job (or housing) on regular terms, so they are channeled into the most exploitative work (or housing) arrangements—on terms that enrich owners by impoverishing the criminalized.

The contributions of criminal legal governance to social inequality come into further view when we incorporate its role in promoting the *collective* conditions that enable predatory inclusion. Take, for instance, how policing continues to sustain the conditions that push many residents of race- and class-segregated neighborhoods into intense forms of exploitation. And consider, too, the roles that police, courts, and jails play as backstops for the predatory practices that flourish inside such neighborhoods—such as by enforcing renter evictions and payments to creditors who have pulled residents into perpetual debt traps.

On top of all this, there are the practices that have received the lion's share of our attention in this book—practices that are carried out under the banner of law and justice and through the workings of criminal legal governance itself. Legal plunder functions in the US today as a powerful engine of social inequality based on exploitation and dispossession. It extracts vast sums of resources from the nation's most oppressed communities, pushing further down people who were already at or near the bottom of the socioeconomic ladder. It delivers these resources to governments and corporations, where they benefit people who were already better off. The spoils of legal plunder fuel corporate profits and enrich shareholders and investors. They flow to private equity firms, banks, and insurance companies. They underwrite middle-class jobs in governments and businesses—as well as regal salaries for affluent executives at the top of the corporate world. By subsidizing a wide range of government costs, they ease the tax burdens of advantaged Americans and allow them to keep greater shares of income and wealth.

Predation and Political Framing Strategies

Beyond its potential to advance inquiry, the concept of predation offers a distinctive basis for framing and fighting extractive criminal legal practices. Indeed, predatory framings have already been adopted by a number of activist and advocacy groups in the field, and even in legislation such as the End Predatory Court Fees Act introduced in the state of New York.[9] How should we think about the strengths and limitations of such framings? To answer this question, we have to evaluate predation in the context of alternatives, as one option in the prevailing repertoire of oppositional frames.

Our goal is not to identify a single "best" approach. The effectiveness of any framing strategy will depend on the challenges that campaigns confront, the actors they aim to influence, and the goals they hope to achieve. An appeal that is effective in one setting (e.g., persuading a public agency head) may fall flat in another (e.g., community organizing) and prove useless in some other setting (e.g., a lawsuit that depends on framing extractive practices so that they fall under a specific category of legal protection). In chapter 10, we stressed the diversity of political arenas and tactics that shape outcomes in antipredation campaigns. Against this backdrop, there are good reasons to value a broad repertoire of framing alternatives.

As a political frame, predation ties extractive criminal legal practices directly to structural inequalities and injustices. It connects them to a wider range of predatory state and market projects and focuses attention on how the plunder of subjugated communities subsidizes dominant groups and institutions. It is first and foremost a *social injustice* frame that foregrounds systemic, intersectional inequalities and emphasizes how they enable and organize extractive projects. In these respects, it can be distinguished (in part or whole) from the most widely deployed oppositional frames in the field.

Punishment frames have inspired and shaped advocacy on monetary sanctions and "the criminalization of poverty."[10] Politically, these frames integrate financial takings into campaigns against mass policing and punishment and help to underscore how extractive practices undermine penological goals and impose penalties and obligations beyond the sentences set forth in criminal laws—a rallying cry that surely resonates with many legally entangled people (and their loved ones) who feel that they have been wrongly "punished." Penal frames are a requirement for Eighth Amendment legal challenges to predatory takings,[11] and they help reformers engage criminal legal officials on familiar terms. Among people who already see policing and punishment through a group-oppression lens (e.g., racism), these frames can effectively connect legal takings to broader social injustices. On their own, however, they do not make this connection. They also entail some significant limits and risks.

By leaning into the politics of punishment, these frames position the fight on a terrain favored by many defenders of predation, who can exploit well-established discourses to stoke public fears and demonize "criminals." As Chloe Thurston and Traci Burch respectively note, efforts to make extractive practices more visible *as forms of punishment* may evoke public support for punitive policies as well as beliefs that "criminals" rather than "taxpayers" should pay for the costs of crime.[12] Such frames also risk reinforcing the fragmentation of struggle discussed in chapter 10. Some forms of criminal justice predation, such as court fines, can easily be framed as punishments, but many are harder to incorporate. It can be a tough sell, for example, to convince policymakers and other important audiences that bail bond premiums and charges for prison phone calls are penal sanctions. Punishment frames also tend to center government entities, making for-profit actors in the field a secondary concern and obscuring connections to other modes of predation that target the same communities (e.g., payday lending).

Fairness frames focus attention on norms of equity and rights to equal treatment and due process. They are particularly useful for promoting procedural changes designed to make institutions live up to well-established ideals and commitments. Advocates often use fairness frames to challenge practices that impose financial burdens in arbitrary or biased ways (across social groups or jurisdictions). Fine-and-fee practices are often charged with being unfair specifically because they impose financial charges and debts on people who lack the ability to pay. Fairness frames have also served as a basis for conflict-of-interest and due-process challenges—for instance, when judges control decisions that help to fund their own courts. Marc Levin, formerly of the conservative reform organization Right on Crime, argued in this regard: "It is time to live up to the guarantees of due process and equal protection enshrined in our Constitution and ensure fines and fees are reasonable, proportionate, and transparent."[13]

The most important risks and limits of such frames flow from their premise—that with the right procedural adjustments, predation can be made *fair*. Indeed, by designating reforms as safeguards of fairness, they may shore up predation by making it seem more legitimate and just. And when fairness arguments produce distinctive protections for subgroups of affected individuals (e.g., those who lack an ability to pay), they risk dividing the people that organizers hope to unite. In this regard, Monica Bell writes that ability-to-pay restrictions are "reminiscent of the emphasis on decarceration for . . . nonviolent, nonserious, and nonsexual offenders. . . . . [R]eformers must be careful not to rely too heavily on implicit distinctions between the blameless and blameworthy . . . and should instead take a more systemic and institutional approach to framing the issue."[14] From an abolitionist perspective, Beth Colgan emphasizes that when such reforms curtail highly offensive excesses, they can shield systemic takings from more fundamental challenges.[15]

Misguided-governance frames appeal to technocratic ideals and rational commitments to changing practices that are shown to be ineffective, inefficient, or counterproductive. They are, in key respects, de-politicizing frames that elevate means-ends logics and cost-benefit calculations. As a result, they can be useful for swaying public managers and other officials who prize rational, evidence-based action. Reformers invoke this type of frame when they argue that monetary sanctions are irrational because they do not produce a good return on investment for government: People who live in poverty can rarely afford to pay off criminal legal debts, and collection efforts often prove costly. In a more criminological vein, some advocates argue that legal debts undermine crime-reduction efforts by creating barriers to reentry and encouraging recidivism.[16]

The wager made by such framing strategies is that appeals to rational goal-seeking can trump contending political forces. It is a questionable bet. After all, the overwhelming evidence that mass incarceration is inefficient, ineffective, costly, and counterproductive for public safety has produced little in the way of meaningful systems change. Efforts to frame predation as an irrational revenue strategy are especially questionable.[17] First, few predatory criminal legal practices can be effectively framed in this way. As we have shown, most generate substantial private and public revenues. Second, in cases where officials have decided that collections do not pay for themselves, they have often worked to develop more efficient or aggressive collection methods (or outsourced the task to for-profit specialists) rather than rolling back their debt-producing practices. This is perhaps the biggest risk of irrationality frames: They may motivate institutional responses that make predation more effective and efficient.

State-versus-market frames fold criminal justice predation into long-standing partisan and ideological narratives—liberal progressive discourses of unregulated corporate greed or conservative broadsides against big-government threats to liberty and property. For this reason, they tend to be especially useful for recruiting partisan allies and persuading elected officials. Working within this frame, Democrats and liberals challenge commercial bail and private prisons, often casting government management or oversight as the solution. Republicans and conservatives condemn practices such as asset forfeiture that, in their view, exemplify "government overreach."[18]

By selectively challenging practices that fit established ideological commitments, state-versus-market frames risk splintering the struggle and bolstering the legitimacy of some predatory arrangements through contrasts with the "bad objects" they single out.[19] Ultimately, they misconstrue the regime they aim to combat. Legal plunder today mostly operates through public–private partnerships. Reforms that target actors on one side of the state–market divide (e.g., commercial bail and for-profit prisons) often pave the way for extractive practices on the other (e.g., government fees for pretrial supervision and penal custody). In this manner, such frames can encourage policy changes that shift the sites and agents of predation but do little to curb the injustices and resource takings experienced by targeted communities.

Poverty frames focus attention on how criminal legal takings generate deprivation and hardship, integrating them into the field of anti-poverty advocacy. Arguments of this form focus on how extractive practices contribute to more severe and entrapping forms of community poverty, criminalize poverty, and intensify the suffering of low-income individuals and families.[20] Such framings can be effective for generating outrage, sympathy, and perceptions of injustice among potential allies. They are also likely to resonate with people who see, in their own lives, how institutions operate to keep them poor and use their poverty against them. Importantly, they also help to draw well-developed networks of anti-poverty organizations and advocates into the fight.

Poverty frames have two major drawbacks, though. First, as they focus on hardships at the bottom of the social order, they risk diverting attention from the top—i.e., the beneficiaries of the revenues generated by predation. Indeed, campaigns framed by poverty have often substituted for or displaced more direct reckonings with structural inequalities in the United States.[21] Second, the historical record—particularly for means-tested welfare programs—suggests that, like punishment frames, poverty frames may move the fight over predation onto unfavorable terrain.[22] Political battles over poverty have long been dominated by discourses that vilify "the undeserving poor," associate them with self-defeating cultural pathologies, and blame their hardships on personal irresponsibility.[23]

Social injustice frames focus attention on shared experiences of group-based inequities, emphasizing their structural roots and assigning responsibility to specific institutions and actors. Among scholars and activists, they are widely seen as essential for mobilizing and sustaining collective action, and in various forms, they have galvanized struggles against domination and oppression around the world.[24] In the fight against legal plunder, they hold a prominent place in the contemporary repertoire of oppositional frames. In chapter 10, for example, we discussed campaigns that frame criminal legal takings as racial injustices and integrate them into broader struggles for racial freedom and justice.

Predation operates as a particular kind of social injustice frame, and a number of its features make it advantageous for the political fight against legal plunder. From the outset, predatory frames focus attention on societal inequalities and structural injustices, emphasizing how they make predatory practices possible and define their targets and beneficiaries. In this manner, they shift the terms of conflict and debate away from the toxic politics of crime and punishment. The targets of plunder are framed not as legally entangled individuals (as in punishment frames) but as subjugated communities—not as disadvantaged and vulnerable people (as in poverty frames) but as groups that are actively exploited and dispossessed on the basis of race, class, gender, and national origin. Moreover, unlike single-axis social injustice frames, predation offers a broad umbrella for pursuing intersectional approaches to activism, advocacy, and coalition building. As we have shown in this book, it is particularly helpful for making gender-based injustices and women from RCS communities more central to the ways people understand and contest criminal justice predation.

Equally important, predatory framings move the agents and beneficiaries of legal plunder toward the center of the political picture. They connect resource stripping at the bottom to revenue generation at the top and, in so doing, focus attention on the predatory partnerships that subsidize government agencies and enrich corporate profiteers, banks, insurance companies, and private equity firms. By emphasizing revenue production, predatory framings also encourage activists and advocates to make vital connections between the fight against legal plunder and struggles over public finance (a topic we return to in the next section). Predation connects criminal legal takings to a wide range of business operations that exploit the same marginalized communities, framing them as variations on the same kind of injustice. It also encourages a politically potent historical perspective on the contemporary regime, tying it to a long line of predatory projects in America that stretches back to slavery and Native dispossession.

Predatory frames have great potential to support community organizing, political mobilization, coalition building, public messaging and media campaigns, and broad efforts to pressure lawmakers into passing legislation. But they also have limitations. In many circumstances, other frames will be more effective for engaging decision-makers on terms they find reasonable, relevant, and persuasive. Arguments that characterize prevailing prison operations as predatory, for example, are unlikely to resonate with many leaders of penal agencies. They are also unlikely to help attorneys convince judges that their rulings should be based on specific legal protections or precedents. Efforts to frame today's regime as part of a longer history of predatory projects can also be counterproductive if they flatten history into a story of endless and unchanging oppression. By making it seem like the political struggles of earlier generations bore little fruit, such narratives risk reinforcing a politics of despair—a "sense that nothing will ever change no matter what some imagined collective 'we' does to try to bring change."[25]

But of course, this need not be the case. As we have shown in earlier chapters, successful political struggles put an end to major forms of predation in earlier eras, and antipredation campaigns are winning a growing number of victories today. Many framing strategies will be needed to build on these successes, perhaps some that we have yet to imagine. As part of this broader repertoire, we believe that predation offers some important advantages for political organizing, strategy, and action.

Toward a Post-Predation Future

In this final section, we reflect on what the analysis presented in this book suggests about the conditions needed to achieve a future free of predation. What guidance can a predatory perspective offer for efforts to make sure that today's regime of legal plunder has no successor and to repair the harms and injustices it has produced? In our introductory chapter, we suggested that putting an end to this regime is likely to require more than what most people mean by "criminal legal reform." It is more compatible with abolitionist agendas that connect battles against policing and penal injustices to larger efforts to transform the social order. Having presented our study in full, we are now in a position to elaborate.

There are significant political limits to approaching extractive criminal legal operations solely as a problem of policing and penal governance. With historical hindsight, most observers today see clearly that Black Codes, discriminatory policing, and convict leasing were not, in their day, distinct matters of law enforcement and punishment, divisible from the Jim Crow political economy that produced and sustained them. Most recognize as well that when reforms shut down one mode of predation in this era (e.g., convict leasing), others took its place (e.g., chain gangs and penal farms). These dynamics may not be as clear in our own time, but they are no less important for understanding and overcoming contemporary forms of legal plunder.

Abolishing criminal justice predation requires confronting how thoroughly it is woven into "core" policing and penal operations and how deeply it is rooted in institutions and interests beyond them. The state and market actors who have clear material and ideological stakes in defending them today include many who have no direct role in policing, adjudication, or punishment. Equally important, today's practitioners of legal plunder have proved to be remarkably nimble and inventive. They have repeatedly found innovative ways to overcome narrowly targeted reforms by reconfiguring their operations.

For these and other reasons, we are skeptical that reform agendas that focus narrowly on isolating and excising specific extractive practices will be enough, on their own, to get the job done. Without question, winning policy changes that curb such practices (and leveraging them to make further advances possible) will be essential for making progress in the years ahead. The most productive of these, if the goal is to *end* predation, will be "non-reformist" reforms—changes to policy and law that scale back predatory operations, weaken and isolate their defenders, undermine their justifications, and help to build political solidarity and power.

Given the tremendous political and institutional advantages of predation's defenders, the kinds of political power needed to end legal plunder are unlikely to emerge from organizing and advocacy efforts that focus solely on extractive modes of policing and punishment. Success will depend on developing a broader, more diverse, and more formidable coalition by expanding the scope of conflict.[26]

In practical terms, this means making concerted efforts to build on what activists and advocates have already done to ground their work in broader justice agendas and collaborate with like-minded organizations in policy arenas closely related to their own. Opportunities for doing so are plentiful. A predatory perspective encourages attention to several in particular.

As we have already suggested, decisions regarding public finance define an especially relevant and important arena of conflict. The restructuring of fiscal arrangements in the 1970s and '80s helped to initiate the rise of new revenue-generating criminal legal practices, and intense budgetary pressures have helped to sustain and expand them since. Today, predatory revenues are used to fill budget holes and subsidize operations across a wide array of government arenas. Institutional dependence on these funds has become a significant obstacle to meaningful reform.

For these reasons, and to ensure that restrictions on predatory modes of provision do not cause legally entangled individuals and their loved ones to lose access to vital goods and services, reformers have good reasons to engage the politics of public finance. Victories that curtail extractive practices often depend on securing compensatory funding for government entities that stand to lose revenue. This is why, as we discussed in chapter 10, advocates and officials in California (2021) and New Jersey (2023) tied their fee-elimination measures to new budget allocations for state agencies and local governments. Abolitionists have a robust history of engagement with budgetary politics. Their "divest/invest" agendas have long focused on defunding police and penal operations *and* investing in alternative models for promoting community safety and social and environmental well-being.[27]

There are also more fundamental reasons to connect contemporary struggles over legal plunder and public finance. Throughout US history, public finance laws, rules, and procedures have served as a basis for predatory racial injustices in their own right, as Andrew W. Kahrl powerfully demonstrates in his book, *The Black Tax: 150 Years of Theft, Exploitation, and Dispossession in America.*[28] Kahrl introduces his book with a capsule summary that foregrounds many of the same themes we have explored in this study.

> *The Black Tax* tells . . . the story of Black people's struggles against local tax systems that forced them to pay more for less and subjected them to heavy penalties and the threat of dispossession when they failed to pay on time. It is the story of how these tax structures were built and maintained and whose interests they served. It is the story of those who exploited the machinery of local tax enforcement, and Black people's vulnerabilities and disadvantages as property owners, to amass wealth and property at their expense; of the riches they accumulated; and of the trail of destruction they left behind. It is the story of how Black Americans resisted exploitation, guarded against predation, and fought for an equitable distribution of public goods and services.[29]

The uses of property taxation for racial exploitation and dispossession, Kahrl shows, persist to the present day. Surveying the broader landscape, Brian Highsmith argues that public finance in the US today is organized to facilitate "the structural violence of municipal hoarding."[30] Jurisdictional boundaries, race and class segregation, and constraints on local taxation and resource transfers combine to shield White wealth from redistribution and thwart "efforts to equitably provide education, infrastructure, public safety, and other critical services."[31] Communities disadvantaged by race and class are forced to endure deprivations of public goods and services, systematic underinvestment, and the financial burdens of regressive municipal funding practices—including criminal legal fines and fees.[32]

In these and other ways, the politics of public finance and legal plunder are already and necessarily entangled. The injustices that advocates are fighting in the two arenas are, in many respects, overlapping, and they offer significant opportunities for political collaboration. There are also good foundations to build on in pursuing this work. Abolitionist groups have developed effective models for doing so and, over the past fifty years, have increasingly focused on public budgets as a basis for analysis and organizing.[33] At the community level, many have become active participants in "People's Budget" coalitions that formulate concrete alternatives to the fiscal priorities and categories of governments.[34] In some cases, such as the statewide coalition Californians United for a Responsible Budget (CURB), organizations fighting to restructure public finance have grown directly out of campaigns to reduce the footprint of penal governance.[35]

Beyond abolitionist efforts, some leading organizations in the fight against legal plunder have become increasingly involved in the politics of public finance. Joanna Weiss, codirector of the Fines and Fees Justice Center, stressed this agenda as she pressed New York officials to lift the state's cap on property taxes in 2019: "When local governments cannot use property taxes to fund the services their residents need, they fill revenue gaps [with criminal legal] fines and fees. . . . Lifting the cap will help prevent the harms [to communities] that come from alternative regressive tax schemes imposed by local governments in the form of fines and fees."[36] Efforts to make such connections have helped to move revenue-generating criminal legal practices onto the agendas of some important policy organizations in the field of public finance, such as the Urban Institute's Tax Policy Center.[37] The Debt Collective connects legal plunder and public finance in a more politically ambitious way by incorporating criminal legal debtors into their broader campaigns against the pervasive injustices of debt production and exploitation in America (see chapter 10). Failures to provide "what should be publicly financed goods" are the common source of such inequities, the group argues, and we can only end them by creating a more just and democratic system of public finance.[38]

Beyond this arena, we have argued throughout this book for the importance of connecting legal plunder to broader structural injustices and pursuing the fight against it on these terms. For many advocacy, activist, and social movement organizations, the struggle against criminal legal takings is fundamentally about achieving justice for people in racially oppressed poor and working-class communities. This vision has proven to be a powerful basis for community organizing and for drawing new activist and advocacy organizations into the fight, including some of the nation's most prominent (e.g., the NAACP). In addition to pursuing more of this work, efforts to assemble a stronger and more intersectional justice coalition can build on a point we have emphasized in this book: criminal justice predation is rife with *gender-based* injustices.

The need for a stronger oppositional coalition is not, however, the primary reason why we see the pursuit of broader justice agendas as essential for putting an end to legal plunder. A predatory perspective identifies criminal legal resource stripping as a particular instance of something more general: the systematic exploitation and dispossession of subjugated communities. It underlines the fundamental connections between criminal justice predation and the structural injustices of oppression, domination, and exclusion. The conditions that give rise to systematic criminal legal takings are the same ones that underwrite other forms of predation, and getting free of them is a project of emancipatory struggle. The Movement for Black Lives has exemplified this agenda, as organizers have incorporated legal plunder into a political project that aims to reconceive and transform "all of the forces that inhibit Black people's ability to live and thrive."[39]

Some advocates may worry that direct ties to such struggles will make campaigns against criminal legal takings too "radical" and, therefore, will be counterproductive for efforts to sway policymakers and win reforms. On this point, it bears repeating that there are good strategic reasons to frame the fight in different ways, depending on immediate audiences and goals. But the meaning of "radical" (going to the roots) underscores why a strong grounding in emancipatory movements is essential. In much of the discourse that surrounds criminal legal takings, discussions of race- and class-based injustices center on *who is targeted*. From this perspective, racial injustice may be seen as an imperative matter for some policy questions and goals but less germane for others. Engagement with it ceases to be optional, however, if we shift the political focus from who is targeted for legal plunder to its enabling conditions—to its roots in structural inequalities and injustices. Shifts in predation have tended to be minimal, or even counterproductive, when reforms have left these roots undisturbed. They have been far more substantial when political struggles have restructured the underlying terms of the social order.

Finally, a predatory perspective highlights opportunities to connect the fight against criminal legal takings to movements for reparations. Expanding the agenda in this way could bring in new allies and shift the terms of conflict to collective injustices. But the reasons to do so run deeper than such strategic considerations. A moral and political reckoning with criminal justice predation calls for more than just fighting to end existing practices. It requires acknowledging the injustices of legal plunder, taking political responsibility for them, and working to effectively repair their harms.

When we began this project, Ta-Nehisi Coates's 2014 article, "The Case for Reparations," loomed large in the ways we thought about predation— and, in fact, was the inspiration for our use of the term "legal plunder."[40] Coates's argument for reparations focuses on how the exploitation and dispossession of Black people has made White wealth, prosperity, and liberal democracy possible in the US. His central theme is theft—through force, deception, and manipulation. "Enslaved Africans [were] plundered of their bodies," he writes, "plundered of their families, and plundered of their labor." The Jim Crow South was "in all facets of society, a kleptocracy . . . the state's regime partnered robbery of the franchise with robbery of the purse." From lands taken through "legal chicanery" to rapacious housing, lending, and banking practices, Coates makes his case for reparations based on the long history of state-sanctioned predation of Black communities.

Over the past decade, a growing number of organizations, activists, and scholars have joined the call for reparations, elaborated justifications for pursuing them, and proposed ways to design and implement such programs. A small but rising number of cities have adopted policies that they designate as reparations, and some states, most notably California, have proposed or created task forces to work on the issue. An idea that was widely dismissed not so long ago has gathered political momentum, risen on the agendas of mainstream justice organizations,[41] and mobilized networks of scholars, policy experts, advocacy organizations, and activist groups.[42]

Focusing especially on Black and Indigenous peoples, the contemporary movement resuscitates and builds on a long tradition of reparations campaigns in America and around the world.[43] Most advocates focus their arguments on the compounding effects of historical injustices and how the many harms inflicted on earlier generations now affect their descendants. Implicitly or explicitly, the leading justifications tend to be based on a line of reasoning similar to Charles Mills's argument that what "racial justice requires is that people not be differentially and invidiously treated by race, and that where such treatment has left a legacy, it should be corrected for."[44] Like Coates, however, most advocates stress that the racial injustices that must be rectified are ongoing—as seen so clearly in this book. In practical terms, reparations agendas typically call for implementing targeted compensatory measures as part of a broader "program of acknowledgment, redress, and closure for grievous injustices."[45]

The growing movement has generated many visions of what compensatory measures might entail. As a result, campaigns against criminal justice predation have a wide range of options for incorporating reparations agendas into their work. In their influential 2020 book, *From Here to Equality*, William A. Darity Jr. and A. Kirsten Mullen place America's staggering Black–White wealth gap at the center of their analysis.[46] To close this gap and move the nation toward racial equality, they argue, reparations must be carried out at the federal level and focus primarily on making direct payments to individuals.

Alternatively, Rashad Williams and Justin Steil advocate for more diverse and localized urban and regional planning initiatives. "Individualistic efforts to redistribute wealth would be beneficial [but] are inadequate to address collective elements of harm," they argue. "Reparative planning offers an opportunity to focus on collective repair."[47] Others advocate for using policies (at various levels of government) to provide free college tuition, forgive student loans, subsidize housing down payments, and support the growth and success of Black-owned businesses—or to eliminate racial inequalities in K–12 public school funding or in healthcare access and outcomes.[48]

The massive amounts of resources plundered through criminal justice predation since the 1980s, in our view, make reparations agendas all the more important. Many people living in RCS communities today have directly experienced grievous harms that, to satisfy the demands of justice, must be acknowledged and remedied. In some cases, government agencies may have records that can be used to estimate how much resource stripping has taken place in a jurisdiction—or at least the amount of public revenue generated. Indeed, such records might even make it possible to pursue reparations from some of the many corporations that have profited so handsomely from legal plunder. Of course, any community investments or individual payments achieved in this way would represent a small fraction of what has been lost and could not undo the damage done. But it would be a meaningful step toward reckoning with a profound injustice, and one with considerable potential to promote and legitimize the broader agendas of the reparations movement.

For all they do to advance the cause of justice, however, compensatory reparations, even sizable ones, can take us only so far. They redistribute resources on a societal terrain that remains geared toward the exploitation and dispossession of subjugated groups. To go further, Olúfẹ́mi Táíwò argues, we must pursue a "constructive" vision of reparations through political projects that define structural injustices as the targets of repair and reparation as the construction of a just world.[49] As Táíwò shows, such visions of repair are not new. They have been developed, debated, and championed by decolonial movements and people engaged in emancipatory struggles for a very long time.

The regime of legal plunder that thrives in America today has ravaged the nation's most oppressed and marginalized communities for decades. What is needed to truly repair its injustices? First and foremost, its predatory operations must be put to an end so that people in such communities do not continue to be stripped of what little they have and forced to suffer its devastating consequences. The nation must also acknowledge and redress the grievous injustices of the regime—considering not only the vast scale of the harms it has caused but also the full depth and breadth of benefits it has produced for dominant groups and institutions. Ultimately, however, the only way to truly rectify the predatory injustices of the past and present is to create a future in which *all* communities can live under conditions of freedom and equality in a just, caring, and democratic social order.

ACKNOWLEDGMENTS

Over the years of working on this project, we accumulated countless personal and professional debts. Generous support and steady encouragement sustained us along the way. Close readings and critical engagements by friends and colleagues pushed us to revise claims, reconsider interpretations, and sharpen arguments. Without the vital work of those who engaged these issues for many years before us, it would have been impossible to research and write *Legal Plunder*. We are especially grateful to Tracey Meares and Vesla Weaver, who organized a small conference in 2015 that allowed us to workshop our early ideas with a brilliant group of participants, urged us to move forward with the project, and provided our first funding for research assistance. From the start, Larry Jacobs insisted on the importance of publishing our project as a book and offered valuable support and guidance.

For careful, thoughtful, and enthusiastic research assistance, we thank Caity Curry, Alejandra Diaz, AshLee Smith, Jack Gramlich, Austin Jenkins, Rebecca Maung, Chase Hobbs-Morgan, Victoria Piehowski, Eric Seligman, Thalya Yanell Reyes, Ryan Steel, Brieanna Watters, Rowan Wylie, Trinity Sitzman, and Nasema Zeerak. Friends and colleagues helped us track down data, encouraged us to keep going, and provided an invaluable source of critiques and suggestions. We give special thanks to Spencer Piston, Karin Martin, Rob Stewart, Sarah Shannon, Chris Muller, Brett Burkhart, Phil Goodman, Marie Gottschalk, Michael Walker, Michelle Phelps, Chris Uggen, Sandy Schram, Forrest Stuart, Sarah Lageson, Jonathan Simon, Andy Papachristos, Noah Zatz, Adam Reich, Beth Colgan, Jeff Selbin, Michael Gibson-Light, Alexes Harris, Kaaryn Gustafson, Chloe Thurston, Brian Highsmith, Lauren-Brooke Eisen, Mary Fainsod Katzenstein, Mitali Nagrecha, Christine Scott-Hayward, Anna Hall, Tommaso Bardelli, and Danica Rodarmel.

We are especially grateful to our superb editor, Sara Doskow, and others at the University of Chicago Press for championing this book, providing thoughtful guidance for our revisions, and bringing it to publication.

It has been a joy to work with you all. Thanks also to the anonymous reviewers for their serious engagement with the book and insightful feedback, which pushed us to tighten and sharpen our analysis. Letta Page, editor extraordinaire, helped us whip the manuscript into shape. Through her efforts, the book became leaner, clearer, and more engaging. Thank you!

The case study presented in chapters 6–8 would not have been possible without the cooperation of A-Team Bail Bonds. We are grateful to the company's owners for allowing Josh to conduct his ethnographic research, and to the staff for sharing the tricks of the trade as well as their perspectives on bail and a host of related matters.

Josh thanks the faculty, staff, and students in the Department of Sociology for their encouragement and friendship. He's grateful to the College of Liberal Arts and the Fink and Talle families for financial support during the writing process. He greatly appreciates Galen, Hannah, and everybody else at East Lake Aikido, his home away from home. He thanks his wonderful family for their unconditional love and support. His pups—Jasper (RIP), Penny (RIP), Hattie, and Izzy—laid by his side (or barked out the window) as he wrote at the kitchen table and read in the captain's chair. He's so grateful for their companionship. Finally, he thanks Letta a million times over for providing constant love, encouragement, and guidance, and filling their home with warm smiles, cheerful laughter, and fresh flowers.

Joe thanks the faculty, students, and staff of the Humphrey School, Political Science, and Sociology for their support and engagement. For friendships and encouragement that sustained him through the research and writing process, he thanks Peter Hoeffel, Jay Burritt, Andrew Kashian, Peter Noble, Noah Levy, Lenn Burnett, and the broader West Bank community. His devoted canine research assistants, Maybelle (RIP) and June Bug, put in long hours and sometimes let him know with an insistent paw when it was time to close the laptop and get some sleep. Eli Soss and Emil Soss grew into young adults during the years it took to write this book, and their love, humor, and support (and questions about the project!) were a gift at every step along the way. Most of all, Joe is grateful to share his life with Kira Dahlk and the seemingly endless supply of love, care, creativity, laughter, companionship, and wisdom that she brings to the world.

APPENDIX

Methodology and Ethics

In this appendix, we discuss methodological and ethical issues related to our case study of commercial bail predation, starting with the ethnographic research that stands at its center.

Ethnographic Research at A-Team

Page's ethnographic research ultimately became the basis for an extended case study of predation in the bail bond industry. But that's not how it began. In fact, Page had been studying the industry and conducting research at A-Team for some time before we ever discussed the concept of predation or the possibility of collaborating on a book project. He initially set out to study bail practices and pretrial processes for other reasons. The topic was attractive, in part, because of Page's long-standing interests in labor and the everyday work of criminal legal governance. In an earlier study of California prison officers and their unions, he had developed a deep appreciation of the ways frontline workers can shape penal policy and practice.[1] The bail sector offered Page an opportunity to extend his interests to a new (and potentially quite different) arena, where street-level actors have considerable autonomy and discretion to make decisions of consequence for people's lives.

It also presented Page with an opportunity to build on his earlier study of how the California Correctional Peace Officers' Association built power, pursued political influence, and reshaped the penal field.[2] The bail bond lobby, largely funded and organized by insurance companies, had become a similarly formidable interest group—rich in resources, well connected, integrated into conservative coalitions, and effective at shaping pretrial policies and industry regulations. Page was eager to study the industry in a way that connected bail lobby work at the top to storefront operations at the bottom.

Indeed, such a study seemed all the more promising in light of the growing focus on privatization among scholars and activists in the field.

A disproportionate amount of attention focused on for-profit prisons, Page noted, but private bail bond businesses had been operating for far longer and dominated their sector to a much greater degree. By investigating how profit motives shaped the structure of the industry, local business operations, and bond agents' practices, Page hoped to produce sector-specific insights that illuminated for-profit criminal legal governance in general.

As Page contemplated these possibilities, he was struck by how little was known about the working world of commercial bail. He kept coming back to something Malcolm Feeley wrote in the groundbreaking 1979 book, *The Process Is the Punishment*: "There has been virtually no scholarly interest in the bail bondsman . . . [and] this neglect and perfunctory dismissal cannot be attributed to the bondsman's lack of importance."[3] Decades later, and amid an outpouring of research on police, courts, community supervision, and prisons, the sentiment still rang true. The industry had grown dramatically, and more and more defendants relied on bonds to secure pretrial release from jail. Yet, the research literature on commercial bail—including its role and significance in the penal state—remained paper thin.

From the start, Page saw the distinctive advantages of grounding his project in ethnographic research, and for this reason, he ultimately decided to seek employment as a bail bond agent. In this position, he could not only observe but also participate in the day-to-day routines of bail work, producing "the most direct evidence on action as the action unfolds in everyday life."[4] On the job, Page would learn about the social, cultural, and material organization of bail work through firsthand experience—his understandings would develop and be tested, time and again, based on his practical need to *effectively* navigate this particular social terrain.

As a method that unfolds over time, participant observation allows the researcher to compare words and deeds and analyze how they vary across actors and settings.[5] Immersive ethnography provides an especially effective way to "observe how people make sense of their worlds, to chart how they ground their ideas in everyday practices and administrative routines."[6] It offers repeated opportunities to explore how people's circumstances and understandings combine to produce (what appear to them as) *sensible reasons* to pursue some choices and actions rather than others. It maximizes the chances of encountering puzzling events that challenge what researchers think they know and push them to pursue unexpected lines of inquiry.[7] Through direct engagement, the researcher learns and, in various ways, embodies the cognitive, emotional, and discursive conditions of participation in the field of social action.[8]

Getting hired as a bail agent took some time. Page needed to find a company owner who would hire him *and* allow his research. Lacking contacts in the industry, Page sent out feelers to colleagues, friends, and acquaintances in several states. Eventually, he received word that a friend of a friend knew a personable owner who was willing to hear Page out. Page was up front about his motivation—to understand the world of bail by participating in it. He presented himself as a curious professor, eager to learn about the industry from his more experienced and knowledgeable coworkers. (Since he knew little about the inner workings of the bond business, this presentation was accurate.) The owner was eager to show him the ropes and explain that bond agents are important service providers, part of a helping profession. After a couple conversations, A-Team's owner agreed to hire Page and allow him to conduct his study.

A-Team is a professional, well-managed, successful business. Page's conversations with lawyers and other companies' agents; consultations of industry, media, and governmental reports; and direct observations all suggested that A-Team did not differ in any fundamental way from most bail businesses in large urban counties. A-Team, however, should not be mistaken for a representative case of commercial bail in the sense that a statistical sample might be representative of a broader population. Commercial bail is a diverse industry, and no single company can be treated as a stand-in for all local bail businesses, accurately revealing in one site what happens everywhere else. Rather, A-Team and Rocksville provided Page with a concrete case of organized actors navigating and grappling with the general conditions of the industry—a productive vantage point for analyzing the broader structures and forces that shape local bond business practices throughout the US. Ethnographic research at A-Team made it possible to investigate, experience, and analyze the day-to-day workings of the street-level bail game in fine-grained detail.

Page's position as a university professor distinguished him from his new coworkers at A-Team, but (perhaps surprisingly) it seemed to facilitate rather than hinder his acceptance into the group. Bail agents tend not to be well respected in the legal field, and media rarely portray them in a favorable light. For some of Page's coworkers, having a professor on staff who valued what they knew and wanted to learn from them became a source of pride. Page's research signaled that their line of work (and their company specifically) was worthy of serious scholarly attention. On several occasions, Page even had to ask his colleagues *not* to introduce him as a professor because he wanted people (such as lawyers and clients) to interact with him like they would any other agent. His coworkers understood and, over time, referred to him as "the professor" less and less.

Other aspects of Page's social position also helped him fit in at A-Team. Like most of his coworkers, Page is White and middle class. Although he has lived in cities for many years, he grew up in the suburbs of Southern California, which made it easier to relate to his colleagues' suburban self-conceptions and routines. Importantly, his physical appearance and interests (especially in sports) read as traditionally masculine; he has an athletic build, practices martial arts, and his arms are covered with tattoos. A-Team is a masculine space. Men made up a majority of the personnel, and most of the agents (women included) were aggressive competitors who ribbed each other, specialized in ribald humor, and claimed not to "take shit" from anyone.

Once he learned the basics of his new job, Page worked hard to demonstrate that he was a serious bail agent and team player. He joined in the same activities as his coworkers. He solicited business at court, worked daytime and nighttime desk shifts, posted bonds at courthouses throughout the state, developed relationships with attorneys, checked warrants, and followed up with defendants who missed court or did not make payments. He also tried to help out coworkers whenever he could—for example, by subbing for them if they needed time off, working undesirable evening shifts, and helping write advertisements for hiring new agents. Fully engaging in the social life of the company was important as well. Page regularly went for lunch or afternoon coffee with coworkers, attended company parties, and exchanged texts with colleagues about bail, sports, television, movies, and life events.

Page also made concerted efforts to blend into the courthouse scene in Rocksville. Following his colleagues' lead, he tried to come across as a legal professional. This was not difficult since his bearing, dress (flat-front pants, button-down shirt, sports coat, and hat), and worn attaché case made him appear a lot like the lawyers in the building. Because he looked and acted the part, friends and family members of defendants were rarely taken aback when he approached them. Most potential clients were initially reticent with Page, and some remained so throughout their interactions with him. But this was normally the case for Page's coworkers as well. Race and class inequalities likely played a significant role (most potential clients were low-income people of color). Perceptions of the bail agent's power contributed to fear and distrust as well. Understandably, many clients see bail bond companies as just another part of the "system." Like welfare workers, court clerks, and cops, bail agents are often seen as people who could use the information that clients provide against them in harmful ways.

Distrust and reticence are usually (and rightly) seen as obstacles to good ethnographic research. In this case, however, Page was not studying bail bond clients or their experiences. He contacted clients only to discuss matters directly related to A-Team's bond services and did not delve into their personal lives. Page's research focused on the working world of bail agents and the practices that bail company personnel use to recruit clients, secure cosigners, collect payments, and so forth. He wanted to understand how agents understood and pursued their work. As we discuss in chapter 7, efforts to ease potential clients' apprehensions and build rapport and trust play a central role in bail agents' recruitment tactics. Page's encounters with wary and reticent clients mirrored the experiences of his coworkers. His efforts to understand why many clients eventually opened up to agents—and even expressed gratitude for their efforts—led to some of his most important insights into the nature of bail bond work, the meanings it holds for agents, and the legitimizing beliefs that help to sustain it.

With permission from A-Team's owners, Page wrote extensive field notes on and off the job. The rhythms and routines of bail work proved advantageous in this regard. At the office, agents frequently sat at their computers, scrolling through jail rosters, sending out and receiving contracts, or surfing the internet. Page fit right in when he popped open his laptop to take notes. At the courthouse, too, agents often wrote down case details, phone numbers, and other useful information. Sitting in the court "pews," they took notes on legal pads or printouts of the "first appearance" docket. So, there was nothing unusual about Page writing notes of his own. He was often able to jot down direct quotes and detailed descriptions of courthouse scenes and events as they unfolded in real time. In addition, Page made significant use of audio field notes. In situations where note-writing was impractical or inappropriate (e.g., at lunch with coworkers), he could briefly step away to record observations on his phone. Audio notes also proved useful for documenting Page's emotions and states of mind during particular events. Listening back to the recordings—which captured not only his words but also telling changes in his voice and breathing—returned Page in a *physical* way to key moments in his fieldwork, even years later.

Guided by Loïc Wacquant's writings on "carnal sociology" and "enactive ethnography," Page paid close attention to his own emotions—not just those of the people he was studying—throughout his fieldwork.[9] By continually reflecting on how he felt in the field, he gained critical insights into the "habitus" of the street-level bail game. The rush he felt when he landed relatively large bonds, for example, felt familiar from his time playing competitive soccer as a teenager and softball as an adult. Now, as then, he was thrilled to beat the competition, help his team win, and receive recognition from his teammates. An insecure novice not so long ago, these moments testified that he had learned the trade well and become accepted among his peers. His exhilaration was also evidence that he had become invested in the bail game and internalized the relentless drive that pushes agents to constantly check jail rosters, work their networks, and answer phone calls during meals and in the middle of the night.

Page saw the injustices of the bail industry all too clearly, first as a scholar and now as a participant, too. This recognition frequently led to more painful and complicated emotions, both on and off the job. But Page was not surprised when he felt disconcerted or went through bouts of sadness or outrage. He had anticipated as much from the outset. In the doing, however, his participatory research had produced something more unexpected—a taste for the "hustle" and pride at winning the game. Page paid close attention to these feelings, not only to limit the risks they posed but also as an ongoing development that required explanation. In this manner, Page came to understand more clearly how the structural conditions of street-level bail work cultivated motivations, dispositions, and emotional investments: the intensely competitive nature of the market, commission-based pay schemes that require agents to hustle just to make a living, sales competitions that pitted A-Team agents against one another, managerial surveillance and exhortations to "always be closing," and the struggle for positive recognition among people who engage in the stigmatized and disavowed forms of labor that Everett Hughes called "dirty work."[10]

Casing the Study

Page's research began as a study of commercial bail and the pretrial process; it became a study of criminal justice predation, situated at the street level of a particular sector of extractive operations (i.e., the bail bond industry). This transition occurred through a process that one of us (Soss) has described as *casing* a study. This process, which can occur at any point in a research project, involves revisiting and reimagining what one's study might best be treated as a case *of*—how it might be fruitfully analyzed and theorized in different ways.[11] A shift in casing "allows the researcher to put the study into dialogue with a different set of empirical phenomena, creating new standpoints for interpretation; new paths for generalization; and new terms for relational, processual, or comparative analysis."[12] The re-casing was a social process from the start, sparked by political events and a thought-provoking workshop invitation and then developed through a series of coffee shop conversations between the two of us.

In 2015, we were both asked to participate in a workshop at Yale Law School titled "Deconstructing Ferguson: How Social Institutions, Policy, and Law Shape American Civic Identity and Experience." The organizers, Tracy Meares and Vesla Weaver, asked participants to step away from their current projects and write a fresh "idea brief" for discussion at the workshop. We considered several ideas, but with our attention focused on Black Lives Matter protests and a bombshell report recently released by the US Department of Justice, we kept returning to questions raised by revelations that police and courts in Ferguson, Missouri had been using racially targeted fine-and-fee practices to generate municipal revenues on a vast scale. Timing mattered in a second way as well: We had both recently read and admired Richard Young and Jeffrey Meiser's analysis of how race served as the basis for a "dual state," *predatory* for some and *liberal-contractual* for others, in the early American republic. Drawing on Young and Meiser's work, we wrote a brief that framed Ferguson's revenue-generating practices as part of a broader *contemporary* development: the rise of "predatory" modes of criminal legal governance across the US that siphoned resources from oppressed communities and turned them into sizable streams of public and private revenue.

Participants at the workshop asked tough questions, but they were enthusiastic about the brief and urged us to consider writing a book. Afterward, Meares and Weaver offered further encouragement and even supplied funding for our first research assistant. We continued to pursue and refine the ideas laid out in our brief, eventually abandoning the concept of a "predator state" (for reasons discussed in our Introduction) in favor of developing a different kind of analytic framework focused on *predatory relations and practices.*

Page's research at A-Team guided and grounded our earliest discussions, and one day he suggested drawing on it to write a case study of bail predation for the book. Soss was initially hesitant, worrying that the new project might "hijack" a nearly completed research effort, but Page allayed his concerns by outlining plans to pursue parts of his original agenda in separate publications. So, we began to talk in a more focused way about how commercial bail operates as a site of predatory relations and practices, how it works as part of a more expansive network of extractive criminal legal operations, and how Page's ethnographic research might make distinctive contributions to a broader study of criminal justice predation in America today.

While Page continued to pursue his initial research interests, we were now asking new questions and applying different analytic frames to what he had experienced and observed as a bail agent. We tried to learn all that we could from the study of A-Team and Rocksville by interrogating it, at various levels of abstraction, as a case of predatory relations and practices, a case of bail-based predation, a case of implementation processes that convert predatory designs into practices, and a case for studying the kinds of discourses that help to legitimize predation. We also began to see how Page's research offered unique opportunities to explore questions that were beyond our reach elsewhere in the book, such as how street-level practices are organized and improvised in effective ways, how practitioners understand and manage their relations with legally entangled people, and how race, class, and gender organize and orient legal plunder *in the doing.*

In chapters 6–8, we explore these and other issues through an extended case study of bail predation, anchored in Page's ethnographic research. Drawing on the writings of Michael Burawoy and Clyde Mitchell, Mario L. Small discusses two meanings of the term "extended" in this context.[13] In one sense, it refers to a case study in which "researchers analyze a particular social situation in relation to the broader social forces shaping it."[14] Researchers ask how social, cultural, and material structures shape action at the field site; how actors exercise agency in consequential ways amid the social forces in which they are embedded; and what research at the site can contribute to our understanding of how these broader structures operate in the social order. In a second sense, the term "extended" refers to a case study that is carried out over a substantial period of time, allowing for analysis of how actors understand and respond to "a series of situations" and how relevant social processes develop, unfold, and culminate. Both meanings describe the approach we adopt in our extended case study of bail predation.

Our "re-casing" of Page's ethnographic study in terms of *predation* was eased considerably by the fact that he had been taking field notes on relevant themes all along. From the outset, he had identified exploitation and profit-generating practices as important dimensions of his larger study of commercial bail and pretrial processes. Early in his fieldwork, Page also began to note parallels between the ways that bail businesses and courts imposed financial charges. At A-Team, defendants routinely complained about hefty court fines and fees and the steep charges they had to pay for various conditions of pretrial release (such as electronic monitoring and drug and alcohol testing). These observations prompted conversations about how public and private actors collaborate in criminal legal governance and often extract resources in similar ways. On the job at A-Team, Page had learned how courts and bail companies depend on one another and how, in their predatory operations, they exhibit a similar logic of practice.

In fact, this is just one of the many ways that Page's ethnographic research shaped and informed the larger study presented in this book. Page's observations of how gender structured predatory practices in the bail field pushed us to explore this dynamic in other arenas. As Page described the various companies that hawked their wares to bond businesses, trying to tap into the profitable world of commercial bail, we began to think about how revenue-seeking actors try to "piggyback" on extractive operations in other criminal legal arenas—and how this process works to intensify and multiply predatory takings as a whole. The diversity of legitimizing rationales that Page encountered among street-level practitioners—and the ways they differed from the defenses emphasized by the bail industry lobby—encouraged us to analyze how legal plunder may be supported by multiple (and sometimes contradictory) discourses and how justifications can vary across arenas and levels of practice.

Importantly, Page's research also served as a steady reminder of how an analysis of predatory relations and practices can be distorted by assumptions that participating actors are and must be "predators." This sort of character-defining label—designating a *type* of person—clashed with Page's experiences of his coworkers, the diversity of their behaviors at work, and the complex mixtures of beliefs, values, and intentions guiding their actions. Even the most aggressive and deceptive agents at A-Team regularly gave clients a break and treated them with respect and sympathy. They often spoke with pride about the care and service they offered to distressed clients. Many felt conflicted about their jobs and vacillated between different ways of making sense of it. As we explain in chapters 7 and 8, attention to these sorts of complexities is essential for understanding how bail predation works and how its practitioners sustain a sense that what they do is acceptable and worthwhile. It also underscores that no matter what Page and his coworkers believed or intended, or how well they treated or supported their clients, they operated within a business model—a *structure* of relations and practices—designed to exploit the desperate circumstances of accused individuals and their loved ones for profit.

The Ethics of Ethnographic Bail Research

An ethnographic study based on participation in the bail industry raises important questions of research ethics. After all, we argue that the industry operates in a predatory manner and should be understood as a site of significant injustice. We detail how street-level businesses and bond agents leverage the conditions of pretrial incarceration (and all the fears, needs, and vulnerabilities that come with it) to generate profits. Was it ethical for Page to pursue ethnographic research by working as a bail bond agent?

Conventional guidelines for research ethics—adopted by professional associations, universities, government agencies, and the like—generally focus on research procedures and the potential for studies to expose "human subjects" to risks or harms that would not exist in their absence.[15] From this perspective, several features of the project merit note. The project received formal approval from the University of Minnesota's Institutional Review Board (IRB) for research ethics. Working at A-Team, Page was paid commissions from sales, but he did not keep any as personal income. Aside from a portion used to pay for research assistance early in the project (until he received a grant), he donated all of his after-tax earnings to community organizations. We use pseudonyms for all individuals, organizations, and locations, and we have taken steps to ensure that none of the details we report can be used to identify A-Team, its staff, or its clients. On the job, Page tried to conform to company expectations and the prevailing norms and practices of his more experienced colleagues, minimizing the chances that his presence could significantly alter the experiences of clients or coworkers. (To the best of our knowledge, Page's research did not disrupt or change how A-Team carried out its business, compared to the periods before and after his employment or relative to the counterfactual of A-Team hiring a novice bail agent who was not conducting research.)

The ethical questions at hand, however, go beyond the specifics of Page's *research*. Was it ethical for Page to *participate* in the commercial bail industry? Conventional criteria for research ethics offer little guidance for addressing this sort of question because, in an important sense, they are one-sided. They focus overwhelmingly on the design and conduct of research, paying little or no attention to dilemmas and responsibilities that operate prior to or outside the study itself. In most textbook discussions and professional guidelines, where there is no research, there can be no problem of research ethics. Matters of ethical consequence arise only once we "intervene" through the act of research itself.

In contrast, scholars who adopt interpretive and critical approaches to social science tend to start with the assumption that researchers are already implicated in—are already, in an important sense, *participating* in—the social worlds they study, even if they elect not to study them. From this perspective, ethical dilemmas and responsibilities must be contemplated in a more balanced way, as a basis for evaluating action and inaction alike. As the scholarship on "bystander phenomena" makes clear, a decision to stay on the sidelines, declining to get involved when confronted with an atrocity or injustice, is in some cases a significant abdication of ethical and political responsibility.[16] Guided by political theorists such as Iris Marion Young and Clarissa Hayward, we begin from the premise that people who participate in, benefit from, and are positioned to act upon unjust arrangements have a political responsibility to "normatively evaluate [these structural injustices], analyze how they share responsibility with others for shaping and reshaping them, and act together with those others to change the relevant structures in justice-promoting ways."[17]

Throughout this book, we argue that predatory practices that strip resources from subjugated communities subsidize the quality of life that relatively advantaged Americans experience. They generate corporate and individual wealth, create middle-class jobs, underwrite state and societal institutions, ease the tax burdens of middle- and upper-class citizens, and more. This is to say, those of us who do not work within or get pulled into the nation's criminal legal institutions are *not* nonparticipants; we just participate on terms that make it easy to maintain social, spatial, and cognitive distance from our involvement and responsibility.

Indeed, as employees of the University of Minnesota, we make our living by directly participating in an institution that benefits from predation. After President Abraham Lincoln signed the Morrill Act in 1862, the federal government granted the university 4,631 acres of Daḳota lands taken through violence and deception.[18] In its early years, the university used funding from a known slave owner to build "Old Main," the campus's first building and symbolic "heart."[19] Today, the university purchases furniture and laundry services from MINNCOR, the state department of corrections' prison industries program.[20] The university's recreation and wellness center has used incarcerated laborers to erect a "sports dome" during winters so college students can participate in recreational activities without exposure to the elements.[21]

By working at A-Team, Page made his involvement in and responsibility for criminal justice predation explicit, becoming a direct participant in the bail industry in order to bring its practices to public light and clarify how bail predation is enacted and legitimized at the street level. The research was motivated, in part, by the ethical and political responsibility to *do something* in response to the bail industry's ongoing invisibility in scholarship and in society as a whole. Page pursued his participatory study because it appeared to offer the best way to understand the work itself—and thus, to develop a critical and effective analysis of how bail-based predation is organized and carried out.

If Page had forgone this research, the bail industry would have been no less predatory; the distribution of its harms would have been altered in no meaningful way; and our responsibility for the industry's injustices, while certainly less visible and direct, would have remained. Sometimes ethically complex research—inserting ourselves into troubling forms of social action in a more overt way—is worth pursuing precisely because it offers a way to take responsibility for societal injustices that are already being carried out in our names and to the benefit of those of us who occupy relatively advantaged social positions.

No formula for cost-benefit accounting can generate a summary yes-or-no ethical grade for such research. Nor can the procedure-centered judgments of the University of Minnesota's IRB, which approved this "human subjects" research, be seen as the final word on the complex ethical questions involved. In ethnographic research, as in much of social life, participation is a subject that must be wrestled with on moral terms that go beyond professional research ethics guidelines. The bail industry in the US today presents us with no easy answers as we endeavor, both as scholars and citizens, to understand how it works, explain what it does, and put an end to its injustices.

NOTES

Introduction

1. Patrick Irving, "Prisoners like Me Are Being Held Hostage to Price Hikes," *New York Times*, November 2, 2022, https://www.nytimes.com/2022/11/02/opinion/inflation-prison.html. All of the quotes in the next three paragraphs are from this editorial.

2. Peter Wagner and Bernadette Rabuy, *Following the Money of Mass Incarceration* (Prison Policy Initiative, 2017), https://www.prisonpolicy.org/reports/money.html.

3. "Executive Order 14006 of January 26, 2021, Reforming Our Incarceration System to Eliminate the Use of Privately Operated Criminal Detention Facilities," *Compilation of Presidential Documents* (2021); Jocelyn Rosnick, "Orange Is the New Black Tackles Prisons for Profit," ACLU Ohio, June 17, 2016, https://www.acluohio.org/en/news/orange-new-black-tackles-prisons-profit.

4. US Department of Justice Civil Rights Division, *Investigation of the Ferguson Police Department*, March 4, 2015, 14, https://www.justice.gov/sites/default/files/opa/press-releases/attachments/2015/03/04/ferguson_police_department_report.pdf; Ta-Nehisi Coates, "The Gangsters of Ferguson," *Atlantic*, March 5, 2015, https://www.theatlantic.com/politics/archive/2015/03/The-Gangsters-Of-Ferguson/386893/.

5. Brandon Stahl, "Philando Castile Was Caught Up in a Cycle of Traffic Stops, Fines," *Star Tribune*, July 17, 2016, https://www.startribune.com/castile-lived-in-a-cycle-of-traffic-stops-fines/387046341/.

6. The quote from Ms. Castile is available here: News on Purpose, "Remembrance of Philando Castile Rally," filmed July 6, 2020, at St. Anthony Village City Hall & Community Center, St. Anthony, MN, Facebook video, 3:22:58, https://m.facebook.com/newsonpurpose/videos/remembrance-of-philando-castile-rally/3031165067002164/?_rdr.

7. Jennifer Gonnerman, "Before the Law," *New Yorker*, September 29, 2014, https://www.newyorker.com/magazine/2014/10/06/before-the-law.

8. Gonnerman, "Before the Law."

9. Shawn Carter, "Jay Z: For Father's Day, I'm Taking On the Exploitative Bail Industry," *Time*, June 16, 2017, https://time.com/4821547/jay-z-racism-bail-bonds/.

10. Carter, "Jay Z."

11. David Montgomery, "Sandra Bland, It Turns Out, Filmed Traffic Stop Confrontation Herself," *New York Times*, May 7, 2019, https://www.nytimes.com/2019/05/07/us/sandra-bland-video-brian-encinia.html.

12. See, e.g., Sara Mayeux, "The Idea of 'The Criminal Justice System,'" *American Journal of Criminal Law* 45, no. 1 (2018): 55–94, https://scholarship.law.vanderbilt.edu/faculty-publications/898; John Pfaff, *Locked In: The True Causes of Mass Incarceration and How to Achieve Real Reform* (Basic Books, 2017), 70.

13. See, e.g., Alexes Harris, *A Pound of Flesh: Monetary Sanctions as Punishment for the Poor* (Russell Sage Foundation, 2016); Alexes Harris, Heather Evans, and Katherine Beckett, "Drawing Blood from Stones: Legal Debt and Social Inequality in the Contemporary United States," *American Journal of Sociology* 115, no. 6 (May 2010): 1753–99, https://www.jstor.org/stable/10.1086/651463.

14. See, e.g., Lauren-Brooke Eisen, *Inside Private Prisons: An American Dilemma in the Age of Mass Incarceration* (Columbia University Press, 2018); David Shichor and Michael J. Gilbert, *Privatization of Criminal Justice: Past, Present, and Future* (Routledge, 2001).

15. See, e.g., Ariel Jurow Kleiman, "Nonmarket Criminal Justice Fees," *Hastings Law Journal* 72 (2021): 517; Henry Ordower, J. S. Onesimo Sandoval, and Kenneth Warren, "Out of Ferguson: Misdemeanors, Municipal Courts, Tax Distribution, and Constitutional Limitations," *Howard Law Journal* 61, no. 1 (2016).

16. See, e.g., Mary Fainsod Katzenstein and Maureen R. Waller, "Taxing the Poor: Incarceration, Poverty Governance, and the Seizure of Family Resources," *Perspectives on Politics* 13, no. 3 (September 2015): 638–56, https://doi.org/10.1017/S153759271500122X; Jackie Wang, *Carceral Capitalism* (Semiotext(e), 2018).

17. Keeanga-Yamahtta Taylor, *Race for Profit: How Banks and the Real Estate Industry Undermined Black Homeownership* (University of North Carolina Press, 2019).

18. Devah Pager, *Marked: Race, Crime, and Finding Work in an Era of Mass Incarceration* (University of Chicago Press, 2009).

19. Loïc Wacquant, "Deadly Symbiosis: When Ghetto and Prison Meet and Mesh," *Punishment & Society* 3, no. 1 (2001): 105, https://doi.org/10.1177/1462474011222876.

20. Graham Rayman and Reuven Blau, *Rikers: An Oral History* (Random House, 2023).

21. On RCS communities, see Joe Soss and Vesla Weaver, "Police Are Our Government: Politics, Political Science, and the Policing of Race-Class Subjugated Communities," *Annual Review of Political Science* 20 (2017): 565–91, https://doi.org/10.1146/annurev-polisci-060415-093825.

22. See, e.g., Greta R. Krippner, *Capitalizing on Crisis: The Political Origins of the Rise of Finance* (Harvard University Press, 2011).

23. Wendy Brown, *Undoing the Demos: Neoliberalism's Stealth Revolution* (Zone Books, 2015).

24. For a discussion of analytic sites and vantage points, see Thea Riofrancos, "From Cases to Sites: Studying Global Processes in Comparative Politics," in *Rethinking Comparison: Innovative Methods for Qualitative Political Inquiry*, ed. Erica S. Simmons and Nicholas Rush Smith (Cambridge University Press, 2021).

25. See, e.g., Matthew Desmond, *Poverty, by America* (Crown Books, 2023).

26. On police and prison abolition, see, e.g., Michael J. Coyle and David Scott, eds., *The Routledge International Handbook of Penal Abolition* (Routledge, 2021); Angela Y. Davis, Gina Dent, Erica R. Meiners, and Beth E. Ritchie, *Abolition. Feminism. Now* (Haymarket Books, 2022); Mariame Kaba and Andrea J. Richie, *No More Police: The Case for Abolition* (New Press, 2022).

27. See, e.g., Mohamed Shehk, Pilar Weiss, Rachel Foran, Sharlyn Grace, and Woods Ervin, *On the Road to Freedom: An Abolitionist Assessment of Pretrial and Bail Reforms* (Critical Resistance and Community Justice Exchange, June 2021).

28. Critical Resistance, "Reformist Reforms vs. Abolitionist Steps to End Imprisonment," *Community Resource Hub*, accessed September 23, 2022, https://communityresourcehub.org/resources/reformist-reforms-vs-abolitionist-steps-in-policing/.

29. See, e.g., Beth A. Colgan, "Beyond Graduation: Economic Sanctions and Structural Reform," *Duke Law Journal* 69 (April 2020): 1550.

30. See, e.g., Daniel Béland, Andrea Louise Campbell, and R. Kent Weaver, *Policy Feedback: How Policies Shape Politics* (Cambridge University Press, 2022).

31. Jacob S. Hacker, "Between the Waves: Building Power for a Public Option," *Journal of Health Politics, Policy, and Law* 46, no. 4 (2021): 535–47.

32. Mayeux, "The Idea of 'The Criminal Justice System.'"

33. Erica Bryant, "Why We Say 'Criminal Legal System,' Not 'Criminal Justice System,'" Vera Institute of Justice, December 1, 2021, https://www.vera.org/news/why-we-say-criminal-legal-system-not-criminal-justice-system.

34. Robin Steinberg, *The Courage of Compassion: A Journey from Judgment to Connection* (Optimism Press, 2023), 2.

Chapter One

1. Alexes Harris, *A Pound of Flesh: Monetary Sanctions as Punishment for the Poor* (Russell Sage Foundation, 2016); Peter Edelman, *Not a Crime to Be Poor: The Criminalization of Poverty in America* (New Press, 2017).

2. Mary Pattillo and Gabriela Kirk, "Layaway Freedom: Coercive Financialization in the Criminal Legal System," *American Journal of Sociology* 126, no. 4 (January 2021): 896, https://doi.org/10.1086/712871.

3. Lisa Wedeen, *Authoritarian Apprehensions: Ideology, Judgment, and Mourning in Syria* (University of Chicago Press, 2019); Jennifer L. Hochschild, "Disjunction and Ambivalence in Citizens' Political Outlooks," in *Reconsidering the Democratic Public*, ed. G. E. Marcus and R. L. Hanson (Pennsylvania State University Press, 1993), 187–210.

4. Devah Pager, Rebecca Goldstein, Helen Ho, and Bruce Western, "Criminalizing Poverty: The Consequences of Court Fees in a Randomized Experiment," *American Sociological Review* 87, no. 3 (February 2022): 533, https://doi.org/10.1177/0003122422107783.

5. Mallory E. SoRelle, *Democracy Declined: The Failed Politics of Consumer Financial Protection* (University of Chicago Press, 2020), 255.

6. Boaz Moselle and Benjamin Polak, "A Model of a Predatory State," *Journal of Law, Economics, and Organization* 17, no. 1 (April 2001): 1–33, https://ssrn.com/abstract=832264; Cameron G. Thies, "The Political Economy of State Building in Sub-Saharan Africa," *Journal of Politics* 69, no. 3 (August 2007): 716–31, https://doi.org/10.1111/j.1468-2508.2007.00570.x; Kenneth Kalu, Olajumoke Yacob-Haliso, and Toyin Falola, eds., *Africa's Big Men: Predatory State-Society Relations in Africa* (Routledge, 2018).

7. Douglass North, *Structure and Change in Economic History* (W. W. Norton, 1981).

8. Thies, "The Political Economy," 717.

9. Boaz Moselle and Benjamin Polak, "A Model of a Predatory State," 1–33.

10. Charles Tilly, "War Making and State Making as Organized Crime," in *Bringing the State Back In*, ed. Peter Evans, Dietrich Rueschemeyer, and Theda Skocpol (Cambridge University Press, 1985).

11. For a "dual-state" adaptation, see Richard Young and Jeffrey Meiser, "Race and the Dual State in the Early American Republic," in *Race and American Political Development*, ed. Joseph Lowndes, Julie Novkov, and Dorian T. Warren (Routledge, 2008), 31–58.

12. Kimberly J. Morgan and Ann Shola Orloff, eds., *The Many Hands of the State: Theorizing Political Authority and Social Control* (Cambridge University Press, 2017).

13. Max Weber, *Economy and Society: An Outline of Interpretive Sociology* (University of California Press, 1978 [1922]).

14. Dalton Conley, *Being Black, Living in the Red: Race, Wealth, and Social Policy in America* (University of California Press, 2010).

15. Charles Tilly, *Durable Inequality* (University of California Press, 1999).

16. Keeanga-Yamahtta Taylor, *Race for Profit: How Banks and the Real Estate Industry Undermined Black Homeownership* (University of North Carolina Press, 2019).

17. Louise Seamster and Raphaël Charron-Chénier, "Predatory Inclusion and Education Debt: Rethinking the Racial Wealth Gap," *Social Currents* 4, no. 3 (2017): 199–200, https://doi.org/10.1177/2329496516686620.

18. Henry-Louis Taylor Jr., "Disrupting Market-Based Predatory Development: Race, Class, and the Underdevelopment of Black Neighborhoods in the U.S.," *Journal of Race, Ethnicity and the City* 1, nos. 1–2 (2020): 16–21, https://doi.org/10.1080/26884674.2020.1798204.

19. Douglas Massey and Nancy Denton, *American Apartheid: Segregation and the Making of the Urban Underclass* (Harvard University Press, 1993); Richard Rothstein, *The Color of Law: The Forgotten History of How Our Government Segregated America* (Liveright, 2017); Taylor, *Race for Profit*.

20. Kenneth B. Clark, *Dark Ghetto: Dilemmas of Social Power* (Harper & Row, 1965); Loïc Wacquant, "Deadly Symbiosis: When Ghetto and Prison Meet and Mesh," *Punishment & Society* 3, no. 1 (2001): 95–133, https://doi.org/10.1177/1462474012228276.

21. Chloe Thurston, *At the Boundaries of Homeownership: Credit, Discrimination, and the American State* (Cambridge University Press, 2018); Beryl Satter, *Family Properties: How the Struggle over Race and Real Estate Transformed Chicago and Urban America* (Picador, 2010).

22. Wendell E. Pritchett, "The 'Public Menace' of Blight: Urban Renewal and the Private Uses of Eminent Domain," *Yale Law & Policy Review* 21, no. 1 (2003): 1–52.

23. Steven M. Graves, "Landscapes of Predation, Landscapes of Neglect: A Location Analysis of Payday Lenders and Banks," *Professional Geographer* 55, no. 3 (2003): 303–17, https://doi.org/10.1111/0033-0124.5503017; Megan Doherty Bea, "Relational Foundations of an Unequal Consumer Credit Market: Symbiotic Ties Between Banks and Payday Lenders," *Journal of Consumer Affairs* 57, no. 1 (2023): 320–45, https://doi.org/10.1111/joca.12501.

24. Tilly, *Durable Inequality*, 10; Matthew Desmond and Nathan Wilmers, "Do the Poor Pay More for Housing? Exploitation, Profit, and Risk in Rental Markets," *American Journal of Sociology* 124, no. 4 (2019): 1090–1124, https://doi-org.ezp3.lib.umn.edu/10.1086/701697.

25. William Baude, "Rethinking the Federal Eminent Domain Power," *Yale Law Journal* 122, no. 7 (2013): 1738–1825, https://ssrn.com/abstract=2270442; Siddhant Issar, "Theorising 'Racial/Colonial Primitive Accumulation': Settler Colonialism, Slavery and Racial Capitalism," *Race & Class* 63, no. 1 (2021): 23–50, https://journals.sagepub.com/doi/10.1177/0306396821996273.

26. Onur Ulas Ince, "Primitive Accumulation, New Enclosures, and Global Land Grabs: A Theoretical Intervention," *Rural Sociology* 79, no. 1 (2013): 104–31, https://doi.org/10.1111/ruso.12025; Nikhil Pal Singh, "On Race, Violence, and So-Called

Primitive Accumulation," *Social Text* 34, no. 3 (2016): 27–50, https://doi.org/10.1215/01642472-3607564.

27. Nancy Fraser, "Expropriation and Exploitation in Racialized Capitalism: A Reply to Michael Dawson," *Critical Historical Studies* 3, no. 1 (Spring 2016): 166–67, https://doi.org/10.1086/685814.

28. Pritchett, "The 'Public Menace' of Blight."

29. Robert Nichols, *Theft Is Property! Dispossession and Critical Theory* (Duke University Press, 2020).

30. Nichols, *Theft Is Property*, 8, 34.

31. On relational analysis, see Mustafa Emirbayer, "Manifesto for a Relational Sociology," *American Journal of Sociology* 103, no. 2 (September 1997): 281–317, https://doi.org/10.1086/231209; Donald Tomaskovic-Devey and Dustin Avent-Holt, *Relational Inequalities: An Organizational Approach* (Oxford University Press, 2019); Tilly, *Durable Inequality*.

32. Alexander Wendt, "On Constitution and Causation in International Relations," *Review of International Studies* 24, no. 5 (December 1998): 101–18, https://www.jstor.org/stable/20097563.

33. Ella Baker and Marvel Cooke, "The Bronx Slave Market," *The Crisis*, November 1935, 330.

34. Baker and Cooke, "The Bronx Slave Market," 340.

35. Destin Jenkins and Justin Leroy, "Introduction: The Old History of Capitalism," in *Histories of Racial Capitalism*, ed. Destin Jenkins and Justin Leroy (Columbia University Press, 2021), 1–26.

36. Jodi Melamed, "Racial Capitalism," *Critical Ethnic Studies* 1, no. 1 (2015): 76–85, https://doi.org/10.5749/jcritethnstud.1.1.0076; Michael Dawson, "Why Race and Capitalism Not Racial Capitalism," March 25, 2021, https://c4ejournal.net/2021/03/26/michael-dawson-why-race-and-capitalism-not-racial-capitalism-2021-c4ej-27/; Satam Virdee, "Racialized Capitalism: An Account of Its Contested Origins and Consolidation," *Sociological Review* 67, no. 1 (2019): 3–27, https://doi-org.ezp1.lib.umn.edu/10.1177/0038026118820293.

37. Gargi Bhattacharyya, *Rethinking Racial Capitalism: Questions of Reproduction and Survival* (Rowman & Littlefield, 2018).

38. Ta-Nehisi Coates, "The Case for Reparations," *Atlantic*, June 2014, https://www.theatlantic.com/magazine/archive/2014/06/the-case-for-reparations/361631/.

39. Manning Marable, *How Capitalism Underdeveloped Black America* (South End Press, 1983), 2.

40. Patrick Wolfe, *Traces of History: Elementary Structures of Race* (Verso, 2016); Bhattacharyya, *Rethinking Racial Capitalism*.

41. Jenkins and Leroy, *Histories of Racial Capitalism*; Michael C. Dawson, "Hidden in Plain Sight: A Note on Legitimation Crises and the Racial Order," *Critical Historical Studies* 3, no. 1 (March 1, 2016): 143–61, https://doi.org/10.1086/685540; Fraser, "Expropriation and Exploitation."

42. Melamed, "Racial Capitalism," 76–85; Jenkins and Leroy, *Histories of Racial Capitalism*.

43. Tithi Bhattacharya, *Social Reproduction Theory: Remapping Class, Recentering Oppression* (Pluto Press, 2017); Sylvia Federici, *Revolution at Point Zero: Housework, Reproduction, and Feminist Struggle* (PM Press, 2012).

44. Fraser, "Expropriation and Exploitation"; Dawson, "Hidden in Plain Sight"; Nancy Fraser, "Behind Marx's Hidden Abode: For an Expanded Conception of

Capitalism," *New Left Review* 896 (March 2014): 55–72, https://newleftreview.org/issues/ii86/articles/nancy-fraser-behind-marx-s-hidden-abode.pdf.

45. Evelyn Nakano Glenn, *Forced to Care: Coercion and Caregiving in America* (Harvard University Press, 2010); Jacqueline Jones, *Labor of Love, Labor of Sorrow: Black Women, Work, and the Family, from Slavery to the Present* (Basic Books, 2010).

46. Dawson, "Hidden in Plain Sight."

47. On RCS communities, see Joe Soss and Vesla Weaver, "Police Are Our Government: Politics, Political Science, and the Policing of Race-Class Subjugated Communities," *Annual Review of Political Science* 20 (2017): 565–91, https://doi.org/10.1146/annurev-polisci-060415-093825. On the gendered social organization of care, see Glenn, *Forced to Care.*

48. All quotations in this paragraph are from Michael Dawson and Emily Katzenstein, "Articulated Darkness: White Supremacy, Patriarchy, and Capitalism in Shelby's *Dark Ghettos," Journal of Political Philosophy* 27 (2019): 264.

49. George Lipsitz, "What Is This Black in the Black Radical Tradition," in *Futures of Black Radicalism,* ed. Gaye Theresa Johnson and Alex Lubin (Verso, 2017), 108–19.

50. W. E. B. Du Bois, *Black Reconstruction in America: An Essay Toward a History of the Part Which Black Folk Played in the Attempt to Reconstruct Democracy in America, 1860–1880* (Free Press, 1998 [1935]); Lipsitz, "What Is This Black," 108–19; Robin D. G. Kelley, *Freedom Dreams: The Black Radical Imagination* (Beacon Press, 2003).

51. Shauna Sweeney, "Gendering Racial Capitalism and the Black Heretical Tradition," in Jenkins and Leroy, *Histories of Racial Capitalism,* 53–83; Françoise N. Hamlin, *Crossroads at Clarkdale: The Black Freedom Struggle in the Mississippi Delta After World War II* (University of North Carolina Press, 2014); Angela Davis, "Reflections on the Black Woman's Role in the Community of Slaves," *Massachusetts Review* 13, no. 1/2 (1972): 81–100, https://www.jstor.org/stable/2088201.

52. Henry-Louis Taylor Jr., "The Urban Process and City Building Under Racial Capitalism," *Journal of Race, Ethnicity and the City* 5, no. 1 (2023): 95–105, https://doi.org/10.1080/26884674.2023.22794313.

53. David Roediger, *Class, Race, and Marxism* (Verso, 2017), 103.

54. Kevin Bruyneel, *Settler Memory: The Disavowal of Indigeneity and the Politics of Race in the United States* (University of North Carolina Press, 2021), 1–20.

55. Walter L. Hixson, *American Settler Colonialism: A History* (Palgrave MacMillan, 2013); Nick Estes, *Our History Is the Future: Standing Rock versus the Dakota Access Pipeline, and the Long Tradition of Indigenous Resistance* (Verso, 2019).

56. Sweeney, "Gendering Racial Capitalism," 66; Sylvian Diouf, *Slavery's Exiles: The Story of the American Maroons* (New York University Press, 2014).

57. Du Bois, *Black Reconstruction in America,* 49–75.

58. Issar, "Theorising 'Racial/Colonial Primitive Accumulation'"; Wolfe, *Traces of History.*

59. K-Sue Park, "Race, Innovation, and Financial Growth: The Example of Foreclosure," in Jenkins and Leroy, *Histories of Racial Capitalism,* 27.

60. Barbara Fields, "Slavery, Race, and Ideology in the United States of America," *New Left Review,* May/June 1990; David Brion Davis, *The Problem of Slavery in the Age of Revolution, 1770–1823* (Oxford University Press, 1999 [1975]); Max Carocci and Stephanie Pratt, eds., *Native American Adoption, Captivity, and Slavery in Changing Contexts* (Palgrave Macmillan, 2012).

61. Patrick Wolfe, "Land, Labor, and Difference: Elementary Structures of Race," *American Historical Review* 106, no. 3 (2001): 866–905, https://doi.org/10.2307/

2692330; Robert F. Berkhofer Jr., *The White Man's Indian: Images of the American Indian from Columbus to the Present* (Vintage Books, 1979).

62. Wolfe, *Traces of History*, 52.

63. Barbara Fields, "Ideology and Race in American History," in *Region, Race, and Reconstruction: Essays in Honor of C. Vann Woodward*, ed. J. M. Kousser and J. M. McPherson (Oxford University Press, 1982), 143–77.

64. Patrick Wolfe, "Race and the Trace of History: For Henry Reynolds," in *Studies in Settler Colonialism: Politics, Identity, and Culture*, ed. Fiona Bateman and Lionel Pilkington (Palgrave Macmillan, 2011), 273.

65. Evelyn Nakano Glenn, "Settler Colonialism as Structure: A Framework for Comparative Studies of U.S. Race and Gender Formation," *Sociology of Race and Ethnicity* 1, no. 1 (2015): 52–72, http://dx.doi.org/10.1177/2332649214560440; Wolfe, "Land, Labor, and Difference," 866–905.

66. Glenn, "Settler Colonialism as Structure," 52–72.

67. Patricia Hill Collins, *Black Feminist Thought: Knowledge, Consciousness, and the Politics of Empowerment*, 2nd ed. (Routledge, 2014); Micki McElya, *Clinging to Mammy: The Faithful Slave in Twentieth Century America* (Harvard University Press, 2007).

68. Patrick Wolfe, "Nation and MiscegeNation: Discursive Continuity in the Post-Mabo Era," *Social Analysis* 36 (October 1994): 93–152, https://www.jstor.org/stable/23171805; Berkhofer Jr., *The White Man's Indian.*

69. Rayna Green, "The Pocahontas Perplex: The Image of Indian Women in American Culture," *Massachusetts Review* 16, no. 4 (Autumn 1975): 698–714, https://www.jstor.org/stable/25088595; Michael Paul Rogin, *Ronald Reagan, the Movie: And Other Episodes in Political Demonology* (University of California Press, 1988).

70. Patrick Wolfe, "Settler Colonialism and the Elimination of the Native," *Journal of Genocide Research* 8, no. 4 (2006): 387, https://doi.org/10.1080/14623520601056240; Ian Haney Lopez, *White by Law: Legal Construction of Race*, 2nd ed. (New York University Press, 2006).

71. Sweeney, "Gendering Racial Capitalism," 60.

72. Wolfe, "Land, Labor, and Difference"; Berkhofer Jr., *The White Man's Indian.*

73. Wolfe, "Settler Colonialism and the Elimination of the Native," 388.

74. Ann M. Carlos, Donna M. Feir, and Angela Redish, "Indigenous Nations and the Development of the U.S. Economy: Land, Resources, and Dispossession," *Journal of Economic History* 82, no. 2 (2022): 516–55, https://doi.org/10.1017/S0022050722000080.

75. Young and Meiser, "Race and the Dual State," 43.

76. Young and Meiser, "Race and the Dual State," 40.

77. Young and Meiser, "Race and the Dual State," 42.

78. Park, "Race, Innovation, and Financial Growth," 28.

79. Park, "Race, Innovation, and Financial Growth," 28.

80. Park, "Race, Innovation, and Financial Growth," 28; K-Sue Park, "Money, Mortgages, and the Conquest of America," *Law and Social Inquiry* 41, no. 4 (2016): 1006–35, http://dx.doi.org/10.1111/lsi.12222.

81. Du Bois, *Black Reconstruction in America*, 5.

82. Edward E. Baptist, *The Half Has Never Been Told: Slavery and the Making of American Capitalism* (Basic Books, 2014); Walter Johnson, *River of Dark Dreams: Slavery and Empire in the Cotton Kingdom* (Harvard University Press, 2013).

83. Thomas Piketty and Gabriel Zucman, "Capital Is Back: Wealth-Income Ratios in Rich Countries 1700–2010," *Quarterly Journal of Economics* 129, no. 3 (August 2014): 1300–1302, https://doi.org/10.1093/qje/qju018.

84. Caitlin Rosenthal, *Accounting for Slavery: Masters and Management* (Harvard University Press, 2018).

85. Sidney W. Mintz, *Sweetness and Power: The Place of Sugar in Modern History* (Penguin, 1986).

86. Harriet A. Washington, *Medical Apartheid: The Dark History of Medical Experimentation on Black Americans from Colonial Times to the Present* (Anchor Books, 2006), 26, 54.

87. Don E. Fehrenbacher, *The Slaveholding Republic: An Account of the United States Government's Relation to Slavery* (Oxford University Press, 2001); Young and Meiser, "Race and the Dual State."

88. Young and Meiser, "Race and the Dual State," 42.

89. Young and Meiser, "Race and the Dual State," 33.

90. David Waldstreicher, *Slavery's Constitution: From Revolution to Ratification* (Hill and Wang, 2009), 3; Fehrenbacher, *The Slaveholding Republic*; David F. Ericson, *Slavery in the American Republic: Developing the Federal Government, 1791–1861* (University Press of Kansas, 2011).

91. Young and Meiser, "Race and the Dual State," 37–39; Aziz Rana, *The Two Faces of American Freedom* (Harvard University Press, 2014).

92. Ira Katznelson, "Flexible Capacity: The Military and Early American Statebuilding," in *Shaped by War and Trade*, ed. Ira Katznelson and Martin Shefter (Princeton University Press, 2002), 104.

93. Katznelson, "Flexible Capacity," 91.

94. Robin Einhorn, *American Taxation, American Slavery* (University of Chicago Press, 2006).

95. Robin Einhorn, *Tax Aversion and the Legacy of Slavery* (University of Chicago Press, 2006), https://press.uchicago.edu/Misc/Chicago/194876.html.

96. Joel Olson, *The Abolition of White Democracy* (University of Minnesota Press, 2004).

97. Edmund S. Morgan, "Slavery and Freedom: The American Paradox," *Journal of American History* 59, no. 1 (1972): 28, https://doi.org/10.2307/1888384.

98. Morgan, "Slavery and Freedom," 28.

99. Morgan, "Slavery and Freedom," 29.

100. Rogers M. Smith, *Civic Ideals: Conflicting Visions of Citizenship in US History* (Yale University Press, 1997).

101. Adam Dahl, *Empire of the People: Settler Colonialism and the Foundations of Modern Democratic Thought* (University Press of Kansas, 2018).

102. Aziz Rana, "American Democracy and Its Imperial Roots," *LPE Project* (blog), April 19, 2022, https://lpeproject.org/blog/american-social-democracy-and-its-imperial-roots/.

103. Judith N. Shklar, *American Citizenship: The Quest for Inclusion* (Harvard University Press, 1991).

104. Danielle Allen, "Invisible Citizens: Political Exclusion and Domination in Arendt and Ellison," *Nomos* 46 (2005): 28–76.

105. Cristina Beltrán, *Cruelty as Citizenship: How Migrant Suffering Sustains White Democracy* (University of Minnesota Press, 2020).

106. Olson, *The Abolition of White Democracy*.

107. Du Bois, *Black Reconstruction in America*, 700.

108. Jeff Goodwin, "Black Reconstruction as Class War," *Catalyst* 6, no. 1 (2022): 52–95, https://catalyst-journal.com/2022/06/black-reconstruction-as-class-war.

109. Olson, *The Abolition of White Democracy.*

110. Bernadette Atuahene, "A Theory of Stategraft," *New York University Law Review* 98, no. 1 (2023): 1–48.

111. Tonya L. Brito et al., "Racial Capitalism in the Civil Courts," *Columbia Law Review* 122, no. 5 (2022): 1243–86, https://columbialawreview.org/content/racial -capitalism-in-the-civil-courts/.

112. Nichols, *Theft Is Property*; Hixson, *American Settler Colonialism.*

113. Ben Brucato, "Fabricating the Color Line in a White Democracy: From Slave Catchers to Petty Sovereigns," *Theoria: A Journal of Social and Political Theory* 61, no. 141 (2014): 39.

114. Alex Vitale, *The End of Policing* (Verso, 2017), 44.

115. Kelly Lytle Hernández, *City of Inmates: Conquest, Rebellion, and the Rise of Human Caging in Los Angeles, 1771–1965* (University of North Carolina Press, 2017), 35.

116. Hernández, *City of Inmates*, 36.

117. Office of Indian Affairs, Washington, DC, *Annual Report of the Commissioner of Indian Affairs (1881)*, https://digital.library.wisc.edu/1711.dl/3YVW4ZRARQT7J8S, xvii–xviii. We are grateful to Brieanna Watters for bringing this document and quote to our attention.

118. Ben Brucato, "Policing Race and Racing Policing: The Origin of US Police in Slave Patrols," *Social Justice* 47, no. 3–4 (2020): 126, https://www.jstor.org/stable/ 27094596.

119. Brucato, "Policing Race and Racing Policing," 130.

120. Brucato, "Policing Race and Racing Policing," 130–31.

121. Vitale, *The End of Policing*, 47.

122. Eric Foner, *Reconstruction* (Harper Perennial Modern Classics, 2015), 203.

123. Foner, *Reconstruction*, 201.

124. Christopher Muller and Daniel Schrage, "The Political Economy of Incarceration in the Cotton South, 1910–1925," *American Journal of Sociology* 127, no. 3 (2021), https://doi-org.ezp2.lib.umn.edu/10.1086/718045.

125. Douglas Blackmon, *Slavery by Another Name: The Re-Enslavement of Black Americans from the Civil War to World War II* (Anchor Books, 2008), 53.

126. Oshinsky, *Worse Than Slavery* (Free Press, 1996), 21.

127. Oshinsky, *Worse Than Slavery*, 21; Muller and Schrage, "The Political Economy of Incarceration in the Cotton South, 1910–1925."

128. Geeta Chowdhry and Mark Beeman, "Situating Colonialism, Race, and Punishment," in *Race, Gender, and Punishment: From Colonialism to the War on Terror*, ed. Mary Bosworth and Jeanne Flavin (Rutgers University Press, 2007), 26.

129. Chowdhry and Beeman, "Situating Colonialism, Race, and Punishment," 26.

130. Foner, *Reconstruction*, 200.

131. Ida B. Wells, *Crusade for Justice: The Autobiography of Ida B. Wells* (University of Chicago Press, 1970), 63.

132. Stewart E. Tolnay and E. M. Beck, *A Festival of Violence: An Analysis of Southern Lynchings* (University of Illinois Press, 1995).

133. Naomi Murakawa, "Ida B. Wells on Racial Criminalization," in *African American Political Thought: A Collected History*, ed. Melvin L. Rogers and Jack Turner (University of Chicago Press, 2021), 224.

134. Isabel Wilkerson, *The Warmth of Other Suns: The Epic Story of America's Great Migration* (Penguin Random House, 2011).

135. Massey and Denton, *American Apartheid*, 28–29.

136. Loïc Wacquant, "A Janus-Faced Institution of Ethnoracial Closure: A Sociological Specification of the Ghetto," in *The Ghetto: Contemporary Global Issues and Controversies*, ed. Ray Hutchison and Bruce D. Haynes (Routledge, 2012), 8.

137. Wacquant, "A Janus-Faced Institution of Ethnoracial Closure," 7.

138. Vitale, *The End of Policing*, 48.

139. Monica Bell, "Anti-Segregation Policing," *New York University Law Review* 95, no. 3 (2020): 717, https://ssrn.com/abstract=3610953. See also Robert Blauner, "Internal Colonialism and Ghetto Revolt," *Social Problems* 16, no. 4 (1969): 404, https://doi.org/10.2307/799949.

140. James Baldwin, "Fifth Avenue, Uptown," *Esquire*, October 16, 2007 (July 1960), https://www.esquire.com/news-politics/a3638/fifth-avenue-uptown/.

141. Elise C. Boddie, "Racially Territorial Policing in Black Neighborhoods," *University of Chicago Law Review* 89, no. 2 (2022): 477–98, https://ssrn.com/abstract=4050958.

142. Clark, *Dark Ghetto*, 28.

143. Mehrsa Baradaran, *The Color of Money: Black Banks and the Racial Wealth Gap* (Belknap Press, 2017), 110.

144. Simon Balto, *Occupied Territory: Policing Black Chicago from Red Summer to Black Power* (University of North Carolina Press, 2019), 73.

145. Balto, *Occupied Territory*, 73.

146. Balto, *Occupied Territory*, 76.

147. Warren Wright, "The Big Steal," in *Colonialism in Modern America: The Appalachian Case*, ed. H. M. Lewis, L. Johnson, and D. Askins (Appalachian Consortium Press, 1978), 161–75.

148. John Gaventa, *Power and Powerlessness: Quiescence and Rebellion in an Appalachian Valley* (University of Illinois Press, 1980), 89.

149. Alex Gourevitch, "Police Work: The Centrality of Labor Repression in American Political History," *Perspectives on Politics* 13, no. 3 (2015): 762–73.

150. Vitale, *The End of Policing*, 40.

151. Rebecca M. McLennan, *The Crisis of Imprisonment: Protest, Politics, and the Making of the American Penal State, 1776–1941* (Cambridge University Press, 2008), 28–29.

152. Roger A. Ekirch, *Bound for America: Convict Transportation to Colonial America* (Oxford University Press, 1987), 58.

153. McLennan, *The Crisis of Imprisonment*, 28.

154. Ekirch, *Bound for America*, 27.

155. Malcolm Feeley, "Entrepreneurs of Punishment: The Legacy of Privatization," *Punishment & Society* 4, no. 3 (2002): 328–29, https://doi.org/10.1177/14624742400426770; Ekirch, *Bound for America*, 3.

156. McLennan, *The Crisis of Imprisonment*, 29.

157. Alan Atkinson, "The Free-Born Englishman Transported: Convict Rights as a Measure of Eighteenth-Century Empire," *Past & Present* 144 (1994): 106, https://www.jstor.org/stable/651144; McLennan, *The Crisis of Imprisonment*, 29.

158. Ekirch, *Bound for America*, 151; McLennan, *The Crisis of Imprisonment*, 30; Atkinson, "The Free-Born Englishman Transported," 102.

159. Atkinson, "The Free-Born Englishman Transported," 100; Ekirch, *Bound for America*, 152.

160. Atkinson, "The Free-Born Englishman Transported," 100; Ekirch, *Bound for America*, 152.

161. Blackmon, *Slavery by Another Name*, 56.

162. Blackmon, *Slavery by Another Name*, 56.

163. Oshinsky, *Worse Than Slavery*, 33–35; Robert Perkinson, *Texas Tough: The Rise of America's Prison Empire* (Metropolitan Books, 2010), 88–89.

164. See, e.g., Matthew J. Mancini, *One Dies, Get Another: Convict Leasing in the American South, 1866–1928* (University of South Carolina Press, 1996).

165. Alex Lichtenstein, *Twice the Work of Free Labor: The Political Economy of Convict Labor in the New South* (Verso, 1996), 3.

166. Lichtenstein, *Twice the Work of Free Labor*, 4.

167. Christopher Muller, "Exclusion and Exploitation: The Incarceration of Black Americans from Slavery to the Present," *Science* 374 (2021): 282–86.

168. Lichtenstein, *Twice the Work of Free Labor*, 5.

169. Oshinsky, *Worse Than Slavery*, 60.

170. Oshinsky, *Worse Than Slavery*, 57.

171. Lichtenstein, *Twice the Work of Free Labor*, xviii.

172. Perkinson, *Texas Tough*, 98–99.

173. Sarah Haley, *No Mercy Here: Gender, Punishment, and the Making of Jim Crow Modernity* (University of North Carolina Press, 2016), 68.

174. Haley, *No Mercy Here*, 67.

175. Talitha L. LeFlouria, "'Under the Sting of the Lash': Gendered Violence, Terror, and Resistance in the South's Convict Camps," *Journal of African American History* 100, no. 3 (June 1, 2015): 366–84, https://doi.org/10.5323/jafriamerhist.100 .3.0366.

176. Phillip Goodman, Joshua Page, and Michelle Phelps, *Breaking the Pendulum: The Long Struggle over Criminal Justice* (Oxford University Press, 2017), chap. 2.

177. Goodman, Page, and Phelps, *Breaking the Pendulum*, chap. 2.

178. Michelle Jones and Lori Record, "Magdalene Laundries: The First Prisons for Women in the United States," *Journal of the Indiana Academy of the Social Sciences* 17, no. 1 (2014): 166, https://sites.tufts.edu/stslunch/files/2018/03/jones-record.pdf.

179. Jones and Record, "Magdalene Laundries," 176, 166.

180. Jones and Record, "Magdalene Laundries," 166–67.

181. McLennan, *The Crisis of Imprisonment*, 58.

182. McLennan, *The Crisis of Imprisonment*, 99.

183. McLennan, *The Crisis of Imprisonment*, 66.

184. McLennan, *The Crisis of Imprisonment*, 105, emphasis in original.

185. McLennan, *The Crisis of Imprisonment*, 111.

186. McLennan, *The Crisis of Imprisonment*, 113.

187. McLennan, *The Crisis of Imprisonment*, 113.

188. McLennan, *The Crisis of Imprisonment*, 233–38; ACLU and The Global Human Rights Clinic at the University of Chicago (GHRC), *Captive Labor: Exploitation of Incarcerated Workers* (June 15, 2022), 26–27, https://www.aclu.org/report/captive -labor-exploitation-incarcerated-workers.

189. Feeley, "Entrepreneurs of Punishment," 333.

190. McLennan, *The Crisis of Imprisonment*, 236–37.

191. Oshinsky, *Worse Than Slavery*, 109.

192. Oshinsky, *Worse Than Slavery*, 110.

193. H. Claire Brown, "How Corporations Buy—and Sell—Food Made with Prison Labor," *The Counter*, May 18, 2021, https://thecounter.org/how-corporations-buy-and-sell-food-made-with-prison-labor/.

194. J. Thorsten Sellin, *Slavery and the Penal System* (Quid Pro Books, 2016 [1976]), 173; Feeley, "Entrepreneurs of Punishment," 333.

195. Oshinsky, *Worse Than Slavery*, 155.

196. Perkinson, *Texas Tough*, 125.

197. Robert T. Chase, "Cell Taught, Self Taught: The Chicano Movement Behind Bars—Urban Chicanos, Rural Prisons, and the Prisoners' Rights Movement," *Journal of Urban History* 41, no. 5 (September 2015): 841, https://doi.org/10.1177/0096144215589949.

198. Chase, "Cell Taught, Self Taught," 841.

199. Chase, "Cell Taught, Self Taught," 841.

200. Hernández, *City of Inmates*, 36.

201. Hernández, *City of Inmates*, 47.

202. Hernández, *City of Inmates*, 60.

203. Lichtenstein, *Twice the Work of Free Labor*, 181.

204. Benjamin Weber, *American Purgatory: Prison Imperialism and the Rise of Mass Incarceration* (New Press, 2023), 85, 89.

205. Weber, *American Purgatory*, 105, emphasis in original.

206. Stephanie Dawn Hinnershitz, *Lessons from the Incarceration and Forced Labor of Japanese Americans During World War II* (Scholars Strategy Network, 2018), https://scholars.org/contribution/lessons-incarceration-and-forced-labor-japanese-americans-during-world-war-ii.

207. Hinnershitz, *Lessons from the Incarceration*.

208. Daniel Engber, "Prisoners Are Fighting Mudslides?," *Slate*, January 12, 2005, https://slate.com/news-and-politics/2005/01/why-prisoners-are-fighting-mudslides.html.

209. Volker Janssen, "When the 'Jungle' Met the Forest: Public Work, Civil Defense, and Prison Camps in Postwar California," *Journal of American History* 96, no. 3 (2009): 703, https://www.jstor.org/stable/25622475.

210. Janssen, "When the 'Jungle' Met the Forest"; Goodman, Page, and Phelps, *Breaking the Pendulum*, chap. 2.

211. Janssen, "When the 'Jungle' Met the Forest," 705.

212. Janssen, "When the 'Jungle' Met the Forest," 712–13.

213. Janssen, "When the 'Jungle' Met the Forest," 714.

214. Jessica Mitford, *Kind and Usual Punishment: The Prison Business* (Alfred A. Knopf, 1973), 167–68.

215. Washington, *Medical Apartheid*, 259–62; Mitford, *Kind and Usual Punishment*, 144–45.

216. Allen Hornblum, *Acres of Skin: Human Experiments at Holmesburg Prison* (Routledge, 1999), 263.

217. Hornblum, *Acres of Skin*, 262.

218. Washington, *Medical Apartheid*, 260.

219. Hornblum, *Acres of Skin*, 26.

220. Mitford, *Kind and Usual Punishment*, 143; Bernard E. Harcourt, "Making Willing Bodies: The University of Chicago Human Experiments at Stateville Penitentiary," *Social Research* 78, no. 2 (2011): 444, https://doi.org/10.1353/sor.2011.0045.

221. Harcourt, "Making Willing Bodies," 454–55.

222. Washington, *Medical Apartheid*, 250.

223. Gary Lee, "Prisoner Irradiation Probed," *Washington Post*, November 20, 1994, https://www.washingtonpost.com/archive/politics/1994/11/20/prisoner-irradiation-probed/908d0102-0021-409c-a0a0-71f0700b3721/.

224. Mitford, *Kind and Usual Punishment*, 145.

225. Hornblum, *Acres of Skin*, chap. 8.

226. Hornblum, *Acres of Skin*, 240; Keramet Reiter, "Experimentation on Prisoners: Persistent Dilemmas in Rights and Regulations," *California Law Review* 97, no. 2 (2009): 514.

227. Jessica Mitford, "Experiments Behind Bars: Doctors, Drug Companies, and Prisoners," *Atlantic*, January 1973, https://www.theatlantic.com/magazine/archive/1973/01/experiments-behind-bars-doctors-drug-companies-and-prisoners/664718/.

228. Reiter, "Experimentation on Prisoners," 514.

229. Mitford, *Kind and Usual Punishment*, 143.

230. Washington, *Medical Apartheid*, 249; Mitford, *Kind and Usual Punishment*, 148–49.

231. Lee, "Prisoner Irradiation Probed."

232. Hornblum, *Acres of Skin*, 242.

233. Reiter, "Experimentation on Prisoners."

234. See, e.g., Heather Ann Thompson, *Blood in the Water: The Attica Uprising of 1971 and Its Legacy* (Pantheon, 2016).

235. Reiter, "Experimentation on Prisoners," 518.

236. See, e.g., Amy Gutmann, *Liberal Equality* (Cambridge University Press, 1980); Ronald Dworkin, "What Is Equality? Part 3: The Place of Liberty," *Iowa Law Review* 73, no. 1 (1987): 1–54, https://heinonline.org/HOL/P?h=hein.journals/ilr73&i=13.

237. Carole Pateman and Charles W. Mills, *Contract and Domination* (Polity Press, 2007).

238. Charles Mills, "Liberalism and the Racial State," in *State of White Supremacy: Racism, Governance, and the United States*, ed. M.-K. Jung, J. H. Costa Vargas, and E. Bonilla-Silva (Stanford University Press, 2011), 27–28.

239. Smith, *Civic Ideals*; Rogers and Turner, *African American Political Thought*.

240. Rogin, *Ronald Reagan, the Movie*, 136.

241. Carole Pateman, *The Sexual Contract* (Polity Press, 1988); Charles Mills, *The Racial Contract* (Cornell University Press, 1997); Pateman and Mills, *Contract and Domination*.

242. Mills, "Liberalism and the Racial State," 30.

243. Mills, "Liberalism and the Racial State," 32; Charles Mills, "Intersecting Contracts," in *Contract and Domination*, 165–99.

244. Charles Mills, "The Domination Contract," in *Contract and Domination*, 87.

245. Rana, *The Two Faces of American Freedom*, 12.

246. Rana, *The Two Faces of American Freedom*, 51.

247. See, e.g., Rogin, *Ronald Reagan, the Movie*, 146–48.

248. Rana, *The Two Faces of American Freedom*, 106–7.

249. Carole Pateman, "The Settler Contract," in *Contract and Domination*, 35–36.

250. Rogin, *Ronald Reagan, the Movie*, 163, 46.

251. Rogin, *Ronald Reagan, the Movie*, 47.

252. Ashley Jardina and Spencer Piston, "The Politics of Racist Dehumanization in the United States," *Annual Review of Political Science* 26 (2023): 369–88; Charles Mills, "Liberalism and the Racial State," 39; Rogin, *Ronald Reagan, the Movie*, 46.

253. Walter Johnson, "A Nettlesome Classic Turns Twenty-Five," *Commonplace* 1, no. 4 (July 2001), http://commonplace.online/article/a-nettlesome-classic-turns-twenty-five/.

254. Cherokee Nation v. Georgia, 30 U.S. (5 Pet.) 1 (1831).

255. David Roediger, *Race, Class, and Marxism*, 107.

256. David Roediger, *Race, Class, and Marxism*, 105.

257. David Roediger, *Race, Class, and Marxism*, 103.

258. Mills, "Liberalism and the Racial State," 33.

259. Charles Mills, "Contract and Social Change," in *Contract and Domination*, 13.

260. Carole Pateman, "Race, Sex, and Indifference," in *Contract and Domination*, 155.

261. Pateman, "Race, Sex, and Indifference," 162.

Chapter Two

1. Sarah Stillman, "Taken," *New Yorker*, August 5, 2013, https://www.newyorker.com/magazine/2013/08/12/taken; "Morrow v. City of Tenaha, et al.—Plaintiff Biographies," ACLU, August 14, 2012, accessed October 13, 2022, https://www.aclu.org/other/morrow-v-city-tenaha-et-al-plaintiff-biographies.

2. On RCS communities, see Joe Soss and Vesla Weaver, "Police Are Our Government: Politics, Political Science, and the Policing of Race-Class Subjugated Communities," *Annual Review of Political Science* 20 (2017): 565–91, https://doi.org/10.1146/annurev-polisci-060415-093825.

3. Terance D. Miethe and Hong Lu, *Punishment: A Comparative Historical Perspective* (Cambridge University Press, 2005).

4. Beth A. Colgan, "Reviving the Excessive Fines Clause," *California Law Review* 102, no. 2 (April 2014): 277.

5. Colgan, "Reviving the Excessive Fines Clause."

6. Douglas Blackmon, *Slavery by Another Name: The Re-Enslavement of Black Americans from the Civil War to World War II* (Anchor Books, 2008).

7. Christopher Muller, "Exclusion and Exploitation: The Incarceration of Black Americans from Slavery to the Present," *Science* 374 (2021): 282–86.

8. Wayne A. Logan and Ronald F. Wright, "Mercenary Criminal Justice," *University of Illinois Law Review* 4 (2014): 1175–1226, https://ir.law.fsu.edu/articles/163.

9. Logan and Wright, "Mercenary Criminal Justice," 1182.

10. Michael Willrich, *City of Courts: Socializing Justice in Progressive Era Chicago* (Cambridge University Press, 2003).

11. Nicholas R. Parillo, *Against the Profit Motive: The Salary Revolution in American Government* (Yale University Press, 2013), 255–94.

12. Willrich, *City of Courts*, 28.

13. Parillo, *Against the Profit Motive*, 259.

14. Parillo, *Against the Profit Motive*, 267.

15. Colgan, "Reviving the Excessive Fines Clause."

16. Parillo, *Against the Profit Motive*, 272–94.

17. Michael Armstrong, "Police Corruption: An Historical Overview," *New York Law School Law Review* 40, no. 1/2 (1995): 59–64.

18. See, e.g., Rebecca M. McLennan, *The Crisis of Imprisonment: Protest, Politics, and the Making of the American Penal State, 1776–1941* (Cambridge University Press, 2008), chap. 4–5.

19. Eric Blumenson and Eva Nilsen, "Policing for Profit: The Drug War's Hidden Economic Agenda," *University of Chicago Law Review* 65, no. 1 (Winter 1998): 75.

20. Blumenson and Nilsen, "Policing for Profit," 75.

21. Caleb Nelson, "The Constitutionality of Civil Forfeiture," *Yale Law Journal* 125 (2015–2016): 2465–66.

22. Nelson, "The Constitutionality of Civil Forfeiture," 2471–72.

23. Nelson, "The Constitutionality of Civil Forfeiture," 2476.

24. Matt Powers, "John Oliver on Civil Forfeiture: 'This Is So Much Worse than We Thought,'" Institute for Justice, February 16, 2016, http://ij.org/john-oliver-on-civil-forfeiture-this-is-so-much-worse-than-we-thought/.

25. Alice W. Dery, "Overview of Asset Forfeiture," *Business Law Today*, June 2012, https://www.americanbar.org/groups/business_law/publications/blt/2012/06/02_dery/.

26. Stillman, "Taken."

27. Michelle Alexander, *The New Jim Crow: Mass Incarceration in the Age of Colorblindness* (New Press, 2010), 72.

28. Alexander, *The New Jim Crow*, 77.

29. Blumenson and Nilsen, "Policing for Profit," 51.

30. Blumenson and Nilsen, "Policing for Profit," 42–56.

31. Alexander, *The New Jim Crow*, 77.

32. Alexander, *The New Jim Crow*, 78.

33. J. Mitchell Miller and Lance H. Selva, "Drug Enforcement's Double-Edged Sword: An Assessment of Asset Forfeiture Programs," *Justice Quarterly* 11, no. 2 (1994): 318.

34. Blumenson and Nilsen, "Policing for Profit," 40. See also Miller and Selva, "Drug Enforcement's Double-Edged Sword."

35. Blumenson and Nilsen, "Policing for Profit," 67.

36. Blumenson and Nilsen, "Policing for Profit," 67–68.

37. Blumenson and Nilsen, "Policing for Profit," 68.

38. Sandra Guerra Thompson, "Did the War on Drugs Die with the Birth of the War on Terrorism? A Closer Look at Civil Forfeiture and Racial Profiling After 9/11," *Federal Sentencing Reporter* 14, no. 3–4 (2001–2002): 149.

39. Blumenson and Nilsen, "Policing for Profit," 63.

40. Blumenson and Nilsen, "Policing for Profit," 63.

41. Stillman, "Taken"; Gene Callahan and William Anderson, "The Roots of Racial Profiling," *Reason*, August/September 2001, https://reason.com/2001/08/01/the-roots-of-racial-profiling-2/.

42. Blumenson and Nilsen, "Policing for Profit," 64.

43. Miller and Selva, "Drug Enforcement's Double-Edged Sword," 318.

44. Michael Sallah, Robert O'Harrow Jr., Steven Rich, and Gabe Silverman, "Stop and Seize," *Washington Post*, September 6, 2014, https://www.washingtonpost.com/sf/investigative/2014/09/06/stop-and-seize/; Robert O'Harrow Jr., Steven Rich, and Shelly Tan, "Asset Seizures Fuel Police Spending," *Washington Post*, October 11, 2014, https://www.washingtonpost.com/sf/investigative/2014/10/11/asset-seizures-fuel-police-spending/.

45. Sallah et al., "Stop and Seize."

46. Sallah et al., "Stop and Seize."

47. Sallah et al., "Stop and Seize."

48. Robert O'Harrow Jr., Michael Sallah, and Steven Rich, "Police Intelligence Targets Cash: Reports on Drivers, Training by Firm Fueled Law Enforcement Aggressiveness," *Washington Post*, September 7, 2014, https://www.washingtonpost.com/sf/investigative/2014/09/07/police-intelligence-targets-cash/.

49. Sallah et al., "Stop and Seize."

50. Sallah et al., "Stop and Seize."

51. O'Harrow, Sallah, and Rich, "Police Intelligence Targets Cash."

52. O'Harrow, Sallah, and Rich, "Police Intelligence Targets Cash."

53. O'Harrow, Sallah, and Rich, "Police Intelligence Targets Cash."

54. Christopher Ingraham, "Drug Cops Took a College Kid's Savings and Now 13 Police Departments Want a Cut," *Washington Post*, June 30, 2015, https://www.washingtonpost.com/news/wonk/wp/2015/06/30/drug-cops-took-a-college-kids-life-savings-and-now-13-police-departments-want-a-cut/.

55. Ingraham, "Drug Cops Took a College Kid's Savings."

56. Lisa Knepper, Jennifer McDonald, Kathy Sanchez, and Elyse Smith Pohl, *Policing for Profit: The Abuse of Civil Asset Forfeiture*, 3rd ed. (Institute for Justice, December 2020), 5, https://ij.org/report/policing-for-profit-3/.

57. Dick M. Carpenter II, Lisa Knepper, Angela C. Erickson, and Jennifer McDonald, *Policing for Profit: The Abuse of Civil Asset Forfeiture*, 2nd ed. (Institute for Justice, November 2015), 6, https://www.aclu-il.org/sites/default/files/wysiwyg/policing-for-profit-2nd-edition.pdf.

58. Christopher Ingraham, "Law Enforcement Took More Stuff from People than Burglars Did Last Year," *Washington Post*, November 23, 2015, https://www.washingtonpost.com/news/wonk/wp/2015/11/23/cops-took-more-stuff-from-people-than-burglars-did-last-year/.

59. Ram Subramanian, Jackie Fielding, Lauren-Brooke Eisen, Hernandez Stroud, and Taylor King, *Revenue over Public Safety: How Perverse Financial Incentives Warp the Criminal Justice System* (Brennan Center for Justice, July 6, 2022), 8–9 (table 1), https://www.brennancenter.org/our-work/research-reports/revenue-over-public-safety. Data is not included for Alabama, Alaska, Arkansas, Kansas, North Dakota, Ohio, and Vermont.

60. ACLU of Pennsylvania, *Guilty Property: How Law Enforcement Takes $1 Million in Cash from Innocent Philadelphians Every Year—and Gets Away with It* (June 2015), 5, https://www.aclupa.org/en/publications/guilty-property-how-law-enforcement-takes-1-million-cash-innocent-philadelphians-every.

61. Joel Handley, Jennifer Helsby, and Freddy Martinez, "Inside the Chicago Police Department's Secret Budget," *Chicago Reader*, September 29, 2016, https://chicagoreader.com/news-politics/inside-the-chicago-police-departments-secret-budget/.

62. Carpenter et al., *Policing for Profit*, 14.

63. Sallah et al., "Stop and Seize."

64. Brief for ACLU et al. as Amici Curiae at 25–26, *Timbs v. Indiana*, 139 S. Ct. 682 (2019) (No. 17-1091).

65. Diane Jennings, "Lawmakers Eye Reforms for Texas Asset Forfeitures," *Dallas Morning News*, February 28, 2011, https://web.archive.org/web/20190826181504/https://www.dallasnews.com/news/texas/2011/02/28/lawmakers-eye-reforms-for-texas-asset-forfeitures/.

66. Handley, Helsby, and Martinez, "Inside the Chicago Police."

67. Natalia Alamdari, "Using Loophole, Seward County Seizes Millions from Motorists Without Convicting Them of Crimes," *Flatwater Free Press*, June 15, 2023, https://flatwaterfreepress.org/using-loophole-seward-county-seizes-millions-from-motorists-without-convicting-them-of-crimes/.

68. Laurien Rose, "Police Chief Ken Burton Calls Forfeiture Funds 'Pennies from Heaven,'" *Maneater*, November 27, 2012, https://web.archive.org/web/20220319220755/https://themaneater.com/police-chief-ken-burton-calls-forfeiture -funds-pen/.

69. ACLU of California's Criminal Justice and Drug Policy Project, *Civil Asset Forfeiture: Profiting from California's Most Vulnerable* (May 2016), https://www .aclunc.org/docs/aclu_california_civil_asset_forfeiture_report.pdf; Rebecca Vallas, Tracey Ross, Todd Cox, Jamal Hagler, and Billy Corriher, *Forfeiting the American Dream: How Civil Asset Forfeiture Exacerbates Hardship for Low-Income Communities and Communities of Color* (Center for American Progress, April 2016), 5, https://cdn.americanprogress.org/wp-content/uploads/2016/04/01060039/ CivilAssetForfeiture-reportv2.pdf.

70. C. J. Ciaramella, "Poor Neighborhoods Hit Hardest by Asset Forfeiture in Chicago, Data Shows," *Reason*, June 13, 2017, https://reason.com/2017/06/13/poor -neighborhoods-hit-hardest-by-asset/.

71. Vallas et al., *Forfeiting the American Dream*; ACLU of California, *Civil Asset Forfeiture*; Anna Lett, Nathaniel Cary, and Mike Ellis, "TAKEN: How Police Departments Make Millions by Seizing Property," *Greenville News*, January 27, 2019, https:// www.greenvilleonline.com/in-depth/news/taken/2019/01/27/civil-forfeiture-south -carolina-police-property-seizures-taken-exclusive-investigation/2457838002/; Jackson Smith, "Dirty Money and Financial Inequality in North Philadelphia," *Theoretical Criminology* 28, no. 1 (2024): 50–69.

72. John Schuppe, "Officer Mistook Philando Castile for a Robbery Suspect, Tapes Show," *NBC News*, July 12, 2016, https://www.nbcnews.com/news/us-news/officer -thought-philando-castile-was-robbery-suspect-tapes-show-n607856.

73. Schuppe, "Officer Mistook Philando Castile."

74. Mark Berman, "Diamond Reynolds Agrees to $800,000 Settlement Stemming from Philando Castile's Death," *Washington Post*, November 29, 2017, https://www .washingtonpost.com/news/post-nation/wp/2017/11/29/diamond-reynolds-agrees-to -800000-settlement-stemming-from-philando-castiles-death/.

75. Brandon Stahl, "Philando Castile Was Caught Up in a Cycle of Traffic Stops, Fines," *Star Tribune*, July 17, 2016.

76. Eyder Peralta and Cheryl Corley, "The Driving Life and Death of Philando Castile," NPR, July 15, 2016, https://www.npr.org/sections/thetwo-way/2016/07/ 15/485835272/the-driving-life-and-death-of-philando-castile.

77. Kameel Stanley, "How Riding Your Bike Can Land You in Trouble with the Cops—If You're Black," *Tampa Bay Times*, April 18, 2015 (updated June 21, 2021), https://www.tampabay.com/news/publicsafety/how-riding-your-bike-can-land-you -in-trouble-with-the-cops---if-youre-black/2225966.

78. Mary Wisniewski, "'Biking While Black': Chicago Minority Areas See the Most Bike Tickets," *Chicago Tribune*, March 17, 2017, http://www.chicagotribune.com/ news/local/breaking/ct-chicago-bike-tickets-minorities-0319-20170317-story.html.

79. Civil Rights Division of the US Department of Justice, *Investigation of the Baltimore City Police Department* (US Department of Justice, August 10, 2016), 50, https://cdn0.vox-cdn.com/uploads/chorus_asset/file/6915773/DOJ_Baltimore_Police _Department.0.pdf.

80. Karin D. Martin, Bryan L. Sykes, Sarah Shannon, Frank Edwards, and Alexes Harris, "Monetary Sanctions: Legal Financial Obligations in US Systems of Justice," *Annual Review of Criminology* 1 (January 2018): 482.

81. Angela LaScala-Gruenewald and Leslie Paik, "Legal Financial Obligations in the United States: A Review of Recent Research," *Sociology Compass* 17, no. 5 (2023): e13070.

82. Michael W. Sances and Hye Young You, "Who Pays for Government? Descriptive Representation and Exploitative Revenue Sources," *Journal of Politics* 79, no. 3 (2017): 1090–94; Rebecca Goldstein, Michael W. Sances, and Hye Young You, "Exploitative Revenues, Law Enforcement, and the Quality of Government Service," *Urban Affairs Review* 56, no. 1 (2018): 5–31.

83. Tax Policy Center, *Briefing Book: A Citizen's Guide to the Fascinating (Though Often Complex) Elements of the Federal Tax System*, accessed October 24, 2022, https://www.taxpolicycenter.org/briefing-book/what-are-sources-revenue-local-governments.

84. Tax Policy Center, *Briefing Book*.

85. Tax Policy Center, *Briefing Book*.

86. Dan Kopf, "The Fining of Black America," *Priceonomics*, June 24, 2016, https://priceonomics.com/the-fining-of-black-america/.

87. Sances and You, "Who Pays for Government?," 1091.

88. Soss and Weaver, "Police Are Our Government," 570.

89. James Forman Jr., *Locking Up Our Own: Crime and Punishment in Black America* (Farrar, Straus and Giroux, 2017), 155.

90. Peralta and Corley, "Driving Life and Death"; Laura Schenker, David Sylvan, Jean-Louis Arcand, and Ravi Bhavnani, "Segregation and 'Out-of-Placeness': The Direct Effect of Neighborhood Racial Composition on Police Stops," *Political Research Quarterly* 76, no. 4 (2023): 1646–60, and 1656.

91. Charles R. Epp, Steven Maynard-Moody, and Donald P. Haider-Markel, *Pulled Over: How Police Stops Define Race and Citizenship* (University of Chicago Press, 2014).

92. "New NYCLU Report Finds NYPD Stop-and-Frisk Practices Ineffective, Reveals Depth of Racial Disparities," New York Civil Liberties Union, May 9, 2012, https://www.nyclu.org/en/press-releases/new-nyclu-report-finds-nypd-stop-and-frisk-practices-ineffective-reveals-depth-racial.

93. Ciaramella, "Poor Neighborhoods Hit Hardest"; Vallas et al., *Forfeiting the American Dream*.

94. US Commission on Civil Rights, *Targeted Fines and Fees Against Communities of Color: Civil Rights and Constitutional Implications* (September 2017), 7, https://www.usccr.gov/pubs/2017/Statutory_Enforcement_Report2017.pdf.

95. Radley Balko, "How Municipalities in St. Louis County, Mo., Profit from Poverty," *Washington Post*, September 3, 2014, https://www.washingtonpost.com/news/the-watch/wp/2014/09/03/how-st-louis-county-missouri-profits-from-poverty/?utm_term=.7e893e846b52.

96. US Department of Justice Civil Rights Division, *Investigation of the Ferguson Police Department*, March 4, 2015, https://www.justice.gov/sites/default/files/opa/press-releases/attachments/2015/03/04/ferguson_police_department_report.pdf.

97. Henry Ordower, J. S. Onesimo Sandoval, and Kenneth Warren, "Out of Ferguson: Misdemeanors, Municipal Courts, Tax Distribution, and Constitutional Limitations," *Howard Law Journal* 61, no. 1 (2016): 18.

98. Ordower, Sandoval, and Warren, "Out of Ferguson," 147.

99. Stephen Bingham, Mari Castaldi, Elisa Della-Piana, Michael Herald, Dana Isaac, Alex Kaplan, Meredith Desautels, Antionette Dozier, Kristina Harootun, Brittany Stonesifer, and Theresa Zhen, *Stopped, Fined, Arrested: Racial Bias in Policing and Traffic Courts in California* (East Bay Community Law Center, April 2016), 4, http://ebclc.org/wp-content/uploads/2016/04/Stopped_Fined_Arrested_BOTRCA.pdf.

100. Alex Bender, Stephan Bingham, Mari Castaldi, Elisa Della-Piana, Meredith Desautels, Michael Herald, Endria Richardson, Jesse Stout, Theresa Zhen, *Not Just a Ferguson Problem: How Traffic Courts Drive Inequality in California* (Lawyers' Committee for Civil Rights of the San Francisco Bay Area, 2015), https://lccrsf.org/wp-content/uploads/2021/05/Not-Just-a-Ferguson-Problem-How-Traffic-Courts-Drive-Inequality-in-California-2015.pdf.

101. Min Su, "Taxation by Citation? Exploring Local Governments' Revenue Motive for Traffic Fines," *Public Administration Review* 80, no. 1 (2019): 36–45.

102. Chuck DeVore, "Police-Collected Fines, Fees and Forfeitures: How Does Your City Rank?," *Forbes*, October 26, 2016, https://www.forbes.com/sites/chuckdevore/2016/10/26/police-collected-fines-fees-and-forfeitures-how-does-your-city-rank/#4a8065cd2520.

103. Melissa Sanchez and Sandhya Kambhampati, "How Does Chicago Make $200 Million a Year on Parking Tickets? By Bankrupting Thousands of Drivers," *Mother Jones*, February 27, 2018, https://www.motherjones.com/crime-justice/2018/02/how-does-chicago-make-200-million-a-year-on-parking-tickets-by-bankrupting-thousands-of-drivers/.

104. Sanchez and Kambhampati, "How Does Chicago."

105. Sanchez and Kambhampati, "How Does Chicago."

106. Melissa Sanchez and Elliott Ramos, "Chicago Hiked the Cost of Vehicle Sticker Violations to Boost Revenue. But It's Driven More Low-Income, Black Motorists into Debt," *ProPublica*, July 26, 2018, https://www.propublica.org/article/chicago-vehicle-sticker-law-ticket-price-hike-black-drivers-debt.

107. Sanchez and Ramos, "Chicago Hiked the Cost."

108. Lauren Nolan, *The Debt Spiral: How Chicago's Vehicle Ticketing Practices Unfairly Burden Low-Income and Minority Communities* (Woodstock Institute, June 2018), 2; Maura Ewing, "Should States Charge Low-Income Residents Less for Traffic Tickets?," *Atlantic*, May 13, 2017, https://www.theatlantic.com/politics/archive/2017/05/traffic-debt-california-brown/526491/.

109. Kasey Henricks and Ruben Ortiz, "The Irrelevance of Innocence: Ethnoracial Context, Occupational Differences in Policing, and the Tickets Issued in Error," *Socius* 8 (2022): 2, 7.

110. Henricks and Ortiz, "The Irrelevance of Innocence," 15.

111. Henricks and Ortiz, "The Irrelevance of Innocence," 14.

112. US DOJ, *Investigation of the Ferguson Police Department*, 14.

113. Show-Me Institute, "David Stokes Interviews Ferguson Mayor James Knowles," February 9, 2014, https://www.youtube.com/watch?v=EosnUNmIC20.

114. US DOJ, *Investigation of the Ferguson Police Department*.

115. Travis Madsen and Phineas Baxandall, *Caution: Red Light Cameras Ahead: The Risks of Privatizing Traffic Law Enforcement and How to Protect the Public* (US PIRG Education Fund, October 2011), https://uspirg.org/reports/usp/trafficcamreport.

116. Madsen and Baxandall, *Caution*.

117. Lee Fang, "How Police and Traffic Light Companies Are Conspiring to Give You More Tickets," *AlterNet*, June 5, 2012, https://www.alternet.org/2012/06/how_police_and_traffic_light_companies_are_conspiring_to_give_you_more_tickets/.

118. David Kidwell, "Redflex to Pay $20 Million to Chicago to Settle Lawsuit over Red-Light Camera Bribery," *Chicago Tribune*, February 6, 2017, https://www.chicagotribune.com/news/watchdog/redlight/ct-red-light-cameras-lawsuit-settled-met-20170206-story.html.

119. Kidwell, "Redflex to Pay."

120. Nolan, *The Debt Spiral*, 7.

121. Fran Spielman, "Company That Took Over Red-Light Camera Program After Scandal Gets New Contract," *Chicago Sun Times*, July 11, 2018, https://chicago .suntimes.com/business/company-that-took-over-red-light-camera-program-after -scandal-gets-new-contract/.

122. Eumi K. Lee, "Monetizing Shame: Mugshots, Privacy, and the Right to Access," *Rutgers University Law Review* 70 (2018): 563–64.

123. Lee, "Monetizing Shame," 586, 594.

124. Samantha Schmidt, "Owners of Mugshots.com Accused of Extortion: They Attempted 'to Profit off of Someone Else's Humiliation,'" *Chicago Tribune*, May 18, 2018, https://www.chicagotribune.com/business/ct-biz-mugshot-website-owners -extortion-20180518-story.html.

125. Lee, "Monetizing Shame," 569.

126. First Amended Class Action Complaint, Gabiola et al. v. Sarid et al., No. 16-cv-02076 (Circuit Court of Cook County, IL, filed August 24, 2016), https://www .courthousenews.com/wp-content/uploads/2017/08/Mug.Illinois.pdf.

127. Office of the Attorney General, "Attorney General Becerra Announces Criminal Charges Against Four Individuals Behind Cyber Exploitation Website," California Department of Justice, press release, May 16, 2018, https://oag.ca.gov/ news/press-releases/attorney-general-becerra-announces-criminal-charges-against -four-individuals.

128. Alexes Harris, "The Cruel Poverty of Monetary Sanctions" (white paper, *The Society Pages*, March 4, 2014), https://thesocietypages.org/papers/monetary-sanctions/.

129. Joseph Shapiro, "As Court Fees Rise, the Poor Are Paying the Price," NPR, May 19, 2014, https://www.npr.org/2014/05/19/312158516/increasing-court-fees -punish-the-poor.

130. Jessie Van Berkel, "Minnesota's Criminal Justice Fees Often Fall Hardest on Poor," *Star Tribune*, May 3, 2021, https://www.startribune.com/minnesota-s-criminal -justice-fees-often-fall-hardest-on-poor/600050762/.

131. Alicia Bannon, Mitali Nagrecha, and Rebekah Diller, *Criminal Justice Debt: A Barrier to Reentry* (Brennan Center for Justice, New York University School of Law, 2010), 30, http://www.brennancenter.org/sites/default/files/legacy/Fees%20and %20Fines%20FINAL.pdf.

132. Alexes Harris, *A Pound of Flesh: Monetary Sanctions as Punishment for the Poor* (Russell Sage Foundation, 2016), 43.

133. Nicholas Miller, "You Have the Right to an Attorney, but It Might Cost You," *The Nation*, October 30, 2023, https://www.thenation.com/article/society/public -defender-fees/.

134. Marea Beeman, Kellianne Elliott, Rosalie Joy, Elizabeth Allen, and Michael Mrozinski, *At What Cost? Findings from an Examination into the Imposition of Public Defense Fees* (National Legal Aid and Defender Association [NLADA], July 2022), 5.

135. Jessica Feierman, Nadia Mozaffar, Naomi Goldstein, and Emily Haney-Caron, *The Price of Justice: The High Cost of "Free" Counsel for Youth in the Juvenile Justice System* (Juvenile Law Center, 2018), 3, https://debtorsprison.jlc.org/documents/JLC -Debtors-Paying-for-Justice.pdf.

136. Miller, "You Have the Right to an Attorney"; Lauren Gill and Weihua Li, "If You Can't Afford an Attorney, One Will Be Appointed. And You May Get a Huge Bill," *Marshall Project*, February 12, 2024, https://www.themarshallproject.org/2024/02/ 12/miranda-rights-indigent-defense-iowa; Beeman et al., *At What Cost?*

137. Beeman et al., *At What Cost?*, 19.

138. Gill and Li, "If You Can't Afford an Attorney."

139. Miller, "You Have the Right to an Attorney."

140. Gill and Li, "If You Can't Afford an Attorney."

141. Helen A. Anderson, "Penalizing Poverty: Making Criminal Defendants Pay for Their Court-Appointed Counsel Through Recoupment and Contribution," *University of Michigan Journal of Law Reform* 42, no. 2 (2009): 360.

142. Michael Kaufman and Andrés Kwon, eds., *Paying for Justice: The Human Cost of Public Defense Fees* (ACLU of Southern California, 2017), 2.

143. John D. King, "Privatizing Criminal Procedure," *Georgetown Law Review* 107, no. 3 (2019): 579.

144. King, "Privatizing Criminal Procedure," 588.

145. Joshua Vaughn, "In Pennsylvania, Defendants Pay a Fee Just to Plead Guilty," *The Appeal*, August 29, 2018, https://theappeal.org/in-pennsylvania-defendants-pay-a-fee-just-to-plead-guilty/.

146. Vaughn, "In Pennsylvania."

147. Maura Ewing, "Want to Clear Your Record? It'll Cost You $450," *Marshall Project*, May 31, 2016, https://www.themarshallproject.org/2016/05/31/want-to-clear-your-record-it-ll-cost-you-450.

148. ACLU Brief at 6, *Timbs v. Indiana* (see note 64 above).

149. Fines and Fees Justice Center, *Assessments and Surcharges: A 50-State Survey of Supplemental Fees* (December 13, 2022), https://finesandfeesjusticecenter.org/articles/assessments-and-surcharges-a-50-state-survey-of-supplemental-fees/.

150. Marcus Nieto, *Who Pays for Penalty Assessment Programs in California?* (California Research Bureau, February 2006), accessed October 25, 2022, https://web.archive.org/web/20200210230117/https://csgjusticecenter.org/wp-content/uploads/2013/07/2006-CA-report.pdf.

151. Mac Taylor, *Improving California's Criminal Fine and Fee System* (Legislative Analyst's Office, January 2016), http://www.lao.ca.gov/Publications/Report/3322.

152. Taylor, *Improving California's Criminal Fine and Fee System*, 6.

153. Alexes Harris, Beth Huebner, Karin Martin, Mary Pattillo, Becky Pettit, Sarah Shannon, Bryan Sykes, Chris Uggen, and April Fernandes, *Monetary Sanctions in the Criminal Justice System: A Review of Law and Policy in California, Georgia, Illinois, Minnesota, Missouri, New York, North Carolina, Texas, and Washington* (Lauran and John Arnold Foundation, 2017).

154. Trial Court Funding Commission (TCFC), *Trial Court Funding Commission Final Report* (State of Michigan TCFC, September 6, 2019), 7, https://www.michigan.gov/-/media/Project/Websites/treasury/Reports/TCFC_Final_Report_962019_9-16-2019.pdf?rev=1fedbe221d224bf5978880216acbb06d.

155. Harris, *A Pound of Flesh*, 42.

156. Harris et al., *Monetary Sanctions in the Criminal Justice System*, 19.

157. Harris et al., *Monetary Sanctions in the Criminal Justice System*, 19.

158. Alexandra Natapoff, *Punishment Without Crime: How Our Massive Misdemeanor System Traps the Innocent and Makes America More Unequal* (Basic Books, 2018), 117.

159. Martin et al., "Monetary Sanctions," 473.

160. Brief for Professors as Amici Curiae at 7–8, *Timbs v. Indiana*.

161. Professors Brief at 5, *Timbs v. Indiana*.

162. Alexes Harris, Heather Evans, and Katherine Beckett, "Drawing Blood from Stones: Legal Debt and Social Inequality in the Contemporary United States,"

American Journal of Sociology 115, no. 6 (May 2010): 1770, https://www.jstor.org/stable/10.1086/651463.

163. Ebony Ruhland, Bryan Holmes, and Amber Petkus, "The Role of Fines and Fees on Supervision," *Criminal Justice and Behavior* 47, no. 10 (2020): 1244–63.

164. Natapoff, *Punishment Without Crime*, chap. 5.

165. Feierman et al., *The Price of Justice*, 19.

166. Brittany Friedman and Mary Pattillo, "Statutory Inequality: The Logics of Monetary Sanctions in State Law," *RSF: The Russell Sage Foundation Journal of the Social Sciences* 5, no. 1 (2019): 185; Karin Martin, "Monetary Myopia: An Examination of Institutional Response to Revenue from Monetary Sanctions for Misdemeanors," *Criminal Justice Policy Review* 29, nos. 6–7 (2019): 630–62.

167. Principles of Law, Policing, "Policing for the Purposes of Revenue Generation," accessed February 2, 2024, https://www.policingprinciples.org/chapter -1/1-10-policing-for-the-purposes-of-revenue-generation/.

168. Bannon, Nagrecha, and Diller, *Criminal Justice Debt*, 30.

169. Becky Johnson, "Schools Sue State for Diverting Education Funding to Inmates," *Smoky Mountain News*, December 2, 2015, https://smokymountainnews .com/archives/item/16799-schools-sue-state-for-diverting-education-funding-to -inmates.

170. Bannon, Nagrecha, and Diller, *Criminal Justice Debt*, 17.

171. Bannon, Nagrecha, and Diller, *Criminal Justice Debt*, 17.

172. Alexes Harris, Tyler Smith, and Emmi Obara, "Justice 'Cost Points': Examination of Privatization Within Public Systems of Justice," *Criminology and Public Policy* 18, no. 2 (2019): 347; Bannon, Nagrecha, and Diller, *Criminal Justice Debt*, 17.

173. Harris, *A Pound of Flesh*, 53.

174. Devin Fergus, *Land of the Fee: Hidden Costs and the Decline of the American Middle Class* (Oxford University Press, 2018).

175. Mary Childs, "Private-Debt Market Already Has Growing Pains," *Barron's*, March 21, 2018, https://www.barrons.com/articles/private-debt-market-already-has -growing-pains-1521641578.

176. Jacob S. Hacker, *The Great Risk Shift: The New Economic Insecurity and the Decline of the American Dream* (Oxford University Press, 2006).

177. Greta Krippner, *Capitalizing on Crisis: The Political Origins of the Rise of Finance* (Harvard University Press, 2011); Fergus, *Land of the Fee*.

178. Mallory E. SoRelle, *Democracy Declined: The Failed Politics of Consumer Financial Protection* (University of Chicago Press, 2020); Susanne Soederberg, "The US Debtfare State and the Credit Card Industry: Forging Spaces of Dispossession," *Antipode* 45, no. 2 (2012): 493–512.

179. Mehrsa Baradaran, *The Color of Money: Black Banks and the Racial Wealth Gap* (Belknap Press, 2017).

180. Chloe N. Thurston, *At the Boundaries of Homeownership: Credit, Discrimination, and the American State* (Cambridge University Press, 2018); Keeanga-Yamahtta Taylor, *Race for Profit: How Banks and the Real Estate Industry Undermined Black Homeownership* (University of North Carolina Press, 2019).

181. Soederberg, "The US Debtfare State."

182. Edward Gramlich, *Subprime Mortgages: America's Latest Boom and Bust* (Urban Institute Press, 2007).

183. Michael Feola, "Blood from a Turnip: Debt, Race, and Expropriation in Penal Capitalism," *Theory & Event* 23, no. 4 (2020): 877–901; Louise Seamster, "Black Debt,

White Debt," *Contexts* 18, no. 1 (2019): 30–35; Pew Charitable Trusts, "Payday Lending in America" (series of reports, 2015), http://www.pewtrusts.org/en/research -and-analysis/collections/2014/12/payday-lending-in-america.

184. Employee Benefits Research Institute, *How Is Debt Different by Race and Ethnicity*, January 7, 2021, https://www.ebri.org/docs/default-source/fast-facts/ff -375-debtbyrace-7jan21.pdf.

185. Seamster, "Black Debt, White Debt," 33.

186. Seamster, "Black Debt, White Debt," 33.

187. IBISWorld, "Debt Collection Agencies in the US—Market Size 2005–2029," January 10, 2023, https://www.ibisworld.com/industry-statistics/market-size/debt -collection-agencies-united-states/.

188. Childs, "Private-Debt Market."

189. "CFPB Survey Finds over One-in-Four Consumers Contacted by Debt Collectors Feel Threatened," Consumer Financial Protection Bureau (CFPB), January 12, 2017, https://www.consumerfinance.gov/about-us/newsroom/cfpb-survey-finds -over-one-four-consumers-contacted-debt-collectors-feel-threatened/; Erik Clark, "Debt Collectors in the US You Need to Know," *National Bankruptcy Forum*, October 22, 2021, http://www.natlbankruptcy.com/top-debt-collectors/.

190. Clark, "Debt Collectors"; CFPB, "CFPB Survey Finds."

191. US Government Accountability Office (GAO), "Credit Cards: Fair Debt Collection Practices Act Could Better Reflect the Evolving Debt Collection Marketplace and Use of Technology," *Report to Congressional Requesters*, GAO-09-748, September 2009, 41, https://www.gao.gov/new.items/d09748.pdf.

192. Paul Kiel, "So Sue Them: What We've Learned About the Debt Collection Lawsuit Machine," *ProPublica*, May 5, 2016, https://www.propublica.org/article/so -sue-them-what-weve-learned-about-the-debt-collection-lawsuit-machine.

193. Kiel, "So Sue Them."

194. ACLU, *A Pound of Flesh: The Criminalization of Private Debt* (2018), 5, https:// www.aclu.org/report/pound-flesh-criminalization-private-debt.

195. Paul Kiel and Annie Waldman, "The Color of Debt: How Collections Suits Squeeze Black Neighborhoods," *ProPublica*, October 8, 2016, https://www.propublica .org/article/debt-collection-lawsuits-squeeze-black-neighborhoods.

196. ACLU, *A Pound of Flesh*.

197. ACLU, *A Pound of Flesh*.

198. ACLU, *A Pound of Flesh*, 5.

199. ACLU, *A Pound of Flesh*, 5.

200. Lea Shepard, "Creditors' Contempt," *BYU Law Review* 2011, no. 5 (December 1, 2011): 1509.

201. ACLU, *A Pound of Flesh*, 18.

202. ACLU, *A Pound of Flesh*, 10.

203. ACLU, *A Pound of Flesh*, 5.

204. ACLU, *A Pound of Flesh*, 5.

205. Jim Gallagher, "Payday Lenders Use Courts to Create Modern Debtors' Prison," *St. Louis Post-Dispatch*, August 19, 2012, http://www.stltoday.com/business/ local/payday-lenders-use-courts-to-create-modern-debtors-prison/article_f56ca6aa -e880-11e1-b154-0019bb30f31a.html.

206. Both quotations can be found in ACLU, *A Pound of Flesh*, 18.

207. ACLU, *A Pound of Flesh*, 16–18.

208. ACLU, *A Pound of Flesh*, 6–7.

209. Elvin Wyly and C. S. Ponder, "Gender, Age, and Race in Subprime America," *Housing Policy Debate* 21, no. 4 (2011): 529–64.

210. Matthew Desmond and Nathan Wilmers, "Do the Poor Pay More for Housing? Exploitation, Profit, and Risk in Rental Markets," *American Journal of Sociology* 124, no. 4 (2019): 1090–1124, https://doi-org.ezp3.lib.umn.edu/10.1086/701697.

211. Matthew Desmond, *Evicted: Poverty and Profit in the American City* (Crown Books, 2016).

212. Nick Graetz, Carl Gershenson, Peter Hepburn, and Matthew Desmond, "A Comprehensive Demographic Profile of the US Evicted Population," *Proceedings of the National Academy of Sciences* 120, no. 41 (2023): e2305860120.

213. Eli Hager, "Can You Go to Jail for Not Paying Rent?," *Marshall Project*, April 16, 2015, https://www.themarshallproject.org/2015/04/16/can-you-go-to-jail-for -not-paying-rent.

214. Hager, "Can You Go to Jail for Not Paying Rent?"

215. Alec MacGillis, "Baltimore's 'Kushnerville' Tenants File Class Action Against Landlord," *ProPublica*, September 27, 2017, https://www.propublica.org/article/ baltimore-kushnerville-tenants-file-class-action-against-landlord; Aaron C. Davis and Shawn Boburg, "At Sean Hannity Properties in Working-Class Areas, an Aggressive Approach to Rent Collection," *Washington Post*, May 11, 2018, https://www .washingtonpost.com/investigations/at-hannitys-properties-in-low-income-areas -an-aggressive-approach-to-rent-collection/2018/05/10/964be4a2-4eea-11e8-84a0 -458a1aa9ac0a_story.html.

216. Davis and Boburg, "At Sean Hannity Properties."

217. Public Citizen, "Nursing Homes Often Do Not Report Private Equity Firms Among Their Owners," September 1, 2022, https://www.citizen.org/news/nursing -homes-often-do-not-report-private-equity-firms-among-their-owners/.

218. Hilary Hanson, "93-Year-Old Woman Spends 2 Nights in Jail After Eviction from Senior Housing," *Huffington Post*, December 16, 2017, https://www.huffingtonpost.com/entry/93-year-old-woman-arrested-rent_us _5a314874e4b091ca26849ee3.

219. "Child Support Pass-Through and Disregard Policies for Public Assistance Recipients," National Conference of State Legislatures, May 29, 2020, http://www.ncsl .org/research/human-services/state-policy-pass-through-disregard-child-support.aspx.

220. "Citizen's Guide to U.S. Federal Law on Child Support Enforcement," US Department of Justice, updated May 28, 2020, https://www.justice.gov/criminal-ceos/ citizens-guide-us-federal-law-child-support-enforcement.

221. Noah D. Zatz, "A New Peonage? Pay, Work, or Go to Jail in Contemporary Child Support Enforcement and Beyond," *Seattle University Law Review* 39, no. 3 (2016): 933.

222. Lynne Haney, *Prisons of Debt: The Afterlives of Incarcerated Fathers* (University of California Press, 2022).

223. Tonya L. Brito, "Fathers Behind Bars: Rethinking Child Support Policy Toward Low-Income Noncustodial Fathers and Their Families," *Journal of Gender, Race & Justice* 15 (2012): 619.

224. Mary Fainsod Katzenstein and Maureen R. Waller, "Taxing the Poor: Incarceration, Poverty Governance, and the Seizure of Family Resources," *Perspectives on Politics* 13, no. 3 (September 2015): 638–56, https://doi.org/10.1017/ S153759271500122X.

225. Haney, *Prisons of Debt.*

226. Katzenstein and Waller, "Taxing the Poor," 645.

227. See, e.g., Devah Pager, Rebecca Goldstein, Helen Ho, and Bruce Western, "Criminalizing Poverty: The Consequences of Court Fees in a Randomized Experiment," *American Sociological Review* 87, no. 3 (2022): 529–53, https://doi.org/10.1177/0003122422107783.

228. Harris, *A Pound of Flesh*, 90, 94.

229. Harris, *A Pound of Flesh*, 92.

230. Harris, *A Pound of Flesh*, 94.

231. Melissa Sanchez and Sandhya Kambhampati, "How Does Chicago Make $200 Million a Year on Parking Tickets? By Bankrupting Thousands of Drivers," *Mother Jones*, February 27, 2018, https://www.motherjones.com/crime-justice/2018/02/how-does-chicago-make-200-million-a-year-on-parking-tickets-by-bankrupting-thousands-of-drivers/.

232. Harris, Smith, and Obara, "Justice 'Cost Points,'" 344.

233. Professors Brief at 16, *Timbs v. Indiana.*

234. Mike Maciag, "Addicted to Fines," *Governing*, August 19, 2019, https://www.governing.com/archive/gov-addicted-to-fines.html.

235. Elaine S. Povich, "Unpaid Court Fines? That Could Get Your Water Shut Off," *Governing*, April 11, 2019, https://www.governing.com/topics/finance/sl-fines-fees-utilities-cities.html.

236. Bannon, Nagrecha, and Diller, *Criminal Justice Debt.*

237. Subramanian et al., *Revenue over Public Safety*, 31.

Chapter Three

1. Alex Brizee, "'This Case Is Tragic': Abused Caldwell Woman Sentenced for Murder of Stepfather," *Idaho Statesman*, June 8, 2023, https://www.idahostatesman.com/news/local/crime/article276243706.html.

2. Barbara Owen, James Wells, and Jocelyn Pollock, *In Search of Safety: Confronting Inequality in Women's Imprisonment* (University of California Press, 2017).

3. Brizee, "'This Case Is Tragic.'"

4. Brizee, "'This Case Is Tragic.'"

5. "Caldwell Woman Sentenced to Prison for 2nd Degree Murder," press release, Canyon County, Idaho, June 8, 2023, https://www.canyoncounty.id.gov/caldwell-woman-sentenced-to-prison-for-2nd-degree-murder/.

6. Jeremy Travis and Bruce Western, "The Era of Punitive Excess," Arnold Ventures, April 13, 2021, https://www.arnoldventures.org/stories/the-era-of-punitive-excess.

7. On RCS communities, see Joe Soss and Vesla Weaver, "Police Are Our Government: Politics, Political Science, and the Policing of Race-Class Subjugated Communities," *Annual Review of Political Science* 20, no. 1 (2017): 565–91, https://doi.org/10.1146/annurev-polisci-060415-093825.

8. Adam Reich, "From Hard Labor to Market Discipline: The Political Economy of Prison Work, 1974–2022," *American Sociological Review* 89, no. 1 (2024): 139.

9. Reich, "From Hard Labor," 127.

10. Reich, "From Hard Labor," 139; Eric Seligman and Geert Dhondt, "Prison Labor in U.S. State Prisons, 1974–2016: New Slavery or Enforced Idleness," working paper, 2024.

11. Wendy Sawyer and Peter Wagner, *Mass Incarceration: The Whole Pie* (Prison Policy Initiative, March 14, 2023), https://www.prisonpolicy.org/reports/pie2023.html.

12. Erin Hatton, ed., *Labor and Punishment: Work in and out of Prison* (University of California Press, 2021).

13. Erin Hatton, "Forced Laborers," *Inquest*, June 9, 2023, https://inquest.org/forced-laborers/.

14. ACLU and The Global Human Rights Clinic at the University of Chicago (GHRC), *Captive Labor: Exploitation of Incarcerated Workers*, June 15, 2022, 23, https://www.aclu.org/report/captive-labor-exploitation-incarcerated-workers.

15. Reich, "From Hard Labor," 18; The term "prison housework" is from Noah Zatz, "Working at the Boundaries of Markets: Prison Labor and the Economic Dimension of Employment Relationships," *Vanderbilt Law Review* 61, no. 3 (2008): 918.

16. Erin Hatton, "Working Behind Bars: Prison Labor in America," in Hatton, *Labor and Punishment*, 21.

17. ACLU and GHRC, *Captive Labor*, 16.

18. Reich, "From Hard Labor," 143.

19. Reich, "From Hard Labor," 18.

20. ACLU and GHRC, *Captive Labor*, 10.

21. Lisa Collier, *Agribusiness at the Department of Criminal Justice* (Texas State Auditor's Office, March 2021), https://sao.texas.gov/SAOReports/ReportNumber?id =21-016.

22. Jamiles Lartey, "The Food on Your Table, Brought to You by Prison Labor," *Marshall Project*, February 3, 2024, https://www.themarshallproject.org/2024/02/03/food-prison-labor-walmart-target.

23. Robin McDowell and Margie Mason, "Prisoners in the US Are Part of a Hidden Workforce Linked to Hundreds of Popular Food Brands," Associated Press, January 29, 2024, https://apnews.com/article/prison-to-plate-inmate-labor-investigation -c6f0eb4747963283316e494eadf08c4e.

24. ACLU and GHRC, *Captive Labor*, 34.

25. McDowell and Mason, "Prisoners in the US."

26. Philip Goodman, "'Another Second Chance': Rethinking Rehabilitation Through the Lens of California's Prison Fire Camps," *Social Problems* 59, no. 4 (2012): 437–58.

27. Reich, "From Hard Labor," 28.

28. ACLU and GHRC, *Captive Labor*, 38.

29. Tracey Kyckelhahn, *State Corrections Expenditures, FY 1982–2010* (Bureau of Justice Statistics, 2012 [Revised 2014]), 1, https://bjs.ojp.gov/library/publications/ state-corrections-expenditures-fy-1982-2010.

30. Breanna Edwards, "La. Sheriff Furious at New Laws Allowing for Release of 'Good,' Nonviolent Inmates Because 'We Use Them to Wash Cars,'" *The Root*, October 12, 2017, http://www.theroot.com/la-sheriff-furious-at-new-laws-allowing-for-release -of-1819395204.

31. Dani Anguiano, "US Prison Workers Produce $11bn Worth of Goods and Services for Pittance," *Guardian*, June 15, 2022, https://www.theguardian.com/us-news/ 2022/jun/15/us-prison-workers-low-wages-exploited.

32. ACLU and GHRC, *Captive Labor*, 30, 39–41.

33. Hatton, "Working Behind Bars," 24.

34. Eli Hager, "Prisoners Who Fight Wildfires in California: An Insider's Look," *Marshall Project*, August 20, 2015, https://www.themarshallproject.org/2015/08/19/prisoners-who-fight-wildfires-in-california-an-insider-s-look.

35. Matt Wotus and Monte Plott, "California Inmates Help Battle Raging Wildfires," CNN, October 18, 2017, https://www.cnn.com/2017/10/13/us/california-fires-inmate-firefighters/index.html.

36. "Wildland Firefighter Salary in California," Indeed, accessed June 9, 2023, https://www.indeed.com/salaries/Wildland-Firefighter-Salaries,-California; Wotus and Plott, "California Inmates."

37. Jamie Lowe, "The Incarcerated Women Who Fight California's Wildfires," *New York Times Magazine*, August 31, 2017, https://www.nytimes.com/2017/08/31/magazine/the-incarcerated-women-who-fight-californias-wildfires.html.

38. Lowe, "The Incarcerated Women."

39. CA Corrections (@CACorrections), "Today, more than 2,000 volunteer inmate firefighters, including 58 youth offenders, are battling wildfire flames throughout CA. Inmate firefighters serve a vital role, clearing thick brush down to bare soil to stop the fire's spread. #CarrFire #FergusonFire #MendocinoComplex," Twitter (now X), July 31, 2018, 6:40 p.m., https://twitter.com/CACorrections/status/1024439641221419008.

40. Reich, "From Hard Labor," 143.

41. Reich, "From Hard Labor," 143.

42. ACLU and GHRC, *Captive Labor*, 29.

43. ACLU and GHRC, *Captive Labor*, 39.

44. ACLU and GHRC, *Captive Labor*, 39–40.

45. Christian Parenti, *Lockdown America: Police and Prisons in the Age of Crisis* (Verso, 1999), 232–33.

46. Quoted in ACLU and GHRC, *Captive Labor*, 29.

47. Keri Blakinger, "Some Prison Programs Lose Money—Even When Prisoners Work for Pennies," *Marshall Project*, September 2, 2021, https://www.themarshallproject.org/2021/09/02/some-prison-labor-programs-lose-money-even-when-prisoners-work-for-pennies.

48. UNICOR, *Factories with Fences: 85 Years Building Brighter Futures*, 2018, 31.

49. Hatton, "Working Behind Bars," 24.

50. McDowell and Mason, "Prisoners in the US."

51. ACLU and GHRC, *Captive Labor*, 31.

52. ACLU and GHRC, *Captive Labor*, 10.

53. Hatton, "Forced Laborers."

54. US Bureau of Justice Assistance, "Prison Industry Enhancement Certification Program," program brief, August 2018, 2, https://bja.ojp.gov/sites/g/files/xyckuh186/files/Publications/PIECP-Program-Brief_2018.pdf.

55. Danielle Kaeble, *Probation and Parole in the United States, 2021* (Bureau of Justice Statistics, February 2023), 1.

56. Noah Zatz, "The Carceral Labor Continuum: Beyond the Prison Labor/Free Labor Divide," in Hatton, *Labor and Punishment*, 150.

57. Noah Zatz, Tia Koonse, Theresa Zhen, Lucero Herrera, Han Lu, Steven Shafer, and Blake Valenta, *Get to Work or Go to Jail: Workplace Rights Under Threat* (UCLA Institute for Research on Labor and Employment, March 2016), UCLA School of Law, Public Law Research Paper No. 16-24, 2.

58. Jamie Peck and Nik Theodore, "Carceral Chicago: Making the Ex-Offender Employability Crisis," *International Journal of Urban and Regional Research* 32, no. 2 (2008): 251–81.

59. Josh Seim and David J. Harding, "Parolefare: Post-Prison Supervision and Low-Wage Work," *RSF: The Russell Sage Foundation Journal of the Social Sciences* 6, no. 1 (2020): 173–95; Dallas Augustine, "Coerced Work During Parole: Prevalence, Mechanisms, and Characteristics," *Criminology* 61, no. 3 (2023): 546–81.

60. Gretchen Purser, "'You Put up With Anything': On the Vulnerability and Exploitability of Formerly Incarcerated Workers," in Hatton, *Labor and Punishment*, 216.

61. Gretchen Purser, "'Still Doin' Time': Clamoring for Work in the Day Labor Industry," *WorkingUSA* 15 (2012): 406.

62. Purser, "'Still Doin' Time,'" 407.

63. Susila Gurusami, "Working for Redemption: Formerly Incarcerated Black Women and Punishment in the Labor Market," *Gender & Society* 31, no. 4 (2017): 433–56.

64. Sarah Picard, Jennifer A. Tallon, Michela Lowry, and Dana Kralstein, *Court-Ordered Community Service: A National Perspective* (Center for Justice Innovation, 2019), "Summary," 1, https://www.innovatingjustice.org/sites/default/files/media/document/2019/Community_Service_Summary_10312019.pdf.

65. Daniel Hatcher, *Injustice Inc: How America's Justice System Commodifies Children and the Poor* (University of California Press, 2023), 94–95.

66. Zatz et al., *Get to Work or Go to Jail*, 3.

67. The statement is quoted by Hatcher, *Injustice Inc.*, 94, and is posted at https://doc.mo.gov/programs/community-service (accessed on March 14, 2024).

68. "Community Service," *United States Probation and Pretrial Services, New Hampshire*, accessed October 9, 2022, http://www.nhp.uscourts.gov/community-service.

69. Amy Julia Harris and Shoshana Walter, "They Thought They Were Going to Rehab. They Ended up in Chicken Plants," *Reveal*, October 4, 2017, https://revealnews.org/article/they-thought-they-were-going-to-rehab-they-ended-up-in-chicken-plants/.

70. Harris and Walter, "They Thought They Were Going to Rehab."

71. Brett Story, *Prison Land: Mapping Carceral Power Across Neoliberal America* (University of Minnesota Press, 2019), 80.

72. Ram Subramanian, Jackie Fielding, Lauren-Brooke Eisen, Hernandez Stroud, and Taylor King, *Revenue over Public Safety: How Perverse Financial Incentives Warp the Criminal Justice System* (Brennan Center for Justice, July 6, 2022), 21–22, https://www.brennancenter.org/our-work/research-reports/revenue-over-public-safety.

73. Subramanian et al., *Revenue over Public Safety*, 21–22.

74. Lauren-Brooke Eisen, "Paying for Your Time: How Charging Inmates Fees Behind Bars May Violate the Excessive Fines Clause," *Loyola Journal of Public Interest* 15, no. 2 (Spring 2014): 319–42.

75. April D. Fernandes, Brittany Friedman, and Gabriela Kirk, "Forcing People to Pay for Being Locked Up Remains Common," *Washington Post*, May 2, 2022, https://www.washingtonpost.com/outlook/2022/05/02/forcing-people-pay-being-locked-up-remains-common/.

76. April D. Fernandes, Brittany Friedman, and Gabriela Kirk, "Homepage," Captive Money Lab, accessed March 11, 2023, https://www.captivemoneylab.org/; Fernandes et al., "Forcing People to Pay."

77. Steve Mills and Todd Lighty, "State Sues Prisoners to Pay for Their Room, Board," *Chicago Tribune*, November 30, 2015, https://www.chicagotribune.com/2015/11/30/state-sues-prisoners-to-pay-for-their-room-board/. April D. Fernandes, Brittany Friedman, Gabriela Kirk, "The 'Damaged' State vs. the 'Willful' Nonpayer: Pay-to-Stay and the Social Construction of Damage, Harm, and Moral Responsibility in a Rent-Seeking Society," *RSF: The Russell Sage Foundation Journal of the Social Sciences* 8, no. 1 (January 2022): 82–105.

78. Alexandra Alter, "A Prisoner Got a Book Deal. Now the State Wants Him to Pay for His Imprisonment," *New York Times*, February 17, 2018, https://www.nytimes.com/2018/02/17/books/curtis-dawkins-graybar-hotel-prisoner-book-deal.html.

79. Leah A. Plunkett, "Captive Markets," *Hastings Law Journal* 65, no. 1 (2013): 101–2; Stephanie Campos-Bui, Jeffrey Selbin, Hamza Jaka, Tim Kline, Ahmed Lavalais, Alynia Phillips, and Abby Ridley-Kerr, *Making Families Pay: The Harmful, Unlawful, and Costly Practice of Charging Juvenile Administrative Fees in California* (Policy Advocacy Clinic, UC Berkeley School of Law, March 2017), https://www.law.berkeley.edu/wp-content/uploads/2015/12/Making-Families-Pay.pdf.

80. Dara Lind, "At Least 2 States Let Prisons Charge the Families of Dead Ex-Prisoners for Their Food and Health Care," *Vox*, October 16, 2015, https://www.vox.com/2015/5/26/8660001/prison-jail-cost.

81. Lind, "At Least 2 States."

82. Alison Bo Andolena, "Can They Lock You Up and Charge You for It? How Pay-to-Stay Corrections Programs May Provide a Financial Solution for New York and New Jersey," *Seton Hall Journal of Legislation and Public Policy* 35, no. 1 (2010): 94–129.

83. Fox Butterfield, "Many Local Officials Now Make Inmates Pay Their Own Way," *New York Times*, August 13, 2004, http://www.nytimes.com/2004/08/13/us/many-local-officials-now-make-inmates-pay-their-own-way.html. For additional examples of county profits from pay-to-stay, see Mary Fainsod Katzenstein and Maureen R. Waller, "Taxing the Poor: Incarceration, Poverty Governance, and the Seizure of Family Resources," *Perspectives on Politics* 13, no. 3 (September 2015): 643, https://doi.org/10.1017/S153759271500122X.

84. Alter, "A Prisoner Got a Book Deal."

85. Andolena, "Can They Lock You Up?," 107.

86. ACLU of Ohio, *In Jail and in Debt: Ohio's Pay-to-Stay Fees* (Fall 2015), 7, https://www.acluohio.org/en/jail-debt. Information on the 70/30 revenue split between Intellitech and counties is from Jessica Lussenhop, "The US Inmates Charged per Night in Jail," *BBC News Magazine*, November 9, 2015, https://www.bbc.com/news/magazine-34705968.

87. Lussenhop, "The US Inmates Charged per Night in Jail."

88. Jennnifer Steinhauer, "For $82 a Day, Booking a Cell in a 5-Star Jail," *New York Times*, April 29, 2007, http://www.nytimes.com/2007/04/29/us/29jail.html. On the Seal Beach facility, see Alysia Santo, Victoria Kim, and Anna Flagg, "Afraid of Jail? Buy an Upgrade: How California's Pay-to-Stay Jails Create a Two-Tiered Justice System," *Marshall Project*, March 9, 2017, https://www.themarshallproject.org/2017/03/09/afraid-of-jail-buy-an-upgrade.

89. Worth Rises, *The Prison Industry: How It Started. How It Works. How It Harms* (Worth Rises, 2020), 59.

90. Catherine Akenhead, "How States Can Take a Stand Against Prison Banking Profiteers," *George Washington Law Review* 85, no. 4 (2017): 1224–62, https://www.gwlr.org/wp-content/uploads/2018/01/85-Geo.-Wash.-L.-Rev.-1224.pdf.

91. Daniel Wagner, "Meet the Prison Bankers Who Profit from the Inmates," *Time*, September 30, 2014, https://time.com/3446372/criminal-justice-prisoners-profit/; Akenhead, "How States Can Take a Stand."

92. Quoted in Akenhead, "How States Can Take a Stand," 1236.

93. Wagner, "Meet the Prison Bankers."

94. Wagner, "Meet the Prison Bankers."

95. Stephen Raher, "The Multi-Millon Dollar Market of Sending Money to an Incarcerated Loved One," *Prison Policy Initiative* (blog), January 18, 2017, https://www.prisonpolicy.org/blog/2017/01/18/money-transfer/.

96. Wagner, "Meet the Prison Bankers."

97. Akenhead, "How States Can Take a Stand," 1228, 1233.

98. "Minnesota Department of Corrections," JPay, accessed March 25, 2024, http://www.jpay.com/Agency-Details/Minnesota-Department-of-Corrections.aspx. For rates in other states and counties, see "Availability & Pricing," JPay, accessed March 25, 2024, http://www.jpay.com/Pavail.aspx.

99. Wagner, "Meet the Prison Bankers"; Oklahoma Watch, "Prison Bankers Exact Fees, Profits from Families," February 17, 2015, accessed October 28, 2019, http://oklahomawatch.org/2015/02/17/prison-bankers-exact-fees-profits-from-families/.

100. Minnesota Department of Corrections, "MN Money Order Deposit Form," JPay, accessed March 11, 2024, https://www.jpay.com/moneyOrderForms/MN%20Money%20Order%20Deposit%20Form%20DOC%20ENG.pdf.

101. Stephen Raher, "Paging Anti-Trust Lawyers: Prison Commissary Giants Prepare to Merge," *Prison Policy Initiative* (blog), July 5, 2016, https://www.prisonpolicy.org/blog/2016/07/05/commissary-merger/; Jim Runkle, "Contract for Commissary Services at Prison Accepted," *The Express*, August 14, 2015, http://www.lockhaven.com/news/local-news/2015/08/contract-for-commissary-services-at-prison-accepted/.

102. Wagner, "Meet the Prison Bankers"; Tommaso Bardelli, Zach Gillespie, and Thuy Linh Tu, "Surviving Austerity: Commissary Stores, Inequality and Punishment in the Contemporary American Prison," *Punishment & Society*, 25, no. 4 (2023): 971.

103. Stephen Raher, *The Company Store: A Deeper Look at Prison Commissaries* (Prison Policy Initiative, May 2018), https://www.prisonpolicy.org/reports/commissary.html.

104. Raher, "Paging Anti-Trust Lawyers"; Wagner, "Meet the Prison Bankers"; Eric Markowitz, "Making Profits on the Captive Prison Market," *New Yorker*, September 4, 2016, https://www.newyorker.com/business/currency/making-profits-on-the-captive-prison-market.

105. Timothy Williams, "The High Cost of Calling the Imprisoned," *New York Times*, March 30, 2015, https://www.nytimes.com/2015/03/31/us/steep-costs-of-inmate-phone-calls-are-under-scrutiny.html.

106. Drew Kukorowski, Peter Wagner, and Leah Sakala, *Please Deposit All of Your Money: Kickbacks, Rates, and Hidden Fees in the Jail Phone Industry* (Prison Policy Initiative, May 2013), 2, https://www.prisonpolicy.org/phones/please_deposit.pdf.

107. Victoria Law, "$15 for 15 Minutes: How Courts Are Letting Prison Phone Companies Gouge Incarcerated People," *The Intercept*, June 16, 2017, https://theintercept.com/2017/06/16/fcc-prison-phone-call-rates-court-deregulate-trump/; Kukorowski, Wagner, and Sakala, *Please Deposit*, 5.

108. Ann E. Marimow, "FCC Made a Case for Limiting Cost of Prison Phone Calls. Not Anymore," *Washington Post*, February 5, 2017, https://www.washingtonpost

.com/local/public-safety/fcc-made-a-case-for-limiting-cost-of-prison-phone-calls-not
-anymore/2017/02/04/9306fbf8-e97c-11e6-b82f-687d6e6a3e7c_story.html.

109. PR Newswire, "Securus Provides over $1.3 Billion in Prison, Jail and Government Funding over the Last 10 Years," October 31, 2014, https://www
.prnewswire.com/news-releases/securus-provides-over-13-billion-in-prison-jail-and
-government-funding-over-the-last-10-years-281105252.html.

110. Lauren-Brooke Eisen, *Inside Private Prisons: An American Dilemma in the Age of Mass Incarceration* (Columbia University Press, 2018), 73.

111. Frannie Kelley, "Drakeo's Acclaimed Album Highlights How Much Prisons Profit from Phone Calls," NPR (*All Things Considered*), August 28, 2020, https://www
.npr.org/2020/08/28/906807077/prison-telecom-business-indicted-by-rap-album
-recorded-in-jail; Greg Roumeliotis, "Platinum Equity Nears Deal to Buy Prison Phone Company Securus: Sources," Reuters, May 16, 2017, https://www.reuters
.com/article/us-securus-tech-m-a-abrypartners/platinum-equity-nears-deal-to-buy
-prison-phone-company-securus-sources-idUSKCN18C2FU; "Securus Technologies, Inc. Completes Transaction to Acquire JPay Inc.," Abry Partners, July 31, 2015, https://abry.com/securus-technologies-inc-completes-transaction-to-acquire-jpay
-inc/.

112. Roumeliotis, "Platinum Equity Nears Deal."

113. Stephen Raher, *You've Got Mail: The Promise of Cyber Communication in Prisons and the Need for Regulation* (Prison Policy Initiative, January 21, 2016), https://www.prisonpolicy.org/messaging/report.html.

114. Raher, *You've Got Mail.*

115. Eisen, *Inside Private Prisons*, 75.

116. Bernadette Rabuy and Peter Wagner, *Screening Out Family Time: The For-Profit Video Visitation Industry in Prisons and Jails* (Prison Policy Initiative, January 2015), https://www.prisonpolicy.org/visitation/report.html.

117. Rabuy and Wagner, *Screening Out Family Time.*

118. Rabuy and Wagner, *Screening Out Family Time*; Brian Alexander, "When Prisoners Are a 'Revenue Opportunity,'" *Atlantic*, August 10, 2017, https://www
.theatlantic.com/business/archive/2017/08/remote-video-visitation/535095/.

119. Gabrielle A. Perry, "In Prison, Having Your Period Can Put Your Life in Danger," *Washington Post*, https://www.washingtonpost.com/opinions/2022/03/25/
prison-period-danger-health-risks-sexual-abuse/.

120. Anne Stuhldreher, "Jail Stores Should Provide Low-Priced Necessities, Not Generate Punitive Profits," *Spotlight*, September 2, 2020, https://spotlightonpoverty
.org/spotlight-exclusives/jail-stores-should-provide-low-priced-necessities-not
-generate-punitive-profits/.

121. Michael Gibson-Light, "Ramen Politics: Informal Money and Logics of Resistance in the Contemporary American Prison," *Qualitative Sociology* 41 (2018): 200.

122. Bardelli et al., "Surviving Austerity," 962.

123. Mack Finkel and Wanda Bertram, "More States Are Signing Harmful 'Free Prison Tablet' Contracts," *Prison Policy Initiative* (blog), March 7, 2019, https://www
.prisonpolicy.org/blog/2019/03/07/free-tablets/.

124. Wagner, "Meet the Prison Bankers"; David M. Reutter, "Florida Prisoners Get Tablets, Lose $11.3 Million in Digital Music," *Prison Legal News*, February 4, 2019, https://www.prisonlegalnews.org/news/2019/feb/4/florida-prisoners-get-tablets-lose
-113-million-digital-music/.

125. Kaitlin Peterson, "No Right to Read: Profiteering Corporations Creep into Prison Libraries," *People's World*, December 22, 2020, https://www.peoplesworld.org/article/no-right-to-read-profiteering-corporations-creep-into-prison-libraries/; Mia Armstrong, "Return to Sender: No More Mailing Books to Inmates in Pennsylvania," *Slate*, September 19, 2018, https://slate.com/technology/2018/09/pennsylvania-prisons-ban-book-donations-ebooks.html; Stephen Raher, "The Wireless Prison: How Colorado's Tablet Computer Program Misses Opportunities and Monetizes the Poor," *Prison Policy Initiative* (blog), July 6, 2017, https://www.prisonpolicy.org/blog/2017/07/06/tablets/.

126. Worth Rises, *The Prison Industry*, 62.

127. Worth Rises, *The Prison Industry*, 63; Amadou Diallo, "'Release Cards' Turn Inmates and Their Families into Profit Stream," Malta Justice Initiative, accessed January 2, 2025, http://maltajusticeinitiative.org/release-cards-turn-inmates-and-their-families-into-profit-stream/.

128. Diallo, "'Release Cards.'"

129. Rabuy and Wagner, *Screening Out Family Time*.

130. Hanna Kozlowska, "Prison Communications Company Securus Will No Longer Require Jails to Ban In-Person Visits," *Quartz*, May 9, 2015 (updated July 20, 2022), https://qz.com/400055/prison-communications-company-securus-will-no-longer-require-jails-to-ban-in-person-visits/.

131. Class Action Complaint for Injunctive Relief and Damages, M. M. et al. v. Sheriff Mat King et al. (31st Cir. Ct., Michigan, March 14, 2014), 57, https://civilrightscorps.org/wp-content/uploads/2024/03/St.ClairCounty-Complaint.pdf.

132. Class Action Complaint, *M. M. v. King*, 60.

133. Class Action Complaint, *M. M. v. King*, 57.

134. Tommaso Bardelli, Ruqaiyah Zarook, and Derick McCarthy, "How Corporations Turned Prison Tablets into a Predatory Scheme," *Dissent*, March 7, 2022, https://www.dissentmagazine.org/online_articles/corporations-prison-tablets-predatory-scheme; Tonya Riley, "'Free' Tablets Are Costing Prison Inmates a Fortune," *Mother Jones*, October 5, 2018, https://www.motherjones.com/politics/2018/10/tablets-prisons-inmates-jpay-securus-global-tel-link/.

135. JPay, "Joshua—it's time to try VideoGram" (email received by Joshua Page, September 14, 2016).

136. JPay, "10% Off of Stamp Purchases—a Holiday Treat!" (email received by Joshua Page, December 5, 2017).

137. Taylor Elizabeth Eldridge, "The Big Business of Prisoner Care Packages," *Marshall Project*, December 21, 2017, https://www.themarshallproject.org/2017/12/21/the-big-business-of-prisoner-care-packages.

138. Eldridge, "Prisoner Care Packages."

139. Eldridge, "Prisoner Care Packages."

140. Isabel Arriagada, "Prison, Technology, and Consumption: A Visual Study of the Use of Electronic Commerce Strategies in the Inmate Package Industry," *Theoretical Criminology* 27, no. 3 (2023): 457–80.

141. Arriagada, "Prison, Technology, and Consumption."

142. Arriagada, "Prison, Technology, and Consumption," 463–66.

143. Arriagada, "Prison, Technology, and Consumption," 463.

144. Eisen, *Inside Private Prisons*, 72.

145. Michael Sorkin, "Drawing the Line: Architects and Prisons," *The Nation*, August 27, 2013, https://web.archive.org/web/20190809133059/https://www

.thenation.com/article/drawing-line-architects-and-prisons/; Eric Schlosser, "The Prison-Industrial Complex," *Atlantic*, December 1998, http://www.theatlantic.com/magazine/archive/1998/12/the-prison-industrial-complex/304669/.

146. James Kilgore, "Even in Government-Run Prisons, the Profiteering off of Human Lives Is Staggering," *Truthout*, October 4, 2015, https://truthout.org/articles/even-in-government-run-prisons-the-profiteering-off-of-human-lives-is-staggering/.

147. Eisen, *Inside Private Prisons*, 76.

148. Natalie Delgadillo, "Maggots with a Side of Dirt? What Privatization Does to Prison Food," *Governing*, January 26, 2018, http://www.governing.com/topics/public-justice-safety/gov-private-food-service-prisons-aramark-trinity-ohio-michigan.html.

149. James Kilgore, "Five Corporations You've Never Heard of Are Making Millions from Mass Incarceration," *Truthout*, January 19, 2015, https://truthout.org/articles/five-corporations-you-ve-never-heard-of-making-millions-from-mass-incarceration/.

150. Eli Hager and Alysia Santo, "Inside the Deadly World of Private Prisoner Transport," *Marshall Project*, July 6, 2016, https://www.themarshallproject.org/2016/07/06/inside-the-deadly-world-of-private-prisoner-transport.

151. Hager and Santo, "Private Prisoner Transport."

152. Quoted in Hager and Santo, "Private Prisoner Transport."

153. Hager and Santo, "Private Prisoner Transport."

154. Eisen, *Inside Private Prisons*, 72.

155. Eisen, *Inside Private Prisons*, 65.

156. Eisen, *Inside Private Prisons*, 65.

157. Nzong Xiong, "Private Prisons: A Question of Savings," *New York Times*, July 13, 1997, https://www.nytimes.com/1997/07/13/business/private-prisons-a-question-of-savings.html.

158. Xiong, "Private Prisons."

159. Eisen, *Inside Private Prisons*, 145–47; Richard Culp, "The Rise and Stall of Prison Privatization: An Integration of Policy Analysis Perspectives," *Criminal Justice Policy Review* 16, no. 4 (2005);

160. Eisen, *Inside Private Prisons*, 147; Culp, "The Rise and Stall of Prison Privatization," 426–27.

161. Eisen, *Inside Private Prisons*, 145.

162. Eisen, *Inside Private Prisons*, 147.

163. Eisen, *Inside Private Prisons*, 149.

164. Eisen, *Inside Private Prisons*, 148–49.

165. Eisen, *Inside Private Prisons*, 139.

166. Eunice Hyunhye Cho, "Unchecked Growth: Private Prison Corporations and Immigrant Detention, Three Years into the Biden Administration," ACLU, August 7, 2023, https://www.aclu.org/news/immigrants-rights/unchecked-growth-private-prison-corporations-and-immigration-detention-three-years-into-the-biden-administration.

167. Detention Watch Network, *Banking on Detention: Local Lockup Quotas and the Immigrant Dragnet* (2015); *Criminal: How Lockup Quotas and "Low-Crime Taxes" Guarantee Profits for Private Prison Corporations* (In the Public Interest, September 2013), https://www.inthepublicinterest.org/wp-content/uploads/Criminal-Lockup-Quota-Report.pdf.

168. Richard A. Oppel Jr., "Private Prisons Found to Offer Little in Savings," *New York Times*, May 18, 2011, https://www.nytimes.com/2011/05/19/us/19prisons.html.

169. Marie Gottschalk, *Caught: The Prison State and the Lockdown of American Politics* (Princeton University Press, 2014), 70.

170. Fines and Fees Justice Center Reform Alliance (FFJCRA), *50 State Survey: Probation and Parole Fees: A State-by-State Look at the Scope of Probation and Parole Fees and the Consequences for Failure-to-Pay* (May 2022), 8, https://finesandfeesjusticecenter.org/articles/50-state-survey-probation-and-parole-fees/.

171. FFJCRA, *50 State Survey*, 5. The 1990 figure is from Joseph Shapiro, "As Court Fees Rise, the Poor Are Paying the Price," NPR, May 19, 2014, https://www.npr.org/2014/05/19/312158516/increasing-court-fees-punish-the-poor.

172. FFJCRA, *50 State Survey*, 5.

173. FFJCRA, *50 State Survey*, 9.

174. Alexes Harris, Beth Huebner, Karin Martin, Mary Pattillo, Becky Pettit, Sarah Shannon, Bryan Sykes, Chris Uggen, and April Fernandes, *Monetary Sanctions in the Criminal Justice System: A Review of Law and Policy in California, Georgia, Illinois, Minnesota, Missouri, New York, North Carolina, Texas, and Washington*, Report to Lauran and John Arnold Foundation (2017), 171.

175. Wendy Sawyer, *The High Cost of Probation Fees in Massachusetts* (Prison Policy Initiative, December 8, 2016), https://www.prisonpolicy.org/probation/ma_report.html.

176. Harris et al., *Monetary Sanctions in the Criminal Justice System*, 192.

177. Lee Romney, "Private Diversion Programs Are Failing Those Who Need Help the Most," *Reveal*, May 31, 2017, https://www.revealnews.org/article/private-diversion-programs-are-failing-those-who-need-help-the-most/; Sheila Dewan and Andrew W. Lehren, "After a Crime, the Price of a Second Chance," *New York Times*, December 12, 2016, https://www.nytimes.com/2016/12/12/us/crime-criminal-justice-reform-diversion.html.

178. Dewan and Lehren, "After a Crime."

179. Dewan and Lehren, "After a Crime."

180. Romney, "Private Diversion Programs"; Dewan and Lehren, "After a Crime."

181. Dewan and Lehren, "After a Crime."

182. Romney, "Private Diversion Programs."

183. The revenue figure is from ACLU, *A Pound of Flesh: The Criminalization of Private Debt* (2018), 29, https://www.aclu.org/report/pound-flesh-criminalization-private-debt; The quoted part of the sentence is from Romney, "Private Diversion Programs."

184. John Rappaport, "Criminal Justice, Inc.," *Columbia Law Review* 118, no. 8 (2018): 19–20, https://columbialawreview.org/content/criminal-justice-inc-2/.

185. Jessica Pishko, "'Restorative Justice' for Shoplifting? A Court Calls It Extortion," *Marshall Project*, October 30, 2017, https://www.themarshallproject.org/2017/10/30/restorative-justice-for-shoplifting-a-court-calls-it-extortion; Leon Neyfakh, "Let's Make a Deal," *Slate*, February 26, 2015, http://www.slate.com/articles/news_and_politics/crime/2015/02/shoplifting_at_whole_foods_or_bloomingdale_s_pay_corrective_education_company.html.

186. Neyfakh, "Let's Make a Deal."

187. Rappaport, "Criminal Justice, Inc."

188. Neyfakh, "Let's Make a Deal."

189. Neyfakh, "Let's Make a Deal."

190. Pishko, "'Restorative Justice' for Shoplifting?"

191. Rappaport, "Criminal Justice, Inc.," 1.

192. Joe Palazzolo and Sarah Nassauer, "Wal-Mart Stops Shoplifting Diversion Program That Court Described as Extortion," *MarketWatch*, December 21, 2017, https://www.marketwatch.com/story/wal-mart-stops-shoplifting-diversion-program -that-court-described-as-extortion-2017-12-21.

193. Chris Albin-Lackey et al., *Profiting from Probation: America's "Offender-Funded" Probation Industry* (Human Rights Watch, February 5, 2014), https://www.hrw .org/report/2014/02/05/profiting-probation/americas-offender-funded-probation -industry.

194. Eisen, *Inside Private Prisons*, 45.

195. Beth Schwartzapfel, "Probation-for-Profit Just Got Less Profitable," *Marshall Project*, April 13, 2017, https://www.themarshallproject.org/2017/04/13/probation -for-profit-just-got-less-profitable.

196. Harris et al., *Monetary Sanctions in the Criminal Justice System*, 48.

197. ACLU, *A Pound of Flesh*, 26.

198. Sarah Stillman, "Get Out of Jail, Inc." *New Yorker*, June 16, 2014, https:// www.newyorker.com/magazine/2014/06/23/get-out-of-jail-inc.

199. Stillman, "Get Out of Jail, Inc."

200. Albin-Lackey et al., *Profiting from Probation*, 52.

201. Albin-Lackey et al., *Profiting from Probation*, 52.

202. Anat Rubin, "A Record of Trouble," *Marshall Project*, April 11, 2015, https:// www.themarshallproject.org/2015/04/11/a-record-of-trouble.

203. Steve Contorno, "Why Is a Florida For-Profit Prison Company Backing Bipartisan Criminal Justice Reform?," *Tampa Bay Times*, December 7, 2018, https:// www.tampabay.com/florida-politics/buzz/2018/12/07/why-is-a-florida-for-profit -prison-company-backing-bipartisan-criminal-justice-reform/.

204. Carl Takei, "Private Prison Giant CoreCivic's Wants to Corner the Mass Incarceration 'Market' in the States," ACLU Smart Justice, November 7, 2017, https:// www.aclu.org/blog/smart-justice/mass-incarceration/private-prison-giant-corecivics -wants-corner-mass.

205. Christopher Ingraham, "Private Prison Stocks Collapse After Justice Department Promises to Phase Them Out," *Washington Post*, August 18, 2016, https:// www.washingtonpost.com/news/wonk/wp/2016/08/18/private-prison-stocks -collapse-after-justice-department-promises-to-phase-them-out/.

206. Sally Q. Yates, "Reducing Our Use of Private Prisons," (memorandum for the acting director, Federal Bureau of Prisons, August 18, 2016), https://www.justice .gov/archives/opa/file/886311/download.

207. Donald Cohen, "U.S. DOJ Says It Will End Use of Private Prisons," *In the Public Interest*, August 18, 2016, https://www.inthepublicinterest.org/u-s-doj-says-it -will-end-use-of-private-prisons/.

208. Keith Humphreys, "Private Prisons Aren't That Big a Deal," *Washington Post*, August 23, 2016, https://www.washingtonpost.com/news/wonk/wp/2016/08/23/ private-prisons-arent-that-big-a-deal/.

209. Juleyka Lantigua-Williams, "Feds End Use of Private Prisons, but Questions Remain," *Atlantic*, August 18, 2016, https://www.theatlantic.com/politics/archive/ 2016/08/end-of-private-prison-contracts-with-federal-government/496469/.

210. Maurice Chammah, "What You Need to Know About the Private Prison Phase-Out," *Marshall Project*, August 18, 2016, https://www.themarshallproject .org/2016/08/18/what-you-need-to-know-about-the-private-prison-phase-out; Roque Planas, "The Department of Justice Will Still Rely on Private Prisons in a Big

Way," *Huffington Post*, August 24, 2016, https://www.huffpost.com/entry/justice -department-private-prisons_n_57bca9b1e4b00d9c3a1a7e19.

211. Hadar Aviram, "Are Private Prisons to Blame for Mass Incarceration and Its Evils? Prison Conditions, Neoliberalism and Public Choice," *Fordham Urban Law Review* 42, no. 2 (2006): 438.

212. Hadar Aviram, *Cheap on Crime: Recession-Era Politics and the Transformation of American Punishment* (University of California Press, 2015), chap. 7.

Chapter Four

1. See, e.g., Ruth Wilson Gilmore, *Golden Gulag: Prisons, Surplus, Crisis, and Opposition in Globalizing California* (University of California Press, 2007); Georg Rusche and Otto Kirchheimer, *Punishment and Social Structure* (Routledge, 2003); Alessandro De Giorgi, "Punishment and Political Economy" in *The SAGE Handbook of Punishment and Society*, ed. Jonathan Simon and Richard Sparks (SAGE Publications, 2013), 40–59; Dario Melossi, Máximo Sozzo, and José Brandariz García, eds., *The Political Economy of Punishment Today: Visions, Debates and Challenges* (Routledge, 2017).

2. Daniel Béland, Andrea Lousie Campbell, and R. Kent Weaver, *Policy Feedback* (Cambridge University Press, 2023).

3. See, e.g., David Harvey, *A Brief History of Neoliberalism* (Oxford University Press, 2005); Wendy Brown, *Undoing the Demos: Neoliberalism's Stealth Revolution* (Zone Books, 2015).

4. All quotations are from Nancy Fraser, "Expropriation and Exploitation in Racial Capitalism: A Reply to Michael Dawson," *Critical Historical Studies* 3, no. 1 (2016): 176.

5. Greta Krippner, *Capitalizing on Crisis: The Political Origins of the Rise of Finance* (Harvard University Press, 2011).

6. The Debt Collective, *Can't Pay, Won't Pay: The Case for Economic Disobedience and Debt Abolition* (Haymarket Books, 2020); Susanne Soederberg, "The US Debtfare State and the Credit Card Industry: Forging Spaces of Dispossession," *Antipode* 45, no. 2 (2012): 493–512.

7. On RCS communities, see Joe Soss and Vesla Weaver, "Police Are Our Government: Politics, Political Science, and the Policing of Race-Class Subjugated Communities," *Annual Review of Political Science* 20, no. 1 (2017): 565–91, https://doi .org/10.1146/annurev-polisci-060415-093825.

8. Devin Fergus, *Land of the Fee: Hidden Costs and the Decline of the American Middle Class* (Oxford University Press, 2018).

9. For all practices described in this paragraph, see Daniel Hatcher, *The Poverty Industry: The Exploitation of America's Most Vulnerable Citizens* (New York University Press, 2016).

10. Nancy Brune, Geoffrey Garrett, and Bruce Kogut, "The International Monetary Fund and the Global Spread of Privatization," *IMF Staff Papers* 51, no. 2 (2004): 195–219; Harvey, *A Brief History of Neoliberalism*.

11. Harvey, *A Brief History of Neoliberalism*.

12. Karol Yearwood, *The Privatised Water Industry in the UK: An ATM for Investors* (Public Services International Research Unit, 2018); Harvey, *A Brief History of Neoliberalism*.

13. Brown, *Undoing the Demos*; Sanford Schram and Marianna Pavlovskaya, eds., *Rethinking Neoliberalism: Resisting the Neoliberal Regime* (Routledge, 2018).

14. David E. Osborne and Ted Gaebler, *Reinventing Government: How the Entrepreneurial Spirit Is Transforming the Public Sector* (Penguin Books, 1992).

15. Gernod Gruening, "Origins and Theoretical Basis of New Public Management," *International Public Management Journal* 4, no. 1 (2001): 1–25; Joe Soss, Richard C. Fording, and Sanford F. Schram, *Disciplining the Poor: Neoliberal Paternalism and the Persistent Power of Race* (University of Chicago Press, 2011), chap. 9.

16. Nicholas F. Jacobs, Desmond King, and Sidney M. Milkis, "Building a Conservative State: Partisan Polarization and the Redeployment of Administrative Power," *Perspectives on Politics* 17, no. 2 (2019): 453–69.

17. Charles R. Ring, *Probation Supervision Fees: Shifting Costs to the Offender* (Massachusetts General Court Research Bureau, 1998), 1.

18. Charles Tilly, "War Making and State Making as Organized Crime," in *Bringing the State Back In*, ed. Peter B. Evans, Dietrich Rueschemeyer, and Theda Skocpol (Cambridge University Press, 1985), 169–91.

19. Katherine Beckett, *Making Crime Pay: Law and Order in Contemporary American Politics* (Oxford University Press, 1997); Bernard E. Harcourt, *The Illusion of Free Markets: Punishment and the Myth of Natural Order* (Harvard University Press, 2011).

20. Jackie Wang, *Carceral Capitalism* (Semiotext(e), 2018), 83.

21. Radley Balko, *Rise of the Warrior Cop: The Militarization of America's Police Forces* (PublicAffairs Books, 2013).

22. Stuart Schrader, *Badges Without Borders: How Global Counterinsurgency Transformed American Policing* (University of California Press, 2019).

23. Nikhil Pal Singh, *Race and America's Long War* (University of California Press, 2017), 9.

24. David Harvey, *The New Imperialism* (Oxford University Press, 2003); Harvey, *A Brief History of Neoliberalism*.

25. David Vine, "'We're Profiteers': How Military Contractors Reap Billions from U.S. Military Bases Overseas," *Monthly Review* (July 1, 2014), https://monthlyreview.org/2014/07/01/were-profiteers/.

26. Jonathan Simon, *Governing Through Crime: How the War on Crime Transformed American Democracy and Created a Culture of Fear* (Oxford University Press, 2007); Kaaryn S. Gustafson, *Cheating Welfare: Public Assistance and the Criminalization of Poverty* (New York University Press, 2011).

27. William Lyons, *The Politics of Community Policing: Rearranging the Power to Punish* (University of Michigan Press, 1999); Forrest Stuart, *Down, Out, and Under Arrest: Policing and Everyday Life in Skid Row* (University of Chicago Press, 2016).

28. Loïc Wacquant, *Punishing the Poor: The Neoliberal Government of Social Insecurity* (Duke University Press, 2009).

29. Ana Swanson, "A Shocking Number of Mentally Ill Americans End Up in Prison Instead of Treatment," *Washington Post*, April 30, 2015, https://www.washingtonpost.com/news/wonk/wp/2015/04/30/a-shocking-number-of-mentally-ill-americans-end-up-in-prisons-instead-of-psychiatric-hospitals/.

30. Bruce Western, *Homeward: Life in the Year After Prison* (Russell Sage Foundation, 2018), 7, 61.

31. Mary Fainsod Katzenstein and Maureen R. Waller, "Taxing the Poor: Incarceration, Poverty Governance, and the Seizure of Family Resources," *Perspectives*

on Politics 13, no. 3 (September 2015): 638, 648, https://doi.org/10.1017/
S153759271500122X. The latter phrase quotes Thomas Edsall.

32. Alicia Bannon, Mitali Nagrecha, and Rebekah Diller, *Criminal Justice Debt: A Barrier to Reentry* (Brennan Center for Justice, New York University School of Law, 2010), 30, http://www.brennancenter.org/sites/default/files/legacy/Fees%20and %20Fines%20FINAL.pdf.

33. Henry Ordower, J. S. Onesimo Sandoval, and Kenneth Warren, "Out of Ferguson: Misdemeanors, Municipal Courts, Tax Distribution, and Constitutional Limitations," *Howard Law Journal* 61, no. 1 (2016): 18.

34. On this interplay, see, e.g., Jacob S. Hacker and Paul Pierson, "After the Master Theory: Downs, Schattschneider, and the Rebirth of Policy-Focused Analysis," *Perspectives on Politics* 12, no. 3 (2014): 643–62.

35. Jacob S. Hacker and Paul Pierson, *American Amnesia: How the War on Government Led Us to Forget What Made America Prosper* (Simon & Schuster, 2017), 214.

36. M. Margaret Conway, "PACs and Congressional Elections in the 1980s," in *Interest Group Politics*, ed. Allan J. Cigler and Burdett A. Loomis (CQ Press, 1986), 73.

37. See, e.g., Hacker and Pierson, *American Amnesia*; Patrick J. Akard, "Corporate Mobilization and Political Power," *American Sociological Review* 57, no. 5 (1992).

38. Thomas Byrne Edsall and Mary D. Edsall, *Chain Reaction: The Impact of Race, Rights, and Taxes on American Politics* (W. W. Norton, 1991); Sara Diamond, *Roads to Dominion: Right-Wing Movements and Political Power in the United States* (Guilford Press, 1995).

39. Monica Prasad, *Starving the Beast: Ronald Reagan and the Tax Cut Revolution* (Russell Sage Foundation, 2018).

40. Emmanuel Saez and Gabriel Zucman, *The Triumph of Injustice: How the Rich Dodge Taxes and How to Make Them Pay* (W. W. Norton, 2019).

41. Prasad, *Starving the Beast*.

42. Edsall and Edsall, *Chain Reaction*.

43. Kasey Henricks and David G. Embrick, *State Lotteries: Historical Continuity, Rearticulations of Racism, and American Taxation* (Routledge, 2017), 55; Randolph Hohle, *Race and the Origins of American Neoliberalism* (Routledge, 2015).

44. William Darity Jr. et al., *What We Get Wrong About Closing the Racial Wealth Gap* (Samuel DuBois Cook Center on Social Equity, Insight Center for Community Economic Development, 2018), https://narrowthegap.org/images/documents/Wealth -Gap---FINAL-COMPLETE-REPORT.pdf; Meg Wiehe, Emanuel Nieves, Jeremie Greer, and David Newville, *Race, Wealth, and Taxes* (Institute on Taxation and Economic Policy, 2018).

45. Joseph E. Lowndes, *From the New Deal to the New Right: Race and the Southern Origins of Modern Conservatism* (Yale University Press, 2008).

46. Jesse Jackson Jr., "Reagan: A Legacy of States' Rights," *The Nation*, June 17, 2004, https://www.thenation.com/article/archive/reagan-legacy-states-rights/.

47. Jackson, "Reagan."

48. Ronald Reagan, "Speech at Neshoba County Fair," August 3, 1980, accessed August 7, 2019, https://www.youtube.com/watch?v=5I-JZwEPRzs&t=5s.

49. John Donahue, *Hazardous Crosscurrents: Confronting Inequality in an Era of Devolution* (The Century Foundation, 1999).

50. Dale Krane, Carol Ebdon, and John Bartle, "Devolution, Fiscal Federalism, and Changing Patterns of Municipal Revenues: The Mismatch Between Theory and

Reality," *Journal of Public Administration Research and Theory* 14, no. 4 (October 2004): 513–33.

51. *Cities and the Future of Public Finance: A Framework for Public Discussion* (National League of Cities, 2003).

52. Daniel R. Mullins and Michael A. Pagano, "Local Budgeting and Finance: 25 Years of Developments," *Public Budgeting and Finance* 25, no. 4 (2005): 5.

53. Mullins and Pagano, "Local Budgeting and Finance," 5.

54. Mullins and Pagano, "Local Budgeting and Finance," 5.

55. John Shannon, "The Return to Fend-for-Yourself Federalism: The Reagan Mark," *Intergovernmental Perspective* 13 (Summer/Fall 1987): 34–37.

56. David O. Sears and Jack Citrin, *Tax Revolt: Something for Nothing in California* (Harvard University Press, 1985).

57. Isaac William Martin, *The Permanent Tax Revolt: How the Property Tax Transformed American Politics* (Stanford University Press, 2008); Kim Rueben and Megan Randall, *Tax and Expenditure Limits: How States Restrict Revenues and Spending* (Urban Institute Press, 2017).

58. Daniel R. Mullins and Bruce A. Wallin, "Tax and Expenditure Limitations: An Introduction and Overview," *Public Budgeting and Finance* 24, no. 4 (2004): 2–3.

59. Rueben and Randall, *Tax and Expenditure Limits*; Mullins and Wallin, "Tax and Expenditure Limitations," 2–15.

60. Susan K. Urahn et al., *The Local Squeeze: Falling Revenues and Growing Demand for Services Challenge Cities, Counties, and School Districts* (Pew Charitable Trusts, 2012), https://www.pewtrusts.org/-/media/assets/2012/06/pew_cities_local-squeeze_report.pdf.

61. Jamie Peck, "Austerity Urbanism," *City* 16, no. 6 (2012): 632.

62. Peck, "Austerity Urbanism"; David B. Miller and Terry Hokenstad, "Rolling Downhill: Effects of Austerity on Local Government Social Services in the United States," *Journal of Sociology and Social Welfare* 41, no. 2 (2014): 93–108.

63. David Harvey, "From Managerialism to Entrepreneurialism: The Transformation in Urban Governance in Late Capitalism," *Geografiska Annaler: Series B, Human Geography* 71, no. 1 (1989): 3–17.

64. Destin Jenkins, *The Bonds of Inequality: Debt and the Making of the American City* (University of Chicago Press, 2021); Jackie Wang, *Carceral Capitalism* (Semiotext(e), 2018).

65. Alex Schafran, "Discourse and Dystopia, American Style: The Rise of 'Slumburbia' in a Time of Crisis," *City* 17, no. 2 (2013): 130–48.

66. Andrew J. Haile, "Sin Taxes: When the State Becomes the Sinner," *Temple Law Review* 82 (2009–2010): 1041–70.

67. Henricks and Embrick, *State Looteries*, 103.

68. Statista, "U.S. State and Local Lottery Revenue 1977–2021," July 5, 2024, https://www.statista.com/statistics/249128/us-state-and-local-lottery-revenue/.

69. Michael Makowsky, *A Proposal to End Regressive Taxation Through Law Enforcement* (Hamilton Project, March 2019), https://www.hamiltonproject.org/assets/files/Makowsky_PP_20190314.pdf.

70. Karin D. Martin, "Monetary Myopia: An Examination of Institutional Response to Revenue from Monetary Sanctions for Misdemeanors," *Criminal Justice Policy Review* 29, nos. 6–7 (2018): 637.

71. Akheil Singla, Charlotte Kirschner, and Samuel B. Stone, "Race, Representation, and Revenue: Reliance on Fines and Forfeitures in City Governments,"

Urban Affairs Review 56, no. 4 (2020); Rebecca Goldstein, Michael W. Sances, and Hye Young You, "Exploitative Revenues, Law Enforcement, and the Quality of Government Service," *Urban Affairs Review* 56, no. 1 (2018): 5–31; Michael W. Sances and Hye Young You, "Who Pays for Government? Descriptive Representation and Exploitative Revenue Sources," *Journal of Politics* 79, no. 3 (2017): 1090–94; Michael D. Makowsky, Thomas Stratmann, and Alexander T. Tabarrok, "To Serve and Collect: The Fiscal and Racial Determinants of Law Enforcement," *Journal of Legal Studies* 48, no. 1 (2019): 189–216.

72. Michael Leachman et al., *Advancing Racial Equity with State Tax Policy* (Center on Budget and Policy Priorities, November 15, 2018).

73. Josh Pacewicz and John N. Robinson III, "Pocketbook Policing: How Race Shapes Municipal Reliance on Punitive Fines and Fees in the Chicago Suburbs," *Socio-Economic Review* 19, no. 3 (July 2021): 976, https://doi.org/10.1093/ser/mwaa029.

74. Pacewicz and Robinson, "Pocketbook Policing," 986.

75. Pacewicz and Robinson, "Pocketbook Policing," 996.

76. Pacewicz and Robinson, "Pocketbook Policing," 977.

77. Chet Bowie, *Prisoners 1925–1981* (Bureau of Justice Statistics, December 1982), https://www.bjs.gov/content/pub/pdf/p2581.pdf; Paige M. Harrison and Allen J. Beck, *Prisoners in 2005* (Bureau of Justice Statistics, 2007).

78. Phyllis Jo Baunach and Susan A. Kline, *Jail Inmates, 1985* (Bureau of Justice Statistics, July 1987), https://www.bjs.gov/content/pub/pdf/ji85.pdf; Darrell K. Gillard and Allen J. Beck, *Prison and Jail Inmates, 1995* (Bureau of Justice Statistics, 1996), https://www.bjs.gov/content/pub/pdf/PJI95.PDF; Paige M. Harrison and Allen J. Beck, *Prison and Jail Inmates at Midyear 2005* (Bureau of Justice Statistics, May 2006), https://www.bjs.gov/content/pub/pdf/pjim05.pdf.

79. Jake Horowitz et al., *Probation and Parole Systems Marked by High Stakes, Missed Opportunities* (Pew Charitable Trusts, September 25, 2018), https://www.pewtrusts.org/en/research-and-analysis/issue-briefs/2018/09/probation-and-parole-systems-marked-by-high-stakes-missed-opportunities.

80. Preeti Chauhan et al., *Trends in Misdemeanor Arrest Rates in New York*, Report Presented to the Citizens Crime Commission (John Jay College of Criminal Justice, October 2014).

81. Alexandra Natapoff, *Punishment Without Crime: How Our Massive Misdemeanor System Traps the Innocent and Makes America More Unequal* (Basic Books, 2018).

82. Lea S. Gifford, *Justice Expenditure and Employment in the United States, 1995* (Bureau of Justice Statistics, November 1999), 1, https://static.prisonpolicy.org/scans/bjs/jeeus95.pdf.

83. Diane Whitmore Schanzenbach, Ryan Nunn, Lauren Bauer, Audrey Breitwieser, Megan Mumford, and Greg Nantz, *Twelve Facts About Incarceration and Prisoner Reentry* (Hamilton Project, October 21, 2016), https://www.hamiltonproject.org/charts/corrections_spending_per_capita.

84. *Federal Prison System Shows Dramatic Long-Term Growth* (Pew Charitable Trusts, February 2015), https://www.pewtrusts.org/en/research-and-analysis/fact-sheets/2015/02/federal-prison-system-shows-dramatic-long-term-growth.

85. *Fact Sheet: Trends in U.S. Corrections* (Sentencing Project, updated May 2021), https://www.sentencingproject.org/wp-content/uploads/2016/01/Trends-in-US-Corrections.pdf.

86. Christian Henrichson, Joshua Rinaldi, and Ruth Delaney, *The Price of Jails: Measuring the Taxpayer Cost of Local Incarceration* (Vera Institute of Justice, May 2015), 5, https://www.vera.org/downloads/publications/price-of-jails.pdf.

87. Tracy Kyckelhahn, *Justice Expenditure and Employment FY 1982–2007: Statistical Tables* (Bureau of Justice Statistics, December 2011), 6.

88. Kyckelhahn, *Justice Expenditure*, 5.

89. Lauren-Brooke Eisen, *Inside Private Prisons: An American Dilemma in the Age of Mass Incarceration* (Columbia University Press, 2018).

90. Frances Kahn Zemans, *Court Funding*, prepared for the American Bar Association Standing Committee on Judicial Independence (August 2003); American Bar Association (ABA) Task Force on Preservation of the Justice System, *Report to the House of Delegates* (August 2004), 1, https://static.prisonpolicy.org/scans/aba/aba_report_to_the_house_of_delegates.pdf; ABA Task Force on Preservation of the Justice System, *Report to the House of Delegates* (2011), https://static.prisonpolicy.org/scans/aba/aba_report_to_the_house_of_delegates.pdf.

91. Marie Gottschalk, *Caught: The Prison State and the Lockdown of American Politics* (Princeton University Press, 2016), 27.

92. ABA Task Force, 2004 Report.

93. Michael C. Campbell and Heather Schoenfeld, "The Transformation of America's Penal Order: A Historicized Political Sociology of Punishment," *American Journal of Sociology* 118, no. 5 (2013): 1375–1423.

94. Campbell and Schoenfeld, "The Transformation of America's Penal Order," 1405.

95. Andrea Louise Campbell, "Policy Makes Mass Politics," *Annual Review of Political Science* 15, no. 1 (2012): 333–51; Paul Pierson, *Dismantling the Welfare State? Reagan, Thatcher, and the Politics of Retrenchment* (Cambridge University Press, 1994); Joshua Page, *The Toughest Beat: Politics, Punishment, and the Prison Officers Union in California* (Oxford University Press, 2011).

96. Page, *The Toughest Beat*.

97. Joshua Page, Heather Schoenfeld, and Michael Campbell, "To Defund the Police, We Have to Dethrone the Law Enforcement Lobby," *Jacobin*, July 4, 2020, https://jacobin.com/2020/07/defund-police-unions-law-enforcement-lobby.

98. John Pfaff, *Locked In: The True Causes of Mass Incarceration and How to Achieve Real Reform* (Basic Books, 2017), 70.

99. David Ball, "Pay-for-Performance in Prison: Using Healthcare Economics to Improve Criminal Justice," *Denver Law Review* 94, no. 3 (2017): 467.

100. Franklin E. Zimring and Gordon Hawkins, *The Scale of Imprisonment* (University of Chicago Press, 1991), 211–15.

101. Pfaff, *Locked In*.

102. Mona Lynch, "Mass Incarceration, Legal Change, and Locale: Understanding and Remediating American Penal Overindulgence," *Criminology and Public Policy* 10, no. 3 (2011): 673–98.

103. See, e.g., Brown v. Plata, 563 U.S. 493 (2011).

104. Paul LaCommare, "Generating New Revenue Streams," *Police Chief* 77 (2010): 22–30.

105. LaCommare, "Generating New Revenue Streams," 22.

106. LaCommare, "Generating New Revenue Streams," 23.

107. LaCommare, "Generating New Revenue Streams," 28.

108. Theda Skocpol, *Protecting Soldiers and Mothers: The Political Origins of Social Policy in the United States* (Harvard University Press, 1992), 58.

109. Heather Schoenfeld, *Building the Prison State: Race and the Politics of Mass Incarceration* (University of Chicago Press, 2018); Anna Gunderson, *Captive Market: The Politics of Private Prisons in America* (Oxford University Press, 2022).

110. Eisen, *Inside Private Prisons*.

111. Eisen, *Inside Private Prisons*, 74; Eric Schlosser, "The Prison-Industrial Complex," *Atlantic*, December 1998, http://www.theatlantic.com/magazine/archive/1998/12/the-prison-industrial-complex/304669/.

112. Eisen, *Inside Private Prisons*, 74.

113. Wacquant, *Punishing the Poor*, 168.

114. Eisen, *Inside Private Prisons*, 187.

115. Sean Nicholson-Crotty, "The Politics and Administration of Privatization: Contracting Out for Corrections Management in the United States," *Policy Studies Journal* 34, no. 1 (2004): 45.

116. Peter Wagner, "Prison Profiteers Use Campaign Contributions to Buy Contracts," *Prison Policy Initiative* (blog), November 25, 2015, https://www.prisonpolicy.org/blog/2015/11/25/gtl_in_orange/.

117. Wagner, "Prison Profiteers Use Campaign Contributions."

118. Michael Cohen, "How For-Profit Prisons Have Become the Biggest Lobby No One Is Talking About," *Washington Post*, April 28, 2015, https://www.washingtonpost.com/posteverything/wp/2015/04/28/how-for-profit-prisons-have-become-the-biggest-lobby-no-one-is-talking-about/.

119. Eisen, *Inside Private Prisons*, 158.

120. Alexander Hertel-Fernandez, *State Capture: How Conservative Activists, Big Businesses, and Wealthy Donors Reshaped the American States—and the Nation* (Oxford University Press, 2019).

121. Eisen, *Inside Private Prisons*, 232–33.

122. Schlosser, "The Prison-Industrial Complex."

123. Eisen, *Inside Private Prisons*, 191.

124. Eisen, *Inside Private Prisons*, 194–95.

125. Graham Kates, "John Kelly Joins Board of Company Operating Largest Shelter for Unaccompanied Migrant Children," CBS News, May 3, 2019, https://www.cbsnews.com/news/john-kelly-joins-board-of-caliburn-international-company-operating-largest-unaccompanied-migrant-children-shelter/.

126. Hugh Heclo, *Modern Social Politics in Britain and Sweden: From Relief to Income Maintenance* (Yale University Press, 1974).

127. Peter Hall, "Policy Paradigms, Social Learning and the State: The Case of Economic Policymaking in Britain," *Comparative Politics* 25, no. 3 (1993): 275–96.

128. Ben Conarck, "Prison Phone Provider Accuses Florida Dept. of Corrections of Using Inmates' Families as a Slush Fund," Jacksonville.com, January 30, 2019, https://www.jacksonville.com/news/20190130/prison-phone-provider-accuses-florida-dept-of-corrections-of-using-inmates-families-as-slush-fund.

129. Conarck, "Prison Phone Provider Accuses."

130. Wacquant, *Punishing the Poor*.

131. Loïc Wacquant, "Crafting the Neoliberal State: Workfare, Prisonfare, and Social Insecurity," *Sociological Forum* 25, no. 2 (2010): 197–220.

132. Wacquant, "Crafting the Neoliberal State," 198.

133. Wacquant, *Punishing the Poor*, 4, original emphasis removed.

134. Loïc Wacquant, "Deadly Symbiosis: When Ghetto and Prison Meet and Mesh," *Punishment & Society* 3, no. 1 (2001): 15, https://doi.org/10.1177/14624740122228276, original emphasis removed.

135. Wacquant, "Deadly Symbiosis," 112.

136. Wacquant, "Deadly Symbiosis," 97.

137. Wacquant, *Punishing the Poor*, 184–85.

138. Jan Rehmann, "Hypercarceration: A Neoliberal Response to 'Surplus Population,'" *Rethinking Marxism* 27, no. 2 (2015): 303–11.

139. See, e.g., Christian Parenti, *Lockdown America: Police and Prisons in the Age of Crisis* (Verso, 1999), 238.

140. William H. Sewell, *Logics of History: Social Theory and Social Transformation* (University of Chicago Press, 2005), 81–123.

141. Christian Parenti, *Lockdown America*, 238.

Chapter Five

1. GTL, "Transforming Correctional Facilities Through Technology," accessed November 17, 2022, https://www.gtl.net/gtl-tablet-solutions/.

2. GTL, "Transforming Correctional Facilities."

3. Dana Milbank, "When You Drown the Government in the Bathtub, People Die," *Washington Post*, April 10, 2020.

4. Joseph Fenton, "A Private Alternative to Public Prisons," *Prison Journal* 65, no. 2 (1985): 42, 46.

5. William Jefferson Clinton, "State of the Union Address," January 23, 1996, U.S. National Archives and Records Administration: The White House, accessed November 17, 2022, https://clintonwhitehouse4.archives.gov/WH/New/other/sotu.html.

6. Archie B. Carroll, "Corporate Social Responsibility: Evolution of a Definitional Construct," *Business & Society* 38, no. 3 (1999): 268–95.

7. David Sadler and Stuart Lloyd, "Neo-Liberalising Corporate Social Responsibility: A Political Economy of Corporate Citizenship," *Geoforum* 40, no. 4 (2009): 613 and 615.

8. Adam Lindgreen and Valérie Swaen, "Corporate Social Responsibility," *International Journal of Management Reviews* 12, no. 1 (2010): 1–7.

9. Paul Pierson and Theda Skocpol, eds., *The Transformation of American Politics: Activist Government and the Rise of Conservatism* (Princeton University Press, 2007); John Kenneth Galbraith, *American Capitalism: The Concept of Countervailing Power* (Houghton Mifflin, 1952).

10. David Sadler and Stuart Lloyd, "Neo-Liberalising Corporate Social Responsibility," 613, 618, and 620.

11. Anna Gunderson, *Captive Market: The Politics of Private Prisons in America* (Oxford University Press, 2022).

12. Quoted in Alexis M. Durham III, "The Privatization of Punishment: Justification, Expectations, and Experience," *Criminal Justice Policy Review* 30, no. 1 (1989): 51.

13. Lauren-Brooke Eisen, *Inside Private Prisons: An American Dilemma in the Age of Mass Incarceration* (Columbia University Press, 2018), 65.

14. Quoted in Durham, "The Privatization of Punishment," 53.

15. E. S. Savas, *Privatization and Public-Private Partnership* (Chatham House, 2000).

16. Mary Sigler, "Private Prisons, Public Functions, and the Meaning of Punishment," *Florida State University Law Review* 38, no. 1 (2010): 149–78.

17. Francis Allen, "Criminal Justice, Legal Values and the Rehabilitative Ideal," *Journal of Criminal Law and Criminology* 50, no. 3 (1959): 226.

18. Michelle S. Phelps, "Rehabilitation in the Punitive Era: The Gap Between Rhetoric and Reality in U.S. Prison Programs," *Law & Society Review* 45, no. 1 (2011): 53–54.

19. Francis T. Cullen, "The Privatization of Treatment: Prison Reform in the 1980's," *Federal Probation* 50, no. 1 (March 1986): 13, 15.

20. Jeremy Travis, *But They All Come Back: Facing the Challenges of Prisoner Reentry* (Urban Institute Press, 2005).

21. Joe Soss, Richard C. Fording and Sanford F. Schram, *Disciplining the Poor: Neoliberal Paternalism and the Persistent Power of Race* (University of Chicago Press, 2011).

22. Devlin Barrett, "Prison Firm CCA Seeks to Reduce Number of Repeat Offenders," *Wall Street Journal*, September 12, 2014, https://www.wsj.com/articles/prison-firm-cca-seeks-to-reduce-number-of-repeat-offenders-1410561176.

23. Eisen, *Inside Private Prisons*.

24. Colin Lecher, "Criminal Charges: Prison Phones Are a Predatory Monopoly. One Family Fought Back and Won," *The Verge*, accessed November 17, 2022, https://www.theverge.com/a/prison-phone-call-cost-martha-wright-v-corrections-corporation-america.

25. Daniel Wagner, "Meet the Prison Bankers Who Profit from the Inmates," *Time*, September 30, 2014, https://time.com/3446372/criminal-justice-prisoners-profit/.

26. Wagner, "Meet the Prison Bankers."

27. "G4S Chief Says More Policing Will Go Private," BBC, June 21, 2012, https://www.bbc.com/news/uk-18533980.

28. G4S Global, "Our ESG Commitment," accessed January 2, 2025, https://www.g4s.com/social-responsibility/our-csr-commitment.

29. Wendy Brown, *Undoing the Demos: Neoliberalism's Stealth Revolution* (Zone Books, 2015); John Clarke, "Dissolving the Public Realm? The Logics and Limits of Neo-Liberalism," *Journal of Social Policy* 33, no. 1 (January 2004): 27–48.

30. Matthew A. Crenson and Benjamin Ginsberg, *Downsizing Democracy: How America Sidelined Its Citizens and Privatized Its Public* (Johns Hopkins University Press, 2002).

31. Brittany Friedman, April D. Fernandes, and Gabriela Kirk, "'Like If You Get a Hotel Bill': Consumer Logic, Pay-to-Stay, and the Production of Incarceration as a Public Commodity," *Sociological Forum* 36, no. 3 (September 2021): 735–57.

32. Alexes Harris, *A Pound of Flesh: Monetary Sanctions as Punishment for the Poor* (Russell Sage Foundation, 2016), 83.

33. Ebony L. Ruhland, Jason P. Robey, Ronald P. Corbett Jr., and Kevin R. Reitz, *Exploring Supervision Fees in Four Probation Jurisdictions in Texas* (Robina Institute of Criminal Law and Criminal Justice, 2017), 4, https://robinainstitute.umn.edu/sites/robinainstitute.umn.edu/files/2022-02/robina_fee_summary_report_web4.pdf.

34. Devin Fergus, *Land of the Fee: Hidden Costs and the Decline of the American Middle Class* (Oxford University Press, 2018).

35. Timothy Williams, "The High Cost of Calling the Imprisoned," *New York Times*, March 30, 2015, https://www.nytimes.com/2015/03/31/us/steep-costs-of-inmate-phone-calls-are-under-scrutiny.html; David Shapiro, "Price Gouging in Prisons," ACLU, August 10, 2010, https://www.aclu.org/news/smart-justice/price-gouging-prison.

36. Kevin Bliss, "Securus Technologies Rebrands as Aventiv," *Prison Legal News*, January 9, 2020, 48, https://www.prisonlegalnews.org/news/2020/jan/9/securus-technologies-rebrands-aventiv/.

37. Global Tel*Link Corporation (GTL), *Comments of Global Tel*Link Corporation*, In the Matter of Rates for Interstate Inmate Calling Services, WC Docket. No. 12-375, Federal Communications Commission, March 20, 2020, 5, https://ecfsapi.fcc.gov/file/10320044006894/GTL%20comments%20(3-20-20).pdf.

38. GTL, *Comments of Global Tel*Link Corporation*, 2.

39. Stephen A. Raher, *Rates for Interstate Inmate Calling Services*, 12-375 (Federal Communications Commission, April 22, 2013), 3–4, https://ecfsapi.fcc.gov/file/7022289970.pdf.

40. GTL, *Comments of Global Tel*Link Corporation*, 2.

41. Brett R. Whittling, "GTL Explains eTablets for Jail Inmates," *Clarion News*, August 10, 2017, republished by GTL, accessed November 20, 2022, https://www.gtl.net/wp-content/uploads/2017/08/The-Clarion-News-GTL-Tablets-08-10-2017.pdf.

42. Wendy Brown, *Undoing the Demos*.

43. Jacob S. Hacker, *The Great Risk Shift: The New Economic Insecurity and the Decline of the American Dream* (Oxford University Press, 2006), 8.

44. B. J. Brown and Sally Baker, *Responsible Citizens: Individuals, Health and Policy Under Neoliberalism* (Anthem Press, 2012), 4.

45. Brown, *Undoing the Demos*.

46. Julie Guthman, "Teaching the Politics of Obesity: Insights into Neoliberal Embodiment and Contemporary Biopolitics," *Antipode* 41, no. 5 (October 2009): 1111, 1116.

47. Lynne Haney, *Prisons of Debt: The Afterlives of Incarcerated Fathers* (University of California Press, 2022); Daniel Martinez HoSang and Joseph E. Lowndes, *Producers, Parasites, Patriots: Race and the New Right-Wing Politics of Precarity* (University of Minnesota Press, 2019).

48. Loïc Wacquant, "Three Pernicious Premises in the Study of the American Ghetto," *International Journal of Urban and Regional Research* 21, no. 2 (December 2002): 348.

49. Stephanie McCormick, letter at para. 2, June 16, 2016, Texas Collection Improvement Program Comments, July 2016, accessed November 20, 2022, https://www.documentcloud.org/documents/3012378-CIP-Comments.html#document/p1/a313990.

50. Lisa Myrtle, email re: "Proposed Changes to the Collections Improvement Program," dated July 21, 2016, Texas Collection Improvement Program Comments, July 2016, https://www.documentcloud.org/documents/3012378-CIP-Comments.html#document/p43/a313969.

51. Brittany Friedman and Mary Pattillo, "Statutory Inequality: The Logics of Monetary Sanctions in State Law," *RSF: The Russell Sage Foundation Journal of the Social Sciences* 5, no. 1 (February 2019): 183–84.

52. Friedman and Pattillo, "Statutory Inequality," 19, emphases in original.

53. Carole Pateman, "Race, Sex, and Indifference," in *Contract and Domination* (Polity Press, 2007).

54. US Department of Justice (US DOJ) Civil Rights Division, *Investigation of the Ferguson Police Department*, March 4, 2015, https://www.justice.gov/sites/default/files/opa/press-releases/attachments/2015/03/04/ferguson_police_department_report.pdf.

55. Joe Soss, Richard C. Fording, and Sanford F. Schram, *Disciplining the Poor*.

56. Harris, *A Pound of Flesh*.

57. German Lopez, "Slavery or Rehabilitation? The Debate About Cheap Prison Labor, Explained," *Vox*, September 7, 2015, https://www.vox.com/2015/9/7/9262649/prison-labor-wages.

58. UNICOR, *Federal Prison Industries, Inc: Fiscal Year 2019 Annual Management Report* (US Department of Justice, 2019), https://www.unicor.gov/publications/reports/FY2019_AnnualMgmtReport.pdf.

59. Colleen Curry, "Whole Foods, Expensive Cheese, and the Dilemma of Cheap Prison Labor," *Vice News*, July 21, 2015, https://www.vice.com/en_us/article/59ebjd/whole-foods-expensive-cheese-and-the-dilemma-of-cheap-prison-labor.

60. Joseph Broadus et al., *A Successful Prisoner Reentry Program Expands: Lessons from the Replication of the Center for Employment Opportunities* (MDRC, January 2016), iii, 5–6, https://americorps.gov/sites/default/files/evidenceexchange/CEO_PrisonerReentryReport_508_1.pdf.

61. Harris, *A Pound of Flesh*, 83.

62. "Fighting the Drug War in Pennsylvania," *United States Attorneys Bulletin* 38, no. 5 (May 15, 1990): 101.

63. US v. Property Known as 6109 Grubb Road, 890 F.2d 659 and 665–66 (3d Cir. 1989) (Greenberg, J., dissenting), emphasis added.

64. Stefan D. Cassella, "Forfeiture Is Reasonable, and It Works," *The Federalist Society: Criminal Law and Procedure Practice Group Newsletter* 1, no. 2 (May 1, 1997), https://fedsoc.org/commentary/publications/forfeiture-is-reasonable-and-it-works.

65. Naomi Murakawa, *The First Civil Right: How Liberals Built Prison America* (Oxford University Press, 2014); Elizabeth Hinton, *From the War on Poverty to the War on Crime* (Harvard University Press, 2017).

66. Sarah Lustbader, "Joe Biden's Role in Mass Incarceration Was No 'Mistake': It Was Politics," *The Appeal*, April 25, 2019, https://theappeal.org/politicalreport/joe-bidens-role-in-mass-incarceration-was-no-mistake-it-was-politics/.

67. Congressional Record, "Legislative Business," August 24, 1994, https://www.govinfo.gov/content/pkg/CREC-1994-08-24/html/CREC-1994-08-24-pt1-PgH21.htm.

68. Chris Calton, "How a Young Joe Biden Became the Architect of the Government's Asset Forfeiture Program," *Fee*, March 9, 2019, https://fee.org/articles/how-a-young-joe-biden-became-the-architect-of-the-governments-asset-forfeiture-program/.

69. Christian Britschgi, "In the Space of One Minute, Joe Biden Defends the Death Penalty for Drug Dealers, Asset Forfeiture, and Mandatory Minimums," *Reason*, April 4, 2019, https://reason.com/2019/04/04/joe-biden-defends-death-penalty-for-drug/.

70. Anne Larason Schneider and Helen Ingram, *Policy Design for Democracy* (University Press of Kansas, 1997). On "criminalized people and communities," see Matthew Clair, "Criminalized Subjectivity: Du Boisian Sociology and Visions for Legal Change," *Du Bois Review* 18, no. 2 (2021): 289–319.

71. David Garland, *The Culture of Control: Crime and Social Order in Contemporary Society* (University of Chicago Press, 2001), 102.

72. Khalil Gibran Muhammad, *The Condemnation of Blackness: Race, Crime, and the Making of Modern Urban America* (Harvard University Press, 2011).

73. James Q. Wilson and Richard J. Hernstein, *Crime and Human Nature* (Simon & Schuster, 1985).

74. William J. Bennett, John J. DiIulio Jr., and John P. Walters, *Body Count: Moral Poverty . . . and How to Win America's War Against Crime and Drugs* (Simon & Schuster, 1996).

75. John J. DiIulio, "Fill Churches, Not Jails: Youth Crime and 'Superpredators,'" Brookings Institution, February 28, 1996, https://www.brookings.edu/testimonies/fill -churches-not-jails-youth-crime-and-superpredators/.

76. Franklin D. Gilliam Jr. and Shanto Iyengar, "Super-Predators or Victims of Neglect? Framing Effects in Juvenile Crime Coverage," in *Framing American Politics*, ed. Karen Callaghan and Frauke Schnell (University of Pittsburgh Press, 2005), 149–50.

77. Loïc Wacquant, *Punishing the Poor: The Neoliberal Government of Social Insecurity* (Duke University Press, 2009).

78. Steve Benen, "Jeff Sessions to Face Tough Questions over Civil Asset Forfeiture," MSNBC, December 28, 2016, http://www.msnbc.com/rachel-maddow -show/jeff-sessions-face-tough-questions-over-civil-asset-forfeiture.

79. US DOJ, *Investigation of the Ferguson Police Department*.

80. Jacob Sullum, "Anti-Theft Measure," *Reason*, June 30, 1999, https://reason .com/1999/06/30/anti-theft-measure/; Ira Glasser, "Forfeiting Property and More," *New York Times*, February 24, 1999, https://www.nytimes.com/1999/02/24/ opinion/forfeiting-property-and-more.html.

81. Jude McCulloch and Sharon Pickering, "Suppressing the Financing of Terrorism," *British Journal of Criminology* 45, no. 4 (April 2005): 470–86.

82. Andrew Ayers, "The Financial Action Task Force: The War on Terrorism Will Not Be Fought on the Battlefield," *New York School Journal of Human Rights* 18, no. 3 (Summer 2002): 449–59. The quotations are from pp. 458–59.

83. Ronald Takaki, *A Different Mirror: A History of Multicultural America*, rev. ed. (Back Bay Books, 2008); Lisa Lowe, *Immigrant Acts: On Asian American Cultural Politics* (Duke University Press, 1997).

84. Walter A. Ewing, Daniel E. Martínez, and Rubén G. Rumbaut, *The Criminalization of Immigration in the United States* (American Immigration Council, July 13, 2015), https://www.americanimmigrationcouncil.org/research/criminalization -immigration-united-states.

85. Melina Juárez, Bárbara Gómez-Aguiñaga, and Sonia P. Bettez, "Twenty Years After IIRIRA: The Rise of Immigrant Detention and Its Effects on Latinx Communities Across the Nation," *Journal on Migration and Human Security* 6, no. 1 (November 2018): 74–96.

86. Priscilla Huang, "Anchor Babies, Over-Breeders, and the Population Bomb: The Reemergence of Nativism and Population Control in Anti-Immigration Policies," *Harvard Law & Policy Review* 2, no. 2 (2008): 385–406.

87. Bianca E. Bersani, "An Examination of First and Second Generation Immigrant Offending Trajectories," *Justice Quarterly* 31, no. 2 (February 2012): 315–43, https:// doi.org/10.1080/07418825.2012.659200.

88. Philip Bump, "Surprise! Donald Trump Is Wrong About Immigrants and Crime," *Washington Post*, July 2, 2015, https://www.washingtonpost.com/news/the -fix/wp/2015/07/02/surprise-donald-trump-is-wrong-about-immigrants-and-crime/.

89. Stacy Fernández, "Texas Sheriff at White House Briefing: If Criminal Immigrants Are Released 'Drunks' Will 'Run over Your Children,'" *Texas Tribune*, October 10, 2019, https://www.texastribune.org/2019/10/10/texas-tarrant-county -sheriff-bill-waybourn-speaks-white-house/.

90. Linda Qiu, "The Many Ways Trump Has Said Mexico Will Pay for the Wall," *New York Times*, January 11, 2019, https://www.nytimes.com/2019/01/11/us/ politics/trump-mexico-pay-wall.html.

91. Hamed Aleaziz, "The Trump Administration Wants to Charge Immigrants Nearly $1,000 to Appeal Deportation Cases," *Buzzfeed News*, September 17, 2019, https://www.buzzfeednews.com/article/hamedaleaziz/trump-administration -immigrant-fees-increase-court-appeals.

92. Hamed Aleaziz, "The Trump Administration Will Start Charging Immigrants Fees for Applying for Asylum," *Buzzfeed News*, July 31, 2020, https://www .buzzfeednews.com/article/hamedaleaziz/trump-administration-asylum-application -fees.

93. Rachel Morris, "Trump Got His Wall, After All," *Huffington Post*, November 24, 2019, https://www.huffpost.com/highline/article/invisible-wall/. On administrative burdens, see Pamela Herd and Donald P. Moynihan, *Administrative Burden: Policymaking by Other Means* (Russell Sage Foundation, 2019).

94. Harris, *A Pound of Flesh*, 26.

95. Harris, *A Pound of Flesh*, 96; US Government Accountability Office (GAO), *Federal Criminal Restitution: Most Debt Is Outstanding and Oversight of Collections Could Be Improved* (Publication GAO-18-203, February 2, 2018), https://www.gao.gov/ products/gao-18-203.

96. Harris, *A Pound of Flesh*, 94.

97. Committee on Criminal Justice Operations et al., *New York Should Re-Examine Mandatory Court Fees Imposed on Individuals Convicted of Criminal Offenses and Violations* (New York City Bar, 2018), 4, https://www.nycbar.org/member-and-career -services/committees/reports-listing/reports/detail/new-york-should-re-examine -mandatory-court-fees#_ftnref19.

98. Department of Justice, "Justice Department Honors Asset Forfeiture Program Team with the Crimes Victims' Financial Restoration Award," Press Release No. 18- 475, April 13, 2018, https://www.justice.gov/opa/pr/justice-department-honors-asset -forfeiture-program-team-crimes-victims-financial-restoration.

99. Garland, *Culture of Control*, 143.

100. "Summary of Megan's Law," *California Megan's Law Website, State of California Department of Justice, Office of the Attorney General*, accessed November 20, 2022, https://web.archive.org/web/20220815184652/https://www.meganslaw.ca .gov/About.aspx.

101. National Institute of Justice, "The Overlap Between Those Committing Offenses Who Also Are Victims: One Class of Crime Victim Rarely Seeks or Receives Available Services," March 11, 2021, https://nij.ojp.gov/topics/articles/overlap -between-those-committing-offenses-who-also-are-victims-one-class-crime.

102. Garland, *Culture of Control*, 143.

103. Jonathan Simon, *Governing Through Crime: How the War on Crime Trans- formed American Democracy and Created a Culture of Fear* (Oxford University Press, 2007).

104. Sarah Stillman, "Taken," *New Yorker*, August 5, 2013, https://www .newyorker.com/magazine/2013/08/12/taken.

105. Fox Butterfield, "Many Local Officials Now Make Inmates Pay Their Own Way," *New York Times*, August 13, 2004, https://www.nytimes.com/2004/08/13/us/many-local-officials-now-make-inmates-pay-their-own-way.html.

106. Wendy Sawyer and Peter Wagner, *Mass Incarceration: The Whole Pie* (Prison Policy Initiative, March 14, 2023), accessed January 21, 2024, https://www.prisonpolicy.org/reports/pie2023.html.

107. Tim Helldorfer, "Guest Column: Anti-Forfeiture Bills Threaten Drug Task Forces," *Commercial Appeal*, February 14, 2016, http://www.commercialappeal.com/opinion/local/guest-column-anti-forfeiture-bills-threaten-drug-task-forces-2b713e3e-68b2-220d-e053-0100007f92df-368756121.html.

108. Michael Wetzel, "Jail Fees Hurt Inmates' Loved Ones, Help County Budgets," *The Advertiser*, November 21, 2019, https://www.moultonadvertiser.com/news/local/article_b6554ca0-0c64-11ea-9766-0792682d6205.html.

109. Charles Ring, *Probation Supervision Fees: Shifting Costs to the Offender* (Research in Brief, 88-2, Massachusetts Legislative Research Bureau, 1988), 9, 17.

110. Timothy Pachirat, *Every Twelve Seconds: Industrialized Slaughter and the Politics of Sight* (Yale University Press, 2011).

111. Pachirat, *Every Twelve Seconds*, 5.

112. Vesla Weaver, Gwen Prowse, and Spencer Piston, "Too Much Knowledge, Too Little Power: An Assessment of Political Knowledge in Highly-Policed Communities," *Journal of Politics* 81 (2019): 1153–66.

113. Mary Fainsod Katzenstein and Maureen R. Waller, "Taxing the Poor: Incarceration, Poverty Governance, and the Seizure of Family Resources," *Perspectives on Politics* 13, no. 3 (September 2015): 638–56, https://doi.org/10.1017/S153759271500122X.

114. Nicholas Carnes and Noam Lupu, "The Economic Backgrounds of Politicians," *Annual Review of Political Science* 26, no. 1 (2023): 253–70.

115. Jacob Hacker, "Privatizing Risk Without Privatizing the Welfare State: The Hidden Politics of Social Policy Retrenchment in the United States," *American Political Science Review* 98, no. 2 (May 2004): 243–60; Pepper D. Culpepper, *Quiet Politics and Business Power: Corporate Control in Europe and Japan* (Cambridge University Press, 2010).

Chapter Six

1. Joshua Page, *The Toughest Beat: Politics, Punishment, and the Prison Officers Union in California* (Oxford University Press, 2011), chap. 4.

2. "A-Team" and "Rocksville" are both pseudonyms.

3. Timothy Schnacke, *Fundamentals of Bail: A Resource Guide for Pretrial Practitioners and a Framework for Pretrial Reform* (National Institute of Corrections, 2014), 91.

4. The industry generated $2.4 billion in revenue in 2023. Demetrios Berdousis, "Bail Bond Services in the US," *IBISWorld*, September 2023, 32.

5. Thea Riofrancos, "From Cases to Sites: Studying Global Processes in Comparative Politics," in *Rethinking Comparison: Innovative Methods for Qualitative Political Inquiry*, ed. Erica S. Simmons and Nicholas Rush Smith (Cambridge University Press, 2021), 107–26.

6. Timothy Schnacke, Michael Jones, and Claire Brooker, *The History of Bail and Pretrial Release* (Pretrial Justice Institute, 2011), 4–5. Nineteen have constitutional

provisions that stipulate a right to bail except in capital cases. Another twenty-two "have right to bail provisions that have been amended to expand preventive detention" for people charged with certain types of crimes, such as "violent offenses" and "sex offenses." Amber Widgery, "Pretrial Release Eligibility" (National Conference of State Legislatures, 2022), accessed January 12, 2022, http://www.ncsl .org/research/civil-and-criminal-justice/pretrial-release-eligibility.aspx.

7. Kellen Funk and Sandra G. Mayson, "Bail at the Founding," *Harvard Law Review*, forthcoming, University of Pennsylvania Law School, Public Law Research Paper No. 23011, 72.

8. Funk and Mayson, "Bail at the Founding," 72.

9. Schnacke, *Fundamentals of Bail*, 41.

10. Schnacke, *Fundamentals of Bail*, 26.

11. Leary v. United States, 224 U.S. 567 (1912).

12. F. E. Devine, "How American Commercial Bail Developed Differently from Other Common Law Countries," *International Journal of Comparative and Applied Criminal Justice* 18, no. 1–2 (1994): 265–76.

13. Council of Economic Advisers (CEA), *Fines, Fees, and Bail: Payments in the Criminal Justice System That Disproportionately Impact the Poor* (2015), 6, https:// obamawhitehouse.archives.gov/sites/default/files/Page/files/1215_cea_fine_fee_bail _issue_brief.pdf.

14. CEA, *Fines, Fees, and Bail*, 6.

15. Patrick Liu, Ryan Nunn, and Jay Shambaugh, *The Economics of Bail and Pretrial Detention* (Hamilton Project, December 2018), 9, https://www.hamiltonproject.org/ assets/files/BailFineReform_EA_121818_6PM.pdf.

16. Brian A. Reaves, *Felony Defendants in Large Urban Counties, 2009: Statistical Tables* (Bureau of Justice Statistics, 2013), 2–3, https://bjs.oPage.gov/content/pub/ pdf/fdluc09.pdf.

17. On the politics of bail from the 1980s forward, see Joshua Page and Christine S. Scott-Hayward, "Bail and Pretrial Justice in the United States: A Field of Possibility," *American Review of Criminology* 5 (2022): 91–113.

18. Forrest Dill, "Discretion, Exchange and Social Control: Bail Bondsmen in Criminal Courts," *Law & Society Review* 9, no. 4 (Summer 1975): 642. See Stack v. Boyle, 342 U.S. 1, 7–8 (1951).

19. John S. Goldkamp, "Danger and Detention: A Second Generation of Bail Reform," *Journal of Criminal Law and Criminology* 76, no. 1 (1985): 1–74.

20. James A. Allen, "'Making Bail': Limiting the Use of Bail Schedules and Defining the Elusive Meaning of Excessive Bail," *Journal of Law and Policy* 25, no. 2 (2017): 653.

21. Malcolm Feeley and Jonathan Simon, "The New Penology: Notes on the Emerging Strategy of Corrections and Its Implications," *Criminology* 30, no. 4 (1992): 449–74; Samuel R. Wiseman, "Pretrial Detention and the Right to Be Monitored," *Yale Law Journal* 123, no. 5 (2014): 1344–1404.

22. David May et al., "Going to Jail Sucks (And It Really Doesn't Matter Who You Ask)," *American Journal of Criminal Justice* 39 (2014): 250–66; Michael Walker, *Indefinite: Doing Time in Jail* (Oxford University Press, 2022).

23. Will Dobbie, Jacob Goldin, and Crystal Yang, "The Effects of Pre-Trial Detention on Conviction, Future Crime, and Employment: Evidence from Randomly Assigned Judges," *American Economic Review* 108, no. 2 (2018): 201–40; Arpit Gupta, Christopher Hansman, and Ethan Frenchman, "The Heavy Costs of High Bail: Evidence from Judge Randomization," *Journal of Legal Studies* 45, no. 2 (June 1, 2016):

471–505; Megan T. Stevenson, "Distortion of Justice: How the Inability to Pay Bail Affects Case Outcomes," *Journal of Law, Economics, and Organization* 34, no. 4 (2018): 511–42.

24. Aviva Shen, "Bail Money Funds Louisiana Courts. Now This Powerful Industry Is Fighting Reform," *Guardian*, December 14, 2016, https://www.theguardian.com/us -news/2016/dec/14/new-orleans-criminal-justice-system-bail-bonds.

25. Christine S. Scott-Hayward and Henry F. Fradella, *Punishing Poverty: How Bail and Pretrial Detention Fuel Inequalities in the Criminal Justice System* (University of California Press, 2019), 28.

26. Bernadette Rabuy and Daniel Kopf, *Detaining the Poor: How Money Bail Perpetuates a Cycle of Poverty and Jail Time* (Prison Policy Initiative, 2016), 7.

27. Steven Durlauf, "The Memberships Theory of Poverty: The Role of Group Affiliations in Determining Socioeconomic Outcomes," in *Understanding Poverty*, ed. Sheldon Danziger and Robert Haveman (Harvard University Press, 2002), 392–416.

28. CEA, *Fines, Fees, and Bail*, 6.

29. The website for the Professional Bail Agents of the United States (PBUS) explains: "Unless you are independently wealthy and live in one of the states that allow personal surety, sometimes called pocket bondsmen or property bail agents, you must be appointed by an insurance company to write bail bonds." "About Bail— How to Become a Bail Agent," accessed January 16, 2022, https://www.pbus.com/ Page/3; Color of Change and ACLU, *Selling Off Our Freedom: How Insurance Companies Have Taken Over Our Bail System* (ACLU, May 5, 2017), 22.

30. Shane Bauer, "Inside the Wild, Shadowy, and Highly Lucrative Bail Industry," *Mother Jones*, May/June 2014, https://www.motherjones.com/politics/2014/06/bail -bond-prison-industry/.

31. Color of Change and ACLU, *Selling Off Our Freedom*, 9; Kayla James, "How the Bail Bond Industry Became a $2 Billion Business," *Global Citizen*, January 31, 2019, https://www.globalcitizen.org/en/content/bail-bond-industry-2-billion-poverty/.

32. Color of Change and ACLU, *Selling Off Our Freedom*, 22.

33. Dill, "Discretion, Exchange and Social Control," 646.

34. Bauer, "Inside the Wild, Shadowy, and Highly Lucrative Bail Industry."

35. Studies and reports routinely support this claim, as does Page's research experience. See, e.g., Bauer, "Inside the Wild, Shadowy, and Highly Lucrative Bail Industry"; Dill, "Discretion, Exchange and Social Control"; The Pretrial Justice Institute, *Rational and Transparent Bail Decision Making: Moving from a Cash-Based to a Risk-Based Process* (National Institute of Corrections, March 2012), http:// www.safetyandjusticechallenge.org/wp-content/uploads/2015/05/Rational-and -Transparent-Bail-Decision-Making.pdf; Scott-Hayward and Fradella, *Punishing Poverty*, 57; The Justice Policy Institute, *For Better or For Profit: How the Bail Bonding Industry Stands in the Way of Fair and Effective Pretrial Justice* (September 2012), 27, https://justicepolicy.org/wp-content/uploads/justicepolicy/documents/_for_better_or _for_profit_.pdf; Wendy Sawyer, *All Profit, No Risk: How the Bail Industry Exploits the Legal System* (Prison Policy Initiative, October 2022), https://www.prisonpolicy.org/ reports/bail.html.

36. Alysia Santo, "When Freedom Isn't Free: The Bail Industry Wants to Be Your Jailer," *Marshall Project*, February 23, 2015, https://www.themarshallproject.org/ 2015/02/23/buying-time.

37. Critics charge that monetary bail contributes to jail overcrowding and fiscal problems because poor people cannot afford the services of bail companies. They also insist that more people would be released if courts employed risk assessments and

required defendants adhere to nonmonetary conditions, like checking in with pretrial staff and submitting to drug tests.

38. Bail bond company websites provide bonding fee information for counties in multiple states, including Alabama, Arkansas, Colorado, Louisiana, Mississippi, New Jersey, Tennessee, and Utah. Examples include A&S Bail Bonding Co., Inc. (http:// www.asbailbonding.com/services.html), Triple R Bail Bonds (https://triplerbailbonds .com/how-bail-works/), Good to Go Bail Bonds (https://goodtogobailbonds.com/ aurora-bail-bonds/), Statewide Bail Bonds (https://www.statewidebailbond.com/ links-resources.html), Mississippi Bonding Co. (https://www.msbonding.com/how-to -pay), Bail Depot (https://www.baildepotnj.com/what-is-bail-), All n One Bail Bonds (https://allnonebail.com/2022/07/no-money-down-bail-bonds/), and Bad Boy Bail Bonds, Utah (https://badboysbailbondsutah.com/bad-boys-bail-bonds-reflects-on-ten -years-in-business/).

39. Kim Chandler, "Alabama Senate Approves Bill to Raise Court Costs, Bail Bond Fees," AL.com, May 17, 2012, https://www.al.com/spotnews/2012/05/alabama _senate_approves_bill_t_3.html.

40. Bauer, "Inside the Wild, Shadowy, and Highly Lucrative Bail Industry"; Dill, "Discretion, Exchange and Social Control"; Pretrial Justice Institute, *Rational and Transparent Bail Decision Making*; Scott-Hayward and Fradella, *Punishing Poverty*, 57; Justice Policy Institute, *For Better or For Profit*; Sawyer, *All Profit, No Risk*.

41. Malcolm M. Feeley, *The Process Is the Punishment: Handling Cases in a Lower Criminal Court* (Russell Sage Foundation, 1979), 106; The Financial Justice Project, *Do the Math: Money Bail Doesn't Add Up for San Francisco* (Office of the Treasurer and Tax Collector, June 2017), 11, https://sftreasurer.org/sites/default/files/2019-09/2017.6 .27%20Bail%20Report%20FINAL_2.pdf; Sawyer, *All Profit, No Risk*.

42. For more examples of how courts rely on bail bond companies, see Page and Scott-Howard, "Bail and Pretrial Justice," 99.

43. Dill, "Discretion, Exchange and Social Control," 665.

44. William Ahee et al., *Moving Beyond Money: A Primer on Bail Reform* (Criminal Justice Policy Program at Harvard Law School, 2016), 17.

45. American Bar Association (ABA), *Privatization of Services in the Criminal Justice System*, June 2020, 8–9, https://www.americanbar.org/groups/legal_aid_indigent _defense/indigent_defense_systems_improvement/publications/privatization-of -services-in-the-criminal-justice-system/.

46. Shima Baradaran Baughman, "Costs of Pretrial Detention," *Boston University Law Review* 97, no. 1 (January 2017): 1–29.

47. Jail Advertising Network (JAN), "About Us," accessed December 10, 2022, http://www.jailadvertisingnetwork.com/about-us.

48. JAN, "Advertisers," accessed January 16, 2022, http://www .jailadvertisingnetwork.com/Advertisers/.

49. JAN, "Advertisers."

50. Ruby Renteria, "A Monopoly on Information: How Advertising in Jails Is Problematic for Defendants," *Criminal Law & Policy*, April 15, 2016, https:// crimlawandpolicy.wordpress.com/2016/04/15/a-monopoly-on-information-how -advertising-in-jails-is-problematic-for-defendants/.

51. JAN, "Customer Testimonials," accessed January 16, 2022, https://www .jailadvertisingnetwork.com/testimonial/jail-facility-3.html.

52. JAN, "About Us."

53. Color of Change and ACLU, *Selling Off Our Freedom*, 41, 43; Justice Policy Institute, *For Better or For Profit*, 27.

54. See also David Davis, "Good People Doing Dirty Work: A Study of Social Isolation," *Symbolic Interaction* 7, no. 2 (Fall 1984): 233–47.

55. American Bail Coalition (ABC), *October Newsletter*, organizational newsletter, October 2010, 2, accessed December 13, 2022, https://web.archive.org/web/20140712114124/http://www.asc-usi.com/userfiles/BailResources/ABC_Newsletter%20V1.pdf.

56. Alexander Hertel-Fernandez, *State Capture: How Conservative Activists, Big Businesses, and Wealthy Donors Reshaped the American States—and the Nation* (Oxford University Press, 2019).

57. ABC, *October Newsletter*, 2.

58. Justice Policy Institute, *For Better or For Profit*, 33.

59. ABC, *October Newsletter*.

60. The National Association of Pretrial Services Agencies (NAPSA), *The Truth About Commercial Bail Bonding in America* 1, no. 1 (August 2009).

61. Bauer, "Inside the Wild, Shadowy, and Highly Lucrative Bail Industry."

62. Anne Kim, "Time to Abolish Cash Bail," *Washington Monthly*, January 3, 2017, https://washingtonmonthly.com/magazine/januaryfebruary-2017/time-to-abolish-cash-bail/.

63. Cindy Chavez et al., *Consensus Report on Optimal Pretrial Justice* (County of Santa Clara Bail and Release Work Group, 2016), https://www.sccgov.org/sites/ceo/Documents/bail-release-work-group.pdf.

64. Shadd Maruna, Dean Dabney, and Volcan Topalli, "Putting a Price on Prisoner Release: The History of Bail and a Possible Future for Parole," *Punishment & Society* 14, no. 3 (2012): 317.

65. Maruna, Dabney, and Topalli, "Putting a Price on Prisoner Release," 318.

66. Santo, "When Freedom Isn't Free"; Charles Davis, "For Now, California Bails on Bail Reform," *American Prospect*, August 30, 2017, http://prospect.org/article/now-california-bails-bail-reform.

67. ABA, "Frequently Asked Questions About Pretrial Release Decision Making," accessed May 17, 2021, https://www.ncsc.org/_data/assets/pdf_file/0015/1572/faq_pretrial_justice-1.ashx.pdf.

68. Marie Gottschalk, *Caught: The Prison State and the Lockdown of American Politics* (Princeton University Press, 2015), 76–77; Thanithia Billings, "Private Interest, Public Sphere: Eliminating the Use of Commercial Bail Bondsmen in the Criminal Justice System," *Boston College Law Review* 57, no. 4 (2016): 1337–66.

69. NAPSA, *The Truth About Commercial Bail*, 5.

70. Bauer, "Inside the Wild, Shadowy, and Highly Lucrative Bail Industry."

71. American Legislative Exchange Council (ALEC), *The State Factor: Criminals on the Street: A Citizen's Right to Know*, January 2009, 5, accessed December 13, 2022, https://web.archive.org/web/20161011125801/https://www.alec.org/app/uploads/2009/01/2009-01-State-Factor-bailbond.pdf.

72. NAPSA, *The Truth About Commercial Bail*, 4–5.

73. PBUS, "Support H.R. 2152," accessed December 13, 2022, http://www.pbus.com/?Page=legislation2152.

74. Alan Feuer, "New Jersey Is Front Line in a National Battle over Bail," *New York Times*, August 21, 2017, https://www.nytimes.com/2017/08/21/nyregion/new-jersey-bail-reform-lawsuits.html.

75. Feuer, "New Jersey Is Front Line."

76. Color of Change and ACLU, *Selling Off Our Freedom*, 40–43.

77. Alwyn Scott and Suzanne Barlyn, "U.S. Bail Insurers Spend Big to Keep Defendants Paying," *Reuters*, March 7, 2021, accessed January 18, 2023, https://www.reuters.com/article/us-usa-insurance-bail-jails-insight/u-s-bail-bond-insurers-spend-big-to-keep-defendants-paying-idUSKBN2BI1BP.

78. Color of Change and ACLU, *Selling Off Our Freedom*, 42–43.

79. Jerry Watson, General Counsel for the ABC, used the term "perfect storm" when describing challenges to commercial bail during a speech at a meeting of the American Legislative Exchange Council in 2007. Although Watson used this years ago, it still describes the industry's view. ALEC, "Jerry Watson, American Bail Coalition, Speaks at ALEC Meeting: Part 1," filmed July 25–27, 2007, at the Annual Meeting of the American Legislative Exchange Council, Philadelphia, PA, accessed December 13, 2022, https://www.youtube.com/watch?v=O8nUeJmdf0g.

80. The Editorial Board, "Cash Bail's Lonely Defender," *New York Times*, August 25, 2017, https://www.nytimes.com/2017/08/25/opinion/cash-bails-lonely-defender.html.

81. Jesse Lee Peterson, "SB 10 Ignores the Reality of California's Inner Cities," *Fox & Hounds*, July 14, 2017, https://www.foxandhoundsdaily.com/2017/07/sb-10-ignores-reality-californias-inner-cities/.

82. Nicholas Wachinski, "Creating Public/Private Partnership Based Solutions to the Problems Currently Facing the Criminal Justice System," *American Bail Coalition* (blog), accessed February 7, 2018, http://www.americanbailcoalition.org/current-initiatives-and-projects/pub.

83. ABC, "ABC Calls for Approval of Ban-the-Box and Fair-Chance Policies," October 14, 2014, https://ambailcoalition.org/abc-calls-for-approval-of-ban-the-box-and-fair-chance-policies/.

84. Don Stemen and David Olson, "Is Bail Reform Causing an Increase in Crime?" (Harry Frank Guggenheim Foundation Research and Policy Brief, January 2023), https://www.hfg.org/hfg_reports/bail-reform-2023/.

85. Lisa Foderaro, "New Jersey Alters Its Bail System and Upends Legal Landscape," *New York Times*, February 6, 2017, https://www.nytimes.com/2017/02/06/nyregion/new-jersey-bail-system.html.

86. "SB 10 Bail Reform: No Justice for Victims or Poor Communities," *Digital Journal*, 10, accessed February 21, 2018, http://www.digitaljournal.com/pr/3452237.

87. Color of Change, "Tell Congress: Put People over Bail Industry Profits," accessed March 25, 2023, https://act.colorofchange.org/sign/BailBonds/, emphasis in original.

88. The Bail Project, "After Cash Bail: A Framework for Reimagining Pretrial Justice," January 14, 2020, https://bailproject.org/after-cash-bail/.

89. Joe Forward, "Provisions Allowing Bail Bondsmen Could Be on the Horizon," *Inside Track* (newsletter of the State Bar of Wisconsin), May 1, 2013, https://www.wisbar.org/NewsPublications/InsideTrack/Pages/Article.aspx?Volume=5&Issue=9&ArticleID=10740.

90. Rob Wildeboer, "New Law Limits Bail Profits Cook County Can Take from Poor," WBEZ Chicago, August 25, 2015, https://www.wbez.org/shows/wbez-news/new-law-limits-bail-profits-cook-county-can-take-from-poor/430b3da2-9749-4f0e-aac8-ff9fb01996e8.

91. The Civic Federation, "Elimination of Cash Bail in Illinois: Financial Impact Analysis," October 21, 2022, 1, https://www.civicfed.org/eliminationofcashbailinillinois.

92. Critical Resistance, "On the Road to Freedom: An Abolitionist Assessment of Pretrial and Bail Reforms," June 2021, 11, https://criticalresistance.org/wp-content/uploads/2021/08/OnTheRoadToFreedom_FINAL_June2021-compressed.pdf.

93. Ahee et al., *Moving Beyond Money*, 17.

94. E. E. Schattschneider, *The Semi-Sovereign People: A Realist's View of Democracy in America* (Holt, Rinehart and Winston, 1960).

95. The Bail Project, "After Cash Bail."

Chapter Seven

1. Steven Williams Maynard-Moody and Michael Craig Musheno, *Cops, Teachers, Counselors: Stories from the Front Lines of Public Service* (University of Michigan Press, 2003); Michael Lipsky, *Street-Level Bureaucracy: Dilemmas of the Individual in Public Service*, 30th Anniversary Expanded (Russell Sage Foundation, 2010).

2. Pierre Bourdieu, *Outline of a Theory of Practice*, trans. Richard Nice (Cambridge University Press, 1977), 78.

3. Demetrios Berdousis, "Bail Bond Services in the US," *IBISWorld*, September 2023, 26.

4. Faith M. Deckard, *Bonded: How Commercial Bail Entangles Families Through Money and Risk* (forthcoming PhD diss., University of Texas at Austin); Daniel J. Freed and Patricia M. Wald, "Bail in the United States, 1964" (working paper, National Conference on Bail and Criminal Justice, 1964), 33.

5. Zhen Zeng, *Jail Inmates in 2016* (Bureau of Justice Statistics, February 2018), https://www.bjs.gov/content/pub/pdf/ji16.pdf. Mary T. Phillips found that in New York City, 83 percent of cosigners were family members, and mothers, followed by sisters, "cosigned for bonds far more than anyone else" [Mary T. Phillips, *Making Bail in New York City: Commercial Bonds and Cash Bail* (New York City Criminal Justice Agency, 2011), 20].

6. Lynne Haney, *Prisons of Debt: The Afterlives of Incarcerated Fathers* (University of California Press, 2022).

7. Ronald Goldfarb, *Ransom: A Critique of the American Bail System* (Harper & Row, 1965); Forrest Dill, "Bail and Bail Reform: A Sociological Study" (PhD diss., University of California, Berkeley, 1972); Malcolm M. Feeley, *The Process Is the Punishment: Handling Cases in a Lower Criminal Court* (Russell Sage Foundation, 1979).

8. Agents rarely attend misdemeanor court because judges generally release low-level defendants with no or low monetary bail.

9. Legislative Program Review and Investigations Committee, "Regulatory Practices" in *Bail Services in Connecticut*, December 2003, https://www.cga.ct.gov/2003/pridata/Studies/Bail_Final_Report.htm.

10. Tracey Kaplan, "More than 30 Bail Bondsmen Targeted in Sting," *Mercury News* (blog), August 28, 2015, https://www.mercurynews.com/2015/08/28/more-than-30-bail-bondsmen-targeted-in-sting/.

11. Sarah Esther Lageson, "Crime Data, the Internet, and Free Speech: An Evolving Legal Consciousness," *Law & Society Review* 51, no. 1 (2017): 8–41.

12. David Garland, *The Culture of Control: Crime and Social Order in Contemporary Society* (University of Chicago Press, 2001).

13. Loïc Wacquant, *Punishing the Poor: The Neoliberal Government of Social Insecurity* (Duke University Press, 2009) chap. 7.

14. Karl Polanyi, *The Great Transformation: The Political and Economic Origins of Our Time*, 2nd ed. (Beacon Press, 2001; originally published 1944).

15. Mark Granovetter, "Economic Action and Social Structure: The Problem of Embeddedness," *American Journal of Sociology* 91, no. 3 (November 1, 1985): 495.

16. Jan L. Flora, Jeff Sharp, Cornelia Flora, and Bonnie Newton, "Entrepreneurial Social Infrastructure and Locally Initiated Economic Development in the Nonmetropolitan United States," *Sociological Quarterly* 38, no. 7 (1997): 623–45.

17. Feeley, *The Process Is the Punishment*, 106.

18. State of New Jersey Commission of Investigation, *Inside Out: Questionable and Abusive Practices in New Jersey's Bail-Bond Industry*, May 2014, 2–3, https://www.nj.gov/sci/pdf/BailReportSmall.pdf.

19. Forrest Dill, "Bail and Bail Reform," 72; See also: Goldfarb, *Ransom*, 114–15.

20. Marcel Mauss, *The Gift: The Form and Reason for Exchange in Archaic Societies*, trans. W. D. Halls (W. W. Norton, 2000).

21. Carole Pateman and Charles W. Mills, *Contract and Domination* (Polity Press, 2007).

22. Larry Welborn, "Bail Bondsman Charged in Business Referral Scheme," *Orange County Register*, July 1, 2010, https://www.ocregister.com/2010/07/01/bail-bondsman-charged-in-business-referral-scheme/; Ken Paxton, "Bail and Bail Bond Regulation," Office of the Attorney General, February 20, 2023, https://www.texasattorneygeneral.gov/opinions/categories/1036.

23. Dan Barto, *You Arrested Me for What? A Bail Bondsman's Observations of Virginia's Criminal Justice System* (Dan Barto Publishing, 2015), 27.

24. Elinor Ochs and Lisa Capps, "Narrating the Self," *Annual Review of Anthropology* 25, no. 1 (October 1996): 19–43.

25. Jennifer L. Hochschild, "Disjunction and Ambivalence in Citizens' Political Outlooks," in *Reconsidering the Democratic Public*, ed. G. E. Marcus and R. L. Hanson (Pennsylvania State University Press, 1993), 187–210; Christopher M. Federico and Ariel Malka, "The Psychological and Social Foundations of Ideological Belief Systems," in *The Oxford Handbook of Political Psychology*, 3rd ed., ed. Leonie Huddy et al. (Oxford University Press, 2023), 601–48.

26. Carole Pateman, "Race, Sex, and Indifference," in *Contract and Domination*; Lisa Wedeen, *Authoritarian Apprehensions: Ideology, Judgment, and Mourning in Syria* (University of Chicago Press, 2019).

27. Anna Merritt, Daniel Effron, and Benoît Monin, "Moral Self-Licensing: When Being Good Frees Us to Be Bad," *Social and Personality Psychology Compass* 4/5 (2010): 344.

28. Philip Bond, David K. Musto, and Bilge Yilmaz, "Predatory Mortgage Lending," *Journal of Financial Economics* 94, no. 3 (December 1, 2009): 412–27, https://doi.org/10.101/j.jfineco.2008.09.011.

29. Martha S. Feldman, Brian T. Pentland, Luciana D'Adderio, Katharina Dittrich, Claus Rerup, David Seidl, eds., *Cambridge Handbook of Routine Dynamics* (Cambridge University Press, 2021).

Chapter Eight

1. James C. Scott, *Seeing like a State: How Certain Schemes to Improve the Human Condition Have Failed* (Yale University Press, 1999), 76.

2. On social kinds, see Sally Haslanger, "What Are We Talking About? The Semantics and Politics of Social Kinds," *Hypatia* 20, no. 4 (2005): 10–26.

3. Evelyn Nakano Glenn, *Forced to Care: Coercion and Caregiving in America* (Harvard University Press, 2010).

4. E.g., Bruce Western, *Punishment and Inequality in America* (Russell Sage Foundation, 2006).

5. William H. Frey, "The Nation Is Diversifying Even Faster than Predicted, According to New Census Data," Brookings Institution, July 1, 2020, https://www.brookings.edu/research/new-census-data-shows-the-nation-is-diversifying-even-faster-than-predicted/; Zhen Zeng, *Jail Inmates in 2021: Statistical Tables* (Bureau of Justice Statistics, December 2022), https://bjs.ojp.gov/library/publications/jail-inmates-2021-statistical-tables#:~:text=At%20midyear%202021%2C%20about%2049,%2C%20and%2014%25%20were%20Hispanic.

6. Stephen Demuth, "Racial and Ethnic Differences in Pretrial Release Decisions and Outcomes: A Comparison of Hispanic, Black, and White Felony Arrestees," *Criminology* 41, no. 3 (2003): 873–908; Stephen Demuth and Darrell Steffensmeier, "The Impact of Gender and Race-Ethnicity in the Pretrial Release Process," *Social Problems* 51, no. 2 (2004): 222–42; Traci Schlesinger, "Racial and Ethnic Disparity in Pretrial Criminal Processing," *Justice Quarterly* 22, no. 2 (2005): 170–92; Meghan Sacks, Vincenzo A. Sainato, and Alissa R. Ackerman, "Sentenced to Pretrial Detention: A Study of Bail Decisions and Outcomes," *American Journal of Criminal Justice* 40, no. 3 (2014): 661–81.

7. On RCS communities, see Joe Soss and Vesla Weaver, "Police Are Our Government: Politics, Political Science, and the Policing of Race-Class Subjugated Communities," *Annual Review of Political Science* 20 (2017): 565–91, https://doi.org/10.1146/annurev-polisci-060415-093825.

8. Loïc Wacquant, *The Invention of the "Underclass": A Study in the Politics of Knowledge* (Polity Press, 2022).

9. Steven A. Tuch and Michael Hughes, "Whites' Racial Policy Attitudes in the Twenty-First Century: The Continuing Significance of Racial Resentment," *Annals of the American Academy of Political and Social Science* 634, no. 1 (March 1, 2011): 134–52.

10. Glenn, *Forced to Care*, 6.

11. Joan C. Tronto, *Caring Democracy: Markets, Equality, and Justice* (NYU Press, 2013).

12. Joan C. Tronto, *Moral Boundaries: A Political Argument for an Ethic of Care* (Routledge, 1993).

13. Leopoldina Fortunati, *The Arcane of Reproduction: Housework, Prostitution, Labor and Capital* (Autonomedia, 1995).

14. Fortunati, *The Arcane of Reproduction*; Glenn, *Forced to Care*; Asha Banerjee, Elise Gould, and Marokey Sawo, *Setting Higher Wages for Child Care and Home Health Care Workers Is Long Overdue* (Economic Policy Institute, 2021).

15. In a study of bail in New York City, Mary T. Phillips found that mothers, followed by sisters, "cosigned for bonds far more than anyone else" (22). *Commercial Bail Bonds in New York City: Characteristics and Implications* (New York Criminal Justice Agency, Inc., April 2011), https://www.nycja.org/assets/BailBonds11.pdf. See also The Minnesota Justice Research Center, *The Wide-Reaching Consequences of the Pre-Trial System in Hennepin County* (September 23, 2023).

16. Miriam Forman-Brunell, *Babysitter: An American History* (New York University Press, 2009).

17. C. Wright Mills, "Situated Actions and Vocabularies of Motive," *American Sociological Review* 5, no. 6 (1940): 904–13.

18. On the social construction of target groups, see Anne Larason Schneider and Helen Ingram, *Policy Design for Democracy* (University Press of Kansas, 1997).

19. Carole Pateman, "Race, Sex, and Indifference," in *Contract and Domination* (Polity Press, 2007).

20. Miranda Fricker, *Epistemic Injustice: Power and the Ethics of Knowing* (Oxford University Press, 2007), 1.

21. Elijah Anderson, *Code of the Street: Decency, Violence, and the Moral Life of the Inner City* (W. W. Norton, 1999).

22. Ludwig Wittgenstein, *Philosophical Investigations: The English Text of the Third Edition* (Prentice Hall, 1968), 23; Ludwig Wittgenstein, *The Blue and Brown Books* (Harper Torchbooks, 1965), 69.

23. Wittgenstein, *Philosophical Investigations*, 132.

24. On Wittgenstein and interpretive ethnography, see Frederic Charles Schaffer, *Elucidating Social Science Concepts: An Interpretivist Guide* (Routledge, 2015).

25. Demuth, "Racial and Ethnic Differences"; Demuth and Steffensmeier, "Impact of Gender and Race-Ethnicity"; Schlesinger, "Racial and Ethnic Disparity"; Sacks, Sainato, and Ackerman, "Sentenced to Pretrial Detention."

Chapter Nine

1. Jacqueline Cogdell DjeDje, *History of Trinity Baptist Church 1917–2012* (Trinity Baptist Church of Florida, accessed June 3, 2021), 1–14, http://www.trinitybaptistchurchofla.org/PDF/History-of-Trinity-Baptist-Church.pdf.

2. Jenifer Warren, "Inmates' Families Pay Heavy Price for Staying in Touch," *Los Angeles Times*, February 16, 2002, https://www.latimes.com/archives/la-xpm-2002-feb-16-me-gouge16-story.html.

3. Warren, "Inmates' Families Pay."

4. Warren, "Inmates' Families Pay."

5. Joint Committee on Prison Construction and Operations, *Payphones in Prison Facilities* (Senate Publications, 2002), 47.

6. Joint Committee on Prison Construction, *Payphones*, 50.

7. Joint Committee on Prison Construction, *Payphones*, 47.

8. Warren, "Inmates' Families Pay."

9. Joint Committee on Prison Construction, *Payphones*, 7.

10. James Sterngold, "California Stunned to Find $20 Billion Hole in Budget," *New York Times*, May 12, 2002, https://www.nytimes.com/2002/05/12/us/california-stunned-to-find-20-billion-hole-in-budget.html.

11. Joint Committee on Prison Construction, *Payphones*, 24.

12. Joint Committee on Prison Construction, *Payphones*, 37.

13. On RCS communities, see Joe Soss and Vesla Weaver, "Police Are Our Government: Politics, Political Science, and the Policing of Race-Class Subjugated Communities," *Annual Review of Political Science* 20, no. 1 (2017): 565–91, https://doi.org/10.1146/annurev-polisci-060415-093825.

14. Evelyn Nakano Glenn, "Constructing Citizenship: Exclusion, Subordination, and Resistance," *American Sociological Review* 76, no. 1 (2011): 1–24.

15. Gordon W. Allport, *The Nature of Prejudice* (Addison-Wesley, 1954), 470.

16. Donald P. Moynihan and Joe Soss, "Policy Feedback and the Politics of Administration," *Public Administration Review* 74, no. 3 (2014): 326.

17. Karin Martin, Bryan Sykes, Sarah Shannon, Frank Edwards, and Alexes Harris, "Monetary Sanctions: Legal Financial Obligations in US Systems of Justice," *Annual Review of Criminology* (January 2018): 476.

18. Quoted in Alexandra Natapoff, *Punishment Without Crime: How Our Massive Misdemeanor System Traps the Innocent and Makes America More Unequal* (Basic Books, 2018), 133.

19. Natapoff, *Punishment Without Crime*, 142.

20. Alicia Bannon, Mitali Nagrecha, and Rebekah Diller, *Criminal Justice Debt: A Barrier to Reentry* (Brennan Center for Justice, New York University School of Law, 2010), 30, http://www.brennancenter.org/sites/default/files/legacy/Fees%20and %20Fines%20FINAL.pdf.

21. John L. Worrall, "Addicted to the Drug War: The Role of Civil Asset Forfeiture as a Budgetary Necessity in Contemporary Law Enforcement," *Journal of Criminal Justice* 29, no. 3 (2001): 182.

22. See, e.g., Noah Zatz, "The Carceral Labor Continuum: Beyond the Prison Labor/Free Labor Divide," in *Labor and Punishment: Work in and out of Prison*, ed. Erin Hatton (University of California Press, 2021), 133–78.

23. Mike Maciag, "Addicted to Fines," *Governing*, August 19, 2019, https://www .governing.com/archive/gov-addicted-to-fines.html.

24. Trial Court Funding Commission (TCFC), *Trial Court Funding Commission Final Report* (State of Michigan TCFC, September 6, 2019), 7, 15, 24, https://www .michigan.gov/-/media/Project/Websites/treasury/Reports/TCFC_Final_Report _962019_9-16-2019.pdf?rev=1fedbe221d224bf5978880216acbb06d.

25. TCFC, *Final Report*, 8.

26. Governor Whitmer, *HB 5488 Signing Letter*, Office of the Governor of Michigan, September 17, 2020, https://content.govdelivery.com/attachments/MIEOG/2020/ 09/17/file_attachments/1548703/HB%205488%20Signing%20Letter.pdf.

27. For examples from other jurisdictions, see Ram Subramanian, Jackie Fielding, Lauren-Brooke Eisen, Hernandez Stroud, and Taylor King, *Revenue over Public Safety: How Perverse Financial Incentives Warp the Criminal Justice System* (Brennan Center for Justice, July 6, 2022), 13, https://www.brennancenter.org/our-work/research -reports/revenue-over-public-safety.

28. Brief of the Michigan District Judges Association as Amicus Curiae at 15, People v. Cameron, MSC No. 155849 (Mich., July 10, 2019).

29. Michigan District Judges Brief at app. C, *People v. Cameron*.

30. Michigan District Judges Brief at 15, *People v. Cameron*, see attachments.

31. Ebony L. Ruhland, Jason P. Robey, Ronald P. Corbett Jr., and Kevin R. Reitz, *Exploring Supervision Fees in Four Probation Jurisdictions in Texas* (Robina Institute of Criminal Law and Criminal Justice, 2017), 4, https://robinainstitute.umn.edu/sites/ robinainstitute.umn.edu/files/2022-02/robina_fee_summary_report_web4.pdf.

32. Ruhland et al., *Exploring Supervision Fees*, 4.

33. Ruhland et al., *Exploring Supervision Fees*, 4.

34. Josh Pacewicz and John N. Robinson III, "Pocketbook Policing: How Race Shapes Municipal Reliance on Punitive Fines and Fees in the Chicago Suburbs," *Socio-Economic Review* 19, no. 3 (July 2021): 975–1003, https://doi.org/10.1093/ser/mwaa029.

35. Michigan District Judges Brief at 15, *People v. Cameron*.

36. Michigan District Judges Brief at 15, *People v. Cameron*.

37. Roger S. Magnusson, "The Devil's Choice: Re-Thinking Law, Ethics, and Symptom Relief in Palliative Care," *Journal of Law, Medicine and Ethics* 34, no. 3 (2006): 559–69.

38. Subramanian et al., *Revenue over Public Safety*, 13.

39. Karin D. Martin, "Monetary Sanctions Thwart Access to Justice," *Stanford Law Review Online* 75 (June 2023): 89–103.

40. See, e.g., Maura Ewing, "Want to Clear Your Record? It'll Cost You $450," *Marshall Project*, May 31, 2016, https://www.themarshallproject.org/2016/05/31/want-to-clear-your-record-it-ll-cost-you-450.

41. Jennnifer Steinhauer, "For $82 a Day, Booking a Cell in a 5-Star Jail," *New York Times*, April 29, 2007, http://www.nytimes.com/2007/04/29/us/29jail.html.

42. US DOJ, *Dear Colleague Letter to Courts Regarding Fines and Fees for Youth and Adults* (Office of the Associate Attorney General, April 20, 2023), https://www.justice.gov/opa/pr/justice-department-issues-dear-colleague-letter-courts-regarding-fines-and-fees-youth-and.

43. US DOJ, *Dear Colleague Letter*, 7.

44. US DOJ, *Dear Colleague Letter*, 10–11.

45. Caliste v. Cantrell, No. 18-30954, slip op. at 12 (5th Cir. 2019).

46. *Investigation of the Ferguson Police Department* (Civil Rights Division of the US Department of Justice, March 4, 2015), 2, https://www.justice.gov/sites/default/files/opa/press-releases/attachments/2015/03/04/ferguson_police_department_report.pdf.

47. Chad Cotti, Bryan Engelhardt, and Matt Richie, "Government Funding Incentives and Felony Charge Rates," *Journal of Crime and Justice* 45, no. 2 (2021): 243–57.

48. Both studies are described in Subramanian et al., *Revenue over Public Safety*, 13.

49. Beth A. Colgan, "Fines, Fees, and Forfeitures," *Criminology, Criminal Justice, Law & Society* 18, no. 3 (2017): 209.

50. Matthew Menendez, Michael F. Crowley, Lauren-Brooke Eisen, and Noah Atchison, *The Steep Costs of Criminal Justice Fees and Fines: A Fiscal Analysis of Three States and Ten Counties* (Brennan Center for Justice, 2019).

51. Menendez et al., "The Steep Costs of Criminal Justice Fees and Fines," 9.

52. Subramanian et al., *Revenue over Public Safety*, 13.

53. Brenden Beck, "Police Killings and Reliance on Fine-and-Fee Revenue," *RSF: The Russell Sage Foundation Journal of the Social Sciences* 9, no. 2 (2023): 175.

54. Devon W. Carbado, "Blue-on-Black Violence: A Provisional Model of Some of the Causes," *Georgetown Law Journal* 104, no. 6 (2016): 1479.

55. Bernadette Atuahene and Timothy Hodge, "Stategraft," *Southern California Law Review* 91, no. 2 (2018): 263–302.

56. Jessica Silver-Greenberg and Shaila Dewan, "When Bail Feels Less like Freedom, More like Extortion," *New York Times*, March 31, 2018, https://www.nytimes.com/2018/03/31/us/bail-bonds-extortion.html; The Justice Policy Institute, *For Better or For Profit: How the Bail Bonding Industry Stands in the Way of Fair and Effective Pretrial Justice* (September 2012), 40–41, https://justicepolicy.org/wp-content/uploads/justicepolicy/documents/_for_better_or_for_profit_.pdf.

57. Silver-Greenberg and Dewan, "When Bail Feels Less like Freedom"; Southern Poverty Law Center, "SPLC Lawsuit: Bail Bond Companies Charged Illegal Fees Used Bounty Hunters to Kidnap Clients, Extort Money," June 19, 2021, https://www.splcenter.org/news/2017/06/19/splc-lawsuit-bail-bond-companies-charged-illegal-fees-used-bounty-hunters-kidnap-clients.

58. Chris Albin-Lackey et al., *Profiting from Probation: America's "Offender-Funded" Probation Industry* (Human Rights Watch, February 5, 2014), 49, https://www.hrw

.org/report/2014/02/05/profiting-probation/americas-offender-funded-probation
-industry.

59. "Does Probation for Profit Criminalize Poverty?," NPR (*All Things Considered*), February 7, 2014, https://www.keranews.org/2014-02-07/does-probation-for-profit
-criminalize-poverty.

60. Madison Pauly, "Mississippi's Prison Bribery Scandal Is in the Past, but the State Still Hasn't Learned Its Lesson," *Mother Jones*, February 6, 2019, https://www
.motherjones.com/politics/2019/02/mississippi-corrections-corruption-bribery
-private-prison-hustle/; Celia Perry, "Probation Profiteers: In Georgia's Outsourced Justice System, a Traffic Ticket Can Land You in a Deep Hole," *Mother Jones*, July/
August 2008, https://www.motherjones.com/politics/2008/07/probation-profiteers/.

61. Jon Schuppe, "Pennsylvania Seeks to Close Books on 'Kids for Cash' Scandal," NBC News, August 12, 2015, https://www.nbcnews.com/news/us-news/pennsylvania
-seeks-close-books-kids-cash-scandal-n408666.

62. Justice Policy Institute, *For Better or For Profit*, 42; Melissa Bailey, "Clerk Gets Probation in Bail Bond Scandal," *New Haven Independent*, September 22, 2008, https://www.newhavenindependent.org/index.php/archives/entry/clerk_gets
_probation_in_bail_bond_scandal/.

63. The cases described in this paragraph are documented in Nick Sibila, "Senator Blasts Asset Forfeiture 'Slush Fund' US Marshals Used for Granite Countertops, Salaries," *Forbes*, September 28, 2017, https://www.forbes.com/sites/
instituteforjustice/2017/09/28/senator-blasts-asset-forfeiture-slush-fund-us-marshals
-used-for-granite-countertops-salaries/?sh=7b2bf007437c.

64. Robert B. Cialdini, "Social Influence and the Triple Tumor Structure of Organizational Dishonesty," in *Codes of Conduct: Behavioral Research into Business Ethics*, ed. D. M. Messick and Anne E. Tenbrunsel (Russell Sage Foundation, 1996), 44–58; Jonathan Pinto, Carrie R. Leana, and Frits K. Pil, "Corrupt Organizations or Organizations of Corrupt Individuals? Two Types of Organization-Level Corruption," *Academy of Management Review* 33, no. 3 (2008): 685–709.

65. Jerry Lambe, "Federal Court: Cops Accused of Stealing $225,000 from Suspects Are Immune from Lawsuit," *Law & Crime*, September 7, 2019, https://
lawandcrime.com/high-profile/federal-court-cops-accused-of-stealing-225000-in
-property-from-suspects-are-immune-from-lawsuit/.

66. Mara H. Gottfried, "Report: Some Metro Gang Strike Force Members Seized Property for Personal Use," *Twin Cities Pioneer Press*, August 19, 2009, https://www
.twincities.com/2009/08/19/report-some-metro-gang-strike-force-members-seized
-property-for-personal-use/.

67. Andrew M. Luger and John Egelhof, *Report of the Metro Gang Strike Force Review Panel* (Minnesota Legislature, August 20, 2009), 3, https://www.leg.mn.gov/
docs/2009/other/090834.pdf.

68. Color of Change and ACLU, *Selling Off Our Freedom: How Insurance Companies Have Taken Over Our Bail System* (ACLU, May 5, 2017), 34–35; Lauren-Brooke Eisen, *Inside Private Prisons* (Columbia University Press, 2018), 160, 193–94; Shane Bauer, "My Four Months as a Private Prison Guard," *Mother Jones*, July/August 2016, https://www.motherjones.com/politics/2016/06/cca-private-prisons-corrections
-corporation-inmates-investigation-bauer/; Albin-Lackey et al., *Profiting from Probation*, 57, 61, 66.

69. Camila Domonoske, "Alabama Sheriff Legally Took $750,000 Meant to Feed Inmates, Bought Beach House," NPR, March 14, 2018, https://www.npr.org/sections/

thetwo-way/2018/03/14/593204274/alabama-sheriff-legally-took-750-000-meant-to
-feed-inmates-bought-beach-house.

70. Erwin Chemerinsky remarks that judges have "absolute immunity for their
judicial acts, but not for their administrative acts." Prosecutors have "absolute
immunity for their prosecutorial acts, but not for investigative, and not for
administrative acts." "Prosecutorial Immunity," *Touro Law Review* 14, no. 4 (1999):
1643–44.

71. Harlow v. Fitzgerald, 457 U.S. 800 (1982).

72. Billy Binion, "Cops Accused of Stealing over $225,000 Can't Be Sued, Thanks
to Qualified Immunity," *Reason*, September 20, 2019, https://reason.com/2019/09/
20/court-rules-fresno-police-accused-of-stealing-over-225000-protected-by-qualified
-immunity-and-cant-be-sued-fourth-amendment/.

73. Vesla M. Weaver and Gwen Prowse, "Racial Authoritarianism in U.S.
Democracy," *Science* 369, no. 6508 (2020): 1176–78, https://doi.org/10.1126/science
.abd7669.

74. David Alan Sklansky, "Police and Democracy," *Michigan Law Review* 103, no. 7
(2005): 1699–1830.

75. Magdalena Bexell and Ulrika Mörth, eds., *Democracy and Public-Private
Partnerships in Global Perspective* (Palgrave Macmillan, 2010); John Forrer et al.,
"Public–Private Partnerships and the Public Accountability Question," *Public
Administration Review* 70, no. 3 (May/June 2010): 475–84.

76. American Bar Association Working Group on Building Public Trust in the
American Justice System, *Privatization of Services in the Criminal Justice System*
(American Bar Association, June 2020), 27, https://www.americanbar.org/content/
dam/aba/administrative/legal_aid_indigent_defendants/ls-sclaid-def-aba-privatizaton
-report-final-june-2020.pdf.

77. Katie Rose Quandt, "Pennsylvania County Owes $67 Million After Man Finds
Arrest Records on Mugshots.com," *The Appeal*, April 27, 2019, https://theappeal.org/
pennsylvania-county-owes-67-million-after-man-finds-arrest-records-on-mugshots
-com/.

78. Eisen, *Inside Private Prisons*, 128–30.

79. Human Rights Defense Center to the Honorable Sheila Jackson Lee, *Re: H.R.
1980—Private Prison Information Act of 2017*, July 11, 2017, 1–5, https://www
.humanrightsdefensecenter.org/media/publications/PPIA%20support%20letter
%202017%20final%207-11-17.pdf.

80. Michael Gibson-Light and Josh Seim, "Punishing Fieldwork: Penal Domination
and Prison Ethnography," *Journal of Contemporary Ethnography* 49, no. 5 (2020):
666–90.

81. Bauer, "My Four Months as a Private Prison Guard."

82. Eisen, *Inside Private Prisons*, 180–81.

83. Brian Gran and William Henry, "Holding Private Prisons Accountable:
A Socio-Legal Analysis of 'Contracting Out' Prisons," *Social Justice* 34, no. 3–4 (2007):
176.

84. Joel Handley, Jennifer Helsby, and Freddy Martinez, "Inside the Chicago
Police Department's Secret Budget," *Chicago Reader*, September 29, 2016, https://
chicagoreader.com/news-politics/inside-the-chicago-police-departments-secret
-budget/.

85. Eric Blumenson and Eva Nilsen, "Policing for Profit: The Drug War's Hidden
Economic Agenda," *University of Chicago Law Review* 65, no. 1 (Winter 1998): 112.

86. Radley Balko, "A Louisiana DA Will Let You Out of Your Community Service Obligation—If You Donate to His Nonprofit," *Washington Post*, November 1, 2019, https://www.washingtonpost.com/opinions/2019/11/01/louisiana-da-will-let-you -out-your-community-service-obligation-if-you-donate-his-nonprofit/.

87. Jason Pohl and Michael Finch II, "How Sacramento Sheriff Used Inmate Welfare Fund for Cameras, Fencing—and a Tahoe Resort," *Sacramento Bee*, July 13, 2021, https://www.msn.com/en-us/news/crime/how-sacramento-sheriff-used-inmate -welfare-fund-for-cameras-fencing-and-a-tahoe-resort/ar-AAM6Bz2.

88. Mary Fainsod Katzenstein, Nolan Bennett, and Jacob Swanson, "Alabama Is US: Concealed Fees in Jails and Prisons," *UCLA Criminal Justice Law Review* 4, no. 1 (2020): 265–67.

89. On the conditions described in this sentence and the next, see Mary Pattillo and John N. Robinson III, "Poor Neighborhoods in the Metropolis," in *The Oxford Handbook of the Social Science of Poverty*, ed. David Brady and Linda M. Burton (Oxford University Press, 2016), 341–68; Robert J. Sampson, *Great American City: Chicago and the Enduring Neighborhood Effect* (University of Chicago Press, 2013); Douglas S. Massey, "Segregation in 21st Century America," *Journal of Catholic Social Thought* 15, no. 2 (2018): 235–60.

90. See, e.g., William A. Darity and A. Kirsten Mullen, *From Here to Equality: Reparations for Black Americans in the Twenty-First Century*, 2nd ed. (University of North Carolina Press, 2022).

91. Louise Seamster, "Black Debt, White Debt," *Contexts* 18, no. 1 (2019): 33.

92. Arpit Gupta, Douglas Swanson, and Ethan Frenchman, *The High Cost of Bail: How Maryland's Reliance on Money Bail Jails the Poor and Costs the Community Millions* (Maryland Office of the Public Defender, November 4, 2016), 4, https://www.nmcourts.gov/wp-content/uploads/2020/11/High_Cost_of_Bail_ _Maryland.pdf.

93. Mathilde Laisne, Jon Wool, and Christian Henrichson, *Past Due: Examining the Costs and Consequences of Charging for Justice in New Orleans* (Vera Institute of Justice, 2017), 18.

94. Robert Stewart, Brieanna Watters, Veronica Horowitz, Ryan Larson, Brian Sargent, and Christopher Uggen, "Native Americans and Monetary Sanctions," *RSF: The Russell Sage Foundation Journal of the Social Sciences* 8, no. 2 (2022): 152.

95. Kate O'Neill, Ian Kennedy, and Alex Harris, "Debtors' Blocks: How Monetary Sanctions Make Between-Neighborhood Racial and Economic Inequalities Worse," *Sociology of Race and Ethnicity* 8, no. 1 (2022): 57.

96. Brief for ACLU et al. as Amici Curiae at 30, *Timbs v. Indiana*, 139 S. Ct. 682 (2019) (No. 17-1091); Heather Hunt and Gene Nichol, *Court Fines and Fees: Criminalizing Poverty in North Carolina* (North Carolina Poverty Research Fund, Winter 2017), 1–34; Katherine Beckett and Alexes Harris, "On Cash and Conviction: Monetary Sanctions as Misguided Policy," *Criminology and Public Policy* 10, no. 3 (August 2011): 517.

97. Steven Mello, "Speed Trap or Poverty Trap? Fines Fees, and Financial Wellbeing," (job market paper, November 14, 2018), https://mello.github.io/files/ jmp.pdf.

98. Board of Governors of the Federal Reserve System, *Report on the Economic Well-Being of U.S. Households in 2019, Featuring Supplemental Data from April 2020* (Federal Reserve, May 2020), https://www.federalreserve.gov/publications/files/ 2019-report-economic-well-being-us-households-202005.pdf.

99. Andrea Bopp Stark and Geoffrey Walsh, *Clearing the Path to a New Beginning: A Guide to Discharging Criminal Justice Debt in Bankruptcy* (National Consumer Law Center, October 2020), https://www.nclc.org/images/pdf/criminal-justice/Rpt_Bankruptcy_and_CJ_Debt.pdf; Abbye Atkinson, "Consumer Bankruptcy, Nondischargeability, and Penal Debt," *Vanderbilt Law Review* 70, no. 3 (2017): 917–83.

100. Hunt and Nichol, *Court Fines and Fees*, 7.

101. ACLU Brief at 15, *Timbs v. Indiana*.

102. Neil L. Sobol, "Charging the Poor: Criminal Justice Debt and Modern-Day Debtors' Prisons," *Maryland Law Review* 75, no. 2 (2016): 520.

103. Elaine S. Povich, "Unpaid Court Fines? That Could Get Your Water Shut Off," *Governing*, April 11, 2019, https://www.governing.com/topics/finance/sl-fines-fees-utilities-cities.html.

104. Sam Lew, "San Francisco Tows Cars over Unpaid Tickets, Even When People Are Living in Them," *Talk Poverty*, March 16, 2020, https://talkpoverty.org/2020/03/16/san-francisco-tows-cars-homeless/.

105. Eli Hager, "Debtors' Prisons, Then and Now: FAQ," *Marshall Project*, February 24, 2015, https://www.themarshallproject.org/2015/02/24/debtors-prisons-then-and-now-faq.

106. Campbell Robertson, "For Offenders Who Can't Pay, It's a Pint of Blood or Jail Time," *New York Times*, October 19, 2015, https://www.nytimes.com/2015/10/20/us/for-offenders-who-cant-pay-its-a-pint-of-blood-or-jail-time.html.

107. Ilya Slavinski and Kimberly Spencer-Suarez, "The Price of Poverty: Policy Implications of the Unequal Effects of Monetary Sanctions on the Poor," *Journal of Contemporary Criminal Justice* 37, no. 1 (2021): 53.

108. Alexes Harris, Beth Huebner, Karin Martin, Mary Pattillo, Becky Pettit, Sarah Shannon, Bryan Sykes, and Chris Uggen, *United States Systems of Justice, Poverty and the Consequences of Non-Payment of Monetary Sanctions: Interviews from California, Georgia, Illinois, Minnesota, Missouri, Texas, New York, and Washington* (Laura and John Arnold Foundation, November 8, 2017), 28, http://www.monetarysanctions.org/wp-content/uploads/2018/01/Monetary-Sanctions-2nd-Year-Report.pdf; Leslie Paik and Chiara Packard, *Impact of Juvenile Justice Fines and Fees on Family Life: Case Study in Dane County, WI* (2019), 1–33, https://debtorsprison.jlc.org/documents/JLC-Debtors-Prison-dane-county.pdf.

109. Alabama Appleseed Center for Law and Justice, University of Alabama at Birmingham Treatment Alternatives for Safer Communities, Greater Birmingham Ministries, and Legal Services Alabama, *Under Pressure: How Fines and Fees Hurt People, Undermine Public Safety, and Drive Alabama's Racial Wealth Divide* (2018), 1–62, https://www.alabamaappleseed.org/wp-content/uploads/2018/10/AA1240-FinesandFees-10-10-FINAL.pdf.

110. Ruhland et al., *Exploring Supervision Fees*, 2.

111. Sandra Blanco et al., *Costs of Injustice: How Criminal System Fees Are Hurting Los Angeles County Families* (ACLU of Southern California, November 2019), 13, https://www.aclusocal.org/en/publications/costs-injustice-how-criminal-system-fees-are-hurting-los-angeles-county-families.

112. Federal Reserve, *Report on the Economic Well-Being of U.S. Households*.

113. Justice Policy Institute, *For Better or For Profit*, 3–47; "How to Get Funding with Bad or No Credit," Bail Bonds Costa Mesa, accessed September 11, 2022, http://www.bailbonds-costa-mesa.com/financing-bail-bonds-costa-mesa/; "Your Options for

Covering the Cost of a Bail Bond," *Woods Bail Bonds* (blog), April 17, 2019, http://woodsbailbonds.com/blog/your-options-for-covering-the-cost-of-a-bail-bond/.

114. Joe Valenti and Eliza Schultz, "How Predatory Debt Traps Threaten Vulnerable Families," Center for American Progress, October 6, 2016, https://www.americanprogress.org/issues/economy/reports/2016/10/06/145629/how-predatory-debt-traps-threaten-vulnerable-families/.

115. Daniel J. Boches, Brittany T. Martin, Andrea Giuffre, Amairini Sanchez, Aubrianne L. Sutherland, Sarah K. S. Shannon, "Monetary Sanctions and Symbiotic Harms," *RSF: The Russell Sage Foundation Journal of the Social Sciences* 8, no. 2 (2022): 98–115.

116. Alabama Appleseed et al., *Under Pressure*; Color of Change and ACLU, *Selling Off Our Freedom*.

117. Color of Change and ACLU, *Selling Off Our Freedom*, 31. See also Patrick Griffin et. al, *Paying in Advance: Perceptions of Monetary Bail in Illinois* (Loyola Chicago, Center for Criminal Justice, April 7, 2023), https://loyolaccj.org/blog/paying-in-advance.

118. Saneta deVuono-powell, Chris Schweidler, Alicia Walters, and Azadeh Zohrabi, *Who Pays? The True Cost of Incarceration on Families* (Ella Baker Center, Forward Together, Research Action Design, 2015), 14.

119. See, e.g., Bruce Western, *Homeward: Life in the Year After Prison* (Russell Sage Foundation, 2018), 118; Alice Goffman, *On the Run: Fugitive Life in an American City* (University of Chicago Press, 2014), 113.

120. DeVuono-powell et al., *Who Pays?*, 1–12.

121. Alabama Appleseed et al., *Under Pressure*, 35.

122. DeVuono-powell et al., *Who Pays?*, 14.

123. Dara Lind, "At Least 2 States Let Prisons Charge the Families of Dead Ex-Prisoners for Their Food and Health Care," *Vox*, October 16, 2015, https://www.vox.com/2015/5/26/8660001/prison-jail-cost.

124. Beckett and Harris, "On Cash and Conviction," 523, emphasis added.

125. Brief for Professors as Amici Curiae at 12–13, *Timbs v. Indiana*.

126. Professors Brief at 12–13, *Timbs v. Indiana*.

127. Paik and Packard, *Case Study in Dane County*, 1–33; Beckett and Harris, "On Cash and Conviction," 523; Bannon, Nagrecha, and Diller, *Criminal Justice Debt*, 29.

128. Paik and Packard, *Case Study in Dane County*.

129. Douglas N. Evans, *The Debt Penalty: Exposing the Financial Barriers to Offender Reintegration* (John Jay College of Criminal Justice, August 2014), 1–24, https://jjrec.files.wordpress.com/2014/08/debtpenalty.pdf.

130. Marcel Mauss, *The Gift: The Form and Reason for Exchange in Archaic Societies*, trans. W. D. Halls (W. W. Norton, 2000).

131. Carol B. Stack, *All Our Kin: Strategies for Survival in a Black Community* (Harper & Row, 1975).

132. Donald Braman, *Doing Time on the Outside: Incarceration and Family Life in Urban America* (University of Michigan Press, 2004), 87.

133. Mitali Nagrecha, Mary Fainsod Katzenstein, and Estelle Davis, *When All Else Fails, Fining the Family* (Center for Community Alternatives: Innovative Solutions for Justice, 2017), 1–31, https://www.prisonpolicy.org/scans/communityalternatives/criminal_justice_debt.pdf; Julie E. Miller-Cribbs and Naomi B. Farber, "Kin Networks and Poverty Among African Americans: Past and Present," *Social Work* 53, no. 1 (2008): 43–51, https://doi.org/10.1093/sw/53.1.43.

134. Alexes Harris, *A Pound of Flesh: Monetary Sanctions as Punishment for the Poor* (Russell Sage Foundation, 2016), 70; Alexes Harris and Tyler Smith, "Monetary Sanctions as Chronic and Acute Health Stressors: The Emotional Strain of People Who Owe Court Fines and Fees," *RSF: The Russell Sage Foundation Journal of the Social Sciences* 8, no. 2 (2022); Alabama Appleseed et al., *Under Pressure*, 4.

135. Foster Cook, *The Burden of Criminal Justice Debt in Alabama* (Jefferson County's Community Corrections Program, 2014), 19, https://www.prisonpolicy.org/scans/ uabtasc/the_burden_of_criminal_justice_debt_in_alabama-_part_1_main_report.pdf.

136. Weaver and Prowse, "Racial Authoritarianism in U.S. Democracy"; On the social sources and effects of haunting, see Avery Gordon, *Ghostly Matters: Haunting and the Sociological Imagination* (University of Minnesota Press, 1997).

137. Harris and Smith, "Monetary Sanctions as Chronic and Acute Health Stressors."

138. Elizabeth Sweet, Arijit Nandi, Emma K. Adam, and Thomas W. McDade, "The High Price of Debt: Household Financial Debt and Its Impact on Mental and Physical Health," *Social Science & Medicine* 91 (August 2013): 94.

139. Breanne Rae Pleggenkuhle, "The Effect of Legal Financial Obligations on Reentry Experiences" (PhD diss., University of Missouri-St. Louis, 2012), 118.

140. Harris et al., *United States Systems of Justice*, 34.

141. Harris et al., *United States Systems of Justice*, 34–35.

142. Devah Pager, "The Mark of a Criminal Record," American Journal of Sociology 108, no. 5 (March 2003): 937–75.

143. Professors Brief at 11, *Timbs v. Indiana*.

144. ACLU Brief at 15, *Timbs v. Indiana*.

145. Michele Cadigan and Gabriela Kirk, "On Thin Ice: Bureaucratic Processes of Monetary Sanctions and Job Insecurity," *RSF: The Russell Sage Foundation Journal of the Social Sciences* 6, no. 1 (March 2020): 124.

146. Jenny Landon, "Why the Senate Should Pass the Driving for Opportunity Act," *Prison Policy Initiative* (blog), July 22 2020, https://www.prisonpolicy.org/blog/ 2020/07/22/driving_for_opportunity/; Alex Bender et al., *Not Just a Ferguson Problem: How Traffic Courts Drive Inequality in California* (Lawyers' Committee for Civil Rights of the San Francisco Bay Area), 4–29, accessed September 12, 2022, https://lccr .com/wp-content/uploads/Not-Just-a-Ferguson-Problem-How-Traffic-Courts-Drive -Inequality-in-California-4.20.15.pdf.

147. Henry Grabar, "Too Broke to Drive," *Slate*, September 27, 2017, https://slate .com/business/2017/09/state-lawmakers-have-trapped-millions-of-americans-in-debt -by-taking-their-licenses.html.

148. "New Report Finds New York Has Severe Racial Disparities in Traffic Enforcement and Driver's License Suspensions," Fines and Fees Justice Center, February 18, 2020, https://finesandfeesjusticecenter.org/2020/02/18/new-report -finds-new-york-has-severe-racial-disparities-in-traffic-enforcement-and-drivers-license -suspensions/.

149. Bender et al., *Not Just a Ferguson Problem*, 4–29; Austen Erblat, "South Florida Still Has Racial Disparities in Driver's License Suspensions, Report Says," *South Florida Sun Sentinel*, December 3, 2019, https://www.sun-sentinel.com/community/fl-cn -south-florida-drivers-license-suspensions-20191203-bnbvfjx3jrba3apjho46l2i6wi -story.html; Jessie Van Berkel, "Minnesota's Criminal Justice Fees Often Fall Hardest on Poor," *Star Tribune*, May 3, 2021, https://www.startribune.com/minnesota-s -criminal-justice-fees-often-fall-hardest-on-poor/600050762/.

150. Mario Salas and Angela Ciolfi, *Driven by Dollars: A State-by-State Analysis of Driver's License Suspension Laws for Failure to Pay Court Debt* (Legal Aid Justice Center, Fall 2017), 9.

151. Marc Levin, "Guest Opinion: Driver's Licenses Are Necessary. Stop Suspending Them," *Deseret News*, February 19, 2020, https://www.deseret.com/ opinion/2020/2/19/21135355/utah-drivers-license-suspend.

152. Sam Stockard, "No License? No Way Out of Debt," *Murfreesboro Post*, September 21, 2017, https://www.murfreesboropost.com/news/no-license-no-way -out-of-debt/article_c1906688-c2e9-5966-9430-8f722013f5ed.html; Fred Robinson et al. v. David W. Purkey, U.S. District Court, Middle District of Tennessee, Nashville Division, Case No. 3:17-cv-01263 (June 11, 2018), https://www.govinfo.gov/ content/pkg/USCOURTS-tnmd-3_17-cv-01263/pdf/USCOURTS-tnmd-3_17-cv-01263 -3.pdf.

153. Cadigan and Kirk, "On Thin Ice," 121.

154. Cadigan and Kirk, "On Thin Ice," 122.

155. On debt and labor discipline, see Genevieve LeBaron, "Reconceptualizing Debt Bondage: Debt as a Class-Based Form of Labor Discipline," *Critical Sociology* 40, no. 5 (2014): 763–80.

156. Harris, *A Pound of Flesh*, 120.

157. Beth A. Colgan, "The Excessive Fines Clause: Challenging the Modern Debtors' Prison," *UCLA Law Review* 65, no. 1 (2018): 64–65.

158. Alex Piquero and Wesley Jennings, "Research Note: Justice System–Impacted Financial Penalties Increase the Likelihood of Recidivism in a Sample of Adolescent Offenders," *Youth Violence and Juvenile Justice* 15, no. 3 (2017): 325–40.

159. On desistance and reentry, see Bianca E. Bersani and Elaine Eggleston Doherty, "Desistance from Offending in the Twenty-First Century," *Annual Review of Criminology* 1 (2018): 311–34.

160. Our formulation here follows Judith N. Shklar, *American Citizenship: The Quest for Inclusion* (Harvard University Press, 1991).

161. Glenn, "Constructing Citizenship," 1.

162. Glenn, "Constructing Citizenship," 1–2.

163. Evelyn Nakano Glenn, *Unequal Freedom: How Race and Gender Shaped American Citizenship and Labor* (Harvard University Press, 2002); Glenn, "Constructing Citizenship."

164. See Margaret Somers, *Genealogies of Citizenship: Markets, Statelessness, and the Right to Have Rights* (Cambridge University Press, 2008).

165. See, e.g., Sidney Verba, Kay Lehman Schlozman, and Henry Brady, *Voice and Equality: Civic Voluntarism in American Politics* (Harvard University Press, 1995); Jan E. Leighley and Jonathan Nagler, *Who Votes Now? Demographics, Issues, Inequality, and Turnout in the United States* (Princeton University Press, 2013).

166. Jamila Michener, *Fragmented Democracy: Medicaid, Federalism, and Unequal Politics* (Cambridge University Press, 2018); Joe Soss, Richard C. Fording, and Sanford F. Schram, *Disciplining the Poor: Neoliberal Paternalism and the Persistent Power of Race* (University of Chicago Press, 2011).

167. See, e.g., Cathy J. Cohen and Michael Dawson, "Neighborhood Poverty and African American Politics," *American Political Science Review* 87, no. 2 (1993): 286–302.

168. Traci Burch, *Trading Democracy for Justice: Criminal Convictions and the Decline of Neighborhood Political Participation* (University of Chicago Press, 2013).

169. Robert J. Sampson, "Collective Efficacy Theory: Lessons Learned and Directions for Future Inquiry," in *Taking Stock: The Status of Criminological Theory*, ed. Francis T. Cullen, John Paul Wright, and Kristie R. Blevins (Transaction, 2006), 149–67.

170. Sarah K. Bruch and Joe Soss, "Schooling as a Formative Political Experience: Authority Relations and the Education of Citizens," *Perspectives on Politics* 16, no. 1 (2018): 36–57; Andrea Louise Campbell, "Policy Makes Mass Politics," *Annual Review of Political Science* 15 (2012): 333–51.

171. Amy E. Lerman and Vesla M. Weaver, *Arresting Citizenship: The Democratic Consequences of American Crime Control* (University of Chicago Press, 2014); Soss and Weaver, "Police Are Our Government."

172. Bennett Capers, "Rethinking the Fourth Amendment: Race, Citizenship, and the Equality Principle," *Harvard Civil Rights–Civil Liberties Law Review* 46, no. 1 (2011): 24.

173. Benjamin Justice and Tracey L. Meares, "How America's Criminal Justice System Educates Citizens," *Annals of the American Academy of Political and Social Science* 651, no. 1 (2014): 162.

174. Here, we extend the conclusions of a broader literature on the lessons people in RCS communities tend to take away from their criminal legal encounters. See Lerman and Weaver, *Arresting Citizenship*; Charles R. Epp, Steven Maynard-Moody, and Donald P. Haider-Markel, *Pulled Over: How Police Stops Define Race and Citizenship* (University of Chicago Press, 2014).

175. Here, we draw on and extend analyses on criminal legal governance and citizenship. See, e.g., Lerman and Weaver, *Arresting Citizenship*; Epp, Maynard-Moody, and Haider-Markel, *Pulled Over*; Rueben Miller and Forrest Stuart, "Carceral Citizenship: Race, Rights and Responsibility in the Age of Mass Supervision," *Theoretical Criminology* 21, no. 4 (2017): 532–48.

176. For details, see "The Portals Policing Project," *Shared Studios* (blog), June 12, 2019, https://www.sharedstudios.com/blog-posts/2019/6/12/the-portals-policing -project.

177. All quotations are taken from Vesla M. Weaver, "I Call That a Ransom: Theorizing Distribution, 'Stategraft' and Expendability Among Policed Americans," presentation at Harvard Law School: Progressing Reforms of Fines and Fees, September 12, 2019. Presentation slides on file with the authors. See also Leslie Paik, Andrea Giuffre, Alexes Harris, and Sarah Shannon, "The Long Reach of Juvenile and Criminal Legal Debt: How Monetary Sanctions Shape Legal Cynicism and Adultification," *Children and Youth Services Review* 154 (2023): 107121.

178. Ilya Slavinski, "A Sketchy Business: Misdemeanor Courts as Sites of Political Socialization," working paper.

179. Monica C. Bell, "Police Reform and the Dismantling of Legal Estrangement," *Yale Law Journal* 126, no. 7 (2017): 2057.

180. Michael Feola, "Blood from a Turnip: Debt, Race, and Expropriation in Penal Capitalism," *Theory & Event* 23, no. 4 (2020): 890; see also Jackie Wang, *Carceral Capitalism* (Semiotext(e), 2018), 189.

181. See, e.g., Andrea Giuffre and Beth M. Huebner, "Unpredictable and Monetized Contact with the Police: Race, Avoidance Behaviors, and Modified Activity Spaces," *Criminology* 61, no. 2 (2023): 234–69.

182. Salas and Ciolfi, *Driven by Dollars*.

183. John Eligon, "Stopped, Ticketed, Fined: The Pitfalls of Driving While Black in Ferguson," *New York Times* August 6, 2019, https://www.nytimes.com/2019/08/06/us/black-drivers-traffic-stops.html.

184. Erin Hatton, *Coerced: Work Under the Threat of Punishment* (University of California Press, 2020).

185. Meagan Day, "Workers Are Being Told to Shut Up and Work: An Interview with Eric Hatton," *Jacobin*, June 20, 2020, https://jacobin.com/2020/06/erin-hatton-coerced-interview.

186. Day, "Workers Are Being Told to Shut Up."

187. Hatton, *Coerced*, 128.

188. Frederick F. Wherry, Kristin S. Seefeldt, and Anthony S. Alvarez, *Credit Where It's Due: Rethinking Financial Citizenship* (Russell Sage Foundation, 2019).

189. David Graeber, *Debt: The First 5,000 Years* (Melville House, 2011); Paula Chakravartty and Denise Ferreira da Silva, "Accumulation, Dispossession, and Debt: The Racial Logic of Global Capitalism—An Introduction," *American Quarterly* 64, no. 3 (2012): 361–85.

190. Feola, "Blood from a Turnip," 882.

191. See, e.g., Mary Sarah Bilder, "The Struggle over Immigration: Indentured Servants, Slaves, and Articles of Commerce," *Missouri Law Review* 61 (1996): 743–84.

192. Elizabeth F. Cohen, *Semi-Citizenship in Democratic Politics* (Cambridge University Press, 2009).

193. Harris, *A Pound of Flesh*, 17.

194. Harris, *A Pound of Flesh*, 73.

195. Bannon, Diller, and Nagrecha, *Criminal Justice Debt*.

196. Anna Wolfe and Michelle Liu, "Think Debtors Prisons Are a Thing of the Past? Not in Mississippi," *Marshall Project*, January 9, 2020, https://www.themarshallproject.org/2020/01/09/think-debtors-prisons-are-a-thing-of-the-past-not-in-mississippi.

197. Harris, *A Pound of Flesh*, 3.

198. Harris, *A Pound of Flesh*, 3.

199. See, e.g., Bannon, Diller, and Nagrecha, *Criminal Justice Debt*.

200. Bryan L. Adamson, "Debt Bondage: How Private Collection Agencies Keep the Formerly Incarcerated Tethered to the Criminal Justice System," *Northwestern Journal of Law & Social Policy* 15, no. 3 (2020): 309.

201. See, e.g., Brittan Friedman, "Carceral Immobility and Financial Capture: A Framework for the Consequences of Racial Capitalism Penology and Monetary Sanctions," *UCLA Criminal Justice Law Review* 4, no. 1 (2020): 177–84.

202. Eli Hager, "Victim Restitution Payments for Childhood Crimes Often Linger into Adulthood, Analysis Finds," *Washington Post*, June 11, 2019, https://www.washingtonpost.com/national/victim-restitution-payments-for-childhood-crimes-often-linger-into-adulthood-analysis-finds/2019/06/11/e88de6ca-86de-11e9-a870-b9c411dc4312_story.html; Paik et al., "The Long Reach of Juvenile and Criminal Legal Debt."

203. Beth A. Colgan, "Wealth-Based Penal Disenfranchisement," *Vanderbilt Law Review* 72, no. 1 (2019): 60.

204. Bannon, Diller, and Nagrecha, *Criminal Justice Debt*, 29.

205. Michael Morse, "The Future of Felon Disenfranchisement Reform: Evidence from the Campaign to Restore Voting Rights in Florida," *California Law Review* 109, no. 3 (2021): 1143–97.

206. Lawrence Mower and Langston Taylor, "In Florida, the Gutting of a Landmark Law Leaves Few Felons Likely to Vote," *ProPublica*, October 7, 2020, https://www.propublica.org/article/in-florida-the-gutting-of-a-landmark-law-leaves-few-felons-likely-to-vote.

207. Daniel Perle, "Ex-Felons Face Long Odds, Long Wait to Restore Voting Rights," KTAR News, May 11, 2019, https://ktar.com/story/2569485/ex-felons-face-long-odds-long-wait-to-restore-voting-rights/?eType=EmailBlastContent&eId=d15402e3-a6df-47dd-bd30-eacea405f84d.

208. Arizona Legislature, "Driving or Actual Physical Control While Under the Extreme Influence of Intoxicating Liquor; Trial by Jury; Sentencing; Classification," accessed June 22, 2021, https://www.azleg.gov/ars/28/01382.htm.

209. "Voter Identification Requirements | Voter ID Laws," National Conference of State Legislatures, July 15, 2021, https://www.ncsl.org/research/elections-and-campaigns/voter-id.aspx.

210. Connor Sheets, "Too Poor to Vote: How Alabama's 'New Poll Tax' Bars Thousands of People from Voting," *Guardian*, October 4, 2017, https://www.theguardian.com/us-news/2017/oct/04/alabama-voting-poll-tax.

211. Sam Levine, "Alabama Blocked a Man from Voting Because He Owed $4," *Guardian*, February 27, 2020, https://www.theguardian.com/us-news/2020/feb/27/alabama-voting-rights-alfonzo-tucker.

212. Shklar, *American Citizenship*.

213. Karin Martin and Anne Stuhldreher, "These People Have Been Barred from Voting Today Because They're in Debt," *Washington Post*, November 8, 2016, https://www.washingtonpost.com/posteverything/wp/2016/11/08/they-served-their-time-but-many-ex-offenders-cant-vote-if-they-still-owe-fines/.

214. Joint Committee on Prison Construction, *Payphones*, 59.

215. Governor Gray Davis, *SB 1978 Bill: Vetoed September 30, 2000* (California Legislature, 2000), http://www.leginfo.ca.gov/pub/99-00/bill/sen/sb_1951-2000/sb_1978_vt_20000930.html. Telecom companies paid the state of California $35 million in 2001, roughly 40 percent of prison phone revenue. Warren, "Inmates' Families Pay."

216. Warren, "Inmates' Families Pay."

217. Warren, "Inmates' Families Pay."

218. Joint Committee on Prison Construction, *Payphones*, 40.

219. Joint Committee on Prison Construction, *Payphones*, 43.

220. Joint Committee on Prison Construction, *Payphones*, 39.

221. Joint Committee on Prison Construction, *Payphones*, 43.

222. Joint Committee on Prison Construction, *Payphones*, 40.

223. Hannah L. Walker, *Mobilized by Injustice: Criminal Justice Contact, Political Participation, and Race* (Cambridge University Press, 2020).

224. California Legislature, *SB 81 Bill* (January 17, 2007), http://www.leginfo.ca.gov/pub/07-08/bill/sen/sb_0051-0100/sb_81_bill_20070824_chaptered.html.

225. Nick Gerda, "Why LA County Supervisors Want to Make Jail Phone Calls Free," *LAist*, July 25, 2023, https://laist.com/news/criminal-justice/la-county-jail-phone-calls-fees-board-of-supervisors-inmate-welfare-fund-recidivism-public-safety.

226. "California Department of Corrections and Rehabilitation Announces Reduced Cost of Telephone Calls for Incarcerated Population," California Department of Corrections and Rehabilitation (CDRC), March 1, 2021, https://www.cdcr.ca.gov/news/2021/03/01/california-department-of-corrections-and-rehabilitation-announces-reduced-cost-of-telephone-calls-for-incarcerated-population/.

227. Erika Martin, "California Cuts Cost of State Inmate Phone Calls, Will Expand Prisoners' Access to Tablets," KTLA, March 1, 2021, https://ktla.com/news/california/california-cuts-cost-of-state-inmate-phone-calls-will-expand-prisoners-access-to-tablets/.

228. CDRC, "CDCR Launches Free Audio Calls," news release, December 30, 2022, https://www.cdcr.ca.gov/news/2022/12/30/cdcr-launching-free-audio-calls-for-incarcerated-population/.

Chapter Ten

1. Matt Keyser, "He Languished in Jail for Nearly a Year. Now He's the Face of California's Bail Reform," Arnold Ventures, August 9, 2021, https://www.arnoldventures.org/stories/he-languished-in-jail-for-nearly-a-year-now-hes-the-face-of-californias-bail-reform.

2. *In re Kenneth Humphrey*, on Habeas Corpus (Court of Appeal of the State of California, First Appellate District, March 25, 2021).

3. KQED News Staff and Wires, "S.F. Man Whose Case Upended California's Bail System Wins Release," May 14, 2018, https://www.kqed.org/news/11666269/s-f-man-whose-case-upended-californias-bail-system-wins-release.

4. *In re Kenneth Humphrey*, on Habeas Corpus (Court of Appeal of the State of California, First Appellate District, January 25, 2018), 3.

5. "District Attorney Asking Supreme Court to Review Bail Hearing," *SFGate*, March 30, 2018, https://www.sfgate.com/news/bayarea/article/District-Attorney-Asking-Supreme-Court-To-Review-12795460.php.

6. *In re Kenneth Humphrey*, on Habeas Corpus (Supreme Court of California, March 25, 2021), 2–3.

7. Civil Rights Corps (@CivRightsCorps), "This landmark ruling is one of the most important decisions in recent history in terms of racial justice and #massincarceration." Twitter (now X), March 25, 2021, 1:18 p.m.

8. Nigel Duara, "What the Failure of Prop. 25 Means for Racial Justice in California," *Cal Matters*, November 20, 2020, https://calmatters.org/justice/2020/11/what-the-failure-of-prop-25-means-for-racial-justice-in-california/.

9. For ease of style, all references to "predation" and "antipredation" in this chapter refer specifically to criminal justice predation.

10. On RCS communities, see Joe Soss and Vesla Weaver, "Police Are Our Government: Politics, Political Science, and the Policing of Race-Class Subjugated Communities," *Annual Review of Political Science* 20, no. 1 (2017): 565–91, https://doi.org/10.1146/annurev-polisci-060415-093825.

11. Keith Bentele and Erin O'Brien, "Jim Crow 2.0? Why States Consider and Adopt Restrictive Voter Access Policies," *Perspectives on Politics* 11, no. 4 (2013): 1088–1116; Frances Fox Piven, Lorraine C. Minnite, and Margaret Groarke, *Keeping Down the Black Vote* (New Press, 2009).

12. Kay Lehman Schlozman, Sidney Verba, and Henry E. Brady, *The Unheavenly Chorus: Unequal Political Voice and the Broken Promise of American Democracy* (Princeton University Press, 2012); Dara Z. Strolovitch, *Affirmative Advocacy: Race, Class, and Gender in Interest Group Politics* (University of Chicago Press, 2007).

13. Sidney Verba, Kay Lehman Schlozman, and Henry Brady, *Voice and Equality: Civic Voluntarism in American Politics* (Harvard University Press, 1995); Jan E. Leighley and Jonathan Nagler, *Who Votes Now? Demographics, Issues, Inequality, and Turnout in the United States* (Princeton University Press, 2013).

14. E. E. Schattschneider, *The Semi-Sovereign People: A Realist's View of Democracy in America* (Holt, Rinehart and Winston, 1960); Peter Bachrach and Morton S. Baratz, *Power and Poverty: Theory and Practice* (Oxford University Press, 1970).

15. Martin Gilens, *Affluence and Influence: Economic Inequality and Political Power in America* (Princeton University Press, 2012); Larry Bartels, *Unequal Democracy: The Political Economy of the New Gilded Age*, 2nd ed. (Princeton University Press, 2017).

16. Nathan J. Kelly, *America's Inequality Trap* (University of Chicago Press, 2019).

17. Zoltan L. Hajnal, *Dangerously Divided: How Race and Class Shape Winning and Losing in American Politics* (Cambridge University Press, 2020).

18. Hajnal, *Dangerously Divided*, 22.

19. Frances Fox Piven, "Low-Income People and the Political Process," in *The Politics of Turmoil*, ed. R. A. Cloward and F. F. Piven (Pantheon Books, 1974); Velsa M. Weaver and Gwen Prowse, "Racial Authoritarianism in U.S. Democracy," *Science* 369, no. 6508 (2020): 1176–78, https://doi.org/10.1126/science.abd7669.

20. Elizabeth Hinton, Julilly Kohler-Hausmann, and Vesla M. Weaver, "Did Blacks Really Endorse the 1994 Crime Bill?," *New York Times*, April 13, 2016, https://www.nytimes.com/2016/04/13/opinion/did-blacks-really-endorse-the-1994-crime-bill.html.

21. Elizabeth Hinton, *From the War on Poverty to the War on Crime: The Making of Mass Incarceration in America* (Harvard University Press, 2017); Naomi Murakawa, *The First Civil Right: How Liberals Built Prison America* (Oxford University Press, 2014).

22. Paul Frymer, *Uneasy Alliances: Race and Party Competition in America* (Princeton University Press, 2010).

23. Daniel Béland, Andrea Louise Campbell, and R. Kent Weaver, *Policy Feedback: How Policies Shape Politics* (Cambridge University Press, 2022).

24. Lauren-Brooke Eisen, *Inside Private Prisons: An American Dilemma in the Age of Mass Incarceration* (Columbia University Press, 2018), 164–65.

25. James Mahoney, "Path Dependence in Historical Sociology," *Theory and Society* 29, no. 4 (2000): 507–48.

26. Peter K. Enns, Nathan J. Kelly, Jana Morgan, Thomas Volscho, and Christopher Witko, "Conditional Status Quo Bias and Top Income Shares: How U.S. Political Institutions Have Benefited the Rich," *Journal of Politics* 76, no. 2 (2014): 289–303.

27. Lisa L. Miller, "Checks and Balances, Veto Exceptionalism, and Constitutional Folk Wisdom: Class and Race Power in American Politics," *Political Research Quarterly* 76, no. 4 (2023): 1604–18, https://journals.sagepub.com/doi/abs/10.1177/10659129231166040.

28. Mark Peterson, "Health Reform and the Congressional Graveyard," in *Healthy, Wealthy, and Fair: Health Care and the Good Society*, ed. J. A. Morone and L. R. Jacobs (Oxford University Press, 2005), 205–34.

29. James A. Morone, "Diminishing Democracy in Health Policy: Partisanship, the Courts, and the End of Health Politics as We Knew It," *Journal of Health Politics, Policy, and Law* 45, no. 5 (2020): 758.

30. Lisa L. Miller, *The Perils of Federalism: Race, Poverty, and the Politics of Crime Control* (Oxford University Press, 2008).

31. Peter K. Enns, *Incarceration Nation: How the United States Became the Most Punitive Democracy in the World* (Cambridge University Press, 2016).

32. Albert O. Hirschman, *The Rhetoric of Reaction: Perversity, Futility, Jeopardy* (Belknap Press, 1991).

33. Ned Oliver, "$5 Medical Copays—Equivalent to as Much as 18 Hours of Labor Behind Bars—Suspended at Va. Prisons," *Virginia Mercury*, February 20, 2020, https://www.virginiamercury.com/2020/02/20/5-medical-copays-equivalent-to-as -much-as-18-hours-of-labor-behind-bars-suspended-at-va-prisons/.

34. Dan Frosch and Ben Chapman, "New Bail Laws Leading to Release of Dangerous Criminals, Some Prosecutors Say," *Wall Street Journal*, February 10, 2020, https://www.wsj.com/articles/bail-reform-needs-reform-growing-group-of-opponents -claim-11581348077.

35. Daphne Jordan, "Senator Daphne Jordan: 'Welcome to Albany's "Bizzaro World," Where Senate Democratic Majority Wants a Higher Minimum Wage for Incarcerated Criminals,'" New York State Senate, February 7, 2019, https://www .nysenate.gov/newsroom/press-releases/daphne-jordan/senator-daphne-jordan -welcome-albanys-bizzaro-world-where.

36. Adam H. Johnson, "Police and Sheriff's Departments Join Media Campaign Against Bail Reform in New York State," *The Appeal*, January 27, 2020, https:// theappeal.org/upstate-police-and-sheriff-departments-join-media-campaign-against -bail-reform-in-new-york-state/; James Lartey, "New York Rolled Back Bail Reform. What Will the Rest of the Country Do?," *Marshall Project*, April 23, 2020, https:// www.themarshallproject.org/2020/04/23/in-new-york-s-bail-reform-backlash-a -cautionary-tale-for-other-states.

37. Lartey, "New York Rolled Back Bail Reform."

38. Luis Ferré-Sadurní and Jesse McKinley, "'We Can't Spend What We Don't Have': Virus Strikes N.Y. Budget," *New York Times*, April 2, 2020, https://www .nytimes.com/2020/04/02/nyregion/coronavirus-ny-state-budget.html.

39. Tiana Herring, "Releasing People Pretrial Doesn't Harm Public Safety," *Prison Policy Initiative* (blog), November 17, 2020, https://www.prisonpolicy.org/blog/ 2020/11/17/pretrial-releases/.

40. For a classic analysis, see Theodore J. Lowi, *The End of Liberalism: The Second Republic of the United States* (W. W. Norton, 1969).

41. Daniel Carpenter, "Institutional Strangulation: Bureaucratic Politics and Financial Reform in the Obama Administration," *Perspectives on Politics* 8, no. 3 (2010): 825–46, https://doi.org/10.1017/S1537592710002070.

42. Michael Lipsky, *Street-Level Bureaucracy: Dilemmas of the Individual in Public Service*, 30th Anniversary Expanded (Russell Sage Foundation, 2010); Michael Lipsky, "Bureaucratic Disentitlement in Social Welfare Programs," *Social Service Review* 58, no. 1 (1984); Mitali Nagrecha, Sharon Brett, and Colin Doyle, "Court Culture and Criminal Law Reform," *Duke Law Journal* 69 (2020): 84–113.

43. Anna Simonton, "Defunding Police: Atlanta Shows Politicians' Promises Don't Equal Change," *Scalawag*, June 9, 2020, https://scalawagmagazine.org/2020/06/cash -bail-atlanta/.

44. Simonton, "Defunding Police."

45. Alicia Virani, Stephanie Campos-Bui, Rachel Wallace, Cassidy Bennett, and Akruti Chandrayya, *Coming Up Short: The Unrealized Promise of "In re Humphrey"* (UCLA School of Law Bail Practicum and the UC Berkeley School of Law Policy Advocacy Clinic, October 2022).

46. Annabel Adams, "California Bail Reform Efforts Coming Up Short, According to Study by UCLA Law, Berkeley Law," *UCLA Newsroom*, October 26, 2022, https:// newsroom.ucla.edu/releases/california-bail-reform-progress-humphrey-decision.

47. Virani et al., *Coming Up Short*, 23.

48. Joshua Page and Christine S. Scott-Hayward, "Bail and Pretrial Justice in the United States: A Field of Possibility," *Annual Review of Criminology* 5 (2022): 91–113.

49. Donald P. Moynihan and Pamela Herd, *Administrative Burden: Policymaking by Other Means* (Russell Sage Foundation, 2019).

50. Theresa Zhen, "(Color)Blind Reform: How Ability-to-Pay Determinations Are Inadequate to Transform a Racialized System of Penal Debt," *NYU Review of Law & Social Change* 43, no. 1 (2019): 175–222; Beth A. Colgan, "Beyond Graduation: Economic Sanctions and Structural Reform," *Duke Law Journal* 69 (April 2020): 1529–83.

51. Zhen, "(Color)Blind Reform," 188.

52. Bianca Bruno, "Feds Sue California over Ban on Private Prisons," Courthouse News Service, January 24, 2020, https://www.courthousenews.com/feds-sue-california-over-ban-on-private-prisons/.

53. Maura Ewing, "A Judicial Pact to Cut Court Costs for the Poor," *Atlantic*, December 25, 2017, https://www.theatlantic.com/politics/archive/2017/12/court-fines-north-carolina/548960/; Joseph Neff, "No Mercy for Judges Who Show Mercy," *Marshall Project*, November 29, 2017, https://www.themarshallproject.org/2017/11/29/no-mercy-for-judges-who-show-mercy.

54. C. J. Ciaramella, "Federal Judge Rules That Albuquerque's Asset Forfeiture Created an Unconstitutional Profit Incentive," *Reason*, July 30, 2018, https://reason.com/2018/07/30/federal-judge-rules-albuquerques-asset-f/.

55. Tony Messenger, "Messenger: Lawsuit Seeks to Protect Federal Disability Income from Covering Court Fees," *St. Louis Post-Dispatch*, February 24, 2021, https://www.stltoday.com/news/local/columns/tony-messenger/messenger-lawsuit-seeks-to-protect-federal-disability-income-from-covering-court-fees/article_0dcf772d-1ce8-5ebb-b4c0-6e0b30a8c721.html.

56. "Schmitt Argues Court Should Allow Enforcement of Senate Bill 5 Provisions in St. Louis County," *Missouri Times*, January 30, 2020, https://themissouritimes.com/schmitt-argues-court-should-allow-enforcement-of-senate-bill-5-provisions-in-st-louis-county/.

57. Alex Kornya et al., "Crimsumerism: Combating Consumer Abuses in the Criminal Legal System," *Harvard Civil Rights–Civil Liberties Law Review* 54, no. 1 (Winter 2019): 215, https://harvardcrcl.org/wp-content/uploads/sites/10/2019/03/Crimsumerism.pdf.

58. Murray Edelman, *Politics as Symbolic Action: Mass Arousal and Quiescence* (Academic Press, 1971).

59. William A. Gamson, "Constructing Social Protest," in *Social Movements and Culture*, ed. Hank Johnson and Bert Klandermans (University of Minnesota Press, 1995), 85–106.

60. William A. Gamson, "Injustice Frames," in *The Wiley-Blackwell Encyclopedia of Social and Political Movements* (Wiley-Blackwell, 2013), 1.

61. Gamson, "Injustice Frames," 1.

62. Gamson, "Injustice Frames," 1.

63. Hannah Walker, *Mobilized by Injustice: Criminal Justice Contact, Political Participation, and Race* (Oxford University Press, 2020).

64. Walker, *Mobilized by Injustice*, 52.

65. Erica S. Simmons, *Meaningful Resistance: Market Reforms and the Roots of Social Protest in Latin America* (Cambridge University Press, 2016), 3.

66. Aldon D. Morris, *The Origins of the Civil Rights Movement: Black Communities Organizing for Change* (Free Press, 1986).

67. Walker, *Mobilized by Injustice*, 126.

68. Walker, *Mobilized by Injustice*, 38.

69. Walker, *Mobilized by Injustice*, 126.

70. Critical Resistance, "Bail Flyer 2017," August 23, 2018, http://criticalresistance.org/bail_takeaways_flyer/; Critical Resistance, "On the Road to Freedom: An Abolitionist Assessment of Pretrial and Bail Reforms," June 2021, http://criticalresistance.org/on-the-road-to-freedom-an-abolitionist-assessment-of-pretrial-and-bail-reforms/.

71. *Critical Resistance*, "Bail Flyer 2017."

72. Michael Levitin, "The Triumph of Occupy Wall Street," *Atlantic*, June 10, 2015, https://www.theatlantic.com/politics/archive/2015/06/the-triumph-of-occupy-wall-street/395408/.

73. David S. Meyer and Nancy Whittier, "Social Movement Spillover," *Social Problems* 41, no. 2 (1994): 277–98.

74. Debt Collective, *Can't Pay, Won't Pay: The Case for Economic Disobedience and Debt Abolition* (Haymarket Books, 2020), 2–3.

75. Debt Collective, *Can't Pay, Won't Pay.*

76. Deva R. Woodly, *Reckoning: Black Lives Matter and the Democratic Necessity of Social Movements* (Oxford University Press, 2022); Keeanga-Yamahtta Taylor, *From #BlackLivesMatter to Black Liberation* (Haymarket Books, 2016).

77. "A Vision for Black Lives: Policy Demands for Black Power, Freedom, and Justice," The Movement for Black Lives, accessed September 21, 2022, https://web.archive.org/web/20210603134622/http://whitesforracialequity.org/wp-content/uploads/2017/07/BLM-vision-booklet.pdf.

78. Color of Change, "About Color of Change," accessed September 21, 2022, https://colorofchange.org/about/.

79. Charles Tilly, *Contentious Performances* (Cambridge University Press, 2008).

80. Vera Institute of Justice, "The State of Bail: A Breakthrough Year for Bail Reform," 2017, https://www.vera.org/state-of-justice-reform/2017/bail-pretrial; Page and Scott-Hayward, "Bail and Pretrial Justice."

81. "Harris County, TX: Bail," Civil Rights Corp, accessed September 21, 2022, https://civilrightscorps.org/case/harris-county-tx-bail/.

82. Civil Rights Corp, "Harris County, TX: Bail."

83. O'Donnell v. Harris County, 251 F. Supp. 3d 1052, 1122 (S.D. Tex. 2017) (memorandum and opinion setting out findings of fact and conclusions of law, 7).

84. Brandon L. Garrett and Sandra Guerra Thompson, "Monitoring the Misdemeanor Bail Reform Consent Decree in Harris County, Texas," *Judicature* 105, no. 2 (Duke University School of Law, 2021), https://judicature.duke.edu/wp-content/uploads/2021/09/BailReform_Summer2021-1.pdf.

85. Garrett and Thompson, "Monitoring the Consent Decree," 4.

86. "For the First Time in California, Appeals Court Says Bail Companies Must Follow Consumer Protection Laws, Prohibits Debt Collection of $38M," Lawyers' Committee for Civil Rights of the San Francisco Bay Area, December 29, 2021, https://lccrsf.org/pressroom_posts/for-the-first-time-in-california-appeals-court-says-bail-companies-must-follow-consumer-protection-laws-prohibits-debt-collection-of-38m/.

87. Ariel Nelson et al., *Commercialized (In)justice Litigation Guide: Applying Consumer Laws to Commercial Bail, Prison Retail, and Private Debt Collection* (National Consumer Law Center, June 2020), https://www.nclc.org/images/pdf/criminal-justice/WP_Litigation_Guide.pdf.

88. On venue bias and venue shopping, see, e.g., Frank Baumgartner and Bryan Jones, *Agendas and Instability in American Politics*, 2nd ed. (University of Chicago Press, 2009).

89. Alaska, California, Colorado, Illinois, New Mexico, New Jersey, and New York.

90. Glenn A. Grant, *Report to the Governor and the Legislature* (New Jersey Courts, 2019), 26, https://www.njcourts.gov/courts/assets/criminal/cjrannualreport2019.pdf.

91. Michael Hill, "Bond Industry Reeling from Bail Reform," *NJ Spotlight News*, January 13, 2017, https://www.njspotlightnews.org/video/bond-industry-reeling-bail-reform/.

92. Colin Doyle, "Chesa Boudin's New Bail Policy Is Nation's Most Progressive. It Also Reveals Persistence of Tough-on-Crime Norms," *The Appeal*, January 30, 2020, https://theappeal.org/politicalreport/chesa-boudin-cash-bail-predictions/.

93. Keri Blakinger, "The Beto Effect: Transforming Houston's Criminal Justice System," *Marshall Project*, February 25, 2020, https://www.themarshallproject.org/2020/02/25/the-beto-effect-transforming-houston-s-criminal-justice-system.

94. See, e.g., Sharlyn Grace, "Organizers Change What's Possible," *Inquest*, September 23, 2021, https://inquest.org/organizers-change-whats-possible/.

95. Jocelyn Simonson, *Radical Acts of Justice: How Ordinary People Are Dismantling Mass Incarceration* (New Press, 2023), chap. 3.

96. *The Bail Project Annual Report 2021* (The Bail Project, 2021), 12, https://bailproject.org/wp-content/uploads/2021/11/the_bail_project_annual_report_2021_web.pdf.

97. Angelina Chapin, "The Bail-Fund Windfall: The Minnesota Freedom Fund Raised Too Much Money," *New York Magazine*, May 25, 2021, https://nymag.com/intelligencer/2021/05/minnesota-freedom-fund-bail-fund.html.

98. David Dagan and Steven Teles, *Prison Break: Why Conservatives Turned Against Mass Incarceration* (Oxford University Press, 2016), 55, 144–45.

99. "Civil Forfeiture Reforms on the State Level," Institute for Justice, accessed January 14, 2022, https://ij.org/legislative-advocacy/civil-forfeiture-legislative-highlights/.

100. Anne Teigen and Lucia Bragg, "Evolving Civil Asset Forfeiture Laws," National Conference of State Legislators, February 2018, https://www.ncsl.org/research/civil-and-criminal-justice/evolving-civil-asset-forfeiture-laws.aspx.

101. All information in this paragraph comes from Institute for Justice, "Civil Forfeiture Reforms on the State Level."

102. Nelson et al., *Commercialized (In)justice Litigation Guide*.

103. Evan Mealins, "Ivey Signs Civil Asset Forfeiture Law," *Alabama Political Reporter*, June 13, 2019, https://www.alreporter.com/2019/06/13/ivey-signs-civil-asset-forfeiture-law/.

104. Sarah Stillman, "Jeff Sessions and the Resurgence of Civil-Asset Forfeiture," *New Yorker*, August 15, 2017, https://www.newyorker.com/news/news-desk/jeff-sessions-and-the-resurgence-of-civil-asset-forfeiture.

105. Stillman, "Jeff Sessions and the Resurgence."

106. "City Announces Settlement in Civil Forfeiture Class Action Suit," City of Philadelphia, September 18, 2018, https://www.phila.gov/2018-09-18-city -announces-settlement-in-civil-forfeiture-class-action-suit/.

107. "Philly DA for the People," accessed September 21, 2022, https://www .phillydaforthepeople.org/; Molly Tack-Hooper, "The Reports of Civil Asset Forfeiture's Death in Philadelphia Have Been Greatly Exaggerated," *ACLU* (blog), September 26, 2018, https://www.aclu.org/blog/criminal-law-reform/reforming -police/reports-civil-asset-forfeitures-death-philadelphia-have.

108. C. J. Ciaramella, "Philadelphia Will Dismantle Its Asset Forfeiture Program and Pay $3 Million to Victims," *Reason*, September 18, 2018, https://reason.com/ 2018/09/18/philadelphia-will-dismantle-its-asset-fo/.

109. Max Marin, "Philly DA Report Card: The Promises Krasner Kept (or Didn't) in His First Term," *Billy Penn*, April 25, 2021, https://billypenn.com/2021/04/25/ krasner-philadelphia-district-attorney-election-cash-bail-wrongful-convictions/; Jackson Smith, "Ending Civil Forfeiture in Philadelphia," *Jacobin*, September 28, 2018, https://jacobin.com/2018/09/larry-krasner-philadelphia-civil-forfeiture -reforms.

110. Lisa Soronen, "*Timbs v. Indiana* Civil Forfeiture Case Won't Have Much Impact," *NCLS Blog*, April 10, 2019, https://www.ncsl.org/blog/2019/04/10/timbs -vs-indiana-civil-forfeiture-case-wont-have-much-impact.aspx; see also "*Timbs v. Indiana*," *Harvard Law Review* 133, no. 1 (November 8, 2019): 342–51, https:// harvardlawreview.org/2019/11/timbs-v-indiana/.

111. Wayne A. Logan, "*Timbs v. Indiana*: Toward the Regulation of Mercenary Criminal Justice," *Federal Sentencing Reporter* 32, no. 1 (2019): 3–7, https://papers .ssrn.com/sol3/papers.cfm?abstract_id=3455645.

112. "Ending the Punishment of Poverty: Supreme Court Rules Against High Fines and Civil Asset Forfeiture," Democracy Now!, February 21, 2019, https://www .democracynow.org/2019/2/21/ending_the_punishment_of_poverty_supreme.

113. Emma Andersson, "The Supreme Court Didn't Put the Nail in Civil Asset Forfeiture's Coffin," *ACLU* (blog), March 15, 2019, https://www.aclu.org/blog/ criminal-law-reform/reforming-police/supreme-court-didnt-put-nail-civil-asset -forfeitures.

114. Free to Drive, "Free to Drive Story Map," May 22, 2023, https://www .freetodrive.org/maps/#page-content.

115. Class Action Complaint at 56 (ECF No. 1), Samantha Jenkins et al. v. City of Jennings, Case No. 4:15-cv-00252-CEJ (E.D. Mo., February 8, 2015), available at https://civilrightscorps.org/wp-content/uploads/2021/06/ wYKQspsMSBm2bYn2QnhF.pdf.

116. Alec Karakatsanis, *Usual Cruelty: The Complicity of Lawyers in the Criminal Injustice System* (New Press, 2019), 6.

117. Tony Messenger, *Profit and Punishment: How America Criminalizes the Poor in the Name of Justice* (St. Martin's Press, 2021), 28.

118. Livia Albeck-Ripka, "Ferguson, Mo., Agrees to Pay $4.5 Million to Settle 'Debtors' Prison Suit," *New York Times*, February 2024, https://www.nytimes.com/ 2024/02/29/us/missouri-ferguson-settlement.html.

119. Christina Mendez, Jeffrey Selbin, and Gus Tupper, "Blood from a Turnip: Money as Punishment in Idaho," *Idaho Law Review* 57 (2021): 794; Civil Rights Corps, "New Orleans, LA: Debtors' Prison," February 23, 2022, https://civilrightscorps.org/

case/new-orleans-la-debtors-prison/; David Reutter, "Settlement Ends Montgomery, Alabama Debtor's Prison," *Prison Legal News*, February 3, 2016, https://www .prisonlegalnews.org/news/2016/feb/3/settlement-ends-montgomery-alabama -debtors-prison/; ArchCity Defenders, "Federal Court Approves $3.25 Million Settlement in Debtors' Prison Lawsuit Against Maplewood, Town near Ferguson," press release, April 6, 2023, https://www.archcitydefenders.org/for-immediate -release-federal-court-approves-3-25-million-settlement-in-debtors-prison-lawsuit -against-maplewood-town-near-ferguson/.

120. Jeffrey Selbin, "Juvenile Fee Abolition in California: Early Lessons and Challenges for the Debt-Free Justice Movement," *North Carolina Law Review* 98, no. 2 (2020): 404, 409.

121. Alexander Kaplan, Ahmed Lavalais, Tim Kline, Jenna Le, Rachel Draznin-Nagy, Ingrid Rodriguez, Jenny Van Der Heyde, Stephanie Campos-Bui, and Jeffrey Selbin, "High Pain, No Gain: How Juvenile Administrative Fees Harm Low-Income Families in Alameda County, California," *SSRN Electronic Journal,* January 1, 2016, https://doi.org/10.2139/ssrn.2738710.

122. Jacyln E. Chambers, Karin D. Martin, and Jennifer L. Skeem, *Eliminating Fees in the Alameda County Juvenile Justice System Meaningfully Reduced Financial Burdens on Families* (California Policy Lab, November 2021).

123. Stephanie Campos-Bui, *Debt-Free Justice: A Bottom-up Approach to Ending Juvenile Fees* (Shriver Center on Poverty Law, 2018), 14.

124. Stephanie Campos-Bui, Jeffrey Selbin, Hamza Jaka, Tim Kline, Ahmed Lavalais, Alynia Phillips, and Abby Ridley-Kerr, *Making Families Pay: The Harmful, Unlawful, and Costly Practice of Charging Juvenile Administrative Fees in California* (Policy Advocacy Clinic, UC Berkeley School of Law, March 2017), http://dx.doi.org/ 10.2139/ssrn.2937534.

125. Campos-Bui, *Debt-Free Justice*, 28.

126. Debt Free Justice, "California," accessed January 4, 2025, https:// debtfreejustice.org/location/california.

127. American Legislative Exchange Council, "Elimination of Youth Justice Fines and Fees Act," August 28, 2023, https://alec.org/model-policy/elimination-of-youth -justice-fines-and-fees-act/.

128. Personal communication with Jeffrey Selbin, Clinical Professor of Law and Faculty Director of the Policy Advocacy Clinic, UC Berkeley School of Law, January 3, 2024.

129. Messenger, *Profit and Punishment*, 38.

130. Shannon Prather, "Ramsey County Eliminates Nearly $700,000 in Criminal Fines and Fees," *Star Tribune*, April 14, 2020, https://www.startribune.com/ramsey -county-eliminates-nearly-700-000-in-criminal-fines-and-fees/569640712/.

131. Dana Difilippo, "Governor Murphy's Budget Plan Pitches Ending Fees for Clients of Public Defenders," *New Jersey Monitor*, February 28, 2023, https:// newjerseymonitor.com/2023/02/28/governor-murphys-budget-plan-pitches-ending -fees-for-clients-of-public-defenders/.

132. "Financial Justice Project Accomplishments," Office of the Treasurer and Tax Collector, accessed September 22, 2022, https://sfgov.org/financialjustice/financial -justice-project-accomplishments/.

133. Sukey Lewis, "S.F. Superior Court Forgives More than $32 Million in Unpaid Court Fees," KQED, August 23, 2018, https://www.kqed.org/news/11688518/s-f -superior-court-forgives-more-than-32-million-in-unpaid-court-fees.

134. Aravind Boddupalli and Kim S. Rueben, "Inequitable Criminal Legal Fines and Fees Are Ripe for State Reforms," Urban Institute, October 11, 2022, https://www.urban.org/urban-wire/inequitable-criminal-legal-fines-and-fees-are-ripe-state-reforms.

135. End Justice Fees, "About," accessed March 19, 2024, https://endjusticefees.org/.

136. US Department of Justice, *Dear Colleague Letter to Courts Regarding Fines and Fees for Youth and Adults* (Office of the Associate Attorney General, April 20, 2023), https://www.justice.gov/opa/pr/justice-department-issues-dear-colleague-letter-courts-regarding-fines-and-fees-youth-and.

137. Glenn Thrush, "Justice Dept. Presses Local Courts to Reduce Fines," *New York Times*, April 20, 2023, https://www.nytimes.com/2023/04/20/us/politics/justice-dept-courts-fines.html.

138. "San Francisco Announces All Phone Calls from County Jails Are Now Free," Office of the Mayor, August 10, 2020, https://sfmayor.org/article/san-francisco-announces-all-phone-calls-county-jails-are-now-free.

139. "New Racial and Economic Justice Ordinance Puts Permanent End to Generating Revenue from Incarcerated People and Their Families," Office of the Treasurer and Tax Collector, June 3, 2020, https://sfgov.org/financialjustice/whats-new/san-francisco-introduces-people-over-profits-ordinance.

140. "The Financial Justice Project," Office of the Treasurer and Tax Collector, accessed September 22, 2022, https://sfgov.org/financialjustice/.

141. Worth Rises, "Campaigns," accessed April 29, 2024, https://worthrises.org/ourcampaigns.

142. Peter Wagner and Wanda Bertram, *State of Phone Justice 2022: The Problem, the Progress, and What's Next* (Prison Policy Initiative, December 2022), https://www.prisonpolicy.org/phones/state_of_phone_justice_2022.html.

143. American Bar Association Working Group on Building Public Trust in the American Justice System, *Privatization of Services in the Criminal Justice System* (American Bar Association, June 2020), 16, https://www.americanbar.org/content/dam/aba/administrative/legal_aid_indigent_defendants/ls-sclaid-def-aba-privatizaton-report-final-june-2020.pdf.

144. Connecticut General Assembly, "Public Act No. 21-54: An Act Concerning the Establishment of a Social Equity Council, the Definition of 'Cannabis,' and the Establishment of a Small Business Equity Loan Program," https://www.cga.ct.gov/2021/ACT/PA/PDF/2021PA-00054-R00SB-00972-PA.PDF.

145. The Financial Justice Project, *People over Profits: A Truly Free, No Cost Tablet Program for Incarcerated People in San Francisco*, May 31, 2023, https://sfgov.org/financialjustice/reports/people-over-profits-truly-free-no-cost-tablet-program-incarcerated-people-san-francisco.

146. Worth Rises, "We're winning the fight for prison phone justice" (email, July 29, 2021).

147. Wanda Bertram, "Since You Asked: What's Next for Prison and Jail Phone Justice Now That the Martha Wright-Reed Just and Reasonable Communications Act Is Law?," *Prison Policy Initiative* (blog), January 19, 2023, https://www.prisonpolicy.org/blog/2023/01/19/martha-wright-reed-act/.

148. Bertram, "Since You Asked."

149. Worth Rises, "Tell Congress and the FCC to Regulate the Prison Telecom Industry," Connecting Families, accessed September 22, 2022, https://connectfamiliesnow.com/federalaction.

150. Trung T. Phan, "He Was Facing Life in Prison. Now He's the CEO of the 'Instagram for the Incarcerated,'" *The Hustle*, January 30, 2021, https://thehustle.co/he-was-facing-life-in-prison-now-hes-the-ceo-of-the-instagram-for-the-incarcerated/.

151. Kavontae Smalls, "Former Inmate Turned Entrepreneur Hopes His Mobile App Will Reduce Recidivism Rate," *Atlanta Black Star*, April 3, 2022, https://atlantablackstar.com/2022/04/02/former-inmate-turned-entrepreneur-hopes-his-mobile-app-will-reduce-recidivism-rate/.

152. Jennifer Zabasajja, "Can a Nonprofit Disrupt the Pricey Prison Phone Industry?," *Bloomberg*, September 8, 2021, https://www.bloomberg.com/news/articles/2021-09-08/nonprofit-aims-to-disrupt-pricey-prison-telecom-industry.

153. Eisen, *Inside Private Prisons*, chap. 6.

154. Worth Rises, "About Us," accessed September 22, 2022, https://worthrises.org/aboutus/.

155. Stephen Caruso, "State Employee Retirement Board Balks at Investing in Prison-Linked Private Equity Firm," *Pennsylvania Capital-Star*, September 27, 2019, https://www.penncapital-star.com/blog/state-employee-retirement-board-balks-at-investing-in-prison-linked-private-equity-firm/.

156. Lee DeVito, "Comedian Samantha Bee Blasts Detroit Pistons Owner Tom Gores over Role in Prison Phone Call Injustice," *Detroit Metro Times*, May 6, 2021, https://www.metrotimes.com/news/comedian-samantha-bee-blasts-detroit-pistons-owner-tom-gores-over-role-in-prison-phone-call-injustice-27069851.

157. Kim Bellware, "Detained Immigrants Were Paid Candy or $1 a Day for Labor. They're Owed $17 Million, a Jury Says," *Washington Post*, October 30, 2021, https://www.washingtonpost.com/nation/2021/10/30/immigrant-detainee-minumum-wage/; Madison Pauly, "A Private Prison Company Just Lost a Major Battle over $1-Per-Day Wages for Immigrant Workers," *Mother Jones*, October 28, 2021, https://www.motherjones.com/crime-justice/2021/10/ice-detention-immigration-geo-group-core-civic-lawsuit/.

158. Alice Speri, "The Largest Prison Strike in U.S. History Enters Its Second Week," *The Intercept*, September 16, 2016, https://theintercept.com/2016/09/16/the-largest-prison-strike-in-u-s-history-enters-its-second-week/; German Lopez, "America's Prisoners Are Going on Strike in at Least 17 States," *Vox*, August 22, 2018, https://www.vox.com/2018/8/17/17664048/national-prison-strike-2018.

159. "#EndTheException," accessed September 22, 2022, https://endtheexception.com/; Abolish Slavery National Network, "About," accessed September 22, 2022, https://abolishslavery.us/about/.

160. "#EndTheException," accessed April 28, 2024, https://endtheexception.com/.

161. "Alabama: 1 of 5 States to Decide on Slavery Loopholes for Prison Labor in Upcoming Election," Associated Press, AL.com, October 20, 2022, https://www.al.com/news/2022/10/alabama-1-of-5-states-to-decide-on-slavery-loopholes-for-prison-labor-in-upcoming-election.html.

162. On the relationship between tactical diversity and social movement success, see Aldon Morris, "Birmingham Confrontation Reconsidered: An Analysis of the Dynamics and Tactics of Mobilization," *American Sociological Review* 58, no. 5 (1993): 635; Susan Olzak and Emily Ryo, "Organizational Diversity, Vitality and Outcomes in the Civil Rights Movement," *Social Forces* 85, no. 4 (2007): 1561–91.

163. Mariame Kaba, *We Do This 'Til We Free Us: Abolitionist Organizing and Transforming Justice* (Haymarket Books, 2021).

164. Woodly, *Reckoning*; Frances Fox Piven, *Challenging Authority: How Ordinary People Change America* (Rowman & Littlefield, 2006).

165. Mihir Chaudhary, Gwen Prowse, and Vesla M. Weaver, "A People's Abolition: How Policed Communities Describe and Enact Liberatory Futures," *Social Science Quarterly* 102, no. 7 (2021): 3058–72; Robin D. G. Kelley, *Freedom Dreams: The Black Radical Imagination* (Beacon Press, 2003).

166. Chaudhary, Prowse, and Weaver, "A People's Abolition," 3071.

167. On transformational organizing, see Hahrie Han, *How Organizations Develop Activists: Civic Associations and Leadership in the 21st Century* (Oxford University Press, 2014).

168. Jocelyn Simonson, "Bail Nullification," *Michigan Law Review* 115, no. 5 (2017): 603.

169. Simonson, *Radical Acts of Justice*, 41.

170. "Emancipate NC," Emancipate NC, accessed September 24, 2022, https://emancipatenc.org/.

171. "Freedom Fighter Bail Fund," Emancipate NC, accessed September 24, 2022, https://emancipatenc.org/freedom-fighter-bond-fund/.

172. Simonson, *Radical Acts of Justice*, 41.

173. Peter B. Edelman, "Criminalization of Poverty: Much More to Do," *Duke Law Journal* 69 (April 2020): 114–36.

174. On jail watching, see, e.g., Maurice Chammah, "Their Unlikely Alliance Began at a Whataburger. Can They Reform a Texas Jail?," *Marshall Project*, July 1, 2020, https://www.themarshallproject.org/2020/07/01/their-unlikely-alliance-began-at-whataburger-can-they-reform-a-texas-jail. On court watching, Simonson, *Radical Acts of Justice*, chap. 3.

175. Nagrecha, Brett, and Doyle, "Court Culture."

176. Ann Chih Lin, *Reform in the Making: The Implementation of Social Policy in Prison* (Princeton University Press, 2000).

177. Margaret E. Keck and Kathryn Sikkink, *Activists Beyond Borders: Advocacy Networks in International Politics* (Cornell University Press, 1998).

178. Fines and Fees Justice Center, "About Us," accessed April 28, 2024, https://finesandfeesjusticecenter.org/.

179. Prison Policy Initiative, "About the Prison Policy Initiative," accessed0 September 24, 2022, https://www.prisonpolicy.org/about.html.

180. "Tell Them You Love Them (with Bianca Tylek)," *Pod Save the People*, podcast audio, Crooked Media, January 12, 2021, https://crooked.com/podcast/tell-them-you-love-them-with-bianca-tylek/.

181. On expanding the scope of conflict, see, e.g., Schattschneider, *The Semi-Sovereign People*; Baumgartner and Jones, *Agendas and Instability in American Politics*.

182. Amanda Tattersall, *Power in Coalition: Strategies for Strong Unions and Social Change* (Cornell University Press, 2010).

183. Woodly, *Reckoning*, 49.

184. Woodly, *Reckoning*, 24–30.

185. Woodly, *Reckoning*, 89–126.

186. Debt Collective, *Can't Pay, Won't Pay*, 61.

187. Debt Collective, *Can't Pay, Won't Pay*, 14.

188. Dana Froberg and Morgan Duckett, "The Slow Death of a Prison Profiteer: How Activism Brought Securus to the Brink," *The Appeal*, April 4, 2024,

https://theappeal.org/securus-bankruptcy-prison-telecom-industry/?mc_cid =
99e51d1529&mc_eid = UNIQID.

189. Froberg and Duckett, "The Slow Death of a Prison Profiteer."

190. Frannie Kelley, "Drakeo's Acclaimed Album Highlights How Much Prisons
Profit from Phone Calls," NPR (*All Things Considered*), August 28, 2020, https://www
.npr.org/2020/08/28/906807077/prison-telecom-business-indicted-by-rap-album
-recorded-in-jail.

191. Simonson, *Radical Acts of Justice*, xiv.

192. Philip Goodman, Joshua Page, and Michelle Phelps, *Breaking the Pendulum:
The Long Struggle over Criminal Justice* (Oxford University Press, 2017), 13.

193. Simonson, *Radical Acts of Justice*, ix.

194. Woodly, *Reckoning*, 7.

195. Keeanga-Yamahtta Taylor, "From Small Victories to Larger Battles," *Boston
Review*, March 1, 2016, https://www.bostonreview.net/forum_response/keeanga
-yamahtta-taylor-kelley-black-struggle-campus-protest/.

196. Woodly, *Reckoning*, chap. 4.

197. Amna Akbar, "An Abolitionist Horizon for (Police) Reform," *California Law
Review* 108, no. 6 (2020): 1781–1846.

198. All quotes in this paragraph are from Froberg and Duckett, "The Slow Death
of a Prison Profiteer."

Conclusion

1. Becket Adams, "The Loots in Ferguson Have Caused That Community and the
Nation a Great Deal of Harm," *Washington Examiner*, August 18, 2014, https://www
.washingtonexaminer.com/opinion/1142595/the-looters-in-ferguson-have-caused
-that-community-and-the-nation-a-great-deal-of-harm/.

2. David Garland, *The Culture of Control: Crime and Social Order in Contemporary
Society* (University of Chicago Press, 2001).

3. Jonathan Simon, *Governing Through Crime: How the War on Crime Transformed American Democracy and Created a Culture of Fear* (Oxford University Press,
2007); Garland, *Culture of Control*; Loïc Wacquant, *Punishing the Poor: The Neoliberal
Government of Social Insecurity* (Duke University Press, 2009).

4. Bruce Western and Katherine Beckett, "How Unregulated Is the U.S. Labor
Market? The Penal System as a Labor Market Institution," *American Journal of
Sociology* 104, no. 4 (1999): 1030–60.

5. Forrest Stuart, *Down, Out, and Under Arrest: Policing and Everyday Life in Skid
Row* (University of Chicago Press, 2016); Carolyn Sufrin, *Jailcare: Finding the Safety
Net for Women Behind Bars* (University of California Press, 2017); Garland, *Culture of
Control*.

6. This discussion parallels efforts to re-envision and reframe the boundaries of
"punishment" and the interdisciplinary field of "punishment and society." See, e.g.,
Kelly Hannah-Moffat and Mona Lynch, eds., special issue, "Theorizing Punishment's
Boundaries," *Theoretical Criminology* 16, no. 2 (2012).

7. E.g., Devah Pager, "The Mark of a Criminal Record," *American Journal of
Sociology* 108, no. 5 (2003): 937–75; Bruce Western, *Punishment and Inequality in
America* (Russell Sage Foundation, 2006); Sara Wakefield and Christopher Uggen,
"Incarceration and Stratification," *Annual Review of Sociology* 36, no. 1 (2010):
387–406.

8. Sarah Brayne, "Surveillance and System Avoidance: Criminal Justice Contact and Institutional Attachment," *American Sociological Review* 79, no. 3 (2014): 367–91.

9. Jack Arpey, "New York Lawmakers and Advocates Seek to Eliminate 'Predatory' Court Fees," *Spectrum News*, March 29, 2024, https://spectrumlocalnews.com/nys/central-ny/politics/2024/03/29/push-to-eliminate-court-fees.

10. Alexes Harris, *A Pound of Flesh: Monetary Sanctions as Punishment for the Poor* (Russell Sage Foundation, 2016); Peter Edelman, *Not a Crime to Be Poor: The Criminalization of Poverty in America* (New Press, 2017).

11. Beth A. Colgan, "Reviving the Excessive Fines Clause," *California Law Review* 102, no. 2 (April 2014): 277–350.

12. Traci R. Burch, "Fixing the Broken System of Financial Sanctions," *Criminology and Public Policy* 10, no. 3 (2011): 539–45; Chloe Thurston, "Hidden Fees? The Hidden State Framework and the Reform Prospects for Systems of Monetary Sanctions," *UCLA Criminal Justice Law Review* 4, no. 1 (2020): 283–92.

13. Quoted in Fair and Just Prosecution, *Fines, Fees, and the Poverty Penalty* (2017), 6, https://www.fairandjustprosecution.org/staging/wp-content/uploads/2017/11/FJPBrief_Fines.Fees_.pdf.

14. Monica C. Bell, "Hidden Laws of the Time of Ferguson," *Harvard Law Review Forum* 132, no. 1 (2018): 10.

15. Beth A. Colgan, "Beyond Graduation: Economic Sanctions and Structural Reform," *Duke Law Journal* 69 (April 2020): 1529–83.

16. See, e.g., Michele Cadigan, Alexes Harris, and Tyler Smith, "Monetary Sanctions Are a Barrier to Successfully Addressing Mass Incarceration," *USAPP Blog* (London School of Economics), September 12, 2023, https://blogs.lse.ac.uk/usappblog/2023/09/12/monetary-sanctions-are-a-barrier-to-successfully-addressing-mass-incarceration/.

17. On the limited value of cost-efficiency framings of legal financial obligations, see FrameWorks Institute, "Framing Advocacy on Fines and Fees Reform," 2018, https://www.frameworksinstitute.org/wp-content/uploads/2020/03/fines-and-fees-reform-framebrief-2018.pdf.

18. See, e.g., Jason Pye, Luke Hogg, and Josh Withrow, *From High Seas to Highway Robbery: How Civil Asset Forfeiture Became One of the Worst Forms of Government Overreach* (FreedomWorks Foundation), accessed September 24, 2022, https://fw-d7-freedomworks-org.s3.amazonaws.com/FWF%20-%20Issue%20Brief%20-%20CAF%20-%20Pye-v3.pdf.

19. Jennifer C. Nash and Samantha Pinto, "Everybody's Maybes: Reproducing Feminism's Bad Objects," *South Atlantic Quarterly* 122, no. 3 (2023): 421–30, https://doi.org/10.1215/00382876-10643945.

20. See, e.g., Edelman, *Not a Crime to Be Poor.*

21. For a discussion of this substitution dynamic and an effort make inequality and exploitation central to the poverty frame, see Matthew Desmond, *Poverty, by America* (Crown Books, 2023).

22. See, e.g., Michael B. Katz, *In the Shadow of the Poorhouse: A Social History of Welfare in America* (Basic Books, 1986); Frances Fox Piven and Richard A. Cloward, *Regulating the Poor: The Functions of Public Welfare* (Viking Books, 1993).

23. See, e.g., Michael B. Katz, *The Undeserving Poor: America's Confrontation with Poverty* (Oxford University Press, 2013); Joe Soss, Richard C. Fording, and Sanford F. Schram, *Disciplining the Poor: Neoliberal Paternalism and the Persistent Power of Race* (University of Chicago Press, 2011).

24. William A. Gamson, "Constructing Social Protest," in *Social Movements and Culture*, ed. Hank Johnson and Bert Klandermans (University of Minnesota Press, 1995), 85–106.

25. Deborah Gould, "Political Despair," in *Politics and the Emotions: The Affective Turn in Contemporary Political Studies*, ed. S. Thompson and P. Hoggett (Bloomsbury, 2012), 95.

26. E. E. Schattschneider, *The Semi-Sovereign People: A Realist's View of Democracy in America* (Holt, Rinehart and Winston, 1960).

27. Jocelyn Simonson, *Radical Acts of Justice: How Ordinary People Are Dismantling Mass Incarceration* (New Press, 2023), 127–52.

28. Andrew W. Kahrl, *The Black Tax: 150 Years of Theft, Exploitation, and Dispossession in America* (University of Chicago Press, 2024), 7.

29. Kahrl, *The Black Tax*, 4.

30. Brian Highsmith, "The Structural Violence of Municipal Hoarding," *American Prospect*, July 6, 2020, https://prospect.org/civil-rights/the-structural-violence-of-municipal-hoarding/.

31. Brian Highsmith, "The Bondholders' Veto: Fiscal Federalism and Local Democracy," Law and Political Economy Project, September 9, 2021, https://lpeproject.org/blog/the-bondholders-veto-fiscal-federalism-and-local-democracy/.

32. Brian Highsmith, "On Reimagining State and Local Budgets in an Abolitionist Moment," Law and Political Economy Project, June 15, 2020, https://lpeproject.org/blog/on-reimagining-state-and-local-budgets-in-an-abolitionist-moment/.

33. Simonson, *Radical Acts of Justice*, 132.

34. Simonson, *Radical Acts of Justice*, 127–52.

35. Highsmith, "On Reimagining."

36. Joanna Weiss, "New York State Testimony: The Regressive Tax Burden," testimony before the New York State Committee, February 6, 2019, Fines and Fees Justice Center, https://finesandfeesjusticecenter.org/content/uploads/2019/02/2.11-NYS-State-Testimony_02072019.pdf.

37. Aravind Boddupalli and Kim S. Rueben, "Inequitable Criminal Legal Fines and Fees Are Ripe for State Reforms," *Urban Wire*, October 11, 2022, https://www.urban.org/urban-wire/inequitable-criminal-legal-fines-and-fees-are-ripe-state-reforms; Aravind Boddupalli, Tracy Gordon, and Lourdes Germán, *More Than Fines and Fees: Incorporating Equity into City Revenue Strategies* (Urban Institute, December 1, 2021), https://www.urban.org/research/publication/more-fines-and-fees-incorporating-equity-city-revenue-strategies.

38. Debt Collective, *Can't Pay, Won't Pay: The Case for Economic Disobedience and Debt Abolition* (Haymarket Books, 2020), 14.

39. Deva R. Woodly, *Reckoning: Black Lives Matter and the Democratic Necessity of Social Movements* (Oxford University Press, 2022), 49.

40. Ta-Nehisi Coates, "The Case for Reparations," *Atlantic*, June 2014, https://www.theatlantic.com/magazine/archive/2014/06/the-case-for-reparations/361631/.

41. See, e.g., NAACP, "Reparations," 2019, https://naacp.org/resources/reparations.

42. See, e.g., African-American Redress Network, "Promoting Reparation Efforts," accessed January 4, 2025, https://redressnetwork.org/.

43. Robin D. G. Kelly, *Freedom Dreams: The Black Radical Imagination*, Twentieth Anniversary Edition (Beacon Press, 2022), 110–34; Olúfẹ́mi O. Táíwò, *Reconsidering Reparations* (Oxford University Press, 2022).

44. Charles W. Mills, "Contract of Breach: Repairing the Racial Contract," in *Contract and Domination* (Polity Press, 2007), 121–22.

45. William A. Darity Jr. and A. Kirsten Mullen, *From Here to Equality: Reparations for Black Americans in the Twenty-First Century*, 2nd ed. (University of North Carolina Press, 2022), 2.

46. Darity and Mullen, *From Here to Equality*.

47. Rashad Williams and Justin Steil, "The Past We Step into and How We Repair It," *Journal of the American Planning Association* 89, no. 4 (2023): 586–87, https://doi.org/10.1080/01944363.2022.2154247.

48. Rashawn Ray and Andre Perry, *Why We Need Reparations for Black Americans* (Brookings Institution, 2020), https://www.brookings.edu/articles/why-we-need-reparations-for-black-americans/; Mary T. Bassett and Sandra Galeo, "Reparations as a Health Priority—A Strategy for Ending Black-White Health Disparities," *New England Journal of Medicine* 383, no. 22 (2020): 2101–3, https://www.nejm.org/doi/full/10.1056/NEJMp2026170; Preston C. Green III, Bruce D. Baker, and Joseph O. Oluwole, "School Finance, Race, and Reparations," *Washington and Lee Journal of Civil Rights and Social Justice* 27, no. 22 (2021): 483–558.

49. Táíwò, *Reconsidering Reparations*.

Appendix

1. Joshua Page, *The Toughest Beat: Politics, Punishment, and the Prison Officers Union in California* (Oxford University Press, 2011).

2. Joshua Page, "Punishment and the Penal Field," in *The Handbook on Punishment and Society*, ed. J. Simon and R. Sparks (Sage, 2012), 152–66.

3. Malcolm M. Feeley, *The Process Is the Punishment: Handling Cases in a Lower Criminal Court* (Russell Sage Foundation, 1979), 96–97.

4. Paul Lichterman, "Seeing Structure Happen: Theory-Driven Participant Observation," in *Methods of Social Movement Research*, ed. Bert Klandermans and Suzanne Staggenborg (University of Minnesota Press, 2002), 120–21.

5. Lisa Weeden, "Ethnography as Interpretive Enterprise," in *Political Ethnography: What Immersion Contributes to the Study of Power*, ed. Edward Schatz (University of Chicago Press, 2009); Colin Jerolmack and Shamus Khan, "Talk Is Cheap: Ethnography and the Attitudinal Fallacy," *Sociological Methods & Research* 43, no. 2 (2014): 178–209.

6. Weeden, "Ethnography as Interpretive Enterprise," 85.

7. Peregrine Schwartz-Shea and Dvora Yanow, *Interpretive Research Design: Concepts and Processes* (Routledge, 2012), 24–44.

8. Loïc Wacquant, *Body and Soul: Notebooks of an Apprentice Boxer*, Expanded Anniversary Edition (Oxford University Press, 2022).

9. Wacquant, *Body and Soul*; Loïc Wacquant, "For a Sociology of Flesh and Blood," *Qualitative Sociology* 38, no. 1 (2015): 1–11.

10. Everett C. Hughes, "Good People and Dirty Work," *Social Problems* 10, no. 1 (1962): 3–11.

11. Joe Soss, "On Casing a Study Versus Studying a Case," in *Rethinking Comparison: Innovative Methods for Qualitative Political Inquiry*, ed. Erica S. Simmons and Nicholas Rush Smith (Cambridge University Press, 2021), 84–106.

12. Soss, "On Casing a Study," 89.

13. Mario L. Small, "How Many Cases Do I Need? On Science and the Logic of Case Selection in Field-Based Research," *Ethnography* 10, no. 1 (2009): 5–38.

14. Small, "How Many Cases," 19.

15. Vickie A. Miracle, "The Belmont Report: The Triple Crown of Research Ethics," *Dimensions of Critical Care Nursing* 35, no. 4 (2016): 223–28.

16. Todd L. Pittinsky and Nicole Diamante, "Global Bystander Nonintervention," *Peace and Conflict: Journal of Peace Psychology* 21, no. 2 (2015): 226–47.

17. Clarissa Hayward, "Responsibility and Ignorance: On Dismantling Structural Injustice," *Journal of Politics* 79, no. 2 (2017): 398; Iris Marion Young, *Responsibility for Justice* (Oxford University Press, 2011).

18. Ana Radelat, "University of Minnesota Grapples with Reparation Demands from Tribes Who Say They Were Victims of Land Grabs," *MinnPost*, July 13, 2023, https://www.minnpost.com/national/2023/07/university-of-minnesota-grapples-with -reparation-demands-from-tribes-who-say-they-were-victims-of-land-grabs/.

19. The Journal of Blacks in Higher Education, "The University of Minnesota's Historical Ties to Slavery," November 16, 2019, https://jbhe.com/2019/11/the -university-of-minnesotas-historical-ties-to-slavery/; James Lileks, "What Happened to Old Main, the Former Heart of the University of Minnesota Campus?," *Star Tribune*, September 15, 2020, https://www.startribune.com/what-happened-to-old-main-the -former-heart-of-the-university-of-minnesota-campus/572415622/.

20. Estelle Timar-Wilcox, "Students, Activists Protest U of M Prison Labor Purchases," *MPR News*, February 9, 2024, https://www.mprnews.org/story/2024/02/ 09/protesters-want-u-of-m-to-stop-buying-from-prison-labor-company.

21. Twin Cities Daily Planet, "Principles of Less Eligibility: The Human Cost of Prison Labor, Part II," January 24, 2018, https://www.tcdailyplanet.net/principles-of -less-eligibility-the-human-cost-of-prison-labor-part-ii/.

INDEX

CHICAGO STUDIES IN AMERICAN POLITICS
A series edited by Susan Herbst, Lawrence R. Jacobs, Adam J. Berinsky, and Frances Lee; Benjamin I. Page, editor emeritus

Series titles, continued from front matter:

Partisan Hostility and American Democracy: Explaining Political Divisions and When They Matter
by James N. Druckman, Samara Klar, Yanna Krupnikov, Matthew Levendusky, and John Barry Ryan

Respect and Loathing in American Democracy: Polarization, Moralization, and the Undermining of Equality
by Jeff Spinner-Halev and Elizabeth Theiss-Morse

Countermobilization: Policy Feedback and Backlash in a Polarized Age
by Eric M. Patashnik

Race, Rights, and Rifles: The Origins of the NRA and Contemporary Gun Culture
by Alexandra Filindra

Accountability in State Legislatures
by Steven Rogers

Our Common Bonds: Using What Americans Share to Help Bridge the Partisan Divide
by Matthew Levendusky

Dynamic Democracy: Public Opinion, Elections, and Policymaking in the American States
by Devin Caughey and Christopher Warshaw

Persuasion in Parallel: How Information Changes Minds about Politics
by Alexander Coppock

Radical American Partisanship: Mapping Violent Hostility, Its Causes, and the Consequences for Democracy
by Nathan P. Kalmoe and Lilliana Mason

Neither Liberal nor Conservative: Ideological Innocence in the American Public
by Donald R. Kinder and Nathan P. Kalmoe

Strategic Party Government: Why Winning Trumps Ideology
by Gregory Koger and Matthew J. Lebo

Post-Racial or Most-Racial? Race and Politics in the Obama Era
by Michael Tesler

The Politics of Resentment: Rural Consciousness in Wisconsin and the Rise of Scott Walker
by Katherine J. Cramer

Legislating in the Dark: Information and Power in the House of Representatives
by James M. Curry

Why Washington Won't Work: Polarization, Political Trust, and the Governing Crisis
by Marc J. Hetherington and Thomas J. Rudolph

Who Governs? Presidents, Public Opinion, and Manipulation
by James N. Druckman and Lawrence R. Jacobs

Trapped in America's Safety Net: One Family's Struggle
by Andrea Louise Campbell

Arresting Citizenship: The Democratic Consequences of American Crime Control
by Amy E. Lerman and Vesla M. Weaver

How the States Shaped the Nation: American Electoral Institutions and Voter Turnout, 1920–2000
by Melanie Jean Springer

White-Collar Government: The Hidden Role of Class in Economic Policy Making
by Nicholas Carnes

How Partisan Media Polarize America
by Matthew Levendusky

Changing Minds or Changing Channels? Partisan News in an Age of Choice
by Kevin Arceneaux and Martin Johnson

The Politics of Belonging: Race, Public Opinion, and Immigration
by Natalie Masuoka and Jane Junn

The Partisan Sort: How Liberals Became Democrats and Conservatives Became Republicans
by Matthew Levendusky

Democracy at Risk: How Terrorist Threats Affect the Public
by Jennifer L. Merolla and Elizabeth J. Zechmeister

In Time of War: Understanding American Public Opinion from World War II to Iraq
by Adam J. Berinsky

Agendas and Instability in American Politics, Second Edition
by Frank R. Baumgartner and Bryan D. Jones

The Party Decides: Presidential Nominations Before and After Reform
by Marty Cohen, David Karol, Hans Noel, and John Zaller

The Private Abuse of the Public Interest: Market Myths and Policy Muddles
by Lawrence D. Brown and Lawrence R. Jacobs

Same Sex, Different Politics: Success and Failure in the Struggles over Gay Rights
by Gary Mucciaroni